Beethoven
Piano Sonatas Op. 90–Op. 111

Their Creation, Origins and Reception History
Incorporating
Contextual Accounts of Beethoven and His Contemporaries

BEETHOVEN
As depicted by the life mask taken by Franz Klein in 1812
(derived from a copy in the author's possession)

BEETHOVEN

PIANO SONATAS
OP. 90–OP. 111

THEIR
CREATION ORIGINS
AND
RECEPTION HISTORY

Incorporating contextual accounts of
Beethoven and his contemporaries

Terence M. Russell

Jelly Bean Books

The right of Terence Russell to be identified as the
Author of the Work has been asserted by him in accordance
with the Copyright, Designs and Patents Act 1988.

Copyright © Terence M. Russell 2022

Published by
Jelly Bean Books
136 Newport Road
Cardiff
CF24 1DJ

ISBN: 978-1-915439-11-6

www.candyjarbooks.co.uk

All rights reserved.
No part of this publication may be reproduced, stored in a
retrieval system, or transmitted at any time or by any means,
electronic, mechanical, photocopying, recording or otherwise
without the prior permission of the copyright holder. This book is
sold subject to the condition that it shall not by way of trade or
otherwise be circulated without the publisher's prior consent in any
form of binding or cover other than that in which it is published.

CONTENTS

AUTHOR'S NOTE	I
INTRODUCTION	IX
EDITORIAL PRINCIPLES	XXXIX
BEETHOVEN'S FINANCIAL TRANSACTIONS	XLI
BEETHOVEN: PIANO SONATAS	
Piano Sonata in minor, Op. 90	1
Piano Sonata in A major, Op. 101	41
Piano Sonata in B-flat major, Op. 106 *The Hammerklavier*	103
Piano Sonata in E major, Op. 109	222
Piano Sonata in A-flat major, Op. 110	264
Piano Sonata in C minor, Op. 111	320
BIBLIOGRAPHY	394
INDEX	424
ABOUT THE AUTHOR	435

AUTHOR'S NOTE

I have cherished the idea of making a study of the life and work of Beethoven for many years. This statement requires a few words of personal reflection. I first encountered Beethoven in my early piano lessons — Minuet in G major, WoO 10, No. 2. At the same time I became acquainted with his piano pupil Carl Czerny — *Book One, Piano Studies*. My heart sank when I discovered the rear cover advertised a further *99* books in the same series — scales, arpeggios studies for the left hand, studies for the right hand — all the way to his Op. 824! By coincidence, my *Czerny Book One* was edited by Alec Rowley — who had the same surname as my music teacher. In my childish innocence, I often wondered why *he himself* never appeared to give me a lesson!

In my teenage years I found myself drawn ever closer to Beethoven's music in the manner that ferromagnetic materials are ineluctably held captive in the sway of a magnetic field. The impulse to which I yielded is well described in words the conductor Bruno Walter gave in one of his rare public addresses: 'It is my belief that young people at that age are more easily impressed by what is heroic and grandiose; that they more easily understand works of art in which passionate feelings are violently uttered in raised accents, and that the lighter sounds of cheerfulness are less impressive to them.' I do indeed recall the stirring effect made on me on first hearing the Overture *Egmont*, the unfolding drama of the Fifth Symphony and the declamatory opening chords of the *Emperor* Piano Concerto.

I resolved to read everything I could about Beethoven, starting with Marion Scott's pioneering English-language study of the composer in the *Master Musicians series*. My father took out a subscription for me for *The Gramophone* magazine, enabling me to read reviews of the new 'LP' recordings — none of which though I could afford! The LP was then — 1950s — beginning to supplant the 78 rpm shellac records, stacks of which could be purchased for as little as six pence each in 'old' money. At this same time I had the privilege of hearing Beethoven's music performed by the *Hallé Orchestra* under the baton of Sir John Barbirolli, and experienced the *Carl Rosa Opera Company* perform the composer's only opera *Fidelio*; I borrowed the piano-reduction score from the City Library to become better acquainted with this moving work — only to find the score's fists full of notes were well beyond my capabilities. Nonetheless, since then *Fidelio's* every note has been woven into my DNA. I also recall the period when the *London Promenade Concerts* were designated 'Friday night is Beethoven night'.

Through these influences I resolved to visit Vienna to see where Beethoven had lived and worked. But how? The support for such travel was beyond the means of my family. Fortunately in my final year at school (1959) an opportunity presented itself. I saw a poster that stated *WUS — World University Service* — required volunteers to work in the Austrian town of Linz to help relocate refugees who were living there in improvised wooden shacks — displaced and dispossessed victims of the Second World War. To those participating all expenses would be paid together with free accommodation — in one of the crumbling wooden shacks! From Linz, I planned to make my way to Vienna.

I applied to *WUS* and, despite being a mere school-leaver, I was accepted. The *WUS* authorities doubtless reasoned the building-trade skills I had acquired during my secondary education in the building department of a technical school would be useful. This proved to be the case. At the refugee camp I dug trenches and was allowed to assist as a bricklayer. All about me were wide-eyed children eager to help but mostly getting in the way. I recall one afternoon when a reporter from *The Observer* newspaper paid a visit to our construction site to gather material for an article he was writing on European post-war recovery — he generously admired my trenches and brickwork!

Of lasting significance was another visit, this time from a Belgian priest. He took a group of us to the nearby *Mauthausen* Concentration Camp, recently opened as a silent and solemn memorial to those who had perished there. It was a deeply moving experience. Years later I learned of the views of the ardent Beethovenian Sir Michael Tippet. After the horrors of the *Holocaust*, he posed the question for mankind: 'What price Beethoven now?' He posited: 'Could we any longer find solace in Beethoven's setting of Schiller's *Ode to Joy* and its utopian vision — "Be embraced you Millions"?'

My refugee contribution duly came to end and Vienna beckoned. On arrival there I found scenes reminiscent of *The Third Man* and *Harry Lime*. I recall, for example, encountering cobblestones piled high in the streets waiting to be replaced after having been disturbed by the heavy armoured vehicles that had so recently passed over them. But Vienna was welcoming. I visited the houses where Beethoven had lived and worked and paused outside others associated with him that were identified by a commemorative plaque and the Austrian flag. A particularly memorable occasion was attending a recital in the great salon within the palace of Beethoven's noble patron Prince Lobkowitz – the very one where the *Eroica* Symphony had been premiered. Ultimately, my steps led me to the composer's first resting place in the *Währinger Ortsfriedhof*. I paid silent homage to the great man and, as I did so, discovered nearby the resting place of Franz Schubert to whom Beethoven was an endless source of admiration and inspiration.

I felt a youthful impulse to discover yet more about Beethoven and his music. But absorption in musicology would have to take second place. My chosen career beckoned in the guise of architecture – 'the mother of the arts' and 'the handmaid of society'. There was room though for Beethoven's music and from that time on it has been my constant companion through attendance at recitals, in concerts and music-making in the home. And at home a reproduction of Franz Kline's 1812 study of the composer has greeted me each day for more than half a century.

On my retirement from a career in architectural practice, research and university teaching, the opportunity finally presented itself for me to devote time to researching Beethoven musicology. Having attained my eightieth year also emboldened me to make progress with my good intentions!

With these autobiographical remarks outlined I will say a few remarks about my working method – see also the comments made in *Editorial Principles*.

As a member of staff of The University of Edinburgh, I had the good fortune to have access to the *Reid Music Library*, formed from a nucleus of books bequeathed by General John Reid and augmented over the years by such custodians as Sir Donald Francis Tovey, sometime *Reid Professor of Music* and renowned Beethoven scholar. Over a period of three years, I made a survey of the many works in the Reid collection. I consulted each item in turn making records on paper slips — many hundreds — that I deemed to be relevant for my researches. I confined my searches to book-publications, as reflected in my accompanying bibliography. All of this was quite some years ago, the cut-off date for my researches being 2007. Beyond this date I have not surveyed any further works. I am mindful though that Beethoven musicology and related publication continue to be a major field of endeavour in the manner of the proverbial 'ever rolling stream'.

In the intervening years since completing my archival researches, personal tribulations associated with family illness and bereavement slowed my progress in giving expression to my projected intentions. Latterly, however, with renewed energy, and more time at my disposal, I have been able to make progress. My studies take the form of a set of monographs. These trace the creation origins and reception history of each of Beethoven's piano sonatas and string quartets. The resulting texts also incorporate contextual accounts of Beethoven and his contemporaries. Also included in my musicological surveys are two related Beethoven anthologies. The set of monographs in question, identified by short title, are:

Beethoven: An anthology of selected writings.
Beethoven: The piano sonatas: An anthology of selected writings.

The Piano Sonatas:
Op. 2–Op. 28
Op. 31–Op. 81A
Op. 90–Op. 111

The String Quartets:
Op. 18, Nos. 1–6
Op. 59, Nos. 1–3 (Razumovsky); Op. 74 (The Harp);
 Op. 95 (Quartetto Serioso)
Op. 127, Op. 132 and Op. 130 (Galitzin)
Op. 131, Op. 135; Grosse Fuge, Op. 133 and Op. 134
 (Fugue transcription)

I provide further information about these studies in the introduction to each individual monograph. Suffice it for me to state here the basic premise upon which my work is founded. I believe it is rewarding, concerning the life of a great artist, to find connections between who he *was* and what he *did*; in Martin Cooper's words 'between his personality, as expressed on the one hand in human relationships, and on the other in artistic creation'. (*Beethoven, The Last Decade*) That is not to say I consider it essential to the enjoyment of Beethoven's music to know this or that fact about it. His music can be enjoyed, as millions do, with — in Robert Simpson's apt phrase —'an innocent ear', for what it is and how it reaches out to us in purely musical terms without any prejudging of its merits based upon extra-musicological facts.

I must make a further point. I am mindful that a scholar who ventures into a field of study that is not rightly his may be regarded with some suspicion. In this regard I can but ask the reader to place his or her trust in me in the following way. I have attempted to bring to my work the care which publishers and their desk editors have required of me in my book writings relating to architecture — listed elsewhere.

As inferred, it is now more than sixty years since I paid homage to Beethoven in Vienna's *Währinger Ortsfriedhof* and my warmth of feeling towards the composer and his music have grown with the passing of the years. My studies are not intended to be propaedeutic — that would be pretentious. However, if in sharing with others what I have to say contributes to their knowledge and understanding of the composer, and thereby increases their own feelings towards him and his works, my own pleasure in bringing my work to completion will be all the more enhanced.

It is perhaps fitting that my studies should appear in Beethoven's 250th Anniversary Year — I must confess more by chance than design!

When Beethoven arrived in Vienna, he was unknown. He was armed though with a note of encouragement from his youthful friend and benefactor Count Ferdinand Waldstein. It contained the often-quoted words: 'Receive Mozart's spirit from Haydn's hands.' Some forty years later Beethoven passed away in the House of the black-robed Spaniards at 200 *Alservorstädter*, the *Glacis* where he had lived since the autumn of 1825. Soldiers had to be called to secure the doors to the inner courtyard of the house from the pressure of onlookers. His body was blessed in the *Alservorsttädt Parish Church*, schools were closed and perhaps as many as 10,000 people formed a funeral procession — an honour ordinarily reserved for monarchs. The *Marcia Funebre* from the composer's Op. 26 Piano Sonata was performed at the funeral ceremony. Franz Grillparzer read the funeral oration. Franz Schubert, who, as remarked in life so admired Beethoven, was one of the pallbearers. The composer's mortal remains were lowered into a simple vault. Beethoven now belonged to history.

Dr Terence M. Russell
Edinburgh 2020

INTRODUCTION

The subjects of this study are the creation origins and reception history of Beethoven's piano sonatas. It is one of three that broadly correspond with the generally accepted periods into which the compositions of the composer's maturity are held to conform and which have been described as 'imitative', 'heroic' and 'introspective'. In our first study, the piano sonatas Opp. 2 – 28 are considered; in the second, the piano sonatas Opp. 31 – 81a; and in the third, the piano sonatas Opp. 90 – 111. Conformably with these studies are two companion works *Beethoven: An Anthology of Selected Writings* and *Beethoven: The Piano Sonatas: An Anthology of Selected Writings*. The former of these provides the reader with texts and quotations that position Beethoven as a figure in the history of culture and humankind. The latter is a more focused study that brings together over-arching views concerning the piano sonatas as expressed by composers, musicologists and performing artists. The reader, with a particular interest in Beethoven's keyboard music, will find the survey-writings contained in this anthology will also serve as an introduction to the three sets of piano-sonata studies.

Beethoven was one of the foremost virtuoso pianists of his day. His piano pupil Ferdinand Ries considered his powers of invention, when improvising at the keyboard, 'to be matchless with regard to the wealth of ideas which poured forth, the moods to which he surrendered and the challenges he imposed upon himself'. It is not surprising, therefore, that throughout his life Beethoven turned to the piano sonata as a vehicle for exhibiting pianistic display and the expression of intense musical felling. Only in his closing years did he leave off from writing piano sonatas in favour of the medium of the string quartet.

The collection of writings presented here, derive from the piano-sonata compositions of Beethoven's so-called third period. They take the form of extended essays that may serve the reader as a source of reference — in the manner of programme notes to a recital. Accordingly, the remarks relating to each piano sonata are 'free standing' and can be read independently. That said they are also interlinked by the events unfolding in the composer's life. An attempt has been made, therefore, to interrelate the individual essays so that they may be read as a continuous narrative — in typical book fashion. A summary outline of this narrative is provided in the Index for each individual piano sonata. Thereby the reader is provided not only with a guide to the contents discussed in each sonata-text but also has an over-arching time-line of the principal events bearing on Beethoven's life and work.

By way of an introduction to the individual essays, the following is a summary-outline of the compositions included in this part of our survey:

Three years elapsed before Beethoven returned to the medium of piano-sonata composition since Muzio Clementi's publication of the Piano Sonata Op. 81a in London in 1811. A further year would pass before the completion and publication of the Piano Sonata in E minor, Op. 90; it is as though Beethoven had been taking a sabbatical from writing keyboard sonatas. These circumstances pose the question as to which of Beethoven's creative periods does the Op. 90 belong, within the traditionally accepted stylistic division of his music into the three periods, namely, 'early', 'middle' and 'late'. Beethoven authorities are divided on this proposition. Michael Broyles, with others, accepts it is difficult to determine whether Op. 90 belongs to the second or third period but suggests both the Piano Sonatas Op. 90 and Op.106 'draw attention to the gradual stylistic evolution that begins with the *Eroica*'. Barry Cooper proposes the first fruits of Beethoven's revitalised impulse to compose works for the keyboard, found expression in what he describes as 'highly intimate works' such as the Piano Sonata Op. 90, the Sonata for Piano and Cello, Op. 102 and the pioneering through-composed song cycle *An die ferne Gelibte*, Op. 98. Denis Matthews places Op. 90 'on the threshold of Beethoven's third-period style' and, in similar fashion, Maynard Solomon categorises the piece as being 'a transitional work' but one that incorporates 'intimations of late Beethoven' alongside other near contemporaneous compositions such as the Violin Sonata, Op. 96, and the string quartets, Op. 74 and Op. 95.

Op. 90 is one of the composer's more intense and concentrated works with a performing time of less than fifteen minutes. Its expressive musical nature has disposed commentators to believe it displays 'an acute awareness of the inner life and of its quests'. Musicologist Oscar Bie avers: 'It is a work which, like all these last sonatas, is never thought of as a "piece", but stands before us in one transparency, laying bare the innermost fibres of the man.' The music is more romantic than that found in earlier of the composer's piano sonatas and is considered to anticipate the sound-world inhabited by much of the music of Franz Schubert — his *Rondo* in A for Piano Duet, D 951 is one such example.

According to Beethoven's early biographer Anton Schindler, the first movement of Op. 90 is to be regarded as a 'contest' between the head and the heart, and the second movement to be 'a form of dialogue' with a loved one. Today some authorities are inclined to dismiss Schindler's claims on the grounds he is thought to have fabricated many of his assertions to suit his own ends. Others find Schindler's metaphors useful insofar as they capture, in the case of the Op. 90, the essence of the contrasts between the work's two movements. Donald Tovey, for example, states: '[The] whole point of this Sonata lies in the contrast between a movement full of passionate and lonely energy and a movement devoted to the utmost luxuriance of lyric melodies developed in rondo form. Alongside this expressive nature of the composition, Beethoven confronts the would-be performer with considerable technical challenges; several passages, for example require a span of a tenth.

At the period of composition of the Piano Sonata Op. 90, Beethoven was at the apogee of his public fame. This corresponded with the Congress of Vienna that was convened with the eventual defeat of Napoleon Bonaparte. Although now largely overlooked, Beethoven achieved considerable celebrity with his so-called Battle Symphony — *Wellington's Victory* and the Cantata *Der glorreiche Augenblick* — *The Glorious Moment*. He was also in demand to have his likeness taken by such artists as Louis Letronne, Blasius Höfel, Joseph Mähler, and Johann Christoph Heckel. At this time Beethoven was disposed to make greater use of the German language in the presentation of his compositions. Accordingly, in the Op. 90 he heads the first movement *Mit Lebhafttigkeit und durchaus mit Empfindung und Ausdruck* — 'With life/vivacity and with feeling and expression throughout', and the final movement *Nicht zu geschwind und sehr singbar vorgetragen* — 'Not too fast, and to be played very songfully/in a very singable manner'.

In the spring of 1815, Beethoven's publisher Sigmund Anton Steiner announced the forthcoming appearance of the Piano Sonata, Op. 90 in the Viennese press: '[All] connoisseurs and friends of composition will certainly welcome this Sonata as Beethoven has not written anything for piano for quite a while ... [This] new piece does not need appraisal as it does not lack ingenuity, harmony and art so typical of [this composer] of [this] time.'

Beethoven worked on the A major Piano Sonata, Op. 101 in the summer of 1816. At the time he was residing at the spa town of Baden, just south of Vienna, in search of good health — one of his eternal preoccupations. With the Piano Sonata in A major we find Beethoven on the threshold of his last creative period, a period when he was intent on seeking a new style and of enriching his compositions with greater contrapuntal significance. Whilst the compositions of Beethoven's late period may have been perplexing to his contemporaries, they are now considered as being imbued with 'deep inner significance' that sets them apart from his earlier works. With regard to Beethoven's writing for the piano, the last five piano sonatas — with which the Op. 101 commences the series — together with the *Diabelli* Variations and the Bagatelles Op. 126, take piano music to new levels of feeling and intensity of spiritual expression that many would agree have not been surpassed in the history of western music. Collectively, these works have been described as 'one of the pillars of Beethoven's creative achievement of his last years' (Maynard Solomon). We find the composer absorbed by fugal writing and variation form alongside the exploitation of new pianistic sonorities, made possible by technical developments in the extension of the keyboard; for example a low E was now possible. The trill in Beethoven's hands enters the very soul of the music. In the A major Piano Sonata, Beethoven begins a process he will take even further in his last works for the keyboard. He elevates the trill from being a mere decorative ornament, consisting of the rapid alternation of two adjacent notes, to a transcendental, soul-elevating miniature sound world, imbued with feeling and significance.

In his pioneering study *Ludwig van Beethoven Leben und Schaffen* (1859), the German composer, musical theorist and critic Adolph Bernhard Marx was disposed to describe the A major Piano Sonata in the following terms: 'The innermost and most secret stirrings of a tender soul, to whom the desire alone is granted, not its realisation, only the flights of fancy, nor tangible aims or pithy deeds — how difficult is it to catch what it says, and to bring to a light that shall not offend it.' Fellow compatriot Ernst von Elterlein expressed similar thoughts: 'This Sonata ... belongs to those works whose meaning is more-or-less lost in words and can only be suggested.' And for Romain Rolland: 'With this Sonata we reach the third period of Beethoven's works, that in which reflection and philosophy play such a great part.' Nearer to our own time Paul Bekker has likened the A major Piano Sonata to a 'sonata poem' that in part looks back to the Piano Sonata in E-flat major, Op, 27, No. 1 — *quasi una fantasia* — but which has now much evolved in its free, 'fantastic' treatment of sonata form. A possible indicator of Beethoven's evolving disposition to romantically conceived music, may be inferred from a cryptic entry in his

Tagebuch (Diary) of 1816 in which he wrote: 'Only as before again at the piano [to make] my own fantasies — despite my hearing problems.'

At the period of composition of the Piano Sonata Op. 101, Beethoven was anxious to adopt German-language terminology in his music. Accordingly, he wrote to his publisher Sigmund Anton Steiner that he wished the designation *Hammerklavier* to replace *Pianoforte*. When the composition was duly published in February 1817, Steiner struck a compromise. The Title Page announced: '*Sonate pour le PIANO-FORTE — für das HAMERKLAVIER*'. Steiner did, however, adopt the composer's German designations for the work's individual movements; these provide clues to the nature of the composition. Thus, in the first movement, we have *Etwas lebhaft und mit der innigsten Empfindung* ('With innermost feeling'); in the second movement, *Lebhaft, marschmässig* ('Quick, like a march'); in the third movement, *Langsam und sehnsuchtsvoll* ('Slow and full of yearning'); and in the fourth movement, *Geschwind, doch nicht zu sehr, und mit Entschlossenheit* ('Quickly, but not too fast and with decision'). In addition to his promotion of the adoption of the German language, by means of which to convey feeling and expression in music, Beethoven was also becoming interested in the potential of the newly invented metronome. This was then being pioneered in Paris by its co-inventor Johann Mälzel (Maelzel). Beethoven saw the device as a means by which to better convey his intentions with respect to the tempo at which the music should be taken — thereby reducing the scope for its misinterpretation. Beethoven started to supply metronome indications to his scores from this time — it must be said not always consistently and to the continuing perplexity of modern-day interpreters of his music.

We have a description of Beethoven as recollected in the diary of the physician Dr. Karl von Bursy. He paid a visit to the composer in the summer of 1816 and left the following account: 'He is short, but sturdy-looking with grey hair ... and fiery eyes ... full of intense life. He asked me to speak loudly as his hearing is very bad ... He has not been well for some time.' Beethoven told Bursy: 'I always work at several things at once, and take up first one then the other ... He often strikes the piano with his first so violently that the room resounds.' References to the effects of Beethoven's loss of hearing occur throughout his correspondence over the period 1815–17. For instance, in the summer of 1815 he wrote to Johann Xaver Brauchle, a minor composer who was then employed as the tutor to the children of the Countess Anna Maria Erdödy – an accomplished pianist and one of Beethoven's many aristocratic, women-friend admirers. Beethoven confided to Brauchle: 'I am not well ... more sensitive than all other mortals, and tormented by my poor hearing. I often feel only *pain* in the society of others [Beethoven's italics].' Misfortune was to envelope Beethoven twofold when he was awarded the guardianship of his nephew Karl. It proved to be a disaster for Karl, his mother, and significantly for Beethoven. The many months – years – he expended on litigation, to say nothing of Karl's attempted suicide, resulted not only in his loss of composure but also distracted him from his creative work. His failure to complete his Tenth Symphony may be attributable to these harrowing circumstances.

The originality and artistry enshrined within the Op. 101 Piano Sonata were not lost upon the reviewer commissioned to write about the piece in the October 1817 issue of the *Allgemeine musikalische Zeitung*: 'This latest product which *Beethoven* presents to us, delivers us continued proof of his inexhaustible inventiveness, of his profound artistry, of his lively imagination, of his universal genius! ... Truly, here, in his 101st work, we are filled with admiration and renewed high esteem, when we, thus, with the great painter of soul-images, walk along never-tread-on paths, virtually following Ariadne's thread along labyrinth-like trails, where here, a fresh brook might whisper to us and there, we will be faced by a bold rock, where here, a sweet, fragrant flower attracts us and there, a thorny path might frighten us off.' The reviewer concludes: '[This] work of art ... while small in size, is great, truly great in content, and the unassuming shell of which might hide many a jewel.'

Notwithstanding such fulsome praise as the foregoing, we detect a measure of the aloofness, if not downright hostility, to Beethoven's later piano music as conveyed in an account from the writings of Beethoven's early biographer Wilhelm von Lenz. He has this to say of his experience of the reception of the composer's late piano sonatas when he was in Paris in 1828: 'The last five [Opp. 101, 106, 109, 110 and 111] passed for the monstrous abortions of a German idealist who did not know how to write for the piano.' In England, notably in London, Beethoven's chamber works were also being received with caution. We learn this from Charles Neate who had recently been appointed a Director of The Philharmonic Society. Writing to Beethoven in 1816, he explained the difficulty he was having in promoting the composer's two Cello Sonatas Op. 102: 'I have offered your sonatas to several publishers, but they thought them too difficult, and said they would not be saleable.' More optimistically he adds: '[When] I shall have played them to a few professors, their reputation will naturally be increased by their merits.'

Beethoven himself acknowledged his A major Piano Sonata was difficult to perform. Writing of the interpretive challenges posed by the work, Eric Blom suggests: 'There are difficulties demanding brilliant playing ... and the writing has the ingenuity of the completely self-possessed master; but it is due precisely to this self-possession that Beethoven is now able to concentrate his whole creative mind on emotional expression in the most poetical terms of which music is capable.' Acknowledging the technical challenges confronting the would-be performer, Alfred Brendel remarks: '[To] convey [the] sense of security, of happiness, is very hard in pianistic terms ... I would call it the most difficult sonata to play well ... And how much Op. 101, in particular, needs a confident and initiated player.' To assist the pianist to confront the technical challenges of interpreting the Piano Sonata Op. 101, Beethoven's pupil Carl Czerny is cryptic; he urges the performer to be 'quick and resolute'. Donald Tovey, with a touch of sardonic humour — and enjoying a sustained metaphor — likened grappling with the technical challenges posed by the A major Piano Sonata to rock climbing. He comments that the best he can do is to offer the student 'a foothold or hand-hold here and there' and that, despite what he characterises as 'the marvellous progress of modern pianoforte technique',

Whilst on a walk to Mödling in the summer of 1818, Beethoven's pupil Carl Czerny relates Beethoven told him: 'I am writing a sonata now that is going to be my greatest. He was referring to his majestic Piano Sonata in B-flat major, Op.106 *The Hammerklavier.* In this composition Beethoven consciously challenges pianists as he acknowledged when he further remarked, with a touch of irony, 'he was giving them something to do'. Its thirty-page score (or thereabouts) and its 1200 bars (or thereabouts) have a playing time of typically forty-five minutes — twice the length of its immediate predecessor Op. 101 and equal to that of several of the composer's orchestral compositions. Little wonder it has been described as: 'The grandest sonata ever composed, of colossal dimensions, a real giant, symphonically conceived and framed throughout.' Writing in the *Special Issue* of the *Musical Times* (Death Centenary, 1927), the contributor commented: 'The mighty work in B flat, Op. 106, is of course the greatest test of the executant's powers, but it is far more than this, for in it we are brought into contact with one of the greatest of poets, and it is perhaps the most faithful and lifelike of all the portraits of the master's soul.' In his survey of Beethoven's piano sonatas, Edwin Fischer expressed similar feelings: 'In this work, in *one* creation of the spirit, a mortal man has portrayed and sublimated all the facts of life, its rigours, injustices, joys, its heavenly consolations, the temporal and the external, the conceivable and the inconceivable.' In her pioneering study of the composer, Marion Scott considered the contrapuntal devices and intellectual power Beethoven brings forth in this work have the capacity to overwhelm one 'like the statements of an astronomer about the power of the universe'. In his discussion of developments in the history of Western music, the French composer and musicologist André Hodeir asserts that scores such as *The Hammerklavier* Sonata and the String Quartet Op. 127 'constitute a singular event in the course of human thought, a kind of forward leap — one might almost speak of a mutation — which has never occurred in the history of any other civilization'.

Beethoven commenced work on the B-flat major Sonata sometime in November-December of 1817. By April of the following year the first two movements were well in hand with the sonata as a whole being through-composed later in May. With the Piano Sonata Op. 106 Beethoven returned to the traditional four-movement structure. More than this, it is the only sonata since Op. 28 to have the characteristic pattern of a fast movement, a slow movement, a scherzo and finale — although not in that particular order. We also find Beethoven investing traditional musical forms in new guises such as brusque humour, the exploration of modal harmony and the reinvention of the fugue. Through these processes, in the words of Martin Geck: 'Beethoven demonstrated the power of traditional musical techniques to convey emotion. The result, full as it is of technical difficulties, is impressive and as forceful as it is mysterious.'

In the great B-flat Major Sonata, Beethoven confronts the pianist with considerable musicological pedagogy. Through its four movements there are no fewer than forty key changes; except for that of four sharps, every key signature is employed up to six sharps and six flats. Nevertheless Anton Schindler, Beethoven's amanuensis and biographer, records the trouble Beethoven took to ensure his piano writing was 'pianistic' and lay within the capabilities of the performer. That said, the *Hammerklavier* Sonata, alongside the *Diabelli* Variations, remains one of the most technically and emotionally challenging solo works in the piano repertory. It is pre-eminently a 'professional' composition — a work intended for the concert pianist the scale of which, combined with its structural complexity and sustained emotional demands, place it beyond the capabilities of the amateur.

Although the Piano Sonata Op. 101 has a claim to be known as the *Hammerklavier* Sonata, with the passing of time this association has been lost and the expression *Hammerklavier* is now the exclusive preserve of the Piano Sonata Op. 106. Beethoven dedicated it to his patron and benefactor the Archduke Rudolph. Amongst the surviving sketches for the sonata, now preserved in the archives of the Gesellschaft der Musikfreunde in Vienna, is a leaf bearing drafts for a work to celebrate his pupil's birthday titled 'Kantate für Orchester und Chor auf den Text: "Vivat, vivat

Rudolfus".' The declamatory opening chords of the B flat Sonata are considered to have their origins in this projected choral work. From its inception, commentators have likened the rugged grandeur of the B-flat major Piano Sonata to an orchestral composition. Richard Wagner contemplated orchestrating the piece and Felix Weingartner did so; the resulting stilted ponderosity though has won few adherents.

The German (Viennese) edition was duly announced: 'Great Sonata for the *Hammerklavier*. Dedicated to His Imperial Highness and Eminence, the Most Gracious, Most Reverend Archduke Rudolph of Austria, Cardinal and Archbishop of Olmütz ... in deepest reverence by Ludwig van Beethoven. Op. 106.' Simultaneously, Beethoven's publisher Matthias Artaria announced in the *Wiener Zeitung*: 'Now we shall put aside all the usual eulogies which would be superfluous anyway for the admirers of Beethoven's high artistic talent, thereby meeting the composer's wishes at the same time; we note only in a few lines that this work, which excels above all other creations of this master not only through its most rich and grand fantasy but also in regard to artistic perfection and sustained style, will mark a new period in Beethoven's pianoforte works.' The English (London) edition appeared in 1819. Eager to secure his fee (of 26 pounds sterling) Beethoven sanctioned the publication of the Sonata in a variety of forms; this seems almost heretical today given the carefully wrought nature of his creation.

Despite Artaria's enthusiasm, the composition was largely neglected in the composer's lifetime. Beethoven's later music, such as the B flat Sonata, appears to have alienated him from the music fraternity. This can be detected from a review that appeared shortly after his death in an issue of the influential *Allgemeine musikalische Zeitung* for April 1829. The music critic accuses Beethoven of having become 'melancholic and gloomy' as he withdrew more and more from the external world, no longer able to hear his own music. He accuses Beethoven of 'piling idea upon idea' and of 'stretching human capacities to — and at times almost beyond — their limits'. Franz Liszt is usually accorded the honour of giving the first public performance of the Op. 106 Sonata in two recitals he gave in 1836 at the Salle Érard in Paris. Hector Berlioz, in his capacity as a writer on music, recalled the event in the June issue of the *Revue et gazette musicale.* He writes: 'Never, perhaps, has this great artist excited the Parisian world to such a degree'. Berlioz considered Liszt to be an exponent of 'the great modern school of piano-playing'. In support of his contention he enthused: 'I appeal to the judgement of all those who have heard him play the great *Hammerklavier* Sonata, that sublime poem which until now has been the riddle of the Sphinx for almost every pianist.'

It is a measure of the standing in which the B-flat major Piano Sonata is now held that, notwithstanding the formidable challenges it presents to the performer, it has served as a vehicle for the world's greatest pianists to showcase their skills, in much the same way as Shakespeare's most celebrated roles have earned the respect and attention of the leading actors of their day. Donald Tovey described the ending of the B-flat major Piano Sonata as, 'the final cataclysm that brings the great work to an end that seems to sum up all that is noble in man'. Igor Stravinsky declared the Op. 106 'will always be new music'.

Musicologist Oskar Bie likens the last three of Beethoven's thirty-two piano sonatas to 'three flowers [that] bloom in this late garden'. Each of these he maintains is a unique document: 'the "playing" Sonata [Op. 109], the "landscape" Sonata [Op. 110], and the "life" Sonata [Op. 111]'. He adds: 'The first is on the heights of pure technique, the second is a clarified objective picture, the third is pure subjective inwardness.' These three sonatas have also been described as a trilogy insofar as they are complimentary to each other. The present writer recalls the occasion when thee three sonatas were performed in sequence as if they were one long, unfolding piece — a challenge both performer and audience!

Within the composer's newly found warmth of expression, they share conciseness and compression of form as well as imbuing traditional musical processes, such as sonata form, with the medium of the fugue and variation. These compositions reveal a kind of narrative design and directional process across the individual movements in which the finale is the consummation, ultimately reaching what has been describes as 'fulfilment in culminations of lyric euphoria'. Op. 109 'withdraws into an inner world', Op. 110 'ends in euphoric self-immolation', while Op. 111 'surrenders in silence'. In this trilogy Beethoven sets aside the symphonic breadth of the Op. 106 and is content to return to the smaller dimensions of his Opp. 90 and 101.

Edwin Fischer considered the Piano Sonata Op. 109 possessed 'the charm and luminosity of an old sweetheart met again after twenty years, with the same noble features but spiritualized and more transparent'. Following the impassioned *Hammerklavier* Sonata, Marion Scott likens the E major, Op. 109 to a 'heaven of the island of the blest'. With regard to its artistic merit, Donald Tovey pronounced the composition to be 'one of the profoundest things in music'. Alongside its depth of feeling, he believed it manifests an elegiac quality that may reflect, subconsciously or otherwise, the manner in which Beethoven, at the period of its composition, was seeking to find greater order, stability and consolation in his own life, and to endow these same qualities in other compositions to which his mind was also turning, notably, his *Missa Solemnis*. This is also the view of Romain Rolland who felt moved to remark: '[This] Sonata [has] a high place amongst the happiest conceptions of the master.'

The three Piano Sonatas, Opp. 109, 110 and 111 were a response to a commission from the Berlin music publisher Adolph (Adolf) Martin Schlesinger, a founder member of the influential *Berliner Allgemeine musikalische Zeitung*. He requested them in the spring of 1820 — doubtless to enhance the prestige of his business. Beethoven worked on all three between 1820–22, although his progress was impaired by protracted illness. With work on the E major Piano Sonata complete, Beethoven turned his mind to its dedicatee Maximiliane Brentano, the daughter of the wealthy Frankfurt merchant Franz Brentano. Immortality was duly conferred upon Maximiliane when the Piano Sonata in E major, Op. 109 appeared with her name inscribed on the Title Page: 'SONATA/ *für das Pianoforte/ componirt und/ dem Fräulein Maximiliane Bretano/ gewidmet/ von/* LUDVIG van BEETHOVEN./ 109 *Werk*/ No 1088 [Schlesinger] ...'.

Czerny describes the first movement to be 'more like a fantasia, than a sonata' and of the atmosphere prevailing in the music he considered it to have 'a very noble, calm, but dreamy character'. The second movement, marked *Prestissimo*, follows on from the first with scarcely a moment's pause 'with stamping basses and an excited ascending theme ... interpolated with yearning motives'. Commentators are universal in their admiration of Beethoven's achievement in the third movement. This includes one of the composer's most remarkable sets of variations that are praised for their depth and originality of expression. Beethoven constructs six variations on a melody he marks *mezzo voce*, the opening harmonies of which hover in the tenor and bass registers of the keyboard creating an effect 'not sensuous but spiritual, not a caress but a moment of withdrawal of the soul within itself'.

Although persistent ill-health and deafness had made Beethoven a reclusive figure at the period of composition of the Piano Sonata, Op. 109, his reputation was nonetheless high and widespread. By way of illustration of the this, a music critic writing in a contemporary issue of the Stuttgart *Morgenblatt für gebilete Stände* (which then enjoyed a wide circulation) enthused: 'Our Beethoven ... is, we may say, among musicians what Goethe is among poets ... It is impossible to give an adequate description of Beethoven's free, simple, and hermit-like life. He is entirely devoted to art, and his only tribute to society is the fruit of his genius ... It is a gala day when, to his many enthusiastic admirers, he appears with the power and inspiration of an Orpheus.' Beethoven was also mentioned in the 24 July 1820 issue of the *Allgemeine musikalische Zeitung*. He is compared allegorically with the poets of classical antiquity: 'Beethoven descended on a demonic bridge from the Elysian Fields [the Greek mythological heaven to which only the great and good were admitted] into the Cocytus [the Greek river of lamentation] and manipulated the human heart like Arion [Corinthian poet] did on the zither so that all the strings resounded.'

Writing of Beethoven's final achievement in the genre of the piano sonata, musicologist Matthew Rye states: 'By the time of his last three sonatas ... [Beethoven] had turned the medium from what originally had been an early form of home entertainment into a profound, deeply personal statement. All three seem to inhabit a world away from the world, going beyond the mere exploration of pianistic technique to express something inward and introspective in Beethoven's creative personality.'

Eric Blom regarded the Piano Sonata in A-flat major, Op. 110 as being one of the gentlest of Beethoven's creations that, for all its 'dark colour' and 'inexpressible warmth', he likened to 'a summer evening after sunset'; he saw it as following on, but leaving behind, the thunder of Op. 106. This sonata found musicologist Oscar Bie similarly disposed to comment: 'Butterflies and sun-glitter are the accompaniment. A wholesome strength mounts up and cheerfully wings its way. In a pause of meditation it comes to rest; and from the contemplation rises the old eternal lamentation of man.' Like its predecessor, the A-flat major belongs to the lyrical and intimate domain rather than the outwardly expressive bravura of the *Hammerklavier* and the Op. 111 that closes the Opp. 109–111 trilogy. Writing of Beethoven's last three sonatas, the medically qualified musicologist Anton Neumayr comments: 'In these sonatas, we hardly think of compositional technique, but simply purest expression – outbreaks of passion at its most fierce and the most intimate metamorphosis of the soul.' Reflecting on Beethoven's late music piano-music, and the illness with which he had to contend during the period of its composition, Marion Scott comments: 'Nothing rouses a stronger sense of Beethoven's greatness than the nature of the music which he brought with him out of tribulation.' In this context she identifies the Piano Sonata in E major, Op. 109 (1820), the A-flat major, Op. 110 (1821) and the C minor, Op. 111 (1822). Beethoven authority David Wyn Jones cites Beethoven's preoccupation with great works in the opening years of the 1820s, listing the *Missa Solemnis* and the *Diabelli* Variations alongside the last three piano sonatas. He reflects: 'As a creative artist, Beethoven was totally engrossed in the questing musical language of these works, a language that placed the capabilities of the performer and the predilections of the listener aside in favour of the integrity of the compositional process.' The French philosopher turned musicologist Romain Rolland found autobiographical references in the A-flat major Sonata: 'In this sonata, we have as it were a terrible combat against misfortune, then a return to life and hope, not in a calm pious prayer, but in an exultant hymn of joy triumphant.' Rolland also drew attention to the manner in which 'Beethoven has gone a step further in the direction of welding the whole sonata into one piece'. In his modern-day account, Charles Rosen expresses similar views: 'No sonata of Beethoven is more tightly unified by the recurrence of the same or similar motifs throughout the work, and by the clear desire of the composer that the movements succeed each other without a pause. At the same time, no work has movements of such disparate emotional character.'

Beethoven designates the first movement *Moderato cantabile molto espressivo* 'at a moderate speed in a singing style, very expressively'. Writing about the composer's instructions to the performer, Eric Blom makes the observation that Beethoven is more explicit in this respect in his later compositions than in his earlier ones. He reasons: 'The less he was able to hear, it seems, the more anxious he grew to let the player know how his music should sound, not only in the matter of tempo and dynamics, but in that of meaning.' To give added significance to the expressive qualities Beethoven wishes the performer to contribute to his music, he adds the expression *con amabilità* 'with loveableness' at the very opening of the movement. Thereby he wished the music to sound 'amiable' and to reveal 'warmth and depth of feeling'. Carl Dahlhaus finds the lyricism he believes 'shapes and colours' the thematic material in some of the composer's later works, is manifestly evident in the Piano Sonata Op. 110 and Paul Bekker considered 'grace and sensibility dominate the movement' with 'very little dark shading' whose effect 'resembles the dawn of a brilliant day, the course of which is still unknown'. Carl Czerny characterised the movement as being: 'A very lovely piece, and replete with feeling.' Writing in the *Berliner Allgemeine musikalische Zeitung*, not long after the work's composition, Friedrich Bernard Marx remarked: 'The first movement shows what a great composer can make out of the simplest material.'

Beethoven marks the second movement *Molto allegro*, an indication to play the movement 'in a quick, lively tempo — very swift'. Not surprising, therefore, that although not designated as such, the movement has the character of a scherzo. Beethoven in fact identified only one movement of his late piano sonatas with the term *scherzo*, namely the second movement of the *Hammerklavier* Sonata, Op. 106. In the words of Ernst von Elterlein: 'Here we have the quintessence of a playful, frolicsome *scherzo*.' Charles Rosen is in agreement, contending: 'The *scherzo* is humorous, folksy, sometimes brutal, and even sardonic.'

The final movement of Op. 110 is considered to be one of the composer's most original conceptions for the medium of the piano sonata. It is in effect a double movement insofar as it combines two slow and two fast sections of markedly different character and within which cross-references and allusions to each other occur. Here we have passion music — a complex of Baroque forms in which *ariosi* and fugues are interwoven. Musicologist David Dubal invited Alfred Brendel to comment on Beethoven's adoption of fugal writing in the Op. 110, prompting the following response: '[The] complexity of the last two movements of *ariosos* and fugues that return and interlock has Baroque features. Beethoven was not only an innovator in his late years, he also went back to earlier periods of music and took as much as he could from them, transforming the material to serve his purpose.' Beethoven's manner, as expressed in the A-flat major Piano Sonata, disposed Maynard Solomon to reflect more generally on the composer's style and ideals as exemplified in his late period: 'In the late works, his archetypal patterns retain their impress: struggle is sublimated into ecstasy ... chaos strives for lucid formation ... victorious conclusion are incessantly sought after and discovered as in the *Grosse Fuge*, the Piano Sonata Op. 110 and the finale of the Quartet in C-sharp minor, Op. 131.'

In his *Beethoven: A Critical Biography* (1913), the French composer and teacher Vincent d'Indy argued it was Beethoven's adoption of the fugue in his late music that did much to 'revivify the languishing form' and was 'the point of departure of a new system of musical structure' that was, nonetheless, 'solidly based upon classical tradition'. In his survey *A History of Keyboard Literature* (1996), Stewart Gordon singles out the manner in which the fugue in the closing pages of the A-flat major sonata 'undergoes a metamorphosis'. In Phillip Downs' analysis: 'Fugal devices of various kinds ... give way to a concluding, ecstatically manic extension of the fugue subject treated now homophonically as each stretch of endless melody with each cadence becoming the start of the next phrase.' We give the last word here to Donald Tovey: 'Like all Beethoven's visions this fugue absorbs and transcends the world.'

Impressions of Beethoven, as he appeared at the period of composition of the Piano Sonata Op. 110, have been left by a number of his contemporaries; all are poignant. Wilhelmine Schröder-Devrient was a young opera singer who, in 1821, sang the challenging role of Leonora in Beethoven's revised opera *Fidelio* that had not been performed for several years. Beethoven himself insisted on directing the dress rehearsal from which occasion Wilhelmine left the following account: 'Beethoven sat in the orchestra and waved his baton above the heads of us all ... With confusion written on his face, with more than earthly enthusiasm in his eye, swinging his baton to and fro with violent motions, he stood in the midst of the playing musicians and did not hear a single note!' In the years 1820–22, the English statesman Sir John Russell travelled extensively in Europe and published an account of his journeys in *A Tour in Germany and Some of the Southern Provinces of the Austrian Empire.* In this he makes reference to Beethoven's appearance: 'The carelessness of his dress gives him a savage appearance; his features are marked and prominent; his eyes expressive; his hair, which looks as if it had not been touched by comb or scissors for some years, falls over his broad brow in a disorderly mass, being comparable only to the serpents on Medusa's head.' Another pen-portrait of Beethoven derives from a meeting Gioacchino Rossini had with the composer in 1822. Rossini was then being lionised in Vienna through the popularity of his *Il Barbiere di Seviglia.* He describes how he could barely master his emotions as he mounted the stairs to Beethoven's lodgings. He continues: 'When the door opened, I found myself in a sort of attic terribly disordered and dirty ... The portraits of Beethoven which we know, reproduce fairly well his physiognomy. But what no etcher's needle could not express was the indefinable sadness spread over his features — while from under heavy eyebrows his eyes shone as from out of caverns and, though small, seemed to pierce one.'

Writing in *Music and Letters* on the occasion of Beethoven's Death Centenary (1927), the Scottish classical musician and educator Sir John B. McEwan expressed the opinion: 'In the case of the Sonata in A flat, Op. 110 ... it is impossible for the receptive and sympathetic mind not to be moved to reactions which are determined in emotional significance by the musical expression, and which convince by logic far transcending mere intellectual operations.'

Op. 111 is Beethoven's farewell to the pianoforte sonata. Thereafter he confided his innermost thoughts to the medium of what would be his last great string quartets and the *Missa Solemnis*. This sonata is considered by some to be unrivalled in original beauty and 'an inexhaustible well of the purest wonderment, a glittering crown of stars to all who seek after pure musical forms' (Ernst von Elterlein). Eric Blom saw the Piano Sonata in C minor as a summation of the whole experience Beethoven had gathered throughout his quarter-of-a-century preoccupation with the medium. In similar fashion Edwin Fischer found the composer's Op. 111 to be nothing less than 'a summing-up of Beethoven's whole nature, a testament of his spiritual world which left nothing [more] for him to say in the form of the piano sonata'. In his more recent study of Beethoven's piano sonatas, William Kinderman asserts: 'Beethoven's last piano sonata is a monument to his conviction that solutions to the problems facing humanity lie ever within our grasp if they can be recognised for what they are and be confronted by models of human transformation.'

In the Op. 111 Sonata, Beethoven reverts once more to the key of C minor with which so much of his dramatic music is associated. Some have argued, in the context of his writing for the piano, the first movement of the *Pathétique* Sonata, written years previously, provides a distant glimpse of what lay ahead and what is to be found in the first movement of Op. 111. Structurally, like its predecessors Opp. 54, 78 and 90, the C minor is conceived in two movements. In her commentary to Beethoven's adoption of a two-part format, Jane Coup elaborates on the manner in which the ensuing music unfolds in a palette of contrasts: 'The contrasts between the two mammoth foundations [i.e. movements] are striking; fiery allegros versus serene adagios;

tightly-knit sonata form versus exploratory variations; the dark key of C minor versus the tranquil key of C major; compressed fugal writing versus improvisatory wandering; in essence, the concrete world of man versus the ethereal realm of spirituality.' Donald Tovey, with others, has positioned the Piano Sonata Op. 111 alongside the composer's Op. 106 for technical difficulty. Performing artists have long recognised the challenges posed by the work's virtuoso traits such as its semiquaver passages in octaves and rapid climbs and descents over the whole range of the keyboard.

On 27 May 1823, the *Wiener Zeitung* cryptically announced a sonata as 'newly arrived' — taken to be a reference to Beethoven's Op. 111. The German edition was dedicated to the composer's patron the Archduke Rudolph: 'SONATA/pour le/Piano-Forte/Composée *et trés respecteusement Dediée*/à *Son Altesse Impériale Monseigneur*/L'Archduc Rodolphe d'Autriche/*Cardinal Prince Archevêque d'Olmütz etc., etc.*/par' L: van [Louis De] BEETHOVEN/ *Oeuvre 111.*' Eager to earn an additional fee, Beethoven instructed his former pupil Ferdinand Ries to negotiate an English edition with Muzio Clementi's London-based publishing house, Clementi having already brought out the first English editions of the piano sonatas Opp. 78, 79 and 81a. This time the work was dedicated to Antonie (Antonia) Brentano for whom Beethoven had a deep affection. For her part, Antonie revered Beethoven both as a composer and as a man remarking that he walked 'like a God among mortals'. Clementi's Title Page reads: 'GRAND SONATA/Composed for the/Piano Forte/and Dedicated to/Madame Antonia de Brentano/ By/L. v. BEETHOVEN/ ... /London/ Published by Clementi & Co.'

To add to Antonie Brentano's recollections of Beethoven, we have further descriptions of him. In November 1822 Louis Schlösser made Beethoven's acquaintance.

He was then a twenty-two year old musician residing in Vienna receiving instruction in composition from Salieri. Beethoven was living in a relatively poor district of Vienna known as the *Wiedener* suburb. Schlösser describes Beethoven's apartment as being rather undecorated with a large, four-square oak table and various chairs presenting a somewhat untidy aspect. On the table lay books, pens, pencils, music-paper a metronome and an ear trumpet. In another room Schlösser noticed the Broadwood piano that Beethoven had received a few years previously as a personal gift from the English piano maker John Broadwood. Schlösser found Beethoven preoccupied at his writing desk and had to stamp with his feet to secure his attention. He writes of the composer's 'characteristic head' with its 'surrounding mane of heavy hair ... the furrowed brow of a thinker ... profoundly serious eyes ... [and] ... the amiably smiling expression'. Schlösser attempted to convers with the composer using an ear trumpet but Beethoven laid it aside complaining 'it agitated his nerves too greatly'. Conversation between the two continued by Schlösser writing his thoughts on paper — as by then had become Beethoven's custom. Schlösser records how he left the composer feeling 'the day felt like a beautiful dream'.

In the autumn of 1823, Carl Maria von Weber had occasion to visit Beethoven and wrote to his wife of their meeting: '[Beethoven] received me with the most touching affection; he embraced me at least six or seven times in the heartiest fashion, full of enthusiasm ... We spent the noon hour together, very merrily and happily.' Later in life Weber's son Max recalled his father telling him how he had entered a bare, almost poverty-stricken room: 'The chamber was in the greatest disorder. Music, money, articles of clothing lay on the floor ... the grand piano [probably the Broadwood], which was open, was thick with dust'. Weber likened Beethoven in appearance to King Lear: 'His hair was thick, grey and bristly, here and there altogether white ... like in his [later] portraits ... beneath the bushy eyebrows ... small radiant eyes beamed mildly out'. Weber, like Beethoven, was small in stature but he describes how the eminent composer 'towered cyclopean' above him.

Beethoven designates the first movement of the Piano Sonata Op. 111 *Maestoso*, 'stately, dignified and majestic'. With regard to its interpretation, he adds the tempo marking *Allegro con brio ed appassionato*, 'at a fast tempo, with spirit and energetic/expressive'. The opening five bars have been likened to 'a cry of agony' to which Beethoven responds with five further bars where he seems to be looking 'with tender amazement at his own human wretchedness, turning it in his hands as though to discover its meaning'. Alfred Brendel considers the manner of the opening to be one of 'angry revolt' that at the same time provides 'a thematic seed' for the whole sonata. He also finds a parallel 'psychologically and materially' with Schubert's song setting of Heine's *Der Atlas*. The reader will recall Atlas was the Titan who was condemned to bear the burdens of the world upon his shoulders. Brendel's suggestion is doubly appropriate, considering that at the period Beethoven was composing the C minor Sonata, his mind was also occupied with the *Choral* Symphony with its moving evocation of mankind and joy to its millions.

The pervasive atmosphere of the first movement of Op. 111 has captivated audiences from the time of its inception. Writing of the work in the April 1824 edition of the *Allgemeine musikalische Zeitung*, the reviewer commented on the work's 'powerful, passionate impulsiveness that hardly stops for a moment ... and which drives everything restlessly forward'. Beethoven authority Henry Krehbiel adopts loftier imagery: 'With the first movement of this

Sonata [Beethoven] carries us to the theatre in which the last scene in Goethe's *Faust* plays — the higher regions of this sphere, where earth and heaven meet as they seem to do at times in the high Alps.' With regard to interpretation Carl Czerny, probably the first ever to perform the work, writes: 'This first movement of Beethoven's last sonata, belongs to his greatest, and must be performed with all power, bravura and impassioned emotion, which the tragic character, as well as the difficulty of the passages requires.' Edwin Fischer exhorts: 'The first *movement, Maestoso,* should be begun in the grand manner ... something approaching the opening of the Piano Sonata Op. 106.' He invites the performer to regard the music as the embodiment of life's struggle and for its relentless figuration to be 'chiselled out with steely fingers'. We catch a glimpse of how Franz Liszt may have sounded in his performance of the C minor Piano Sonata, in a letter Richard Wagner wrote on 15 February 1857 to the daughter of Princess Wittgenstein: 'Whoever had frequent occasion to hear Liszt play Beethoven ... must surely have always been struck with the fact there was no question here of *re-production*, but of genuine *production.*' [italics added] Although Chopin was not one of Beethoven's foremost champions, it is known he admired the C minor Sonata, passages of which appear to have found expression in his own *Revolutionary Etude*. With passion and fervour spent, Beethoven closes the first movement with a softly expressed ending that he marks *pp* — *pianissimo*. Thereby, in Barry Cooper's words, the ending 'prepares the ear for the serenity of the *Arietta*' that is to follow and thereby 'we now enter a new world — one of inner, spiritual contemplation'.

As a guide to the interpretation of the second movement, Beethoven writes at the head of the score *Adagio molto semplice e cantabile*, 'slowly, very simply and songlike'.

Charles Rosen argues this is not a description of the music but a direction to the performer to bear in mind that 'simplicity is necessary to bring out what is already there'. The second movement disposed the critic of the *Berliner Allgemeine musikalische Zeitung* to view the music as 'a most extraordinary vision'. He interpreted it as representing the death of a great man. Adopting imagery typical of the period, he proclaimed: 'Do not the harmonies of the theme swell like the music of a distant funeral procession echoing through the night? And in the second part we hear the sounds of the grave. Then the pall-bearers in long veils and friends, the friends weeping quietly come nearer and nearer ... I hear through the pealing bells the last heavy breathing of the dying man.' Later nineteenth-century commentators were no less fulsome in their estimation of the depth of feeling Beethoven invested in the C minor Piano Sonata. Friedrich Bernard Marx speaks of the composition 'as a theme of deep feeling, overflowing with tender, profound melancholy, developed with the utmost regularity but with ever increasing richness, now subdued, now pleasantly stirred, but returning to the elegiac primary tone of feeling, then rousing up with new courage'. He elaborates: 'It seems as if we had an echo from the loftiest ideal and spiritual regions, the language, which is simply untranslatable into words, of the soul soaring to the heavenly regions with fervent and holy rapture.' From Cosima Wagner's Diary of 25 September 1877, we gain an insight into her husband's estimation of the composition: 'R. says that were he to try to visualize Beethoven "in all his starry glory", he would surely think of the second movement of Op. 111 (*Adagio* with variations); he knows nothing more ecstatic, he says, yet at the same time it is never sentimental.'

The variations to which Wagner makes reference have been described as unfolding in a sequence of transformations that elevate the music to 'a higher plane of consciousness'. In the Piano Sonata Op. 109, Beethoven had established a precedent for the adoption of the variation form to close a final movement. In the C minor Sonata he extends this principle even further. In his estimation of Beethoven's achievement, Henry Krehbiel invokes imagery once more from Goethe's *Faust*: '[We] hear the song of *Pater Profundis*, and thence we begin the ascent to the celestial realms above. The variations are the songs of the *Pater Ecstaticus, Blessed Boys, Penitents* and *Angels*, who soar higher and higher, carrying with them the immortal soul of *Faust*.' For the British music critic Samuel Langford, the variations that draw the C minor Piano Sonata to a close, were the embodiment of perfection: 'The final variations approach so nearly to a mechanical perfection that the contemplation of its neatness almost brings a shudder ... where shall we find music more divinely separated from the mechanical than in those first variations? ... Those various transitions and ranges of emotions for the height and parallel of which we could go nowhere in poetry but to the *Paradiso* of Dante.'

The coda that finally draws the sonata to a close emanates from the variations and assumes an identity of its own in which Beethoven makes unprecedented use of the trill. In Philip Radcliffe's estimation, the trills and shimmering demisemiquavers elevate the music 'to the empyrean' — the highest heaven in ancient cosmologies occupied by the element of fire. Beethoven gives us 'ethereal textures that music had never known before' and 'time seems to stand still'.

Of Beethoven's final achievement in the genre of the piano sonata, Eric Blom commented: 'To write about this farewell to the sonata for the piano is to come as near an attempt at describing the indescribable as anyone can possible be faced with.'

We take leave of the composer by recalling an incident in his life shortly after publication of the Piano Sonata in C minor, Op. 111. On 24 February 1824, twenty-eight signatories sent the composer a fulsome letter expressing their esteem of him and his works. The signatories included several of the composer's publishers, Carl Czerny (Beethoven's former piano pupil and pianistic pedagogue), Anton Diabelli (composer and music publisher), Prince Eduard and Count Moritz Lichnowsky (respectively nephew and brother of Prince Carl Lichnowsky (Beethoven's friend and patron), and Andreas Streicher (piano manufacturer and long-time friend of Beethoven). Collectively, Beethoven's devotees remark: 'Out of the wide circle of reverent admirers that surround your genius in your native city, a small number of disciples and lovers of art approach you today to express long-felt wishes.' They place him on a level with Haydn and Mozart and affirm: 'Beethoven's name and his creations belong to all contemporaneous humanity and every country that opens a sensitive heart to art.'

TMR

EDITORIAL PRINCIPLES

By its very nature a study of this kind draws extensively on the work of others. Every effort has been made to acknowledge this in the text by indicating words quoted or adapted with single quotation marks. Wherever possible, for the sake of consistency, I have retained the orthography of quoted texts making only occasional silent changes of spelling and capitalization. Deleted words are identified by means of three ellipsis points ... and interpolations are encompassed within square brackets [ ]. Quoted words, phrases and longer cited passages of text remain the intellectual property of their copyright holders.

I address the reader in the second person notwithstanding that the work is my own. It follows that I must bear the responsibility for any errors of misunderstanding or misinterpretation for which I ask the reader's forbearance. A collaboration I must acknowledge is the help I received from the librarians of the Reid Music Library at the University of Edinburgh. Over the three-year period it took me to compile my reference sources, they served me with unfailing courtesy, often supplying me with twenty or more books at a time. In converting my manuscript into book format, I wish to thank my editorial coordinator, William Rees, for his support and painstaking care. I would also like to thank Shaun Russell for his work designing the cover for each of the nine volumes.

My admiration for Beethoven provided the initial impulse to commence this undertaking and has sustained me over the several years it has taken to bring my enterprise to completion. That said, I am no Beethoven idolater. I am mindful of the danger that awaits one who ventures to chronicle the work of a great artist. I believe it was Sigmund Freud who suggested that biographers may become so disposed to their subject, and their emotional involvement with their hero, that their work becomes an exercise in idealisation. In response to such a charge let me say. First, I am no biographer. I do however make occasional reference to Beethoven's personal life and his relationships with his contemporaries. Second, I acknowledge Beethoven has his detractors. Accordingly, I have not shrunk from allowing dissentient voices, critical of Beethoven and his work, to be heard. These, however, are few and are silenced amidst the adulation that awaits the reader in support of the endeavours of one of humanity's great creators and one who courageously showed the way in overcoming personal adversity.

TMR

BEETHOVEN'S FINANCIAL TRANSACTIONS

Beethoven's negotiations with his music publishers make many references to his compositions. Today they are recognised for what they are — enduring works of art — but referred to in his business correspondence they appear almost as though they were mere everyday commodities — for which he required an appropriate remuneration. Beethoven resented the time he had to devote to the business-side of his affairs. He believed an agency should exist, for fellow artists such as himself, from which a reasonable sum could be paid for the work (composition) submitted, leaving more time for creative enterprises. In the event Beethoven, like Mozart before him, had to deal with publishers largely on his own. Beethoven, though, did benefit in his business dealings from the help he received from his younger brother Kasper Karl (Caspar Carl). From

1800, Carl worked as a clerk in Vienna's Department of Finance in which capacity he found time to correspond with publishers to offer his brother's works for sale and — importantly — to secure the best prices he could. In April 1802 Beethoven wrote to the Leipzig publishers Breitkopf & Härtel: '[You] can rely entirely on my brother who, in general, attends to my affairs.' Whilst Carl promoted Beethoven's interests with determination, he appears to have lacked tact and made enemies. For example, Beethoven's piano pupil Ferdinand Ries — who for a while also helped the composer with his business negotiations — is on record as describing Carl as being 'the biggest skinflint in the world'. The currencies most referred to in Beethoven's correspondence are as follows:

- silver gulden and florin: these were interchangeable and had a value of about two English/British shillings
- ducat: 4 1/2 gulden/florins: valued at about nine shillings
- louis d'or: This gold coin was adopted during the Napoleonic wars and the French occupation of Vienna and Austria more widely. It had a value of about two ducats or approximately twenty shillings or one-pound sterling.

Beethoven was never poor — in the romantic sense of 'an artist starving in a garret'. On arriving in Vienna in 1792, he was fortunate to receive financial support from his patron Prince Karl Lichnowsky who conferred on him an annuity of 600 florins that he maintained for several years. Between the months of February and July of 1796, Beethoven undertook a concert tour taking in Prague, Dresden, Leipzig and Berlin. He was well received and wrote to his other younger brother Nikolaus Johann: 'My art is winning me friends and what more do I want? ... I shall make a good deal of money.' Later on, in 1809, Napoleon Bonaparte's youngest brother Jérôme Bonaparte offered Beethoven an appointment at his Court with the promise of an income of 4,000 florins. Alarmed at the prospect of losing Beethoven — now the most celebrated composer in Europe — three of Vienna's most notable citizens, namely, the Archduke Rudolph (Beethoven's only composition pupil), Prince Kinsky and Prince Lobkowitz settled on the composer the same sum of 4,000 florins. Inflation, however, brought about by the Napoleonic wars, soon eroded its value; personal misfortune to Lobkowitz and Kinsky also took its toll.

Beethoven undoubtedly had to work hard to secure a reasonable standard of living. Notwithstanding, despite his occasional straitened circumstances, he contributed generously to the needs of others. For example, he allowed his works to be performed free of charge at charitable concerts; in 1815 his philanthropy earned for him the honour of Bürgerrecht — 'freedom of the City'.

Beethoven earned a great deal of money when his music was performed, to considerable acclaim, at several concerts held in association with the Congress of Vienna (1814-15). He did not though benefit from it personally; he invested it on behalf of his nephew Karl. It is one of the misfortunes of Beethoven's life that in money-matters he was culpably improvident. This is poignantly evident in a letter he wrote on 18 March 1827 to the Philharmonic Society of London just one week before his death; the Society had made him a gift of £100. He sent the Society 'his most heartfelt thanks for their particular sympathy and support'.

TMR

'We must take art as it is given to us, with such limitations and even defects as it may show. No work is quite flawless, if it comes to that, and without limitations is unthinkable, as it is undesirable without artificialities ... [It] is for us to accept great works as their creators meant them, and believe in them as they are. That is what distinguishes them from small, casual art.'

Eric Blom, *Beethoven's pianoforte sonatas discussed*, 1938.

PIANO SONATA IN E MINOR, OP. 90

'The two sonatas Op. 90 and 111 ... are tone poems, and the master having apparently said all that he had to say, stopped.'

John South Shedlock, *Beethoven's Pianoforte Sonatas: the Origin and Respective Values of Various Readings*, 1918, p. 174.

'[Op. 90] with its motivic concentration on the main idea in the first movement and its lyrical finale that extends to a "heavenly length" in Schubertian fashion, is quite as subtle and original in its way as Op. 78 or 81a.'

William S. Newman, *The Sonata in the Classic Era*, 1963, p. 526.

'It is a work which, like all these last sonatas, is never thought of as a "piece", but stands before us in one transparency, laying bare the innermost fibres of the man.'

Oskar Bie, *A History of the Pianoforte and Pianoforte Players*, 1966, p. 17.

'The sonata as a whole has something in common with Opus 111. The first movement is about human struggle. And the second movement has a lot to do with the sadness of farewell.'

Claudio Arrau in: *Joseph Horowitz, Conversations with Arrau*, 1982, p. 168.

'[Its] two movements, E minor and E major, make an unusually satisfying whole: Hans von Bülow likened their contrast to speech and song, while others have suggested prose and poetry.'

Denis Matthews, *Beethoven*, 1985, pp. 93–4.

'[Although] Op. 90 is short, it shows the direction the composer's writing is to take, one that is borne of acute awareness of the inner life and of its quests. Expressive values in the music are placed in ever-increasing control over all other aspects.'

Stewart Gordon, *A History of Keyboard Literature: Music for the Piano and its Forerunners*, 1996, p. 180.

'[The] whole point of this sonata lies in the contrast between a movement full of passionate

and lonely energy and a movement devoted to
the utmost luxuriance of lyric melodies developed in rondo form.'

Donald Francis Tovey, *A companion to Beethoven's pianoforte sonatas*, revised by Barry Cooper, *Piano Sonata Op. 90*, [1931], 1998, p. 198.

'The E minor Piano Sonata, Op. 90, resembles
the middle-period piano sonatas in being highly
dramatic; it differs from them in being concentrated rather than expansive, and in using themes
which combine trenchancy with a *song-like lyricism*.'

Jeremy Dibble, *Charles Villiers Stanford: Man and Musician*, 2002, p. 648.

Three years elapsed before Beethoven returned to the medium of piano-sonata composition, since, that is, Muzio Clementi's publication of his Piano Sonata Op. 81a in London in February 1811 — and a further year would pass before the completion and publication of the Piano Sonata in E minor, Op. 90. It is as though Beethoven had been 'taking a sabbatical from writing keyboard sonatas' and the composer's compositional silence applied also to the writing of string quartets. When we recall that Beethoven had completed the Op. 81a Piano Sonata in late 1809, the time-interval between that work and his new creation, the Piano Sonata Op. 90, is even greater.

These circumstances pose the question as to which of Beethoven's creative periods does the Op. 90 belong? — within the traditionally accepted stylistic division of his music into the three periods, 'early', 'middle' and 'late' or 'first', 'second' and 'third'. Beethoven scholars and authorities are divided on this proposition. Michael Broyles, with others, accepts it is difficult to determine whether Op. 90 belongs to the second or third period but suggests both the Piano Sonatas Op. 90 and Op.106 'draw attention to the gradual stylistic evolution that begins with the *Eroica*'. He further observes how the E minor Sonata's style, with its 'emphasis upon declamatory rhetoric and individual expression', is more akin to what he describes as 'Beethoven's post-*Eroica* approach.[ii] In defining the boundaries between Beethoven's musical periods, Barry Cooper draws attention to the consequences of the composer's depression, promoted by the realization of his unrequited love, the further deterioration to his hearing and his enforced withdrawal from society. Cooper proposes the first fruits of Beethoven's revitalised impulse to compose found expression in what he describes as 'highly intimate works' such as the Piano Sonata Op. 90, the Sonata for Piano and Cello, Op. 102 and the pioneering through-composed song cycle *An die ferne Gelibte*, Op. 98. He also cites the manner in which the two-movement structure of Op. 90 foreshadows that of the composer's last Piano Sonata, Op. 111 – implying the extent to which the E minor Piano Sonata possesses an inclination to Beethoven's final period.[iii] Denis Matthews places Op. 90 'on the threshold of Beethoven's third-period style'[iv] and, in similar fashion, Maynard Solomon categorises the piece as being 'a transitional work' but one that incorporates 'intimations of late Beethoven' alongside other near contemporaneous compositions such as the Violin Sonata, Op. 96, and the string quartets, Op. 74 and Op. 95.[v] When musicologist David Dubal invited Alfred Brendel to consider the Op. 90 as an 'inaugural work' that prepares for the composer's third period, Brendel, quite independently of Solomon, responded in the same manner: 'It is one of the pieces that prepares for the period. I would also like to mention the Op 74 Quartet and the F minor Quartet, Op. 95.'[vi] Matthew Rye is unequivocal: 'Although Beethoven had written nothing for the piano for the last five years, the Sonata, Op. 90 (1814), has more kinship with the last group of masterpieces written between 1816 and 1822 (Opp. 101, 106, 109, 110 and 111) than to earlier works in the cycle.'[vii]

To take our discussion further, we recall how Beethoven once remarked to the English pianist and composer Charles Neate that 'he never worked without having a picture in mind' (Piano Sonata Op. 2, No. 1).[viii] This remark is relevant to our present discussion since it is alleged (we shall discuss the origins of the allegation shortly) that the Piano Sonata Op. 90, like its precursor the Op. 81a, has a programmatic basis. Within this scheme of things, the first movement of Op. 90 is to be regarded as a 'contest' between the head and the heart, and the second movement to be a form of 'dialogue' with a loved one. To shed light on these suggestions, and their implications for the music, we must briefly reflect on Beethoven's connections with the Lichnowsky family.

We have seen previously (Piano Sonatas Op. 2, Nos. 1–3) that Prince Karl Lichnowsky had been one of Beethoven's most generous patrons; shortly after the young composer had arrived in Vienna, he had conferred upon him an annual stipend of 600 florins. Karl died on 15 April 1814 without ever being reconciled with Beethoven after their falling out – see Piano Sonata Op. 57. Lichnowsky's wife the Countess Maria – an accomplished pianist – was also well disposed to Beethoven and did much to persuade him at the period we have under consideration, to revise his Opera *Fidelio*.[ix] Moreover, the Count's sister, Countess Henriette, also fell under Beethoven's spell and duly received the dedication to the composer's Rondo in G, Op.

51, No. 2. But it is to the Count's younger Brother, Count Moritz Lichnowsky, to whom we need to direct our attention.

Moritz Lichnowsky, like his older brother, had studied with Mozart and became not only one of Beethoven's patrons but also one of his staunchest friends. Born in 1771 he was therefore an exact contemporary of Beethoven, and their close proximity in age may have contributed to the bonds of friendship that lasted until the composer's death — Moritz lived another ten years after Beethoven. An early expression of Beethoven's feeling for the young Count is discerned in a letter he wrote on 8 April 1803 to his publisher Breitkopf & Härtel stating: '[You] would do me a great kindness if on the grand variations [Op. 35] you would omit entirely the *dedication to the Abbé Stadler* and insert instead this dedication which I am now quoting, namely: *Dediées etc. A Monsieur le Comte Lichnowsky.* He is the brother of Prince Lichnowsky and only recently did me an unexpected kindness; and at the moment I have no other opportunity of doing something to please him.'[x] Ten years later we find Beethoven writing (21 September 1814) in similarly effusive terms, this time to Moritz Lichnowsky himself. He first thanked the Count for 'always showering kindnesses upon him' and then remarks: 'I am now telling you that a *sonata* of mine [Op. 90] will soon appear *and that it is dedicated to you* [Beethoven's italics].' He adds: 'I wanted to give you a surprise, although this dedication has been intended for you for a very long time. But your letter yesterday has made me disclose this to you now.'[xi] It is possible that the dedication Beethoven was planning was connected with some financial recognition he was hoping to receive from the British for his patriotic *Wellington's Sieg* (*Wellington's Victory*) — in which the Count may have played a part.[xii]

We turn now to the circumstances that have led to the

two movements of the Op. 90 Piano Sonata being characterised, respectively, as a contest between the head and heart (first movement) and a form of dialogue with a loved one (second movement). Moritz Lichnowsky had a relationship with a singer-actress by the name of Josepha (Johanna) Stummer; she is frequently, and mistakenly, described as being a dancer. Johanna was not of noble birth but must have been a singer of some accomplishments; for example, she sang the role of Donna Elvira in Mozart's *Don Giovanni* and was a member of the Gesellschaft der Musikfreunde. In 1814 Johanna bore Moritz a child whilst his wife, the Countess Maria Castiglione-Faleta, was still alive. Following the death of the Countess, the two subsequently married (1820) — contrary to the family's wishes; Johanna was considered as being beneath the Counts station.[xiii]

Beethoven's biographer Anton Schindler alleges that, with the dedication of the Op 90 Piano Sonata to his friend in mind, Beethoven offered to explain to the Count the 'inner significance' of the music. Schindler claims Beethoven had set the Count's love-story to music and that the two movements could be described as: 'Conflict between head and heart' [Moritz wrestling with his uncertainty] and 'Conversations with the Beloved' [Moritz and Johanna united in their mutual affections].'[xiv] Thereby, Schindler set in motion a body of programmatic interpretation, bearing on the alleged inner meaning of the E minor Piano Sonata, that endured throughout the nineteenth century and beyond.

Today, authorities are inclined to dismiss Schindler's claims on the grounds he is thought to have fabricated the story to suit his own ends — much as he did in connection with his 'read Shakespeare' allegations in connection with the 'meaning' of the *Tempest* Sonata (see Piano Sonata Op. 31, No. 2). Beethoven's early biographer Adolph Bernhard Marx is one of many who harboured suspicions regarding the veracity of Schindler's anecdote, dismissing it at best as a Beethoven joke, 'for it gave no clue to the meaning of the composition'.[xv] Similar doubts also lingered in the mind of musicologist John Fuller-Maitland. Writing on the occasion of Beethoven's Death Centenary he commented: 'I have always wondered what authority there is for the story [i.e. Schindler's anecdote] printed in the "Pop" programme whenever Op. 90, in E minor was played in St. James's Hall.'[xvi] 'Pop' concerts were held regularly on Mondays and Saturdays and, in the words of George Bernard Shaw, 'contributed greatly to the spread and enlightenment of musical taste in England'.

Whatever the truth or otherwise of Schindler's allegations, we have, as William Kinderman has averred, a metaphor 'that draws attention to the contrasting relationship of the paired movements of Op. 90'.[xvii] A hundred years ago, long before Schindler's falsifications had come to light, John Shedlock deciphered Beethoven's intentions in purely musical terms: 'It seems as if [Beethoven] were merely intent on exhibiting strong contrast of mood: agitation and repose, or fierce passion followed by heavenly calm.'[xviii] We give the last words on this aspect of the composition to the eloquence of Eric Blom: 'Lichnowsky's love affair is now a matter of supreme unimportance, and almost as much so are Beethoven's jokes; all that matters is that we have here two wonderfully contrasted movements which do suggest, in a way applicable to mankind at large, some sort of passionate quest attended by a satisfying discovery, some agitating problem followed by a calming solution.'[xix]

We turn next in our consideration of the origins of the Op. 90 Piano Sonata, to circumstances relating to Beethoven's brother Caspar Karl (Carl) and their bearing on how the composition came into being. The reader may recall that from about 1802, until his marriage a few years later, Carl had been assisting his brother with his business negotiations with publishers. Beethoven had written: 'You can rely entirely on my *brother* [Beethoven's italics] – who, in general, attends to my affairs' (Piano Sonata Op. 31, Nos. 1–3). The intervening years had not been kind to Carl though and in 1812 the tuberculosis that he had contracted worsened. Beethoven, as we have seen, often had a troubled relationship with Carl. Although Carl had promoted Beethoven's interests with diligence, he did not always employ the best of tact. Notwithstanding, with the onset of his illness, Beethoven rallied to the support of Carl and his family as we can infer from a letter he wrote to Princess Karoline Kinsky, the wife of the composer's Patron Prince Kinsky who had recently died as a result of a riding accident on 3 November 1812. Beethoven was concerned about the cessation of payments to his Annuity, and the consequences it was having upon his financial circumstances. On 13 February 1813 he explained: 'I have to support entirely an unfortunate sick brother with his family.'[xx]

From Beethoven's correspondence at this time we learn something of his own health – that was ever of concern to him. On 28 February 1812 he complained to his publisher Breitkopf & Härtel: 'My health has again been frequently exposed to some very fierce attacks; and the winter in Vienna destroys nearly all the good which summer usually brings.'[xxi] On 9 August he wrote once more to Breitkopf & Härtel describing the rigours of hydrotherapy: 'My doctor chases me from one spot to another to enable me finally to recover good health ... Hardly have I performed the duty of filling my inside with a large quantity of this water when again I must have my outer surface washed down with it several times.'[xxii] On this occasion Beethoven met the poet Goethe for a second time; we have remarked previously the two had shared each other's company at the spa town of Teplitz (see

Piano Sonata Op. 81a). Beethoven was far from being in awe of the great man of letters and disapproved of his courtly demeanour. He could not help remarking: 'Goethe delights far too much in the court atmosphere, far more than is becoming to a poet.'[xxiii] The following year Beethoven was once more in Baden for reasons of his health and on 27 May he shared his thoughts with his pupil the Archduke Rudolph. He says his consolation is the fine weather: 'Baden ... is still very empty so far as people are concerned; but all the more fully and lavishly is Nature decked out in her profusion of and ravishing beauty'; there are hints here of the *Pastoral* Symphony and 'awakening of cheerful feelings upon arrival in the countryside'.

At the same time that Beethoven was assisting Carl and his wife Johanna, he became on friendly terms with the music publisher Sigmund Anton Steiner. In 1812, Steiner established a publishing firm in Vienna and shortly afterwards went into partnership with the art and music dealer Tobias Haslinger – with whom Beethoven was to enjoy a warm an extended relationship. To assist Beethoven with his brother's needs, Steiner made a loan to him of 1500 florins that was quite a considerable sum – the equivalent of the composer's annual Annuity payments from his patrons. Beethoven was in effect a bondsman to his brother's debt and assumed responsibility for discharging the loan. He did so in a novel way. He agreed to provide Steiner with a new piano sonata for his own use – i.e. profit – for a period of three months, together with granting his firm the first option on a selection of his future compositions. The piano sonata in question was the E minor, Op. 90.[xxiv]

Doubtless Steiner was eager to accept Beethoven's terms in order to progress his firm's business and, not least, to have Vienna's most celebrated composer on his books. Steiner's move was shrewd and profitable. He established a ten-year working relationship with Beethoven, virtually supplanting the composer's former publisher Breitkopf & Härtel, and, in the years coming, brought out all his major compositions in the sequence Op. 90 – Op. 117.[xxv]

Before moving on with our discussion of the Op. 90 Piano Sonata we should take leave of Casper Carl. Believing his days to be numbered, he made Beethoven the co-guardian of his son Karl, and thereby set in motion a series of events that would cast a shadow over the composer that would prove to be almost as debilitating as his deafness and would distract him for months on end from active composition.[xxvi] We reserve reference to these matters for our later discussion of Beethoven's last group of piano sonatas. Carl did in fact pass away on 15 November 1815 and he thereby disappears from our narrative.

Sketches for the E minor Piano Sonata are preserved in the so-called Dessauer Sketchbook. This consists of 82 leaves and was used by Beethoven between March and September of 1814. It was originally owned by the Bohemian composer and collector Josef Dessauer (1798–1876) from whom its name derives. He purchased it when Beethoven's effects were auctioned on 5 November 1827 following his death. In the composer's Birth-Centennial year (1870), Dessauer bequeathed his collection of Beethoven manuscripts, including the sketchbook, to the Gesellschaft der Musikfreunde where it is preserved today in a handsome protective black cover. The Dessauer Sketchbook contains compositional drafts for the first movement of the Op. 90 Piano Sonata at pp. 128–31 and p. 137 and for the second movement at pp. 132–33 and pp. 137–38. It also incorporates studies for revisions to the Opera *Fidelio*, Op. 90 and sketches for the Overture *Namensfeir*, Op. 115.[xxvii] [xxviii]

After completing the sonata sometime in 1814, Beethoven gave the autograph to his friend, patron and composition student the Archduke Rudolf, the inference being that he was not interested in publishing the piece write away.[xxix] However, later on in September, with the work's impending publication in mind, he wrote to the Archduke requesting his manuscript back: 'Since I *must* [Beethoven's italics] publish it.' He reassured his pupil it would not be necessary to have a copy made 'for in a short time I shall have the pleasure of sending you [as was his custom] an engraved copy'.[xxx] It is perhaps a measure of Rudolf's diligence that he could not wait for the composition to be published, and so he promptly set about making a copy of the manuscript dating its completion 16 August 1814. For many years it was just one of several treasures in the Archduke's Library (the *Rudolphinische Bibliothek*) before it, and the entire collection, was subsequently donated to the Gesellschaft der Musikfreunde.[xxxi] Beethoven assisted in the preparation of the autograph that was required to be copied by the engraver. He sometimes adopted his personal system of inserting abbreviations into the text where passages were to be repeated; for example he used a wavy line to indicate these combined with the instruction *come sopra* — 'as previously'.[xxxii]

In the spring of 1815, Steiner, as was the custom of the day, promptly announced the forthcoming appearance of the Op. 90 Piano Sonata in the Viennese press.[xxxiii] Doubtless he was motivated to get the work into print as soon as possible, in part to help his new business enterprise along but also to have the musically inclined public be aware that he was now bringing out the works of the Imperial City's most distinguished composer. In his announcement of the new sonata, Steiner virtually provided his own, albeit brief, review of the work: '[All] connoisseurs and friends of composition will certainly welcome this sonata as Beethoven has not written anything for piano for quite a while.' He continues; '[This] new piece does not need appraisal as it does not lack ingenuity, harmony and art so typical of [this composer] of [this] time.'[xxxiv]

On 1 February 1815 Beethoven began what was in effect his first business transactions with his new publisher; he negotiated the sale of pianoforte arrangements of his Seventh and Eighth Symphonies.[xxxv] The manuscript of the Op. 90 Piano Sonata was now evidently in Steiner's possession, since Beethoven requested its temporary return on 21 March at the request of his pupil the Archduke Rudolf; perhaps Rudolf wanted to correct the copy he had made of the composition the previous year?[xxxvi] However, Beethoven soon requested it back to facilitate his own proof reading.[xxxvii] These circumstances serve to remind us of the demands imposed on Beethoven by the business side of his creative work — and their implications for his finances. To underline the point, we pause here for a moment in our discussion and give typical illustrations of the costs Beethoven incurred in bringing his works into being, i.e. converting his manuscript-texts into fair-copy to be ready either for performance or for submission to his publishers.

We learn something of the costs of copying from a letter Beethoven's received from his copyist Wenzel Schlemmer (see Piano Sonata Op. 53); Schlemmer wrote this on 28 February 1814. He sent Beethoven a bill for copying out some of the orchestral parts for his Seventh and Eighth Symphonies that had been performed at Beethoven's benefit concert held on 24 February in Vienna's Grosser Redoutensaal — the first occasion the Eighth Symphony had been performed. On this occasion Schlemmer copied out 452 sheets at 12 kreuzer per sheet; that worked out at 90 florins and 24 kreuzer.[xxxviii] Later in the year, on 30 November, Schlemmer sent a further bill for copying out the score — orchestral and vocal parts — for the Cantata *Der glorreiche*

Augenblick (see below). This entailed copying 1, 468 full sheets at 15 kreuzer per sheet, a total cost to the composer of 367 florins and 7 kreuzer. Schlemmer had now raised his charges to 15 kreuzer per sheet, doubtless in recognition of the added work entailed in copying out the full-score parts.[xxxix] We can infer what these Viennese money-values of the day meant to Beethoven from two of his more or less contemporaneous letters. Sometime in late February 1812, Beethoven requested his friend Nikolaus Zmeskall to purchase for him a repeater pocket watch for which he was prepared to pay 40 ducats — about 160 florins (compare this with the 90 florins for Schlemmer's first bill). And from a letter dated 21 September 1813, we know Beethoven was paying a manservant about 25 florins a month.[xl] We know also when Beethoven was away from Vienna taking the water-cures at Baden, the cost to him of hiring a piano was 34 florins a month.[xli] Beethoven clearly needed all the income he could earn but, as we shall shortly remark, his financial fortunes were about to improve — very considerably.

A letter of Beethoven's of 20 May reveals how involved he was becoming with Steiner and of his growing recognition overseas. He requested the return of the manuscript of his Seventh Symphony, Op. 92 and his String Quartet, Op. 95 explaining: 'Some foreigners have turned up here [unidentified]; and I can't refuse to let them see some of my recent compositions.'[xlii] In the same month (29 May) Anton Diabelli, who was now working for Steiner as his proof reader, had discovered several errors in the engraving of the Op. 90 Sonata, prompting Beethoven to request the return of his autograph so that he could make the required corrections.[xliii]

On 27 June Beethoven confirmed with Steiner that he had listed the errors necessary for the correction of the copperplate engraving of the work and that he had handed these to Steiner's business partner Tobias Haslinger. Errors had occurred in the misinterpretation of Beethoven's abbreviations, despite Diabelli's valiant endeavours to obviate these; Diabelli was a sharp-eyed proof reader whose vigilance even intimidated his colleagues. In his amusing way, Beethoven remarks in his covering letter that if there are any more such mistakes the publishers will be severely punished! Beethoven adopted quasi military-terms when negotiating with Steiner. He appointed himself as 'Generalissimo in Thunder and Lightening' and Anton Diabelli as 'Chief Provost Marshal Diabolus Diabelli'. Steiner was accorded the status of 'Lieutenant General' and his partner Haslinger was designated his 'Adjutant'. In due course Diabelli would become a publisher in his own right and earn immortality by being the instigator of Beethoven's majestic, so-called, *Diabelli Variations* Op. 120.[xliv]

The Piano Sonata E minor, Op. 90 duly appeared in June 1815 as: *'Sonate für das Pianoforte, gewidmet dem Hochgebornen Herrn Grafen Moritz von Lichnowsky, von Ludwig van Beethoven. Eigenthum des Verlegers, Wien bei S. A. Steiner.'* The cover bears Steiner's Catalogue No. 2350 with the price marked at *3f* — 3 florins?[xlv] A further edition was published by Nikolaus Simrock of Bonn that bears the same announcement, the price being indicated this time as '3 Francs'.[xlvi] This was the first appearance on the Title Page of a composition by Beethoven presented in the German language, including *Ludwig* instead of the French adaptation *Louis*. This was testimony to Beethoven's wish to promote his music styled in his mother tongue — to which we make further reference shortly. An English edition of the Op. 90 Piano Sonata later appeared from the London printing house of Muzio Clementi, consistent with his earlier pioneering of the composer's piano works (see Piano Sonata Op. 78).[xlvii] Also worthy of mention is that the Op. 90 Piano Sonata is thought to be one of the very few of Beethoven's piano sonatas to be performed in public, in Vienna, in the composer's lifetime.[xlviii]

Steiner's hubris in announcing the Op. 90 Piano Sonata with such confidence proved to be justified. The contributor to the respected *Allgemeine musikalische Zeitung* enthused: 'With much pleasure the reviewer calls to attention this new sonata. It is one of the most simple, melodious, expressive, intelligible and mild among all [the sonatas] for which we are indebted to Beethoven.'[xlix] However, it is evident Beethoven's music was still being regarded with some caution – for being too ahead of musical convention – since even this reviewer could not resist inserting a wounding dart, commenting: '[The] high originality, which sometimes borders on the peculiar, characterises all the works of this composer.'[l] Schindler was characteristically fulsome in praise of his master's latest achievement: 'When we consider the medium and nature of the compositions preceding this sonata (the Seventh and Eighth Symphonies, the *Battle* Symphony and the Cantata *Der glorreiche Augenblick)*, we are filled with amazement at the deep tenderness and intimacy of this newest composition in contrast to its predecessors' energy and power.'[li] Nearer our own time the philosopher Theodor Adorno, in his estimation of the Op. 90 Piano Sonata, felt disposed to quote Goethe's dictum: 'Life has value only insofar as it has a consequence.' He considered this maxim to be perfectly suited to the evaluation of music, in general, and, in particular, he regarded Beethoven's *An die Ferne Geliebte*, and the composer's compositions from Op. 90 to Op. 101, to inhabit what he describes as 'this landscape'.[lii]

By the time Beethoven had completed his Op. 90, Napoleon Bonaparte's star had waned and, moreover, the French occupation of Vienna – and with it the sound on the streets of the French language – had given rise to some antipathy to things foreign. As Donald Tovey remarks: 'The native language of Bonaparte was out of favour when this sonata was written, and soon the very word *pianoforte* became disowned by the German language. Such are the faint sounds of war that reach the summit of Parnasus!'[liii] Tovey also remarks on the 'wave of chauvinism' that affected patriotic musicians such as Beethoven at this time, a tendency that may have further disposed him to want to make ever-greater use of the German language in the presentation of his compositions.[liv] We have seen already how Beethoven had insinuated the German expressions *Lebewohl* and *Wiederschen* into his Piano Sonata, Op. 81a and he was clearly determined to take this procedure further in his Op. 90. Picking up on Tovey's remark concerning the expression *pianoforte*, as we shall see in our discussions of his last group of piano sonatas, Beethoven would indeed endeavour to eschew the term *piano* altogether in favour of *hammerklavier*. For the present he was content in the Op. 90, to preface its two movements with detailed German expressions – to which we make later reference – whilst retaining Italian for the performer's interpretive directions within the movements.[lv]

In adopting a two-movement structure for the Op. 90, Beethoven was following the precedent he had established in his Piano Sonatas Op. 54 and Op. 78. Whilst the composition does not, in Cooper's estimation, 'exhibit ... startling novelties' he is of the view it offers 'a new solution for a two-movement structure; an energetic first movement and a more lyrical finale – approximately the reverse of the pattern in Op. 78'.[lvi] In the estimation of some authorities, the composition's highly contrasting two movements – heightened by the transformation from E minor to E major – anticipate the composer's later style.[lvii] Matthew Rye, for example, draws attention to the parallels to be found between the Op. 90 and the minor-major contrast of the two movements of the composer's Piano Sonata Op. 111.[lviii] In our discussion of the Op. 81a Piano Sonata, we drew attention to Edwin Fischer's endorsement of Beethoven's skill in interweaving and interrelating his material, processes he finds at work again here in the E minor Sonata. This time he detects: 'Rhythms and motifs [that] undergo metamorphoses producing patterns which differ externally but are inwardly related.' His supporting imagery is captivating: 'Like the nymph who is turned into a laurel tree or a reed, the divine soul lives on within the new form.'[lix]

Tovey found 'passion', 'energy' and 'nobility' in the E minor Sonata,[lx] sentiments closely allied to William Newman's take on the music: 'It is an exceptionally introspective work, which followed several patriotic works appropriate to the restored freedom in Vienna, and which developed alongside the revision of *Fidelio*.'[lxi] With regard to Beethoven's compositional procedures, we have previously drawn attention to Cooper's identification with what he terms 'the composer's E-flat phase' (Piano Sonata Op. 81a) and, in his discussion of the Op. 90, he elaborates these thoughts drawing attention to the manner in which he considers Beethoven found 'certain key combinations particularly effective in producing well-rounded characters for works'. He cites examples of compositions and their specific movements, set in E major moving to E minor and vice versa, including Op. 2, No. 3; Op. 14, No. 1; Op. 59, No. 2; Op. 90; and Op. 109.[lxii] Oskar Bie contends there are moments, such as in the first movement of Op. 90, when Beethoven's pianistic sound 'stands at the very doors of verbal speech', enshrined in such of his keyboard characteristics as 'pauses, leaps [and] syncopations'.[lxiii] A hundred years before him, the German composer, musical theorist and critic Adolph Bernhard Marx expressed similar thoughts, albeit in a more elaborate and enigmatic reading of the composer's intentions: 'It [Op. 90] is one of those pictures which seem to look at us with inquiring questioning glances: they are going to speak out quite clearly and — words fail them; as if our art had periods, when it is, as it were, suspended between mere sound and definite expression, when one expects every moment to hear the solving word, but it is always withheld.'[lxiv]

We close this part of our prefatory remarks with less abstract thoughts. There is general agreement amongst Beethoven scholars the E minor Piano Sonata, Op. 90 is more romantic than his earlier sonatas.[lxv] Others cite the manner in which Beethoven anticipates the sound-world of his young contemporary Franz Schubert, especially in the closing passages of the final movement. Edward Cone is one such, drawing attention to Schubert's Rondo in A for Piano Duet, D 951 that he persuasively demonstrates takes as its model the finale from the E minor Piano Sonata.[lxvi] Before turning our attention to the individual movements of the sonata, we give consideration to other aspects of Beethoven's life and work at the period under discussion — arguably the most auspicious period in the composer's lifetime when he was at the height of his public celebrity.

The apogee of Beethoven's fame corresponded with the Congress of Vienna that was held following the eventual defeat of Napoleon. The victorious powers (Russia, Great Britain, Europe and Prussia) invited the other states of Europe to send plenipotentiaries to Vienna to attend an extended peace conference that lasted from November 1814 until June 1815. Beethoven's contribution took the form of a benefit concert (gala concert) that was held on 29 November 1814 before an illustrious audience in Vienna's Grosser Redoutensaal. The programme included a performance of his recently composed Seventh Symphony, an orchestral version of *Wellington's Victory – The Battle Symphony –* and, specially composed for the occasion, the Cantata *Der glorreiche Augenblick – The Glorious Moment.* Of these compositions, only the Seventh Symphony has retained its place — and a distinguished one — in today's concert repertoire, the others having all but disappeared as the events that gave them their inception have faded from memory and, it must be said, for their possessing little enduring musical merit. However, at the time Beethoven's two latter-named compositions were well received. Beethoven composed a version of the *Battle Symphony* for the so-called panharmonicon (a form of elaborate musical box) invented by the Court Mechanician (clock maker) Johann Nepomuk Mälzel (Maelzel). In entering into such an enterprise Beethoven may be said to have been following in the footsteps of Mozart who composed his two celebrated Fantasias K. 594 and K. 608 for mechanical organ. The audience on the night of 29 November — and that at two repeat performances later in December — greatly enjoyed the composer's re-worked orchestral version of his original score for the *Battle Symphony,* that now included drum rolls, trumpet fanfares, simulated canon discharges and patriotic renderings of *God Save the King* and *Rule Britannia* — a case perhaps of *Ad captandum vulgus?*[lxvii]

Beethoven set the music of his Cantata *Der glorreiche Augenblick* to a text by Aloys Weissenbach. He was by training and vocation an army physician and surgeon but wrote extensively in the capacity of poet and dramatist — his critics consider he was rather more dramatist than poet. The writer and editor Karl Bernhard later made revisions to Weissenbach text at Beethoven's request. Beethoven needed Bernhard to help him make sense of Weissenbach turgid text that opens: 'Here ye the clang of captives' chains.'[lxviii] Beethoven never allowed the score of the Cantata to be published in his lifetime, probably aware of its low artistic merit; it was not published until ten years after his death in 1837 as his Op. 136.

Doubtless the acclaim Beethoven's music received at the concerts held in connection with the Congress of Vienna did much to promote the wider recognition of his work. Amongst the more discerning of the composer's supporters, mention should be made of the writer, critic and composer Ernst Theodor Hoffman. He is credited with being a polemicist for the Romantic Movement and a pioneering advocate of Beethoven's music, being drawn particularly to the stormy side of his works. Writing in 1813, in the December edition of the *Zeitung für die elegante Welt*, he remarks: 'Thus Beethoven's instrumental music opens up to us ... the realm of the monstrous and the immeasurable. Burning flashes of light shoot through the deep night of this realm, and we become aware of giant shadows that surge back and forth, driving us into narrower and narrower confines until they destroy us.'[lxix] Hoffman was not alone in making such fanciful observations. In July the following year, similar sentiments were expressed in the *Allgemeine musikalische Zeitung*. The reviewer first compared Beethoven's sense of irony with that of Shakespeare's and Goethe's and then enthused: 'This true, poetic irony, gentle, but often also piercing and terrible, hovers over many of his most splendid productions. Indeed, frequently a deep, repressed rage speaks to us from his music, but let us not forget that it is a pure, holy rage.'[lxx]

It was perhaps the success Beethoven was having in the concert hall that emboldened Vienna's theatre directors to approach him with a plan to revive his opera *Leonora*. Beethoven duly consented provided that he was allowed to revise his creation. The playwright Georg Friederich Treitschke was called in to make the much-needed changes to the libretto and the new enterprise, under the guise of *Fidelio*, was performed on 23 May 1814 to considerable acclaim. Louis Spohr recalls in his memoirs: 'In this new form the opera had a resounding success and experienced a long run to full houses. At the first performance the composer was recalled again and again and was once more the object of general attention.'[lxxi] Such was the work's popularity it was performed before the several foreign heads of state who had assembled to take part in the Congress. For the first time in his life Beethoven had a considerable amount of money at his disposal. He invested this in bank shares but not for his own use; he kept the money, almost intact, for the rest of his life to provide an inheritance for his nephew Karl.[lxxii]

With his newly found celebrity came requests for fresh Beethoven portraits. The first of these was commissioned by Artaria & Co. who were still one of the composer's principal publishers. They engaged the fashionable French artist Louis Letronne to make a drawing of Beethoven to form the basis for a copperplate engraving. Letronne was in Vienna at the period of the Congress and took the likenesses of several of the monarchs and statesmen who had come to the imperial city to take part in the event. Blasius Höfel made the eventual engraving but found Letronne's initial study to be unsatisfactory and had to request Beethoven to sit for a second time. Beethoven agreed but complained: 'I consider sitting to be a kind of penance ... O God, how plagued one is when one has such an awkward face as myself.'[lxxiii] Höfel's likeness was well received, even Beethoven approved and had several copies made for his closest friends. He sent one to his old friend Gerhard Wegeler and another to Antonia Brentano – a plausible candidate for the composer's *Immortal Beloved* – with the accompanying note: 'I am sending you a copper engraving on which my face is stamped. Several people maintain that in this picture they can discern my soul quite clearly.'[lxxiv] The Leipzig-based *Allgemeine musikalische Zeitung* also used Höfel's likeness of Beethoven as a frontispiece for an edition of their periodical.[lxxv]

In August the following year (1815) Joseph Mähler painted a second portrait of Beethoven. The reader may recall that between 1804–5 Mähler had made a highly romanticised study of the composer in an Arcadian setting (see Piano Sonata Op. 53). Mähler's new study is more severe than that of Höfel's and the composer's eyes convey a distant almost trance-like expression.[lxxvi] Mention may be made of one further portrait of the composer from this period, namely that taken also in 1815 by Johann Christoph Heckel. This may not be the most flattering study of Beethoven ever taken, but, according to contemporary opinion, it was considered to be one of the best portraits of the composer ever made.[lxxvii] It certainly shows, in the words of H. C. Robbins Landon, 'the same stubborn, rebellious and square-jawed Beethoven that we know to be truthful from the mask'.[lxxviii] Landon is of course referring to the plaster likeness taken of Beethoven in 1812 by Franz Klein (see Piano Sonata Op. 81a). Heckel's portrait was commissioned by the Streicher family of piano-makers to grace the walls of their piano rooms; it is now in the possession of the Library of Congress.

It is somewhat remarkable that Beethoven had been able to conduct his opera *Fidelio* on 23 May (1814) since we learn from an account of how only the previous month (11 April) he had taken the piano part in the first performance of his *Archduke* Trio, Op. 97. The *demon monster* – Beethoven's failing hearing – had evidently finally secured the composer in his grasp. This we infer from an account left by Louis Spohr. Carl Czerny sets the scene in his recollection that 'a new grand trio had then been a subject of conversation among Beethoven's friends, though no one had [yet] heard it'. Beethoven had evidently been persuaded to take part in the first performance. Perhaps the reason for this was that his charitable inclinations may have been roused since the proceeds of the event were destined for a military charity; such altruistic enterprises were always close to the composer's heart. Spohr's recollections make painful reading: 'It was not a treat, for, in the first place, the piano was badly out of tune, which Beethoven minded not a little, since he did not hear it; and secondly, on account of his deafness there was scarcely anything left of the virtuosity of the artist which had formerly been so greatly admired.' He elaborates, remarking how Beethoven hammered the keys so loud in the *forte* passages the strings rattled.[lxxix] Ignaz Moscheles also attended the concert and has left a similar account: 'Apart from the spirit, his actual playing gave me less satisfaction because it was neither clean nor precise, yet I could still notice many traces of a once great virtuosity which I had long recognized in his compositions.'[lxxx] A few weeks later Beethoven — the former keyboard virtuoso who had so captivated audiences in the salons of his patrons — took part in a further performance of the Trio; he would never again perform in public.

Further evidence of the extent to which Beethoven's hearing had deteriorated, and how it was affecting him socially, is apparent from the recollections of the pianist Johann Wenzel Tomaschek. We have remarked how Tomaschek had heard Beethoven play sometime in 1798 and how his playing had 'stirred him strangely to the depths of his soul' (Piano Sonata Op. 2, No. 2). On 10 October 1814, Tomaschek paid the composer a further visit. The following is an extract from his account: 'The unfortunate man was especially hard of hearing this day, so that one had to scream rather than talk to be understood. The reception room in which he greeted me was anything but splendidly furnished and, incidentally, was as disordered as his hair. Here I found an upright piano and on its music-rack the text of a cantata (*Der glorreiche Augenblick*) by Weissenbach; on the keys lay a lead-pencil with which he sketched out his work; and beside it on a scribbled sheet of music-paper I found a number of the most divergent ideas, jotted down without any connection, the most heterogeneous individual details elbowing each other, just as they had come to his mind.'[lxxxi]

Nepomuk Mälzel, whom we have already encountered in connection with the panharmonicon, attempted to alleviate Beethoven's impediment by devising for him a number of hearing aids — ear trumpets; these are perhaps the most poignant of all the composer's surviving possessions. Mälzel evolved a number of designs. The first was a conical-shaped device made from copper; another was a piped-shaped trumpet with a perforated cover — to keep out insects!; and two others were of similar design but supplied with a headpiece to help bear their weight. They are thought to have been of little use but Beethoven continued to place his trust in future innovations but from which he did not live to benefit.[lxxxii]

We redirect our attention now from the events of the Congress of Vienna and Beethoven's personal circumstances, to further considerations of the Op. 90 Piano Sonata.

On 16 February 1816 a farewell concert was held for the cellist Joseph Linke. He had been a member of Count Razumowsky's personal string quartet, was on friendly terms with Beethoven and had taken part in the first performance of the Archduke Trio to which we have just made reference. It is probable Beethoven wrote his two Cello Sonatas Op. 102 with Linke in mind, but they were eventually dedicated to the Countess Marie von Erdödy, a friend and confidante of the composer. Alexander Thayer comments that at Linke's farewell concert a new pianoforte sonata was included in the programme that is thought to have been the Piano Sonata in E minor. The pianist on this occasion was Stainer von Felsburg. A reviewer of the concert later reported: '[A] new pianoforte sonata by this master [Beethoven] heard here for the first time, surprises all of his numerous admirers.'[lxxxiii] This takes us now to our remarks bearing on the composition's two movements.

Consistent with his growing desire to make fuller use of the German language in the designations to his compositions, Beethoven heads the first movement: *Mit Lebhafttigkeit und durchaus mit Empfindung und Ausdruck*. This can be freely translated as: *With life/vivacity and with feeling and expression throughout*, or, in Italian, as: *Con vivacità e sempre con sentinento ed espressione – Animato e sempre con sentinento ed espressione*. These, and other variants, are adopted in contemporary editions of the composition. Words typically used by commentators to describe the mood prevailing within the first movement include 'mysterious' ... 'aggravated' ... 'restless' ... 'thoughtful'.[lxxxiv] There is 'intensity' here and 'great rhythmic variety' that give an impression 'of alternating fierceness and exhaustion'.[lxxxv] Charles Rosen describes the movement as 'despairing and impassioned ... laconic almost to the point of reticence'.[lxxxvi] Ernst von Elterlein, perhaps with thoughts of Schindler's marriage anecdote in view, believed the music revealed 'a noble mind and energetic character, [showing] what the force of eloquence can do in combating distressing doubts and fears'. In support, he cites the words of the nineteenth-century Beethoven scholar Adolph Bernhard Marx: 'A restless aspiration – that is always encountering obstacles, but never quite exhausted, though it often timidly retreats in despair — an alternation of resolution and yielding, of pressing forward and drawing back — such is the character of the whole movement.' Elterlein elaborates, yielding to the impulse of nineteenth-century Romanticism: 'The aim is not attained, and the soul has a foreboding of this while it struggles; the tone, therefore, often rises to poignancy and painful bitterness, but at the end the trouble seems to disappear in quiet submission to the inevitable.'[lxxxvii]

The opening three bars are seminal, imparting a 'driving force' that pervades the whole movement.[lxxxviii] The music may be romantically conceived but its construction has earned fulsome praise: 'The formal construction of the movement is masterly, a production of the utmost artistic ripeness, exquisitely finished even to the smallest details.'[lxxxix] Matthews' endorsements are like-minded: 'There is plenty of brain-work in [the] first movement, of which the re-emergence of the opening subject, out of the decorative semiquavers of the development by a process of changing note-values, is a classic example.'[xc] In Kinderman's estimation, the construction of this E minor movement is 'highly integrated not only in its motivic and rhythmic relations but in its form'.[xci] Rosen is succinct, describing the opening as 'lean'.[xcii] Michael Broyles also finds the first movement to be 'remarkably concise' and cast in sonata form that closely follows 'Classical practice in tonal activity'. He suggests what distinguishes this movement from earlier sonatas is 'the nature of the motion' expressed through 'a large number of motives encompassing great rhythmic variety'.[xciii] Eric Blom also pays tribute to the composer's powers of invention here: 'Never did Beethoven's inexhaustible gift of managing transitions, in a new way, manifest itself more simply and astonishingly.'[xciv]

Paul Bekker found an 'almost superabundant polyphony' in the first movement that, outwardly, he believed corresponded in build with older dance rondos such as that found in the composer's Op. 31. But there, he maintained, the comparison ends as Beethoven confers 'a new and more noble significance ... upon the old form by melodic expression and it becomes the medium of a pure lyricism far surpassing the mere entertainment associated with the older rondos'. He likens the whole to a 'deeply spiritual song-melody' that is repeated over and over again 'like a strophe' that is 'thrown into high relief by curious episodes and contrasted effects, till it completes a circle and returns to the beginning once more'. His final verdict: 'It is one of the most artistically perfect, simple movements which Beethoven ever wrote.'[xcv]

As we turn to views of performance and interpretation, a technical consideration arises. At the period when Beethoven composed the sonata, although the piano had made considerable advances he was still confined to a keyboard that did not go beyond a low F. As Rosen, with others, observes there are passages in the music that clearly require a low E — for example at bar 214. With modern-day instruments in mind he sanctions the alteration of Beethoven's score to utilise the E that Beethoven could not.[xcvi]

Restrained and romantic as the first movement may be, it confronts the performer with technical challenges such as the need to span a tenth at bars 17–21 and the requirement for occasional crossing of hands, as occur between bars 132–143.[xcvii] Carl Czerny, the first to publish written guidance on the interpretation of Beethoven's piano sonatas — learned directly from the composer — elucidates: 'This remarkably beautiful sonata obtains its full effect by the rapid, unrestrained time; by the brilliant, but light performance of the passages; by the correct observance of the stated marks of expression and by the *cantabile* of the melodies, as well as by marking all the notes which are drawn from them.'[xcviii] Tovey encourages the performer to adopt a uniform tempo with the admonition: 'Most of the technical difficulties are greatly aggravated by the prevalent habit of hurrying where there are no semi-quavers.' He asks for the flow of the movement to be maintained without 'patchiness' occasioned by any 'lack self-control'.[xcix] Cooper believes the movement calls for 'feeling and expression throughout'.[c]

Although Anton Schindler has been censured for his mischief in making elaborate claims concerning the meaning implicit in the Piano Sonata, Op. 90 — with implications for its interpretation — this should not prejudice us to all that he has to say about Beethoven's music. With this in mind, we give him the final words here in which he sets out one of his characteristically fervent paeans of praise: 'Consider the form of the first movement of the first sonata in F minor, how different it is from the form of the first movement of the Sonata in E-flat major, Op. 7! And how different again are the first movements of the Sonata in C minor Op. 10 and of the *Pathétique* Op. 13, and so on through the wonderfully inspired Sonatas Op. 57 (F minor), Op. 90 (E minor), Op. 101 (A major), right up to the last! Each one different, and yet the master leads us by way of his form along such a sure, clear path that requires little imagination, provided the performance is adapted to the content, to retain the thread of the poetry without losing it for even an instant.'[ci]

By way of further affirmation of his wish to adopt the German language, Beethoven heads the final movement: *Nicht zu geschwind und sehr singbar vorgetragen — Not too fast, and to be played very songfully/in a very singable manner — Non troppo presto e molto cantabile*. Tovey allows himself here to be influenced by Schindler's assertion that the final movement is intended to convey feelings of 'Happy conversations with the beloved' and, thereby, considers Beethoven turns from the 'raillery' of the first movement (a further indirect allusion to Schindler) 'to modestly smiling congratulations'.[cii] The opening is characterised by a 'rich melodious theme, full of earnestness' inviting both performer and listener to imagine 'the most varied and joyful images [hovering], as it were, around the chief figure'.[ciii] The melody is perhaps the most 'singable' to be found in any of Beethoven's piano-sonata movements and is doubtless the reason for his caution: *'Nicht zu geschwind und sehr singbar vorgetragen'.*[civ] One commentator enthuses Beethoven's melody is 'one of the loveliest tunes ever written'.[cv] When Beethoven's instructions are followed the movement 'displays an unhurried, song-like quality that is more characteristic of Schubert than Beethoven' (see later).[cvi]

Even if Schindler may have exaggerated his claims regarding the allegorical foundation for this music, one authority at least believes Beethoven has given us what he describes as a 'heart-idyll'.[cvii] Schindler discerned 'intimacy' in the music that he thought 'would be hard to find in any work preceding it'.[cviii] The second movement is a rondo, 'proceeding leisurely'[cix] and 'flowing with spacious lyricism'.[cx] For Rosen the rondo has 'the amiability of many Mozart finales' though with what he describes as 'a much more up-to-date cantabile style'.[cxi] There are those who consider the rondo repeats itself too much without undergoing any significant transformation. Tovey is one who comes to Beethoven's defence. He first cites Hubert Parry's definition of a rondo as 'the frequent and desirable return of a melody of great beauty' — a condition Tovey believed Beethoven's rondo admirably fulfils. He outlines the basis for his convictions: 'Tastes may differ about the desirability of hearing the beautiful melody of the rondo of Op. 90 three times unvaried in full, with its own self-repetitions, and a fourth time as a duet between treble and bass, plus a compressed final version in the coda, making ten times in all ... It so happens that the whole thing is compressed into six and a half minutes ... no other composer is a match for him in power of compression.'[cxii]

Bie considers Beethoven embraces the parts of the rondo theme 'frugally'.[cxiii] Cooper expresses the same idea but in more conventional musical terms, remarking on Beethoven's spare use of counterpoint, that in his estimation places this sonata 'closer to Schubert and the early Romantics'.[cxiv] For all its simplifications, the movement is not lacking in invention. Fischer likens Beethoven's 'interwoven style' to an organic form: 'It is splendid, the way Beethoven abbreviates, twists and transforms the third bar where it reappears in its first shape. Such things make us feel that Nature's laws of organic growth are reproduced on the spiritual level — we are reminded even of the inoculation of plants by way a secondary theme is grafted onto simple, strong, primary material.'[cxv] With regard to Beethoven's pianistic devices, Broyles highlights the manner in which the: '[The rondo theme] is set with simple arpeggio accompaniment and is redolent with sensuously placed thirds and octaves.'[cxvi] The trill assumes significance in the final movement, with portends of later — and greater — things to come. As Jeremy Dibble observes: 'Into this rondo Beethoven introduces streams of trills, written out in semiquavers; and we shall see [in the composer's final piano sonatas] that trills came to have a peculiar significance for Beethoven in his last years.'[cxvii] Wilfrid Mellers describes the period of creation of the Op. 90 as the composer's 'transitional years' and associates Op. 90 with the 'radiant lyricism' of the Violin Sonata Op. 96. Both the Op. 90 and Op. 96 Mellers suggests, in a moving phrase, 'seem to attain the peace of earthly love; and perhaps their trills suggest that for

Beethoven at least, earthly love was a necessary step towards heavenly'.[cxviii]

In his discussion of Beethoven's endings, Adorno comments: 'All Beethoven's closing sections are *satisfying* [Adorno's italics], even the tragic ones'. None, he remarks, 'add a question'; he then cites the Op. 90 whose close he describes as 'curious' — perhaps he meant 'enigmatic'?[cxix] Matthews is not enigmatic: '[The Op. 90] closes with the most delicately wrought of all sonata endings.'[cxx]

The influence Beethoven exerted on Schubert in the E minor Piano Sonata has been mentioned. Kinderman is unequivocal about this: 'The second, final movement, is the most Schubertian movement in Beethoven, a luxurious rondo dominated by many appearances of a spacious cantabile theme.'[cxxi] Some have also detected anticipations of Mendelsohn in Beethoven's writing; Blom, for example, considers this to be especially true of Beethoven's opening bars.[cxxii] For Matthews: '[The] rondo ... is a piece Mendelsohn would have been proud to call 'song without words.'[cxxiii]

We close our discussion of Beethoven's Piano Sonata in E minor, Op. 90 with a selection of remarks bearing on the performance and interpretation of the music, taking as our starting point recollections of the playing of Baroness Dorothea von Ertmann. We have encountered Dorothea previously in our discussions of Piano Sonatas Op. 2, Nos. 1–3, Op. 13 and Op. 27, No. 2. The reader will recall Dorothea had received instruction in piano from Beethoven himself. Notwithstanding her amateur status, Schindler considered: '[This] poetess excelled in the expression of the charming and naïve, and also of the deep and the sentimental ... she never overstepped the bounds of what she recognized as her limitations when playing for connoisseurs.' It is to Dorothea von Ertmann that Schindler bestows credit for 'keeping alive' Beethoven's piano sonatas in the first two decades of the nineteenth century. We gain additional insights into the quality of Dorothea's playing from further of Schindler's remarks that link her to our present discussion. 'She grasped intuitively the most hidden subtleties of Beethoven's works with as much sureness as if they had been written-out before her eyes ... If the listener forgot to breathe during the mysterious Largo in the Trio in D major, Op. 70, she would have him sighing for love in the second movement of the Sonata in E minor, Op. 90. She would play the recurring theme of this movement differently each time, sometimes flatteringly, sometimes caressingly, sometimes in a melancholy vein. By such wiles this artist was able to play with her audience.'[cxxiv]

In his commentary to the Op. 90 Piano Sonata, Kinderman cites Schindler's recollections of the playing of Dorothea Ertmann, to which he contributes his own thoughts: 'The main theme is scarcely varied in the rondo, yet sensitive performance can endow the repetition of the theme with ever new shadings and detail.'[cxxv] Czerny, like Dorothea Ertmann, learned the piano sonatas directly under the composer's tutelage and makes the following propaedeutic remarks with regard to the final movement of Op. 90: 'The utmost sweetness and feeling is here required, which can be produced by a delicate touch, fine *cantabile*, and a light performance of the quicker notes. As the theme is frequently repeated, the player must each time endeavour to deliver it with a different gradation of tone, but always with delicacy. The time must not be dragging, and in certain passages the liveliness may be increased.'[cxxvi] Edwin Fischer draws attention to Hans von Bülow's remark that Beethoven had headed the final movement '*Nicht zu geschwind und sehr singbar vorgetragen*' for a good reason, namely, to deter the amateur pianist from rattling through the music as though it were merely another *rondeaux brilliant*. His own advice is: 'The tempo must remain flowing, however, and in place of the rather indefinite and involved German speaking words a better direction for the many non-German speaking players would be something like *Allegretto cantabile* or *amabile*.'[cxxvii] Egerton Lowe urges the performer to become acquainted with other of the composer's music: 'To get the right *atmosphere* of this lovely movement it is helpful to play other Beethoven movements in the same key.' Lowe's additional observations are worthy of remark: 'Again and again we find a feeling of affinity between works of his in the same key. He chose that of E major for the slow movement of the Sonata in C, Op. 2, No. 3; for the first and last movements of the Sonata in E, Op. 14, No. 1; and for the second subject of the *Waldstein* Sonata.'[cxxviii]

Arthur Rubinstein's recollections of his student days connect us to the Piano Sonata Op. 90 and give a hint of his views of the music and his thoughts about its performance. In the summer of 1910, when he was twenty-three years old, he took part in a piano competition held in St. Petersburg; it was named in honour of his namesake, the great Beethovenian Anton Rubinstein — the prize was two thousand rubbles. We let the youthful Rubinstein take up the tale: 'The Beethoven sonata ... worried me a great deal by its shortness and its ineffective, inconclusive ending. The first movement is magnificent and moving but the last has a too-much repeated, beautiful theme which dies out at the end.' At this point Rubinstein recalls that his teacher, Professor Barth, was given to recollecting how Anton Rubinstein 'touched people to tears with this movement'. Bearing this in mind he continues: 'I played this sonata with all my heart, giving a new and stronger meaning to every repetition of the lovely melody.' Notwithstanding his endeavours, the first prize went to a fellow student by the name of Alfred Hoehen — to the accompaniment of a combination of boos interspersed with bravos. Rubinstein received 'a special first prize' — but no financial reward. In his reminiscences he generously acknowledged Hoehen's achievement; his programme had included the arduous *Hammerklavier* Piano Sonata (see our later discussions) disposing Rubinstein to concede: 'He won by merit.'[xxix]

Professor, Sir Donald Francis Tovey is peremptory: 'Players who feel bored by [the Piano Sonata in E minor, Op 90] should really leave Beethoven, early, middle or late, alone.'[xxx]

---

[i] This expression is derived from Stewart Gordon, 1996, p. 180.

[ii] Michael Broyles, 1987, pp. 229–30.

[iii] Barry Cooper, 1991, pp. 198–9.

[iv] Denis Matthews, 1985, pp. 93–4.

[v] Maynard Solomon, 1988, p. 119.

[vi] Alfred Brendel in conversation with David Dubal in: David Dubal, 1985, p. 108.

[vii] Matthew Rye, *Notes to the BBC Radio Three Beethoven experience*, Friday 10 June 2005, www.bbc.co.uk/radio3/Beethoven

[viii] Neate was in Vienna in the summer of 1815 and soon became on friendly terms with Beethoven; the anecdote connecting the two doubtless derives from this time. Neate had brought with him an order from the Philharmonic Society of London for three new overtures (Opp. 113, 115 and 117), for which Beethoven was to receive 75 guineas. Neate, who lived to the great age of 93, had difficulty in obtaining a British publisher for the overtures. See: Barry Cooper, 1991, pp. 49–50. On his departure in 1816, as a mark of affection, Beethoven gave Neate a copy of his Violin Concerto. For a fuller account of Charles Neate's relationship with Beethoven, see: Peter Clive, 2001, pp. 245–6.

[ix] A measure of Beethoven's regard for Maria Lichnowsky is his dedication to her of his piano arrangement of the ballet music *Die Geschöpfe des Prometheus*, Op. 43.

[x] Beethoven had been planning to dedicate his set of *Fifteen Variations* to the Abbé (Maximilian) Stadler who was highly respected in musical circles but had a change of mind in favour of Moritz Lichnowsky. The source for the letter cited is Emily Anderson, 1961, Vol. 1, Letter No. 72, pp. 88–9. See also: H. C. Robbins Landon, 1992, p. 79.

[xi] Emily Anderson, 1961, Vol. 1, Letter No. 498, pp. 470–1.

[xii] William Kinderman, Liner notes to *Beethoven: The complete sonatas*, (Philips) 1996, pp. 31–3.

[xiii] Peter Clive, 2001, pp. 206–8. It is now known Schindler forged an entry in support of his allegations in one of Beethoven's conversation books that the composer used when his deafness precluded normal conversation. For Barry Cooper's doubts regarding the authenticity of Schindler's story, see: Donald Francis Tovey, *A companion to Beethoven's pianoforte sonatas*, revised by

Barry Cooper, *Piano Sonata Op. 90*, [1931], 1998, footnote 31 to p. 258.

[xiv] Anton Felix Schindler, *Beethoven as I knew him*, edited by Donald W. MacArdle and translated by Constance S. Jolly from the German edition of 1860, 1966, footnote to p. 210.

[xv] As quoted in Ernst von Elterlein, 1898, p. 88.

[xvi] John Fuller-Maitland, *Special Issue* [Death Centenary], *The Musical Times*, London, Vol. VIII, No. 2, 1927, p. 221.

[xvii] William Kinderman, Liner notes to *Beethoven: The complete sonatas*, (Philips) 1996, pp. 31–3.

[xviii] John South Shedlock, 1918, p. 174.

[xix] Eric Blom, *Pianoforte Sonatas Op. 78, Op. 90 and Op. 111*, The Beethoven Society, Volume One (undated — c.1938), pp. 15–19.

[xx] Emily Anderson, 1961, Vol. 1, Letter No. 403, pp. 402–3. Beethoven's claim to be supporting his brother and family 'entirely' may be an exaggeration. See: Peter Clive 2001, pp. 20–2.

[xxi] Emily Anderson, 1961, Vol. 1, Letter No. 351, pp. 359–60.

[xxii] For a modern-day interpretation of how Beethoven may have appeared, when taking the waters, see the illustration by the artist-sculptor Donna Dralle reproduced in the website text *The unheard Beethoven* to the Theme with Variation in A, Hess 72.

[xxiii] Emily Anderson, 1961, Vol. 1, Letter No. 380, pp. 383–4, Beethoven House, Digital Archives, Library Document, Sammlung H. C. Bodmer, HCB Br 103.

[xxiv] *Ibid*, pp. 352–5.

[xxv] For an insight into Beethoven's working relationship with Steiner and his partner Haslinger, see: Emily Anderson, 1961, Vol. 2, Letter No. 527, pp. 495–6.

[xxvi] Carl assigned the partial custodianship of his son Karl to Beethoven in the form of a deposition to the Vienna Imperial Court. See: Emily Anderson, 1961, Vol. 2, Document No. 171, pp. 6–7. On 12 April 1813, Carl further affirmed his brother Beethoven should assume the guardianship of his son in a letter to the Court (Imperial Court Landrecht). This only compounded the future strained relationships between the composer, his sister-in-law and his nephew Karl. See: Theodore Albrecht, 1998, Vol. 2, letter No. 171, pp. 7.

[xxvii] Douglas Porter Johnson, editor, 1985, p. 73 and pp. 224–229.

[xxviii] Barry Cooper, 1990, p. 91. Despite its relatively late opus number, the Overture *Namensfeir*, Op. 115 is contemporaneous with the Piano Sonata Op. 90.

[xxix] For a brief account of the publication history of the E minor Piano Sonata see: Beethoven House, Digital Archives, *Sonate für Klavier e-Mol, Op. 90*.

[xxx] Emily Anderson, 1961, Vol. 1, Letter No. 492, p. 466.

[xxxi] This information is reproduced, together with supporting historical information, in the Augener Edition of *Beethoven's Piano Sonatas*, No. 8030, London (undated). See also: Edwin Fischer, 1959, p. 96. Given its authenticity, authorities consider the Archduke's copy of the E minor Piano Sonata to be a valuable historical document.

[xxxii] For a facsimile reproduction of the Autograph, see: Beethoven House, Digital Archives, *Sonate für Klavier e-Mol*, Op. 90. The Autograph is now held in a private London collection, see: Barry Cooper, 1991, p. 189.

[xxxiii] Cooper suggests the publication announcement of the Op. 90 Piano Sonata

may have been made later in the year. See: Barry Cooper, 1991, pp. 24–5. Perhaps Steiner made more than one publication announcement?

xxiv Beethoven House, *Digital* Archives, Library Document *Sonate für Klavier e-Mol*, Op. 90.

xxv Emily Anderson, 1961, Vol. 2, Letter No. 527, pp. 495–6. Beethoven had been working on the composition of the Seventh and Eighth Symphonies in May of 1812 as is evident from a letter he wrote to his then publisher Breitkopf and Härtel (24 May) in which he states: 'I am now composing three new symphonies.' The reference to a third symphony may be the Ninth. See: Emily Anderson, 1961, Vol. 2, Letter No. 370, p. 372.

xxvi Emily Anderson, 1961, Vol. 2, Letter No. 535, p. 505.

xxvii *Ibid*, Vol. 2, Letter No. 537, p. 506.

xxviii Theodore Albrecht, translator and editor, 1996, Vol. 2, Letter No. 182, pp. 30–1.

xxix *Ibid*, Vol. 2, Letter No. 194, pp. 52–3.

xl Emily Anderson, 1961, Vol. 2, Letter No. 430, pp. 424–5.

xli *Ibid*, Vol. 2, Letter No. 420, p. 416.

xlii *Ibid*, Vol. 2, Letter No. 542, p. 510.

xliii *Ibid*, Vol. 2, Letter No. 543, pp. 510–11.

xliv *Ibid*, Vol. 2, Letter No. 545, pp. 513–4. See also: Beethoven House, Digital Archives, *Sonate für Klavier e-Mol, Op. 90*.

xlv This information is also reproduced, together with supporting historical information, in the Augener Edition of Beethoven's Piano Sonatas, No. 8030, London (undated).

xlvi Beethoven House, Digital Archives, Library Document, Sammlung H. C. Bodmer, HCB C Md 53, 17.

xlvii Alan Tyson, 1963, footnote 1 to p. 23.

xlviii There is uncertainty as to which of the very few of Beethoven's piano sonatas were played in public during his lifetime. The piano sonata in question may have been the composer's Op. 101 – see: Maynard Solomon, 1977, p. 128. It is known the Funeral March from Op. 26 was performed in Boston in 1819.

xlix As quoted in: William S. Newman, 1963, p. 526. Newman makes the observation that the changing (favourable) attitude to Beethoven's music may be credited to the musically inlined public '[catching] up a little more with Beethoven'.

l Robin Wallace, 1986, p. 93.

li Anton Felix Schindler, *Beethoven as I knew him*, edited by Donald W. MacArdle and translated by Constance S. Jolly from the German edition of 1860, 1966, p. 209.

lii Theodor W. Adorno, 1998, p. 82.

liii Harold Craxton and Donald Francis Tovey, [1931], p. 93.

liv Donald Francis Tovey, *A companion to Beethoven's pianoforte sonatas*, revised by Barry Cooper, *Piano Sonata Op. 90*, [1931], 1998, p. 198.

lv Beethoven never entirely abandoned the use of Italian directions, sporadically combining them, for instance, in the piano sonatas Op. 101 and 109. See, for example, the observations of Stewart Gordon, 1996, p. 125 and p. 180.

lvi Barry Cooper, 2000, p. 232.

lvii See for example: Michael Broyles, 1987, pp. 229–234.

lviii Matthew Rye, *Notes to the BBC Radio Three Beethoven experience*, Friday 10 June 2005, www.bbc.co.uk/radio3/Beethoven

lix Edwin Fischer, 1959, p. 95.
l Donald Francis Tovey, *A companion to Beethoven's pianoforte sonatas*, revised by Barry Cooper, *Piano Sonata Op. 90*, [1931], 1998, p. 198.
lxi William S. Newman, 1963, p. 526.
lxii Barry Cooper, 1990, p. 125.
lxiii Oskar Bie, 1966, p. 169.
lxiv As quoted by Ernst von Elterlein, 1898, p. 99.
lxv See, for example: Barry Cooper, 2000, p. 232.
lxvi Edward C. Cone, *Schubert's Beethoven*, in: Paul Henry Lang, 1971, pp. 277–91. Cone draws attention to Schubert's debt to Beethoven's design and his 'adherence to Beethoven's formal procedures'. In particular he reveals how Schubert's Rondo opening 'is a four-hand transcription of Beethoven's solo writing' and the extent to which 'both themes exhibit the same uncommon form'.
lxvii The original title of the *Battle Symphony* is *Wellington's Sieg, oder Die Schlact bei Vittoria*. It was first performed on 8 December 1813 at a charity concert in the great hall of the University of Vienna. Also on the programme was Beethoven's Seventh Symphony. The concert was such a success it was repeated four days later, contributing to the composer's public celebrity and bringing in receipts of 4000 florins for the war-wounded. Mälzel persuaded Beethoven to write music for his panharmonicon – originally described as *mechanical trumpeter* – following the wave of patriotism that swept Vienna when news of Wellington's victory reached the city. Ownership of copyright of the orchestral version of the composition subsequently erupted in a protracted quarrel between Beethoven and Mälzel.
lxviii Several verses of the text to *Der glorreiche Augenblick* are reproduced in Elliot Forbes, editor, *Thayer's life of Beethoven*, 1967, pp. 593–4. Thayer condemns Weissenbach's text for being 'stilted in style ... absurdly prosaic ... and nowhere with a spark of poetic fire to illuminate its dreary pages'. To be more sympathetic to Weissenbach, he shared Beethoven's affliction in being hard of hearing.
lxix As recollected in: Jack Sullivan, editor, *Words on music: from Addison to Barzun*, 1990, pp. 116–9.
lxx Quoted in: Wayne M. Senner, Robin Wallace and William Meredith, editors, 1999, p. 42.
lxxi As quoted by Henry Pleasants, editor and translator, *The musical journeys of Louis Spohr*, 1961, p. 101.
lxxii An indication of the business side of Beethoven's nature is revealed in entries he made in one of his sketchbooks. He clearly hoped to repeat the success he was having in Vienna with his opera at other notable theatres including Carlsruhe, Darmstadt, Frankfurt, Gratz, Hamburg, and Stuttgart. He hoped to make 15 ducats in gold from each of these. In the event, none of the theatres he approached performed *Fidelio* in his lifetime. See: Theodore Albrecht, translator and editor, 1996, Vol. 2, Letter No. 184, pp. 34–6.
lxxiii Beethoven House, Digital Archives, Library Document, Sammlung H. C. Bodmer, HCB BBr 69.
lxxiv For the reference to Gerhard Wegeler see: Emily Anderson, 1961, Vol. 2, Letter No. 661, p. 602 and for the reference to Antonia Brentano, see: Emily Anderson, 1961, Vol. 2, Letter No. 607, pp. 557–8.
lxxv Beethoven House, Digital Archives, Library Document, B 2315 and B 9/a. Following on from Höfel, the portrait was re-engraved the following year by Karl Traugott.

[lxxvi] At least three versions of Mähler's portrait exist, one copy of which is owned by the *Gesellschaft der Muisk freunde.* See: Beethoven House, Digital Archives, Library Document B 2388a and H. C. Robbins Landon, 1970, pp. 12–13 and plate 9.

[lxxvii] As remarked by Maynard Solomon, 1970, p. 153.

[lxxviii] H. C. Robbins Landon, 1970, p. 10, plate 13.

[lxxix] As quoted in: Elliot Forbes, editor, *Thayer's life of Beethoven*, 1967, pp.577–8.

[lxxx] As quoted by Maynard Solomon, 1970, p. 151.

[lxxxi] Oscar George Theodore Sonneck, *Beethoven: impressions of contemporaries*, 1927, pp. 100–1.

[lxxxii] Beethoven's hearing aids are illustrated on the Beethoven House, Digital Archives, Library Document, R 2. See also Derek Melville in: Denis Arnold and Nigel Fortune, editors, 1973, plate 8.

[lxxxiii] As quoted in: Elliot Forbes, editor, *Thayer's life of Beethoven*, 1967, p. 641, note 14. Stainer von Felsburg is known to have performed a number of Beethoven's works for piano, including his first Piano Concerto. As remarked in the text, it is thought the Op. 90 Piano Sonata was the only one of Beethoven's piano sonatas to be performed in public during the composer's lifetime. Remarking on this, the music critic Hanslick says: 'Beethoven's piano sonatas failed to appear on concert programmes, not because they were by Beethoven but because they were piano sonatas.' He goes on to explain that at that time piano sonatas were considered suitable only for performance in the home, not in public. Quoted by Donald W. MacArdle in: Anton Felix Schindler, *Beethoven as I knew him*, edited by Donald W. MacArdle and translated by Constance S. Jolly from the German edition of 1860, 1966, p. 340, footnote 145.

[lxxxiv] Oskar Bie, 1966, pp. 178–9.

[lxxxv] Philip Radcliffe, *Piano music*, in: Gerald Abraham, editor, *The age of Beethoven, 1790-1830*, 1982, p. 346.

[lxxxvi] Charles Rosen, 1976, p. 403.

[lxxxvii] Ernst von Elterlein, 1898, p. 100.

[lxxxviii] Edwin Fischer, 1959, p. 95.

[lxxxix] Ernst von Elterlein, 1898, p. 100.

[xc] Denis Matthews, 1985, pp. 93–4.

[xci] William Kinderman, Liner notes to *Beethoven: The complete sonatas*, (Philips) 1996, pp. 31–3.

[xcii] Charles Rosen, 2002, p. 208.

[xciii] Michael Broyles, 1987, p. 229.

[xciv] Eric Blom, *Pianoforte Sonatas Op. 78, Op. 90 and Op. 111*, The Beethoven Society, Volume One (undated, c.1938), pp. 15–19.

[xcv] Paul Bekker, 1925, p. 128.

[xcvi] Charles Rosen, 2002, p. 210

[xcvii] This aspect of performance is mentioned particularly by Ernst von Elterlein, 1929, p. 126.

[xcviii] Carl Czerny in: Paul Badura-Skoda, 1970, p. 52.

[xcix] Harold Craxton and Donald Francis Tovey, [1931], p. 93.

[c] Barry Cooper, 2000, p. 232.

[ci] Anton Felix Schindler, *Beethoven as I knew him*, edited by Donald W. MacArdle and translated by Constance S. Jolly from the German edition of 1860, 1966, p. 405.

[cii] Donald Francis Tovey, *A companion to Beethoven's pianoforte sonatas*, revised by Barry Cooper, *Piano Sonata Op. 90*, [1931], 1998. In fairness to Tovey, it should be noted that he was commenting on Beethoven's piano sonatas at a time when Schindler's falsifications had not yet come to light.

[ciii] Ernst von Elterlein, 1898, p. 101.

[civ] This is the view of Egerton C. Lowe, 1929, pp. 126–7.

[cv] Jeremy Dibble, in: *Charles Villiers Stanford: man and musician*, 2002, p. 648.

[cvi] Barry Cooper, 2000, p. 232.

[cvii] Ernst von Elterlein, 1898, p. 101.

[cviii] Anton Felix Schindler, *Beethoven as I knew him*, edited by Donald W. MacArdle and translated by Constance S. Jolly from the German edition of 1860, 1966, p. 209.

[cix] Gordon Stewart, 1996, p. 180.

[cx] Michael Broyles, 1987, p. 232.

[cxi] Charles Rosen, 2002, p. 210.

[cxii] Donald Francis Tovey, *The forms of music: musical articles from The Encyclopaedia Britannica*, 1944, p. 122.

[cxiii] Oskar Bie, 1966, p. 179.

[cxiv] Barry Cooper, 2000, p. 232.

[cxv] Edwin Fischer, 1959, p. 96.

[cxvi] Michael Broyles, 1987, p. 229.

[cxvii] Jeremy Dibble, 2002, p. 648.

[cxviii] Wilfrid Howard Mellers, 1957, pp. 70–1.

[cxix] Theodore Adorno, 1998, p. 52.

[cxx] Denis Matthews, 1985, pp. 93–4.

[cxxi] Wiliam Kinderman, Liner notes to *Beethoven; The complete sonatas*, Philips, 446 909-2.

[cxxii] Eric Blom, *Pianoforte Sonatas Op. 78, Op. 90 and Op. 111*, The Beethoven Society, Volume One (undated, c.1938), pp. 15–19.

[cxxiii] Denis Matthews, 1985, pp. 93–4.

[cxxiv] Anton Felix Schindler, *Beethoven as I knew him*, edited by Donald W. MacArdle and translated by Constance S. Jolly from the German edition of 1860, 1966, p. 10. Schindler's closing remarks are of particular interest bearing on what he has to say about Dorothea's interpretation of the repeated passages in the rondo that some have criticised for being too repetitious.

[cxxv] William Kinderman, Liner notes to *Beethoven: The complete sonatas*, (Philips) 1996, pp. 31–3.

[cxxvi] Carl Czerny as quoted in: Paul Badura-Skoda, 1970, p. 52.

[cxxvii] Edwin Fischer, 1959, p. 96.

[cxxviii] Egerton C. Lowe, 1929, p. 127.

[cxxix] Arthur Rubinstein, 1973, pp. 338–9.

[cxxx] Harold Craxton and Donald Francis Tovey, [1931], p. 94.A performance of the E minor Piano Sonata, Op. 90 was recorded on 16 December 1970 in honour of Beethoven's Bicentennial by Jörg Demus on Beethoven's restored Broadwood piano. Source: Ann P. Basart, *The sound of the fortepiano: A discography of recordings on early pianos:* Berkley, Fallen Leaf Press, 1985.

PIANO SONATA IN A MAJOR, OP. 101

'This sonata ... belongs to those works whose meaning is more or less lost in words and can only be suggested.'

Ernst von Elterlein, *Beethoven's Pianoforte Sonatas: Explained for the Lovers of the Musical Art*, 1898, p. 102.

'With this sonata we reach the third period of Beethoven's works, that in which reflection and philosophy play such a great part.'

Romain Rolland, *Beethoven and Handel*, 1917, p. 160.

'For its length, Op. 101 is perhaps the most difficult, both intellectually and technically, of all Beethoven's later works.'

Harold Craxton, and Donald Francis Tovey, *Beethoven: Sonatas for Pianoforte*, [1931], p. 113.

> '[And] then, in 1816, the sonata in A major, Op. 101, earliest of the great five of the period. By now Beethoven had completed his colouration of cyclic form with lyric hues and grace: his mind turned towards a harder task — nothing less than the conquest of the highly specialized province of contrapuntal music for harmonic expression. The two most intellectual forms in music — the fugue and the sonata — were to be brought into unity, for his new ethical message exceeded the capacities of lyric form.'

Marion M. Scott, *Beethoven: The Master Musicians Series*, 1940, p. 145.

> 'The whole piece should sound like a continuous fantasia. This sonata demands everything: lyrical feeling, rhythm, absorption and virtuosity. The work is only for mature souls and affords greater interpretive difficulties than the Sonatas Op. 109, 110 and Op. 111.'

Edwin Fischer, *Beethoven's Pianoforte Sonatas: a Guide for Students & Amateurs*, 1959, p. 97.

> 'In Op. 101 an unparalleled height of thematic development is attained.'

Oskar Bie, *A History of the Pianoforte and Pianoforte Players*, 1966, p. 179.

'Late Beethoven is at the same time enigmatic and extremely obvious. The boundary is doubtless marked by the Piano Sonata Op. 101, a work of the highest, of inexhaustible beauty.'

Theodor W. Adorno, *Beethoven: the Philosophy of Music; Fragments and Texts*, 1998, p. 136.

'The sonata displays an elevated, somewhat esoteric style typical of Beethoven's final period, continuing the pattern set by the Cello Sonatas the previous year, with its polyphonic textures and unusual structure.'

Barry Cooper, *Beethoven: The Master Musicians Series*, 2000, p. 252.

'Op, 101 marks a fundamental change in Beethoven's sonatas. Formerly, the sum of the movements resulted in a perfect balance. Now, the dynamic, development aspect of his composing takes hold over the entire work.'

Alfred Brendel, *Alfred Brendel on Music: Collected Essays*, 2001, p. 82.

With the Piano Sonata in A major, Op. 101, we find Beethoven on the threshold of his last creative period, a period when he was intent on seeking a new style and of enriching his compositions with greater contrapuntal significance.[i] Whilst the compositions of Beethoven's late period may have been perplexing to his contemporaries, they are now considered as being imbued with 'deep inner significance' that sets them apart from his earlier works.[ii]

With regard to Beethoven's writing for the piano, the last five piano sonatas — with which the Op. 101 commences the series — together with the *Diabelli* Variations, take piano music to deeper levels of expression and intensity of spiritual expression that many would agree have not been surpassed in the history of western music. In her essay *Memory and invention at the threshold of Beethoven's late style*, Elaine Sisman writes: 'One key to Beethoven's late style ... is offered by the works that, as it were, swing open its door. By linking invention, which speaks of present and future, with memory, which invokes the past, Beethoven's new, complex teleology moves cyclic works not in a straight line toward a goal, but through a process of finding the right place for revelatory recollections.'[iii] This rather challenging statement requires a few words of amplification. Sisman is remarking how Beethoven, in his late compositions, developed a procedure of recalling (*revelatory recollections*) previously heard themes and motives in the later movements of a work (*invention*). Consider for example how, in the Ninth Symphony, Beethoven recalls themes from the first three movements before allowing the music to progress to its majestic conclusion. The Piano Sonata in A major, Op. 101 may be said to portend such procedures through the manner in which themes heard at the start are recalled, almost wistfully, later on. This would become a hallmark in the hands of later Romantics. By way of illustration we may cites the *idée fixe* that Hector Berlioz introduces recurrently in his *Symphonie Fantastique* — premiered, remarkably, a mere three years after Beethoven's death. By means of this device, Berlioz conjures up the vision of his beloved Henrietta (Herriet) Smithson. At the period of composition of Beethoven's twenty-eighth piano sonata, his musicological invention was, if not revolutionary, a startling innovation. For this reason more than one commentator has described the work as being a 'fantasy-sonata'.[iv] In much the same spirit, in his pioneering study *Ludwig van Beethoven Leben und Schaffen* (1859), the German composer, musical theorist and critic Adolph Bernhard Marx was disposed to describe the A major Piano Sonata in the following terms: 'The innermost and most secret stirrings of a tender soul, to whom the desire alone is granted, not its realisation, only the flights of fancy, nor tangible aims or pithy deeds — how difficult is it to catch what it says, and to bring to a light that shall not offend it.'[v] In his overview of the A major Piano Sonata, Barry Cooper makes a distinction between the enduring value of Beethoven's music in comparison with the more ephemeral works being produced by his contemporary Viennese salon composers. He underlines this observation, saying: 'The notion of composing works for posterity, to be preserved like museum-pieces, seems never to have been far from Beethoven's thoughts.'[vi] The Op. 101 then, to recall Sisman's imagery once more, if not fully swinging open the door to the composer's late style, presses hard against it.

In our discussion of the Piano Sonata Op. 81a, we remarked on Beethoven's emerging lyricism and how this corresponded with the period when he was beginning to set folksong arrangements for George Thomson in Edinburgh. These are enchanting works, infused with simple melodies, the manipulation of which it is tempting to speculate may have disposed the composer to find a greater sense of lyricism in his more substantial, contemporaneous compositions. In this context other works worthy of mention. In addition to the Piano Sonata Op. 81a may be include the following: the String Quartet in E-flat major, Op. 74 — with its pizzicato allusions to the harp (perhaps the most romantic of all instruments giving the quartet its nickname); the Piano Fantasia, Op. 77 — written out in an almost experimental, improvisatory manner; the Piano Sonata in F-sharp major, Op. 78 — the light and tender character of which we have noted previously; the heartfelt song cycle *An die ferne Geliebte* (Op. 98); and the Cello Sonata Op. 102 that Beethoven provisionally titled *Free Sonata*. As Stephen Rumph remarks: 'Beethoven discovered an intimate tone that departs from the monumental, hortatory temper of his heroic manner. These gentle works, which open a new space for leisurely melody, show a genuinely Romantic shift from drama to lyrical reflection.'[vii]

Paul Bekker suggests Beethoven brought the fruits of his evolving musical style to bear upon the pianoforte in what he describes as 'the last sonata-poems for the solo instrument'. He positions the A major Piano Sonata at the opening of the series which, as regards the principles upon which it is constructed, he maintains looks back to the Piano Sonata in E-flat major, Op, 27, No. 1 that, the reader will recall, Beethoven had subtitled *Quasi una fantasia*. However, Beethoven's style had evolved greatly since 1801–2, the period of composition of the E-flat major Sonata, and, with the Piano Sonata Op. 101, he no longer felt the need to prepare the performer and listener for the mood prevailing in the music by the adoption of such an expression. Commenting on Bekker's observations, Eric Blom comments: '[Op. 101] is quite as much a *Sonata quasi una fantasia* as the earlier works which Beethoven actually called so. The reason why he no longer used the term by 1816 is that he came to take the free, fantastic treatment of the sonata form for granted. Bekker is right to suggest that Op. 101 has a great formal affinity with the very first work so designated by the composer, the Sonata in E-flat major, Op. 27, No.1.' Blom then adds, mindful of Beethoven's progress: '[S]piritually Op. 27 and Op. 101 are as far apart as they are in years.'[viii]

Whilst in the Piano Sonata Op. 101, Beethoven disposes of the expression *Sonata quasi una fantasia* he does, however, preface each movement with descriptions — significantly in the German language (see later) — by means of which to characterise the nature of the music. Thus, in the first movement, we have *Etwas lebhaft und mit der innigsten Empfindung* (With innermost feeling); in the second movement, *Lebhaft, marschmässig* (Quick, like a march); in the third movement, *Langsam und sehnsuchtsvoll* (Slow and full of yearning); and in the fourth movement, *Geschwind, doch nicht zu sehr, und mit Entschlossenheit* (Quickly, but not too fast and with decision). To quote Bekker again: '[The] programme of the fantasia is [thereby] completely expressed, and completely expressive of Beethoven.'[ix]

A possible indicator of Beethoven's evolving disposition to romantically conceived music, may be inferred from a cryptic entry in his *Tagebuch* (Diary) of 1816 in which he wrote: 'Only as before again at the piano [to make] my own fantasies — despite my hearing problems.'[x] In her Interpretation of these words, Sisman suggests Beethoven's self-exhortation was perhaps a means of urging himself, through his writing for the keyboard, to adopt a fantasy style as a means of compensating himself for no longer being able to improvise at the piano, as he had done years before when he had been lionised in Vienna's salons. In the works we have cited above, Sisman argues Beethoven's music becomes 'self-referential' in which he plays with the boundaries of movements that contain passages which can be characterised by words such as 'reminiscence' and 'recall'.[xi] Reflecting on the nature of the Piano Sonata Op. 101, Alfred Brendel comments: 'Altogether, this sonata had great impact on Romantic composers; the second movement affected Schuman's style more than anything else by Beethoven, and the *cantabile* lyricism of the first ... left clear traces in

Mendelsohn's [Piano] Sonata Op. 6.'[xii]

To return to the spirit of our opening remarks, Maynard Solomon describes Beethoven's last five piano sonatas and the *Diabelli* Variations — to which he adds the Bagatelles Op. 126 — as 'one of the pillars of Beethoven's creative achievements of his last years'. In their working out he draws attention to the manner in which Beethoven fuses fugal writing and variation form with sonata form as a means 'to the formulation of his new musical thought'.[xiii] To Solomon's formulation we might add the composer's searching for new sonorities — alongside technical developments applied to the extension of the keyboard — and his adoption of the trill that is no longer a mere decorative device but is inherent to the very soul of the music. In her pioneering *Master Musicians* study of Beethoven, Marion Scott found grandeur of conception in the composer's last five piano sonatas and highlights their 'breadth and majesty of symphonic thought' and how they simultaneously embrace the 'intimacy and unworldliness of chamber music'.[xiv] We reserve our concluding generalisations here for Cooper: 'The last five [piano] sonatas, spread over a period of seven years, contain, like the string quartets, a spiritual quality which transcends such considerations as form. Although they are considered as a group they differ greatly ... they display a great diversity of expression: the strength and flamboyant defiance of the *Hammerklavier* Sonata, Op. 106, ranging through the anguish of Op. 111, the warmth of Op. 110 and the intimacy of Op. 101.'[xv]

In his characterisation of the Op. 101 Sonata, Theodor Adorno considers the music inhabits a landscape such as that imagined by the German Romantic painter Caspar David Friederich.[xvi] Perhaps his most well known painting depicts a young man upon a rocky precipice contemplating a sea of mist — from which the picture derives its name. This image will be familiar to Schubertians as it is frequently used in association with his *Wanderer Fantasy* D. 489 of 1816 – making it contemporaneous with Beethoven's own piano music. Many commentators have sought to capture in words, the mood prevailing within the A major Piano Sonata. Oskar Bie calls to mind: 'An unearthly sweep of music, born tone-by-tone [that] rolls over us ... air-built scaffolding. It is the streaming forth of the most inward intuition of tone.'[xvii] Romain Rolland believed: 'The whole work is entirely happy and presents an untroubled mind.'[xviii] In a moving passage Wilfrid Mellers proposes the music 'seem[s] to attain the peace of earthly love; and perhaps [its] trills suggest that for Beethoven at least, earthly love was a necessary step towards heavenly'.[xix] For Brendel, the A major Piano Sonata is not an exuberant work: 'It does not belong to the line of spiritual dramas that "wrestle with the elements" or "quarrel with fate". All the happiness, all the power and assurance with which the sonata is imbued are imparted with supreme composure.'[xx]

We have remarked that in the period 1793–94 Beethoven received formal instruction in counterpoint from the learned theorist and contrapuntist Johann Albrechtsberger (see Piano Sonatas, Op. 2, Nos. 1–3). In the following decade, fugal elements and procedures found their way into several of the composer's works such as: the String Quartets, Op. 18 (1801); the Piano Variations and Fugue, Op. 35 (1802); choruses from the Cantata *Christ on the Mount of Olives*, Op. 85 (1803); the Funeral March from the *Eroica* Symphony, Op. 55 (1805); the Mass in C, Op. 86 (1807); and the finale to the String Quartet, Op. 59, No. 3 (1808). In his survey of Beethoven's contrapuntal achievements at this time, Solomon reflects: 'Beethoven ... came to maturity in an antipolyphonic age [and] reinstated the polyphonic principle as a rival of ... the sonata principle.'[xxi]

Beethoven's absorption in counterpoint continued in the next decade, with increased impetus as contrapuntal procedures became ever more prominent in his music — 'a distillation of musical thought where every note is an essential note'; consider, for example, the *Allegretto* of the Seventh Symphony, Op. 92 (1811–12).[xxii] A later generation would also be seized by such feeling, taking as its credo 'Back to Bach'. This remark points us appositely to related considerations that bear directly upon the A major Piano Sonata.

We have noted that Beethoven commenced tuition lessons in composition with the Archduke Rudolph sometime in 1809 (see Piano Sonata Op. 81a). With this course of instruction in mind, he requested his publisher Tobias Haslinger to provide him with a selection of works on music theory. With characteristic diligence Beethoven set about copying and annotating dozens of studies for his pupil — many of which still survive.[xxiii] It is tempting to suggest this absorption in musicological pedagogy may have further disposed him to absorb the very principles he was inculcating into his own music — in much the same way as his preoccupation with George Thomson's folksong settings may have imparted to it a melodic character. With regard to Beethoven's developing interest in counterpoint, Rolland has the following to say: 'One cannot help connecting his use of fugue in many of his later works with his later phase. But it was not the fugue of Bach, but one filled with sublimity and mysticism in which he attempted to render the spiritual force more and more concentrated, the meaning sometimes becomes completely dissipated in his attempt to grasp and hold it.'[xxiv] These later works would include the Cello Sonata, Op. 102, No. 2 (1815) and the *Hammerklavier* Piano Sonata, Op. 106 (1818). Of the A major Piano Sonata, Bie enthuses: 'In Op. 101 an unparalleled height of thematic development is attained ... The sonata exhibits thematic [feeling] in all its forms ... rhythmical motives are plentiful ... the smoothly flowing six-eight time ... the vigorous dotted quaver and semiquaver of the *Vivace*.'[xxv]

In our study of the Piano Sonata Op. 90 we commented that a farewell concert was given in February 1816 for the cellist Joseph Linke, a friend of Beethoven's and a member of Count Razumowsky's personal string quartet. We recall this circumstance one more. A review of the concert appeared in the *Allgemeine musikalische Zeitung* in which it was reported: '[A] new pianoforte sonata by this master [Beethoven] heard here for the first time, surprises all of his numerous admirers.'[xxvi] Beethoven's biographer Anton Schindler, writing of the event years later, recalled the sonata in question was the Op. 101. Authorities now though doubt Schindler's assertion since, as we shall shortly remark, the Autograph of the A major Sonata bears a later date than that of the concert.[xxvii] Less ambiguous is that very few indeed of Beethoven's piano sonatas were performed in public in the composer's lifetime. We learn something of this from the recollections of Franz Liszt. In 1876 Liszt wrote of the period, from about 1821, when he commenced his studies with Carl Czerny — himself a pupil of Beethoven. Liszt, like Czerny, was ten years old when he began his studies although even by then his remarkable powers were much in evidence — in fact Czerny complained Liszt had learned too much too soon. Liszt tells us: 'Many of Beethoven's sonatas were known and profoundly admired, especially the *Pathétique*, *Moonlight* and *Appassionata*, but it wasn't the custom to play them in public. Not until after Beethoven's death did his works circulate everywhere.'[xxviii] A measure of the aloofness, if not downright hostility, to Beethoven's later piano music is conveyed in an account from the writings of Beethoven's early biographer Wilhelm von Lenz. He has this to say of his experience of the reception of the composer's late piano sonatas when he was in Paris in 1828: 'The last five [Opp. 101, 106, 109, 110 and 111] passed for the monstrous abortions of a German idealist who did not know how to write for the piano. People only understood Hummel & Co.'[xxix] A measure of the time it took for Beethoven's late piano music to reach the ears of even the musically informed, can be inferred from a diary entry of Giacomo Meyerbeer dating from 1862. He writes: 'With Cornelie [?] to Hans von Bülow's concert which was devoted to piano music [including] Beethoven's Sonata in A major, Op. 101 which I had never heard before, a gifted glorious work, particularly the first elegiac movement and the third or fourth, which is a fugue.'[xxx] In passing we may observe that Hans von Bülow, now largely remembered as a conductor, was, together with Franz Liszt, a pioneer in promoting the awareness of Beethoven's late piano sonatas to a wider public in the nineteenth century.

We remarked above that although in the Piano Sonata Op. 101 Beethoven disposes of the expression *Sonata quasi una fantasia*, he makes use of German-language expressions by means of which to characterise the nature of the music. This was not something entirely new for him. We have seen, in connection with the Piano Sonata Op. 81a, the significance the composer attached to the German words *Lebewohl* and *Wiederschen* as indicating his inclination to use German titles and expression marks in preference to the conventional Italian. Similarly, we have noted how, in his Piano Sonata Op. 90, his desire to make fuller use of the German language found expression in the headings he provided in each of its two movements. In other of his works Beethoven had also experimented in this direction, and had even coined some substitute words, such as '*Luftsang* for *aria*, *Kreisfluchstück* for *canon*, and *Grundsang* for *bass*'.[xxxi]

More generally, Anton Schindler records that by 1816 German terms were being used in music journals as well as being adopted by other composers.[xxxii]

Beethoven may have been induced to promote his native language, at least in part, in response to national promptings to do so. We learn from Schindler that the suggestion had gone out, sometime in 1817, that German composer's should substitute German terms in their music in place of Italian.[xxxiii] Doubtless this was in response to the resurgence of national spirit felt across Europe in the period 1816–17 in the wake of the Napoleonic wars. In our commentary on the circumstances surrounding the composition of the Piano Sonata Op. 90, we have seen how keenly Beethoven identified with the changing political sentiments in his patriotic *Wellington's Sieg* (*Wellington's Victory*) and the Cantata *Der glorreiche Augenblick* (The Glorious Moment). It is not surprising therefore that he should want to adopt the German vernacular so readily in musical terminology in preference to the internationally accepted Italian terms.

We discuss the compositional origins of the A major Piano Sonata shortly. Suffice it to say here that by 1817 Beethoven was well in hand with the completion of the work. Consequently, with characteristic impetuosity, he wrote to his publisher Sigmund Anton Steiner to ensure the Title Page of his new composition should give expression to his desired German-language reforms. He writes, in the humorous, quasi-militaristic style he customarily adopted in his dealings with Steiner: '[We] are resolved and hereby resolve that from henceforth on all our works, on which the title is German, instead of pianoforte *Hammerklavier* shall be used ... Hence our most excellent L[ieutenan]t G[enera]l and his Adjutant and all others whom it may concern, are to comply with these orders immediately and see that they are carried out.'[xxxiv] In the event, despite the energetic nature of Beethoven's exhortations, his request was not entirely fulfilled — see later.

A further consideration should be briefly mentioned here in connection with Beethoven's enthusiasm for the adoption of the term *Hammerklavier*, in preference to *Pianoforte*. Keyboard instruments were undergoing considerable transformation at the period in question, and would continue to do so to the end of the composer's life. Beethoven never intended the designation *Hammerklavier* to be a mere substitution for *Pianoforte*. Rather, he wished to use terminology that better conveyed the new sonority he was imparting to his piano music and the new type of sound production by hammers actuated from the keyboard — quintessentially well suited to the massive pianism he was to reveal in his next great work for the keyboard, the Piano Sonata Op. 106, universally known simply as *The Hammerklavier*. Of related interest is what Beethoven's former pupil Carl Czerny has to say on the subject of the changes underway regarding the transformation of keyboard instruments. In an address he gave to the students of the August Eberhard Müller's Piano School he remarked: '[The] fortepianos themselves are every year refined with new inventions and improvements, and it is as yet impossible to predict when this complicated instrument will finally be perfected ... [At] the same rate [as the technical improvements] the virtuosi of our time in their playing as well as in their compositions, have brought about a perfection to the handling of the instrument, and a versatility to any performance, that one could not have imagined.'[xxxv]

Beethoven's efforts to bring about reform in the adoption of the German language in music proved in vain. We have just remarked on its permanent association with the great Piano Sonata in B-flat major. Beyond that the term found little acceptance. As we shall see, even the Piano Sonata Op. 101 appeared with *both* 'Hammerklavier' and 'Pianoforte' on its Title Page and the three final Piano Sonatas Opp. 109, 110 and 111 were all designated as being for the Pianoforte. Perhaps the challenge of creating great works and bringing about philological reforms at the same time proved too much, even for Beethoven.

Beethoven dedicated the Piano Sonata Op. 101 to Baroness Dorothea von Ertmann; she has appeared in our accounts on a number of occasions and we have cause to call her to mind once more. She was eleven years younger than Beethoven and by the age of sixteen was familiar with several of his contemporary keyboard works, including the Piano Sonata Op. 2, No. 1. In 1803 an article appeared in the Berlin periodical *Der Freimüthige* in which Ertmann's playing was praised for its 'amazing precision, clarity and delicacy'. Thayer states: '[All] contemporary authorities agree [she was] if not the greatest player of [Beethoven's] works, at least the greatest of her sex.' It is from about 1803 that Dorothea made the personal acquaintance of the composer who, shortly afterwards, and impressed by her playing, felt disposed to send her a greeting card with the salutation: 'To the Baroness Ertmann on New Year's Day 1804 from your friend and admirer Beethoven.'[xxxvi] Schindler considered Ertmann's interpretation of Beethoven's piano music to be without equal, revealing a natural grasp 'of even the most hidden subtleties'. He adds: 'She knew how to give each phrase the motion of its particular spirit, how to move artistically from one phrase to the next, so that the whole seemed a motivated unity.' In Schindler's estimation: 'She was a conservatoire all by herself.' It appears her playing was distinguished by its intimacy and expressiveness rather than by showy physicality. It is known she declined to perform any work that did not suite her style, following her self-imposed maxim: 'Not everything is appropriate for everyone.'xxxvii Dorothea was apparently a pianist who made up for her lack of physical strength by the sensitivity of her playing. According once more to Schindler's testimony, it was as a consequence of her championing of Beethoven's piano sonatas, in later years, that did much to save them from neglect and helped them to maintain their place in the repertoire.xxxviii As several commentators have concluded, given the poetic nature of Ertmann's style of performance — and the personal regard Beethoven had for her playing — it is not surprising he should dedicate his A major Piano Sonata to her, imbued as it is with so many of the pianistic qualities to which she was so intuitively inclined.

Musicologist Nicolas Slonimsky remarks: 'There is a tendency among biographers to seek romantic implications in every dedication Beethoven made to a woman.'xxxix With regard to the dedication of his Op. 101 to Dorothea von Ertmann, the composer's actions are known to be free from such sentiments; she was happily married to Baron Stephan von Ertmann an Austrian army officer who eventually held the rank of lieutenant-field marshal. On a visit to Milan in 1831, Mendelsohn paid a visit to the Ertmann's where they were then residing. He wrote of the experience to his sister Fanny. Dorothea performed the C-sharp minor Piano Sonata for him that he found to be full of expression — if somewhat exaggerated. Baron Ertmann was, however, apparently moved to tears by his wife's playing and when they later dined, he appeared in full-dress military uniform — complete with all his medals! Concerning Mendelssohn's opinion of Dorothea's playing, it should be borne in mind she was by then aged fifty, was living a relatively reclusive life outside of the music salons and had not regularly practised the piano. The views of Dorothea's husband Stefan are also of interest; he told Mendelssohn there was no public enthusiasm in Milan at this time for Beethoven's music.[xl]

Sketches for the A major Piano Sonata appear in the so-called Scheide Sketchbook, named after its former owner William Scheide; it is now a prized possession of the William Scheide Library at Princeton, New Jersey. Beethoven made use of this sketchbook between March 1815 and May 1816. Today it consists of 56 leaves but may originally have contained a further 24, some of which are now housed in other collections in Berlin, Bonn, London (The British Library) and Washington. In addition to drafts for the Op. 101, the sketchbook reveals, in typical Beethoven fashion, ideas for a number of other works. These include outlines for the song cycle *An die ferne Geliebte* (Op. 98) and the Sonata for Cello and Piano in D major (Op. 102, No. 2). Rather tantalisingly, the sketchbook also contains evidence for an unfinished piano concerto.[xli]

One of the miscellaneous leaves, now in the archive of the Beethoven House in Bonn, reveals ideas for the sonata's first and last movements. Of interest, and of some significance, is Beethoven's writing on this sheet the expression 'augmentation'. This may be seen as a typical example of one of Beethoven's self-exhortations, in this case to dispose him to the contrapuntal style of writing that is evident in the work's final movement. In his commentary to these sketches, Sieghard Brandenburg maintains: 'The two outer movements compliment each other, the first movement *mit innigsten Empfindung* and the last movement with its contrapuntal techniques, similar to those of a fugue.' He adds: 'Clearly the two poles between which the musical activity is played-out were decided upon at an early stage ... The old model prelude-fugue, antithetically sharpened, was probably the starting point for the composition.'[xlii]

Given their shared ownership of the Scheide Sketchbook, it is not surprising the composer's Op. 101 and Op. 102 should posses similar features in their musical structures. In the opinion of Charles Rosen: 'The similarities are so striking, the form so eccentric, that it would seem as if Beethoven considered the structure an experimental one that he wanted to essay with two different kinds of material.'[xliii] Other commentators remark on the manner in which the Op. 101 adopts 'the closely-woven four-movement scheme of the cello sonatas and something of their fugal propensities'.[xliv] Eric Blom in his discussion of Beethoven's technical mastery, as evident in his writing for the keyboard, argues this was a means to poetic expression in music of the highest level: 'The means by which this is attained through manipulation of the composer's craft, and put into logical shape by his instinctive knowledge of how to handle and adjust form, came to him quite naturally by this time [1816], provided that he was seized by the fever of irresistible inspiration, as in this glorious work.'[xlv]

Of Beethoven's originality Edwin Fischer contends: 'Here, in Op. 101, the form is still rather open; but the way one thing grows out of another, the way the sonata is hidden, as the structure of a tree is concealed by the foliage, the way the syncopated notes become the very pulse of the work — all this is quite unique.'[xlvi] Stewart Gordon invokes similar imagery in what he describes as, 'Beethoven's penchant for regarding the sonata as an umbrella under which other structures might flourish [and which finally] gives birth in this work to the inclusion of a fugue.'[xlvii] In his notes to the Piano Sonata Op. 101, written on the occasion when all of Beethoven's works were broadcast without interruption within a single week, Matthew Rye alerted listeners in similar manner to these aspects of the work: 'It shares with the *Hammerklavier* and the summatory Opp. 109–111 a desire to weld together the form of sonata with the contrapuntal principles of canon and fugue.'[xlviii] The other device that helps to bind the movements together is one we have mentioned already, namely, Beethoven's innovatory procedure of recalling themes heard in one movement later on in another. In Cooper's words: 'The resulting structure of the sonata, with increased fragmentation, is counterbalanced by a greater sense of continuity between each section.'[xlix]

A further characteristic of the structure of the Op. 101 is Beethoven's exploitation of the extended keyboard that was becoming available to him at the period of the work's conception, a circumstance to which we have made previous reference. Philip Radcliffe comments on this: 'As the compass of the keyboard expanded, Beethoven made use of all possible variety of colour, sometimes concentrating on its extreme registers. The result is often less euphonious than the later works of Clementi and Dussek, but has a strongly individual character. At the same time an increasing interest in counterpoint leads to more and more subtlety of detail.'[l]

Beethoven worked on the A major Piano Sonata in the summer of 1816 which he spent at the spa town of Baden, south of Vienna. Progress with the composition was delayed for a number of reasons. These included having to devote time to what we may describe as the composer's bread-and-butter works that included the large-scale March for Military Wind Band, WoO 24 (3 June 1816), the score of which includes parts for eight trumpets and six horns.[li] Moreover, George Thomson was urging Beethoven to work on more of his folk-song settings, based on airs from other countries than Scotland, including Poland, Russia, Spain and Venice.[lii]

By November 1816 the sonata was completed and the following year the music was in print but its presentation was not yet to Beethoven's satisfaction.[liii] He had detected errors in the proofs and requested his manuscript to be returned from the publishers — Anton Steiner and his partner Tobias Haslinger — so that he could make the required corrections.[liv] Beethoven had also been giving more thought to the adoption of the German language and how the sonata should be described on the Title Page. This is clear from the surviving autograph where it can be seen Beethoven has tentatively written 'Neue Sonate für Ham ... ', the inference being — in leaving the word 'Ham' incomplete — he had not quite decided whether he should name the sonata *Hammer-Klavier* or *Hammer-Flügel*.[lv]

In a subsequent letter to Haslinger (simply dated January 1817) he enthuses: 'Quite by chance I have hit on the following: "Sonata/for the Pianoforte/or — — Hämmer-Clavier/composed and/dedicated to/the Baroness Dorothea [von] Ertmann/née Graumann/by L. v. Beethoven".' He was mindful the Title Page might already have been engraved, in the conventional manner adopting the French language, and so added: 'I shall pay *for the new title*, i.e., *it will be engraved at my expense*, or this title will be reserved *for another new sonata which I shall compose*.' [Beethoven's italics] The reference to 'another new sonata' is almost certainly The *Hammerklavier* Piano Sonata, Op. 106 on which he commenced work later in the autumn. Beethoven urged Haslinger 'to observe the strictest silence about the dedication' since he wanted it to be a surprise for its dedicatee.[lvi] A few days later he berated Haslinger with a further letter stating: '*Sonate* must be printed in German letters — Musée musical should be given first in German, for example, Musikalisches Museum, and underneath this, Musée musical, or printed in German only, Sonata des Museums für Klavie-rmusik, etc.'[lvii] Not satisfied, he wrote to Haslinger once more: 'In regard to the title, a linguist should be consulted as to whether *Hammer* or *Hämmer-Klavier* or, possibly *Hämmer-Flügel* should be inserted. Be sure to let me see the title for my approval.'[lviii] Beethoven was active himself in seeking guidance from reputable authorities regarding the promotion of the German language in music. One such was Wilhelm Hebenstreit, a writer and journalist who interested himself in various contemporary movements, such as the abolition of finding substitutes for foreign terms in favour of their German equivalents. Also, in his correspondence with Haslinger, it appears Beethoven had been receiving advice from Hebenstreit on this subject although the outcome of which is not clear.[lix]

Yet another letter followed from Beethoven, this time to Andreas Steiner, which requires a few words of explanation. A notice of a performance of the Seventh Symphony had recently appeared in the *Wiener Musikzeitung* in which the reviewer had pronounced the work 'difficult to perform'. This was the very symphony, upon hearing which, Weber is alleged to have remarked: 'The extravagances of this genius have now reached the *non plus ultra*, and Beethoven must be quite ripe for the madhouse.'[lx] Beethoven, who was not indifferent to the criticism of his music, could not resist writing to Anton Steiner — with tongue in cheek — with a proposal for the name of his new sonata: 'As for the title of the new sonata, all you need do is to transfer to it the title which the *Wiener Musikzeitung* gave to the Symphony in A, i.e. "The sonata that is difficult to perform".' He adds: 'Difficult is a relative term, e.g. what seems difficult to one person will seem easy to another, and that therefore the term has no precise meaning ... *what is difficult is also beautiful, good, great and so forth* ... everyone will realize that this is *the most lavish* praise that can be bestowed, since what is difficult *makes one sweat* [Beethoven's italics]'.[lxi] There are suggestions here in what Beethoven has to say in the words Shakespeare gives to Prospero in *The Tempest*: '[Too] light winning make the prize light.'

When the sonata was eventually published, Haslinger was once more approached by Beethoven who requested a copy for the dedicatee who was about to leave Vienna.[lxii] It appears Haslinger duly obliged, since on 23 February 1817 Beethoven sent Dorothea an engraved copy of the sonata with the accompanying note: 'MY DEAR AND BELOVED DOROTHEA/ CAECILIA: Please accept now what was often intended for you and what may be to you a proof of my devotion both to your artistic aspirations and to your person.' In designating Dorothea as *Caecilia*, Beethoven was likening her to *Cecilia* the patron saint of music; note also his use of capital letters by way of emphasising the warmth of his feelings.[lxiii]

Notwithstanding Beethoven's many letters to Steiner and Haslinger, when the A major Piano Sonata was duly published, in February 1817, the Title Page still made reference to the pianoforte: '*Sonate pour le PIANO-FORTE – für das HAMER-KLAVIER, des MUSEUMS FÜR KLAVIER-MUSIK, verfast und der Freiin Dorothea Ertmann, geborne Graumann, gewidmet von Ludwig van Beethoven. 101 Werk. Eigenthum der Verlerger, WIEN, bei S. A. Steiner & Co.*'[lxiv] As can be seen, the composer's efforts to promote the German language were not entirely in vain; Steiner had included the required *HAMER-KLAVIER* – although not yet quite in the form as we know it today *Hammerklavier*.[lxv] Also in evidence is Steiner's reference to *des museums für klavier-musik* – in German – as requested by Beethoven. This was the sub-title Steiner gave to a series of publications by means of which he sought to promote works of lasting value, or, as Steiner proclaimed in his original wording, 'only musical products of recognized value, compositions that are particularly distinguished by aesthetically pure design developed with art, charm and clarity'.[lxvi] The A major Piano Sonata was among the first of such compositions to be included in Steiner's 'Museum' and has indeed, as he would have wished, taken its place in the canon of great works for the keyboard — unlike the fate of most other works in Steiner's collection that have remained mere 'cabinet curiosities'. That, however, cannot be said of Franz Schubert's so-called Fantasy Piano Sonata in G major, D. 894 that also appeared in Steiner's Museum series in April 1827.[lxvii]

The originality and artistry enshrined within the Op. 101 Piano Sonata were not lost upon the reviewer commissioned to write about the piece in the October 1817 issue of the *Allgemeine musikalische Zeitung*: 'This latest product which *Beethoven* presents to us, delivers us continued proof of his inexhaustible inventiveness, of his profound artistry, of his lively imagination, of his universal genius! ... Truly, here, in his 101st work, we are filled with admiration and renewed high esteem, when we, thus, with the great painter of soul-images, walk along never-tread-on paths, virtually following Ariadne's thread along labyrinth-like trails, where here, a fresh brook might whisper to us and there, we will be faced by a bold rock, where here, a sweet, fragrant flower attracts us and there, a thorny path might frighten us off.' The reviewer concludes: '[This] work of art ... while small in size, is great, truly great in content, and the unassuming shell of which might hide many a jewel.'[lxviii] We have seen Beethoven himself acknowledged his A major Piano Sonata was difficult to perform. Writing of the interpretive challenges posed by the work, Blom suggests: 'There are difficulties demanding brilliant playing ... and the writing has the ingenuity of the completely self-possessed master; but it is due precisely to this self-possession that Beethoven is now able to concentrate his whole creative mind on emotional expression in the most poetical terms of which music is capable.'[lxix]

Notwithstanding its many virtues, throughout the nineteenth century, and well into the twentieth, the Op. 101 appears to have suffered from neglect. Writing of this, at the time of Beethoven's death-centenary (1927), the distinguished scholar and music critic John Fuller-Maitland stated: 'Op. 101, in A is apt to be overshadowed by the splendour of the others [Opp. 106, 109, 110 and 111] but it could occasionally be heard separately from them, it would be found intensely interesting and characteristic.'[lxx] When in conversation with Alfred Brendel, musicologist David Dubal shared his love of the composition with the acknowledged celebrated interpreter of Beethoven; but suggested: 'It is really not so well-known as the others [i.e., the later sonatas].' Brendel replied: 'It doesn't communicate as well as the later pieces. But it is a wonderful, basically positive, and energetic piece, not a tortured piece.' Acknowledging the technical challenges confronting the would-be performer, he added: 'However, to convey this sense of security, of happiness, is very hard in pianistic terms ... I would call it the most difficult sonata to play well.'[lxxi] In a later essay Brendel recalls the sensitive and informed playing of the composition's original dedicatee, Baroness Dorothea von Ertmann, prompting him to exclaim: 'And how much Op. 101 in particular needs a confident and initiated player!'[lxxii]

Before proceeding to our discussion of the individual movements of the A major Piano Sonata, we briefly consider some of the contextual circumstances bearing down on Beethoven at the period of its creation. This was a time of considerable challenge to his health, wellbeing and everyday circumstances, all of which would, in turn, have consequences for his compositional output — but not on the quality of the creations he would, nonetheless, bring into being. Concerning the latter, the accepted view is to attribute Beethoven's relatively few compositions of his 'late period'

– compared with those of his 'heroic period' – to his progressive loss of hearing and with it the increased social isolation this imposed – depriving him of the stimulation that extemporizing in the salons had once provided. Secondly, affecting his personal circumstances, were his extended, and at times fractious, preoccupations concerning his manoeuvrings to secure the legal custody of his nephew Karl. Finally may be cited Beethoven's worry over financial matters that, it has to be said, were often more imagined than real – bearing in mind the money he had earned, and later invested, at the time of the Congress of Vienna.

Whilst acknowledging Beethoven's personal circumstances had implications for his creative output, it needs to be borne in mind that the nature of the compositions he was now creating imposed greater demands on his time, given their scale and complexity. As William Newman contends: 'These works were not only of relatively great magnitude, both in size and emotional scope, but they continue to lead further and further into obscurities of uncharted techniques, styles, and forms.'[lxiii] Brendel expresses similar thoughts: '[The] influence of biographical events on Beethoven's manner of composition should not be exaggerated: the slowing down in his working procedures may well be explained by the greater density and complexity of his later style.'[lxiv]

References to the effects the loss of hearing meant for Beethoven occur throughout his correspondence over the period 1815–17, both directly and indirectly. For instance, in the summer of 1815 he wrote to Johann Xaver Brauchle, a minor composer who was then employed as the tutor to the children of the Countess Anna Maria Erdödy – an accomplished pianist and one of Beethoven's many aristocratic, women-friend admirers.[lxv] He confides: 'I am not well ... Peevish about many things, more sensitive than all other mortals, and tormented by my poor hearing I often feel only *pain* in the society of others [Beethoven's italics].'[lxxvi] A measure of his concern is further conveyed in a letter he wrote to a certain Herr Riedel (his full name is not given). Riedel was a builder of chamber organs and Beethoven was having difficulty in playing an instrument that Riedel had installed for him. The inference from this is he was searching for an ever more sonorous instrument that he could hear more clearly.[lxxvii]

We have seen in several of our commentaries to other of the composer's piano sonatas, that Beethoven took an active interest in the development of the piano (pianoforte) of his day, often advising instrument makers about their action and offering advice to friends and acquaintances who wanted to purchase an instrument. For example in March 1815, when Beethoven's hearing was still sufficiently intact for him to discern the different qualities of keyboard instruments, he was able to write to Joseph von Varena – a musically and philanthropically inclined lawyer – in the following terms: 'You can have from *Schantz* as good a piano as he is able to supply for the price of 400 gulden.' Johann Schantz was a recognized dealer in fine instruments and was already supplying state-of-the-art pianos with a range of six octaves. Beethoven, ever the businessman, adds: 'There are, however, other excellent makers, I hear, from whom you could purchase a sound and durable instrument for a good deal less.'[lxxviii]

In the following two years, Beethoven's hearing deteriorated considerably and in July 1817 he appealed to Nanette Streicher – a close friend and a founder member of one of Vienna's most celebrated manufacturers of pianos: 'I have a great favour to ask of Streicher [Johann Andreas – Nanette's husband]. Request him on my behalf to be so kind as to adjust one of your pianos for me to suit my impaired hearing. It should be as loud as possible. That is absolutely necessary. It should be as loud as possible.'[lxxix] In August he wrote once more to Nanette asking her to thank Johann for his endeavours with the plea: 'Please ask him to continue his efforts.'[lxxx] Some authorities believe the Streichers' may have supplied Beethoven with a piano having some form of acoustic hood, above the keyboard, so as to reflect back the sound; if this was the case it no longer exists. It is also possible Streicher may have suggested to Beethoven the advantages to his hearing of him using an upright piano. The Vienna-based manufacturer Matthias Muller had developed such an instrument in about 1800. This had something of the appearance of a grand piano, turned upwards, to reveal one straight side and one curved side — earning it the colloquial expression *giraffe-style* of *giraffe-flügel*.[lxxxi]

At the close of 1817 Beethoven appears to have finally come to terms with his impaired hearing — by which we mean he realized it would not improve. In December he wrote once more to Nanette, but this time the subject was ear trumpets. The pioneer of the metronome, Johann Mälzel (Maelzel) had provided Beethoven with a variety of designs (see Piano Sonata Op. 2, Nos. 1—3) and he appears to have sought advice from the Streicher's about one of these. In his letter he asks for its return, with the encouraging remark, 'with its help I have gained a considerable amount of information'.[lxxxii] However, with the passing of time it seems ear trumpets proved to be of little practical benefit. By the following year Beethoven had to make recourse to notebooks — *conversation books* — so that instead of having to yell at him, friends and visitors could write down their thoughts.

We consider next Beethoven's health at the time when he was composing the A major Piano Sonata. Although his relationship with his brother Casper Carl was at times a troubled one — we recall, for example, the occasion when out walking together they had come to blows (see Piano Sonata Op. 31, Nos. 1–3) — nonetheless, he benefited from Carl's assistance on the occasions when he acted on his behalf in his negotiations with publishers. Consequently, when Carl finally succumbed to tuberculosis on 15 December 1815, Beethoven must have felt his brother's loss twofold: first, as an ally in helping him to make progress with his work — although Carl's efforts had lessened in this respect following his marriage; secondly, through the natural bonds of filial affection between close family members. The very next day following Carl's death, Beethoven wrote to his pupil the Archduke Rudolph: Ever since yesterday afternoon I have been lying down exhausted by great exertions necessitated by the very sudden death of my unfortunate brother.'[lxxxiii] Beethoven estimated that during Carl's illness, he had spent upwards of 10,000 gulden on his late brother and family, an amount that was the equivalent to him of ten years' rent.[lxxxiv]

Beethoven's wellbeing continued to be disturbed into the following year as we learn from a letter he wrote on 13 May 1816 to the Countess Erdödy: '[For] the last six weeks I have been in very poor health, so much so that frequently I have thought of my death.' He adds, with characteristic philosophical reflection: 'Man cannot avoid suffering; and *in this respect his strength must stand the test* ... [Beethoven's italics].'[lxxxv] Beethoven's strength was indeed put to the test and a year later we find him once more writing to the Countess (19 June 1817) about his health. He laments being unwell since the previous October and of the number of medications he must take, authorised by a doctor whom he did not trust — 'a wily Italian'. What he regretted most was not being able to go for country walks. He noted in his daybook: 'It is as if every tree spoke to me in the country.

Holy! Holy! Ecstasy in the woods. Who can describe it?'[lxxxvi] Only after several months did Beethoven's doctor allow him to go out, and even then just for a short while. His protracted illness was also having an effect on his creative enterprises, he complained: 'I can compose very little.'[lxxxvii] On 21 August he wrote to his old friend Nikolaus Zmeskall von Domanovecz, a civil servant by profession but known in musical circles as an excellent cellist: 'I often despair and would like to die ... I can foresee no end to my infirmities ... next year I shall not be in London but in my grave.'[lxxxviii]

Beethoven's reference to London requires a few words of explanation. By 1817 his works were being performed there although some were received with caution. For example, the previous year Charles Neate, who had recently been appointed a Director of The Philharmonic Society, wrote to Beethoven on 29 October to explain the difficulty he was having in promoting the composer's two Cello Sonatas Op. 102: 'I have offered your Sonatas to several publishers, but they thought them too difficult, and said they would not be saleable.' More optimistically he adds: '[When] I shall have played them to a few professors, their reputation will naturally be increased by their merits.'[lxxxix] In June 1817 Beethoven's former piano pupil Ferdinand Ries re-kindled the composer's hopes of him paying a visit to England's musical capital. He wrote enthusiastically: 'The Philharmonic Society ... wishes to give you evidence of its great esteem and its gratitude for the many beautiful moments that we have enjoyed in your extraordinarily ingenious works ... I have been commissioned ... to offer you 300 guineas on the following conditions: (1) You are to be here in London next winter; (2) You are to write two grand symphonies for the Philharmonic Society which are to remain its property.'[xc] Although Beethoven had long cherished the idea of paying a visit to London, his protracted illness precluded this. Beethoven did, however, complete one of the requested works – the Ninth Symphony – but its projected companion, a tenth symphony, remained incomplete at the time of his death.

In the early autumn of 1817 Beethoven relocated to Baden where he hoped to benefit by taking the waters, as hydrotherapy was then styled. On 1 September he wrote to his pupil Rudolph once more, remarking on the 'medicines of all kinds and in all forms' he was still taking. He discerned some improvement in his health but acknowledged he 'must abandon the hope of ... making a complete recovery'.[xci] It was not until early November that he felt able to resume his work with something like his former vitality and spirited demeanour.

In his correspondence with Countess Anna Maria Erdödy, Beethoven makes reference to the financial burden of now caring for his nephew Karl – the natural son he never had. Chapters have been written on Beethoven's relationship with Karl, including attempts to superimpose modern-day psychoanalysis. Such detailed considerations lie outside our narrative to which we restrict ourselves to the following summary-remarks.

Casper Carl conferred the custodianship of his son Karl to the composer on 14 November 1814 under the terms of article five of his Will: 'I appoint my brother Ludwig van Beethoven guardian. Inasmuch as he, my deeply loved brother, has often aided me with true brotherly love in the most magnanimous and noblest manner, I expect, with full confidence and with full trust in his noblest heart, that he shall bestow his love and friendship that he showed me also upon Karl, and do all that is possible to promote the intellectual training and welfare of my son.'[xcii] Beethoven persuaded the legal authorities – who were perhaps intimidated by his formidable reputation – to put Karl in his trust, in place of his natural mother, on the grounds of her being considered not a suitable person. Beethoven denigrated his sister-in-law for her alleged illicit, amorous liaisons, referring to her as 'The Queen of the Night' — a thinly veiled allusion to the principal character in Mozart's opera *The Magic Flute*.

These circumstances were a tragedy for all concerned. Karl's mother bitterly contested the court's ruling over the following years, winning back her son at intervals. Beethoven devoted endless time to his nephew; for example, something like sixty letters and notes passed between him and Nanette Streicher, many concerned with the management of his household and Karl's needs — all to the detriment of his creative work. Ultimately, Karl was the most seriously affected by being torn between his mother and an aging, eccentric, hard-of-hearing bachelor. It is not surprising that he made an attempt on his life — to Beethoven's mortification. Fortunately, Karl survived and we can take leave of him in happier circumstances. He eventually joined the army, attained an officer's commission and later married Karoline Naske by whom he had five children. Today his handsome countenance is preserved in an early Daguerreotype.[xciii]

We have a description of Beethoven from the period we are considering, as recollected in the diary of the physician Dr. Karl von Bursy. He paid a visit to the composer in the summer of 1816 and left the following account: 'He is short, but sturdy-looking with grey hair ... and fiery eyes ... full of intense life. He asked me to speak loudly as his hearing is very bad ... He has not been well for some time.' Beethoven told Bursy: 'I always work at several things at once, and take up first one then the other ... He often strikes the piano with his first so violently that the room resounds ... Beethoven seems very anxious about money ... He was pleased to hear that *Fidelio* had been so well received in Berlin ... I saw but little music; some pieces of paper lay on the table.' Bursy remarks how publishers complained Beethoven 'charged monstrously for his compositions'. On a later visit (27 July) Beethoven was not at home and so Bursy left him a message, then temptation overtook him; he left with Beethoven's quill as a souvenir. The *corpus delicti* was 'a constant memorial to his moment of weakness'.[xciv]

Beethoven's illness through 1817 did not entirely subdue his spirit. The Swiss musician, composer and pianist Schnyder von Wartensee (see Piano Sonata Op. 81a) wrote to Beethoven recalling their previous time together in Vienna – the two had first met in 1812. Beethoven responded fulsomely: 'You have remembered that you were once with me in Vienna.' He continued with an exhortation typical of the kind he often imposed upon himself in his notebooks in periods of self-doubt: 'Continue to raise yourself higher and higher into the divine realm of art. For there is no more undisturbed and unalloyed or purer pleasure than that which comes from such an experience.'[xcv]

An event occurred in the autumn of 1815 that should have raised Beethoven's spirits – despite the fact that he was largely immune to flattery. On 16 November, the Magistrates of Vienna's Municipal Council conferred on him 'free civil rights', in effect the Freedom of the City. This honour was in recognition of his philanthropic work as recognised in the wording of the official citation: 'Herr Ludwig van Beethoven ... in the past years [has] not only made available the performance of his musical instrumental compositions free of charge, but also with unpretentious willingness ... and through his humanitarian endeavour ... procured ... such rich proceeds that through it the poor men, women and children, humbled by old age and infirmity, could be provided comfort and alleviation of their destinies ...'.[xcvi] In conferring 'free civil rights' of citizenship on Beethoven in this way, one practical consequence of this noble act on the part of Vienna's Magistrates was to exempt the composer from municipal taxation!

Recognition was bestowed on Beethoven from another quarter that perhaps meant more to him. When issue 18 of the *Allgemeine musikalische Zeitung* appeared on 11 September 1816, it carried a generally favourable review of Beethoven and his music. Interestingly this was based on *An account of the first Edinburgh Music Festival* – the precursor, by a century-and-a-half, of the current Edinburgh International Festival. Beethoven is first compared with Haydn and Mozart. The reviewer acknowledges: '[The] admirable qualities [of] these three famous men are so utterly different in their style and manner.' He continues: 'The first appeared to be more distinguished because of his broad manner and knowledge of effect; the second because of his noble feeling and cultured expression.' Next it is Beethoven's turn: 'With an imagination less ordered and mature than Haydn's and Mozart's, Beethoven seems to posses as much fire and vigour as both. There is a certain wildness and Herculean capturing of imagination that is characteristic of this excellent musician. It is his pleasure to wander about in the regions of darkness and magic and to make the heart shudder with sounds that appear to resound from the inhabitants of an undiscovered land and from whose borders no traveller returns.'[xcvii]

By a remarkable coincidence an entry of 16 June 1816 in the diary of the young Franz Schubert, expresses similar sentiments to the closing passages of the contemporaneous *AmZ* review. Schubert writes of the 'bizzarrerie of current musical trends' and attributes these to the influence of 'one of our greatest living artists ... [who] unites and confuses the tragic and the comic, the pleasant and repulsive without compunction'.[xcviii] Schubert is undoubtedly referring to his hero Beethoven whose music he so admired but which, as his comments imply, he sometimes found difficult to enjoy.

A year later a further tribute to Beethoven appeared in the pages of the *Allgemeine musikalische Zeitung*, this time in the September issue of 1817. Friederike Salzer was a contemporary prolific writer who published more than 600 poems and periodical articles. She clearly admired Beethoven's compositions and set forth her feelings in a sonnet that opens: 'I see heavenly forces intertwine with the world/See beautiful Eden of the first creation blossom/When like Apollo's magic harmonies/The wonderful strings of the master of tones quiver.'[xcix]

These testimonies to and affirmations of Beethoven's creative powers, form a fitting closure to our survey of some of the contextual matters and lifetime circumstances bearing on the composer at the period of gestation and composition of the Piano Sonata in A major, Op. 101. A period, as we have seen, of illness and of mental anguish but above all of which the composer's indomitability of spirit prevailed. We turn now to a consideration of the work's individual movements.

The first movement is headed *Allegretto ma non troppo* that Beethoven — true to his intention of giving fuller expression to the German language — qualifies with the expression *Etwas lebhaft und mit der innigsten Empfindung*. This can be interpreted variously as: 'With innermost feeling'; 'Rather lively and with the warmest feeling'; or 'Somewhat lively, and with the most fervent perception/intimate sentiment/innermost feeling' — all of these terms, and doubtless others, can be found in modern-day commentaries to the movement. Whichever formulation is followed, Beethoven's intentions are clear. From the outset he wishes to convey the music which is about to unfold, is imbued with 'impressions and reveries'. These are the words that, according to Schindler, Beethoven used himself in connection with both the first and third movements.[c] Maynard Solomon, citing Schindler's original German text, suggests a more fitting translation of Beethoven's wording would be 'dreamlike sensations'.[ci]

In interpreting Beethoven's precise meaning by which he sought to characterise the mood prevailing within the first movement, we enter the realms of the subjective and the poetic. The music opens gently, lyrically and, to invoke Solomon once more, 'dreamlike'. For Brendel, the opening is 'a tenderly questioning phrase'.[cii] Rye's response to the opening is to suggest how the work begins subtly, 'almost as if the music had been flowing already'.[ciii] Denis Matthews has a similar take on the opening bars, likening their quiet informality to the experience one has when entering a room in the middle of someone's conversation. He also remarks how well suited Beethoven's expression *mit der innigsten Empfindung* appears to be with what we know of the playing of the sonata's dedicatee, the Baroness Dorothea von Ertmann; as we have noted, her interpretations were intimate rather than virtuosic.[civ] Donald Tovey considered the first movement of the A major Piano Sonata to be 'exquisite' and a demonstration of Beethoven's continuing powers of imagination.[cv] Philosopher and musicologist Theodor Adorno writes how he personally discovered Beethoven's Op. 101 and cherished it as his own. Gripped by the inherent poetic nature of the music, that he characterises as expressing 'resignation', he poses the proposition: 'Is the first movement the model for the prelude to *Tristan*? ... As if the (incomparably condensed) sonata form had become a lyric poem, entirely subjectivized [into] sequences of longing.'[cvi]

Arnold Whittall in his survey of the influences on tradition and innovation in twentieth-century music, singles out what he considers to be central to the spirit of Beethoven's A major Piano Sonata. Writing of its first movement he argues: '[The] mixing of tragic elements endows the pastoral with greater seriousness, and the elevation of style in turn supports the interpretation of the pastoral as a poetic conceit for a spiritual state of innocence (or serenity) subject to the disturbances of ... tragic experience (or remembrance).' Implicit in what he has to say is that Beethoven is, in part, looking back to his Piano Sonata Op 28 that bears the title *Pastoral* and is at the same time moving forward to a newer and deeper style of musical expression.[cvii] Nicolas Slonimsky, is less abstract and likens the music's slow, rhythmical pulse to a barcarole, imagery that for him calls to mind the gentle plash of the gondolier's oars.[cviii]

In our opening prefatory quotation, we cited Ernst von Elterlein's remark on the inadequacy of words to convey feeling in music and how this can only ever be suggested. In that spirit he contends the first movement possesses a 'character of fervent yearning, now timid, now bold'. He then asks: 'Towards what is the desire directed? ... Who can explain it? ... A feeling of mystery runs through these strains, and they are, at least in part, the product of intense individualism.'[cix] Romain Rolland, philosopher, writer and an accomplished interpreter of Beethoven's piano music, found a 'deep poetic vein' for the performer to express.[cx] In his survey of Beethoven's piano sonatas, Gordon reflects: 'The opening movement is transcendental in its lyricism, so much so that pianists have often been known to refer to this sonata as the "most romantic" of the thirty-two.'[cxi] The first movement is tightly compressed and economical in its use of material, and, with a playing time of about four minutes, is one of the shortest opening movements in all of Beethoven's piano sonatas.

In addition to his promotion of the adoption of the German language, by means of which to convey feeling and expression in music, Beethoven was also becoming interested in the potential of the newly invented metronome. He saw this as a means of better conveying a composer's intentions with respect to the tempo at which the music should be taken, and, thereby, of reducing the scope for its misinterpretation. In its October 1813 issue the *Wiener Vatwerländische Blätter* published an article describing a form of chronometer — precursor of the metronome.[cxii] The following year the Dutchman Nikolaus Winkel produced a functioning device that Johann Maelzel soon perfected to achieve the mechanism with which pianists the world over are now familiar. Beethoven's interest was immediately aroused as we can infer from a letter he wrote, sometime in 1815, to his publisher Tobias Haslinger in which he makes reference to his own metronome.[cxiii] Two years later he expressed his views regarding tempo indications to the Viennese conductor and writer on music Ignaz von Mosel — who was also a founder member of the *Gesellschaft der Musikfreunde*. He first refers to the tempo indications currently in use — such expressions as *Allegro* — as being vague and having arisen in what he dismisses as 'the barbarous ages of music'. He next expresses his resolve to bring about changes — the first composer of standing to do so: 'As for me, I have long been thinking of abandoning those absurd descriptive terms, *Allegro, Andante, Adagio, Presto*, and Maelzel's metronome affords us the best opportunity of doing so.'[cxiv] Beethoven was as good as his word and the tempo metronome-indications for all of his published eight symphonies duly appeared in the December 1817 issue of the *Allgemeine musikalische Zeitung*.[cxv]

We remarked in our prefatory comments that a number of single leaves survive separately from their original Scheide

Sketchbook. One of these is now preserved in the Archive of the Beethoven House in Bonn; it reveals Beethoven's preliminary thoughts for the first movement of the Piano Sonata Op 101. Professor Brandenburg provides the following commentary: 'On the reverse, the composer is much further [Beethoven elaborates his ideas]. Here you can see a detailed draft for the first movement. Bars 55—94 are already completely thought out and as they occur in the sonata, but not quite as full and complex as in the finished sonata.'[cxvi]

Matthews pays tribute to Beethoven's powers of invention as he feels they become progressively evident in the first movements of his last five piano sonatas. Notwithstanding that they all follow the conventional sonata pattern, he enthuses: 'But the variety of thought and the flexibility of the form, within chosen bounds, are amazing.' He likens this to 'freedom with strictness' that he regards as being 'a far more potent artistic weapon than freedom uncontrolled'.[cxvii] Speaking in a related way – but more with Beethoven's structural principles in mind – Adorno makes a similar set of generalisations: '[There is] the tendency towards *compression* in late Beethoven; that is, mere indications often stand for groups in the formal schema. The music does not "live out its life" ... The prototype is the first movement of Op. 101, which, in its two pages and with its lyrical tone, carries the weight of a major piece. Something similar [is found] in Opp. 109 and 110 and probably in the first movement of [Op.] 111.'[cxviii]

From the outset, the poetic qualities of the A major Piano Sonata were recognised. The music critic (unidentified) writing in the October 1817 issue of the *Allgemeine musikalische Zeitung* commented: 'The first piece *[movement] (Allegretto, ma non troppo,* or, as the author also describes it in German: *Etwas lebhaft, und mit der innigsten*

Empfindung in A major, 6/8 time) has a simple, childlike and sweet character and contains few, but meaningful, notes and requires an intelligent, sensitive rendition that comes from the performer's innermost [being]. From the following, simple theme, this movement, that contains [only] 102 measures, emerges.' Beethoven's powers of invention are next acknowledged: 'With the highest possible clarity, entirely unadorned, this sweet melody moves along without interruption, always maintained, but presented differently, attaches itself to another, quite strange one, and then appears treated in the following manner, as the lower voice.'[cxix]

Beethoven's pupil Carl Czerny, who studied Beethoven's piano sonatas under the composer's personal direction — and frequently heard him perform them himself — provides the following guidance for the would-be interpreter of the music: 'The importance of this composition, which renders all outward embellishment superfluous, is best displayed by a very soft and sustained delivery, but rich in tone, and by a tranquil performance based on the total effect. It must not be played draggingly, nor disfigured by a fluctuating time.'[cxx] An entry in the diary of Cosima Wagner from 16 November 1874, gives an insight into the interpretation of the music, and a hint of Cosima's feelings about it, when she heard it performed by the celebrated Russian-born pianist Josef Rubinstein — an acquaintance of the Wagner's and not to be confused with his great namesake, and Beethoven interpreter, Anton Rubinstein. Cosima writes: 'Herr Rubinstein plays us the A Major Sonata. The first movement, flowing, ambling along, but at the same time full of sensitivity, is impossible to analyse.'[cxxi]

Nearer to our own time Donald Tovey encourages the performer to observe the following: 'To begin with, notice that Beethoven translates *Allegretto* by *Etwas lebhaft*, "a little lively". *Allegretto* is for him a moderate tempo so near to

Andante ... Yet it is the "cheerful" *(allegro)* or "lively" aspect that he mentions first; qualifying it afterwards by the all-important *"mit der innigsten Empfindung".'* Tovey adds, perhaps somewhat pontifically to modern-day ears: 'Do not be unduly depressed by reflection that your deepest feelings are not equivalent to Beethoven's; there is no deeper expression than that which comes from habitually playing great music faithfully in the full conviction that it is greater than you can realise.'[cxxii]

We conclude our remarks concerning the first movement of the Op. 101 Piano Sonata with reference to reminiscences derived from three great pianists. Our first might well be titled, 'Tribulations of an artist'. It relates to a period just before the outbreak of the Great War, when Artur Schnabel was on a concert tour of what was then East Prussia. We let him take up the tale: 'I remember one place where I played Beethoven's Sonata Op. 101 as the first item. As you know it opens with a very delicate movement. The retired sergeant, who had been selling programmes and tickets at a table behind the last row, counted his takings during this delicate movement, throwing copper and sliver coins onto a china plate which he had ready on his table.' The clatter of the coins proved too much, even for the equably disposed Schnabel; he had to stop the performance and start all over again. He magnanimously reflected that the sergeant was only doing his job and no one had forewarned him.[cxxiii]

The concert pianist Veronica Jochum began her studies in her native Munich, attended the master classes of Edwin Fischer and later studied with Rudolf Serkin. In conversation with the American musicologist David Dubal, she shared with him the following remembrance: 'During his later years, I continued to be intrigued with the [Vladimir] Horowitz mystique. At one concert, he played Beethoven's Sonata

Op. 101, one of the most challenging pieces in the literature. I was deeply moved by this Beethoven playing. The first movement was like a dialogue not only with Beethoven but with God, like an intimate and loving encounter with his Creator.'[cxxiv]

It is difficult, as the idiomatic expression goes, to 'follow that', but we do so with thoughts from Glen Gould that he expressed when he was in conversation with the American writer on music Tim Page. Asked what his feelings were about Beethoven, Gould, known to be somewhat ambivalent towards the composer, replied: '[My] favourite symphony is the Eighth, my favourite movement in all of his sonatas is the opening of Op. 101, and, for me, the *Grosse Fuge* is not only the greatest work Beethoven ever wrote but just about the most astonishing piece in musical literature.'[cxxv]

Turning now to the second movement, Beethoven designates this *Vivace alla Marcia* and once more we encounter his wish to adopt the German language. This time he adds the expression *Lebhaft, marschmässig* – 'Quick, like a march' or 'Lightly, march-like'. As Brendel observes, the original autograph was marked with the additional *zeimlich* – 'quite'/'rather' – but this is now usually omitted.[cxxvi] The march we encounter here replaces the typical Beethoven minuet and scherzo and is combined with a trio section.

The tender restraint of the first movement – Beethoven's 'reveries' – is soon set aside. Bekker considers the *Vivace* belongs to the realm of fantasy to which we have made previous reference. He cites what he describes as the music's 'fleeting, vanishing visions', woven about a lively, rhythmic melody.[cxxvii] Adorno identifies the character and tempo of the second movement with the introduction to the finale of the composer's String Quartet in A minor, Op. 132.[cxxviii] He is not alone in identifying the *alla Marcia* with the medium of the string quartet. Mathews considers Beethoven's writing to have a 'quartet texture' that 'abounds in imitative reposts' and 'canonic two-part writing'.[cxix]

In his commentary to the second movement of the A major Piano Sonata, written at the close of the nineteenth century, Ernst von Elterlein opens with a quotation from Marx (see above), styled in the word-imagery typical of those times: 'Actual deeds are not represented here but the imagination of deeds which may happen, dreamed-of strokes of bold and lofty heroism.' He follows this with his own imagery: 'The effect is almost ethereal, so light, undulating and bright, though not without a certain grandeur; we do not so to speak meet with the tangible, material side of the march measure, which is made subservient to the ideal expression.' With regard to Beethoven's construction, he singles out the music's 'wide skips and abrupt intervals' and the 'simultaneous sounding of the highest and lowest registers.'[cxx] Gordon is like-minded: 'The march ... is full of angular skips, its dotted rhythm underscoring a rough-and-tumble ruggedness.'[cxxi]

The angularity of the music to Sisman's ears is raucous as it ascends and descends over its 'chromatic tetrachord bass'.[cxxii] The energetic character imparted thereby, emphasised by its dotted quavers and semiquavers, suggests to Slonimsky the rhythm of the drumbeat.[cxxiii] Matthews also comments on this aspect of Beethoven's piano writing, with recollections of 'Back to Bach': '[The] vitality [is] maintained, even in the quiet passages, by an all-pervading dotted rhythm that is bandied about between the repeats, though the second half has outgrown itself in the manner of some of Bach's preludes in the Second Book of the "48".'[cxxiv]

The Trio section finds Beethoven in a more pensive mood. Donald Tovey, ordinarily scrupulous to the point or reverential devotion in his urging of the correct adherence to Beethoven's written text, is here prepared to sanction a possible departure from the published score. He cites the views of Gustav Nottebohm, a pioneer in the study and decipherment of Beethoven's sketchbooks, and his pupil the Romanian musicologist Eusabius Mandyczewski — remembered today for his scholarly editing of Schubert's songs and his collected essays *Beethoveniana*. Both suggested the first ten bars of the Trio (55–64) could be repeated, as they believed to be consistent with the composer's original intentions. Of this, Tovey remarks: 'The experiment is well worth trying and it brings out the symmetry that underlies this grotesque and impulsive canonic structure.'[cxxxv]

Commentators have drawn attention to the influence of Beethoven's vigorous *alla Marcia* on the piano writing of Robert Schuman — in particular the middle section of his Fantasy Op. 17. This was written in 1836 in homage to Beethoven and as means of helping to raise funds for a statue in his memory. The statue was eventually (1845) erected — following a major financial contribution from Franz Liszt (the dedicatee of Schuman's Fantasy) — in his hometown of Bonn. Among the many dignitaries taking part in the related celebrations were Queen Victoria and Prince Albert.

The review of this movement in the Allgemeine musikalische Zeitung contains the following passage: 'Vivace alla Marcia, (Lebhaft, marschmässig) in F major, C-time, is completely different from the preceding [movement]. It is entirely held in dotted figures, seldom digresses and is not easy to execute. The Trio, in B major, after which the actual march is repeated, once more, is followed by the lovely motif that will follow here, and it is comprised of the most beautiful imitations.'[cxxxvi]

Carl Czerny, in his commentary to the proper performance of this passage, offers the following guidance: 'Very lively, vehement and energetic ... The *Trio*, on the contrary, extremely soft, and also rather more tranquil.'[cxxxvii] Fischer observes: 'The second movement, *Alla Marcia*, should be played rather in the manner of a string quartet. The independence of the parts leads to overlappings in the rhythm, which are not easy to negotiate within a fixed metre.' He also encourages the strict observation of Beethoven's pedal markings.[cxxxviii] Tovey believed the clue to a convincing rendering of the movement lies in releasing its energy by ensuring that 'all the beats are strongly accented'. He supports this contention by calling to mind the praise that his contemporary Harry Plunket Greene had for the vigour that his fellow Irish jig-players could bestow on their folk music.[cxxxix]

Beethoven designates the third movement *Adagio ma non troppo, con affetto* and once again qualifies his chosen expression in words couched in the German language, *Langsam und sehnsuchtsvoll* – 'Slow and full of yearning' or 'Full of passionate yearning or longing'. The *Adagio* functions as the slow movement of the composition and is not so much an independent movement but is more in the nature of an introduction to the work's finale – as Beethoven had pioneered in the *Introduzione* to his Piano Sonata Op. 53.[cxl] Its effect is like that of a brief extemporisation, the role of which is to prepare for the concluding *Allegro*.[cxli] Beethoven's terseness here is such as to confound those of his critics who have sometimes accused him of being long-winded. With a playing time of less than three minutes it exhibits, in Brendel's words, 'a new attitude towards the miniature'.[cxlii]

Consistent with his German-language descriptions, the music has a yearning quality. Ernst von Elterlein, writing at the close of the nineteenth century, characterised its pervasive mood as: 'A dull sorrow, a gentle complaining, and then again a painful yearning, breathes through these strains.' He metaphorically asks: 'And how is it to be satisfied?' Anticipating the movement's conclusion, he supplies the answer: 'The feelings which we experienced in the first movement take possession of the soul again. And now, behold, a new spirit springs up as it were by magic. Its meaning is confident self-reliance, and buoyant resolution.'[cxliii] Rolland described the *Largo* as being 'permeated with profound feeling'.[cxliv] In a memorable phrase, Matthews likens the music to a 'whispered commentary' that creates a 'grave hushed atmosphere' which is made all the more expressive as Beethoven instructs the piece to be played throughout with the soft pedal — *una corda* — and, moreover, as Matthews further observes, by 'the absence of such expressive devices as crescendos, diminuendos, fortes and pianos'.[cxlv] Brendel adopts similar word-imagery in his description of the music: 'The brief *Adagio* does not sing out its melancholy like the *ariosi* of Op. 110 — played *una corda*, it communes with itself like a whisper, reticent and clear-sighted.'[cxlvi]

In the music's profound calm, Matthews draws a parallel with the choral-like *Adagio* found in Beethoven's Cello Sonata Op. 102, No. 2 that was composed at about the same time as the A major Piano Sonata.[cxlvii] In addition to the music being self-referencing, Rosen detects other stylistic influences. He cites the movement's 'baroque [like] ornamentation' and 'hymn-like texture' and is convinced the ornamentation at bars 14–16 betray Beethoven's youthful study of Bach, in particular the Chromatic Fantasy and Fugue in D minor, BWV 903.[cxlviii] In his commentary to Beethoven's musicianship, William Kinderman describes how, what he calls the 'level of feeling or state of being', is achieved by the manner in which the music is drawn progressively lower in pitch, 'falling through a series of diminished-seventh chords before it drops still further in register'.[cxlix] Musicologist David Dubal suggested to Alfred Brendel that to him (Dubal) the Piano Sonata Op. 101 was something of an enigmatic work and that the third movement was 'in a way, ugly'. Brendel did not fully concur but acknowledged: 'Maybe it doesn't lend itself to the piano so well. It is very much a string-quartet piece, and so is the whole sonata ...'.[cl]

The third movement closes with a passage which, although consisting of a mere seven bars, has considerable musicological and psychological significance that has identified the A major Piano Sonata with the music of the later romantics. We hear a fleeting recollection of the opening theme of the first movement. To our 'innocent ear' — to use Robert Simpson's expression[cli] — such a reiteration of a previously expressed musical idea may today sound commonplace, but, at the period of composition of the Op. 101, Beethoven's innovation was a new departure in piano writing — one that he would further adopt in his penultimate Piano Sonata. Op. 110.[clii] In his *Beethoven et ses trois styles*, Wilhelm von Lenz called the momentary return of the opening movement's first theme as a 'fantastic vision' and before him the Viennese reviewer in the *Allgemeine musikalische Zeitung* called it a 'rhapsodic repetition'.[cliii]

Beethoven had used the procedure of 'thematic recollection' in his pioneering song cycle of 1816 *An die ferne Geliebte*; in this, the vocalist recalls material from the first song in the last. Beethoven follows his own precedent, memorably, in the Ninth Symphony when the vocalist (baritone) dismisses themes heard in the first three movements with the words 'O Freunde, nicht diese Töne!' ('O friends, not these sounds!'), before proceeding to the celebrated 'Ode to Joy' of the final movement. Perhaps a parallel can be drawn here between Beethoven's invention

— and his anticipation of the musical procedures of later composers — and how, similarly, Richard Wagner, in the opening phrase of his opera *Tristan und Isolde* — with the so-called 'Tristan Chord' — was to move traditional harmony towards atonality.

The reviewer of the A major Piano Sonata writing in the *Allgemeine musikalische Zeitung*, was clearly moved by the music: 'It is, so to say, created out of one mould, nothing is too much, nothing is too little; it only consists of a few main ideas, but these have been used extensively, with all contrapuntal artistry that is at the disposal of the master, and with a self-confidence and assurance that bears witness of his study of the old classics, since it is developed thoroughly and strictly.'[cliv]

In his notes to the interpretation of the *Adagio* movement, Czerny emphasises the need for the performer to play with 'intense feeling' and to make full use of the 'shifting pedal' (soft pedal) and 'often with the damper pedal'.[clv] Likewise Fischer: 'The introduction to the last movement — *Adagio ma non troppo* — should be played with the soft pedal — *una corda* ... It must never be allowed to touch the ground of reality, so that after the quotation from the first movement the worldliness and earthiness of the finale may be given full rein.' Fischer also found passages in the *Adagio ma non troppo* to be faintly reminiscent of certain moments in Bach's Chromatic Fantasia and Fugue, BVW 903 — to which we have made previous reference — especially where, in the Bach, patterns of multiple notes are sung to one syllable of text — as known in musicology as melismata.[clvi]

In the printed score, Beethoven gives the direction to the performer *Nach und nach mehrere Saiten* — 'By degrees more strings'. He is referring to the application of the soft pedal, as it was then applicable to the pianoforte-style, keyboard mechanism of his day — when it was possible to shift the hammers from three strings to *one* or *two* strings. Nowadays, on the concert grand, the mechanism shifts the hammers from the *three* strings to *two*, so that, as Lowe in his commentary points out, '*una corda* really means *due corde*.'[clvii] Rosen is unequivocal in his encouragement to the performer to play with feeling and to hold down the soft pedal throughout.[clviii] Tovey, when a mere child, heard Anton Rubinstein play the A major Piano Sonata, and, notwithstanding his tender years later in life was disposed to remark, 'Rubinstein's playing was a thing that can never be forgotten'. Regrettably, all he has to say is that Rubinstein took the movement 'very rhythmically in a *piano* sense'.[clix]

By combining the words of Paul Becker and Philip Radcliffe, we arrive at the final movement: '[The] short, *adagio-intermezzo* (like that in Op. 53), continues in a yearning, mysteriously coloured motive. Reminiscences of the gentle theme of the prelude are introduced, but, at the closing phrase, the composer attains new power. The effort to fight a way through dreams and fancies, spiritual, gay and sentimental by turns, to fully conscious creative activity.'[clx] This creative activity is nothing less than 'the huge, sonata-form finale'.[clxi]

The fourth movement is an *Allegro* that Beethoven indicates is to be played *Geschwind, doch nicht zu sehr, und mit Entschlossenheit*, 'Fast, but not too fast/not excessively so and with determination', or 'Quickly, but not too fast and with decision'. In our opening remarks we made reference to the *Pastoral* Sonata and suggested it was a point of departure for Beethoven to manifest a new poetic feeling in his piano sonata writing. Compositional ideas from other of the composer's earlier works also come to the fore in the A major Piano Sonata that have a bearing on the character of the final movement. Gordon cites, for example, the manner in which the opening movements of the two *fantasy* sonatas

Op. 27, are, like that of the Op. 101, modest in proportions, and show affinities with the A major Piano Sonata by, as it were, 'setting the stage for the importance of the final movement'.[clxii] Brendel's summary-remarks capture the spirit of what is about to unfold: '[The] last movement becomes the climax to which everything leads; it gathers together the forces which in the earlier movements have been pulling in different directions, or surpasses the first movement by the conviction of a superior, and opposite, position, as in Op. 111.'[clxiii]

Adorno regarded the finale of Op. 101 to be prototypical in several ways, including the manner in which Beethoven's writing tends to polyphony and what he characterises as its 'spiritualized counterpoint' and 'extraordinary art'.[clxiv] Commenting on the innovatory nature of the finale, David Dubal, in the conversation he had with Alfred Brendel (see above), prompted the following response from him: 'Yes, it is the first work where the sonata leads towards the last movement as the climax, and that will remain so in the late sonatas.'[clxv] Marx, availing himself of nineteenth-century word imagery, said of the movement as a whole: '[A] rich, refreshing stream of life over which brilliant gleams occasionally flash gaily, courageously, and impetuously, gushes forth.'[clxvi]

The slow movement serves as a foil to the more energetic music that follows in the finale. Matthews remarks how Beethoven had explored such a working-out in his *Waldstein* Piano Sonata, but not, as he comments, 'with such subjective mood-directions as *sehnsuchtsvoll* and *mit Entschlossenheit* — "with yearning" and, for the finale, "with resolution".'[clxvii] Marx is not alone in his description of the music, in responding to its inherent exuberance. Rye deems its contrapuntal writing to be 'joyful', not least in the manner in which it culminates in energetic fugal writing — to be discussed shortly.[clxviii] Von Elterlein considered the music's 'character of buoyant resolution could not be more strikingly represented than by the first subject with its distinctive rhythm'.[clxix] Rosen proposes Beethoven resorts, momentarily, to the vernacular vocal sounds he might have heard as child: 'The movement is an elaborate sonata form and is not only a jocular piece but even bucolic, with yodel motifs in bars 44 to 48.'[clxx] Bekker is more restrained: 'The theme of the closing movement shows rather courageous than joyful determination ... A brooding *fugato* begins in the bass and, mounting, weaves a shadowy dance about a single idea, which, suddenly, with a gesture of elemental force, resumes its former aspect and leads to a jubilant close.'[clxxi]

With respect to the formal construction of the movement, Beethoven employs a profusion of ideas that, in Rosen's estimation, border on the Mozartian.[clxxii] The opening theme dominates throughout the movement but Beethoven subjects it to 'quasi-canonic double counterpoint'[clxxiii] and 'every possible inversion and the most surprising combinations'[clxxiv] in counterpoint that is sometimes 'rough and uncompromising, with bold and exhilarating clashes'.[clxxv]

We recall remarks made previously in connection with Beethoven's search for new sonorities alongside the technical developments then taking place in relation to the extension of the keyboard. These considerations come to the fore in the final movement of the A major Piano Sonata where the music explores limits that go beyond the compass of the typical Haydn-Mozart pianoforte. In the words of one authority: 'Beethoven had once again crossed new boundaries and set new standards.' In this particular case he extended the range of the composition down to bottom E, the lowest note that was then possible on the keyboard instruments of the time. Whilst this was achievable on the more modern pianos of the day, it still confronted Beethoven with the challenge of communicating his intentions to the performer, in the printed copy of the music, since the low E necessitates four ledger lines beneath the usual stave. For the untutored eye, the bottom E would be difficult to read, and, likewise, the same for the notes in the music associated with it. There is evidence Beethoven gave particular thought to the required notation and practised it on the Title Page of the manuscript in pencil and ink. Moreover, on the recto of leaf thirteen in the manuscript, he wrote 'Contra E-problem' (bottom E problem) in pencil on the lowest stave and gave each note a clarifying additional letter with a comment for the engraver: 'N.B: die Buchstaben auch im Stechen drunter gesezt' — 'N.B: the letters [to be] added underneath also in the engraving'. Thereby he sought to make things easier for the performer.[clxxvi]

To make sure his intentions were clear to his publisher, Tobias Haslinger, Beethoven wrote to him requesting he should add alphabet letters to the musical notation at page fifteen, in the final movement, at bars 18, 19, 20 and 21.[clxxvii] Another letter to Haslinger quickly followed, this time exhorting the hapless fellow — styled, albeit it humorously, as 'Second Scoundrel of the Empire': 'In the last movement in the passage where low E appears in the four chords, I should like the letters to be added, namely: E E E E /A Fs Gs A /E E E E.' Furthermore, he added that the explanatory words he had added in his manuscript, in certain places, 'must be noted and inserted'.[clxxviii] It is a tribute to Beethoven's diligence, and Haslinger's patience, that he sent yet a further reminder to ensure mistakes did not arise where the low E occurs in the music and to observe his required letter-indications.[clxxix] In the event, despite Beethoven's many exhortations, his intentions could not be fully implemented. The copper plates, from which the composition was to be printed, were already engraved and for them to be redone would have incurred too great a cost. Beethoven had to be content with his publisher's compromise; Haslinger added the instruction, 'bottom E' where the low note appears for the first time.[clxxx]

The opening theme of the finale is angular — possessed of a 'vigorous, almost gruff vitality'[clxxxi] and, moreover, suggestive of the fugue that will shortly follow.[clxxxii] Precedents for fugal endings in late classical music occur in the works of Haydn — in particular his string quartets — and Mozart, for example the great Adagio and Fugue, K546. Beethoven himself had ventured into the medium in his own chamber works, notably the fugal *Allegro-molto* in the final movement of the third *Razumowsky* String Quartet, Op. 59 and the final movement *Allegro-Fugato* of the Sonata for Cello and Piano, Op. 102, No. 2.[clxxxiii] The fugue in the A major Piano Sonata may be described as 'semi-rigorous', or 'fugato' in terms of strict, orthodox counterpoint, or, as Cooper puts it: 'For a long time this fugato seems almost like a real fugue, with rigorously maintained four-part polyphony, but its tonal scheme is highly unorthodox.'[clxxxiv] However, as Slonimsky cautions, 'Beethoven's fugues were no mere exercises in polyphony'. As a young man, under the guidance of his teachers Johann Albrechtsberger and Joseph Haydn, he had taken great pains to master the art of fugal counterpoint. In the A major Piano Sonata, however, he was setting himself other musical agendas. As he himself remarked: 'To make a fugue requires no particular skill [an exaggeration, as the pains he took with his own apprentice works reveal]. But the imagination ought to assert itself, and a new poetic element should be injected into the traditional form.'[clxxxv]

Matthews describes Beethoven's fugue as 'a superbly cumulative fugal development' in which 'even its playful moods show an intellectual delight in counterpoint'.[clxxxvi]

Beethoven's craftsmanship finds Bie similarly disposed, remarking how: 'The fugue half changes into the rondo, free in all its forms.'[clxxxvii] There is, however, nothing tentative or half-hearted in Beethoven's writing. In Tovey's words: 'The fugue blazes into *forte* and subsides again with a suddenness characteristic of all Beethoven's fugues.'[clxxxviii] The opening figure, which we have described as being 'angular', is used extensively with imitations occurring between bass and treble.[clxxxix] There is perhaps a suggestion here of the style of Handel who Beethoven, at this period, was beginning to so much admire — even remarking on one occasion: 'I would uncover my head, and kneel at his tomb!'[cxc]

We have made previous reference to Beethoven's writing in the A major Piano Sonata as having a string-quartet like character, and this aspect of the music comes to the fore in the final movement: 'The four-voiced texture remains in use throughout the fugue, the approach to the counterpoint is influenced by the use of idiomatic keyboard figurations such as scalar runs and double notes.' We have remarked also on Beethoven availing himself of the freedom given to him through the form of the recently extended keyboard: '[He] seems to take delight in pushing what is physically possible to play on the keyboard to the outer limits.'[cxci]

Mention should be made here of Beethoven's use of the trill. In the A major Piano Sonata; he begins a process he will take much further in the last of his works for the keyboard. Beethoven elevates the trill from being a mere decorative ornament, consisting of the rapid alternation of two adjacent notes, to a transcendental, soul-elevating miniature sound world, imbued with feeling and significance. In his Op. 101, Beethoven is content to let the trill murmur in the bass during the coda or to embellish the fugue alongside its 'comic after-beats' with their false leads and hints of Beethovenian wit.[cxcii] [cxciii]

Once more Beethoven's originality was not lost upon the *Allgemeine musikalische Zeitung*'s reviewer: 'Equally originally, the author arrives at the end in that he lets us hear a motif in one register here, and in two registers there, to which the bass with its pedal tones quietly murmurs. If we succeeded, with this announcement, to prepare the friends of true piano playing to whom *Bach's* school will remain dear forever, for the truly rare degree of pleasures that await them here, our purpose has been fulfilled, and we look forward to a new opportunity at which we will be able to pay tribute to the great composer in a similar manner and to express to him our most sincere respects.'[cxciv]

The reader will recall the reviewer in the *Wiener Musikzeitung* pronounced the A major Piano Sonata 'difficult to perform', and generations of pianists – professional and accomplished amateur alike – have concurred. Kinderman's views are relevant here: 'The depth of synthesis and the richness of allusion in passages such as this [in the final movement] present a special challenge to listener and interpreter alike.'[cxcv] However, Beethoven does not impose technical challenges on the would-be interpreter of his music merely for the sake of it; as Cooper contends: 'The technical difficulties of the movement are part of its underlying aesthetic.'[cxcvi]

To assist the performer confront the technical challenges of performance, Czerny is somewhat cryptic, urging the *Allegro* to be played 'quick and resolute'.[cxcvii] Tovey, with a touch of sardonic wit – and enjoying a sustained metaphor – likened grappling with the technical challenges of the final movement to rock climbing! He comments that the best he can do is to offer the student 'a foothold or hand-hold here and there' and that, despite what he characterises as 'the marvellous progress of modern pianoforte technique', he regrets it is not possible 'to accomplish this climb with the comfort and speed of a funicular railway'. He does make one concession though which is to allow the performer to take the tempo with 'a certain amount of freedom'.[cxcviii]

We draw our remarks to a close in less austere manner with the views of Edwin Fischer. Recalling his personal experience of performing the Piano Sonata in A major, Op. 101, he reflects: 'It is amusing to sense the relief of an audience when instead of the strict fugato, [Beethoven] suddenly goes cheerful again and finishes the piece in gay excitement.'[cxcix]

---

[i] We are here subscribing to the traditional view, first propounded by Conrad von Lenz in his *Beethoven et ses trois styles*, that Beethoven's compositions can be considered as falling into three broad periods, namely, Early, Middle and Late.

[ii] The words quoted are from Egerton C. Lowe, 1929, p. 128. Numerous similar tributes to Beethoven's late style abound in Beethoven musicology.

[iii] Elaine Sisman, *Memory and invention at the threshold of Beethoven's late style*, in: Scott G. Burnham and Michael P. Steinberg editors: *Beethoven and his world*, 2000, pp. 82–3.

[iv] For example, see: Paul Bekker, 1925, pp. 130–1.

[v] As quoted by Ernst von Elterlein, 1898, p. 102.

[vi] Barry Cooper, 2000, p. 252.

[vii] Stephen C. Rumph, 2004, pp. 100–1.

[viii] Eric Blom, 1938, pp. 194–5.

[ix] Paul Bekker, 1925, pp. 130–1.

[x] Beethoven kept a diary from 1812 until 1816 in which he jotted down favourite texts from poems and prose writings, proverbs and aphorism, self-exhortations, and more mundane items such as shopping lists and notes concerning financial matters. See: *Beethoven's Tagebuch*, Beethoven House and Maynard Solomon, 2005, p. 115. I am indebted to the writings of Elaine Sisman (see following) for becoming aware of the words quoted in the main text.

[xi] Elaine Sisman, *Memory and invention at the threshold of Beethoven's late style*, in: Scott G. Burnham and Michael P. Steinberg, editors: *Beethoven and his world*, 2000, pp. 51–3.

[xii] Alfred Brendel, 2001, p. 82.

[xiii] Maynard Solomon, 1977, p. 299.

[xiv] Marion M. Scott, 1940, p. 145.

[xv] Barry Cooper, 1991, p. 242.

[xvi] Theodor W. Adorno, 1998, p. 82.

[xvii] Oskar Bie, 1966, p. 179.

[xviii] Romain Rolland, 1917, p. 161.

[xix] Wilfrid Howard Mellers, 1957, pp. 70–1.

[xx] Alfred Brendel, 2001, p. 82.

[xxi] Maynard Solomon, 1977, pp. 299–300.
[xxii] The words quoted are from Denis Matthews, 1972, p. 179.
[xxiii] See: Beethoven House, Digital Archives, Library Documents, Sammlung H. C. Bodmer, HCB Mh 46a/b/c and 461.
[xxiv] Romain Rolland, 1917, p. 160.
[xxv] Oskar Bie, 1966, p. 179.
[xxvi] As quoted in: Elliot Forbes, editor, *Thayer's life of Beethoven*, 1967, p. 641, note 14.
[xxvii] For a discussion of the concert, and remarks concerning the likely candidates for the actual piano sonata that may have been performed, see: Anton Felix Schindler, *Beethoven as I knew him*, edited by Donald W. MacArdle and translated by Constance S. Jolly from the German edition of 1860, 1966, p. 340, footnote 145.
[xxviii] As recalled in: William S. Newman, 1963, pp. 528–9.
[xxix] Derived from Harold C. Schonberg, 1964, p. 92.
[xxx] Robert Ignatius Letellier, editor and translator, *The diaries of Giacomo Meyerbeer*, 1999-2004, Vol. 4, p. 245.
[xxxi] Nicolas Slonimsky, *The great composers and their works*, edited by Electra Slonimsky Yourke, 2000, p. 174.
[xxxii] Anton Felix Schindler, edited by Donald W. MacArdle and translated by Constance S. Jolly from the German edition of 1860, 1966, p. 478.
[xxxiii] *Ibid*, pp. 667–8.
[xxxiv] Emily Anderson, 1961, Vol. 2, Letter No. 737, p. 654.
[xxxv] Czerny gave his lecture in 1825, by which time the range of the keyboard of some instrument makers had been extended to six and even six-and-a-half octaves. See: Dieter Hildebrandt, 1988, p. 66.
[xxxvi] Elliot Forbes, editor, *Thayer's life of Beethoven*, 1966, p. 412. In addition to her enthusiasm for Beethoven, Dorothea is also known to have been an accomplished interpreter of Bach. See: Peter Clive, 2001, pp. 102–4. A miniature portrait of Dorothea von Ertmann is reproduced in the Beethoven House Digital Archives, Library Document, B 486/b. Shortly after becoming acquainted with Beethoven, Dorothea lost her only child Franz. It is recorded Beethoven was so moved he invited Dorothea to his apartment where he improvised for her on the piano for more than an hour. He is said to have remarked: 'We will now talk to each other in tones.' See, for example: Eric Blom, 1938, p. 194.
[xxxvii] Peter Clive, 2001, pp. 102–4.
[xxxviii] Anton Felix Schindler, edited by Donald W. MacArdle and translated by Constance S. Jolly from the German edition of 1860, 1966, pp. 210–11.
[xxxix] Nicolas Slonimsky, *The great composers and their works*, edited by Electra Slonimsky Yourke, 2000, p. 175.
[xl] Felix Mendelssohn as recollected in, *Letters from Italy and Switzerland*, London: Longman, Green, Longman, and Roberts, 1862, pp. 199–206.
[xli] Douglas Porter Johnson editor, 1985, p. 73.
[xlii] Beethoven House, Digital Archives, Library Document, Sammlung H. C. Bodmer HCB BSk 13/61.
[xliii] Charles Rosen, 2002, p. 212.
[xliv] Dennis Matthews, 1985, p. 55. The words quoted are from this source and are typical of the views expressed by other authorities.
[xlv] Eric Blom, 1938, p. 195.

xlvi Edwin Fischer, 1959, p. 97.
xlvii Stewart Gordon, 1996, pp. 181–2.
xlviii Matthew Rye, *Notes to the BBC Radio Three Beethoven Experience*, Friday 10 June 2005, www.bbc.co.uk/radio3/Beethoven
xlix Barry Cooper, 2000, p. 244.
l Philip Radcliffe, *Piano music* in: *The age of Beethoven, The new Oxford history of music*, Vol. VIII, Gerald Abraham, editor, 1988, p. 354.
li Barry Cooper, 2000, p. 252.
lii See: Theodore Albrecht, translator and editor, 1996, Vol. 2, Letter No. 215, pp. 87–89 and subsequent correspondence.
liii Barry Cooper, 2000, p. 252.
liv Beethoven wrote first to Anton Steiner, see: Emily Anderson, 1961, Vol. 2, Letter No. 744, p. 659 and a little later to Tobias Haslinger, see: Letter No. 746, pp. 659–60.
lv See: John Shedlock, 1918, p. 47.
lvi Emily Anderson, 1961, Vol. 2, Letter No. 742, p. 657.
lvii *Ibid*, Vol. 2, Letter No. 745, p. 659.
lviii *Ibid*, Vol. 2, Letter No. 746, pp. 659–60.
lix *Ibid*, Vol. 2, Letter No. 666, pp. 608–9.
lx The words attributed to Weber are as they appeared (after translation) in the 1840 edition of his biography of the composer. In the 1860 edition he somewhat modifies his remarks, see: Anton Felix Schindler, *Beethoven as I knew him*, edited by Donald W. MacArdle and translated by Constance S. Jolly from the German edition of 1860, 1966, pp. 482–3. For a commentary on Weber's music criticism of Beethoven, see also: Alessandra Comini, *The changing image of Beethoven*, Sunstane Books, 2008, pp. 94–5.
lxi Emily Anderson, 1961, Vol. 2, Letter No. 749, p. 661.
lxii *Ibid*, Vol. 2, Letter No. 763, p. 670.
lxiii *Ibid*, 1961, Vol. 2, Letter No. 764, p. 671.
lxiv See: Beethoven House, Digital Archives, Library Document, Sammlung H. C. Bodmer, HCB C Op. 101. The Beethoven House Archive also illustrates a further edition of the Op. 101 Piano Sonata, once owned by the collector of Beethoven manuscripts Jean van der Spek, bearing his signature, see: Sammlung Jean van der Spek, C Op. 101.
lxv When the A major Piano Sonata was first published in England, in 1820, it was described as being 'for the pianoforte'. Beethoven had to wait until 1823 for his wishes regarding the adoption of the German language to be fulfilled. It was then that an edition of the work appeared described as, *Große Sonata für das Hammerclavier*. See: Dieter Hildebrandt, 1988, pp. 32–3.
lxvi Derived from Barry Cooper, 2000, p. 252.
lxvii Otto Erich Deutsch, 1946, p. 627.
lxviii Elliot Forbes, editor, *Thayer's life of Beethoven*, 1967, p. 641, footnote 14 and William S. Newman, 1963, p. 528.
lxix Eric Blom, 1938, p. 195.
lxx John Fuller Maitland, *Special Issue* [Death Centenary], *The Musical Times*, London, Vol. VIII, No. 2, 1927, p. 222.
lxxi Alfred Brendel in conversation with David Dubal in: David Dubal, *The world of the concert pianist*, 1985, p. 109.
lxxii Alfred Brendel, 2001, p. 82.

[lxxiii] William S. Newman, 1963, p. 527.
[lxxiv] Alfred Brendel, 2001, pp. 79–80.
[lxxv] Peter Clive, 2001, pp. 42–3 and pp. 101–2.
[lxxvi] Emily Anderson, 1961, Vol. 2, Letter No. 550, pp. 519–20. We have seen (Piano Sonata Op. 90) that Beethoven's last public appearance, in the capacity of pianist, was in April 1814 when he had taken part in a disastrous performance of his recently composed *Archduke* Trio, Op. 97.
[lxxvii] Emily Anderson, 1961, Vol. 2, Letter No. 594, p. 545.
[lxxviii] *Ibid*, Vol. 2, Letter No. 536, pp. 505–6. Beethoven was on good terms with Johann Schantz – one of Vienna's leading pianoforte manufacturers – as we learn from a letter he wrote in the spring of 1810 to his friend Baron Ignaz von Gleichenstein: 'I can obtain *an expensive instrument* for a *very low figure.*' [Beethoven's italics]. See: Emily Anderson, Letter No. 255, p. 269, Vol. 1. See also: Beethoven House, Digital Archives, Library Document, Sammlung H. C. Bodmer, HCB BBr 18.
[lxxix] Emily Anderson, 1961, Vol. 2, Letter No. 785, pp. 685–6. Nanette was responsible for many of the business dealings in the family firm, whilst Johann concerned himself with the more technical/manufacturing side of things.
[lxxx] Emily Anderson, 1961, Vol. 2, Letter No. 810, pp. 704–5.
[lxxxi] See: Derek Melville, *Beethoven's Pianos*, in: Denis Arnold and Nigel Fortune, editors, 1973, p. 65.
[lxxxii] Emily Anderson, 1961, Vol. 2, Letter No. 844, p. 726.
[lxxxiii] *Ibid*, Vol. 2, Letter No. 571, p. 532.
[lxxxiv] The sum of 10,000 gulden may have been something of an exaggeration. It is evident, however, Beethoven did spend considerable sums to secure his brother's wellbeing. Later on he incurred medical fees, when his nephew Karl required a hernia operation, as well as bearing the cost of sending him to boarding school. In order to make his own finances more secure, he invested 10,000 florins (gulden) with his music publisher Sigmund Anton Steiner. This earned him an annual interest of 8%. In later years Beethoven made himself unnecessarily poor by denying himself access to his investments in the desire to secure an inheritance for his beloved Karl.
[lxxxv] Emily Anderson, 1961, Vol. 2, Letter No. 633, pp. 577–8.
[lxxxvi] As quoted in: H. C. Robbins Landon 1970, p. 157.
[lxxxvii] Emily Anderson, 1961, Vol. 2, Letter No. 783, pp. 683–4. A facsimile copy of this letter is reproduced in the Beethoven House, Digital Archives, Library Document Sammlung H. C. Bodmer, HCB Br 120.
[lxxxviii] Emily Anderson, 1961, Vol. 2, Letter No. 805, p. 701.
[lxxxix] Theodor Albrecht, 1996, Vol. 2, Letter No. 234, pp. 112–5.
[xc] *Ibid*, Vol. 2, Letter No. 239, pp. 121–4. Beethoven himself sought to promote his own compositions in England. A case in point concerns his then hugely popular *Wellington's Victory* Symphony. He sent a copy of this to the Prince Regent but never received a reply, despite the work being performed several times to London audiences – to great acclaim. To add insult to injury, a piano arrangement was made without Beethoven's consent and without him receiving any royalty payment. See: Emily Anderson, 1961, Vol. 2, Letter No. 546, pp. 514–6.
[xci] Emily Anderson, 1961, Vol. 2, Letter No. 816, pp. 708–9.
[xcii] Derived from Theodore Albrecht, translator and editor, 1996, Vol. 2, document 213, pp. 82–5.

xciii See: Beethoven House, Digital Archives, Library Document, B 204/1. For a miniature of Karl when he was a boy, see: Library Document, Ley Band VII, Nr. 394 a. For an outline of Beethoven's relationship with Karl, see: Hans Conrad Fischer and Erich Kock, pp. 32–3.

xciv Dr. Bursy's diary recollections are given in: Ludwig Nohl, *Beethoven depicted by his contemporaries*, 1880 pp. 150–61.

xcv Emily Anderson, 1961, Vol. 2, Letter No. 803, pp. 699–700.

xcvi The full text of the citation is reproduced in: Theodore Albrecht, translator and editor, 1996, Vol. 2, document 214, pp. 85–6.

xcvii Derived from Wayne M. Senner, Robin Wallace and William Meredith, editors, 1999, Vol. 2, pp. 43–4.

xcviii Quoted by John Daverio in: *The Cambridge companion to Beethoven*, 2000, p. 152.

xcix Derived from Wayne M. Senner, Robin Wallace and William Meredith, editors, 1999, Vol. 1, p. 45.

c Anton Felix Schindler, 1860, English edition, Donald W. MacArdle, 1966, p. 209.

ci Maynard Solomon, 1977, p. 304.

cii Alfred Brendel, 2001, p. 82.

ciii Matthew Rye, *Notes to the BBC Radio Three Beethoven experience*, Friday 10 June 2005, www.bbc.co.uk/radio3/Beethoven

civ Denis Matthews, 1967, p. 45. See also: Denis Matthews, 1972, p. 179.

cv Harold Craxton and Donald Francis Tovey, [1931], Piano Sonata in A major, Op. 101.

cvi Theodor W. Adorno, 1998, pp. 4–5 and p. 126.

cvii Arnold Whittall, 2003, pp. 11–12.

cviii Nicolas Slonimsky, 2000, p. 176.

cix Ernst von Elterlein, 1898, p. 102.

cx Romain Rolland, 1917, pp. 160–1.

cxi Stewart Gordon, 1996, p. 182.

cxii Barry Cooper, 1991, pp. 24–5.

cxiii Emily Anderson, 1961, Vol. 2, Letter No. 587, p. 542.

cxiv *Ibid*, Vol. 2, Letter No. 845, pp. 727–8.

cxv Barry Cooper, 1991, p. 26. Given Beethoven's wish to establish authenticity in the interpretation of his music, an anecdote from the recollections of his pupil Ferdinand Ries is not without its lighter side. Ries, then living in London, endeavoured to secure a reprint of Beethoven's symphonies and wrote to Beethoven asking for the required metronome numbers. These were duly sent to Ries but the letter containing them failed to arrive. Ries, accordingly, requested Beethoven to send them once more. Beethoven obliged, metronomising the symphonies again and sending the numbers off to London. Meanwhile, his first letter had arrived and it turned out Beethoven had given different numbers each time. As reproduced in: Edwin Fischer, 1959, pp. 93–5. In exoneration of Beethoven, however, we need to bear in mind this was a period of some experimentation with the new instrument and doubtless the regularity of the metronome itself was still being established.

cxvi Beethoven House, Digital Archives, Library Document, Sammlung H. C. Bodmer HCB BSk 13/61.

cxvii Denis Matthews, 1967, p. 45.

[cviii] Theodor W. Adorno, 1998, p. 159.
[cix] Derived from Wayne M. Senner, Robin Wallace and William Meredith, editors, 1999, Vol. 2, pp. 43–4.
[cx] Carl Czerny in: Paul Badura-Skoda, 1970, p. 63.
[cxi] Gregor-Dellin and Dietrich Mack, editors, *Cosima Wagner's diaries, Vol. 1 1869–1877*, 1978–1980.
[cxii] Harold Craxton, and Donald Francis Tovey, [1931], p. 113.
[cxiii] Artur Schnabel, 1961, pp. 48–9.
[cxiv] As recollected in: David Dubal, editor, *Remembering Horowitz: 125 pianists recall a legend*, 1993, p. 338.
[cxv] Tim Page, editor, *The Glenn Gould reader*, 1987, p. 102.
[cxvi] Alfred Brendel, 2001, p. 83.
[cxvii] Paul Bekker, 1925, p. 131.
[cxviii] Theodor W. Adorno, 1998, pp. 126–7.
[cxix] Denis Matthews, 1985, p. 94.
[cxx] Ernst von Elterlein, 1898, p. 103.
[cxxi] Stewart Gordon, 1996, p. 182.
[cxxii] Elaine Sisman, *Memory and invention at the threshold of Beethoven's late style*, in: Scott G. Burnham and Michael P. Steinberg, editors, *Beethoven and his world*, 2000, p. 71.
[cxxiii] Nicolas Slonimsky, 2000, p. 176.
[cxxiv] Denis Matthews, 1967, p. 46.
[cxxv] Harold Craxton and Donald Francis Tovey, [1931], p. 115.
[cxxvi] Derived from Wayne M. Senner, Robin Wallace and William Meredith, editors, 1999, Vol. 2, pp. 43–4.
[cxxvii] Carl Czerny in: Paul Badura-Skoda, 1970, p. 63.
[cxxviii] Edwin Fischer, 1959, pp. 97–8.
[cxxix] Harold Craxton and Donald Francis Tovey, [1931], p. 114. The Irish baritone Harry Plunket Greene possessed quite remarkable powers of clarity and diction in his vocal renderings, notable amongst which is his interpretation of Franz Schubert's *Der Leiermann*, 'The Hurdy Gurdy Mann'.
[cxl] See Charles Rosen, 2002, p. 215, Nicolas Slonimsky, *The great composers and their works*, edited by Electra Slonimsky Yourke, 2000, p. 176 and Barry Cooper, 2000, p. 252.
[cxli] Stewart Gordon, 1996, p. 182.
[cxlii] Alfred Brendel, 2001, p. 80.
[cxliii] Ernst von Elterlein, 1898, p. 104.
[cxliv] Romain Rolland, 1917, p. 161.
[cxlv] Denis Mathews, 1967, p. 46.
[cxlvi] Alfred Brendel, 2001, p. 82.
[cxlvii] Denis Matthews, 1985, p. 94. See also: Charles Rosen, 2002, p. 215.
[cxlviii] Charles Rosen, 2002, p. 215. Rosen goes further than the words quoted and asserts that when Beethoven does not sound like Bach he is apt to sound like Chopin.
[cxlix] William Kinderman, *The middle-period sonatas*, in Larry R. Todd, editor, 2004, p. 72.
[cl] David Dubal in conversation with Alfred Brendel, in: David Dubal, *The world of the concert pianist*, 1985, p. 109.
[cli] The Composer and musicologist Robert Simpson coined the expression 'The

cdii innocent ear' in connection with a series of BBC Radio Broadcasts, delivered on the Third Programme, in which he played pieces of music without initially disclosing the name of the composer. By this means he sought to free his listeners of any prior prejudices, for or against the music, by inviting it to be heard with an 'innocent ear'.

cdiii Beethoven's innovation in the A major Piano Sonata was not entirely novel. As Denis Matthews points out: 'He took a backward glance at the *Adagio* in the coda of the Finale in the Piano Sonata Op. 27, No. 1.' See: Denis Matthews, 1967, pp. 46–7.

cdiii As cited in Elaine Sisman, *Memory and invention at the threshold of Beethoven's late style*, in: Scott G Burnham and Michael P. Steinberg, editors, 2000, p. 51.

cdiv Derived from Wayne M. Senner, Robin Wallace and William Meredith, editors, 1999, Vol. 2, pp. 43–4.

cdv Carl Czerny in: Paul Badura-Skoda, 1970, p. 63.

cdvi See Edwin Fischer, 1959, p. 98.

cdvii Egerton C. Lowe, 1929.

cdviii Charles Rosen, 2002, p. 215.

cdix Harold Craxton and Donald Francis Tovey, [1931], Piano Sonata in A major, Op. 101, p. 115.

cdx Paul Bekker, 1925, p. 131.

cdxi Philip Radcliffe, *Piano Music* in: *The Age of Beethoven, The New Oxford History of Music, Vol. VIII*, Gerald Abraham, editor, 1988, p. 340.

cdxii Stewart Gordon, 1996, pp. 181–2.

cdxiii Alfred Brendel, 2001, p. 82.

cdxiv Theodor W. Adorno, 1998, pp. 127.

cdxv David Dubal, 1985, p. 109.

cdxvi As quoted in: Ernst von Elterlein, 1898, p. 105.

cdxvii Denis Matthews, 1967, p. 47.

cdxviii Matthew Rye, *Notes to the BBC Radio Three Beethoven Experience*, Friday 10 June 2005, www.bbc.co.uk/radio3/Beethoven

cdxix Ernst von Elterlein, 1898, pp. 104–5.

cdxx Charles Rosen, 2002, p. 216.

cdxxi Paul Bekker, 1925, pp. 131–2.

cdxxii Charles Rosen, 2002, p. 216.

cdxxiii Philip Radcliffe, *Piano Music* in: *The age of Beethoven, The new Oxford history of music*, Vol. VIII, Gerald Abraham, editor, 1988, p. 347.

cdxxiv Ernst von Elterlein, 1898, pp. 104–5.

cdxxv Philip Radcliffe, *Piano Music* in: *The age of Beethoven, The new Oxford history of music*, Vol. VIII, Gerald Abraham, editor, 1988, p. 347.

cdxxvi Beethoven House, Digital Archives, Library Document, Sonate für Klavier (A-Dur) Op. 101, Autograph, NE 219.

cdxxvii Emily Anderson, 1961, Vol. 2, Letter No. 746, p. 659.

cdxxviii *Ibid*, Vol. 2, Letter No. 747, p. 660.

cdxxix *Ibid*, 1961, Vol. 2, Letter No. 748, pp. 660–1.

cdxxx See: Beethoven House, Digital Archives, Library Document, Sonate für Klavier (A-Dur) Op. 101, Autograph, NE 219.

cdxxxi Stewart Gordon, 1996, p. 184.

cdxxxii As remarked and discussed by Stewart Gordon, 1996, pp. 182–3.

clxxxiii As discussed by Charles Rosen, 2002, p. 217.
clxxxiv Barry Cooper, 2000, p. 252.
clxxxv As quoted in: Nicolas Slonimsky, *The great composers and their works*, edited by Electra Slonimsky Yourke, 2000, p. 177.
clxxxvi Denis Matthews, 1967, p. 47.
clxxxvii Oskar Bie, 1966, p. 179.
clxxxviii Harold Craxton and Donald Francis Tovey, [1931], Piano Sonata in A major, Op. 101, p. 115.
clxxxix See: Egerton C. Lowe, 1929, p. 131.
cxc Elliot Forbes, editor, *Thayer's life of Beethoven*, 1967, p. 871.
cxci Stewart Gordon, 1996, p. 184.
cxcii Philip Radcliffe, *Piano Music* in: *The age of Beethoven, The new Oxford history of music*, Vol. VIII, Gerald Abraham, editor, 1988, p. 340.
cxciii Charles Rosen, 2002, p. 217.
cxciv Derived from Wayne M. Senner, Robin Wallace and William Meredith, editors, 1999, Vol. 2, pp. 43–4.
cxcv William Kinderman, *The middle-period sonatas*, in: Larry R. Todd, editor, 2004, p. 73.
cxcvi Barry Cooper, 2000, p. 253.
cxcvii Carl Czerny in: Paul Badura-Skoda, 1970, p. 63.
cxcviii Harold Craxton and Donald Francis Tovey, [1931], Piano Sonata in A major, Op. 101, p. 113 and p. 116.
cxcix Edwin Fischer, 1959, p. 98. A performance of the A major Piano Sonata, Op. 101 was recorded by Paul Badura-Skoda, on a Conrad Graf Piano of 1824, see: Astrée AS-48. The sonata was also recorded by Malcolm Binns on an Érard Piano of 1818, see: L'Oiseau-Lyre. Source: Ann P. Basart, *The sound of the fortepiano: A discography of recordings on early pianos*. Berkley, Fallen Leaf Press, 1985. The A major Piano Sonata was performed seven times at the National Gallery lunchtime concerts during the Second World War.

PIANO SONATA IN B-FLAT MAJOR, OP. 106
THE HAMMERKLAVIER

'Beethoven once told me during a walk to Mödling, "I am writing a sonata now which is going to be my greatest." It was Op. 106, around 1818.'

Carl Czerny: *On the Proper Performance of all Beethoven's Works for the Piano.* Paul Badura-Skoda, [1846] 1970, p. 10.

'Although this great work incurred — and still incurs [1860] the pedant's cavilling, it is a composition worthy of a Beethoven and, when played with perfect mastery, a clear and comprehensible

> piece of music that requires of its performers a high degree of virtuosity and knowledge of this art form.'

Anton Felix Schindler, *Beethoven as I Knew Him*, edited by Donald W. MacArdle and translated by Constance S. Jolly from the German edition of 1860, 1966, p. 214.

> 'As for the marvellous Sonata Op. 106, it consists of four movements: *Allegro, Scherzo, Adagio, Prelude and Fugue*, which take up seventy printed pages, if not more, and lasts almost an hour. I played it at the age of ten, doubtless very badly, but with passion — without anyone having taught it to me.'

Extract from a letter of Franz Liszt to Princess Carolyne Sayne-Wittgenstein, a Polish-born, intimate friend and confidant, 26 October 1876. Derived from: Adrian Williams, editor and translator, *Franz Liszt: Selected Letters*, 1998, pp. 806–7.

> 'The grandest sonata ever composed, of colossal dimensions, a real giant, symphonically conceived and framed throughout.'

Ernst von Elterlein, *Beethoven's Pianoforte Sonatas: Explained for the Lovers of the Musical Art*, 1898, p. 105.

> 'The work is a battle song, combining the joyous energy of Op. 53 with the demonic passion of Op. 57.'

Paul Bekker, *Beethoven*, 1925, p. 133.

> 'Is it possible to lift this gigantic work of Beethoven's into the symphonic sphere of the orchestra and thus to invest it with that resplendent power, which although inherent to it, cannot be clearly manifested on a keyed instrument by two human hands [even] were they the hands of the greatest master?'

Felix Weingartner, Preface to *Sonate für das Hammerklavier, Op. 106, für Orchestra*, 1926.

> 'The mighty work in B flat, Op. 106, is of course the greatest test of the executant's powers, but it is far more than this, for in it we are brought into contact with one of the greatest of poets, and it is perhaps the most faithful and lifelike of all the portraits of the master's soul.'

John Fuller-Maitland, *Special Issue* [Death Centenary], *The Musical Times*, London, Vol. VIII, No. 2, 1927, p. 222.

> 'B flat, the key of the sonata, is simply B in German notation. Did Beethoven, perchance, intend this colossal work to be typical of himself, an autobiography, in fact, in music?'

Egerton C. Lowe, *Beethoven's Pianoforte Sonatas: hints on their rendering, form, etc., with appendices on definition of sonata, music forms, ornaments, pianoforte pedals, and how to discover keys*, 1929, p. 141.

> 'The student cannot go wrong in assuming, as the most practical basis for his study of Op. 106, that

> Beethoven's imagination is always right, always based on the instrument he uses whatever his opinion as to their capacity, and always at its highest power throughout this particular work.'

Harold Craxton and Donald Francis Tovey, *Piano Sonata in B-flat major, Op. 106*, [1931], p. 136.

> '[There] is plenty of evidence that Beethoven wrestled liked a giant with the overwhelmingly potent material of this sonata, the composition of which might be called a kind of Mount Everest, were it not for the difference that he did actually reach the summit.'

Eric Blom, *Beethoven's Pianoforte Sonatas Discussed*, 1938, p. 203.

> 'The contrapuntal devices and the intellectual power Beethoven put forth overwhelm one like the statements of an astronomer about the power of the universe.'

Marion M. Scott, *Beethoven: The Master Musicians*, 1940, p. 146.

> 'In this work, in *one* creation of the spirit, a mortal man has portrayed and sublimated all the facts of life, its rigours, injustices, joys, its heavenly consolations, the temporal and the external, the conceivable and the inconceivable.'

Edwin Fischer, *Beethoven's Pianoforte Sonatas: a guide for students & amateurs*, 1959, p. 108.

'Then suddenly rises before us the "Grand Sonata" (Op. 106). We recognise no longer the old well-known features. It has assumed the forms of the giant-world; it laughs in its greatness, in its childlikeness. Will it really permit itself to be played by human hands? We are at the mysterious limits of piano music.'

Oskar Bie, *A History of the Pianoforte and Pianoforte Players*, 1966, p. 179.

'By 1819 the *Hammerklavier* was ready. It was the most titanic of all the sonatas, both in gestures and in time-scale, a triumphant enlargement of the four-movement plan to epic proportions.'

Denis Matthews, *Beethoven: piano sonatas*, 1967, p. 47.

'This mammoth sonata resembles the later quartet in the same key in its extraordinary fecundity, huge dimensions, and radical substance. Both works challenge our powers of absorption even now, in fact await full appreciation from a future generation.'

Igor Stravinsky, *Themes and Conclusions*, 1972, p. 272.

'The immensely difficult *Hammerklavier* Sonata, Opus 106, dates from the year 1818 and marks the full revelation of third-period Beethoven. It is a colossal work, not only in length but in the nature of its utterance. Here, he announced, was a sonata that would give pianists something to do,

> "a work that will be played in fifty years' time".'

Christopher Headington, *The Bodley Head History of Western Music*, 1974, p. 173.

> The *Hammerklavier* Sonata of 1817–18 constitutes an overreaching attempt to hold on to the traditional structure by a magnification of time scale and an intensification of contrast.'

Maynard, Solomon, *Beethoven*, 1977, p. 320.

> '[Beethoven] tried to go back to the time of the *Appassionata* in an attempt to give birth to yet another heaven-storming sonata. But he was now beyond such things and far on the way to a spiritual transformation of the highest order ...'.

Claudio Arrau, in: Joseph Horowitz, *Conversations with Arrau*, 1982, p. 244.

> 'Beethoven's *Hammerklavier* Sonata, as music and human musical experience, extends far beyond the written score, a particular moment in history, or any single performance.'

Reginald Byron, *Music, Culture, & Experience: selected papers of John Blacking*, 1995, p.226.

> 'One suspects [in the designation *Hammerklavier*] a vague psychological connection between the imagery of an emerging piano, one gaining in strength and power and tone, and the heroic demands of this work on both the instrument and

the performer ... Technically, the music is as challenging as anything in the literature, and the listener is hurled into a wild panorama of sound and fury, one that stretches the performer and the instrument to the absolute limits.'

Stewart Gordon, *A History of Keyboard Literature: music for the piano and its forerunners*, 1996, pp. 184—188.

'The Op. 106 Sonata offers unusual challenges not only to pianists but to all listeners. It was this work in particular that provoked a crises in the reception of his music. The notion of Beethoven's later music as inaccessible, too difficult, or even incomprehensible arose particularly in reaction to pieces like the fugal finales of Op. 106 and of the [String] Quartet Op. 130 in its original version — the *Grosse Fuge*.'

William Kinderman, *Beethoven*, 1997, p. 202.

'The sonata is the first manifestation of a new departure in Beethoven's late style — one which may be termed gigantism ... In every way, this work is a giant among sonatas.'

Barry Cooper, *Beethoven: The Master Musicians*, 2000, pp. 261—2.

'The *Hammerklavier* Sonata offers ... many stumbling blocks to the pianist. Difficult inner trills uncomfortable crossings of hands at a very close range, so that the fingers collide on a single key, chords demanding unnatural extension, all

> these usages are doubtful inducements to frequent performance.'

Nicolas Slonimsky, *The Great Composers and their Works*: edited by Electra Slonimsky Yourke, 2000, Vol. 1, p. 179.

> 'Even today, this work shows up the outer limits of what a composer of sonatas can accomplish, a performer can control, or a listener can take in. In a magnificent exertion of will, it combines grandeur and delicacy, the grand sweep and extreme density of detail.'

Alfred Brendel, *Alfred Brendel on Music: Collected Essays*, 2001, p. 83.

> 'This work has somewhat suffered from its reputation. Even the name of *Hammerklavier*, which could just as easily have been given to Op. 101, portrays it is massive. It has come to seem more like a monument to be admired than a work to be enjoyed ... I think we ought to abandon the view of this work as a kind of musical mammoth, or a construction comparable to the larger pyramids.'

Charles Rosen, *Beethoven's Piano Sonatas: a short companion*, 2002, p. 219.

> '[The] *Hammerklavier*, though written in the early nineteenth century has nothing to do with what we call "the nineteenth century" but rather is concrete evidence that Beethoven had entered the cosmic realm and plugged into those incred-

ible forces which are the source of human and animal life, solar and stellar life.'

George Rochberg, *The Aesthetics of Survival: a composer's view of twentieth-century music*, 2004, pp. 176–7.

'The Piano Sonata in B-flat major, Op. 106 will always be new music.'

Stephan Playstow, Notes to the BBCs, *Building a Library*, 28 October, 2006. See BBC website *Building a Library*.

It is fitting we should open our account of Beethoven's Piano Sonata in B-flat major, Op. 106, *The Hammerklavier* with an extended set of epigrammatic quotations. These reflect the standing this great work holds in the repertoire of the concert pianist and, indeed, its iconographic status in the realm of keyboard literature. In the words of musicologist Wilfrid Mellers: 'With the *Hammerklavier* Sonata, Op. 106, we cross the threshold into Beethoven's reborn world.'[i] It is a domain in which, to quote Alfred Brendel 'this gigantic work appears to be a triumph of logic without equal'.[ii] [iii] Beethoven was given to saying that he did not care to repeat himself and, as a consequence, with each of his piano sonatas he endeavoured to make new strides and explore new innovations, be they with respect to form, construction, motivic development or an exploration of what is humanly possible for ten fingers to execute on the keyboard. In composing the Piano Sonata Op. 106, he gave full expression to his self-imposed exhortation.

In our previous discussions we have seen that the keyboard itself had been undergoing a form of metamorphosis during the composer's lifetime, as it transformed from the pianoforte into the piano.[iv] With Op. 106,

Beethoven imposed yet further demands on his instrument. It requires a tonal range of some six and a half octaves, over an octave more than the range available to Beethoven on the instruments for which he had composed his earlier piano sonatas.[v] As Nicolas Slonimsky states: 'The extension in length and tonal range are the outward attributes of the inner grandeur of conception, a fullness of development, a complexity of detail, which characterizes the last period of Beethoven's creative life, to which the *Hammerklavier* belongs.'[vi] By any measure, the Piano Sonata in B-flat major stands apart from its predecessors.

In the Piano Sonata Op. 106, Beethoven returned to the four-movement sonata structure that he had first developed almost a quarter of a century previously, with the three sonatas Op. 2, and to which he returned intermittently in his Op. 7, Op. 10, No. 3, Op. 22, Op. 26, Op. 27, No. 1, Op. 28, Op. 31, No. 3, and Op. 101. But, as Stewart Gordon observes: 'In the Op. 106, the concept reaches its zenith.'[vii] Its thirty-page score (or thereabouts) and its 1200 bars (or thereabouts) have a playing time of typically forty-five minutes — twice the length of its immediate predecessor Op. 101 and equal to that of several of the composer's orchestral compositions.[viii] In his consideration of Beethoven's 'late period' disposition to the creation of works on a greater and more expanded scale, Barry Cooper draws a parallel with what we may describe as the composer's earlier *Eroica*-period of composition: 'Just as in 1803, he had begun composing on an enlarged scale after the crisis of Heiligenstadt (see Piano Sonata Op. 28), with works such as the *Eroica* and the *Waldstein* Sonata, so now in 1818 the scale was enlarged again, resulting in a series of works of unprecedented proportions ...'.[ix] These works included the Ninth Symphony, the *Diabelli* Variations and the *Missa solemnis*, the composition of all of which was commenced in the period 1817–19 and each of which share the new realms of scale and ambition that are characteristic of the Piano Sonata Op. 106. 'Beethoven's attempt to unify all the movements of a sonata, developed with Op. 27 and, above all, with the *Appassionata*, attains a new power with the *Hammerklavier*, which will be applied with equal cogency to the last three sonatas.'[x] In the estimation of Ernst von Elterlein: 'The uniform bond which unites the four movements of the sonata is, in my opinion, the ideal grandeur of the conception and execution; the work bears throughout the stamp of originality and boldness.'[xi] Beethoven himself appears to have been aware of the pioneering nature of his new creation when he remarked, on the publication of the work in September 1819: 'Now there you have a sonata that will keep the pianists busy when it is played fifty years hence.'[xii]

In our previous study of the Piano Sonata Op. 101, we remarked Beethoven sought to adopt the German language in his piano sonatas, in preference to the conventional Italian. Writing to his publisher in January 1817 he stated: '[We] are resolved and hereby resolve that from henceforth on all our works, on which the title is German, instead of pianoforte *Hammerklavier* shall be used.'[xiii] The Piano Sonata Op. 101, thereby, has a claim also to be known as the *Hammerklavier* Sonata, but, with the passing of time, this association has been lost and the expression *Hammerklavier* is now the exclusive preserve of the Piano Sonata Op. 106. Eric Blom summarizes the situation in the following amusing way: 'If, therefore, we do not call both these works *Hammerklavier* Sonatas it is simply because we do not call both children by the same name without causing endless confusion.'[xiv,xv]

We know from the recollections of Carl Czerny, that of all his piano sonatas Beethoven preferred the *Appassionata* until he composed the *Hammerklavier* that he then considered to be his greatest.[xvi] Since that time, the musical fraternity has — with few exceptions — agreed with Beethoven and has bestowed fulsome praise on the work. 'It is usually described as monumental and majestic, and at the same time enigmatic or labyrinthine, and it exercises a curious fascination over performers, musicologists and listeners.'[xvii] Beethoven's early biographer Adolph Bernhard Marx described the work in the following terms: 'Both in external proportions and in depth of meaning, the tone poem far over-passes the boundaries which even Beethoven himself had hitherto reached in pianoforte music.'[xviii] In his death-centenary tribute to the composer, the musicologist John Fuller-Maitland wrote: 'The virility of the first movement, the puckish waywardness of the second, the profound loveliness of the slow movement and the originality of the fugue (not forgetting the many points at which the pedants might be shocked), all are the purest Beethoven, and all seem to come from the soul rather than from the brain.'[xix] We discuss the role of the fugue in the *Hammerklavier* Sonata later; suffice it to say here that it is an aspect of the composition singled out for special mention by the French composer and musicologist André Hodeir. In his discussion of developments in the history of Western music, he cites Bach's fugues and Beethoven's String Quartets, describing them as 'pre-figurations of superhuman art'. He adds: 'Scores like Beethoven's *Hammerklavier* Sonata and Twelfth Quartet [Op. 127] constitute a singular event in the course of human thought, a kind of forward leap — one might almost speak of a mutation — which has never occurred in the history of any other civilization.'[xx]

As we shall see in the course of our narrative, the *Hammerklavier* Sonata was composed during a period of considerable personal difficulty for the composer and amidst many tribulations; its creation was nothing less than a triumph over personal adversity. In his estimation of the work, William Kinderman believes Beethoven's suffering — and with it his indomitability of spirit — found their way into the music, prompting him to comment: 'Like the *Eroica*, yet even more profoundly, the *Hammerklavier* Sonata implies an analogous narrative progression of heroic struggle and suffering, leading to a rebirth of creative possibilities.' He concludes: 'The *Hammerklavier* Sonata is concerned with much more than mere beauty; it is profoundly shaped by forces of conflict and tension.'[xxi]

As we shall also see in our later narrative, the *Hammerklavier* Sonata has its critics as well as it admirers. One such dissentient voice can be detected in a diary entry of the American composer George Rochberg, dating from 13 June 1985. Apparently Rochberg had a visitor, to whom he refers simply as 'S', who was finding it difficult to come to terms with Beethoven's challenging creation. He found it 'repellent' and couldn't relate to it 'as a human musical expression'. In his estimation it was evidence of 'an uncaring, unloving attitude on Beethoven's part' despite its brilliance of composition. Along the way 'S' compared the *Hammerklavier* Sonata and its world of 'non-human gestures' to Shakespeare's *King Lear*. Rochberg responded: 'I tried to point out that the only way one could grasp the essence of the *Hammerklavier* Sonata (and the Grand Fugue [Op. 133] and *Missa Solemnis*) was to recognise that it lay beyond the ordinary limits of human culture; and particularly, that despite the fact of Beethoven being an historic personality, such work lies outside of history itself and refuses any of the constraints of the normal historical perspectives.'[xxii][xxiii]

It is a measure of the standing in which the B-flat major Piano Sonata is now held that, notwithstanding the formidable challenges it presents to the performer, it has served as a vehicle for the world's greatest pianists to showcase their skills, in much the same way as Shakespeare's most celebrated roles have earned the respect and attention of the leading actors of their day. Donald Tovey describes Beethoven's treatment of the piano in his Op. 106 as being 'transcendental' and that his imagination of pianoforte tone 'is nowhere at a higher power than in this work'.[xxiv] In his Cramb Lectures of 1925, he elaborated his views, acknowledging the technical difficulties Beethoven's piano writing holds for the interpreter: 'Beethoven is cram full of atrocious passages ... where the difficulty simply seems to make a fool of a player, and you would simply say that it is against the nature of the instrument. As a matter of fact, he is just the kind of composer whose ideas have not been dictated by what he can conveniently play extemporarily, whose ideas are really free, who never forgets the nature and character of his instrument, but certainly forgets that some people may have to practise the passage for four hours a day for six months before it goes.'[xxv]

Alongside the *Diabelli* Variations, the *Hammerklavier* Sonata remains one of the most technically and emotionally challenging solo works in the piano repertory. It is pre-eminently a 'professional' composition. It is a work intended for the concert pianist, the scale of which, combined with its structural complexity and sustained emotional demands, place it beyond the capabilities of the amateur — quite unlike the composer's earlier sonatas (perhaps with a few exceptions). When the sonata was originally published it appears to have so perplexed Beethoven's contemporaries that it failed to secure a review in the music journals — despite the fact that only a few years previously, at the period of the Congress of Vienna, Beethoven had been widely performed and enthusiastically acclaimed. His later compositions, such as the B-flat Sonata, appear to have alienated him as can be detected from a review that appeared shortly after his death in the influential *Allgemeine musikalische Zeitung* of 29 April 1829. The music critic accuses Beethoven of having become 'melancholic and gloomy' as he withdrew more and more from the external world, no longer able to hear his own music. He accuses Beethoven of becoming what he calls 'an eye-composer' who took pleasure in 'inventing odd motives and working them out in an artificial and strange way ... He piled idea upon idea, and on paper they appeared very clear and delighted the eye, but in working them out they often become a *chaotic image*'.[xxvi] In effect, the music critic in question is accusing Beethoven of having become so isolated by deafness that he lived in an idealised sound world where anything was possible even if it stretched human capacities to — and at times almost beyond — their limits. Such an accusation is still heard today in connection with what has been described as the 'terrifyingly challenging' choral writing in the Ninth Symphony.

Critics of late Beethoven suggest he went too far 'in subjugating euphony and considerations of practicality to the demands of his musical conceptions', by which they mean his exploration and invention of 'new sonorities' ... 'new alignments of sound' ... and 'unaccustomed effects'. They assert Beethoven's ideas 'seem too big for human capabilities to express'.[xxvii] This idea is implicit in Ernst Bloch's commentary on the writings of Paul Bekker where he states: 'Bekker is not altogether wrong in his comment that the B-flat major Sonata and *Diabelli* Variations are ultimately unplayable because they are written for an instrument that has never existed and never will exist.' Bekker's contention is that Beethoven's writing does not enshrine 'real sound' but 'incorporeal, purely cerebral abstractions of sound'.[xxviii] Blom, however, offers a contrary view. He takes as his starting point what he calls 'grit', in the moral and intellectual sense. He reminds us that this is the quality we have learnt to value most in Beethoven, as an artist, and believes we must also 'take [Beethoven's] technical grittiness into the bargain [and] look upon it as an essential to our full appreciation of him'. With regard to the *Hammerklavier* Sonata he states: '[The pianist] cannot always have everything his own way, nor do those who are capable of understanding this sonata expect to hear from beginning to end such suavities as could not lend genuine beauty to certain passages for the very good reason that they would rob them of character.' He concludes with the following eloquent summation that has universal and enduring value: 'We must take art as it is given to us, with such limitations and even such defects as it may show. No work is quite flawless, if it comes to that, and art without limitations is unthinkable, as it is undesirable without artificialities ... [It] is for us to accept great works as their creators meant them, and believe in them as they are. That is what distinguishes them from small and casual art.'[xxix]

The *Hammerklavier* Sonata confronts not only the performer but the listener also. As long ago as the 1920s, when, admittedly, the Op. 106 was little known, Fuller-Maitland was disposed to reflect: 'It is undoubtedly a task to listen to the whole sonata if we bring any intelligence to bear upon it, and exhausted human nature must be held accountable if we fail to enter fully into the "heavenly length", as Schuman called the Great Schubert Symphony [No, 9 in C major], of the slow movement.'[xxx] Fuller-Maitland has here singled out the *Adagio sostenuto* that has a playing time of twenty minutes — or more in some interpretations. In his Cornell Lecture *What is music?* (c1955), Vaughan Williams discussed musical form and the manner in which we appreciate sound and in particular melody. What he had to say is germane to our appreciation of Beethoven's extended piano writing: 'Musical form is not a series of mysterious or trade secrets but is simply the development of a power natural to the human ear and the human mind ... When the first note passes to the second, the hearer must not only keep the first note in memory, but co-ordinate it with the second, and so on to the third ... If we did not have these powers, the simplest tune would be meaningless. To appreciate the *Hammerklavier* Sonata or the Ninth Symphony requires exactly the same qualities as the appreciation of the simplest tune ...'.[xxxi]

Much of the tonal landscape and prevailing mood of the *Hammerklavier* Sonata is established by the pervasive adoption of B minor — a tonality Beethoven once described as a 'black key'. In William Kinderman's words: 'B minor functions in the *Hammerklavier* like a focus of negative energy pitted against the B-flat major tonic, creating a dramatic opposition with far-reaching consequences.'[xxxii] When Peter Maxwell Davies was in conversation with the British music critic Paul Griffiths, the subject of key significance in music was mentioned, in part prompted by Davies' then recently composed (1980) Second Symphony. Davies turned the conversation to late Beethoven, known to be a principal source of stimulus to him, and enthused: 'Beethoven ... had very definite feelings associated with C minor, E-flat major, or B major, which he hardly touches, but when he does it's very significant — I'm thinking of the *Hammerklavier* Sonata and that obsessive B which goes down to B flat ...'.[xxxiii]

Beethoven commenced work on the B-flat major Sonata sometime in November-December of 1817. By April of the following year the first two movements were well in hand with the sonata as a whole being through composed later in May.[xxxiv] It was not, however, until the autumn of 1819 that the Viennese edition of the work was ready for publication with an English (London) edition following soon afterwards.

We refer to these circumstances in greater detail in a later part of our account.

A primary source for the creation-origins of the *Hammerklavier* Sonata, regrettably now lost, was the so-called Boldrini Sketchbook. The book took its name from Carlo Boldrini, an employee of Beethoven's publisher Artaria, who probably took possession of it following the sale of Beethoven's effects in 1827. It is believed to have originally consisted of 64 leaves, the principal contents of which were ideas for the first and second movements of Op. 106. It took the form of a pocket sketchbook and was in use from the autumn of 1817 until the spring of 1818. The pioneering Beethoven scholar Gustav Nottebohm made a study of the sketches and concluded the principal contents were, as stated, ideas for the first and second movements. Apparently almost all the sketches and notes were made in pencil with a small number being worked over in ink. Sketchbook drafts in pencil are characteristic of Beethoven as he so often worked outdoors whilst strolling in the countryside. Nottebohm's records suggest the orthography of the sketches was: first movement, pp. 18–88; second movement, pp. 75–128; and third movement, pp.116–27. Interestingly, sketches for the Ninth Symphony occupied pp. 92–109.[xxv] Should the Boldrini Sketchbook ever come to light it would be one of the great musicological finds of the century.

Although the Boldrini Sketchbook is now lost, several leaves of sketches have survived, dating, as we have already mentioned, from the autumn (possibly November but more probably December) of 1817.[xxvi] The surviving loose leaves are of a heterogeneous nature, 44 of which have been identified. These reflect work on the fourth movement; only eight leaves contain sketches for the first three movements.[xxvii] By way of interest, a quarter of an originally large single leaf with sketches for the first movement exists, suggesting, as is so frequently the case with Beethoven memorabilia, that it may have been broken up to create collectors' souvenirs.[xxxviii] Two other sketch sources survive in collations known as Vienna A 44 and Vienna A 45, both of which were previously owned by the collector and musicologist Gustav Nottebohm. Vienna A 44 now forms part of the collections of the Gesellschaft der Musikfreunde. Scholars who have studied these fourteen leaves of sketches believe Beethoven worked on them in the mid-summer of 1818. They belong to the fourth movement but appear to have no particular order regarding their musical content. Vienna A 45 passed from Gustav Nottebohm into the ownership of Johannes Brahms and is now also in the possession of the Gesellschaft der Musikfreunde. It consists of 36 leaves that are thought to derive from April to June of 1818. They reveal ideas relating primarily to the last two movements but include thoughts also for the second movement in the following page sequences: third movement, pp.1–13; fourth movement, pp. 3–5, pp. 14–24, and pp. 28–36; second movement, pp. 20–1.[xxxix]

In his analysis of Gustav Nottebohm's pioneering studies of the composer's sketches, Martin Cooper believes Beethoven's creative process may have jumped about somewhat — in typical Beethovenian fashion as his imagination was seized by various ideas. He remarks: 'During the composition of the first movement, the second and then the third were sketched; and, during the composition of the second and third, the final introduction and fugue were begun.'[xl] Notwithstanding that the surviving sketches indicate some measure of method and order, they also bear testimony to the effort they cost the composer: 'Never had a great master a harder struggle in hewing his material into the shape that satisfied him; but where we have sketches of his to compare with the finished product, we invariably find that the latter is infinitely superior.'[xli] Our reference to Beethoven's imagination being seized by a multiplicity of ideas takes on additional significance with the realization that, great as Beethoven's labours were in fashioning the Op. 106 Piano Sonata into shape, the sketches also reveal his mind turning intermittently to other major endeavours: 'Simultaneously with the sonata, Beethoven was at work on the Ninth Symphony, a Tenth also was before his fancy ...'.[xlii] 'The only surviving handwritten sources for the sonata are the sketches; no autograph score, corrected copy or engraver's model has survived.[xliii] If the autograph score should ever come to light, it would be an even more highly prized musicological treasure than the lost Boldrini Sketchbook.

We have remarked that with the Piano Sonata Op. 106 Beethoven returned to the traditional four-movement structure. More than this, it is the only sonata since Op. 28 to have the traditional four-movement pattern of a fast opening movement, a slow movement, scherzo and finale — although not in that particular order.[xliv] We also find Beethoven investing traditional musical forms in new guises. In the words of one commentator: 'The sonata ... represents the spectacular emergence of many of the themes that were to recur in Beethoven's late period: the reinvention of traditional forms, such as sonata form; a brusque humour; and a return to pre-classical traditions, including an exploration of modal harmony and reinventions of the fugue within classical forms.'[xlv] Through these processes, in the words of Martin Geck: 'Beethoven demonstrated the power of traditional musical techniques to convey emotion. The result, full as it is of technical difficulties, is impressive and as forceful as it is mysterious.'[xlvi]

We consider aspects of Beethoven's constructional procedures later in our discussion of the composition's individual movements. For the moment we make the following brief observations. Mellers regards the Op. 106 Piano Sonata as being 'one of the most titanic of Beethoven's conflict pieces' whose effect owes much to the composer's 'massive percussive writing ... assertive metre ... and [processes of] modulation'.[xlvii] Oskar Bie detects many of Beethoven's characteristic hallmarks in the piano writing: 'Rhythms marked by sharp blows, modulations in thirds, enharmonics ... Narrow-cut successions of chords'; these, he continues, 'are the very hand [hallmarks] of Beethoven.' He also draws attention to Beethoven's searching in the sketches for ways of giving what he calls 'additional upbeats' to the music whereby to 'heighten the eloquence of a theme'.[xlviii] Beethoven's adoption of the interval of a third is central to the fabric on which the sonata is constructed: 'Each of the ... movements and the introduction to the fugue use the third considerably. In this way Beethoven preserves the thematic kinship between the movements.'[xlix] Beethoven confronts the pianist with considerable musicological pedagogy: 'Through the four movements there are no fewer than forty key changes ... Except for that of four sharps, every key-signature is employed up to six sharps and six flats'.[l] Nevertheless Anton Schindler, Beethoven's amanuensis and biographer, ever eager to write in support of the composer, records the trouble Beethoven took to ensure his piano writing was 'pianistic' and lay within the capabilities of the performer, even though he occasionally demands reaches of a tenth. Notwithstanding the extreme deafness that afflicted Beethoven at the period of the composition of the *Hammerklavier* Sonata — and those that followed it — Schindler relates: 'When composing music for the fortepiano, the master would often go to the instrument and try certain passages, especially those that might present difficulties in performance. At such times he was totally oblivious of anyone present. To this circumstance I owe my acquaintance with the complete Sonatas Opp. 106, 109 and 110, and parts of the last movement of Op. 111.'[ii]

Beethoven dedicated the Piano Sonata in B-flat major to his only composition pupil the Archduke Rudolph. Writing to him early in June 1819 he informed him: 'I enclose two pieces which I have written that I had in fact composed ... last year before Your Imperial Highness's name day [the Archduke's birthday that fell on 4 April 1818].' The two pieces were in fact the first two movements of the B-flat Piano Sonata, Op. 106. He adds: 'To the two pieces in my handwriting composed for Y. I. H's name-day, I have added two more, the second of which is a grand *Fugato*, really amounting to a grand sonata, which will soon be published and which was long ago dedicated entirely *in my heart* to Y. I. H.'[iii] It is worth noting here Beethoven regarded the 'grand *Fugato*' — that is the fourth movement — as amounting almost to a sonata on its own, a consideration to which we will return shortly when we discuss Beethoven's proposals for an English edition of the Op. 106 Sonata.

Although the Archduke Rudolph was an accomplished pianist — it has even been remarked he could have had a musical career had he not followed his religious vocation — the technical challenges posed by the *Hammerklavier* Sonata were well beyond his capabilities. This circumstance has prompted Dieter Hildebrandt to make the following remarks: 'With earlier dedications it was possible to imagine that the person so honoured might actually play the piece ... or else have it performed, but this Op. 106 was quite impossible: not only for the son of the emperor but for any pianist far and wide.' He adds with a touch of irony: 'There is something almost lunatic about the dedication to the Austrian Archduke Rudolf, his patron and student — rather as if a sculptor were to dump a rough-cut block of granite at the door of one of his masons.'[liii]

Beethoven sold the *Hammerklavier* Sonata to the Viennese publisher Mathias Artaria for the fee of 100 ducats, about 45 pounds sterling — a considerable sum for a piano sonata; for example a few years later Artaria published the great String Quartet, Op. 130 — in the same key as the Op. 106 Sonata of B-flat major — for the lesser fee of 80 ducats.[liv] Artaria sent the engraved proofs to Beethoven for his inspection and correction on 24 July 1818. He simultaneously announced in the *Wiener Zeitung*: 'Now we shall put aside all the usual eulogies which would be superfluous anyway for the admirers of Beethoven's high artistic talent, thereby meeting the composer's wishes at the same time; we note only in a few lines that this work, which excels above all other creations of this master not only through its most rich and grand fantasy but also in regard to artistic perfection and sustained style, will mark a new period in Beethoven's pianoforte works.'[lv] Beethoven, having checked the proofs of his creation, responded with a letter to Artaria that he sent to him on 1 October from his summer residence in the spa town of Mödling. He first greets his publisher with the salutation: 'Very best castrated/emasculated (without testicles) virtuosi!' — an example of the extent to which his sense of humour could at times descend to the rustic upon his long-suffering associates. That said, Beethoven never allowed his humour to be quite as scatological as is the case in passages of Mozart's correspondence. Beethoven requested, as was his custom, six copies of his published sonata; he was in the habit of distributing copies of his newly published works to close friends, pupils and musicians whom he considered to be in need.[lvi]

The Title Page of the *Hammerklavier* Sonata appeared under both French and German titles. Beethoven gave permission for the wording of the Title Page in a letter to his Vienna publisher Artaria on 31 August 1819. He requested the reference to 'Grosse' Sonata should adopt the German spelling 'β' (= ss) but this could not be adopted since the words in question were to be engraved in capitals, thus 'GROSSE SONATE'. He humorously suggests the composition could be made available in 'Tahiti, India, Greenland and North America'.[lvii] The German edition was subsequently styled: 'GROSSE SONATE für das *Hammerklavier*. Seiner Kais[erlichen] König[lichen] Hoheit und Eminenz, dem Durchlauchtigen Hochwürdigsten Herrn Herrn Erzherzog Rudolph von Oesterreich, Cardinal und Erzbischoff von Olmütz etc. etc. in tiefster gewidmet von Ludwig van Beethoven. 106 Werk. Wien, bei Artaria und COMP.' This may be translated: 'Great Sonata for the *Hammerklavier*. Dedicated to His Imperial Highness and Eminence, the Most Gracious, Most Reverend Archduke Rudolph of Austria, Cardinal and Archbishop of Olmütz , etc. etc. in deepest reverence by Ludwig van Beethoven. Op. 106.'[lviii] It is a measure of Beethoven's standing, in the estimation of Artaria, that at about the same time as his announcement of the Piano Sonata Op. 106 his publishing house also listed all their editions of Beethoven's compositions to date.[lix] Despite Beethoven's insistence on the adoption of German in the Title Page, he returned to Italian inscriptions throughout the music itself.

No contemporaneous review of Op. 106 is known; only the wording of the publication announcement by Artaria from which we have quoted. One later reviewer, writing sometime around 1826, felt disposed to compare the *Hammerklavier* Sonata with the composer's much earlier, and highly popular, Septet in E-flat major, Op. 20. Such was its fame it had become a source of irritation to Beethoven in later life, given that he himself was acutely aware of the extent to which his music had so much advanced. The reviewer in question ruefully observed: 'It is strange that Beethoven declared precisely this work [the Septet] to be one of his least successful. For even if the dimensions are somewhat broad, it is infinitely richer in true beauty than many of his later works, for instance the big Sonata Op. 106.'[lx] Commenting on the relative neglect of Beethoven's late-period compositions, on the part of such review journals as the *Allgemeine musikalische Zeitung*, Nicolas Slonimsky reasons: 'Contemporary critics mistook [the] vastness of design [in the *Hammerklavier* Sonata] and [its] multiplicity of ideas for a confusion in Beethoven's mind in his last years. This picture of the master, almost totally deaf, untidy in his dress, unable to organise his daily life, anxious over his financial insecurity, was projected by such critics onto the music of Beethoven's last period, and the conclusion was drawn that it was the music of decline.'[lxi] Only a few astute commentators were able to discern that a new era was dawning in Beethoven's late music — music that to so many remained strange, unfamiliar and difficult to assimilate.

In addition to his transactions with Artaria, Beethoven also negotiated for an English (London) edition of the Piano Sonata Op. 106 to be brought out with the assistance of his former pupil Ferdinand Ries. He had studied piano with Beethoven in Vienna and from 1813 enjoyed a successful career as a composer-pianist in England. In 1815 Ries was elected a Member of the Philharmonic Society and from this time he acted as Beethoven's unpaid agent in the composer's dealings with his English publishers.[lxii] Beethoven set great store by the sale of his publications in England — not forgetting his extensive dealings with the Edinburgh-based publisher George Thomson. He thereby sought to maximise his income.[lxiii] On 19 March 1818 Beethoven informed Ries he had composed 'a grand sonata for pianoforte solo [Op. 106]' and requested him to put in hand arrangements for its sale to a London publisher. He had been advised by his former acquaintance Cipriani Potter to select the publishing House of Samuel Chappell (co-founded by J. B. Cramer) but Ries was given a free hand in the matter. Beethoven had been on friendly terms with Potter during the latter's stay in Vienna. Potter, an accomplished pianist, later became a central figure in London's concert life premiering the composer's first English performances of the First, Third and Fourth Piano Concertos. In his letter to Ries, Beethoven laments: 'My situation is now so difficult that I have to resort to every means merely to enable me to preserve this dreary life ... unless I want to become a beggar in Vienna.'[lxiv]

On 20 March 1819 Beethoven, eager to see his work in print and error free, sent Ries a comprehensive list of corrections for what would become the first English edition of the sonata. He apologised for there being so many errors — running to several pages. He explained the work had been copied in haste and had not been undertaken by his normal copyist, Wenzel Schlemmer, but by someone else. Schlemmer was the composer's favourite copyist (see Piano Sonatas Opp. 53 and 90) but now had failing sight; to Beethoven's chagrin he died four years later.[lxv] Beethoven explained he was not able to send Ries the tempo indications since his metronome was broken; he had promised these in a letter to Ries of 30 January 1819, undertaking to send them 'within two or three months at the latest'.[lxvi] We discuss Beethoven's (controversial) tempo indications, and their considerable implications, shortly. Beethoven then made the following suggestions: 'Should the sonata not be suitable for London, I could send you another one; or [concerning the Op. 106] you could omit the *Largo* and begin straight away with the fugue, which is the last movement; or you could use the first movement and then the *Adagio*, and then for the third movement the *Scherzo* — and omit entirely No. 4 with the *Largo* and *Allegro risoluto* and let them form the whole sonata. I leave it to you to do what you think best.' Beethoven doubted whether he could in fact write another sonata since he was 'very busy with other things'; these included work on the Ninth and Tenth Symphonies. Regarding the Piano Sonata Op. 106, he confided in Ries: 'The sonata was written in dreadful circumstances, for it is hard to compose almost entirely for the sake of one's daily bread.'[lxvii]

To many commentators Beethoven's suggestions to Ries that an English publisher might bring out the *Hammerklavier* Sonata in a number of alternative forms, seems almost heretical, not least given the carefully wrought nature of his creation. In effect, Beethoven was proposing the English edition could assume one of three possible forms: the first two movements alone; the *Allegro risoluto* by itself without the *Largo*; or the first three movements, with the order of the *Scherzo* and *Adagio* reversed. As Brendel observes, Beethoven's 'unsettling suggestions' have to be considered in their context. Initially, as he remarks, they 'seem to defy sanity' but, from what we have just cited in his letter to Ries, we know Beethoven had a desperate need to earn a fee from his London publisher 'whatever the compromise'.[lxviii] Blom has much the same to say as Brendel: 'How great [Beethoven's] anxiety must have been to see the sonata published on almost any conditions, so long as it was well paid for ... That from Beethoven, on whom we are accustomed to look as the most passionately scrupulous of all composers in matters of form ... His plight must indeed have been a sorry one to bring him to such a pass'.[lxix] William Newman concurs: 'The carte blanche [to Ries] is shocking to everyone who regards the over-all cycles of Beethoven's instrumental music as inviolable wholes in which every last detail is an indispensible factor.'[lxx] Denis Matthews comments in similar fashion: 'Tragic evidence of Beethoven's financial position was his readiness to compromise with a London publisher over the sonata's length by omitting whole movements'.[lxxi]

It is conceivable that considerations, other than financial hardship, may have pre-disposed Beethoven to countenance the publication of his B-flat major Sonata in a modified form by an English publisher. First and foremost, as we have seen, he had the reassurance the 'correct' version was being published by Artaria in Vienna. Did it really matter then, could Beethoven have reasoned, if the London edition was compromised — so long as he received his much-needed fee? Martin Cooper puts the musicological case: 'It is of course theoretically possible that Beethoven wrote the first two movements of Op. 106 together, as the key and subject matter suggest, then wrote separately the great fugue and the *Largo* introduction, and subsequently again the *Adagio*; and their organic connection was no closer in his mind than the organic connection between anyone of them'.[lxxii] Philip Radcliffe suggests doubts in Beethoven's mind may, in part, have disposed him to write to Ries as he did: 'Perhaps because of the vast scale of [the] first movement, Beethoven had curious doubts about the over-all construction of the rest of the sonata, his longest.'[lxxiii] We have also seen, from Beethoven's letter to the Archduke Rudolph, how he regarded the grand *Fugato* as 'really amounting to a grand sonata' — that is an independent work. Commentators have also drawn attention to the fact that Beethoven was prepared to radically amend other of his compositions. In particular they cite the String Quartet in B flat, Op. 130 for which the *Grosse Fuge* was originally composed as its finale and which he later discarded allowing it to be published separately as his Op. 133. John Shedlock, reflecting a century ago on Beethoven's proposals to Ries, felt disposed to comment: 'Considering that the work is very long, it is strange that no pianist at a recital ever seems to have adopted Beethoven's suggestions.'[lxxiv] It is unthinkable today, however, that any pianist of international standing would ever perform the *Hammerklavier* Sonata other than in its accepted published form. We give the last word on this aspect of the creation origins of the *Hammerklavier* Sonata to Charles Rosen: 'It is evident that, since the sonata was to be printed properly soon in Vienna, Beethoven did not much care what the English thought about it, as long as they printed it without delay and he got his payment. The proposals to Ries have no musical interest; they concern only Beethoven's financial dealings.'[lxxv]

Beethoven duly received his English fee for the *Hammerklavier* Sonata, although it appears he had to wait a considerable time for it. He raised the question of his payment with Ries in a letter to him of 25 May 1819 stating: 'Don't forget about the ... sonata and the *money*, I mean to say the *honorarium* ... !!!'[lxxvi] On 10 November he once more urged the matter on Ries complaining: 'I really need a good deal of money.'[lxxvii] Finally, on 6 July 1822, he was in a position to write to his ever-patient interlocutor Ries: 'I received safely the 26 pounds sterling, for which I send you my warmest thanks.' Of related interest is the next part of the letter: 'I have composed two new sonatas for pianoforte solo which are not really very difficult [Piano Sonatas Opp. 110 and 111]. I should be glad if you could obtain the same sum of 26 pounds sterling for these, for I can dispose of them in Germany as well without injuring either the English or German publisher.' This letter also reveals Beethoven had made progress with the Ninth Symphony since he asks Ries: 'Have you any idea what fee the *Harmony Society*

[Philharmonic Society] would offer me for a grand symphony?' He takes leave of Ries on a note of optimism that regrettably would not be fulfilled: 'I am still toying with the idea of going to London, provided my health permits it, perhaps next spring?'[lxxviii]

Following the copyright procedures then in force in England, the Piano Sonata Op. 106 was deposited at Stationer's Hall in London[lxxix] — as Beethoven had suggested, in two parts. The first three movements were titled 'Grand Sonata' and appeared, without opus number, in the sequence I, (*Allegro*), III, (*Adagio*), and II, (*Scherzo*). The last movement was published as 'Introduction and Fugue', also without an opus number. The two parts were received at Stationer's Hall on 1 October 1819, each part making reference to the dedication to 'His Imperial Highness the Archduke Rudolph, of Austria' — although this salutation did not subsequently appear on the published copies. The two parts were again entered at Stationer's Hall on 24 December 1819. Alan Tyson suggests that although the sonata was ready for publication on 1 October 1819 it was postponed, to enable Ries, who was seeing the work through the press, to first ensure that the protocol of the Viennese edition being published first was fulfilled, and, second, to ensure that any corrections received by Ries from Beethoven could still be made.[lxxx] Tyson concludes: 'This makes the true publication date of the English edition 24 December 1819, by which time the dedication had been dropped and a new Title Page engraved, so the work was re-entered.'[lxxxi]

The now, very rare, English first edition of the *Hammerklavier* Sonata — three movement version — has the following Title Page: 'Grand Sonata/for the Pianoforte/Composed by/L. VAN BEETHOVEN./Ent. Sta. Hall — Price 7 [shillings]/London, Printed by/THE REGENT'S HARMONIC INSTITUTION,/(Lower

Saloon, Argyll Rooms)/290.'[lxxxii] The Regent's Harmonic Institution, mentioned here, was founded in 1818 by a group of professional musicians who included J. B. Cramer, Beethoven's former pupil Ferdinand Ries, Sir George Smart and Samuel Wesley. The Institution's distinguished premises were designed by the fashionable Regency architect John Nash. Pamela Willets, in her study of the early English editions of Beethoven's compositions held in the British Museum (British Library), has identified six publishers who also brought out editions of the *Hammerklavier* Sonata. These continued to be in two parts but now bearing the designations 'First Part, Op. 106' and 'Second Part, Op. 106'. Among the early publishers was Ignaz Moscheles who issued the two pieces in his *Complete Edition* of Beethoven's works, giving them his Catalogue Nos. 30 and 31; thereby, it has been conjectured, Moscheles was probably the first person to perform the *Hammerklavier* Sonata in England, albeit in its truncated form. J. B. Cramer and his partners also published an edition about 1838 and a further one in 1844. These circumstances suggest that, notwithstanding the formidable technical challenges posed by the composition, the work nevertheless finding a market.[lxxxiii]

We consider for a moment Beethoven's suggested metronome marks that, as we have remarked, he promised to send to Ries in his letters of 30 January and 20 March 1819; we discuss these in more detail in our commentaries to the first and fourth movements. In our discussion of the Piano Sonata Op. 101 we commented how Beethoven had responded with enthusiasm to the invention of the metronome. An article in the *Wiener Vatwerlänidische Blätter* had even proclaimed the composer's support for Maelzel's instrument: 'Herr Beethoven looks upon this invention as a means with which to secure the performance of his brilliant compositions in all places in the tempos conceived by him, which to his regret have so often been misunderstood.'[lxxxiv] Beethoven now carried his enthusiasm over into the *Hammerklavier* Sonata – the only one of his piano sonatas to be given metronome indications by him. Beethoven was as good as his word and sent Ries the tempo indications for the four movements of the sonata in a letter dated 16 April 1819. They were as follows: first movement, minim = 138; second movement minim = 80; third movement quaver = 92; and fourth movement, *Introduzione*, Largo, quaver = 76 and fugue, minim = 144.[lxxxv] Of equal significance to these metronome markings is Beethoven's additional comment that, despite the Op. 106 Piano Sonata now being fully composed, he wished to add a further bar to the third movement – what would become its first bar. As we shall see, this relatively innocent-sounding remark was to create quite a stir that still has resonance today in commentaries to the composition.

It is now universally acknowledged – with the possible exception of Artur Schnabel (see later) – that Beethoven's tempo indications are unrealistically too fast. In the words of Brendel: 'The metronome marks ... with one exception ... are all hurried, not to say mechanically overdriven. In the first movement particularly, the prescribed tempo cannot be attained, or even approached, on any instrument in the world, by any player at all, be he the devil incarnate, with grievous loss of dynamics, colour and clarity.'[lxxxvi] He offers the following advice to the would-be interpreter: 'If you have in front of you a piece like the *Hammerklavier* Sonata, with Beethoven's own metronome markings, it is important that you first become very well acquainted with the piece in all it has to offer, and only then determine the tempo – not the other way round, starting with the metronome figure and squeezing everything into the tempo it asks for. By doing that you would lose much that is important.'[lxxxvii]

Why did Beethoven set such improbable tempo indications? In answering this question we first recall what Anton Schindler said (see above) about the care Beethoven took to ensure his piano writing was 'pianistic' and lay within the capabilities of the performer. However, as Barry Cooper observes: 'By the time Beethoven started work on the composition of his Op. 106, deafness had all but isolated him from the keyboard, depriving him from being able to confirm the viability of what he had written.'[lxxxviii] It has also been suggested Beethoven's isolation from the world of *real* sound, into the realm of *idealised* sound, may have induced him in his imagination to set quicker metronome markings than he would have adopted had he still been a performing artist.[lxxxix]

There is a further suggestion to offer by way of explaining Beethoven's metronome marks; could he have been stirred into composing a deliberately challenging piano composition in response to one recently published by his contemporary, and celebrated keyboard virtuoso, Johann Nepomuk Hummel? The Hummel work in question is his Piano Sonata in F-Sharp minor, Op. 81. Composed and published in Vienna at about the same time as Beethoven's Op. 106, it confronts the performer with formidable technical challenges that once earned for it the nickname the 'unplayable sonata'. Although with the passage of time it has not secured a permanent place in the piano repertory, as Beethoven authorities have observed (including Wilhelm von Lenz), Hummel's Op. 81 shares many common features with Beethoven's Op. 106. These include 'very fast metronome markings, formidable technical demands, an innovative idiom, and fugal passages in the last movement'.[xc]

We can offer further conjectures. Could Beethoven's metronome have been defective in some way, thereby misleading him? The metronome is a very delicate instrument and contemporary accounts bear testimony to Beethoven's clumsiness. In this context we should bear in mind his numerous changes of address, with his possessions usually being transported on the back of a cart. We have also noted, from the composer's letter to Ries of 20 March 1819, that his metronome was broken. Doubtless also Beethoven could not hear the beats of his metronome, as a consequence of his profound deafness, and had to rely instead on observing the less precise oscillating mechanism. There is the added consideration of his poor eyesight; in his later years when at work Beethoven wore spectacles. This would add to the difficulty of interpreting the small numbers on the metronome's graduated scale.[xci]

We gain an appreciation of the newness of Maelzel's metronome, and with it the help composers required in becoming familiar with it, from a letter the inventor wrote to Beethoven on 19 April 1818. The first part of this letter, however, is in connection with improvements to the design of an ear trumpet on which he had been working in an attempt to alleviate the composer's deafness (see later). Maelzel then can't resist blowing his own trumpet, if the pun may be allowed. He refers to the 'sensation' his metronome was making in France with composers — Maelzel's workshop was in Paris where he had first introduced his instrument — and how Beethoven's own endorsement of it in the *Wiener Vatwerlänidische Blätter* had had 'a mighty effect'. He asserts: '[Composers] do not merely accept the metronomic method of [tempo] designation: rather they want to avail themselves of this [method] *exclusively*... they renounce the Italian words for the interpretation of tempos.' Of interest, especially to exponents of authentic-performance on original instruments, is Maelzel's chart that accompanies his letter. This was designed: 'To give composers a guide to the [tempo] designations from which they may now choose in all meters, depending upon whether the piece of music has a slow, moderate or fast tempo.' Maelzel respectfully adds in his letter: 'It goes without saying that I do not want to give *you* [Beethoven] advice [or] any instruction about it; you know the subject as well as anyone.' Maelzel's chart takes the form of a table giving the scale of the metronome (vertically), on the left side, and suggested tempo indications (horizontally), on the right. Alongside these indications of the traditional Italian terms — *Lento, Moderato, Presto* — are Maelzel's recommended metronome equivalents. At the foot of the table is a list of celebrated composers of the day, including Cherubini, Clementi, Cramer, Paer, Spontini and Beethoven himself, with indications of their own interpretations of the Italian terms alongside Maelzel's metronome equivalents.[xcii]

Of related interest is what Anton Schindler has to say, more generally, about the early metronomes of Beethoven's day. He describes two variants that were in use from about 1815. A superior model took the form of a pyramid about a foot high (30 centimetres) and was calibrated with numbers from 50 to 160. This sold for three louis d'or — the equivalent of about three pounds sterling; on account of its high price it did not find many buyers. A cheaper and smaller version, about eight inches high (20 centimetres), was made especially for the German trade and sold for one louis d'or. The eminent musicologist Perter Stadlen believed he had identified such a metronome as having once belonged to Beethoven, following the sale of the composer's effects in 1827. This metronome was calibrated with numbers from 40 to 208. Schindler remarks: 'The difference between the two types soon gave rise to complaints that any tempo mark was ambiguous unless it specifically stated which of the two machines was implied.'[xciii]

We close this part of our discussion with a further recollection from Schindler that suggests Beethoven, like any other great artist, could exercise the prerogative of changing his mind. Beethoven was asked by the [Royal] Philharmonic Society of London to supply metronome indications for the Ninth Symphony. The list was subsequently mislaid and, to Beethoven's vexation, had to be repeated. The task complete, the original indications were subsequently found and 'showed a difference in all the movements'. Schindler recollects: 'Then the master, losing patience exclaimed; "No more metronome! Anyone who can feel the music right does not need it, and for anyone who can't, nothing is of any use; he runs away with the orchestra anyway".'[xciv]

It is doubtful if Beethoven ever played the *Hammerklavier* Sonata through himself. Carl Czerny was probably the only one to master its great technical difficulties in the composer's lifetime; Thayer informs us that Czerny played the work in Beethoven's presence during the spring of 1819 — Czerny would then be just nineteen years old.[xcv] This is consistent with what Czerny himself has to say in his own recollections of the composer from the period 1818–20. He writes: 'I organized concerts by my pupils every Sunday in my lodgings; they played to a quite selected audience.' On two occasions Beethoven himself was present and consented to perform himself. Of this, Czerny says: '[He] still improvised even then ... everyone was deeply stirred and moved in a wonderful way.' Commenting on Czerny's recollections, Schindler adds: 'Herr Czerny played Op. 106 which he had often studied with [Beethoven] at an earlier time.' He also states: 'In the years after 1818 Beethoven no longer improvised except at home.'[xcvi]

Franz Liszt is usually accorded the honour of giving the first public performance of the Op. 106 Sonata in two recitals he performed in 1836 at the Salle Érard in Paris.[xcvii] Liszt himself tells us how he discovered the *Hammerklavier* Sonata at the unbelievably early age of ten! It is more probable that he 'played with' the sonata rather than having performed it, nevertheless, for a mere child to have the maturity of outlook to engage with such a work is remarkable. Of this, Liszt says: 'My father [his first teacher] wasn't up to it and Czerny [his subsequent teacher] was afraid to put me on such a diet.' In fact, Czerny disapproved of his young protégé's hand position and, more generally, considered his youthful pupil 'had learned too much too soon'.[xcviii]

A possible rival claimant to being the first to play the *Hammerklavier* Sonata, in public, is the Franco-Polish pianist Henri Mortier de Fontaine.[xcix] History has now neglected him but he is described in Grove's *A Dictionary of Music and Musicians* (1900) as being 'possessed of unusual technical ability'. De Fontaine was born in Warsaw in 1816. If we assume he performed the *Hammerklavier* Piano Sonata sometime, say, in the early 1830s, he must still have been only in his late teens. This observation prompts a modern-day anecdote. When the seventeen-year old Daniel Barenboim was asked why he had recorded the *Hammerklavier* Sonata so young, he is alleged to have retorted: 'Well, It's never going to get any easier!'

Two recollections, co-incidentally both from the same year of 1833, connect us with early performances of the *Hammerklavier* Sonata in England. The first reunites us with Cipriani Potter who, at the period in question, was a leading figure at the London (later Royal) Academy of Music. Amongst his pupils was the highly gifted Sterndale Bennett; Mendelsohn said of him: 'I think him the most promising young musician I know.' Potter wished to introduce his pupil, then not quite eighteen-years old, to the *Hammerklavier* Piano Sonata. In sending Bennett to secure a copy of the work from the music shop, his sole direction to his pupil was: 'Go and ask for the sonata that nobody plays.' This, however, proved to be sufficient for the music-seller who duly brought down the work from a dusty high shelf with the aid of a stepladder. According to Bennett's biographer, the pupils of Potter saw in their master a direct link with Beethoven: 'They were, indeed, very proud of this, and would not require [allow] anyone else to explain the great composer to them.'[c] Our second recollection from 1833 connects us with a concert series promoted by Thomas Alsager for a fraternity of music lovers known as the Queen Square Select Society. Alsager was a writer for the *Times* newspaper — and possibly the earliest to give reviews of concerts. Ignaz Moscheles first performed for the Society in 1833 when he played Beethoven's Piano Sonatas Opp. 110 and 111 — amongst the very earliest public performances of these works in England. On 9 March 1845, Moscheles was again invited to play an arduous programme of Beethoven sonatas that included: Op. 31, No. 2; Op. 90; and Op. 106. After the concert Moscheles recorded in his diary: 'I was glad that my powers did not fail me in the B-[flat] major Sonata. In the *Adagio* in F sharp minor my feelings were most powerfully moved, but in the fugue it pained me to find so many extravagances. It contains more discords than concords, and Beethoven seems to me all the while to be saying: "I intend working up a subject in a learned manner, [whether] it may sound well or not".'[d]

As the nineteenth century progressed, the *Hammerklavier* Sonata gradually entered the repertoire, but only slowly. Beethoven's remark that he had composed a sonata 'that would give pianists something to do' and would by played 'in fifty years' time', proved to be accurate. Illustrious names associated with early and mid-nineteenth century performances include: Franz Liszt, Clara Schumann, Hans von

Bülow, Anton Rubinstein, Frederic Lamond and Ferruccio Busoni. We now offer a selection of accounts to illustrate the progress and assimilation of this great composition.

An extract from a letter Felix Mendelssohn wrote to his sister Rebecca, on 25 March 1845 when he was in Frankfort, bears testimony to his versatility as a pianist — and his Puckish sense of humour. 'I came with Friedrich Schlemmer [a lawyer and organist friend] last night at one o'clock from a punch party, where I first played Beethoven's Sonata Op. 106, in B flat, and then drank 212 glasses of punch *fortissimo*; we sang the duet from *Faust* in the Mainz Street, because their was such wonderful moonlight, and today I have rather a headache.'[cii] The correspondence of Sir George Grove sheds light on a long-forgotten young woman pianist, Arabella Goddard, who must have possessed extraordinary pianistic gifts. Despite her English-sounding name, she was born in France. An acknowledged child prodigy, Arrabella studied with Sigismond Thalberg and played before Chopin and Queen Victoria. She made her formal debut in London on 14 April 1853, when age 17, giving a performance of the *Hammerklavier* Sonata. Some authorities, including Grove, considered Goddard's performance to be the first London performance of the work but, as we have seen, this honour may go to Ignaz Moscheles. Be this as it may, Goddard can be credited with bringing performances of Beethoven's late piano sonatas — largely unknown at the time — before the London public, primarily through the series of recitals she gave at the Chrystal Palace in the concert seasons of 1857 and 1858. At these she pioneered playing from memory, then still an innovation. Writing to his sister-in-law Emma Bradley [November?] 1862, Grove enthused about the *Hammerklavier* Sonata in the following terms: 'Why, my dear child, it's the most *awfully difficult* thing! You perhaps don't know what an event it is, having heard it at all. I recollect Miss [Arabella] Goddard played it ... and the extraordinary sensation it made. There is no doubt whatever, it is she we have to thank for Beethoven's latest and most difficult sonatas having become so popular as they now are.'[ciii]

We derive an insight into the early career of the French organist and composer Eugène Gigout, from the time he was a piano pupil of Camille Saint-Saëns. Gigout was still only a schoolboy at the time but, nonetheless, Saint-Saëns, aware of his youthful pupil's precocious abilities, challenged him to learn the *Hammerklavier* Sonata by heart. According to Saint-Saëns: 'He did it very well, hence I gave him my reward. I took him to *Faust*.' Following his success, the youthful Gigout made an attempt at orchestrating the composition but which has not survived. Ever after, Saint-Saëns affectionately referred to Gigout as 'my little 106'.[civ]

The piano-music literature of the nineteenth century inevitably abounds in recollections of the playing of Franz Liszt. He will recur in our later accounts; for now we offer the following reminiscences of his playing. Liszt was Richard Wagner's father-in-law, but it would be wrong to accuse Wagner of misplaced filial devotion in his admiration of Liszt's playing. In his extensive prose writings he says: 'Whoever had frequent occasion to hear Liszt play Beethoven, for instance — particularly in a friendly circle — must have surely been struck with the fact that there was no question here of re-production, but of genuine production ... I ask all who have heard, for instance, Op. 106 or Op.111 of Beethoven's (the two great Sonatas in B and C) played by Liszt in a private circle, what they previously knew of these creations and what they then discovered in them?'[cv]

The German organist, pianist and composer Theodor Kirchner heard Liszt perform the B-flat Sonata on 27 November 1856. He and a number of distinguished guests had assembled in the house of the ardent music lover Herr Bourit, a wealthy merchant of St. Gallen. Liszt was persuaded to play. Kirchner later recorded: 'Now we can truly say that we have witnessed the impossible, for I shall always regard what I have just heard as an impossibility.'[cvi] The English writer, diplomat and journalist William Beatty-Kingston heard Liszt perform on several occasions, including renderings of the piano sonatas Opp. 106 and 111. Of his technique Beatty-Kingston writes, from the period 1869: 'Practice and will had so disciplined his fingers and accustomed them to fulfil infallibly the orders transmitted to them from his brain, that in all probability, the word "difficulty" (in connection with *technique*) had ceased to possess any exact significance, as far as Liszt the executant was concerned.' He adds — in the much same manner as Wagner: 'He who has enjoyed frequent opportunities in a small intimate circle, of hearing Liszt play — Beethoven's music, for example, — must have realised the fact the playing in question was not mere reproduction, but actual *re-creation*'.[cvii]

In his capacity as music critic, George Bernard Shaw regretted not having heard Liszt perform. Writing for the *Dramatic Review* of 10 April 1886, he still held out hopes of hearing the celebrated virtuoso perform. As it was he had to be content with the reviews of Liszt's concerts and anecdotes about him. Shaw referred to Liszt as 'The Favourite of Fortune' and said of him — mindful that Liszt was now an old man: 'We cannot expect him to formally undertake a public performance of Beethoven's Opus 106, his playing of which was ranked by Wagner as a creative effort [see above]; but there is abundant hope he may be tempted to touch the keyboard at some concert at which only his presence can be promised.' He concluded his appreciation saying: '[He] was once a great player, one who far more than any interpreter of his time could play a sonata as the composer thought it, reading into every quaver the intention with which it was written ...'. It so happens that the *Hammerklavier* Piano Sonata was the very last work Liszt ever performed, just before he died in July, a mere two months after Shaw's appreciation of him.[cviii]

Our next set of recollections, regarding celebrated musicians and their connection with the *Hammerklavier* Piano Sonata, draw us closer to our own time.

As a young man the widely acclaimed German-born conductor Otto Klemperer studied piano in Berlin with the intention of becoming a concert pianist. When age twenty he gave a performance of the *Hammerklavier* Sonata that his fellow student Ilse Fromm praised for what she described as Klemperer's 'sense of musical equilibrium'. In 1905 Klemperer entered the Anton Rubinstein piano competition held that year in Paris. The winner was the twenty-one year old Wilhelm Backhaus but opinions amongst the judges were apparently divided. A month later Klemperer entered for the coveted Mendelssohn Prize in Berlin, at that time the foremost competition in Germany. On this occasion he was commended by a jury — that included the violinist Joseph Joachim — for his performance of the *Hammerklavier* Sonata. Although this mighty work was judged to be in keeping with Klemperer's own physical stature — he was 1.96m. tall (six feet five inches), a later meeting with Gustav Mahler determined the young Klemperer's career as an orchestral conductor.[cix]

Arthur Rubinstein's recollections of his student days connect us to the Piano Sonata Op. 106 and give a hint of his views of the music and his thoughts about its performance. In the summer of 1910, when he was twenty-three years old, he took part in a piano competition held in St. Petersburg; it was named in honour of his namesake, the great Beethovenian Anton Rubinstein. Notwithstanding

Rubinstein's endeavours, the first prize went to a fellow student by the name of Alfred Hoehn. Rubinstein generously acknowledged Hoehn's achievement; his programme had included the arduous *Hammerklavier* Piano Sonata. Of Hoehn's performance he says: 'He played this great work magnificently, as a mature master. This music was in him — it sounded as spontaneous as if he had just composed it. I was deeply impressed by the noble conception of the first movement and moved by the simply and beautifully played *Adagio*. The final difficult fugue was splendid; the whole sonata was a masterly performance.' Two days after the competition, Rubinstein and Hoehn performed together, each including the *Hammerklavier* Sonata in his programme. The critics found Rubinstein's interpretation too romantic and that of Hoehn too correct and less exciting. In conversation with his friend, André Diederichs, Rubinstein later declared: 'The truth is we were both right.' When asked to defend this apparent contradiction, Rubinstein replied: '[If] you ask ten famous artists to paint you, your face will be *different* on each picture but the painters will assure you they *interpreted* your face exactly as they see.' Elaborating on his views he added: '[Each] creative work becomes a part of the universe, just like a flower, or human being. Consequently, a sonata sounds *different* to each gifted interpreter. This is the real mission of our particular talents.'∝

In April 1926 Dmitri Shostakovich was accepted on the post-graduate composition course at the Leningrad Conservatoire where he also continued his piano studies. At the preceding Graduate Diploma Examination it was obligatory to play a work from the classical repertoire. His friend Lydia Zhukova recalled the circumstances: 'Two weeks beforehand he still didn't know what he would play. Eventually he chose the *Hammerklavier* Sonata. He said it was inconceivably difficult, and that some of the ninths and tenths were unperformable.' The evening before the examination, Zhukova called round to hear Shostakovich play though the work. She continues: 'He played for me. He was a wonderful pianist, with strong hands and his own precise manner of playing.' Zhukova, however, felt 'sick at heart' regarding Shostakovich's interpretation as being 'only a sketchy performance'. The following day she had cause to revise her opinion, describing her friend and compatriot's playing as exhibiting 'authority and maturity' and 'displaying a symphonic grasp of the whole grandiose work'.[cxi]

Our next pianistic tribute, albeit a brief one, comes from an unexpected source. During the 1950s the twentieth-century modernist composer Alexander Goehr was a pupil of Olivier Messiaen. He recalls the afternoon when Messiaen played the class Beethoven's *Hammerklavier* Sonata, an interpretation he remembers as having been 'absolutely marvellous'.[cxii]

Our final illustration returns us to Wilhelm Backhaus to whom we referred a moment ago when he was at the outset of his career. His name came up when Stephen Kovacevich was in conversation with the musicologist David Dubal. Dubal asked Kovacevich, himself a celebrated interpreter of Beethoven: 'In the Germanic school, did you admire Backhaus?' Kovacevich's response was unequivocal: 'Absolutely. To my mind, Backhaus was the only person who ever truly understood Beethoven's *Hammerklavier* Sonata. Listen to his recordings. It's true he may not be faithful to the text in every instance, but the wildness of what he's attempting to do is quite wonderful.'[cxiii]

From its inception, commentators have likened the rugged grandeur of the B-flat major Piano Sonata to an orchestral composition: 'It is closer to the symphony style than any other late work, with the possible exception of the Ninth Symphony ... Its grandiosity, both in size and tone, suggest symphonic scope.'[cxiv] First and foremost amongst devotees of this belief was the Austrian composer and conductor Felix Weingartner; we should not overlook also Weingartner's prowess as a pianist — he was for a period a pupil of Franz Liszt. Weingartner had the good fortune to be present on the memorable evening when Hans von Bülow played the last five sonatas of Beethoven in one concert. The experience left a lasting impression on the young artist: 'I have heard the monumental "Op. 106" played by the most famous pianists. Never was I able to get rid of the feeling that here was something wanting, that here the spirit of the creator demands more than the instrument chosen is able to give.' Weingartner resolved to undertake an orchestration of the sonata, setting out his beliefs in a manifesto. Since this text is hard to locate, in the standard keyboard literature, we reproduce extracts from it here under the headings as given by Weingartner:

Orchestration a part of the conception:

'On making a close examination of Beethoven's style of writing and construction in this sonata, it becomes more and more difficult that an orchestral conception should not have been present in his mind. Numerous portions resemble the sketch of a symphony, and are transferable forthwith to full score.'

Execution of the orchestration:

'Harmonic additions become necessary when pedal effects have to be taken into consideration, and to some extent ... Beethoven has indicated them.'

Need for restraint:

'The very natural temptation to make full use of the orchestral apparatus for more elaborate thematic and polyphonic combinations had of course to be set aside entirely. In a very few cases, however, it is so clear that Beethoven would have continued a part, if he had had ...

the orchestra at his disposal, that this continuation could be carried out without scruple, especially as it in no way presents a change in the original, but merely an adaptation to the scope of the orchestra.'

Permissible changes:

'Actual changes were necessary only in those two places which Beethoven has indicated in his notation as cadenza-like figures ... as in the ascending run in the *Scherzo*, and to a greater extent in the introduction to the last movement.'

Instrumentation:

'The instrumentation follows the original published by the Academy of Arts of Berlin. [Hans von Bülow made metronomic revisions (changes) here.] The orchestral disposition is the same as that of the Ninth Symphony, without the percussion instruments added there in the choral-finale. The abrupt and frequent changes of key ... made it impossible to entirely do without the use of valve-horns and trumpets ... Thus the present score differs in no essential particular from an original orchestral work by Beethoven.'[cxv]

As may be expected Weingartner's orchestration has not been without its critics for the reason that the only true analogue of the *Hammerklavier* Sonata is, of course, the sonata itself. Blom puts such a point of view: 'Felix Weingartner's orchestral version of Op. 106 is merely an interesting experiment, not a successful substitution. Although it was undertaken because Weingartner honestly felt that it would for the first time reveal the meaning of a sonata not playable without superhuman effort, in performance it is found to do nothing of the kind, precisely because one misses an effort that is part of the very stuff and fibre of a Beethoven.'[cxvi] Pianist Denis Matthews is like-minded: 'When the conductor Felix Weingartner made the experiment of orchestrating the *Hammerklavier* he dispensed with and alleviated its severer technical demands, but also removed the sense of superhuman effort that seems so essential to the character of this colossus of sonatas.'[cxvii] To the Beethovenian purest, these are incontrovertible views. For the more typical music lover, who is not averse to musicological experimentation, an occasional hearing of Weingartner's transcription in the concert hall may still offer a rewarding experience.

We close this part of our account with a brief selection of writings bearing on the interpretation of the Piano Sonata Op. 106.

As befits the majestic scale of the composition, Carl Czerny's notes to the *Hammerklavier* Sonata are the most expansive in his commentaries to Beethoven's thirty-two piano sonatas. Czerny was well aware of the innovatory nature of the B-flat major Piano Sonata and the demands expected of the performer. Accordingly, he draws attention to the challenges posed by the composition: 'At the epoch when Beethoven wrote this, his greatest sonata, he paid little attention to the peculiarities of pianoforte composition, but used every effort in order to produce the effects which he had in view. Hence his latter pianoforte works are so much more difficult, as we frequently have to employ an uncommon mode of fingering, of position and of touch, and as the difficulties must be accomplished in as neat, free and natural a manner, as in other compositions. Consequently, those who would study these latter works, must be already well acquainted with the former compositions of this great master; for the present sonata is the mature fruit of the former blossoms.'[cxviii] We consider what Czerny has to say, bearing on the work's individual movements, in the later parts of our discussion.

Donald Tovey acknowledged, in what he describes as the more 'energetic passages' of this sonata, that there are 'moments of harshness and shrillness more conspicuous than anywhere else in Beethoven'. He urges: 'These must not be bowdlerised. But on the other hand, they must not dominate the player's imagination.' He cautions: '[E]nthusiasts may come to regard the harshness and shrillness as the accredited symbols of Beethoven's style ... his imagination penetrated into every note ... Some passages in Op. 106 are supremely beautiful as examples of pianoforte style; and the student cannot better prepare himself for the task of the whole than by taking such passages into consideration.' Tovey cites, by way of particular illustration, bars 39—68 of the *Adagio*.[cxix]

We recall the time when, towards the end of his career as a concert pianist, Alfred Brendel, doubtless with regret, announced that he would no longer perform the *Hammerklavier* Sonata in public. Perhaps he realized the time had come when he must follow his own advice: 'The player should master endurance as well as boldness, fierce intensity as well as the cool grasp of a panoramic overview.'[cxx]

The late Charles Rosen remarks how Beethoven's indications for *una corda* producing 'its half-whispered sonority ... must have been very moving for a small gathering'. He adds: 'The intended performance of Op. 106 was for a very intimate public. This may seem a curious paradox when one considers the spectacular brilliance of the opening and closing movements. Clearly, we must extend Schnabel's observation that a Beethoven sonata "is greater than any one of its interpretations": it also transcends any venue, any form of presentation, private, public or recorded.'[cxxi]

In the foregoing section of our account we have outlined aspects of the creation origins and reception history of the B-flat major Piano Sonata. In order to better locate this celebrated composition in its place in cultural history, we now direct the next section of our discussion to a consideration of the personal circumstances bearing on the composer during the period of its composition.

In our study of the Piano Sonata Op. 101, we remarked how Beethoven's health had been poor throughout much of 1817. His doctor had confined him indoors, depriving him of his strolls in the countryside that were such a spur to his creative process. In addition he was obliged to take medications 'of all possible kinds', prescribed by a doctor whom he did not trust.[cxxii] Writing on 21 August to his old friend Nikolaus Zmeskall von Domanovecz, a civil servant by profession but known in musical circles as an excellent cellist, he bitterly complained: 'I often despair and would like to die ... I can foresee no end to my infirmities.'[cxxiii] However, by September 1817 he felt sufficiently recovered so as to write to his pupil the Archduke Rudolph that he discerned some improvement in his health.[cxxiv] By November something like his former vitality and spirited demeanour were restored and with them his energies for serious composition.

In the new year of 1818 Beethoven informed Ries that, despite the improvements to his health, he felt obliged once more to postpone his long-projected visit to London; he did not yet fully trust his health and, moreover, he now had additional responsibilities concerning his nephew Karl — which we consider shortly.[cxxv] Later on in May he relocated himself, his Nephew Karl and two servants to the spa town Mödling where, as Thayer relates: 'He began taking the baths two days after his arrival and, the desire and capacity for work soon returning, he took up energetically the Pianoforte Sonata in B-flat.'[cxxvi] He continued to work on the composition through the summer and in June was in sufficiently high spirits to write to his friend Vinzenz Hauschka: 'By the way, my health is much improved.' Hauschka was a civil servant by profession but was more widely known in Vienna as an accomplished musician; for example, he was a founder member of the Gesellschaft der Musikfreunde and on 3 May 1818 he conducted the first movement of the *Eroica* Symphony.[cxxvii]

Whereas Beethoven's illnesses, mostly of an abdominal kind, appear to have responded to the benefits of hydrotherapy, his most precious faculty, his hearing, continued to deteriorate. We have seen (Piano Sonata Op. 101) that in July 1817, Beethoven appealed to the piano makers Johann and Nanette Streicher to provide him with an instrument that should be 'as loud as possible'.[cxxviii] From about February 1818 he was so hard of hearing as to request those having a conversation with him to communicate their thoughts in writing, through the medium of his so-called conversation books. An entry in one such book suggests Beethoven turned to natural remedies to improve his loss of hearing. It records how a visitor informed Beethoven that a certain Dr. H. Graff had a natural remedy for the cure of deafness: 'You take fresh horseradish ... grate it onto cotton cloth, which is quickly rolled up and stuck in the ear.' Anton Neumayr, in his study of Beethoven's many illnesses, also remarks on the composer seeking help from a nature healer called Father Weiss, a Viennese priest who had made a study of the psychology and physiology of the ear. Weiss recommended application of oil in the ears. 'The excellent psychological attention that the good father showed his patient could have given Beethoven confidence [restored his moral].'[cxxix] Beethoven, however, still attempted to benefit from Maelzel's ear trumpets but to ever-lessening advantage, despite the inventor adapting his design to suit the needs of the composer.[cxxx]

What must have been a poignant reminder to Beethoven of his affliction occurred in the autumn of 1818 when he received an invitation to perform his Piano Concerto in

E-flat, Op. 73; a concert was planned to take place later in the year at Vienna's Grosser Redoutensaal. He declined since by then he was quite unable to hear an orchestra, let alone co-ordinate his playing with that of other instrumentalists; his last public attempt to do so was in 1814 when he played the piano part in his so-called *Archduke* Trio, Op. 97. This proved to be disastrous; his fortissimos had jangled the piano's strings and his pianissimos were inaudible — to the mortification of those present who, ten years previously, had marvelled in the salons at the composer's keyboard virtuosity (see Piano Sonata Op. 90). Mindful of his limitations, Beethoven requested his former pupil Carl Czerny to take his place. Czerny, however, was now making his own way in the world and declined on the grounds he was giving piano lessons for up to twelve hours a day 'to the neglect of his own playing'.[cxxxi]

By 1818 Beethoven had assumed the custody of his nephew Karl, the only son of his brother Kaspar (Caspar) Karl, recently deceased, and of his sister-in-law Johanna, who Beethoven had persuaded the courts to regard as unfit for her son's upbringing (see Piano Sonata Op. 101). Karl was then aged twelve and initially Beethoven derived contentment and pleasure from the boy's company. On 23 January he wrote to Nanette Streicher telling her his nephew had arrived to stay with him and how happy he was, remarking 'every moment he shows his love and affection for me'.[cxxxii] A measure of Beethoven's devotion is that he spent long hours encouraging Karl with his study of music and piano practice. However, as 1818 progressed, little short of a tragedy for all concerned unfolded. The details of Beethoven's progressively tortured relationship with his nephew fall outside the scope of our narrative but, insofar as they form a backdrop to the creation origins of the B-flat major Piano Sonata, they require some acknowledgement.

In January 1818, Karl left the boarding school where he had been studying in order to live with his uncle; for the continuation of his education Beethoven employed a private tutor. In May, Beethoven and Karl moved to Mödling for the summer months where Karl continued his studies with the village priest. In September, Karl's mother Johanna petitioned the courts to obtain guardianship of her son, only to have her pleas rejected; further appeals by her in October were also dismissed. On 3 December Karl ran away to be with his mother, to Beethoven's acute distress; he even enlisted the assistance of the police to have the boy returned. Beethoven recorded in his diary: 'God help me. Thou seest me deserted by all men, for I do not wish to do wrong, hear my supplication, only for the future to be with my Karl, since the possibility shows itself nowhere. O harsh fate. O cruel destiny, no, no, my unhappy condition will never end.'[cxxxiii]

On the grounds of Karl having run away so as to be with his mother, on 7 December Johanna petitioned Vienna's highest court the *Landrecht* – a court that confined its deliberations exclusively for persons of noble birth. This was duly referred to a lower Court, the *Magistrat*, since Beethoven was deemed in law to be a commoner. His somewhat wily efforts to have the Dutch prefix *van* to his surname to be accepted as equating with the German *von* – signifying noble lineage – was thrown out. The legal wrangling between the parties continued into 1819 and beyond, to the anguish of all concerned.[cxxxiv] A parallel may perhaps be drawn here between the case of Jarndyce and Jarndyce in Charles Dickens's novel *Bleak House* in which a legal case proceeds interminably through the English Court of Chancery, to the detriment of the principal protagonists. Adopting a similar outlook, Cooper reflects: 'Beethoven saw his struggle with his sister-in-law for the guardianship of her son in terms of absolute right and wrong; and the scale which the struggle assumed in his mind was hardly less than that of *Milton's Paradise* Lost.'[cxxxv] Beethoven's relationship with his young nephew had further distressing ramifications, but consideration of these lies outside the scope of our present discussion.

In our opening remarks we stated the composition of the *Hammerklavier* Sonata was a triumph over adversity for Beethoven, given the nature of his many tribulations. Maynard Solomon states the case more prosaically, observing the distraction created by the litigation over the custody of his nephew Karl 'seems not to have had an adverse affect on Beethoven's productivity' He reminds us that in this period (1818–20) he completed the *Hammerklavier* Sonata, began to sketch the *Diabelli* Variations and made substantial progress on the *Missa Solemnis*, completing the *Kyrie*, the *Gloria*, and part of the *Credo* before the end of 1819.[cxxxvi] Perhaps the major compositional casualty, occasioned by the legal disputes over the custody of Karl, was Beethoven's failure to find time to complete his projected Tenth Symphony. As it is we have Berry Cooper to thank for assembling the composer's surviving sketches into a performing version of much the intended music.[cxxxvii]

Throughout 1818 Beethoven maintained contact with his Edinburgh publisher George Thomson, providing him with his requested lyrical folksong settings – which continued to be a valued source of income. However, in a letter to the composer of 22 June, Thomson raised a familiar complaint: 'But alas my good sir! Everyone in the country finds that your works are much too difficult; that there are only a very small number of masters with the greatest skill who will be able to play them.' Thomson had corresponded with 'one of the foremost dealers in London', to seek his opinion and had received the reply: 'Although a great and sublime artist, Beethoven *is not understood*, and his arrangements of your songs is *much too difficult* for the public.' Thomson sought to encourage Beethoven with the thought: '[I] flatter myself that the time is coming when the English will be able to comprehend and truly perceive the great beauties of your works.' As an expedient, he proposed Beethoven should add a flute accompaniment to his song settings, or replace the violin part with one for the flute, thereby to reach out to a wider audience and, in particular, make his song settings 'noticed by the flutists'.[cxxxviii]

An aspect of the composer's life that saw some improvement was a change for the better in his domestic arrangements. Beethoven enlisted the support of Nanette Streicher who intimated she was willing to help with his domestic affairs, without which he conceded, 'everything in that line would be quite hopeless'. He was then paying his kitchen maid 60 gulden a year and 12 kreuzer a day for her 'bread money'. The arrangement with Nanette would last, in one way and another, until Beethoven's death in 1827. Beethoven's relations with his domestic help were turbulent; he mistrusted their honesty and fidelity and doubtless his deafness furthered his suspicions of them.[cxxxix] Amidst his creative work, Beethoven found time to keep his ménage in order by filling the key position of his cook. He dismissed his existing cook 'Baberl' (diminutive of Barbara) on 27 December 1817 and appointed in her place the twenty-two year old 'Peppi' (diminutive of Josephine) who turned out to be a good cook.[cxl]

On 3 July 1818, the Swiss publisher Hans Georg Nägeli wrote to Beethoven seeking his endorsement of a plan to publish an edition of J. S. Bach's Mass in B minor that, along with much other of the composer's choral music, had fallen into neglect.[cxli] In the event Nägeli's edition was not published until 1833, long after Beethoven's death, during which time the youthful Felix Mendelsohn had also commenced his pioneering efforts to bring Bach's choral music — in particular the St. Matthew Passion — before a wider public. Perhaps it was Nägeli's letter that prompted Beethoven, later that month (29 July), to express his views about music to his pupil the Archduke Rudolph. Writing from his summer residence at Mödling he expounds: '[The] older composers render us double service, since there is generally real artistic value in their works (among them, of course, only the *German Händel and Sebastian Bach* possessed genius). But in the world of art, as in the whole of our great creation, *freedom and progress* are the main objectives. And although we moderns are not quite as far advanced in *solidity* as our *ancestors*, yet the refinement of our customs has enlarged many of our conceptions as well.'[cxlii] Beethoven's conceptions were clearly too modern however for Carl Maria von Weber as he appears to suggest in an appreciation he wrote on 23 July in support of the music of Friedrich Fesca, a contemporary violinist and composer. Weber makes the following indirect reference to Beethoven: 'Herr Fesca can be gay, even witty ... He is scrupulous in detail and his music recalls Spohr ... but he is by nature too gentle to seize the listener unexpectedly, as Beethoven does, and suddenly hold him in his giant fist over the edge of a precipice.'[cxliii]

A more measured estimation of Beethoven's music, expressed by a musically inclined visitor — he described himself as being a 'foreign friend of music' — wrote the following in the 26 December 1818 issue of the *Allgemeine musikalische Zeitung*: 'I didn't find *Beethoven's* splendid keyboard compositions as well known here as I had imagined.' This confirms, what is frequently stated, which is that Beethoven's piano sonatas were not performed in public during his lifetime. The unidentified 'friend of music' continues: 'In the beginning this struck me as odd, but soon I became aware of the reasons. *Beethoven's* genius could not be limited to write for the six-octave, key-action implements and ten trained fingers ... He wrote for himself, like *Mozart*, unconcerned about the player, while most of the others, descending from Clementi's school, kept only the instrument in mind.' What the correspondent has to say here confirms an awareness that Beethoven was indeed now writing for the six-and-a-half octave keyboard — as in the case of the *Hammerklavier* Sonata. He concludes: 'For that reason *Beethoven's* masterpieces delight the connoisseur, please more and more often they are listened to, and enchant the non-connoisseur who has heard them a few times. They are difficult, but fortunately for the performer they don't blind and they don't overpower immediately.'[cxliv]

Beethoven probably composed the *Hammerklavier* Sonata with the assistance of the Streichers' 61/2 octave piano that the composition requires. This manufacturer, one of Beethoven's favourite piano makers, took out a patent in 1817 that earned the composer's warm endorsement.[cxlv] Authorities believe the Streichers' latest patent piano may have been the first Viennese instrument to have a true *una corda*. 'It had two pedals to achieve this effect [*una corda*], one for *due corde*, which corresponds to the modern soft pedal, which can strike only two strings, and a second pedal to move the action so that the hammer struck only one string.'[cxlvi] These innovations were not lost to the musically inclined visitor to Vienna. He enthused: 'For the last thirty years every instrument has made gigantic progress.'[cxlvii] Vienna's musically minded public would be similarly inclined to enthuse when news began to circulate of the gift to Beethoven of a magnificent English piano.

On his tour of the continent, Thomas Broadwood, manager of the celebrated firm of John Broadwood & Sons of London, made the acquaintance of Beethoven. Doubtless aware of the prestige it would confer on his business, he put in hand arrangements for one of his latest pianos to be sent as a gift to the composer. We recall how the French manufacturer Sébastien Érard had rendered a similar service to Beethoven, in 1803, when his firm made the composer a gift of one his firm's finest pianos (see Piano Sonata Op. 53). On 27 December 1817, Broadwood selected from his warehouse a six-octave Grand Piano, No. 7362 that was carefully packed in a deal case with a waterproof lining of tin foil; this was then delivered to a Mr. Farlowe of London ready for shipment to Trieste. The choice of particular instrument was in part made by a small group of distinguished musicians of the day. As a measure of their respect and esteem for the recipient, they test-played and signed the piano before it was sent away. The musicians involved in the enterprise were John Baptiste Cramer, Jaques Godfroi, Friedrich Kalkbrenner, Charles Knyvett and Ferdinand Ries. They each inscribed the piano with their signatures alongside the inscription: *Hoc Instrumentum est Thomae Broadwood (Londrini) donum propter ingenium illustrissime Beethoven* — 'This instrument is a proper gift from Thomas Broadwood to the great Beethoven.' Broadwood's own, more prosaic, inscription reads: 'John Broadwood & Sons, Makers of Instruments to His Majesty and the Princesses. Great Pulteney Street, Golden Square, London.[cxlviii]

Beethoven's new Broadwood had a range of six octaves (from the third C below middle C to the third C above), a half octave less than the Streichers' latest instrument, which meant it was unsuitable for the performance of the *Hammerklavier* Piano Sonata. Its case was constructed from Spanish mahogany inlaid with marquetry. It was triple strung and was equipped with a una chord pedal enabling the action to move the keys to the right so that the hammers would strike one string only. The soundboard was thicker than that of equivalent Viennese instruments and the hammers were heavier. These gave the piano a more sonorous tone than its Viennese rivals but at the expense of a heavier action, making the performance of passages requiring great velocity more difficult.[cxlix]

Typical of Broadwood's solicitude towards Beethoven is that he arranged for his own piano tuner, Johann Andreas Stumpff, to travel to Vienna to tune and regulate the piano; significantly, Broadwood refers to his instrument as a *piano*, rather than *pianoforte* of *fortepiano*.[cl] When Beethoven received news of Broadwood's intended gift, he responded fulsomely in a letter of 3 February 1818. He expressed his pleasure at the prospect of receiving the piano that he intended to regard 'as an altar on which to place the beautiful gifts of his spirit before the divine Apollo'. In addition he promised to send Broadwood 'the first fruits of his inspiration on playing it' — an undertaking that, however, he dose not appear to have fulfilled.[cli]

Beethoven received the Broadwood piano in late spring 1818. It had been delayed in Trieste so that the required customs formalities could be completed; Broadwood had born the cost of the freightage but customs dues still had to be paid. Beethoven turned to his friend and patron Count Moritz Lichnowsky to assist him to obtain the necessary exemption, as Beethoven insisted, from payment of the customs duty. Lichnowsky was able to do this by reason of being on friendly terms with the Austrian Minister of Finance. (If we enter into the spirit of Beethoven's penchant for making bad puns, we could say that Lichnowsky was able to pull a few strings!) Given Beethoven's standing in Vienna, these circumstances appear to have been regarded as having something of national significance since the arrival in the Imperial City of Broadwood's instrument was subsequently reported in the *Wiener Zeitung* of 8 June 1818 and the

Vienna Gazette of the Arts: '[The] Broadwood Piano is a true masterpiece, in its interior structure as well as in its outward form, which is chiefly distinguished by its unadorned simplicity, solidity and portability to any place whatsoever.'[clii]

When Beethoven's Broadwood piano arrived it was unpacked by men from Streichers' piano-manufacturing establishment in Vienna and from there it was sent on to the composer, then residing in Mödling. Doubtless Johann and Nanette Streicher were eager to see for themselves the latest product of a rival instrument maker, albeit a foreign one. Ignaz Moscheles and Cipriani Potter were allowed to try out the piano. They confirmed its beautiful tone but Moscheles found the action to be too heavy; not surprising, the piano was out of tune. On a later visit to see Beethoven, Potter remarked on this to the composer whose response was tart: 'That's what they all say; they would like to tune it and spoil it, but they shall not touch it.'[cliii]

Whilst, as Thayer comments, 'Beethoven's delight in the pianoforte must have been great' (p. 695), it is uncertain if its arrival had any direct bearing on the creation origins of the B-flat major Piano Sonata, the sketching of which was well in hand by the time of its arrival. Some authorities concede it may have assisted Beethoven to try out passages of the composition, in the later stages of its working-out, bearing in mind though, as remarked, the Broadwood had a limited range of six octaves.[cliv]

Whilst visitors to Vienna around 1818 may have been surprised not to hear Beethoven's piano sonatas played in public, the footsteps of artists continued to make their way to his rooms. This may be taken as a measure of his artistic standing and celebrity, despite the fact that he was now a reclusive figure, seldom to be seen in public — other than at eating houses or when strolling about the countryside. Three likenesses of Beethoven were taken at the period when he worked on the composition of the *Hammerklavier* Sonata. The recollections of their creators convey impressions of the composer at this time.

The painter August von Kloeber met Beethoven in the summer of 1818 when he called on the composer who, as remarked, was at this time residing at Mödling with his nephew Karl. Kloeber had made a prior arrangement to take a likeness of Beethoven who was thought to be more amenable to such an undertaking whilst away sojourning in the countryside. Kloeber recalls: 'He was very deaf, and if I wished to say anything, I had to either write it down or speak into his ear trumpet, unless his *Famulus* [Karl], a young relative of about twelve years of age, ... shouted the words in his ear.' As the artist began his work Karl was required to practice the piano — the Broadwood that had recently been given to Beethoven. Kloeber states that despite his deafness Beethoven was attentive to Karl's playing and called out whenever he made an error. Doubtless he kept a close watch on his nephew's hand position and the sonority of his new instrument may have been an aid to his failing hearing. Kloeber continues: 'Beethoven had a very earnest look; his very vivacious eyes were for the most part turned upwards, with a thoughtful and rather a gloomy expression ... His complexion was florid, the skin rather pock-marked, his hair the colour of steel, for the black was already turning grey ... When his hair streamed in the breeze, there was a sort of Ossian-like demonism about him.' Kloeber's portrait of Beethoven was rendered in charcoal-pencil with highlights in white chalk. It is valued for being a true likeness, in contrast to other depictions of a more idealized and declamatory kind. Kloeber created two more studies of the composer: an oil painting portraying him in the countryside in the company of his nephew Karl — regrettably now lost; and a re-working of his original study, this time in chalk and somewhat more idealised and romantic. A lithograph of Kloeber's portrait by Theodor Neu and Carl Fisher, dating from the 1840s, became very popular in the nineteenth century.[clv]

The Austro-Hungarian artist Ferdinand Schimon painted a portrait of Beethoven in the autumn of 1818. Anton Schindler, who was frequently in the composer's company at this time, considered it to be 'the most interesting' and 'full of characteristic truth'. In his typically fulsome manner he enthuses: 'In the rendering of that particular look, the majestic forehead, the dwelling-place of mighty, sublime ideas, of hues, in the drawing of the firmly shut mouth and the chin shaped like a shell, it is truer than any other picture.' This portrait is now in the possession of the Beethoven House in Bonn.[clvi]

Beethoven sat for the artist Joseph Carl Stieler sometime in the spring of 1820. Contemporaries, including Schindler, thought Stieler had made a good likeness. Stieler requested the composer to 'sit as if you were writing' and to add authenticity he introduced manuscript pages of the *Missa Solemnis* on which Beethoven was then at work. Commentators value Stieler's portrait for its thoughtful expression, others though regard it as being somewhat idealized. The music publisher Mathias Artaria later published a lithograph of the portrait that promoted the composer's popularity.[clvii]

Having outlined the creation origins of the Piano Sonata in B-flat major, Op. 106, and made reference to selected aspects of the composer's personal circumstances during the period of its composition, we now direct our attention to the work's individual movements.

The first movement of Piano Sonata Op. 106 is one of Beethoven's large-scale structures. A measure of the expansive nature of the work that is about to unfold is its almost four-hundred bars that have a playing time, despite the movement as a whole being marked *Allegro*, of more than eleven minutes — approaching a quarter of an hour in a more extended interpretation. In the words of Carl Dahlhaus: 'Beethoven overwhelmed the limits of Classical form in his sonata movements by blurring the demarcations between sections and theme-groups and in creating such gigantic structures as the first movements of the *Hammerklavier* Sonata and the Ninth Symphony.'[clviii] In a letter to his friend Nikolaus Zmeskall, Beethoven was once given to exclaim: 'Power is the moral principle of those who excel others, and it is also mine.' In his adaptation of these words, Paul Bekker considers 'the phrase might stand as a text for the first movement of Op. 106'.[clix] For Oskar Bie the first movement in nothing less than: 'An Olympian poem.'[clx] In the estimation of Wilfrid Mellers, in its dynamic energy: 'The first movement in many ways carries on from the Seventh and Eighth Symphonies.'[clxi] 'The first movement is in the determination to speak in the language of invincibility pitted against the truth of a composer whose musical thought constantly pulls towards despair.'[clxii]

Tovey admired the first movement's opening chords 'for euphony in *forte* and *fortissimo* passages', asserting: 'Liszt himself never produced pianoforte chords and colours more gorgeously orchestral.'[clxiii] Igor Stravinsky expressed similar views: 'Much of the first movement could be included in my category of orchestral sonata.'[clxiv] And likewise Michael Broyles: 'The first movement contains a number of symphonic features: the opening gesture ... the broad forte theme ... the wide spacing of the closing theme [with its] simple driving rhythm ... The *Hammerklavier* Sonata is symphonic in conception but thoroughly pianistic in gesture.'[clxv] An entry from the diary of Cosima Wagner (4 November 1872) has direct bearing on the foregoing:

'[Richard] tells me he has been going through the first movement of Beethoven's B-flat Sonata and was quite overwhelmed by the beauty and tenderness and richness of its detail, which passes by in such a way that nobody notices all that has been put into it ... He talks about orchestrating this sonata, in order to make it more accessible.' At this point Wagner himself remarked: 'As it is, only the greatest of virtuosos can play it, but if it were performed as orchestrated by me, a sort of tradition could be established.' Cosima concludes: 'We read though the sonata together with incredible delight, its richness of detail is like flowers hidden in a meadow.'[clxvi]

We have remarked that Beethoven dedicated his Piano Sonata Op. 106 to the Archduke Rudolph. Amongst the surviving sketches for the sonata, now preserved in the archives of the Gesellschaft der Musikfreunde in Vienna, is a leaf bearing drafts for a work to celebrate his pupil's birthday titled 'Kantate für Orchester und Chor auf den Text: "Vivat, vivat Rudolfus".' The opening chords of the sonata are considered to have their origins in this projected choral work.[clxvii] Although the Cantata was later abandoned, both the celebratory spirit of the intended work, and its opening melody, were transferred to the sonata.[clxviii] Matthews remarks: 'The tremendous opening affirmation of the chord of B flat ... related to sketches for a choral greeting to the Archduke — "vivat, vivat Rudolphus" — give a clue to [the movement's] vociferous character and rhythmical impetus.'[clxix]

Ernst von Elterlein likens the opening chords to a 'trumpet call'.[clxx] Igor Stravinsky regarded them as 'a bolt from the blue'.[clxxi] In Blom's estimation of the opening: 'Nothing could be simpler, nothing more impressive ... The figure is stamped on the hearer's mind at once, so that its most elaborate developments later on cannot possibly escape attention.'[clxxii] The music critic Neville Cardus discerned much in the opening chords: 'The famous repeated notes, the poundings in the first movement especially, obviously have extra-musical significance ... When Beethoven repeats his notes or rhythmical stresses, he is not engaged with tonal abstractions. He is hammering out something of human and spiritual significance.'[clxxiii]

The challenge to the pianist is to strike the opening notes clearly and without hesitation. From the time of the sonata's first appearance, the opening chords have been regarded as the pianists' *bête noire*. If Carl Czerny is to believed, he once wrote to Beethoven complaining: 'There's a lady in Vienna who has been practising your B-flat Sonata, Op. 106 for three months, and she still can't play the beginning.'[clxxiv] Beethoven confronts the pianist with a great leap extending from a low B flat in the left hand to a high D in the right hand — a span of more than three octaves. When David Dubal asked Charles Rosen if, from a pianistic point of view, the *Hammerklavier* Sonata was the most difficult work of Beethoven he had studied, Rosen replied: 'Oh, no, I think the *Appassionata* and the *Les Adieux* are more difficult. I think the *Hammerklavier* has that reputation because it has a difficult opening. If you play the opening measures as written, that jump with one hand can be frightening, particularly with stage fright added in.'[clxxv]

Strategies have been suggested to make the opening more amenable to interpretation, but with potential risk to pianistic expression, as Daniel Barenboim explains. 'A difficult passage in a Beethoven sonata may be easier if you divide the notes between the two hands because they are easier to control, but part of the expression, the need to struggle with the difficulty, then gets lost.' He continues: 'For instance, at the beginning of the *Hammerklavier* Sonata the jump from the low B flat to the chord in the left hand is very precarious. It is easy to play the wrong notes in the chord, but if you divide them between the two hands and play the low note with the left hand and the chord with the right, which is easy, the sense of the enormous geographical distance between the bass note and the chord is lost, together with a lot of expression.'[clxxvi] Musicologist Andrea Olmstead discussed the *Hammerklavier* Sonata with the American composer Roger Sessions, prompting him to remark: 'There are passages in Beethoven which sound awkward, because they were meant to ... In a sense the struggle is embodied in the writing and is not meant to be removed. The kind of tension that goes into playing a difficult passage itself communicates to the audience.'[clxxvii]

The sonata's opening notes do not appear to have inhibited the ten-year old Franz Liszt. Recalling his early lessons with his father he relates: 'My father played the spinet ... A piano he bought with difficulty out of his savings: in country districts at that time it was considered an extravagance ... With childish temerity I went so far as to delve enthusiastically into Beethoven's *Hammerklavier* Sonata of which my father was very fond ... I continued to dissect my favourite sonata. What most delighted me was the leap in the bass from B flat to D ... '.[clxxviii]

The opening declamatory chords influenced Mendelssohn's own Piano Sonata in B-flat major, coincidentally also Op. 106, and also that of Brahms's Piano Sonata, Op. 1.[clxxix] When a music critic had the temerity to draw the similarities to the attention of Brahms, he was not amused, anymore than he had been when his First Symphony had been hailed as 'Beethoven's Tenth'. On this occasion, he expostulated: 'Das bemerkt ja schon jeder Esel' — 'Every jackass notices that.'[clxxx]

From the time when Beethoven's manuscripts were auctioned following his death, those that have survived have assumed ever-greater musicological and cultural importance.

This is well illustrated by the following record of events. An isolated sketch in the British Museum (Library), in two-stave piano score, has been identified as belonging to the first movement of the *Hammerklavier* Sonata — identified from the characteristic rhythm of its notation. The leaf was formerly in the possession of Vincent Novello who noted: 'Beethoven's handwriting. Given to me (on the very day that I visited his grave, July 27 1829) by Madame Streiker [Nanette Streicher] ... an old friend of the latter great composer.' Novello later noted on 27 July 1843: 'I have the pleasure of presenting this rare curious specimen of Beethoven's singular mode of making hasty memoranda and indicative sketches (which no one could understand but himself) of his Musical thoughts — for preservation in the Library of the Museum.'[clxxxi]

In addition to arresting the attention of the listener, the sonata's opening chords fulfil important roles in the construction of the movement and its progressive working out. Edwin Fischer likens them to 'the essential germs of the whole movement'.[clxxxii] Likewise Romain Rolland: 'The first movement ... is evolved from the two little germs contained in the first two bars.'[clxxxiii] Blom is fulsome in his recognition of the composer's working method: 'It is Beethoven's masterful way to build up his most complex structures out of the most rudimentary material, as earlier and more familiar examples such as the opening themes of the Third and Fifth Symphonies show as clearly as in this sonata.'[clxxxiv] As the work proceeds, Beethoven constructs his musical structure with the aid of other components: 'Chains of falling thirds provides much of the underlying melodic and harmonic structure of each movement, helping to bind the work into a unified whole ... descending thirds provide much of the tonal architecture.'[clxxxv] More than this: 'Two elements, the tension between the keys of B-flat major and B minor, and the interval of a third, are decisive in the unfolding of the vast design.'[clxxxvi]

In May 1938, Michael Tippett was asked to write a report in anticipation of a congress to be held later in London. Although the anticipated event was the Festival of the International Congress of Contemporary Music, he wrote the following in defence of tonality: 'The artistic use of the tonal system is based on the fact that music whose tonal centres are rising in the scale of fifths produces an effect of ascent (struggle, illumination), while tonal centres descending in the scale of fifths produce an effect of descent (resignation, despair).' He elaborates: 'Beethoven was the great master of these effects. The first movement of the *Hammerklavier* Sonata is a skilfully continuous use of ascent, while the first movement of the *Appassionata* is an equally continuous descent.'[clxxxvii]

The French composer Vincent d'Indy taught for many years at the Paris Conservatoire where his instruction made reference to the works of Beethoven — he published a study of the composer in 1911. One of his pupils recalls: 'His teaching of sonata form stressed the tripartite division of exposition, development, and recapitulation; the exposition in its turn was divided into two main contrasting ideas, masculine and feminine in character, exemplified by the subjects of the first movement of Beethoven's *Hammerklavier Sonata*, Op. 106, forceful and lyrical respectively.'[clxxxviii] This personification of the character of the changing moods of the music, approximates closely to the views of von Elterlein: 'The first movement ... is constructed on two themes: the first displaying boldness, power, pride, decision and magnanimity; the second, womanly gentleness, grace, tenderness, softness and devotion.'[clxxxix]

In our own time Alfred Brendel has found value in word-imagery and metaphors, derived from the visual arts, to better explain his views on music. For Brendel, the word 'composition' has special significance. He asks: 'What constitutes composition?' In response, he makes reference to the Piano Sonata Op. 106: 'The balance of the whole, of all the components — even a picture or a piece of music ... In the *Hammerklavier* Sonata, for example, Beethoven needs the three remaining movements to counterbalance the intrusion of B minor in the first movement.' He adds: 'A piece of music takes place in time. It is a process leading from the beginning to the end, whereas a picture rests in itself, circles, breathes, almost bursts its frame'.[cxc]

The drama of the first movement is not confined to the opening bars: '[The] progress of the movement is carried on with true grandeur, a majestic descent of octaves from the high C follows, and a coruscation of brilliant flashes from the broken chords of the F major chord'.[cxci] Philip Radcliffe believes the first movement has points in common with the finale of Op. 101. In particular he draws attention to the movement's 'long fugal episode in the development and in the final bars a gradual diminuendo which is suddenly brushed aside'. But, he observes, in the Op. 106 Beethoven is working on a larger scale, 'majestic in style and more varied in mood, with an astonishing wealth of ideas'.[cxcii]

We have made reference to the 'chains of thirds' that play such an important role in the construction of the movement. They come to the fore in the development section in which a fugetta descends continuously in thirds, deriving its motivation and material from the imperious opening chords.[cxciii] Theodor Adorno enthuses: 'This is one of the most magnificent passages in Beethoven. It has something gigantic about it — something by which the sense of proportion in relation to the individual body is entirely suspended.'[cxciv]

We have noted that Beethoven's tempo indications, as

signified by his suggested metronome settings, are today considered to be unrealistically too fast. Discussing these the respected interpreter of Beethoven, Wilhelm Kempff, said: 'The erroneous metronome markings can easily lead to this regal movement being robbed of its radiant majesty.'[cxcv] Edwin Fischer felt similarly inclined: 'It is unpleasant on the piano to perform the piece at this tempo.' He further maintained: '[The] rich harmonies after the start of the recapitulation are impossible at the speed Beethoven asks. The listener would fail to grasp the sequences and Beethoven's direction *cantabile* would be impossible to fulfil.'[cxcvi] One of the few artists to perform the *Hammerklavier* Sonata at Beethoven's original tempo indications was Artur Schnabel. Writing of his performance, Martin Cooper states: 'Artur Schnabel decided to take Beethoven at his word and to play the first movement of Op. 106 at the tempo so long considered impossible. He did not wholly convince listeners by his own performance in which the fullness of the fast chordal passages and the wealth of detail in inner parts were not ideally clear, and his example has not been generally followed by subsequent performers, even those with larger hands and greater facility than Schnabel's.'[cxcvii] A less generous commentator than Cooper condemned Schnabel's adherence to Beethoven's stipulations as an act of 'mistaken piety'.

Brendel believes Beethoven's metronome indication for the movement is unworkable 'by any player, and on any instrument'. But, he concedes: 'Let us by all means play this movement "fast and furious" yet leave enough room for its wide range of colour and dynamics to emerge.'[cxcviii] Joseph Horowitz discussed metronome indications with Claudio Arrau and their value as a guide to interpretation in the *Hammerklavier* Sonata. Arrau responded: 'If you play the first movement of the *Hammerklavier* at the metronome tempo, it loses all its majesty.' He revealed he had tried to perform it at Beethoven's metronome tempo but, although he considered it 'feasible', he personally found it to be 'very difficult technically ... almost impossible'. Schnabel thought Carl Czerny's metronome markings (see later) for the sonata deserved respect for being 'the only markings from somebody who actually studied with Beethoven and performed under his influence'. Of these though he accepted – 'they're not too reliable either'. In response to Horowitz's generalization: 'Do you think there is such a thing as a proper tempo for a given piece?' Arrau averred, somewhat laconically: 'There is a proper range, I think. A rather narrow range.'[cxcix]

Charles Rosen did not regard metronome indications as being sacred and believed composers themselves could misjudge them. That said, he recognised in the *Hammerklavier* Sonata 'Beethoven wanted a fast tempo for [the] first movement'. In elaborating his views he comments: 'Suggestions for revising [Beethoven's] 138 have ranged from Felix Wiengartner's insanely slow 80 and Moscheles's 116, more reasonable but somewhat sedate, to Paul Badura-Skoda's proposed reduction of 10–15 per cent which comes out as 120 to 126.' In the context of authentic performance on period instruments he has this to say: 'If one considers this movement has a much lighter character when played on one of Beethoven's instruments, 138 will not appear so unreasonable for many pages of it; it seems to me to be ideal for bars 39 to 63 for example.' He takes issue with 'high-minded pianists' who consider a very fast tempo to be vulgar and equally those who confer on the music 'excessive nobility'. He concludes: 'There is no reason to think that the first movement is majestic; that would go against the grain of most of it. It is not a commemorative work. More than anything else, it is an explosion of energy.'[cc]

Franz Liszt is known to have conferred his own formidable energy on his interpretations of Beethoven. As we draw this section of our discussion to a close, we cite a selection of recollections of his memorable interpretations of the composer's Op. 106. In the summer of 1836 Liszt gave a recital at the Salon Érard in Paris. Hector Berlioz, in his capacity as a writer on music, recalled the event in the June issue of the *Revue et gazette musicale*. He writes: 'Never, perhaps, has this great artist excited the Parisian world to such a degree ...'. Berlioz considered Liszt to be an exponent of 'the great modern school of piano-playing'. In support of his contention he enthused: 'I appeal to the judgement of all those who have heard him play the great *Hammerklavier* Sonata, that sublime poem which until now [1836] has been the riddle of the Sphinx for almost every pianist. Liszt, a new Oedipus, has solved it in a manner which would have made the composer, had he heard it in his grave, thrill with pride and joy.' Berlioz continues in a similarly fulsome manner, paying tribute to Liszt being faithful to the score; he is known, however, on occasions to have added decorative flourishes and double octaves of his own devising. On the evening in question though, Berlioz, who was following the performance from a copy of the score, could detect 'not a single alteration made to what was indicated in the text, not an inflexion or an idea weakened or changed its true meaning.'[cci]

The German composer Wendelin Weissheimer heard Liszt play the *Hammerklavier* Sonata when he was travelling in Germany in the summer of 1858 and has left the following account of his playing: 'Seating himself at the piano ... he began to prelude as the fancy took him, more and more in the manner of Beethoven ... until the principal theme of the opening movement boomed forth in all its splendour, and the colossal work was under way. In such glory might this majestic, overwhelming theme have sprung from the mind of its divine creator himself some forty years earlier, just as it was brought to life again before his astonished audience by the wonder-working hands of Franz Liszt.' Weissheimer, who had been nominated to turn the music pages for Liszt, became so absorbed in his performance that he frequently forgot his place but not, apparently, without distracting Liszt in the least who had the work by heart.[ccii]

What Weissheimer has to say about Liszt preluding before he commenced his performance is consistent with what others also recall concerning Liszt the showman. In his early days he had been disposed to take liberties with Beethoven's scores, adding tremolos, trills and double octaves at will as his powers of extemporization and skill at embellishment took over. However, with the passing of the years, Liszt's respect to observe the wishes of the composer had long become a feature of his interpretations. We discern this in a recollection left by the German composer and chorus-master Siegfried Ochs who was present at one of Liszt's master-classes in 1883 – Liszt was by then aged 73. A pupil performed the *Hammerklavier* Sonata but not to Liszt's satisfaction. Ochs remembers: 'He stressed he had asked countless times for expression marks in Beethoven to be followed not merely to a certain extent but with considerable vigour; that Beethoven made an enormous difference between *piano* and *pianissimo*, and that the distance from *piano* to *forte* was to be regarded as greater in Beethoven than that between *North* and *South* poles.' Finally, Ochs recalls: '[Liszt] sat down at the piano and played the whole of the first part of the sonata himself.' Of his interpretation he records: 'Thus I too came to hear Liszt. Undoubtedly as a pianist he was no longer what he had been in earlier years; old age showed itself unmistakably in his hard touch.' Nevertheless, Ochs continues: 'I realized that so far as the playing of classical music was concerned, a new world was being revealed to me, similar to the one I had experienced during Bülow's rendering of the symphonies.'[cciii]

Carl Czerny himself modified Beethoven's Op. 106 metronome marks. More generally he has the following words of guidance on the interpretation of the first movement: 'The chief difficulty lies in the unusually quick and impetuous time prescribed by the author; also in the performance of the melodious passages, which are in many parts and require to be given strictly *legato*; in the clear delivery of the roulades [embellishments], extensions and skips; and, lastly, in the steadiness which the whole requires. All single difficulties are matter for attention and practice. The comprehension of the entire first movement, which is truly grand and written more in the symphony-style, develops itself by frequent playing, after being properly studied *in the right time.*' [italics added][cciv]

For the would-be interpreter of this challenging movement, Martin Cooper makes the following observations: 'He needs a clear intellectual grasp of the musical events that come to life in what can easily be a bewilderingly kaleidoscopic variety under his hands; and even then the final interpretation of the movement has hardly begun. For having first understood what he is playing and then mastered its physical problems, he must go on to grasp the whole musical significance of the grand design and to render plausible to the listener the extraordinary alternation of defiance and tenderness, the violent contrasts of pitch and dynamics.'[ccv]

We give the final words here to Donald Tovey: 'The movement closes with mutterings of thunder, over which the first theme floats, exultantly at first and then dies away gradually until cut short by two great chords which reveal that the design is accomplished.'[ccvi]

Beethoven designates the second movement *Scherzo: Assai vivace*. In so doing he was establishing a precedent that he would adopt in the Ninth Symphony, sketched, as we have seen, more of less contemporaneously with the Piano Sonata Op. 106. Other comparisons between the two compositions may be made. In reversing the conventional order of the movements in the sonata, as in the symphony, Beethoven may be seen as offering both performer and listener a moment of respite from the expansive music that has just unfolded. Furthermore, in both compositions 'the profound meditations of an *Adagio* demanded postponement'.[ccvii] Perhaps, for reasons of the meditative nature of the three piano sonatas that were to follow the *Hammerklavier*, this was the last time Beethoven used the term *scherzo* in a piano sonata.

The *Scherzo* is light-hearted and plays for less than three minutes. Rosen considered it to be a parody of the main theme of the first movement, especially its last page, particularly in its use of descending thirds.[ccviii] Von Elterlein, writing at the close of the nineteenth century, had a more serious take on the music: 'The second movement ... displays a restless, unstable character, a strange hurrying, a peculiar hunting, fleeting, and crowding ... an unsatisfied longing, but in the so-called trio ... in the following presto, and at the conclusion, a picture of bold, fantastic bizarre humour is depicted, reminding us of the wonderful, strange colouring in the B-flat minor movement.' In support of his views, von Elterlein cites the imagery that Beethoven's early biographer Wilhelm von Lenz invoked in his commentary to the movement. Lenz's recalls lines in Goethe's Faust, the scene where Faust, in the company of Mephistopheles, hastens on his magic stead, and asks: 'Was weben die dort um den Rabenstein?' ('What weave they round the Raven-stone?') ... 'Schweben auf, schweben ab, neigen sich, beugen sich.' ('Hovering up, hovering down, bending low, bearing down.') To which Mephistopheles responds: 'Vorbei!

Vorbei!' ('On! On!'). Perhaps Lenz was drawn to make this connection with the music and Goethe's verses as a consequence of the movement's rhythmic opening four-note motif, suggestive, to some, of the incessant beating of a horse's hooves.[ccix]

In Rolland's estimation: 'The *Scherzo* is fantastic in the extreme', a view shared by Matthews: 'The *Scherzo* of Op. 106 is a strangely whimsical affair, full of quirks ...'.[ccx] But, as Rolland recognised, there is more than mere whimsy at work: 'From the playful mood of the first part it is suddenly plunged into the inexpressible anguish of the minor trio.'[ccxi] Amidst the 'great variety of harmonic and thematic material are 'mysterious swaying harmonies ... a tremolo which shakes itself ... bold chromatic shifting from B to B flat ... the ghostly close ... all these points ... make this work the summit of Beethoven's pianoforte *scherzi*.[ccxii]

One sketch leaf contains drafts for the second and third movements of the sonata, together with other ideas for projected works for piano that Beethoven appears not to have developed.[ccxiii] Study of the sketches reveals Beethoven's preoccupation with accenting the upbeat: 'Once again, Beethoven is concerned with the interval of a third, rising and falling; it would hardly be an exaggeration to say that the whole Scherzo is concerned with this single interval pursued through a rhythmic maze further complicated by strong dynamic contrasts and frequent accentuation ...'.[ccxiv] Tovey regarded the Scherzo as 'one of the simplest movements extant'.[ccxv] Matthew Rye believes, within its small format, 'the brief Scherzo breaks the bounds of the form Beethoven had already himself established in other works, with several changes of tempo and metre and an almost improvisational flow.'[ccxvi]

In Cooper's analysis of Beethoven's compositional procedures, he believes the 'strangeness of feeling' that he discerns in the Trio section of the movement derives from the music being laid out such that bass and treble are sometimes several octaves apart 'with no comfortable "filling" between'. This, as he further comments, 'is common in the works of his last years' a procedure he likens to 'Bach's delight in his high trumpet parts'.[ccxvii] Beethoven provides a pianistic flourish in the *Presto* section of the Scherzo that must have astonished his contemporaries. The tremolo that follows it is no less astonishing: 'It is as [Beethoven] were declaring possession in the *prestissimo* passage of the Scherzo, which runs from an F below the bass clef to a top F four lines above the treble, spanning six full octaves — a range well beyond the capacity of his earlier instruments ...'.[ccxviii] As for its interpretation, Edwin Fischer urges it 'must glide swiftly past like a ghost'.[ccxix]

Concerning the interpretation of the movement more generally, Czerny writes: 'This must be played in an extremely fleet and humorous manner. The Trio (in B-flat minor) harmoniously *legato* and always with a judicious employment of the pedal.'[ccxx]

Tovey throws caution to the wind: 'Do not be afraid of this episode, but let it run as mad as Beethoven obviously intends.'[ccxxi]

Beethoven sets the mood and atmosphere of the third movement by designating it *Adagio sostenuto. Appassionato e con molto sentimento*. It has been described as 'among the greatest — and perhaps indeed the greatest — of all Beethoven's slow movement's' that 'forms the heart of the sonata'.[ccxxii] In Fischer's opinion: 'This twenty-minute colloquy with the piano is perhaps the most beautiful contribution ever made to the literature of our instrument.'[ccxxiii] In the estimation of Rolland: 'The *Adagio* is one of the sublimest things in all music. It certainly reaches heights which transcend the limits of the piano.'[ccxxiv] In Radcliffe's assessment: 'No sonata since Op. 10, No. 3 had had a slow movement of so tragic a character as this ... but the later movement [is] mellower in tone; there are fewer *sforzandi* and cries of protest and it ends in a comparatively resigned mood.'[ccxxv] Adorno was of the opinion that after writing the slow movements of his String Quartets Op. 59, Nos. 1 and 2, Beethoven composed only two further movements of comparable 'weight' and 'sonata-like density', namely the *Largo* of the so-called *Ghost* Trio, Op. 70, and the *Adagio* of the *Hammerklavier* Sonata.[ccxxvi] Barry Cooper also draws parallels with other of the composer's creations: 'It is ... one of his most highly emotional ... and its deeply anguished lyricism derives from the same world as the *Cavatina* in the String Quartet, Op. 130.'[ccxxvii]

The endorsements of musicians past and present and likewise the commentaries of musicologists, bear testimony to the *Adagio* being one of the most profound, spiritual expressions of the composer, bordering on the ethereal and being variously grave, contemplative, passionate and tranquil.[ccxxviii] Claudio Arrau, by way of illustration, described it as 'the profoundest slow movement of [Beethoven's] entire corpus'.[ccxxix] 'As a guardian of spiritual revelation, the movement, like most keepers of the flame, does not give up its truths easily, nor until an earnest quest on the part of the seeker, in this case listener, has been undertaken.' These words, of Stewart Gordon, may be taken as a reference to the ancient fire-worshippers of Azerbaijan. They have contemporary, quasi-religious, spiritual meaning with connotations of communing between humankind and spiritual light and one possessed of sufficient desire and passion to provide creative insights whatever the challenge. Gordon likens the movement to a 'stream of consciousness'.[ccxxx]

Anton Neumayr has studied the relationship between Beethoven's music and his many illnesses. In his remarks, bearing on the *Adagio* of the Piano Sonata Op. 106, he cites the words of the German music theorist Hugo Riemann that are worthy of reiteration: 'It is surly the most moving song of lamentation ever written for the piano. All the deep sorrow which the master's heart had taken unto itself in these years is gathered here and strains to make itself heard ... A more beautiful adagio for the piano has never been written, and we have no reason to hope anything like it will ever occur again.'[ccxxxi] Riemann's contemporary, the musicologist Wilhelm von Lenz, described the movement as 'une immense lamentation, assise sur les ruines de tous les bonheurs', that has been translated as 'an unmeasured wail over the ruin of all happiness', and likened the *Adagio* to 'The mausoleum of the collective anguish of the world'. J. W. N. Sullivan, the Irish-American mathematician and author of *Beethoven: His spiritual development* (1927), writes of the movement as 'the deliberate expression, by a man who knows no reserves, of a cold and immeasurable woe ... as inimical to human existence as the icy heart of some remote mountain lake'. Fischer qualifies this bleak imagery with thoughts of his own, likening the music to 'a passionate argument with God which ends in submission and humility, after the gift of heavenly consolation has been received'. Fisher adds: 'Metaphors and words are only upsetting here, however, and the statement that "Music begins where language ends" is nowhere more applicable.' In support of his remarks, Fischer quotes Beethoven's own words that he wrote in his sketchbook: "Holy peace, how beautiful, how glorious. Here is God, here rest to serve Him."[ccxxxii]

Some commentators believe a choral and song-like character permeates the *Adagio*: 'With the slow movement ... we approach a new conception ... Here we have a sublime song-movement in Italian style, even with quasi-vocal coloratura ... Rhetorical passion dissolves into melody.'[cxxxiii] We have: '[An] *Adagio* sounding the very depths of lamentation and a triumph-song of unconquerable will, such as none Beethoven has attempted to sing either before or since.'[cxxxiv] The music 'has the feeling of a very personal, intimate musing on the simple chordal theme'.[cxxxv] Von Elterlein perceived a devotional character in the music: 'The third movement ... is a painful, ardent, yearning prayer for the light and joy, out of profound sorrow and darkness: a tone poem pervaded by real religious inspiration and devotion.'[cxxxvi] Egerton Lowe considered bars 14–15, in particular, exhibit 'a peculiar *holy charm*' that he urged the performer should play 'with the tenderest possible execution'.[cxxxvii] Tovey was almost reverential in his estimation of Beethoven's achievement: '[The] emotional and dramatic expression and scope of the ... slow movement are far too large to be described by any pen but that of a great poet, and then only if the poet were to work out his own inspirations, leaving it to chance whether they produced a result analogous to the work described.'[cxxxviii]

In his working out of the movement, Beethoven exploits his resourcefulness at writing variations that are celebrated for their 'profundity of personal expression and intricate attention to detail'[cxxxix] and their sense of 'spontaneous creation'.[ccxl] The interval of a third assumes renewed importance in the *Adagio* as Kinderman remarks: 'Beethoven distils the intervallic basis of the whole sonata, reducing the music to a mysterious, underlying level of content consisting wholly of a chain of thirds in the base, accompanied by soft, hesitant chords in the treble.' In this, he finds reminiscences of J.S. Bach.[ccxli] Tonality assumes importance once more in the sonata: 'The *Adagio* is so to speak ... wide as life itself, Michael Angelo like in its strenuous longing for F-sharp major.'[ccxlii] Beethoven's intensity and powers of invention prompted von Elterlein to indulge in typical nineteenth-century word-imagery: 'Darkness, which the exalted forms of light vainly endeavour to pierce, again covers all; for a long time despair and gloom hold fatal sway. But those deep unfathomable strains in F-sharp major are heard again, and produce a sense of bliss, which is heightened by a magical modulation from E flat to F sharp ... Gleams of joy break through in F-sharp major ... what comforting, hopeful restfulness breathes in these sounds!'[ccxliii]

Blom was of the opinion that the more decorative passages in the slow movement may have exerted an influence on aspects of Chopin's style of piano writing; tantalisingly, he leaves it to his readers to agree and to work out what the specific connections might be.[ccxliv] Also with Chopin in mind, some authorities have suggested the form and spirit of Beethoven's *Adagio* anticipate his Ballades. Less ambiguous is the fact that Liszt was so enamoured of the movement that he made a transcription of it for strings — thereby reversing his normal practice of transcribing Beethoven's orchestral works for piano. In the context of connections between different works and their composers, Matthews remarks: 'It is interesting that [the *Adagio's*] rare key of F-sharp minor should also have inspired one of Mozart's profoundest slow movements, the *Adagio* of the famous A major Concerto, K. 488'.[ccxlv] Cooper describes the keyboard writing here in the Op. 106, as having 'hymn-like simplicity' and notes how Beethoven 'has specified the hushed, silvery tone of *una corda mezza voce*'. He quotes Paul Bekker (*Beethoven*, p. 134): '[We] feel the religious atmosphere of the second Mass about us: the mood of consolation, of reliance on supernatural promises, as it exists in the *Benedictus.*'[ccxlvi]

In addition to what we have said previously concerning the sketches for the Piano Sonata Op. 106, mention should be made of a single leaf that contains outlines almost entirely devoted to the third movement.[ccxlvii] A companion single leaf exists that reveals Beethoven's mind gestating ideas for the *Hammerklavier* Piano Sonata alongside drafts for the Ninth Symphony and what was intended to be its successor, the unfinished Tenth. Of particular interest are Beethoven's hand-written notes, outlining his thoughts about the order of movements, their tempo and which key to use.[ccxlviii]

With a performing time approaching twenty minutes, the *Adagio* is Beethoven's longest. Tovey states this fact more eloquently: 'The movement ... is the largest and greatest specimen of its kind. The mere facts of its form imply unusual length, for even the bare outline of that form occupies considerable time if it is to be stated slowly as is inevitable in a slow movement.'[ccxlix] And from Matthews: 'The size of the *Adagio* is in proportion to the breadth and number of its themes, which are unfolded in the fullest sonata form and the fullest range of keyboard eloquence to be found anywhere in the sonatas.'[ccl]

Notwithstanding the expansive scale of the *Adagio*, Fischer considers it unfolds in two sections: '[The] whole of the first part (which includes second and third groups in different keys) is repeated ... What comes in between is not a development but a cadenza in the nature of an improvisation.'[ccli] In von Elterlein's analysis the movement is: 'Simple and intelligible [in all its] grandeur, as are the lofty ideal contents of this the gigantic *Adagio* of pianoforte music, equally clear and simple in its formal construction.'[cclii] Adorno identifies with what we have said previously regarding the song-like character that some believe characterises the *Adagio*: 'The form of the theme is extremely simple: a two-part song form.' He then makes a particularly interesting generalisation: 'The repeated notes, together with the other elements, give rise to the peculiar *speaking* character of the theme. Melody in very late Beethoven becomes alienated from melody, and its logic is that of speech.'[ccliii] In the opinion of Igor Stravinsky: 'The [third] movement is the richest harmonically of all [Beethoven's] sonatas, in so far as that element can be thought of separately.'[ccliv]

On the occasion when Luciano Berio was interviewed by musicologist Rossana Dalmonte, they discussed tendencies in musical thinking that embrace and work towards a totality. Berio first offered some generalisations: 'The successive stages in Beethoven's creative process hardly ever suggest a linear route a discourse that is constructed and perceived "from left to right". If anything, they suggest a total, summated event that sinks into us without any before or after.' He then added, making further reference to Chopin: 'There are pieces by Beethoven, those that I think I know particularly well and to which I feel very close, that I perceive and "feel" globally, without a beginning and an end, lie an organic, non-chronological whole, or a huge process of mutation. I am thinking for example of that ineffable and somewhat labyrinthine meditation, the *Adagio* from Op. 106 (where, amongst other things, there's a glimpse of Chopin in a quite clear *ante litteram* [ahead of one's time] citation).'[cclv]

'What could be more expressive than the upward impulse in the first subject, issuing from the innermost heart!' — asks von Elterlein?[cclvi] Radcliffe agrees: '[The] magnificent stream of floridly beautiful melody that leads from the first to the second subject is one of the most pianistic passages Beethoven ever wrote.'[cclvii] Rosen calls to mind what we have already said about the music being song-like: 'The style of the decoration is fundamentally operatic, but the sonata offered Beethoven an intimacy that the public stage could not accommodate, and he achieved here an intensity greater than any operatic composer has ever imagined.'[cclviii] In his working out of the movement, Beethoven explores the remote key of F-sharp minor through the medium of one of his favourite constructions, a set of variations – regarded as 'justifiably famous for their profundity of personal expression and intricate attention to detail'.[cclix]

We return for a moment to the period when Beethoven was negotiating with Ferdinand Ries for an English edition of the sonata. We recall that on 16 April 1819 he provided Ries with the required metronome markings and, significantly for our present discussion, a request to insert an additional bar to the opening of the third movement. At this, Ries was incredulous. He recalls: 'Artistically a most remarkable thing happened [concerning the Piano Sonata Op. 106] that Beethoven had sent to me in London, so that [it] would be published there at the same time as in Germany. The engraving was finished and I daily expected a letter specifying the day of publication. When the letter arrived, it contained the surprising instruction: "Insert at the beginning of the *Adagio* ... these two notes as an opening measure".' Ries continues: 'I really admit that I began to wonder if my dear old teacher had gone really daft, a rumour which was going about at the time. To add two notes to such a great work, which had been thoroughly reworked and completed half a year ago! And yet I was amazed at the effect of these two notes. Never again could such effective, important notes be added to a completed work, not even if they had been intended from the very beginning.'[cclx]

Paul Lang likens the additions to 'architectural second thoughts' to be added to an already completed edifice, but the effect of which he characterises as 'momentous'.[cclxi] In strictly musicological terms, the notes in question are merely bass notes that ascend from A to C sharp. However, as intimated from the preceding remarks, they are considered to have profound significance. Von Elterlien explains: 'The two bass notes come in ... in the course of [the composition] of the movement, with the closer management of the chief theme – which begins strictly in the second bar – their great importance became evident to the master, and he thus recognised and supplied the want at the beginning of the movement.'[cclxii] Cooper defines their role as 'forging both a link from the end of the previous movement and also subtle motivic connections (rising third followed by falling third) with the first two movements'.[cclxiii] Tovey comments in similar fashion, stating the notes in question have two functions, 'firstly in conjunction with the first two notes of the following theme ... a subtle allusion to the principal figure of the *Scherzo* ... secondly they give new meaning to certain points in the development of the coda'.[cclxiv]

Authorities vie with one another in bestowing praise on the effect of Beethoven's late additions to the *Adagio*. For (Martin) Cooper, they are 'the voice of consolation'.[cclxv] Seeking to underline what he believes to be the deep spiritual nature of this movement, Fischer remarks, reverentially: 'The first bar was added by Beethoven at a late stage. It serves to force the listener on his knees.'[cclxvi] For Radcliffe they are simply 'magical'.[cclxvii] Kinderman is similarly terse, describing the notes as 'mysterious octaves'.[cclxviii] Wilhelm von Lenz resorted to chilling imagery, likening the opening notes to 'two steps towards the grave's side'.[cclxix]

Franz Liszt comes to the fore once more in our recollections of past interpreters of this music. We have noted previously that Hector Berlioz heard him perform in the summer of 1836. Of his rendering of the third movement he writes: 'In the *Adagio* above all ... he remained constantly at the level of the composer's inspiration. No higher praise can be given. I know, but since it is true I cannot say less ... By such a rendition of a work totally misunderstood until now, Liszt has proved that he is the pianist of the future.'[cclxx] The German composer and conductor Wendelin Weissheimer heard Liszt play the *Hammerklavier* Sonata when he was travelling in Germany in the summer of 1858. He compared Liszt's interpretation of the *Adagio* to that of 'a whole orchestra', likening the entry of the second theme to 'the deepest notes of the tuba' and the demisemiquaver figures to 'expressive violin passages'.[cclxxi] Our next recollection of Liszt's playing connects us with the occasion of the first Bayreuth Festival in 1876. Liszt and some close friends were invited to dine at Wagner's *Wahnfried* Villa. After dinner, the conversation turned to Beethoven's late piano sonatas, but Wagner, being fatigued as a consequence of his involvement with the arrangements for the Festival, left the company. At this juncture Liszt spoke about the *Hammerklavier* Sonata, in particular regarding the *Adagio*. To illustrate his remarks he went to the piano and played the movement through. Among the distinguished guests was the Hungarian nobleman Count Albert Apponyi. He relates: 'When the last bars of that mysterious work had died away, we stood motionless.' On hearing Liszt play, Wagner had left his bedroom but respectfully listened in silence until Liszt's playing was concluded. Running down stairs, in his nightshirt, he flung his arms round Liszt's neck and thanked him emotionally in broken phrases, 'for the wonderful gift he had received'.[cclxxii]

The American student of piano Margaret Chanter was introduced to Franz Liszt on the occasion of his sixty-sixth birthday — 22 October 1877. He honoured her by suggesting she should attend one of the master-classes he was then giving; this was an unhoped-for privilege since only a select few were so invited. On the appointed day a young man played the *Hammerklavier* Sonata note-perfect, but not to Liszt's satisfaction. He took the pupil gently by the shoulder, removed him from the piano stool and played through the *Adagio* 'pouring out his soul'. Chanter later recollected: 'I do not think that movement can ever have been played better or have moved any group of people so deeply before of since ... We had been in the Great Presence'.[cclxxiii] Our final recollection of the playing of Liszt derives from another American classical pianist, Carl Lachmund. He studied with Liszt for three years and in his diary reminiscences, for September 1882, he makes reference to a performance by Liszt of the *Hammerklavier* Sonata: 'When he came to the *Adagio* ... his eyes began to water and he seemed to breathe with more difficulty, so ardently did he love the Beethoven slow movements.' Lachmund adds: 'When he had ended, we felt as though we had experienced a vision, as though we had heard angels singing! No one moved, only a slight sigh could be heard from more than one mouth.'[cclxxiv]

Felix Weingartner recalls his days when he was studying piano at the Leipzig Conservatoire under Professor Oskar Paul — Weingartner was then age twenty at the time. According to Weingartner's own account, the announcement of the death of Wagner, on 13 February 1883, affected him deeply. Coincidentally, Weingartner had just completed studying the B-flat major Piano Sonata. To stir him from his melancholy Paul declared: 'You will play it at our next soirée. I have already put your name on the programme, so no protests please.' Weingartner relates: 'I proceeded to concentrate my energies on practising the sonata, which I had neglected for a short period, and soon after accomplished the difficult task successfully. The *Adagio*, so far removed from all worldly things, I silently constituted a memorial to the genius who had so recently left us.'[cclxxv]

We conclude our recollections from the past of celebrated interpreters of the Piano Sonata Op. 106, with two reminiscences from the memoirs of Arthur Rubinstein. The first of these concerns the French pianist Édouard Risler. Notwithstanding his patriotic attachment to the music of his fellow countrymen, Risler was well versed in the German repertoire and gave several major cycles of Beethoven's 32 sonatas in Paris at the Salle Pleyel. He also toured widely and it was when Rubinstein heard Risler play, at a recital in Berlin, that he realized 'he was a serious rival'. Rubinstein adds: 'I heard three of the Risler concerts. He played ... the *Appassionata, Les Adieux* and the great *Hammerklavier.* To this day [1980], I have never heard anybody play these sonatas as beautifully and movingly as Risler. He played them naturally, just as they spoke to him, revealing the highly romantic nature of these masterpieces.' Rubinstein continues: 'I was never convinced by the intellectual and almost pedantic conception ... whereas the *Adagio* of the *Hammerklavier* ... made me cry when played by Risler.' Our second reminiscence recalls a performance Rubinstein himself gave of the *Hammerklavier* Sonata in Vienna early in his career. He refers to the composition as being 'formidable' and 'a stumbling block for the average pianist'. Of his performance he states: 'To hold the listener's attention during the long, calm, majestic *Adagio* was a difficult problem which I seemed to have solved on that evening.' In the audience was Leopold Godowsky; despite never having had a piano lesson in his life — his training was entirely autodidactic — he was the possessor of a formidable technique. After the concert Godowsky praised Rubinstein's rendering of the Op. 106, adding, however: 'But you must practice!'[cclxxvi]

We close our commentary to the third movement of the B-flat major Piano Sonata, with a selection of further remarks bearing on its performance and interpretation.

Vincent d'Indy is reported to have said: 'One must have suffered oneself to dare to attempt the execution of the

Adagio in F-sharp minor.'[cclxxvii] In a footnote to his performing edition of the work, Hans von Bülow warns the aspiring pianist off the movement as off holy ground: 'Almost no other movement of the master's demands such pious and awe-full devotion to do justice to its dolorous nobility. This is no longer a question of "playing the piano": let anyone who cannot "speak" on the keyboard with his whole soul content himself with reading this music.'[cclxxviii]

To those daring to venture on the 'holy ground' of the *Adagio*, Carl Czerny urges the music to be played: 'With the most pensive expression, extremely *legato* and *cantabile*, but in strict time, except where the contrary is indicated.' Recognising the length of the movement, and thereby the demands on the listener's powers of concentration, he adds: 'In this *Adagio*, the player must call forth the whole art of performance, in order that the hearer may not become fatigued from its unusual length.' Czerny reads Beethoven's personal circumstances into the music: 'And yet in all these means, the highly tragic and melancholic character of the whole must be faithfully preserved. Still the excited and varied passages serve greatly to animate this wonderful composition which depicts the feelings of the aged master, oppressed both in body and soul, who occasionally thinks of happier times.'[cclxxix]

Lowe advises Beethoven's designation *Appassionato* may be interpreted as 'full of *affection*' (Lowe's italics).[cclxxx] Commenting on Beethoven's directions, Fischer observes: 'The *Appassionato e con molto sentimento* which Beethoven requires seems to contradict the *mezza voce*, but the contradiction is only apparent, since when we have something to say that comes from the depths of the soul, we lower our voices to a whisper.'[cclxxxi] In this context, Brendel reminds us how performance practice is intimately connected with the quality of sound the piano itself produces in its different registers of *una corda* (one string) and *tutte le corde* (three strings) and, thereby, the need to strictly observe the composer's pedal markings. He remarks: 'On Beethoven's pianos, the quality of the sound produced by the soft pedal was more shadowy and fragile than it is today, a sphere of whispering and subdued *mezza voce* singing.'[cclxxxii] Stravinsky also makes reference to the piano of Beethoven's day: '[Such] pianos were equipped with a pedal which shifted the hammers from three strings to one, thereby effecting a change of tone and weight comparable to a change in registration on an organ or harpsichord.' This, he observes, gave the performer, playing on such an instrument, 'an entire dimension, for the alternation of two timbres and intensities'. Stravinsky perceived the *Adagio* to be 'conceived in dialogue form', and the challenge to the modern-day performer, he maintained, is to capture this 'dialogue' on the modern-day instrument.[ccclxxxiii]

Gordon reminds us the *Adagio* confronts both the player and performer: '[The] work's musical challenges, as represented by the *Adagio sostenuto*, demand that the performer, as well as the listener, enter a world so intensely profound that ... parallels in the [keyboard] literature can scarcely be found.'[ccclxxxiv]

We close our account of the third movement with the thoughts of John Fuller-Maitland, bearing in mind he was writing in 1927 on the occasion of Beethoven's death centenary, when he felt the need to promote the composition: 'I believe that if this wonderful creation [the *Adagio*] were played by itself, it would be more widely recognised as one of the Master's most individual utterances, and the deep poetry that is revealed in its almost formless course would make it the best-loved movement in the whole of the sonatas.'[ccclxxxv]

Beethoven designates the opening to the fourth movement *Largo*. This takes the form of a slow, ethereal-like introduction that serves as a transitional passage to the majestic fugue that is to follow. Beethoven's writing here is in 'a free, harmonious form'.[cclxxxvi] The first bar alone contains thirty-five semiquavers, the second forty, and the tenth eighty-eight.[cclxxxvii] Bie likens the *Largo* to an old-style toccata that 'tries this and that, prelude-wise [in its] striving after fixed forms'.[cclxxxviii] Stephan Playstow makes a comparison with the music's initial opening 'hesitations' and the manner in which the composer, in the Ninth Symphony, momentarily halts the progress of the music with the declamatory words: 'O Freunde, nicht diese Töne!' – 'Oh friends, not these sounds!'[cclxxxix] Gordon characterises the broken chords in the *Largo* to 'a series of fragments' the role of which is to connect the *Adagio* to the concluding fugue and which he believes contribute the composer's desired 'musical stream of consciousness'.[ccxc] In strictly musical terms Tovey describes the introduction as a 'process of *feeling for the keynote of the finale*' [Tovey's italics].[ccxci] When considered as a recitative – albeit a short one, the music is already 'full of meaning ... highly poetic, almost dramatic, [a] prelude ... [that is] powerfully effective' stirring, as Adolph Bernhard Marx says, 'all the regions of the tone world'.[ccxcii] Notwithstanding its short compass, Beethoven's open style of writing in the *Largo* creates 'a sense of timelessness'.[ccxciii] Ferruccio Busoni discussed aspects of originality in music, and the search by composers to liberate themselves from the past, in their search for new forms of expression in music. He cites Beethoven as a case in point: 'Such lust of liberation filled Beethoven, the romantic revolutionary that he ascended one short step on the way leading music back to its loftier self – a short step in the great task, a wide step in his own path. He did not quite reach absolute music, but in certain moments he divined it, as in the introduction to the fugue of the *Hammerklavier*.'[ccxciv]

We have remarked previously on the composer Wendelin Weissheimer's recollections of the playing of Franz Liszt. Of his interpretation of the opening bars of the fourth movement he writes: 'Of the *Largo*, which forms a kind of prelude to the great fugue of the last movement, Liszt made a poem of infinite melancholy, sweet dreaminess, and sudden exultation.'[ccxcv]

Fischer is full of praise for the manner in which Beethoven makes the transition from the third movement to the sonata's finale: 'The way Beethoven leads into the last movement is one of his greatest strokes of genius: leading away from the sublime back to earthly the conflict of the fugue, forgetting bar lines, starting four times over and finally, after the great outburst in A major, attaining F, which he had begun with as in a dream, establishing it now as the dominant of B flat — all this is psychologically magnificent.'[ccxcvi] As the last movement strives to emerge, the music accelerates in pace, transitioning through *allegro* to *prestissimo* until the *Allegro risoluto* is reached that leads to the great fugue.

Beethoven marks the fugue, *Fuga a tre voci, con alcune licenze* — 'Fugue in three voices, with a little licence'. At the very outset, thereby, he prepares the performer to anticipate that the music, which is about to unfold, will not be of a strictly orthodox, contrapuntal kind. The fugue forms a climax to the sonata and, as befitting the grandeur of the composition, it is itself laid out on a monumental scale, approaching 400 bars in length with a typical playing time of between twelve and fifteen minutes. Two centuries after its creation it still has the power to challenge both performer and listener. Bie describes the three-voiced giant fugue as 'the utmost of art for art'.[ccxcvii] In assigning a role to the fugue, Fischer comments: 'The Fugue is difficult to play, certainly, but I believe that Beethoven's intention was not merely to write a fourth movement worthy of the preceding music, but also to give the pianist a rewarding task.' He was critical of those who regarded the fugue 'as a mere contrapuntal exercise', asserting: 'It was, in fact, intended to be a fine-sounding piano-piece of great expressive power — the thematic work is merely the means to an end.' Fischer also considered it required a virtuoso of the standing of Ferruccio Busoni 'to make us feel that the piece is well-written for the instrument'.[ccxcviii]

The great fugue in the closing movement earned Tovey's enduring admiration: 'The finale is so immense in its power and grandeur that I confess I have some difficulty in understanding how any difficulty or any roughness in its effect could prevent the listener from being profoundly moved by it.' For him it was nothing less than: '[The] most terrific movement ever written for the pianoforte ...'.[ccxcix] Von Elterlein posed the question: '[Who] can explain this tone mystery ... [It is enough] if we feel the grandeur of the master's imagination, if we recognise that we have not before us a mere conglomeration of notes and play of sounds, but a deeper meaning runs through all.'[ccc] One commentator has suggested: 'If in the first three parts you have the feeling of divine revelation, through the Fuga in the fourth part, man descends to earth.'[ccci] To other commentators the fugue of the *Hammerklavier* Sonata stands alongside the *Grosse Fuge* that was originally intended for the String Quartet, Op. 133 and equally the *Et Vitam Venturi* fugue in the *Missa Solemnis* — all considered as testimonies to Beethoven's most daring and extensive late explorations of contrapuntal art.

Brendel's remarks serve to remind us that Beethoven's achievement came at personal cost: 'Boundless energy and intellectual rigour have never been coupled at a higher pitch of excitement.' To which he adds: 'Beethoven's special contribution as a fugal composer is the turbulent and frenzied fugue that nearly, but only nearly, defies the strictures of the contrapuntal writing.'[cccii] Rolland likened the composer's counterpoint to 'a struggle of giants, unbridled in its onslaught' and reflected, 'its great licences and amazing contortions have puzzled many minds'.[ccciii] Bie discerns the fugal writing as 'striving to find resolution' which is eventually achieved: 'The three-voiced giant-fugue is the deliverance, in whose retardations the old storm, however, still, conceals itself ... It is the utmost of art for art.'[ccciv]

Beethoven's writing in the final movement of the Piano Sonata Op. 106 is not without its critics. The respected German musicologist Walter Riezler described the fugue as 'overladen to the point of artificiality with all the arts of the fugue'.[cccv] William Newman expressed similar thoughts: 'To some the twelve-minute fugue, with its rich assortment of traditional intellectualisms as well as "alcune licenze", puts Op. 106 in Beethoven's special category of "magnificent failures" — that is, in the company of the "Grosse Fuge" for Quartet or even the choral finale of the Ninth Symphony.'[cccvi] In his discussion of Beethoven's fugue, Wilhelm von Lenz went so far as to quote Ovid's phrase, 'rudis indisgestaque modes' — 'a rude and disordered mass'.[cccvii]

Martin Cooper's observations reminds us the fugue in the *Hammerklavier* Sonata is not a contrapuntal exercise, of the kind Beethoven had written for his teachers years previously, but a composition intended for performance. Moreover, as he further remarks, the final fugue is not just a case of 'playing the piano'; it assumes a 'transcendental technique' on the part of the performer so as to 'confront the further, purely interpretive problems of the movement'. He concludes: 'In fact, the fugue raises in acutest form the question of virtuosity and its justification, not as an end in itself but as means to an end ... The technical difficulty of the music is part of its character, an element as integral as the emotional energy displayed in its carrying out.'[cccviii] Cooper cautions on the wisdom of making a four-hand arrangement of the great fugue in the *Hammerklavier* Sonata. He argues, whereas Beethoven sanctioned, and personally wrote out, a four-hand arrangement of the *Grosse Fuge*, he suggests this would be a mistake in the case of the Op. 106: 'A four-hand arrangement would unquestionably promote clarity and balance, accuracy of accentuation and correct chording; but the element of individual effort and mastery — the experience of a single man [performer] confronting and overcoming what appear overwhelming obstacles — would be lost, and with it something far more important to Beethoven's idea than formal elegance and correctness.'[cccix]

We return once more to the writings of the French musicologist André Hodeir whose views on music we have previously noted. He discusses the history of Western music in the context of equal temperament and the harmonic scale and their consequences for the art of music and how these achievements opened the way 'not only for the eminently "human" works of art in history — *The Saint Matthew Passion* and Beethoven's Ninth Symphony — but for the most abstract, as well — *The Art of the Fugue* and the finale of the *Hammerklavier* Sonata.' He adds: 'These works, born of the marriage between the tonal system and the concept of equal temperament, were far more beautiful than any previous music, and perhaps than any previous work of art.'[cccx]

The newness in Beethoven's writing is known to have perplexed many of his contemporaries and it still resonates today as 'a piece of *new music* among the most uncompromising ever written'.[cccxi] In the opinion of Denis Matthews:

'A few bars chosen at random will illustrate the mental and physical battle that rages and triumphs in the sonata's final fugue. They have a twentieth-century look about them — "contemporary for ever", to borrow Stravinsky's phrase — and they show Beethoven's growing obsession with the trill as a "personality" (see later).'[cccxii]

It is the quality of imagination that is pre-eminent in the closing fugue. 'The spiritual content of this fugue is the fitting compliment to the *Adagio* in the sense that nothing else could have survived. And the greatness of Beethoven is shown in the fact that, having passed through the experience that left him so little to express, he yet expressed so much.'[cccxiii] 'In this fugue, the soul soars into those extra-terrestrial regions where pain is absent and incarnates the victory of the divine over the misery of human existence — a victory Beethoven achieved over himself.'[cccxiv]

The English composer and musicologist Christopher Headington acknowledges Beethoven's debt to Bach, in the final movement, with the qualification: 'But the mood of awe-inspiring striving of the *Hammerklavier* Sonata's finale, fugal though it may be, is world's away from Bach. It is literally aggressive, with its shrilling trills and melodic leaps, in spite of a gentle interlude a little beyond the halfway point which offers a brief respite from the conflict.' He concludes admiringly: '[The] finale is a masterpiece of structure.'[cccxv] Kinderman is like-minded in his estimation of Beethoven's contrapuntal writing: 'The fugue of the *Hammerklavier* seems not to affirm a higher, more perfect or serene world of eternal harmonies, as in Bach's works, but to confront an open universe.'[cccxvi]

Von Elterlein saw Beethoven's 'confrontation' in the following terms: 'A representation of supreme unrest is set before us, so gloomy often that one fancies it is a storm with fiery lightnings and rolling thunder, conjured up by unknown forces, an unchaining of the dark powers.' He further invokes the imagery of Adolph Bernhard Marx who 'perceives the expression of a most deeply agitated spirit, relentlessly swaying two and fro, coloured, softened, and restrained by certain elegiac tones'.[cccxvii] '[It] is a fugue such as never was before or since — a titanic assertion of power. Unity is attained, but after how wild and terrible a struggle. If in the Fifth Symphony Beethoven is in conflict with the forces that threaten the fulfilment of personality, with Fate or Providence or a hostile society, here he is in conflict with himself.'[cccxviii] Bekker characterises the fugue, which he more correctly describes as a *fugato* — by acknowledging Beethoven's own qualification *con alcune licenze* — as 'a series of wild outcries'.[cccxix] For Solomon these impart to the movement its 'aggressive and rebellious thrust ... with its defiant relentless striving (*Allegro risoluto*) to surmount immense obstacles'. He describes its closest analogue as 'the process of birth, the pain-ridden, exultant struggle for emergence — and the passage through the labyrinth from darkness to light from doubt to belief, from suffering to joy'.[cccxx]

We recall Beethoven's assertion that with his *Hammerklavier* Sonata he was consciously challenging pianists by 'giving them something to do'. The remark was not lost on Claudio Arrau who pronounced Beethoven's fugue, 'the most ragingly difficult fugue imaginable, as if to say, "Now that will show you!" '[cccxxi] And Igor Stravinsky who, in his student days had the work under his fingers, was disposed to reflect: 'As for the fugue, it is not only inexhaustible but exhausting.'[cccxxii] Matthews comments: The fugue of the *Hammerklavier* is as formidable a challenge to any player's technique and stamina as it was to Beethoven's hard-won mastery of counterpoint ... both performer and listener must strive to meet the composer's challenges.'[cccxxiii] This was a point Tovey raised in an essay that appeared in the *Musical Gazatte*, No. 8, March 1902. He states: 'Probably one of the most difficult things to enjoy in all music is the fugue in Beethoven's Sonata, Opus 106 (I select it as a thing which I believe can and ought to be enjoyed); and the key to its enjoyment is not a knowledge of the laws of fugue, in general, but a knowledge of Beethoven's Opus 106 – helped no doubt in numberless points by a knowledge of other sonatas and fugues and other musical compositions, but never confused by matter that does not concern Opus 106.'[cccxxiv]

As the surviving sketches indicate, composing the fugue to the Piano Sonata, Op.106 caused Beethoven considerable effort. In his study of them, Nottebohm found Beethoven exploring a great number of fugal subjects 'three of which show characteristics of the theme finally chosen'. Other distinguishing features are the composer's interest in 'the leap of a tenth ... the impetuously descending scale passages ... the all-important trill'.[cccxxv] These are considerations Blom raises in his commentary to the music: '[Beethoven's] fierce tussle with the stuff of music sometimes becomes materially evident in his work, as in the final fugue of the *Hammerklavier* Sonata, where it is reflected in the almost heartbreaking technical efforts the pianist is obliged to make in order to keep the textures clear without detracting from the bigness of tone that is required.'[cccxxvi] In Barry Cooper's discussion of Beethoven's music, in the context of the emerging literary ideals and aesthetic trends of the period, he calls attention to a point we have made previously, that is, the relevance to performance of the manner in which the pianist is seen to overcome the obstacles inherent in the music. He comments: '[In] pieces like the finale of the *Hammerklavier* Sonata or the *Grosse Fuge*, the sense of strain or difficulty placed on the performer and listener alike appears almost to be a calculated part of the aesthetic effect; the music seems at times to court incomprehensibility.'[cccxxvii] Cooper's observations call to mind the occasion when Franz Schubert was attempting to play his technically challenging *Wanderer Fantasy*, D. 760 that he is alleged to have left off, with the remark 'the devil may play it'!

The first eight leaves of the so-called Landsberg 9 Sketchbook, dating from 1818, contain ideas for the fugue of Op. 106. These form part of a miscellany of 36 leaves that came into the possession of the Berlin Royal Library in 1862 together with a collection of manuscripts belonging to their former owner Ludwig Landsberg.[cccxxviii] They provide insights into the composer's working method. Four sides of sketches, now forming part of the Beethoven Archive in Bonn, reveal work on the fugue at an advanced stage. The music is written out in long passages, as distinct from the composer's style of setting down his preliminary thoughts that typically take the form of much shorter ideas and fragments.[cccxxix]

In the autumn of 1939 Roger Sessions delivered the Spencer Trask Lectures at Princeton University. He took as his subject the origins of creative inspiration in music, charting the intellectual progress between 'inspiration' and 'having an idea'. In the course of one of these lectures he made reference to the Piano Sonata Op. 106, from which we have derived the following: 'The inspiration may come in a flash, or as sometimes happens, it may grow and develop gradually.' Sessions had in his possession photostatic copies of several pages of Beethoven's sketches for the last movement of the *Hammerklavier* Sonata which he believed revealed the composer 'carefully modelling then testing in [a] systematic and apparently cold-blooded fashion the theme of the fugue'. He posed the question: 'Where, one might ask, is the inspiration here?' His response was: '[If] the word has any meaning at all, it is certainly appropriate to this movement, with its irresistible and titanic energy of expression, already present in the theme.' He proposed inspiration takes the form 'not of a sudden flash of music, but a clearly envisaged impulse toward a certain goal for which the composer [is] obliged to strive.' Contemplating Beethoven at work on his sketches, Sessions concluded: 'When this perfect realization was attained ... there could have been no hesitation — rather a flash of recognition that this was exactly what he wanted.'[cccxxx]

Any commentary to the fugue in the *Hammerklavier* Sonata would be incomplete without making acknowledgement to the important role assumed by the trill. The conventional role of the trill in classical music was to add decoration to a note, but in the Piano Sonata Op. 106 the device assumes far greater significance. In his Piano Sonata Op, 53, Beethoven had pioneered the use of the sustained trill and he extends this procedure throughout many passages in the fugue. At the outset, just as the fugue is about to get under way, the trill is employed in ever ascending intervals, as though alerting the listener to the drama that is about to unfold — setting the stage as it were 'for the music of high energy, ruggedness, and extreme intensity, all of which [including the adoption of the trill] are magnified as the fugue progresses'.[cccxxxi] At the close of the fugue, the trill is sustained for no fewer than twelve bars. Thereby the purely decorative role of the trill is thoroughly set aside. In the words of one commentator: 'The screaming trills which dominate the theme, and therefore the contrapuntal texture, would seem to express the anguished determination to achieve unity of being.'[cccxxxii]

In his youth Beethoven learned the preludes and fugues of Bach's *Well-Tempered Clavier* from his teacher Christian Gottlob Neefe, an experience that conferred within him a lifelong fascination with fugal and contrapuntal textures. Later, as we have remarked (Piano Sonatas Op. 2, Nos. 1–3), he consolidated his knowledge of counterpoint through the medium of his studies with Johann Albrechtsberger and Joseph Haydn – studies the mastery of which did not apparently come easily to him as is evident from the many pedagogical exercises that survive from this period in the composer's career.[cccxxxiii] Later in life, yielding to the temptation to make one of his puns, he was given to exclaim: 'Nicht Bach, sondern Meer solte er heiβen!' – 'He should not be called stream but rather sea!' – the German word *bach*, meaning a stream. A further measure of Beethoven's admiration for Bach is implicit in the action he took on the occasion when Franz Anton Hoffmeister announced his intention to publish the complete works of J. S. Bach; Beethoven promptly made it known he wished to purchase a set. And in July 1809 he wrote to his publisher Breitkopf & Härtel requesting all the scores he had of Bach, amongst others, that he considered 'should certainly be in the possession of every true artist, not only for the sake of real enjoyment but also for the purpose of study'.[cccxxxiv]

The surviving sketches for the fugue in the *Hammerklavier* Sonata, reveal Beethoven annotating his own ideas alongside extracts from the *Well-Tempered Clavier*. One leaf in particular, thought to date from 1817 and now in the possession of the Beethoven House in Bonn, includes studies that are considered to be preparation for work on the fugue that features so prominently in the fourth movement of Op. 106. The Beethoven House authority commenting on this sketch remarks: 'As with all the composers, from whom Beethoven wished to learn something, he copied out interesting works or solutions to problems.'[cccxxxv] Rosen suggests on this occasion perhaps Beethoven wished 'to remind himself of the [fugal] style'. However, he goes on to remark that Beethoven makes a departure from strict orthodox procedures: 'The style of Bach is rejected: if there is to be counterpoint, it must be made new.'[cccxxxvi] Beethoven's striving to find this newness is evident in his many sketches as the subject of the fugue underwent 'innumerable metamorphoses' before reaching its finale form.[cccxxxvii]

In the fugue to Op. 106 Beethoven was seeking to depart from the traditional concept of the contrapuntal medium as being 'a vehicle for serious and religious thought' and to invest the construction with new levels of imagination and poetical expression.[cccxxxviii] Writing of Beethoven's fugal creation at the close of the nineteenth century, von Elterlein was disposed to observe: '[This] fugue is one of the most difficult exercises of musical art, for the form, modulation, and working out of the themes are so peculiar that the whole is by no means easy to follow; properly speaking, it is rather a strange union of fugue and rondo forms than a pure fugue; but the movement does not, on this account, stand any-theless on an equality with Bach's creations, for contrapuntal art and freedom; only with this difference, that the spirit of the nineteenth century here pervades the form.'[cccxxxix] Nearer to our own time Pierre Boulez, in his discussion of Beethoven's contrapuntal procedures and far-sighted innovations, remarks: 'With Beethoven, the divergence between harmony and counterpoint becomes more marked, and his late works may be considered as expressing a violent conflict between the vertical control of the results of linear superimpositions, and the intervallic exigencies of the melodic lines themselves. By his nature, Beethoven resolves this conflict of techniques dramatically, finding solutions whose boldness was to remain unequalled until the beginning of the twentieth century. As characteristic examples may be mentioned the closing fugue of the Piano Sonata, Op. 106, and the *Grosse Fuge* for string quartet.'[cccxl]

The fugue in the finale is conceived on a large scale. With the exception of the fifteen-bar transitional Largo and twenty-nine bars about half way through — that offer a moment's tranquillity and respite — it accounts for the movement's almost 400 bars.[cccxli] Not only is the fugue large in conception, it is acknowledged for being one of the composer's 'greatest formal preoccupation[s] in [the] late sonatas'.[cccxlii] Ray Longyear writes how 'Beethoven's exuberant delight in displaying his contrapuntal skill culminates in his late works, especially in the fugal finale of the Piano Sonata Op. 106 and the *Grosse Fuge*.'[cccxliii] The six bars that usher in the fugue have been likened to entering as 'on the wings of a storm' and dispersed within them are to be found 'the principal figures of its subject'.[cccxliv] As the fugue progresses it is as though Beethoven wishes to showcase his mastery of counterpoint as he brings into service every conceivable 'learned' contrapuntal device. In the words of Nicolas Slonimsky: 'In it the subject is presented in a variety of transformations, following the Bach tradition, namely in augmentation (played twice as slowly), inversion (playing ascending notes in descending order and vice versa), crab motion (playing the theme backward), and inverted crab motion (which is tantamount to playing the music upside down).'[cccxlv] In addition 'leaps, trills, double notes, sporzandi, octaves and syncopation abound'.[cccxlvi] As Marion Scott reflects: 'During the course of the fugue, Beethoven shows an unerring command of almost every kind of technical device, yet devises a work of great art, which must surely silence all those critics who doubt his power to write a fugue.[cccxlvii]

In the course of writing out the fugue Beethoven must have become aware of the need to insert what we have described as a 'moment's tranquillity and respite' for the relief — albeit temporary — of both performer and listener.

This he provides at bars 250—278 in which, as von Elterlein describes: 'Isolated gleams of light shine through, now and then, and a humorous impulse is often distinctly heard.'[cccxlviii] Musically these bars serve, in Cockshoot's phrase, the equivalent of the military expression, 'reculer pour mieux sauter' — 'draw back in order to leap better'. The pause serves to 'change the atmosphere of the music' for a while enabling the listener to 'consolidate his aural impressions of the fugue so far and prepare for the subject to return with renewed vigour'.[cccxlix] For Rolland, the tranquil bars are nothing less than 'heavenly interludes' that 'transport one into the pure air of the *Sanctus* of the Mass in D'.[cccl] The moment of respite is short-lived: 'From the ruinous breakdown of the last page the opening of the fugue-subject rises like a phoenix from the ashes and we realize that the leap of a tenth harks back to the beginning of the whole sonata. And so, despite all the suffering, the circle closes with a positive affirmation.'[cccli]

Amongst past interpreters of the *Hammerklavier* Sonata, Franz Liszt inevitably vies once more for attention. We recall the recollections of Wendelin Weissheimer when he heard the celebrated virtuoso play the Piano Sonata Op. 106 in the summer of 1858. According to his testimony: 'It was as though ... Beethoven and Liszt had mobilised all their powers to accomplish the gigantic fugal feat — the former in its creation, the latter in the conquest of its immense difficulties. Just as Beethoven, in the inexorable flow of his thoughts, almost entirely forgot he was writing for the piano, so Liszt likewise seemed to forget he was dealing with a limited keyboard instrument; he again played an *orchestra* on it. Thus, shortly before the end of the twelve-page fugue, where the hands of ordinary mortals threaten to drop from the keyboard from sheer exhaustion, he was still able to set before his astounded listeners six *octave trills, with turn*, one after another *in both hands,* instead of the usual simple trills; and yet with such mighty power that it was as though he had just begun and was about to reward the piano, now quivering in all its joints, by dealing it its death blow.' Weissheimer adds: 'There was a saying, then current, that when Liszt was in France, and it was announced he was about to give a concert, "every Érard piano in Paris trembled".'[ccclii]

The Bohemian-born pianist Rudolf Serkin is regarded as one of the foremost interpreters of Beethoven of the twentieth century. However, notwithstanding his pre-eminence, he was in thrall to the playing of Vladimir Horowitz of whose interpretation of the *Hammerklavier* Sonata he writes: 'Horowitz was beyond technique ... in his playing of fast octaves and scales but to which he could add colour and many other things.' Serkin's own rendering of the sonata was justly celebrated, but of Horowitz's playing he remarked: '[He] had never heard such a stunning performance, and the fugue was electrifying.' Despite his consummate possession of the music, Horowitz never performed the *Hammerklavier* Sonata in public.[cccliii]

With regard to modern-day performance practice, few would contest Gordon's contention: '[The sonata's] technical challenges, as represented by the fugue, are unique and among the greatest in keyboard literature.'[cccliv] Metaphorically speaking: 'The fugue is almost unplayable because it is an experience that is almost unattainable.'[ccclv] Radcliffe, in his discussion of the richness and complexity of the fugue, with its three-part writing, augmentation, inversion and cancrizans, was disposed to remark: 'Long and patient study is necessary in order to grasp as a whole the immensely powerful structure of the movement, with its varied tonal scheme and frequently changing moods.'[ccclvi] Edward Cone took the *Hammerklavier* Sonata as the subject of his 1972 Ernst Bloch Lecture, *Participation and Identification*. In the course of this he remarked: 'If music is normally to be heard as composing itself, this music is heard at the stage of pre-composition ... [A] strong histrionic flavour must permeate its performance, but here the pianist is not portraying a composer-performer in the act of public improvisation; instead he must convey the impression of the persona of the sonata trying to order its own musical thoughts so as to arrive at its final self-realization in the fugue.'[ccclvii]

Commenting on the desirable metronome settings for the final movement, Rosen makes two observations: 'The metronome indication for the fugal finale of the *Hammerklavier* Sonata shows us that Beethoven liked his concluding fugues to be difficult to play and to listen to.' He adds: 'The fugato in the development section (Bars 138ff) becomes stodgy at too slow a tempo and benefits from at least 126 or faster. One must remember Beethoven's ... metronome mark was only valid for the first bars and one cannot put a measure to sentiment.'[ccclviii] Tovey advised: '[Keep] the greater part of this fugue within the scale of tone you would expect from a string trio that is not over-exerting itself ... [If] Weingartner's crotchet = 126 be taken as the fundamental tempo, the onrush may often reach Beethoven's crochet = 144.'[ccclix]

Turning next to questions of interpretation, Slonimsky reminds us: '[The] *Grand Fugue* of the finale, presents additional difficulties, necessitating the subtlest possible use of dynamics in order to *orchestrate* the several voices.'[ccclx] To quote Tovey once more: 'Op. 106 is, especially in the fugue, full of strenuous passages which betray the player into exhausting his reserves of tone when he ought not to have reached the percussion stage at all ... What such passages need is the older technique so ... suitable to Beethoven's earlier works, with ready command of a brilliant finger-staccato or non-legato, and a sparing use of pedal except in

Beethoven's characteristic masses of cloudy arpeggio.'[ccclxi] Carl Czerny has time-honoured advice for anyone venturing to play the piano: '[The] present finale is one of the most difficult pianoforte pieces, and can be most suitably studied by first practising it *slowly* and in small portions – line by line, and page by page.' When these precepts have been followed, Czerny reassures the would-be interpreter: 'The performer will himself discover, that it must be played in a very lively and energetic manner – with the observance of all the marks of expression, as well as with the utmost certainty in the bravura passages ... '[ccclxii] Matthews offers words of caution of a different kind: '[Nowadays] the *Hammerklavier* fugue deters fewer and fewer virtuosos: the danger is that one day it may be made to sound too easy. This it must not: the leaping trills and the jagged angles of the counterpoint, with its fierce augmentations and intellectual reversals of the subject, crabwise, are a mental as well as a physical battle.'[ccclxiii]

Professor Sir Donald Tovey once described the ending of Beethoven's Piano Sonata in B-flat major, Op. 106, the *Hammerklavier,* as 'the final cataclysm that brings the great work to an end that seems to sum up all that is noble in man'.[ccclxiv]

---

[i] Wilfrid Howard Mellers, 1957, p. 70.

[ii] Alfred Brendel, 2001, p. 33.

[iii] Alfred Brendel, *The veil of order*: Alfred Brendel in conversation with Martin Meyer, 2002, p. 111.

[iv] We recall an address given by Carl Czerny in 1825 to the students of the August Eberhard Müller's Piano School. He stated: '[The] virtuosi of our time in their playing as well as in their compositions, have brought about a perfection to the handling of the instrument, and a versatility to any performance, that one could not have imagined ... Even the fortepianos themselves are every year refined with new inventions and improvements, and it is as yet impossible to predict when this complicated instrument will finally be perfected.' Source: Dieter Hildebrandt, *Pianoforte: a social history of the piano,* 1988, p. 66.

[v] It is probable Beethoven composed the Piano Sonata Op. 106 with the assistance of Johann and Nanette Streichers' 6 1/2 octave piano that the

v sonata requires. Streichers' piano was then a state-of-the-art instrument by the composer's favourite piano maker. See: Derek Melville *Beethoven's Pianos* in: Denis Arnold and Nigel Fortune editors, *The Beethoven companion*, 1973, p. 47.

vi Nicolas Slonimsky, 2000, p. 178.

vii Stewart Gordon, 1996, p. 184.

viii Although interpretations on record fall outside the scope of our discussion, the following performing times for the Piano Sonata Op. 106 are of interest: Artur Schnabel 1935, 40.55; Vladimir Ashkenazy, 1980, 44.37; Emil Gilels, 1983, 48.47; and Daniel Barenboim, 2005, 50.04. Schnabel is the only pianist to have attempted to record the *Hammerklavier* Sonata adopting Beethoven's original tempo indications — see main text. Source: Basilio Morante, Professor of piano at Conservatorio Superior de Música, Valencia, Spain: *A Panoramic survey of Beethoven's Hammerklavier Sonata, Op. 106*, Website text.

ix Barry Cooper, 2000, p. 261.

x Charles Rosen, 2002, p. 224.

xi Ernst von Elterlein, 1898, 112.

xii These words are cited frequently and probably owe their origin to the recollections of Carl Czerny, the first person to perform the Op. 106. They first appear in the writings of Wilhelm von Lenz, *Beethoven*, Hamburg: Hoffman & Campe., Vol.5, p. 32. We have quoted them from Maynard Solomon, 1977, p. 300.

xiii Emily Anderson, 1961, Vol. 2, Letter No. 737, p. 654.

xiv Eric Blom, 1938, p. 202.

xv Concerning the adoption of the designation *Hammerklavier* for the Piano Sonata Op. 106, a letter written by Franz Liszt to his Polish-born, intimate friend and confident the Princess Carolyne Sayne-Wittgenstein is of interest. Writing to her on 26 October 1876 he remarks: 'I can't tell you exactly why in 1821 Beethoven put this word [*Hammerklavier*] into the title. It had been used on earlier occasions, but has fallen into disuse — just like that of *clevecin*. For years, pianoforte, or simply piano, has been used exclusively. If I'm not mistaken, the *Hammerklavier* was the transition between the harpsichord (preceded by the spinet) and the pianoforte that we know only too well.' Liszt's recollection for dates may have failed him here; in referring to 1821 he probably intended to refer to 1819, the date of publication of the *Hammerklavier* Sonata. Derived from Adrian Williams editor and translator, *Franz Liszt: Selected letters*, 1998, pp. 806–7.

xvi Carl Czerny in: Paul Badura-Skoda, 1970, p. 54.

xvii Basilio Morante, Professor of piano at Conservatorio Superior de Música, Valencia, Spain, *A Panoramic Survey of Beethoven's Hammerklavier Sonata, Op. 106*, Anonymous, *Beethoven: Piano Sonata* Op. 106, Website text, p. 237.

xviii As cited by Ernst von Elterlein, 1898, p. 112.

xix John Fuller-Maitland, *Special Issue* [Death Centenary], *The Musical Times*, London, Vol. VIII, No. 2, 1927, p. 222.

xx André Hodeir, 1975, p. 225.

xxi William Kinderman, 1997, p. 202 and p. 210.

xxii George Rochberg, 2004, pp. 176–7.

xxiii George Rochberg's visitor is not alone in likening Beethoven's *Hammerklavier* Sonata to Shakespeare's tragedy *King Lear*. Oskar Bie invokes related thoughts but in a different frame of mind, likening the sonata to a 'tragedy

xxiii towering heavenwards'. See: Oskar Bie, 1966, p. 173.
xxiv Harold Craxton and Donald Francis Tovey, [1931], *Piano Sonata in B-flat major, Op. 106*, p. 136.
xxv Michael Tilmouth, editor, Donald Francis Tovey: *The classics of music: talks, essays, and other writings previously uncollected*, 2001, p. 502.
xxvi Derived from Wayne M. Senner, Robin Wallace and William Meredith, editors, 1999, Vol. 1, p. 131.
xxvii Donald Jay Grout, and Claude V. Palisca editors, 1998, p. 648.
xxviii Ernst Bloch, 1985, pp. 117–8.
xxix Eric Blom, 1938, pp. 204–5.
xxx John Fuller-Maitland, *Special Issue* [Death Centenary], *The Musical Times*, London, Vol. VIII, No. 2, 1927, p. 222.
xxxi Ralph Vaughan Williams, 1955, p. 11.
xxxii William Kinderman, 1997, p. 202.
xxxiii Paul Griffiths in conversation with Peter Maxwell Davies on 1 February and 2 May 1980, in: Paul Griffiths, *Peter Maxwell Davies*, 1980.
xxxiv For a brief outline of the origins of the Op. 106 Piano Sonata, see: Beethoven House, Digital Archives, Library Document BH 125. See also: Barry Cooper, 1991, pp. 26–7.
xxxv Douglas Porter Johnson, editor, 1985, p. 332 and pp. 348–50. See also: Beethoven House, Digital Archives, Library Document, Sammlung H. C. Bodmer HCB Mh 94 and Barry Cooper, 1991, p. 172.
xxxvi See the historical notes accompanying: Beethoven House, Digital Archives, Library Document, Sammlung, H. C. Bodmer, HCB 6/54.
xxxvii See the historical notes accompanying: Beethoven House, Digital Archives, Library Document, Sammlung H. C. Bodmer, HCB Mh 91.
xxxviii See the historical notes accompanying: Beethoven House, Digital Archives, Library Document, BH 125 and Douglas Porter Johnson, editor, 1985, p. 220.
xxxix Douglas Porter Johnson, editor, 1985, pp. 351–4 (Vienna 45) and pp. 355–7 (Vienna 44).
xl Martin Cooper, 1970, p. 157.
xli Eric Blom, 1938, p. 203.
xlii Elliot Forbes, editor, *Thayer's life of Beethoven*, 1967, p. 714.
xliii Beethoven House, Digital Archives, Library Document, Sammlung, H. C. Bodmer, HCB 6/54 and Library Document BH 125.
xliv Michael Broyles, 1987, p. 226.
xlv Wikipedia, anonymous article: *Beethoven's Piano Sonata Op. 106*.
xlvi Martin Geck, 2003, p. 114.
xlvii Wilfrid Howard Mellers, 1957, p. 70.
xlviii Oskar Bie, 1966, p. 179 and p. 203.
xlix John V. Cockshoot, 1959, p. 71.
l Egerton C. Lowe, 1929, p. 138.
li Anton Felix Schindler, *Beethoven as I knew him*, edited by Donald W. MacArdle and translated by Constance S. Jolly from the German edition of 1860, 1966, p. 270.
lii Emily Anderson, 1961, Vol. 2, Letter No. 948, pp. 813–5. In the same letter Beethoven intimates he is planning a High Mass, the *Missa Solemnis*, to celebrate the Archduke's forthcoming ceremony of solemnization.
liii Dieter Hildebrandt, 1988, pp. 33–4.

liv Peter Clive, 2001, pp. 8–9.
lv Elliot Forbes, editor, *Thayer's life of Beethoven*, 1967, p. 714. With some variation in wording, Artaria's announcement is also published in: *Beethoven's Piano Sonatas*, Augener Edition No. 8030, London, undated. See also: Martin Cooper, 1970, p. 176.
lvi Emily Anderson, 1961, Vol. 2, Letter No. 975, pp. 845–6. For a facsimile reproduction of this letter, see: Beethoven House, Digital Archives, Library Document Sammlung H. C. Bodmer, HCB Br 4.
lvii Emily Anderson, 1961, Vol. 2, Letter No. 962, p. 832. For a facsimile reproduction of this letter, see: Beethoven House, Digital Archives, Library Document N E 44.
lviii Beethoven House, Digital Archives, Library Documents, J. van der Spek, Op. 106; H. C. Bodmer, HCB C Md 38; C106/1 and C106/7. See also: Elliot Forbes, editor, *Thayer's life of Beethoven*, 1967, p. 714; Martin Cooper, 1970, p. 176; see also the historical text to: *Beethoven's Piano Sonatas*, Augener Edition No. 8030, London, undated; and William S. Newman, 1963, p. 532.
lix Beethoven House, Digital Archives, Library Documents, Artaria, 2588.
lx William Kinderman, 1997, p. 106.
lxi Nicolas Slonimsky, 2000, p. 178.
lxii See: Peter Clive, 2001, pp. 284–7.
lxiii For a commentary on Beethoven's dealings with his English publishers see: Pamela J. Willetts, 1970, pp. 30–1. Beethoven's correspondence reveals his negotiations with publishers could at times be somewhat nefarious as he was not averse to arranging the publication rights with two publishers simultaneously, the one not being aware of the other, in order to favour his financial advantage.
lxiv Emily Anderson, 1961, Vol. 2, Letter No.898, pp. 762–3. For a facsimile of this letter, see: Beethoven House, Digital Archives, Library Document NE 211.
lxv Schlemmer was in his sixtieth year at the period of his negotiations with Beethoven. The composer showed much compassion to his favourite copyist, referring to him as 'a poor devil'. See Emily Anderson, 1961, Vol. 2, Letter No. 938, pp. 793–796. For a facsimile of this letter, see: Beethoven House, Digital Archives, Library Document Sammlung Wegeler, W 13.
lxvi Emily Anderson, 1961, Vol. 2, Letter No. 935, pp. 790–1.
lxvii *Ibid*, Vol. 2, Letter No. 939, pp. 797–805. This letter is in two parts: one formed part of the Bodmer Collection, see: Beethoven House, Digital Archives, Library Document Sammlung H. C. Bodmer, HCB Br 198. The other part is now preserved in the Fitzwilliam Museum, Cambridge.
lxviii Alfred Brendel, 2001, p. 85.
lxix Eric Blom, 1938, p. 202.
lxx William S. Newman, 1963, p. 532.
lxxi Denis Matthews, 1967, p. 48.
lxxii Martin Cooper, 1970, p. 164.
lxxiii Philip Radcliffe, *Piano music* in: *The age of Beethoven, The new Oxford history of music*, Vol. VIII, Gerald Abraham, editor, 1988, p. 147.
lxxiv John South Shedlock, 1918, p. 32.
lxxv Charles Rosen, 2002, p. 228. Maynard Solomon should also be quoted here: 'Many scholars believe Beethoven, knowing the sonata was being published correctly in Vienna, did not mind what was done with it in London.' See:

Maynard Solomon, 1977, p. 301.

[lxxv] Emily Anderson, 1961, Vol. 2, Letter No. 944, pp. 808–9. For a facsimile reproduction of this letter, see: Beethoven House, Digital Archives, Library Document Sammlung Wegeler, W 14.

[lxxvi] *Ibid*, 1961, Vol. 2, Letter No. 982, pp. 856–7.

[lxxvii] *Ibid*, 1961, Vol. 2, Letter No. 1084, pp. 953–4. See also: Alan Tyson, 1963, p. 104.

[lxxix] In England at this time the Law of Copyright required eleven copies of newly printed works to be deposited at Stationers' Hall, the London home of the Worshipful Company of Stationers and Newspaper Makers, a Livery Company that regulated the affairs of the printing and publishing industry. See: Piano Sonata Op. 78.

[lxxx] The evidence suggests Ries did in fact play a conspicuous role in the context of reconciling the textual variations between the English and continental editions of the *Hammerklavier* Sonata. See: Alan Tyson, 1963, p. 30 and Paul Badura-Skoda, 1970, p. 63.

[lxxxi] Alan Tyson, 1963, p. 143. See also: William S. Newman, 1963, p. 532.

[lxxxii] *Ibid* p. 102.

[lxxxiii] Pamela J. Willets, 1970, pp. 27–9 and Alan Tyson, 1963, pp. 102–3.

[lxxxiv] Elliot Forbes, editor, *Thayer's life of Beethoven*, 1967, p. 544. The composer Antonio Salieri also endorsed the adoption of the metronome.

[lxxxv] Emily Anderson, 1961, Vol. 2, Letter No. 940, pp. 806–7.

[lxxxvi] Alfred Brendel, 2001, p. 33.

[lxxxvii] Alfred Brendel, 2002, pp. 156–7.

[lxxxviii] Barry Cooper, 1991, p. 282.

[lxxxix] The views expressed here are an adaptation of those of the Swiss musicologist Willy Hesse as outlined in his *Ludwig van Beethoven*, Amadeus Verlag, 1988 (reprint), p. 17. They also owe a debt to Barry Cooper, see preceding reference.

[xc] Basilio Morante, Professor of piano at Conservatorio Superior de Música, Valencia, Spain: *A panoramic survey of Beethoven's Hammerklavier Sonata, Op. 106*, Website text, p. 253.

[xci] For a contemporary account of the issues raised here, see: *Was something wrong with Beethoven's metronome*, Sture Forsén et. al., Notices of the American Smithsonian Society, Vol. 60, No. 9, 2013, pp. 1146–53.

[xcii] Theodore Albrecht, translator and editor, 1996, Vol. 2, Letter No. 248, pp. 136–141. This document is of particular interest insofar as it includes a version of Maelzel's original tempo-indication chart.

[xciii] Anton Felix Schindler, *Beethoven as I knew him*, edited by Donald W. MacArdle and translated by Constance S. Jolly from the German edition of 1860, 1966, p. 425.

[xciv] *Ibid*.

[xcv] Elliot Forbes, editor, *Thayer's life of Beethoven*, 1967, p. 713.

[xcvi] As quoted in: Paul Badura-Skoda, 1970, p. 16 and the editor's note 59.

[xcvii] There are many references to the early performances of the *Hammerklavier* Sonata by Franz Liszt; see for example: Edwin Fischer, 1959, p. 103 and Brian Rees, 1999, p. 29.

[xcviii] Adrian Williams, editor and translator, *Franz Liszt: Selected letters*, 1998, p. 807.

[xcix] Alan Tyson, 1963, p. 105. The reader is referred to the website text *Henri*

    Mortier de Fontaine for an account of this remarkable artist's life and work.
[c] James R. Sterndale Bennett, 1907, pp. 32–3.
[ci] Pamela J. Willets, 1970, pp. 54–5.
[cii] Ferdinand Hiller, *Mendelssohn: Letters and recollections*, 1972, pp. 389–90.
[ciii] Charles L. Graves, 1903, p. 93.
[civ] Brian Rees, 1999, p. 110.
[cv] William Ashton Ellis, *Richard Wagner's prose works: Vol.1, The art-work of the future*, edited and translated by William Ashton Ellis, 1895 p. 240.
[cvi] Adrian Williams, *Portrait of Liszt: by himself and his contemporaries*, 1990, p. 333.
[cvii] *Ibid*, pp. 436–8.
[cviii] Bernard Shaw, *How to become a musical critic*, 1960 (reprint), p. 117.
[cix] Peter Heyworth, *Otto Klemperer, his life and times*, 2 Vols. 1983–1996, derived from Vol. 1, pp. 16–17.
[cx] Arthur Rubinstein, 1973, p. 339 and p. 355.
[cxi] Elizabeth Wilson, *Shostakovich: a life remembered*, 1994, p. 56.
[cxii] Peter Hill, *The Messiaen companion*, 1995, p. 295.
[cxiii] David Dubal, *The world of the concert pianist*, 1985, p. 75.
[cxiv] Michael Broyles, 1987, p. 226.
[cxv] Felix Weingartner, Preface to *Sonate für das Hammerklavier, Op. 106, für Orchestra*, Breitkopf & Härtel, Leipzig, 1926. Charles Rosen was wary of the virtues of attempting to orchestrate Beethoven's Piano Sonata Op. 106 for the reasons he explains: 'The opening bars of the *Hammerklavier* demonstrate the relation between musical idea and instrumental colour. The motif is projected in the first bar over the lower, middle and high registers, encompassing the greatest part of the audible range. In order to function, this projection requires single tone colour in all three registers, preferably a neutral colour as only the piano can give. That is why an attempt, like Weingartner's, to orchestrate this opening is so disastrous: the orchestra needs many instruments and a variety of tone colours to achieve the single, unified gesture of the pianist.' Charles Rosen, 1995, p. 30.
[cxvi] Eric Blom, 1938, p. 205.
[cxvii] Denis Matthews, 1967, p. 97.
[cxviii] Carl Czerny in: Paul Badura-Skoda, 1970, p. 53.
[cxix] Harold Craxton and Donald Francis Tovey, [1931], *Piano Sonata in B-flat major, Op. 106*, p. 136.
[cxx] Alfred Brendel, 2001, p. 83.
[cxxi] Charles Rosen, 2002, p. 225.
[cxxii] As quoted in: H. C. Robbins Landon 1970, p. 157.
[cxxiii] Emily Anderson, 1961, Vol. 2, Letter No. 805, p. 701.
[cxxiv] *Ibid*, 1961, Vol. 2, Letter No. 816, pp. 708–9.
[cxxv] *Ibid*, 1961, Vol. 2, Letter No. 895, pp. 759–60.
[cxxvi] Elliot Forbes, editor, *Thayer's life of Beethoven*, 1967, p. 700 and p. 713.
[cxxvii] Emily Anderson, 1961, Vol. 2, Letter No. 903, pp. 766–7. For a detailed account of Beethoven's health and illnesses at this period see: Anton Neumayr, *Music and medicine*, 1994-1997, pp. 268–9.
[cxxviii] *Ibid*, 1961, Vol. 2, Letter No. 785, pp. 685–6. Nanette was responsible for many of the business dealings in the family firm, whilst Johann concerned himself with the more technical/manufacturing side of things.

cxxix Anton Neumayr, 1994-1997, pp. 289–9. See also: Anton Felix Schindler, *Beethoven as I knew him*, edited by Donald W. MacArdle and translated by Constance S. Jolly from the German edition of 1860, 1966, pp, 62–3.

cxxx Mälzel evolved a number of designs. The first was a conical-shaped device made from copper; another was a piped-shaped trumpet with a perforated cover – to keep insects out!; and two others were of similar design but supplied with a headpiece to help bear their weight. They are thought to have been of little use but Beethoven continued to place his trust in future innovations from which he did not, alas, live to benefit. Beethoven's hearing aids are illustrated on the Beethoven House, Digital Archives, Library Document, R 2. See also: Derek Melville in: Denis Arnold and Nigel Fortune, editors, 1973, plate 8.

cxxxi Emily Anderson, 1961, Vol. 2, Letter No. 910, pp. 775–6. Czerny went on to become one of the most celebrated ad sought-after teachers of piano of his age, writing hundreds of technical studies with the aim of assisting pianists to improve their finger dexterity at the keyboard.

cxxxii *Ibid*, 1961, Vol. 2, Letter No. 886, p. 752.

cxxxiii Peter Charlton, website text: *Works of Ludwig van Beethoven*. For a comprehensive account of Beethoven's *Tegebuch* (diary) see: Maynard Solomon, *Beethoven Essays*, 1990.

cxxxiv For a comprehensive account of the troubled relationship between Beethoven and his nephew Karl, see: Peter Clive, 2001, pp. 17–20.

cxxxv Martin Cooper, 1970, p. 158.

cxxxvi Maynard Solomon, 1977, p. 250.

cxxxvii *Beethoven: First recording of Symphony No. 10 in E flat, 1st movement*; London Symphony Orchestra conducted by Wyn Morris; Carlton Classics; ASIN: B000003YPG.

cxxxviii Theodre Albrecht, translator and editor, 1996, Vol. 2, Letter No. 249, pp. 142–7.

cxxxix Emily Anderson, 1961, Vol. 2, Letter No. 884, pp. 748–9 and Letter No. 885, pp. 750–2.

cxl Theodore Albrecht, translator and editor, 1996, Vol. 2, Letter No. 245, pp. 133–4.

cxli *Ibid*, Vol. 2, Letter No. 250, pp. 147–8.

cxlii Emily Anderson, 1961, Vol. 2, Letter No. 886, pp. 822–3.

cxliii John Hamilton Warrack, 1981, p. 270.

cxliv Derived from Wayne M. Senner, Robin Wallace and William Meredith, editors, 1999, Vol. 1, p. 47.

cxlv Emily Anderson, 1961, Vol. 2, Letter No. 807, pp. 702–3.

cxlvi Derek Melville, *Beethoven's pianos* in: Denis Arnold and Nigel Fortune, editors *The Beethoven companion*, 1973, p. 47 and pp. 50–1. Melville describes a Broadwood piano, No. 8074, similar to Beethoven's in the Colt Collection that he maintains, having played the instruments in question, to be 'a very fine piano and far superior in tone to the four-stringed Graf [another instrument with which Beethoven was familiar]'. He adds: 'There is a similar model in the Germanisches Museum, Nuremburg, but it is not equal to the one in the Colt Collection ... There seems little doubt Beethoven preferred the Broadwood to all his other pianos.'

cxlvii Derived from Wayne M. Senner, Robin Wallace and William Meredith, editors, 1999, Vol. 1, p. 43.

cxlviii Dieter Hildebrandt, 1988, p. 27.

cxlix See: David Wainright, *Broadwood by appointment*, The Book Service, 1982 and Reginald Gerig, *Famous pianists and their technique*, Washington: R. B. Luce, 1974, p. 44. See also: Derek Melville, *Beethoven's pianos* (Plate 4a) in: Denis Arnold and Nigel Fortune, editors, *The Beethoven companion*, 1973.

cl Theodore Albrecht, translator and editor, 1996, Vol. 2, Letter No. 252, pp. 149–50.

cli Emily Anderson, 1961, Vol. 2, Letter No. 891, pp. 755–6. See also: Dieter Hiderbrandt, *Pianoforte: A social history of the piano*, 1988, pp. 87–8 and Edwin Marshall *Good, Giraffes, black dragons and other pianos: a technological history from Cristofori to the modern concert grand*, 1982, pp. 83–8.

clii Emily Anderson, 1961, Vol. 2, Letter, No. 890, pp. 754–5. For a facsimile reproduction of this letter see: Beethoven House, Digital Archives, Library Documents, NE 196. See also: Dieter Hildebrandt, 1988, p. 27.

cliii Elliot Forbes, editor, *Thayer's life of Beethoven*, 1967, p. 695. See also: Derek Melville, *Beethoven's pianos*, in: Denis Arnold and Nigel Fortune, editors, 1973, p. 65.

cliv Dieter Hildebrandt, 1988, pp. 32–3.

clv Ludwig Nohl, *Beethoven depicted by his contemporaries*, 1880, pp. 162–6. For a facsimile reproduction of Kloeber's portrait, see: Beethoven House, Digital Archives, Library Documents NE 168 and B 1.

clvi H. C. Robbins Landon, 1970, p. 16 and plate 11.

clvii *Ibid*, pp. 16–17 and plate 12. See also: Beethoven House, Digital Archives, Library Documents, B 1083/c.

clviii Carl Dahlhaus, *Nineteenth-century music*, Translated by J. Bradford Robinson, 1989, p. 29.

clix Paul Bekker, 1925, p. 133. Bekker refers to 'moral law' rather than 'moral principal'. For the context of Beethoven's quoted words, see: Emily Anderson, 1961, Vol. 1, Letter No. 30, p. 32.

clx Oskar Bie, 1966, p. 170.

clxi Wilfrid Howard Mellers, 1957, p. 70.

clxii Peter Charlton, website text: *Works of Ludwig van Beethoven*.

clxiii Harold Craxton and Donald Francis Tovey, [1931], *Piano Sonata in B-flat major, Op. 106*, p. 136.

clxiv Igor Stravinsky, 1972, p. 272.

clxv Michael Broyles, 1987, p. 226.

clxvi Gregor-Dellin and Dietrich Mack, editors, Cosima *Wagner's diaries, Vol. 1, 1869 - 1877*, 1978–1980, p. 551.

clxvii Edwin Fischer, 1959, p. 103.

clxviii Barry Cooper, 2000, p. 260. The same spirit is also preserved in the declamatory opening to the *Missa Solemnis*.

clxix Denis Matthews, 1967, p. 48 and p. 95.

clxx Ernst von Elterlein, 1898, p. 106.

clxxi Igor Stravinsky, 1972, p. 269. The full quotation reads, 'most players succeed in making the opening of the *Hammerklavier* sound not merely deliberated but *recherché*, which is not, I think, the most fitting way of dealing with a bolt from the blue'.

clxxii Eric Blom, 1938, p. 205.

clxxiii Donald Wright, editor, *Cardus on music: a centenary collection*, 1988, p. 45.

clxxiv For an accessible account of this anecdote see: David Dubal in conversation with Charles Rosen, in: David Dubal, *The world of the concert pianist*, 1985,

p. 273.

[clxxv] David Dubal in conversation with Charles Rosen, in: David Dubal, *The world of the concert pianist*, 1985, p. 273.

[clxxvi] Daniel Barenboim, 1991, p. 27.

[clxxvii] Andrea Olmstead, *Conversations with Roger Sessions*, 1987, pp. 99–100. Donald Tovey was unequivocal here, remarking: 'Nobody has ever had the temerity to suggest that the mighty initial leap should be made easy by taking the chord in the right hand.' Harold Craxton and Donald Francis Tovey, [1931], *Piano Sonata in B-flat major, Op. 106*, p. 137.

[clxxviii] Adrian Williams, *Portrait of Liszt: by himself and his contemporaries*, 1990, p. 2.

[clxxix] Stewart Gordon, 1996, p. 185.

[clxxx] As quoted in: Leonard Stein, 1975, p. 398.

[clxxxi] Pamela J. Willets, 1970, pp. 11–12. The manuscript in question is MS. 14396, f. 30.

[clxxxii] Edwin Fischer, 1959, p. 104.

[clxxxiii] Romain Rolland, 1917, p. 161

[clxxxiv] Eric Blom, 1938, pp. 205–6.

[clxxxv] Barry Cooper, 2000, p. 261.

[clxxxvi] Alfred Brendel, 2001, p. 84.

[clxxxvii] Ian Kemp, *Tippett: the composer and his music*, 1984, p. 90.

[clxxxviii] Andrew Thomson, *Vincent d'Indy and his world*, 1996, pp. 130–1.

[clxxxix] Ernst von Elterlein, 1898, p. 105.

[cxc] Alfred Brendel, in conversation with Martin Meyer in: Alfred Brendel, 2002, p. 74.

[cxci] Ernst von Elterlein, 1898, p. 105.

[cxcii] Philip Radcliffe, *Piano music* in: *The age of Beethoven, The new Oxford history of music*, Vol. VIII, Gerald Abraham editor, 1988, p. 147.

[cxciii] Denis Matthews, 1967, p. 49.

[cxciv] Theodor W. Adorno, 1998, p. 65.

[cxcv] As quoted by Sture Forsén et. al. in: *Was something wrong with Beethoven's metronome?*, Notices of the AMS [American Smithsonian Society], 2013, Vol. 60, No. 9, pp. 1146–53.

[cxcvi] Edwin Fischer, 1959, p. 103.

[cxcvii] Martin Cooper, 1970, p. 159. Regarding the reference in the text to Schnabel's facility at the keyboard, it should be remembered he was slight in physical stature with correspondingly small hands; consequently he had to convert chords, outside his span, into arpeggios.

[cxcviii] Alfred Brendel, 2001, p. 85 and 2002, p. 157.

[cxcix] Joseph Horowitz, *Conversations with Arrau*, 1982, pp. 122–3.

[cc] Charles Rosen, 2002, p .219.

[cci] Adrian Williams, *Portrait of Liszt: by himself and his contemporaries*, 1990, pp. 79–80. The original review appeared in the *Revue et gazette musicale* 12 June 1836.

[ccii] *Ibid*, pp. 342–4. Wendelin Weissheimer was a favourite pupil of Liszt with whom he studied composition.

[cciii] *Ibid*, pp. 620–2.

[cciv] Carl Czerny in: Paul Badura-Skoda, 1970, p. 54.

[ccv] Martin Cooper, 1970, p. 160.

[ccvi] Donald Francis Tovey: *The classics of music: talks, essays, and other writings*

ccvi *previously uncollected*, in: Michael Tilmouth, editor, 2001, p. 53. Tovey's 'two great chords' are worthy of comment. Beethoven requires them to be played *fortissimo* and designates them *ff* – a rare example in his piano-sonata writing. Furthermore, he precedes them with a penultimate bar to be played *pianissimo* that he designates *ppp* – an equally rare example in the piano sonatas.

ccvii Denis Matthews, 1967, p. 49.
ccviii Charles Rosen, 2002, p. 223.
ccix Elterlein Ernst von, 1898, pp. 107–8.
ccx Denis Matthews, 1967, p. 49.
ccxi Romain Rolland, 1917, p. 161.
ccxii Paul Bekker, 1925, 134.
ccxiii Beethoven House, Digital Archives, Library Document, Sammlung H. C. Bodmer, HCB Mh 91.
ccxiv Martin Cooper, 1970, p. 162.
ccxv Michael Tilmouth, editor, Donald Francis Tovey: *The classics of music: talks, essays, and other writings previously uncollected*, 2001, p. 53.
ccxvi Matthew Rye, *Notes to the BBC Radio Three Beethoven experience*, Friday 10 June 2005, www.bbc.co.uk/radio3/Beethoven
ccxvii Martin Cooper, 1970, p. 162.
ccxviii Dieter Hildebrandt, 1988, pp. 32–3.
ccxix Edwin Fischer, 1959, p. 105.
ccxx Carl Czerny in: Paul Badura-Skoda, 1970, p. 54.
ccxxi Harold Craxton and Donald Francis Tovey, [1931], *Piano Sonata in B-flat major, Op. 106*, p. 139.
ccxxii Martin Cooper, 1970, pp. 164–5.
ccxxiii Edwin Fischer, 1959, p. 106.
ccxxiv Romain Rolland, 1916, p. 161.
ccxxv Philip Radcliffe, *Piano music* in: *The age of Beethoven, The new Oxford history of music*, Vol. VIII, Gerald Abraham editor, 1988, p. 147.
ccxxvi Theodor W. Adorno, 1998, p. 88.
ccxxvii Barry Cooper, 2000, p. 262.
ccxxviii Adapted, in part, from Denis Matthews, 1967, p. 50.
ccxxix Joseph Horowitz, *Conversations with Arrau*, 1982, p. 244.
ccxxx Stewart Gordon, 1996, p. 187.
ccxxxi As quoted in: Anton Neumayr, *Music and medicine*, 1994-1997, p. 268.
ccxxxii Edwin Fischer, 1959, p. 106. The quotations attributed to Lenz and Sullivan are derived from Fischer's text.
ccxxxiii Wilfrid Howard Mellers, 1957, p. 71. See also: Stewart Gordon, 1996, p. 186.
ccxxxiv Paul Bekker, 1925, p. 133.
ccxxxv Matthew Rye, *Notes to the BBC Radio Three Beethoven experience*, Friday 10 June 2005, www.bbc.co.uk/radio3/Beethoven
ccxxxvi Ernst von Elterlein, 1898, p. 108.
ccxxxvii Egerton C. Lowe 1929, p. 139.
ccxxxviii Donald Francis Tovey: *The classics of music: talks, essays, and other writings previously uncollected*, in Michael Tilmouth, editor, 2001, p. 55.
ccxxxix Michael Broyles, 1987, p. 228.
ccxl Matthew Rye, *Notes to the BBC Radio Three Beethoven Experience*, Friday

10 June 2005, www.bbc.co.uk/radio3/Beethoven
ccxli William Kinderman, 1997, p. 120.
ccxlii Oskar Bie, 1966, p. 180.
ccxliii Ernst von Elterlein, 1898, pp. 108–9.
ccxliv Eric Blom, 1938, p. 204. If Blom is to be believed, what he has to say is all the more remarkable, since it is well documented that Chopin was not a particular admirer of Beethoven's writing for the piano.
ccxlv Denis Matthews, 1967, p. 50.
ccxlvi Martin Cooper, 1970, p. 166.
ccxlvii Beethoven House, Digital Archives, Library Document, NE 193. For a long time the leaf in question was in a private collection and only came into the possession of the Beethoven House in 1992.
ccxlviii Beethoven House, Digital Archives, Library Document, Sammlung H. C. Bodmer HCB BSk 8/56.
ccxlix Michael Tilmouth, editor, Donald Francis Tovey: *The classics of music: talks, essays, and other writings previously uncollected*, 2001, p. 55.
ccl Denis Matthews, 1967, p. 50.
ccli Edwin Fischer, 1959, p. 106.
cclii Ernst von Elterlein, 1898, pp. 109–10.
ccliii Theodor W. Adorno, 1998, p. 128.
ccliv Igor Stravinsky, 1972, p. 272.
cclv Luciano Berio: *Two interviews with Rossana Dalmonte and Bálint András Varga*, Osmond-Smith, editor and translator, 1985, p. 67.
cclvi Ernst von Elterlein, 1898, p. 108.
cclvii Philip Radcliffe, *Piano music* in: *The age of Beethoven*, *The new Oxford history of music*, Vol. VIII, Gerald Abraham, editor, 1988, p. 148.
cclviii Charles Rosen, 2002, p. 225.
cclix Michael Broyles, 1987, p. 228.
cclx Franz Wegeler, *Remembering Beethoven: the biographical notes of Franz Wegeler and Ferdinand Ries*, 1838–45, reprint 1988, pp. 94–5.
cclxi Paul Henry Lang, 1997, p. 177.
cclxii Ernst von Elterlein, 1898, p. 110.
cclxiii Barry Cooper, 2000, p. vii.
cclxiv Donald Francis Tovey: *The classics of music: talks, essays, and other writings previously uncollected*, in: Michael Tilmouth, editor, 2001, p. 56.
cclxv Martin Cooper, 1970, p. 166.
cclxvi Edwin Fischer, 1959, p. 106.
cclxvii Philip Radcliffe, *Piano music* in: *The age of Beethoven*, *The new Oxford history of music*, Vol. VIII, Gerald Abraham, editor, 1988, p. 147.
cclxviii William Kinderman, 1997, p. 206.
cclxix As quoted in: Ernst von Elterlein, 1898, p. 110.
cclxx The original source is *Revue et gazette musicale* 12 June 1836, as quoted in: Adrian Williams, *Portrait of Liszt: by himself and his contemporaries*, 1990, pp. 79–80.
cclxxi *Ibid*, pp. 342–4.
cclxxii Derived from Alan Walker, *Franz Liszt. Volume 3, The final years, 1861–1886*, 1997, note 41, p. 317. See also: Adrian Williams, 1990, pp. 525–6.

[cclxiii] Adrian Williams, 1990, pp. 551–2.
[cclxiv] *Ibid*, pp. 608–9.
[cclxv] Felix Weingartner, 1937, pp. 88–9.
[cclxvi] Arthur Rubinstein, 1973, p. 159 and p. 399.
[cclxvii] Vincent d'Indy, as quoted in: *Cardus on music: a centenary collection*, Donald Wright, editor, 1988, p. 45.
[cclxviii] Martin Cooper, 1970, p. 165.
[cclxix] Carl Czerny in: Paul Badura-Skoda, 1970, p. 54.
[cclxx] Egerton C. Lowe, 1929, p. 139.
[cclxxi] Edwin Fischer, 1959, p. 106.
[cclxxii] Alfred Brendel, 2001, p. 84.
[cclxxiii] Igor Stravinsky, 1972, pp. 267–8.
[cclxxiv] Stewart Gordon, 1996, p. 184.
[cclxxv] John Fuller-Maitland, *Special Issue* [Death Centenary], *The Musical Times*, London, Vol. VIII, No. 2, 1927, p. 222.
[cclxxvi] Ernst von Elterlein, 1898, p. 111.
[cclxxvii] For an analysis of the construction of the opening bars see: Egerton C. Lowe, 1929, p. 138.
[cclxxviii] Oskar Bie, 1966, p. 180.
[cclxxix] As remarked by Stephan Playstow in his contribution to the BBC series *Building a Library*, The *Hammerklavier* Sonata. For details, see: BBC website *Building a Library*. Solomon expresses similar thoughts: '[Chaos] strives for lucid formation as in the transition to the Fugue of the *Hammerklavier* Sonata and in the opening of the finale of the Ninth Symphony.' Maynard Solomon, 1977, p. 294.
[ccxc] Stewart Gordon, 1996, p. 188.
[ccxci] Michael Tilmouth, editor, Donald Francis Tovey: *The classics of music: talks, essays, and other writings previously uncollected*, 2001, p. 59.
[ccxcii] As quoted by Ernst von Elterlein, 1898, p. 111.
[ccxciii] Barry Cooper, 2000, p. 262.
[ccxciv] Daniel Albrecht, editor, *Modernism and music: an anthology of sources*, 2004, p. 142. The original source is Ferruccio Busoni, *Sketch of a new aesthetic of music*, 1907.
[ccxcv] Adrian Williams, *Portrait of Liszt: by himself and his contemporaries*, 1990, pp. 342–4.
[ccxcvi] Edwin Fischer, 1959, p. 107.
[ccxcvii] Oskar Bie, 1966, p. 180.
[ccxcviii] Edwin Fischer, 1959, pp. 107–8.
[ccxcix] Donald Francis Tovey: *The classics of music: talks, essays, and other writings previously uncollected*, in Michael Tilmouth, editor, 2001, p. 59.
[ccc] Ernst von Elterlein, 1898, p. 110.
[ccci] The origins of this source have not been identified.
[cccii] Alfred Brendel, 2001, p. 84.
[ccciii] Romain Rolland, 1917, p. 162.
[ccciv] Oskar Bie, 1966, p. 180.
[cccv] As quoted in: Maynard. Solomon, 1977, p. 300. The original source is: Walter Riezler, *Beethoven*, with an Introduction by Wilhelm Furtwängler, New York, E. P. Dutton & Co., 1938.
[cccvi] William S. Newman, 1963, p. 530.

ccvii Ernst von Elterlein, 1898, p. 112.
ccviii Martin Cooper, 1970, p. 171.
ccix Barry Cooper, 1991, p. 64.
ccx André Hodeir, 1975, p. 38.
ccxi William Kinderman, 1997, p. 210.
ccxii Denis Matthews, 1972, p. 180.
ccxiii As quoted by Peter Charlton, website text: *The works of Ludwig van Beethoven*. The original quotation is derived from J. W. N. Sullivan, *Beethoven; his spiritual development*, 1927.
ccxiv Anton Neumayr, 1994–97, p. 268.
ccxv Christopher Headington, 1974, p. 173.
ccxvi William Kinderman, 1997, p. 209.
ccxvii Ernst von Elterlein, 1898, p. 111.
ccxviii Alec Harman, with Anthony Milner and Wilfrid Mellers, 1988, p. 649.
ccxix Paul Bekker, 1925, p. 133.
ccxx Maynard Solomon, 1977, p. 300.
ccxxi Joseph Horowitz, *Conversations with Arrau*, 1982, p. 244.
ccxxii Igor Stravinsky, 1972, p. 272.
ccxxiii Denis Matthews, 1967, p. 51.
ccxxiv As quoted in: Michael Tilmouth, editor, Donald Francis Tovey: *The classics of music: talks, essays, and other writings previously uncollected*, 2001, p. 659. Tovey's detailed analysis of the *Hammerklavier* Sonata is given at pp. 43–66.
ccxxv Martin Cooper, 1970, p. 171.
ccxxvi Eric Blom, 1938, p. 204.
ccxxvii Barry Cooper, 1991, p. 64.
ccxxviii Douglas Porter Johnson, editor, 1985, p. 220.
ccxxix See: the commentary to Beethoven House, Digital Archives, Library Document, Sammlung H. C. Bodmer, HCB Mh 93.
ccxxx Edward T. Cone, editor, *Roger Sessions on music: collected essays*, 1979, p. 21. Sessions elaborated his views in a further series of lectures he gave at the Juilliard School of Music in the summer of 1949. In the third of these he remarked: 'In an early sketch for the introduction to the last movement of the *Hammerklavier* Sonata, Beethoven has made brief and obviously rapid notes indicating the general character of the various short episodes that make up the whole passage, and in several cases where the musical line moves from a very low note to a very important high one, he has simply indicated the note of departure and the note of destination, and connected them with a "wavy line". In this way he has indicated in the most rapid fashion the general shape he had in mind. In the final version, the early sketch is entirely recognizable except for the fact that ... the notes of destination have been changed, quite clearly to intensify the whole passage, and the episodes have been elaborated.' Derived from the same source at pp. 54–5.
ccxxxi Stewart Gordon, 1996, p. 188.
ccxxxii Alec Harman, with Anthony Milner and Wilfrid Mellers, 1988, pp. 649–50.
ccxxxiii For a commentary on Beethoven's early grounding in counterpoint see: Barry Cooper, 1991, p. 203.
ccxxxiv Emily Anderson, 1961, Vol. 1, Letter No. 220, pp. 233–6.
ccxxxv Beethoven House, Digital Archives, Library Document, Sammlung H. C. Bodmer, HCB Mh 43.
ccxxxvi Charles Rosen, 2002, p. 227.

cccxxxvi   See: Martin Cooper, 1970, p. 159.
cccxxxvii With acknowledgment to Barry Cooper, 1991, p. 242 and Peter Charlton, *Works of Ludwig van Beethoven*, website text.
cccxxxix   Ernst von Elterlein, 1898, p. 111.
cccxl   Pierre Boulez, 1991, p. 231.
cccxli   Apparently Wagner found the final movement of the *Hammerklavier* Sonata too long for his taste – which is somewhat surprising, given the length of his own music dramas. A diary entry of Cosima Wagner's, from 10 June 1870, recalls when she and her husband fell into conversation: 'We then started talking about Beethoven, and Richard says: "The only time Beethoven was not concise is in the finale of the great B-flat major sonata, which your father [Franz Liszt] alone can play, and in which I get more enjoyment out of his virtuosity than out of what was being played".' It would seem, on this occasion, Cosima did not share her distinguished husband's views since she added: '[It] grieves me to observe that what one of the greatest dose is not always acceptable to another of the greatest, even in his most mature works.' Gregor-Dellin and Dietrich Mack, editors, *Cosima Wagner's diaries, Vol. 1 1869-1877*, 1978-1980, p. 231.
cccxlii   Matthew Rye, *Notes to the BBC Radio Three Beethoven experience*, Friday 10 June 2005, www.bbc.co.uk/radio3/Beethoven
cccxliii   Rey M. Longyear, *Beethoven and Romantic Irony*, in: Paul Henry Lang, 1971, p. 154.
cccxliv   Michael Tilmouth, editor, Donald Francis Tovey: *The classics of music: talks, essays, and other writings previously uncollected*, 2001, p. 60.
cccxlv   Nicolas Slonimsky, *The great composers and their works*, edited by Electra Slonimsky Yourke, 2000, p. 179. For a detailed commentary on Beethoven's compositional procedures in the *Hammerklavier* Sonata, see: John V. Cockshoot, 1959, pp. 70–94.
cccxlvi   Stewart Gordon, 1996, p. 188.
cccxlvii   Marion M. Scott, 1940, p. 145.
cccxlviii Ernst von Elterlein, 1898, p. 111.
cccxlix   John V. Cockshoot, 1959, p. 86.
cccl   Romain Rolland, 1917, p. 162.
cccli   Edwin Fischer, 1959, p. 108.
ccclii   Recalled in: Adrian Williams, *Portrait of Liszt: by himself and his contemporaries*, 1990, pp. 342–4.
cccliii   As recounted in David Dubal, editor, *Remembering Horowitz: 125 pianists recall a legend*, 1993, p. 281.
cccliv   Stewart Gordon, 1996, p. 184.
ccclv   Alec Harman, with Anthony Milner and Wilfrid Mellers, 1988, p. 650.
ccclvi   Philip Radcliffe, *Piano music* in: *The age of Beethoven, The new Oxford history of music*, Vol. VIII, Gerald Abraham, editor, 1988, p. 148.
ccclvii   Edward T. Cone, 1972, p. 130.
ccclviii   Charles. Rosen, 2002, p. 219.
ccclix   Harold Craxton and Donald Francis Tovey, [1931], *Piano Sonata in B-flat major, Op. 106*, p. 141.
ccclx   Nicolas Slonimsky, 2000, p. 179.
ccclxi   Harold Craxton and Donald Francis Tovey, [1931], *Piano Sonata in B-flat major, Op. 106*, p. 136.
ccclxii   Carl Czerny in: Paul Badura-Skoda, 1970, pp. 54–5.
ccclxiii   Denis Matthews, 1967, p. 51.

PIANO SONATA IN E MAJOR, OP. 109

'Beethoven destroyed the symphonic multiplicity of the pianoforte once for all; he carried it back to enlargement upon a single poetic subject (corresponding to improvisation), which he now unfolded with all the force of a sure expression-technique of motive, in a blend of styles of chamber music and improvisation. We have the results in [the] three last sonatas, Opp. 109, 110 and 111.'

Paul Bekker, *Beethoven*, 1925, p. 137.

'Following the terrific *Hammerklavier*, the Sonata in E major, Op. 109, and the Sonata in A-flat major, Op. 110, seem like havens of the islands of the blest.'

Marion M. Scott, Beethoven, The Master Musicians, 1940, p. 146.

> 'The work [Op.109] has the charm and luminosity of an old sweetheart met again after twenty years, with the same noble features but spiritualized and more transparent.'

Edwin Fischer, *Beethoven's Pianoforte Sonatas: a Guide for Students & Amateurs*, 1959, p. 108.

> 'Three flowers bloom in this late garden, three unique documents of a pure masterdom: the "playing" Sonata [Op. 109], the "landscape" Sonata [Op. 110], and the "life" Sonata [Op. 111]. The first is on the heights of pure technique, the second is a clarified objective picture, the third is pure subjective inwardness.'

Oskar Bie, *A History of the Pianoforte and Pianoforte Players*, 1966, p. 180.

> '[In] the last three sonatas of all Beethoven achieved a new conciseness, a new intimacy, a new warmth of heart. Opp. 109, 110 and 111 have been called a trilogy, but it would be safer to call them complimentary; they all have traditional processes — sonata form, variations, fugue — to highly individual ends.'

Denis Matthews, *Keyboard Music*, 1972, p. 180.

> 'This sonata [Op. 109] is like an angel with a

demon in the middle.'

Alfred Brendel in conversation with David Dubal in: David Dubal, *The World of the Concert Pianist*, 1985, p. 110.

> 'The E major Sonata Op. 109, the first of the three sonatas that occupied Beethoven during 1820–21, is also perhaps the most easily perceived of this trio. Like Emmanuel Bach in old age, Beethoven is the consummate master of his material who does not want to do the same thing twice.'

Philip G. Downs, *Classical Music: the Era of Haydn, Mozart, and Beethoven*, 1992, p. 606.

> 'Beethoven composed between 1820 and 1822: the Sonatas in E major, Op. 109, in A-flat major, Op. 110, and in C minor, Op. 111. In these works, issues of contrast and continuity are pursued in unique and far-reaching ways. In their narrative designs, each of these three sonatas ultimately unfold toward a condition of lyric euphoria, which is outwardly manifested in the employment of slow variations as the basis for the finales of Op. 109 and Op. 111.'

William Kinderman, *Contrast and Continuity in Beethoven's Creative Process*, in: Scott G. Burnham, and Michael P. Steinberg, editors, *Beethoven and his World*, 2000, p. 207.

> 'Perhaps the most unusual aspect of the Sonata [Op. 109] is how unassuming on the surface are

> the opening of the first movement and the end
> of the last, how apparently modest, and yet how
> much they demand and reward meditation.'

Charles Rosen, *Beethoven's Piano Sonatas: a Short Companion*, 2002, p. 234.

When Beethoven completed his monumental Piano Sonata Op. 106, in the estimation of many authorities he had reached 'the furthest attainable summit of pianistic expression'. However, with the Mount Everest of piano sonatas conquered, there still remained the equivalent, in mountaineering terms, of the K2 range of summits to surmount. 'Beethoven had achieved a goal; to him no further advance was conceivable. But he had by no means exhausted the possibilities of the most problematic, yet most stimulating, of instruments. He had written his last symphonic concert-sonata, but there remained the fantasia and the chamber sonatas.'[i] In the opinion of Igor Stravinsky: 'The three final sonatas represent a great ventilation in style — what a more Augustan writer would describe as a rediscovery of the classical spirit ... Beethoven's path of discovery tended, at the end, to lead more and more to contrapuntal means, homophonic thematic developments giving way to thematic transformation in variation and fugue.'[ii]

On his final pianistic path of discovery 'Beethoven turned his attention to the three-movement and the two-movement forms, and as such we have his last will and testament as a pianoforte composer, a document which marks not only an end, like Op. 106, but which is significant for the future.'[iii] Beethoven's 'last will and testament' took the form of the Piano Sonatas Opp. 109, 110 and 111. 'All three show Beethoven breaking the bounds of the traditional sonata ... For example, variation technique and fugue usurp the more familiar "sonata form", and the layout of the sonatas has ... become ... more condensed.' In the words of Matthew Rye: 'By the time of his last three sonatas ... [Beethoven] had turned the medium from what originally had been an early form of home entertainment into a profound, deeply personal statement. All three seem to inhabit a world away from the world, going beyond the mere exploration of pianistic technique to express something inward and introspective in Beethoven's creative personality.'[iv]

Beethoven's biographer Anton Schindler states: 'While composing music for the pianoforte, the master would often go to the instrument and try certain passages, especially those that might present difficulties in performance.' Beethoven's pupil Carl Czerny has much the same to say of his teacher: 'Beethoven was accustomed to composing everything with the aid of the piano, and would try out a given passage countless times; one can imagine, then, what a difference it made when his deafness made that impossible. Therefore the uncomfortable keyboard writing of his sonatas, therefore the harshness of the harmony; and as Beethoven himself admitted in confidence, therefore the lack of easy continuity and the departure from the older form.'[v] Schindler's recollections continue: 'At such times he was totally oblivious of anyone present. To this circumstance I owe my acquaintance with the complete Sonatas Opp. 109, 110 and parts of the last Sonata Op. 111.' He alleges Beethoven composed his last three sonatas 'at a single stroke'[vi] but this is an overstatement and should be considered to be more of a rhetorical remark or, as Paul Bekker puts it, *cum grano salis* – 'with a grain of salt' – sceptically.[vii] These three compositions occupied Beethoven over a two-year period. He started work on Op. 109 in the spring of 1820 with the piece being ready to submit to his publisher by the autumn. He then turned his attention to the Bagatelles Op. 119 and the *Missa Solemnis* Op. 123. The Mass should have already been completed in fulfilment of obligations into which the composer had entered in connection with celebrations planned for the enthronement of his pupil Rudolph as Archbishop of Olmütz. Beethoven's sketchbooks reveal him working on the Piano Sonata Op 110 in 1821 and Op. 111 by the beginning of 1822.[viii]

Schindler's remark 'at a single stroke' was in part a response to what a music critic had written about Beethoven in issue XXIII of the *Allgemeine musikalische Zeitung* of 1821. Hearing of Beethoven's pre-occupation with song-settings, the critic wrote: 'Beethoven now busies himself, as Papa Haydn once did, with arrangements of Scottish songs. He is apparently quite incapable of greater accomplishments.' According to Schindler, such rumours, concerning the composer's intellectual exhaustion, 'seemed only to amuse Beethoven' who responded: 'Just wait; you'll soon change your tune!'[ix] In due course the *Allgemeine musikalische Zeitung* did indeed change its tune. Another music critic writing in issue XXVI of the *AmZ* of 1824 made a survey of Beethoven's pianos sonatas in what would be its longest contemporary review of his keyboard compositions. He enthused: 'The composer struck along new paths some thirty years ago.' He acknowledged his works 'engendered hostility on the way' but conceded 'all that is now stilled for today, no other can touch this great spirit'. In particular, he praised 'the structure, melody, harmony, and rhythm' of the last three sonatas. Whilst acknowledging their 'many technical difficulties' he re-assured the would-be performer that 'non of these is insurmountable' — a reassurance, to return to our opening metaphor, that can hardly be offered to those attempting the K2 range![x]

As implied in our opening remarks, Beethoven was no

longer intent upon imparting 'symphonic breadth to his sonata style' but was content to return to the smaller dimensions of the Piano Sonatas Opp. 90 and 101. Nonetheless, his last creations in the genre are now 'infused alternately with a variety of rigorous polyphonic textures and an etherealized improvisatory tone'.[xi] Not only do the last three sonatas have a lesser compass than that of Op. 106, they achieve 'a new conciseness' and 'a new flexibility' and 'bow to no conventional order of events'. Moreover, 'the weight and distribution of the various sections is unique in each case'.[xii] 'Like [Emmanuel] Bach, [Beethoven] enjoys making his sonatas into terse, aphoristic statements, seemingly in free form, but actually strict and traditional in fundamental ways.'[xiii] Beethoven's final sonata trilogy 'embodies other kinds of narrative designs in which the finale becomes the centre of gravity of the whole', thereby projecting 'a directional process that is sustained across the individual movements, ultimately reaching fulfilment in culminations of lyric euphoria'.[xiv] 'Op. 109 withdraws into an inner world, Op. 110 ends in euphoric self-immolation, while Op. 111 surrenders in silence.'[xv] 'The marvellous intellectual texture of these sonatas and the heavenly relevance of all their details, are there for everyone who cares to study them, but it is their surpassing beauty which always shines out in our memories when their names are mentioned.'[xvi]

The E major Piano Sonata does not have the monumental character of its immediate predecessor nor does it pose the same formidable technical challenges. That said, the resourcefulness required of the performer should not be underestimated as Egerton Lowe was at pains to point out: 'Its difficulties are far too great to admit of an off-hand performance, for it requires much mastery of detail, and its beauties and merits hardly appeal to the ordinary student until the whole work has been thoroughly absorbed and the right atmosphere grasped.'[xvii] Lowe was writing in the 1920s since when the standard of technical performance has risen markedly. This, combined with the inherent artistic merit of the Piano Sonata Op. 109, makes it one of the most loved and frequently performed of the composer's last works in the genre. With regard to its artistic merit Donald Tovey pronounced the composition to be 'one of the profoundest things in music'.[xviii] Alongside its depth of feeling it manifests an elegiac quality that may reflect, subconsciously or otherwise, the manner in which Beethoven, at the period of its composition, was seeking to find greater order, stability and consolation in his own life, and to endow these same qualities in other compositions to which his mind was also turning, notably, his *Missa Solemnis*.[xix] This is the view of Romain Rolland who felt moved to remark: '[This] sonata [has] a high place amongst the happiest conceptions of the master ... Written at the age of fifty, it seems possible that he poured into the later instrumental forms much that he felt was beyond the vocal forms of the great Mass in D [*Missa Solemnis*] which was occupying his thoughts at this time.'[xx]

Whilst the E major Sonata is a more technically restrained work than the B-flat major Sonata, it is nonetheless in Glen Stanley's estimation 'equally unconventional'.[xxi] 'The whole sonata is a mixture of styles.'[xxii] In the E major Sonata, Op. 109 'we once more encounter the fantasia-sonata, of which it is an even more striking example than Op. 101'.[xxiii] In his essays on music Alfred Brendel brings into play his pleasure in word-imagery in his description of the E major Piano Sonata: 'The first movement of the Sonata Op. 109 hovers a few inches above the earth: the bass line follows the upper voices as weightlessly as possible. In contrast to this, the bass line of the second movement scrapes into the earth, as it were. The third movement unites earth and air: it both hovers and rests at the same time.'[xxiv]

A major source for the origins of the E major Piano Sonata is the so-called Wittgenstein Sketchbook. Today this consists of 43 leaves and is preserved in the Archives of the Beethoven House in Bonn. The physical appearance of the sketchbook, as evident from stich perforations and residual paper fragments, suggest it may originally have consisted of some 60–64 leaves. Beethoven began using this sketchbook as a source for various compositions from around April–May of 1819 and worked with it well into the following year. Some authorities believe the Wittgenstein Sketchbook may have been in use until as late as May–June 1820, others though suggest a cut-off time nearer to April-May.[xxv]

The history of the sketchbook can be traced to the auction of Beethoven's possessions that took place on 5 November 1827 shortly after his death. It was sold as Lot 63 to the publisher C. A. Spina and a month later it was purchased by Aloys Fuchs, a collector of Beethoven autographs. He subsequently presented it to the youthful Felix Mendelsohn who kept it for only two years before making a gift of the precious document to Ignaz Moscheles. Following his death in 1870, it remained in the possession of the Moscheles family until its sale in 1911 to the wealthy Wittgensteins of Vienna. It is through this association that the sketchbook has acquired its name. Its last private owner was the indefatigable collector of Beethoven memorabilia H. C. Bodmer, to whom Beethovenians owe a debt for bequeathing it to the Beethovenhuas in Bonn, in 1956, thereby making it available for scholarly study.[xxvi]

Those privileged to have personally studied the Wittgenstein Sketchbook suggest Beethoven probably outlined ideas for the first movement of the Op. 109 Piano Sonata on several leaves from the end of the sketchbook; these are amongst those now detached from the original compilation.

Thoughts for the second and third movements occupy pages 35–78. Evidence of Beethoven being able to turn his mind to more than one major work at a time is seen at the start of the sketchbook that includes thoughts for the *Diabelli* Variations, Op. 120.[xxvii]

A further source for the origins of the Piano Sonata Op. 109 is the Artaria 197 Sketchbook that dates from the period March–December of 1821. This sketchbook formed part of the collection of the music publisher Artaria & Co. who had extensive business dealings with Beethoven; for example, at the start of his career they brought out his first set of Piano Sonatas, Op. 2 and towards the end of his life were in negotiations with him to publish his *Missa Solemnis*. The Berlin State Library, now the present-day Berlin Staatsbibliothek, acquired the Artaria 197 Sketchbook in 1911. Authorities have established this sketchbook includes ideas for all three movements of the Piano Sonata Op. 109, which are combined in typical Beethoven fashion with sketches for the first movement of Op. 110 and early ideas for what is thought to be Op. 111.[xxviii] Close examination reveals that concept sketches for what was to become the second movement *Prestissimo* are well represented.[xxix]

The detached miscellaneous leaves that once formed part of the Wittgenstein Sketchbook, today constitute a pocket-book collation known as Bonn BH 107 – as adopted in the Beethoven House Archives system of nomenclature. This was previously owned by Robert Mendelsohn, a distant relation of the composer and consists of 22 leaves. It is thought these represent the period November 1819–April 1820 when the composer was gestating ideas for the *Missa Solemnis*, giving this collation its colloquial name of the *Missa Solemnis* Sketchbook. Sketches are included in it for the first movement of Op. 109 at pp. 39–41 and p. 43.[xxx]

The origins of the three Piano Sonatas, Opp. 109, 110

and 111 arose in response to a commission from the Berlin music publisher Adolph (Adolf) Martin Schlesinger, a founder member of the influential *Berliner Allgemeine musikalische Zeitung*. In the spring of 1820 he requested three sonatas from the composer – doubtless to enhance the prestige of his business.[xxxi] It is worth reflecting how this circumstance is typical of the origins of many of Beethoven's works, the point being that compositions, now so revered, frequently owe their origins not so much to the inner promptings of the composer's creative muse, but evolved in response to such pragmatic requests as Schlesinger's for new works. On this occasion Beethoven, ever in need of money, responded to Schlesinger's request on 30 April 1820: 'I will gladly let you have new sonatas but not at a lower price of 40 ducats each. Hence a work consisting of three sonatas would cost 120 ducats.' In this letter Beethoven tempts Schlesinger with the prospect of composing other works: 'Moreover, we might perhaps undertake several works, even greater ones, perhaps trios or quartets.'[xxxii] Regarding the projected three piano sonatas, Beethoven appears to have met his match in business matters since Schlesinger subsequently negotiated the lower price of 90 ducats for the three proposed sonatas.[xxxiii]

Throughout the early months of 1820 Beethoven endeavoured to make progress with the composition of the three sonatas but, as a consequence of illness, he felt obliged to write to Schlesinger on 20 September in the following terms: 'Everything will [now] go more quickly in the case of the three sonatas – the first is quite ready, save for correcting the copy, and I am working uninterruptedly at the other two – My health is completely restored and I will make every effort to fulfil my obligation to you as soon as possible.'[xxxiv] What Beethoven says here was not strictly true. He was in fact exaggerating his progress, particularly with regard to the

Piano Sonatas Opp. 110 and 111 upon which he did not commence serious work until the autumn and winter of 1821–22.

On 7 March 1821 Beethoven once more wrote to Schlesinger in apologetic terms saying: 'You have probably formed an unfavourable opinion of me. But you will soon think better of me when I tell you that for six weeks I have been laid up with a violent arrack of rheumatism. However, I am better now.' He was able to provide Schlesinger with the details that he wanted to appear on the Title Page of the Op. 109: '[As] to the sonata which you must have received a long time ago, I request you add the following title together with the dedication, namely: "Sonata for the Hammerklavier/composed and/dedicated to/Fräulein Maximiliane Brentano/ Op. 109".' We discuss the dedicatee Maximiliane Brentano shortly. Of interest here is Beethoven's request for the designation *Hammerklavier* to be included on the Title Page, evidence Beethoven still wanted to promote the German language in the presentation of his compositions. In the event Schlesinger appears to have ignored, or overlooked, Beethoven's request since the Piano Sonata Op. 109 duly appeared as being for the *Pianoforte* and not the *Hammerklavier* (see later).

By the summer of 1821 Schlesinger had supplied Beethoven with the proofs of the Piano Sonata Op. 109 but the work had not been done to his satisfaction: 'Thus there are now very many mistakes to correct, including *some really serious ones.*' [Beethoven's italics] In his response to Schlesinger of 7 June, he undertook to have the corrections delivered by mail coach within the week.[xxv] This proved to be too optimistic since it was not until 7 July that Beethoven sent the corrected proofs (no longer surviving) back to his publisher. This letter reveals insight into the efforts Beethoven had to take to ensure his work appeared error-free. He writes: 'In the engraved copy some of the mistakes are marked in red pencil and some in red ink; but the bars are marked off with grey pencil. In the manuscript copy the corrections are indicated in red ink ... and the list of errata is also in red ink.' He then reproaches Schlesinger: '*Let me remind you that an expert* should always lend a hand, for at least two or three proofs will be required before an engraved copy is absolutely identical with the *manuscript copy*.'[xxxvi] [Beethoven's italics] Despite this exhortation textual problems appear to have persisted since, as late as 13 November, Beethoven once more requested Schlesinger to correct errors. Beethoven accepts some of the responsibility: 'My persistent ill health is the reason why everything to a certain extent has become wearisome to me; and that too is what happened in the case of the proof-reading. While I was doing it I was taken ill with jaundice and felt very poorly.'[xxxvii] With his health improving he undertook to complete work on the Piano Sonatas Opp. 110 and 111 'very soon' adding 'what is more copied correctly'. Beethoven makes a closing remark to Schlesinger that sheds light on his working method. He explains that, as a consequence of his poor health, he had to '*draft more fully than* usual'. [Beethoven's emphasis] Now, feeling better, he intimates he is returning to his old ways: 'I merely jot down certain ideas, as I used to do, and when I have completed the whole in my head, everything is written down.'[xxxviii]

With work on the E major Piano Sonata complete, Beethoven turned his mind to its dedicatee Maximiliane Brentano. She was the daughter of the wealthy Frankfurt merchant Franz Brentano and his wife Antonia [Antonie] (née von Birkenstock), the daughter of a civil servant and a noted art collector. The artist Nikolaus Lauer created a pastille likeness of Maximiliane with her father; she was just one of his twelve children.[xxxix] The Brentanos became close friends of Beethoven during their visits to Vienna. Beethoven in particular had a 'tender friendship' with Antonia and is said to have improvised for her on occasions outside her anteroom.[xl] In 1812 Beethoven composed his Piano Trio in B-flat major, WoO 39 for Maximiliane to encourage her with her piano playing. On 6 December 1821, when Maximiliane was nineteen, Beethoven wrote to her announcing his intention to dedicate to her his Piano Sonata Op. 109: 'A dedication!!! Well, this is not one of those dedications that are used and abused by thousands of people. It is the spirit which unites the noble and finer people of this earth and which *time* cannot destroy ... May you sometimes think of me with a feeling of fondness — My most heartfelt wishes.'[xli] Beethoven's sincerity appears to have been too fulsome in the estimation of Maximiliane's father, since on 20 December Beethoven felt obliged to write an apology to him: 'I was too forward in not asking for permission before dedicating one of my compositions to your daughter Maxe. I would like you to regard this work as a token of lasting devotion to you and your whole family.'[xlii]

Immortality was duly conferred upon Maximiliane when the Piano Sonata in E major, Op. 109 appeared with her name inscribed on the Title Page: 'SONATA/ *für das Pianoforte/ componirt und/ dem Fräulein Maximiliane Bretano/ gewidmet/ von/* LUDVIG van BEETHOVEN./ 109 *Werk*/ No 1088 [Schlesinger]/ *Eigenthum der Verlegers/* Berlin/ *In der Schlesinger Buch und Musikhandlung./* Wien/ *bei Artaria & Co. Cappi & Diabelli, Steiner & Co.*'[xliii] A later edition was published in which the Title Page announced the simultaneous publication of the sonata in Vienna, Paris and London.[xliv]

Commenting on the innovatory nature of Beethoven's achievement, in his later compositions, William Drabkin writes: 'By a variety of techniques ... Beethoven breaks down the concept of "movement" in many of his works, and makes the work as a whole the artistic unit of measurement. This means taking in much longer stretches of music at a time ... [the compositions] ... [become] stories told in music.'[xlv] Wilhelm von Lenz, in his pioneering study *Beethoven*, perceived the Op. 109 Piano Sonata as being essentially 'a single movement in several phases (*Bewegungen*) — one and the same idea stated in recitative, teasingly alluded to in the *Vivace*, drained of its lifeblood in the *Prestissimo* and achieving beatitude in the Variations.'[xlvi] A century later Igor Stravinsky came close to saying the same thing, albeit more succinctly, in his observation 'compression is more evident than expression'.[xlvii] In his discussion of Beethoven's departure from the traditional style of expression, as found in his early sonatas compared with the innovations in the late sonatas, Matthew Rye comments how 'the traditional movement "types" are no longer the cast-in-stone sureties of earlier works'.[xlviii] Eric Blom summarised the construction of the E major Sonata in the following terms: 'First we have a slow movement ... then an agitated piece in ... that could by no stretch of the imagination be called a *scherzo*, either in mood or form, and last a set of very elaborate and at the same time free and fantastic variations on a slow melody.'[xlix]

An anecdote connects us with the last piano sonatas of Beethoven and the celebrated interpreter of his works Artur Schnabel. In his recollections he relates: 'A friend of mine in Frankfurt-am-Main was the famous Louis Koch. I mention him because he had one of the finest collections of musical and other precious manuscripts. Each time I went to Frankfurt he invited me to spend hours in his house alone. His housekeeper had instructions to open to me whatever I was interested in. So in that house, quite by myself, I read or played from manuscript works like some of the last Beethoven sonatas and the last three Schubert sonatas. It was an inestimable experience.'[1] A further anecdote takes us back a generation earlier and recalls the legend of the keyboard Franz Liszt. It is derived from a diary entry of Kurd von Schlözer from 14 January 1868 when he was Secretary to the Prussian Legation in Rome — where Liszt was at that time residing. Von Schlözer writes: 'When I visited Liszt one morning recently, he was amusing himself by sitting at a little dummy piano without strings and practising a trill from a Beethoven sonata (Op. 109), which until then he had played his whole life-long with second and third fingers. Now, in later life [Liszt was then in his 57th year], he has taken it into his head to do it with the third and fourth.' Of related interest is the following. At the Paris Exhibition of 1868 the prize — a gold medal — for the finest keyboard instrument was won by a concert grand made by the American manufacturer Chickering, then a rival of Steinway & Co — who were also awarded a gold medal. For publicity purposes Chickering presented their award-winning piano to Liszt. To add to the occasion Frank Chickering, the Company's principal representative in Paris, accompanied the instrument to Italy and presented it to Liszt in person.[ii] This circumstance has a close parallel with the occasion, fifty years before, when Broadwood & Co. presented one of their state-of-the-art instruments to Beethoven (see Piano Sonata Op. 106).

Although persistent ill health and deafness had made Beethoven a reclusive figure, as far as society in general was concerned, his reputation was nonetheless high and widespread. By way of illustration of the latter, the music critic writing in the October issue of the Stuttgart *Morgenblatt für gebilete Stände* (which then had a wide circulation) enthused: 'Our Beethoven ... is, we may say, among musicians what Goethe is among poets ... It is impossible to give an adequate description of Beethoven's free, simple, and hermit-like life. He is entirely devoted to art, and his only tribute to society is the fruit of his genius ... He rarely shows himself to passing and merely inquisitive observers who care for nothing but a few lines in their albums ... It is a gala day when, to his many enthusiastic admirers, he appears with the power and inspiration of an Orpheus.'[lii] Beethoven also received a reference in the 24 July 1820 issue of the *Allgemeine musikalische Zeitung* in which he is compared allegorically with the poets of classical antiquity: 'Beethoven descended on a demonic bridge from the Elysian Fields [the Greek mythological heaven where only the great and good were sent] into the Cocytus [the Greek river of lamentation] and manipulated the human heart like Arion [Corinthian poet] did on the zither so that all the strings resounded.'[liii]

Gala days grew few in number for Beethoven in his later years, for the reasons stated. However, he did occasionally appear in public to conduct his own works as was the case on the evening of 17 January 1819. The Judicial Faculty in Vienna gave a concert for the benefit of widows and orphans, and with his typical generosity Beethoven consented to his A major Symphony being performed; this had become popular with the musically-minded public at the period of the Congress of Vienna. The Swedish poet Per Daniel Atterbom was present and left the following account. '[Beethoven] is short but strongly built ... a lofty commanding forehead, and a countenance bearing not a trace of happiness. His deafness is the main cause of this, for he is now what is called stone deaf. For this reason also he loves solitude and rarely speaks to anyone. He lives on a pension given him by three princes, and composes all kinds of musical works with restless fire and industry. He is also bringing up a poor nephew with much care and affection. He conducted the concert ... where the programme consisted only of his own [works] ... and could bear in his mind [that is, conduct from memory] ... He stood as if on a distant island, directing his dark demonical harmonies with the strangest movements. For instance, Beethoven indicates a *pp* by gently kneeling down and stretching out his arms to the floor; for a *ff*, he springs up like an elastic bow set free, seems to rise above his usual height, and spreads both arms widely out; and between these two extremes he constantly oscillates.'[liv] Anton Schindler was also present at the concert and according to his account it was not the happiest of occasions. '[Beethoven] had agreed to conduct his Symphony in A major at a large benefit concert for the widows and orphans of deceased professors of law.' The performance took place in the auditorium of the University whose acoustics were apparently so poor they made the music sound 'deafening' — to all but the composer. Schindler adds: 'It was all too obvious that the master was no longer capable of conducting his own works.'[lv]

A watercolour-pencil drawing was made of Beethoven by the Viennese artist Joseph Weidner that portrays the composer as he may well have appeared on the night of 17 January 1819; it gives a rear view of him in the act of conducting.[lvi] In the winter of 1819–20 the Viennese sculptor and medal maker Joseph Daniel Böhm made the acquaintance of Beethoven as is evident from references to him in the conversation books of the period. During that time Böhm created small pencil drawings of the composer as he appeared when out walking. They are characteristic of descriptions left by the composer's contemporaries and confirm accounts of him by his close friend Gerhard von Breuning. In his recollections of the composer (1874) he writes: 'He usually wore a hat ... his grey hair ... flying out at both sides ... [his] coattails ... heavily loaded ... not only with a handkerchief ... but also a folded notebook for his compositions ... as well as an octavo conversation book with a thick pencil like those which carpenters often use.'[lvii]

Franz and Antonie Brentano, who we have encountered earlier in connection with the Piano Sonata Op. 109, commissioned the artist Joseph Karl (Carl) Stieler to paint a portrait of Beethoven in the spring of 1820. Stieler required no fewer than four sittings which was unusual for Beethoven who was known to be impatient with portrait painters and would not sit still for more than a few moments at a time. Stieler requested Beethoven to adopt a pose depicting himself 'performing his art', that is, holding a manuscript and pen. Appropriately, the composer is portrayed working on the *Missa Solemnis* with which, as we have seen, he was occupied at the time. Stieler's likeness contributed greatly to the shaping of Beethoven's image in the eyes of later ages, notably as an inspired genius and a central figure in the Romantic movement.[lviii]

Recognition of Beethoven's celebrity came from other sources. On 15 March 1819 Beethoven was conferred Honorary Membership of the Philharmonic Society of Laibach, then in Hapsburg territory. Beethoven had been denied membership in 1808 on the grounds that a referee had complained: 'Beethoven is as full of moodiness as he is devoid of obligingness.' In 1819, however, the Laibach Society re-considered Beethoven's name once more and on this occasion were disposed to remark: '[By] appointing you one of their Honorary Members, ask you, sir, to accept the strongest proof of their most profound admiration.'[lix] Beethoven expressed his thanks in a letter of 4 May 1819, undertaking to send the Society an unpublished composition. There is no evidence though that he fulfilled this intention; instead he may have sent a copy of his *Pastoral* Symphony.[lx] The Styrian Musical Society was founded in 1815 and in 1820 its list of members included Beethoven, alongside such other composers as Diabelli, Moscheles and

Salieri. In 1823 it elected Franz Schubert to its membership, one of the few honours conferred on Beethoven's gifted young contemporary in his lifetime.[lxi]

The correspondence between the composer-conductor Carl Friedrich Zelter and Goethe gives insights into the evolving attitude to Beethoven's music. Writing to his celebrated friend on 19 July 1819, Zelter comments: 'Music is very much appreciated in Vienna, and especial preference being shown to the Italian composers ... Beethoven is exalted to the heavens because he works so hard and is still living; but it is in the works of Haydn that the national sentiment is most truly and perfectly expressed.' Later in the year Zelter met Beethoven where, as we have remarked, he had spent the summer months at Mödling. Of this encounter he wrote to Goethe on 14 September: 'The unhappy man is practically deaf, and I felt almost moved to tears.' Notwithstanding, Zelter adds: 'Beethoven enjoys a reputation which only falls to the lot of eminent men.'[lxii]

On 20 February 1822, Beethoven requested his publisher Schlesinger to send a copy of his recently published Piano Sonata Op. 109 to Dr. Wilhelm Christian Müller in Bremen. It was intended as a gift to an acquaintance he had known for many years. Müller had studied theology but earned his living teaching and writing about music.[lxiii] He and his daughter – who was an accomplished pianist – met Beethoven in October 1820 on their way to Italy; this circumstance may have disposed Beethoven to make Müller the gift of a copy of the E major Piano Sonata. Recalling his experience of music making in Vienna at this period, Müller writes: 'It is incredible to what extent the Viennese are fond of music, especially of proficiency in fortepiano playing. There is a good instrument in every house. At banker Geymüller's we found five by different manufacturers ... We heard several ladies, for example Frau von Mosel, etc.;

Baroness Ertmann, who studied with Beethoven, appeared to excel all in her execution.'[lxiv]

Before turning our attention to the individual movements of the Piano Sonata in E major Op. 109, we close our remarks bearing on its creation origins with reference to an early English performance of the work. Thomas Alsager was a writer on musical matters for *The Times* newspaper, making him one of the earliest English music critics. In addition, from about 1833, he arranged a series of concerts for a fraternity of music lovers known as the *Queen Square Select Society*. These concerts included some remarkably early performances of Beethoven's last piano sonatas. On one such occasion, from 1833, Ignaz Moscheles was called to play the sonatas Opp. 109 and 111. He noted in his diary: 'I found some of my hearers listening with deep devotion, whilst at my own house [where Moscheles often performed for selected audiences] artists seem comparatively indifferent; some certainly moved, while others are scared of the extravagancies of the master, and do not recover their equanimity until I favour them with the more intelligible D minor Sonata [Op. 31, No. 2]'.[lxv]

In our consideration of the individual movements of the E major Piano Sonata, Op. 109, we return for a moment to its creation origins. From the period of the Congress of Vienna (1814–15) Beethoven developed a friendship and working relationship with the librettist Karl Joseph Bernhard; he may have contributed to the composer's Cantata *Der glorreiche Augenblick*, Op. 136 that was written for the occasion. Bernhard also assisted the composer in matters connected with the custody of his nephew Karl. In Beethoven's conversation book for February 1820, Bernhard intimated their mutual acquaintance, the horn player and composer Friedrich Starke, was collecting compositions for a piano tutor. Starke eventually published this in three parts, including contributions from the leading composers of the day, under the title *Wiener Pianoforte-Schule*. Beethoven was already on close terms with Starke and employed him to give piano lessons to his nephew. Bernhard's entry in Beethoven's conversation book was, in effect, a prompt to the composer to make a contribution. As he noted: 'We must give him something.' This refers to the second part of Starke's planned publication which has relevance, albeit indirectly, to the origins of the first movement of the E major Sonata.[lxvi]

Beethoven's duly obliged and composed a short piece for Starke that he entrusted for delivery to him through the offices of Franz Olivia, an administrator who was then acting as the composer's secretary. When Beethoven received the request from Adolf Schlesinger for 'three sonatas' (see previous), it appears Olivia suggested to Beethoven that ideas he had been working on for Starke's piano tutor, might form a point of departure for the first of the requested piano sonatas, namely, Op. 109. The evidence from Beethoven's sketchbook suggests he acted on this suggestion. He retained the piece intended for Starke, to be reworked as the first movement of the E major Sonata, and provided his friend with not one but five short pieces as a gift for New Year's Day 1821. Beethoven later included these pieces as part of his set of Bagatelles, Op. 119, Nos. 7 to 11 inclusive.[lxvii] Starke subsequently expressed his gratitude in the final part of his piano tutor by paying homage to Beethoven as 'a star of the first magnitude in the musical firmament'.[lxviii]

The first movement is cast in three sections that Beethoven designates, *Vivace, ma non troppo – Adagio espressivo – Tempo I.* It opens with what Bekker describes as 'wave-like figures' that may look back to the *vivace* theme of Op. 79.[lxix] The E major Sonata has been described as a 'fantasy sonata' and this aspect of the composition quickly manifests itself in its 'frequent tempo changes' and 'irregular structural features [that] merge into each other'.[lxx] The opening has also been likened to 'a graceful impromptu-like harp-play of broken chords, which twice thicken themselves in recitative songs'.[lxxi] In Brendel's estimation: 'The quasi-improvised, dreamlike first movement suspends gravity ... the bass hovers in syncopation behind the notes of the melody, hardly touching the ground.'[lxxii] Ernst von Elterlein detected the 'wave-like figures' in his own descriptive imagery of the first movement's opening: 'The freest and most natural harmony plays around these fleeting, hovering strains, and the soul appears to lose itself in a fairy dreamlike world. Sometimes the waves seem to rise higher, but they subside again, gently and tranquilly.'[lxxiii] Rolland found the movement to be rhapsodic 'with its light and happy figures'[lxxiv] that William Newman characterised as 'unusual in their tempo change' as they progress from fast to slow.[lxxv]

Almost from the outset, the first movement establishes 'a dual character' in which the *Vivace* and *Adagio* themes are in opposition, 'the latter interrupting the former almost at once'.[lxxvi] A dialogue is thereby established in which the movement's motive, based on a short figure, is 'exchanged by the hands and is pursued until the very last chord of the Coda'.[lxxvii] Von Elterlein found 'grave tones' in the *Adagio*, and invokes Adolph Bernhard Marx's description of them as being 'a sharp pain ... like a stab in the heart' that, in his own words, 'transforms the gentle being, and is followed by a strong ebullition of feeling ... this figure of gloom appears twice, but the lovely images of the dream always regain the mastery, and hover around the soul the more deliciously'.[lxxviii]

One of the most striking features of the first movement is its brevity, having a playing time of typically less than four minutes. Notwithstanding, within its tightly compressed format, Beethoven 'demonstrates ... complete mastery over sonata-allegro form'.[lxix] 'Compression' is the movement's hallmark, a characteristic that the sonata-allegro structure shares with the opening movement of Piano Sonata Op. 101.[lxx] In his analysis of the movement, Barry Cooper suggests clues to its structure may be found in its origins as the planned contribution to Friedrich Starke's piano tutor to which we have made reference. This, he maintains, 'may partly explain its very unusual structure ... Its most striking feature [being] its fantasia-like alternation between *vivace* and *adagio* sections, with three flowing *vivaces* interspersed with two *adagios* that differ from them not only in tempo but in almost every other way — [e.g.] contrasts of dynamism, stasis, [and] irregular rhythm'. These contrasts, Cooper suggests, were perhaps originally conceived by Beethoven to provide pedagogical challenges to learners.[lxxi] Martin Cooper's description of Beethoven's piano writing has affinities with what his namesake has to say: '[The] highly ornamented writing ... is in greatest possible contrast to the extreme simplicity of the opening theme ... suspensions and anticipations suggest ... the reserving of psychic energy, the savouring of contrast and tension before its solution and possibly an emphasis on the syntax of music — its intellectual structure — at the expense of its purely sensuous pleasingness.'[lxxii]

Although in one of his drafts Beethoven himself provisionally labelled a thematic idea as *Fantasie*,[lxxiii] Downs argues, considering the movement as a whole: '[All] the elements of sonata structure are present: the opening *Vivace* serves both as a definition of tonality and a transition to the dominant; the *Adagio* comprises the second tonal area of the form; and at the *Tempo primo* the middle section begins.'[lxxiv] Commenting on this structure Matthew Rye observes: 'If the form seems diffuse, there is at least a sense of unity provided by the thematic material. The arabesque-like figuration of the opening *Vivace* hides within itself the main idea of the *Prestissimo*, as well as the theme of the Variations.'[lxxxv]

The first movement may be seen as a study in the contrast of textures in which the first subject consists of 'seven flashing *Vivace, ma non troppo* bars' in opposition to a second subject of 'seven bars of *Adagio espressivo*' whose 'contrasts in style and texture could hardly be more extreme'.[lxxxvi] Beethoven's textures have been described as 'Baroque-style' whose profile is enhanced by the juxtaposition of contrasting thematic ideas.[lxxxvii] In its emotional range, and with its sequences of interruptions, the music has been compared to the preludes of J. S. Bach.[lxxxviii] Whatever designations and attributions are assigned to the opening, as Brendel remarks: 'The first movement glides along in a singular rhythmic pattern, interrupted by the declamatory second theme in a new tempo and time signature; it has light colours long breath-spans and undulating contours.'[lxxxix] A century before him, Von Elterlein was content to muse: 'Who can say of what peculiar state of feeling this is the outcome? There is something fanciful about the whole plan and construction of the movement; despite its depth of feeling it gives the impression of a free fantasia rather than of a movement in the strict sonata-form.'[xc]

In a retrospective account of the composer's piano music, the critic of the Berlin *Allgemeine musikalische Zeitung* remarked: 'Beethoven could not go on writing forever in the style of his youth, but his admirers could still find much to value in his later works, despite the widespread perplexity which they had caused.' Concerning the E major Piano Sonata, the writer takes issue with the first movement because 'it has not a theme but an emotional state'. He found the whole, despite some beautiful moments, to be 'somewhat disturbing'.[xci] Writing in the April 1824 issue of the Leipzig-based *Allgemeine musikalische Zeitung*, the reviewer was equally cautious in his estimation of the first movement of the Piano Sonata Op. 109. He acknowledged that merely 'reading the notes' — as was customary on the part of reviewers at the time — would not convey a full appreciation of the music; rather, he declared: 'One must hear the entire work in context, performed with understanding.' That said, he found the *Adagio* at the beginning to have a 'melancholy character' though with 'lighter moments'. These he characterised as 'English whims'![xcii]

Czerny described the first movement of the E major Sonata as 'interesting', and subscribed to the view 'it is more like a fantasia, than a sonata'. He singled out the manner in which 'The *Vivace* frequently alternates with *Adagio*.' Of the atmosphere prevailing in the music he considered it to have 'a very noble, calm, but dreamy character'. To the performer he urged: 'The quick passages in the *Adagio* must be played very lightly and dream-like, and the *Vivace* is only effective when given very *legato* and *cantabile*.'[xciii] In his admiration for Beethoven's achievement, Philip Downs describes its closing moments as being 'among the miracles of music in that they make explicit what was implicit in the opening two elements [*Vivace* and *Adagio*]'.[xciv]

In our opening remarks we remarked that the resourcefulness required of the performer should not be underestimated. This is a view shared by Edwin Fischer: 'The opening of the first movement is not easy to play; the rocking, hovering effect must be "described" with small arm movements. Finger technique alone will not obtain the required effect. The difference between the *Vivace* and the *Adagio* is only apparent. The whole thing must be of one piece, like a good improvisation. Every note should be illuminated with golden light.'[xcv]

The second movement, marked *Prestissimo*, follows on

from the first with scarcely a moment's pause 'with stamping basses and an excited ascending theme ... interpolated with yearning motives'.[xcvi] This was the second time only Beethoven had used the expression *prestissimo* in a piano sonata, the first being in the Piano Sonata Op. 10, No. 1. At least two commentators regard the *Prestissimo* as being typical of Beethoven's innovations and departure from tradition, sounding like a scherzo – despite its tempo.[xcvii] William Kinderman contends 'the imaginative, transformational process' lies at the core of Beethoven's creative method. In his discussion of the second movement of the E major Sonata, he first cites Carl Czerny's recollections of how Beethoven, when improvising at the piano, would first strike a few apparently insignificant tones upon which to create an entire musical edifice. He adds: 'Something of this quality can also be discovered in his compositional process for the second movement of Op. 109, in which the rapidly descending triplet figuration ... was developed, step-by-step, into forms familiar to us from the finished work.'[xcviii]

A mood is quickly established feels Brendel 'veering between anger and fear'. We recall what he said about the music hovering just above the earth. Here, he likens it to 'clinging to the ground, yet unable to impose stability as it remains almost entirely rooted in the dominant'.[xcix] 'Fury reigns unchecked [but] only for a few seconds before both hands join in the soft unison declamation of what seems like a message from the world beyond.'[c] Von Elterlein found in this music a distinct character of 'restlessness ... agitation' and of 'dark pursuing' reminding him of the furies chasing Orestes.[ci] Stravinsky regarded the second movement as 'anachronistic', as though it belonged to some other period in time and to be on a different level to the rest of the sonata.[cii] In this context, to return once more to what von Elterlein has to say, he sensed the manner of late Mendelssohn in both the construction and character of the music, the latter for him being distinctly fantasia-like throughout.[ciii] The reviewer, writing in a contemporary issue of the Berlin *Allgemeine musikalische Zeitung*, found the second movement more to his taste than the first regretting 'only that it is so short' but acknowledging it has 'a very excited passion'.[civ]

Brendel describes the movement as 'flickering jagged and jerky' and possessed of diverse rhythms.[cv] It is has 'all the tightly-packed meaning and concentration of contrapuntal thought typical of Beethoven's scherzo's in his last phase'.[cvi] Beethoven, the virtuoso, comes to the fore with a display that, although never quite fugal, relies heavily upon the devices of counterpoint, imitation, canon and contrary-motion between the hands that are required to move progressively to opposite ends of the keyboard.[cvii] All this ultimately prepares the way for a 'passionate restatement of the opening subject and the piece closes in wild, onward-pressing chords'.[cviii] Czerny urges the performer to play 'quickly' and 'passionately' but also with 'a melancholy colouring'.[cix] Tovey, however, sounds a note of caution: 'Until your hands have learnt the habit of declaiming every detail in this movement, do not venture beyond *moderato*: a comfortable walk at two in the bar.'[cx]

In the third movement Beethoven rekindled his wish to establish the adoption of the German language in the descriptions of his compositions, by following its main heading of *Andante, molto cantabile ed espressivo*, with the sub-heading *Gesangvoll, mit innigster Empfindung*. Not only did he thereby seek to fulfil a long-held wish but also, by intensifying the Italian with the additional German, he sought to emphasise to the performer his requirement for the movement to be played 'songful with intense sentiment' or 'with deepest feeling'.[cxi] This movement is considered by many to be the most radical of the three insofar as its structure consists of a theme followed by six variations. In the wider context of the composer's later compositions, the adoption of the variation form is found in other of his works such as the Piano Sonata Op. 111, (pre-eminently) the *Diabelli* Variations, and the String Quartet, Op. 127.

In the E major Piano Sonata, Beethoven's exploration of the possibilities implicit in the medium of the variation form begins to differ radically from his earlier use of this style of musical expression as, for example, in the middle movement of Op. 14, No. 2 and the first movement of Op. 26. As Rye elucidates: 'Where variation movements in early Beethoven sonatas usually kept to the basic pulse and form of the melody, gradually introducing increasingly decorative figuration, in Op. 109 his approach is more wide-ranging.'[cxii] Charles Rosen elaborates on this aspect of the composer's later keyboard works: 'In many of the late variation sets ... there is progressive implication as the variations proceed — not of texture but of conception of the underlying theme. That part of its shape, to which the variations allude, becomes gradually more and more skeletal in nature. There is also a progressive isolation of different aspects of the theme, as if they were being illuminated one by one.'[cxiii] It was not a new departure for Beethoven to close a work with a finale based on variations, he had already done so in his String Quartet Op. 74, the so-called *Harp* Quartet. However, as Blom affirms, 'Beethoven had not before filled the variation form with a significance that made the movement, cast in it, unmistakably the peak of a whole work'.[cxiv]

Commentators are universal in their admiration of Beethoven's achievement in the third movement of the E major Piano Sonata. 'The final movement is one of the composer's most remarkable sets of variations in terms of originality and depth of expression.'[cxv] 'The final movement combines the essence of the first with the aspirations of the second; it both floats along and brings repose.'[cxvi] 'The finale of Op. 109 ... is both emotionally and intellectually the most exacting movement in the work besides being much the longest and most complex. Compared with it the earlier movements are in the nature of introductions, obviously designed to rouse expectation and to create mood in which the variations may come to us both as a surprise and a solace.'[cxvii] 'The restless introductory movement [*Prestissimo*] is followed by an *Andante* conceived in variation form, "singing with intense emotion", expressive of absolute happiness and peace, passionless desire, which finds fulfilment, not in conflict with hostile powers, but in the activities of the creative imagination.'[cxviii] '[The final movement] is closed by the variations on that never-to-be-forgotten melody in E major, which, through reflective romance, cheerful étude-like activity, sober fugues, bright trill-heights, lead back to the captivating simplicity of their theme.'[cxix]

Beethoven constructs the six variations of the last movement on a melody he marks *mezzo voce*, the opening harmonies of which hover in the tenor and bass registers of the keyboard creating an effect 'not sensuous but spiritual, not a caress but a moment of withdrawal of the soul within itself'.[cxx] Commentators are once more universal in their response to Beethoven's achievement, this time to the expressive nature of his elegiac theme. 'The air comes in quietly, but firmly, decidedly, and at the same time very simply; it is a song of deep feeling an emanation of sincere, true restfulness of soul, a happy submission to destiny; such is the feeling it evokes.'[cxxi] Adolph Bernhard Marx called the theme, 'one of those melodies full of holy devotion, in which the soul, in deep abstraction, reflects on the past; does not think, but with the images of the past reflected as in a crystal-clear stream, falls into a reverie with many an afterthought, and many a sigh'.[cxxii] The opening theme has been variously described as being 'like a prayer',[cxxiii] 'choral-like',[cxxiv] 'utterly disarming',[cxxv] possessed of 'supreme beauty',[cxxvi] and 'one of Beethoven's most intimate and touching melodies'.[cxxvii] Commenting on this, Igor Stravinsky remarks: 'Beethoven was apparently so fond of the opus 109 hymn theme that he could hardly bear to abandon it. It reappears in opus 110, in the form in which it breaks out in the "Bach-Partita" Variation (No II).'[cxxviii]

In the variations that follow the serious, choral-like theme undergoes a series of transformations viewed by some as 'startling'[cxxix] and by others as conjuring up 'a series of bright and varied images'.[cxxx] The variations are not only rich in melodic invention, but are possessed of contrapuntal passages that one commentator found to be equal in mastery and ease of manipulation to that which Beethoven had demonstrated in the great fugue to the Piano Sonata Op. 106.[cxxxi] In common with this work, Beethoven breaks new ground; the variations, as a sequence, are longer and cover a wider range of mood than found in the composer's previous piano sonatas. The sense of spaciousness is extended in Variations II, III, V and VI by Beethoven having fully written out his required repeats. Moreover, 'they have a clearly organised scheme'.[cxxxii] Each variation follows the underlying harmony of the main theme together with 'melodic fragments' especially one based on a 'falling major third'.[cxxxiii] Of related interest, and testimony to the composer's powers of invention, is that all six variations share the same key of E major and yet each receives 'a different element or aspect'.[cxxxiv] Regarding the variations as a whole, Egerton Lowe urges the performer: 'Bear always in mind the directions; "In a singing style with the *greatest possible expression*".'[cxxxv]

Variation I – *Molto espressivo* – is a songful melody,

prayer-like, set above a simple bass accompaniment. Its particular style of ornamentation has been compared to similar melodies found in the slow movement of the Ninth Symphony and in the *Benedictus* of the *Missa Solemnis*, upon both of which Beethoven was working at the same time.[cxxxvi] The first variation 'is almost like a new melody, so skilfully is it developed from the previous material'[cxxxvii] — 'a kind of solemn mazurka'.[cxxxviii] The theme of the first variation establishes the context for the subsequent variations that will soon start 'their magnificent and stately progress, surveying what has been and leading us to new heights'. The left-hand accompaniment seems to look forward to the pianistic waltz, although its role here is to establish a sonorous foundation for the melody hovering above.[cxxxix]

In the summer of 1895 (14 June), Sir George Grove had occasion to write to his pupil Louise Heath. In his letter he makes reference to Beethoven's E major Piano Sonata remarking: 'Do things take *hold of you* sometimes? They do so of me quite absurdly. All yesterday from 6 a.m., I was humming, howling, shouting the first variation in the finale of Beethoven's Sonata in E, Op. 109. How lively it is! And also how bold! A variation? Wherein does the likeness to the theme consist? And yet there is no mistaking the resemblance. Look at the 6th and 7th bars. They are only a kind of *excursion* outside of the melody, and how beautiful they are — the A natural and then the A sharp, and then the G sharp further on. Oh dear, it is all magical, I think ...'.[cxl]

Variation II — *Leggermente* — is a 'reminiscence' of the first movement, a form of double variation that both evokes and modifies the material of the *Vivace* and *Adagio*.[cxli] There are 'hints of polyphony'[cxlii] interwoven with 'a light semiquaver outline'[cxliii] that is 'warmly sung and content to dance along with broken chords'[cxliv] whilst occasional 'unearthly trills foreshadow our direction to a higher plain'.[cxlv] Carl Czerny requests the performer to play this variation 'rather animated and softly'.[cxlvi] But not too slowly as Tovey cautions, '*leggermente* does not agree [equate] with dragging'.[cxlvii]

Variation III — *Allegro vivace* — takes the form of a short but 'brilliant technical study'.[cxlviii] With its animation, it 'moves out of the *espressivo* world into that of a two-part invention in double counterpoint' with scalar configurations that serve to outline a series of chord progression more than to outline the original melody.[cxlix] Igor Stravinsky professed not to like this variation, believing it to be the 'weak link' in the set. He accepted it fulfilled its function of providing an element of contrast but considered the underlying theme to be 'inaccessible' and 'too brisk'.[cl] Beethoven's vigorous double counterpoint is like a 'Bach two-part invention' in its deployment of 'fast inverted counterpoint' and 'exaggerated contrary motion' that has affinities with the sonata's second movement.[cli] Czerny encourages the performer here to adopt a 'quick and brilliant' tempo but Tovey once more urges caution on the grounds: 'The bars are so short that this variation will pass in a flash at any reasonably lively tempo.'[clii][cliii]

For Variation IV Beethoven took particular care in stating his instructions to the performer, resorting to both Italian and German: *Un poco meno andante, cioè, un poco più adagio del tema — Etwas langsamer als das Thema.* Modern-day commentators recognise that within its 'warmly spacious and expressive character'[cliv] lies 'one of the composer's most extraordinary inspirations' in which 'expressive arabesques weave intricately through four-voice textures of transparent grace'.[clv] From an earlier generation, the fragments of melody suggested to Hans von Bülow the description of the world of 'angelic activity and contemplation' found in the first monologue to *Faust* (Part I, Act I, lines 96–70): "Wie Himmelskräfte auf und nieder steigen ... Und sich die gold'nen Einer reichen" — 'Like angelic powers that rise and sink and pass from hand to hand the golden vessels.'[clvi]

In his study *Neue Beethoven-Studien und andere Themen* (1967), musicologist Ludwig Misch refers to what he describes as 'the rebirth of fugue from the spirit of the sonata'. Elaborating on this, Maynard Solomon remarks how in his later compositions, and in his need to create different types of musical movements, Beethoven explored the role of such musical devices as 'fughettas, fugatos, canons, and other brief contrapuntal passages'.[clvii] The construction of Variation IV may be viewed in this context in the adoption of its 'free polyphony'[clviii] and 'more elaborately contrapuntal style'.[clix] In this variation Czerny urges the performer to play the music 'tranquil and legato'.[clx] Tovey invites the student to interpret Beethoven's Italian directions as meaning: 'With a little less *go*, that is, with a little more *leisure* than the theme.' He adds: 'Take the Variation as slowly as you can reconcile with a good colour in the second strain.'[clxi]

Variation V — *Allegro ma non troppo* — 'brings canonic writing to the fore' with reminiscences of the second movement.[clxii] A 'fugal texture'[clxiii] is maintained throughout with 'canonical imitations'.[clxiv] The textures are 'vigorous'[clxv] and set up a 'bluff, blunt march-like fugue in three parts'.[clxvi] A running counterpoint of eighth notes adds to the 'already strongly contrapuntal texture'.[clxvii] Stravinsky found this variation more to his liking: 'The contrapuntal fifth variation, like the late-period fugues ... contains most of the sonata's share of "modern" music.'[clxviii]

Variation VI — *Tempo I del tema Cantabile* — brings the E major Piano Sonata, Op. 109 to a close. In so doing, in the opinion of some authorities, Beethoven harnesses his powers of imagination and originality to the forms of previous masters. In Stephen Rumph's estimation: 'The finale of Op. 109 itself pays no small tribute to the *Goldberg Variations*, with the four-square saraband theme, the fluctuating metres and characters of the variations, and the return of the intact theme.'[clxix] Philip Downs believes: 'Beethoven achieves complete freedom within the strictest discipline, bringing to mind a small number of compositions from Emanuel Bach's last years that are clearly the result of extreme compositional rigor but [which] sound like improvisations.'[clxx] And for Egerton Lowe: '[Variation VI] reminds one of the old Handelian Doubles where the notes were halved in value and doubled in number in each successive variation.' Lowe draws particular attention to Handel's *Air with Doubles* in E, popularly known as *The Harmonious Blacksmith*.[clxxi]

In this variation Beethoven sets aside counterpoint initially in favour of a peaceful restatement of the original theme. However, as the music proceeds, it dissolves 'in a shower of continuously diminishing note values and internal trills'[clxxii] and 'a mountain of scales'.[clxxiii] Beethoven's trills progress relentlessly, as though attempting to communicate the idea of something 'unending'[clxxiv] and 'transcendental'.[clxxv] The trills eventually subside and the main theme appears once more in its original form, 'ineffably enhanced in the light of all these adventures'.[clxxvi]

Whatever may be Beethoven's debt to the past, in this final variation he achieves a polyphonic character that establishes the variation's 'inherent simplicity'[clxxvii] and the manner in which the original theme is revisited and 'becomes exquisitely tender in tone, resumes its original form, and the imagery of dreams gives place to utter peace'.[clxxviii] In Martin Cooper's opinion, in this variation Beethoven is exploring territory new not only to the instrument but to the musical imagination itself: '[The] transfiguration of the [original] theme in an atmosphere so rarefied [conveys] the impression of a music that hovers above the world of everyday experience to which it is connected by only the most tenuous of links [and] has no parallel in any earlier work of Beethoven's not even in Op. 106.' He elaborates: 'Whether or no Beethoven himself associated the crystalline, ethereal character of these last pages of Op. 109 with something of the same other-worldliness as that of the *Missa* Solemnis (which he was composing at the same time), the hymn-like character of the original theme is unmistakable when it returns in its original form, bringing an extraordinary reminder to the listener of the distance that he has travelled during the space of these comparatively short six variations.'[cxxix]

---

[i] Paul Bekker, 1925, pp. 136–7.

[ii] Igor Stravinsky, 1972, pp. 272–3.

[iii] Paul Bekker, 1925, pp. 136–7m

[iv] Matthew Rye, *Notes to the BBC Radio Three Beethoven experience*, Friday 10 June 2005, www.bbc.co.uk/radio3/Beethoven

[v] Carl Czerny in: Paul Badura-Skoda, 1970, p. 13.

[vi] Anton Felix Schindler, *Beethoven as I knew him*, edited by Donald W. MacArdle and translated by Constance S. Jolly from the German edition of 1860, 1966, pp. 231–2 and p. 270.

[vii] Paul Bekker, 1925, p. 137.

[viii] For a brief historical outline of the compositional origins of Beethoven's last three Piano Sonatas, see: Beethoven House Digital Archives, Library Document *Sonata für Klavier Op. 109*.

[ix] Anton Felix Schindler, *Beethoven as I knew him*, edited by Donald W. MacArdle and translated by Constance S. Jolly from the German edition of 1860, 1966, pp. 231–2.

[x] Quotations from the *Allgemeine musikalische Zeitung* are derived from William S. Newman, 1963, p. 533.

[xi] Maynard Solomon, 1927, p. 301.

[xii] Denis Matthews, 1967, p. 51.

[xiii] Philip G. Downs, 1992, p. 606.

[xiv] William Kinderman, 1997, p. 120.

[xv] Alfred Brendel, 2001, pp. 85–6.

[xvi] Marion M. Scott, 1940, p. 146.

[xvii] Egerton C. Lowe, 1929, p. 142.

[xviii] Harold Craxton and Donald Francis Tovey, [1931], *Piano Sonata in E major, Op. 109*.

[xix] Some discussion along these lines is made by Peter Charlton in his website text: *Beethoven Piano Sonata Op. 109*.

xx Romain Rolland, 1917, pp. 162–3.

xxi Glen Stanley in: Philip Radcliffe, *Piano music* in: *The age of Beethoven*, *The new Oxford history of music*, Vol. VIII, Gerald Abraham, editor, 1988, p. 348.

xxii Harold Truscott in: Denis Arnold and Nigel Fortune, editors, *The Beethoven companion*, 1973, p. 112.

xxiii Paul Bekker, 1925, p. 137.

xxiv Alfred Brendel, 2001, p. 75.

xxv Barry Cooper believes a date of May–June 1820 is too late and suggests April–May is more probable. See: Barry Cooper, 2000, p. 186.

xxvi A facsimile of the Wittgenstein Sketchbook is reproduced on the Beethoven House, Digital Archives, Library Document, Sammlung H. C. Bodmer HCB BSk 1/49.

xxvii Derived from, Douglas Porter Johnson, editor, *The Beethoven sketchbooks: history, reconstruction, inventory*, 1985, p. 73 and pp. 253–4.

xxviii Douglas Porter Johnson, editor, 1985, pp. 269–70.

xxix William Kinderman in: Scott G. Burnham, and Michael P. Steinberg, editors, 2000, p. 211.

xxx As intimated in the main text, this sketchbook is now preserved in the Beethoven House Digital Archives as Library Document Bh 107. For a discussion of this, see: Douglas Porter Johnson, editor, 1985, p. 332 and pp. 366–7 and Martin Cooper, 1970, pp. 176–7.

xxxi An anonymous artist depicted Adolph Schlesinger that reveals a sturdy-looking countenance. See: Beethoven House, Digital Archives, Library Documents, Ley, Band VI, Nr. 1171.

xxxii Emily Anderson, 1961, Vol. 2, Letter No. 1021, pp. 891–3.

xxxiii *Ibid*, Vol. 2, Letter No. 1024, pp. 894–5.

xxxiv *Ibid*, 1961, Vol. 2, Letter No.1023, p. 902. For a facsimile reproduction of this letter, with German text and commentary, see: Beethoven House, Digital Archives, Library Documents, Sammlung H. C. Bodmer, HCB Br 210.

xxxv Emily Anderson, 1961, Vol. 2, Letter No. 1052, pp. 918–9. For a facsimile reproduction of this letter, with German text and commentary, see: Beethoven House, Digital Archives, Library Documents, NE 88.

xxxvi Emily Anderson, 1961, Vol. 2, Letter No. 1053, pp. 919–10. For a facsimile reproduction of this letter, with German text and commentary, see: Beethoven House, Digital Archives, Library Documents, Sammlung H. C. Bodmer, HCB Br 211.

xxxvii Beethoven had his first attack of jaundice during the summer of 1820 and it persisted well into August. Writing of this, the medical authority Anton Neumayr has the following observations. 'Beethoven liked fish and was particularly fond of oysters. In the conversation books we read time and again about oysters having freshly arrived ... by special mail. It could have been his fondness for fresh oysters that gave him viral hepatitis with jaundice. According to present day scientific understanding, oysters are a common source of infection for the Hepatitis A virus, present in [contaminated] seawater.' See: Anton Neumayr, 1994–1997, pp. 276–7.

xxxviii Emily Anderson, 1961, Vol. 2, Letter No. 1060, pp. 927–8.

xxxix The portrait is reproduced on the Beethoven House, Digital Archives, Library Document B 1946.

xl For biographical details of the Brentano family see: Peter Clive, 2001, pp. 47–51.

xli Emily Anderson, 1961, Vol. 2, Letter No. 1062, pp. 931–2.
xlii *Ibid*, Vol. 2, Letter No. 1064, pp. 933–4. For a facsimile reproduction of this letter, with German text and commentary, see: Beethoven House, Digital Archives, Library Documents, B H 25.
xliii For a facsimile reproduction of the Title Page to the Piano Sonata, Op. 109 see: Beethoven House, Digital Archives, Library Document, Sammlung Jean van der Spek, J. van der Spek C Op. 109 and C Op. 109/3.
xliv See: Beethoven House, Digital Archives, Library Documents, H. C. Bodmer, HCB C Md 53, 18.
xlv William Drabkin in: Barry Cooper, *Beethoven: The master musicians series*, 2000, p. 208.
xlvi Martin Cooper, 1970 p. 177.
xlvii Igor Stravinsky, 1972, p. 273.
xlviii Matthew Rye, *Notes to the BBC Radio Three Beethoven experience*, Friday 10 June 2005, www.bbc.co.uk/radio3/Beethoven
xlix Eric Blom, 1938, p. 224.
l Artur Schnabel, 1961, p. 63.
li Derived, with adaptation, from: Adrian Williams, *Portrait of Liszt: by himself and his contemporaries*, 1990, p. 426.
lii Quoted in: Ludwig Nohl, 1880, pp. 180–1.
liii Derived from Wayne M. Senner, Robin Wallace and William Meredith, editors, 1999, Vol. 2, p. 51. The *AmZ* author's flattering imagery is not entirely inappropriate since Beethoven was an admirer of the authors of classical antiquity, devoted much of his evenings reading about them and their works, and frequently cites them in his letters.
liv As recalled in: Ludwig Nohl, 1880, pp. 172–3.
lv Anton Felix Schindler, *Beethoven as I knew him*, edited by Donald W. MacArdle and translated by Constance S. Jolly from the German edition of 1860, 1966, pp. 231–2.
lvi See: Beethoven House, Digital Archives, Library Documents, HCB Bi 3.
lvii The text quoted is derived from the Beethoven House, Digital Archives, Library Documents, B 47 and 281. These sources also reproduce copies of Böhm's evocative pencil studies.
lviii See: Beethoven House, Digital Archives, Library Documents, B. 2389 and W. 26. Contextual information is also combined with later modernistic interpretations of Stieler's artwork, see, for example: Beethoven House Library Documents B 1083/b/c/g and Peter Clive, 2001, pp. 355–6.
lix See: Theodore Albrecht, translator and editor, 1996, Vol. 2, Letter No. 257, pp. 159–60, note 1.
lx Emily Anderson, 1961, Vol. 2, Letter No. 943, p. 808, note 2.
lxi Otto Erich Deutsch, 1946, pp. 274–5. Deutsch also remarks (pp. 512–13 and pp. 693–7) on two contemporary reviews of Schubert piano sonatas in which his work is compared with that of Beethoven. The first is in connection with Schubert's Piano Sonata in A minor, D. 846 (Op. 42) that was composed in 1825. In the March 1826 issue of the *Allgemeine musikalische Zeitung*, the reviewer comments: '[The sonata] moves so freely and originally within its confines, and sometimes so boldly and curiously, that it might not unjustly have been called a fantasy. In that respect it can probably be compared only with the greatest and freest of Beethoven's sonatas.' We can well imagine with what pleasure Schubert himself must have felt, reading these words, bearing in mind the veneration in which he held his great contemporary.

The second review was devoted to Schubert's Piano Sonata in G major, D. 894 (Op. 78) that he completed in October 1826. In the December 1827 issue of the *Allgemeine musikalische Zeitung*, Schubert is once more compared with Beethoven: 'The composer, who has made for himself a numerous following by not a few excellent songs, is capable of doing the same by means of pianoforte pieces.' Of the Piano Sonata in G major he writes 'he has evidently chosen Beethoven as a model'. At the close of what is an extended piece, the reviewer adds: 'If we have lingered longer over this composition than it is as a rule possible ... we regard ourselves justified by the fact that it comes from an artist who is still young and who has raised the most pleasurable hopes by several works so far.' Alas, this 'young' artist died the following year.

[lii] As recalled in: Ludwig Nohl, 1880, pp. 174–9.

[liii] For a facsimile reproduction of the letter in question, with German text and commentary, see: Beethoven House, Digital Archives, Library Documents, N E 213.

[liv] As recounted in: H. C. Robbins Landon, 1992, pp. 193–4.

[lv] As recalled in: Pamela J. Willets, 1897, pp. 54–5.

[lvi] Elliot Forbes, editor, *Thayer's life of Beethoven*, 1967, pp. 761–2.

[lvii] *Ibid* and Barry Cooper, 2000, pp. 279–80.

[lviii] Peter Clive, 2001, pp.348–9.

[lix] Paul Bekker, 1925, p. 137.

[lx] Phillip G. Downs, 1992, p. 606.

[lxi] Oskar Bie, 1996, p. 180.

[lxii] Alfred Brendel, 2001, p. 86.

[lxiii] Ernst von Elterlein, 1898, p. 113.

[lxiv] Romain Rolland, 1917, pp. 162–3.

[lxv] William Newman, 1963, p. 534.

[lxvi] Denis Matthews, 1967, p. 52.

[lxvii] Glen Stanley in: Scott G Burnham and Michael P. Steinberg, editors, 2000, p. 89.

[lxviii] Ernst von Elterlein, 1898, p. 113.

[lxix] Wikipedia text *Piano Sonata No 30 (Beethoven)*.

[lxx] As discussed by Charles Rosen, 2002, p. 230.

[lxxi] Barry Cooper, 2000, p. 280.

[lxxii] Martin Cooper, 1970, p. 179.

[lxxiii] William Kinderman in: Scott G. Burnham, and Michael P. Steinberg, editors, 2000, p. 210.

[lxxiv] Philip G. Downs, 1992, p. 606.

[lxxv] Matthew Rye, *Notes to the BBC Radio Three Beethoven experience*, Friday 10 June 2005, www.bbc.co.uk/radio3/Beethoven

[lxxvi] Philip Radcliffe, *Piano music* in: *The age of Beethoven, The new Oxford history of music*, Vol. VIII, Gerald Abraham, editor, 1988, p. 348.

[lxxvii] William Kinderman in: Scott G. Burnham, and Michael P. Steinberg, editors, 2000, p. 210.

[lxxviii] Stephen C. Rumph, 2004, p. 112–13.

[lxxix] Alfred Brendel, 2001, p. 86.

[xc] Ernst von Elterlein, 1898, p. 113.

[xci] Robin Wallace, 1986, p. 61.

xcii *Ibid*, p. 39.
xciii Carl Czerny in: Paul Badura-Skoda, 1970, p. 55.
xciv Philip G. Downs, 1992, p. 606.
xcv Edwin Fischer, 1959, pp. 108–9.
xcvi Paul Bekker, 1925, p. 137.
xcvii See by way of illustration: Roman Rolland (1917, pp. 162–3) who did regard the second movement as a scherzo, and Matthew Rye who found the second movement to have 'more of the scherzo' about it as expressed in: *Notes to the BBC Radio Three Beethoven experience*, Friday 10 June 2005, www.bbc.co.uk/radio3/Beethoven
xcviii William Kinderman, *Contrast and continuity in Beethoven's creative process*, in: Scott G. Burnham and Michael P. Steinberg, editors, *Beethoven and his world*, 2000, p. 212.
xcix Alfred Brendel, 2001, p. 86.
c Peter Charlton, website text *Beethoven Piano Sonata Op. 109*.
ci Ernst von Elterlein 1898, p. 114.
cii Igor Stravinsky, 1972, p. 273.
ciii Ernst von Elterlein 1898, p. 114.
civ Robin Wallace, 1986, pp. 61–2.
cv Alfred Brendel, 2001, p. 86.
cvi Martin Cooper, 1970, p. 179.
cvii See the musical analysis by: Philip G. Downs, 1992, p. 608.
cviii Paul Bekker, 1925, p. 137.
cix Carl Czerny in: Paul Badura-Skoda, 1970, p. 66.
cx Harold Craxton and Donald Francis Tovey, [1931], *Piano Sonata in E major, Op. 109*.
cxi The German may be translated in various ways. Our first wording is derived from Martin Cooper, 1970, p. 180 and our second wording is from the introduction to: Harold Craxton and Donald Francis Tovey, [1931], *Piano Sonata in E major, Op. 109*.
cxii Matthew Rye, *Notes to the BBC Radio Three Beethoven experience*, Friday 10 June 2005, www.bbc.co.uk/radio3/Beethoven
cxiii Charles Rosen, 1976, pp. 436–7.
cxiv Eric Blom, 1938, p. 225.
cxv Stewart Gordon, 1996, p. 191.
cxvi Alfred Brendel, 2001, p. 86.
cxvii Eric Blom, 1938, p. 225.
cxviii Paul Bekker, 1925, p. 138.
cxix Oskar Bie, 1966, p. 180.
cxx Martin Cooper, 1970, p. 180.
cxxi Ernst von Elterlein, 1898, p. 115.
cxxii *Ibid*, p. 115.
cxxiii Peter Charlton, website text, *Beethoven Piano Sonata Op. 109*.
cxxiv Stewart Gordon, 1996, p. 190.
cxxv Alfred Brendel in conversation with David Dubal in: David Dubal, *The world of the concert pianist*, 1985, p. 140.
cxxvi Egerton C. Lowe, 1929, p. 144.
cxxvii Denis Matthews, 1967, p. 53.

ccxviii Igor Stravinsky, 1972, p. 273.
ccxix Stewart Gordon, 1996, p. 190.
ccxx Paul Bekker, 1925, p. 137.
ccxxi John Fuller-Maitland, *Special Issue* [Death Centenary], *The Musical Times*, London, Vol. VIII, No. 2, 1927, p. 222.
ccxxii Philip Radcliffe, *Piano music* in: *The age of Beethoven, The new Oxford history of music*, Vol. VIII, Gerald Abraham, editor, 1988, p. 340.
ccxxiii Stewart Gordon, 1996, p. 190.
ccxxiv Martin Cooper, 1970, p. 180.
ccxxv C. Egerton C. Lowe, 1929, p. 144.
ccxxvi Philip G. Downs, 1992, p. 609.
ccxxvii Egerton C. Lowe, 1929, p. 144.
ccxxviii Martin Cooper, 1970, p. 180.
ccxxix Philip G. Downs, 1992, p. 609.
cd Charles L. Graves, *The life & letters of Sir George Grove*, 1903, pp. 421–2.
cdi Egerton C. Lowe, 1929, p. 145 and Philip G. Downs, 1992, p. 609.
cdii Philip Radcliffe, *Piano music* in: *The age of Beethoven, The new Oxford history of music*, Vol. VIII, Gerald Abraham, editor, 1988, p. 340.
cdiii Denis Matthews, 1967, p. 53.
cdiv Quoted with adaptation from Martin Cooper, 1970, p. 181.
cdv Peter Charlton, website text *Beethoven Piano Sonata Op. 109*.
cdvi Carl Czerny in: Paul Badura-Skoda, 1970, p. 66.
cdvii Harold Craxton and Donald Francis Tovey, [1931], *Piano Sonata in E major, Op. 109*.
cdviii Stewart Gordon, 1996, p. 190.
cdix Martin Cooper, 1970, p. 181.
cl Igor Stravinsky, 1972, p. 273.
cli Denis Matthews, 1967, p. 53 and Philip G. Downs, 1992, p. 609.
clii Carl Czerny in: Paul Badura-Skoda, 1970, p. 66.
cliii Harold Craxton and Donald Francis Tovey, [1931], *Piano Sonata in E major, Op. 109*.
cliv Denis Matthews, 1967, p. 53.
clv Charles Rosen, 2002, p. 233.
clvi As quoted in: Martin Cooper, 1970, p. 181.
clvii Maynard Solomon, 1977, p. 299.
clviii Martin Cooper, 1970, p. 181 and Philip G. Downs, 1992, p. 609.
clix Philip Radcliffe, *Piano music* in: *The age of Beethoven, The new Oxford history of music*, Vol. VIII, Gerald Abraham editor, 1988, p. 340.
clx Carl Czerny in: Paul Badura-Skoda, 1970, p. 66.
clxi Harold Craxton and Donald Francis Tovey, [1931], *Piano Sonata in E major, Op. 109*.
clxii Matthew Rye, *Notes to the BBC Radio Three Beethoven experience*, Friday 10 June 2005, www.bbc.co.uk/radio3/Beethoven
clxiii Philip Radcliffe, *Piano music* in: *The age of Beethoven, The new Oxford history of music*, Vol. VIII, Gerald Abraham, editor, 1988, p. 340.
clxiv Egerton C. Lowe, 1929, p. 145.
clxv Denis Matthews, 1967, p. 53.
clxvi Martin Cooper, 1970, p. 181.

[clvii] Philip G. Downs, 1992, p. 609.
[clviii] Igor Stravinsky, 1972, p. 273.
[clix] Stephen C. Rumph, 2004, p. 112–13.
[clx] Philip G. Downs, 1992, p. 609.
[clxi] Egerton C. Lowe, 1929, p. 145.
[clxii] Philip Radcliffe, *Piano music* in: *The age of Beethoven, The new Oxford history of music*, Vol. VIII, Gerald Abraham, editor, 1988, p. 340.
[clxiii] Denis Matthews, 1967, p. 53.
[clxiv] Peter Charlton, website text *Beethoven Piano Sonata Op. 109*.
[clxv] Stewart Gordon, 1996, p. 190.
[clxvi] Denis Matthews, 1967, p. 53.
[clxvii] Charles Rosen, 2002, p. 234.
[clxviii] Paul Bekker, 1925, p. 137.
[clxix] Martin Cooper, 1970, p. 186. A performance of the E major Piano Sonata, Op. 109 was recorded by Paul Badura-Skoda, on a Conrad Graf pianoforte of 1824, see: Astrée AS-48. The sonata was also recorded by Malcolm Binns on a John Broadwood pianoforte of 1814, see: L'Oiseau-Lyre D 185 D3, and by Jörg Demus on Beethoven's Conrad Graf of 1825, see: BASF KHF-20328. Source: Ann P. Basart, *The sound of the fortepiano: A discography of recordings on early pianos*, 1985. See also: notes to the recording by Jörg Demus of the Piano Sonata Op. 109 on BAS-KAF-20328. Source: Edwin Marshall Good, *Giraffes, black dragons, and other pianos: a technological history from Cristofori to the modern concert grand*, Stanford, California: Stanford University Press, 1982 footnote to p. 92. The E major Piano Sonata was performed 16 times at the wartime concerts held at the National Gallery London — second only in popularity to the Piano Sonata Op. 110.

PIANO SONATA IN A-FLAT MAJOR, OP. 110

'Strongly individual states of feeling must have inspired this sonata. In it Beethoven's tone language becomes more and more subjective, if not obscure, and sometimes mysterious; any explanation in words can give but a suggestion as to the meaning which grows increasingly difficult.'

Ernst von Elterlein, *Beethoven's Pianoforte Sonatas: explained for the lovers of the musical art*, 1898, p. 118.

'Here we find Beethoven in his most exalted mood, and it is significant that whilst the main outlines of the sonata form are at the foundation of the piece, he has gone a step further in the direction of welding the whole sonata into one

> piece ... In this sonata, we have as it were a terrible combat against misfortune, then a return to life and hope, not in a calm pious prayer, but in an exultant hymn of joy triumphant.'

Romain Rolland, *Beethoven and Handel*, 1917, pp. 163—4.

> 'Of all the thirty-two sonatas surely this is the most beautiful. One could wish that it had followed instead of preceded Op. 111, so as to have been known as the composer's "swan-song".'

C. Egerton Lowe, *Beethoven's Pianoforte Sonatas: hints on their rendering, form, etc., with appendices on definition of sonata, music forms, ornaments, pianoforte pedals, and how to discover keys*, 1929, p. 146.

> 'And truly, [Op. 110] is one of the gentlest things [Beethoven] ever wrote. For all its dark colour, it has an inexpressible warmth, like a summer evening after sunset. There has been thunder [Op. 106], we know, but we are not asked to remember it here. It will be time enough for that in the next, and last, sonata [Op. 111].'

Eric Blom, *Beethoven's Pianoforte Sonatas Discussed*, 1938, p. 230.

> 'If we call Op. 111 a masculine work, this sonata is feminine, though such descriptions do not go to the heart of the matter.'

Edwin Fischer, *Beethoven's Pianoforte Sonatas: a guide for students & amateurs*, 1959, p. 114.

'We have a landscape in the A-flat major (Op. 110) ... Over the sward rises the tender song. Butterflies and sun-glitter are the accompaniment. A wholesome strength mounts up and cheerfully wings its way. In a pause of meditation it comes to rest; and from the contemplation rises the old eternal lamentation of man.'

Oskar Bie, *A History of the Pianoforte and Pianoforte Players*, 1966, p. 181.

'Like Op. 109 this sonata belongs to the lyrical and intimate rather than the so-called "bravura" category (Opp. 106 and 111), demanding considerable freedom in the treatment of tempo.'

Martin Cooper, *Beethoven: the Last Decade, 1817–27*, 1970, p. 188.

'Essentially monothematic, the sonata Opus 110 ranks, of course, among the most sublime studies of expansion and intention.'

Paul Henry Lang, *The Creative World of Beethoven*, 1971, p. 254.

'[It] cannot be emphasized too strongly that all three of [Beethoven's] last sonatas are closely related to one another: they seem to share something of the same expressive goal, realized through the same formal procedures of variation, fugue, and sonata and utilizing the same medium as the piano.'

Philip G. Downs, *Classical Music: the era of Haydn, Mozart, and Beethoven*, 1992, p. 611.

> 'No sonata of Beethoven is more tightly unified by the recurrence of the same or similar motifs throughout the work, and by the clear desire of the composer that the movements succeed each other without a pause. At the same time, no work has movements of such disparate emotional character.'

Charles Rosen, *Beethoven's Piano Sonatas: a short companion*, 2002, p. 235.

> 'Of all the late sonatas, perhaps Op. 110 in A-flat (1821) reveals the most explicitly transcendental or religious characteristics.'

William Kinderman, *[Beethoven] The Late Sonatas*, in: Larry R. Todd, editor, *Nineteenth-Century Piano Music*, 2004, pp. 72–83.

Reflecting on Beethoven's late music Marion Scott comments: 'Nothing rouses a stronger sense of Beethoven's greatness than the nature of the music which he brought with him out of tribulation.' In this context she identifies the Piano Sonatas in E major, Op. 109 (1820), the A-flat major, Op. 110 (1821) and the C minor, Op. 111 (1822). To these compositions she includes the *Missa Solemnis* in D minor (1823) and the Ninth Symphony (1823) also in D minor adding, 'in which joy is not only shall, but does, "overtake us as a flood".' She concludes: 'Those were his works, full of blessing and consolation.'[1] David Wyn

Jones makes similar reference to Beethoven's preoccupation with great works in the opening years of the 1820s, listing the *Missa Solemnis* and the *Diabelli* Variations alongside the last three piano sonatas. He reflects: 'As a creative artist Beethoven was totally engrossed in the questing musical language of these works, a language that placed the capabilities of the performer and the predilections of the listener aside in favour of the integrity of the compositional process.' In Jones' estimation, in these works 'Beethoven was able to explore to the ultimate degree his duty to his art'.[ii] Also with the composer's late works in mind, Edwin Fischer reflects: 'The style of all three last piano sonatas strongly points towards the last quartets.'[iii]

Recognising the challenging and pioneering nature of Beethoven's late-period music, Donald Grout and Claude Paliscare reminds us: 'Critics have held that in his late works Beethoven went too far in subjugating euphony and considerations of practicality to the demands of musical conceptions, and some attribute this fault to his deafness.' They cite challenging passages in the finale of the Sonata Op. 106, the first sections of the *Grosse Fuge*, the B-major cadenza given to the four soloists in the last movement of the Ninth Symphony, and the *Et vitam venturi* fugue in the *Missa Solemnis*. In their words these compositions 'almost require a miracle to make them "sound" in performance'. Notwithstanding, they uphold the contention: 'The ideas seem too big for human capabilities to express, but whether one approves or condemns these passages, there is not the slightest doubt that Beethoven, even had his hearing been perfect, would have altered a single note, either to spare tender ears among his auditors or to make things easier for the performers.'[iv]

Writing of Beethoven's last three sonatas, the medically qualified musicologist Anton Neumayr comments: 'In these sonatas, we hardly think of compositional technique, but simply purest expression – outbreaks of passion at its most fierce and the most intimate metamorphosis of the soul.' It is well known Beethoven chose to work on a number of compositions at the same time, turning from one to the other. This aspect of the composer's creative process disposed Neumayr to further reflect: 'Just how Beethoven was able to work purposefully on his *Missa Solemnis* all these years and at the same compose his three last great piano sonatas on the side, so to speak, is hard to imagine.'[v] And, we may add, these sonatas were composed amidst the tribulation of sustained and debilitating illness to which we refer later.

With the emotional qualities inherent within the A-flat major piano sonata in mind, the American musicologist and professor of piano Stewart Gordon hypothesizes: 'If Beethoven had written this work twenty years earlier, he might have been consistent and entitled it *quasi una fantasia*, as he did with the Op. 27 pair.' He maintains, features of the composition that suggest this designation are: 'the relatively compact sonata-allegro first movement' (although not, he believes, as condensed as the first movements of either the Op. 101 or the Op. 109); 'the free improvisatory introduction to the third movement'; and the final movement characterised by its 'two strikingly contrasting [and alternating] sections' – an *arioso* and a fugue. Gordon also singles out the manner in which the fugue itself 'undergoes a metamorphosis in the final pages of the work'.[vi] Perhaps it was with these aspects of the composition in mind that disposed Charles Rosen to conjecture: 'One might imagine there is a programme connected with this work, and that is certainly possible.' But he adds the caution: 'There is a scenario to Op. 110, but whether it refers to any event or literary inspiration we do not know, and it would not help us either to play the piece or listen to it if we could find out.'[vii] We detect a hint of trying to find 'meaning' in the work though in a contemporary account of the music that appeared in Issue One of the influential *Berliner Allgemeine musikalische Zeitung*. The reviewer begins by reflecting on the misfortune of Beethoven's deafness under which, as he remarks, 'the composer had laboured for several years'. He then proceeds to interpret the sonata as 'a gentle look backwards to happier times'.[viii] In our own time, the proposition of finding an interaction between an artist's life and his work continues to exercise the minds of musicologists and pianist-performers. For example, the American musicologist Martin Meyer raised this subject with Alfred Brendel, an acknowledged authority on the interpretation of Beethoven's piano works. Brendel conceded there may occasionally be such a connection but qualified his response, saying: 'It is indeed true that Beethoven's A-flat major Sonata Op. 110, composed in 1821, reflects in a certain way — but only in a certain way — the jaundice from which he had just recovered: you have to think of the *Arioso dolente*, the "song of grief", which bears the marking "gradually reviving", as it flows into the inversion of the fugue.' At this point, Brendel asserts, 'the music has psychologically, so to speak, participated in life'.[ix]

As the Piano Sonata Op. 110 progressed through the nineteenth century it featured regularly in recitals. For Bernard Shaw, in the capacity of music critic, its appearance in the London concert season of 1888–89 represented for him 'the highest plane of musical enjoyment'. He heard the work performed by Madame Alma Haas — not to be confused with Dame Myra Hess about whom we remark later. Shaw describes the work as 'exquisite' and Madame Haas' interpretation as 'most beautiful' but the audience's incessant coughing, he lamented, ruined her performance.

Moreover, people had come apparently not to hear the pianist but a then popular baritone of the day — a Mr. Sim Reeves — who shared the platform with the pianist. Shaw's patience eventually gave out and he concluded his review of the concert with one of his typically acerbic observations: '[It] remains a matter of regret that the attendants did not remove them [the offenders] to Piccadilly and treat their ailment there by gently passing a warm steam-roller over their chests!'[x]

Writing in the Beethoven Centenary Issue (1927) of *The Musical Times*, the musicologist John Fuller-Maitland reflected on the interpretation of the A-flat major Piano Sonata by Sir George Grove who was known to have 'a very special love' for the work and who, according to Fuller-Maitland, was never tired of pointing out 'not merely the exquisite suavity of its first movement and the humour of its second, but the marvellous emotional depth of the Adagio' — in which Fuller-Maitland himself considered 'the resources of the soft pedal are so happily used'.[xi] Writing in the contemporaneous issue of *Music and Letters*, the Scottish classical musician and educator Sir John B. McEwan expressed the opinion: 'In the case of the Sonata in A flat, Op. 110 ... it is impossible for the receptive and sympathetic mind not to be moved to reactions which are determined in emotional significance by the musical expression, and which convince by logic far transcending mere intellectual operations.' He continued: 'That we cannot — and need not — connect these emotional reactions with definite ideas or images, matters very little. The parallelism of feeling between us and the Master goes deeper than mere perception of ideas, and involves the profounder and more obscure roots of personality.'[xii]

Menahan Pressler, the pianist member of the *Beaux Art Trio*, discussed Beethoven's late piano sonatas with the musicologist Nicholas Delbanco. He enthused: 'I am always finding so much more in these works — Op. 110, for instance. I can't drink in enough of it. It is so fulfilling, so satisfying to hear the fugue, so organically complete.' Pressler identified with those commentators who regard the piece as being in many ways autobiographical. He substantiated this remark with the observations: 'The first movement is Beethoven the idealist, the second one Beethoven the hedonist, the third is Beethoven full of grief, of despair, of regret, the Beethoven who sings the *klagendes Gesang* ('plaintive song').' He enthused over the work's structure and special moments such as Beethoven's adoption of the G-major chord about which Pressler felt 'one can spend hours building them, hearing them, feeling them'.[xiii]

In our previous discussion of the Piano Sonata Op. 109, we remarked the creation origins of the A-flat major Piano Sonata arose in response to a commission from the Berlin music publisher Adolph (Adolf) Martin Schlesinger, a founder member of the influential *Berliner Allgemeine musikalische Zeitung*. We recall he had met Beethoven in the summer of 1819 and soon became on cordial terms with him. It was in the spring of 1820 that he requested three sonatas from the composer, doubtless to enhance the prestige of his still fledgling business. He also requested 25 song settings for which he was prepared to pay 60 ducats. Beethoven almost always composed in response to such commissions; he was not a 'desk composer', setting down his ideas in response to the inner promptings of his creative muse and then filing them away for some future occasion or outlet. As Barry Cooper remarks: 'Very little was written purely for art's sake or for an audience in an ideal world that he hoped lay somewhere in the future.'[xiv]

On 30 April 1820, Beethoven wrote to Schlesinger accepting his proposal to compose three new sonatas that would become the final trilogy Opp. 109, 110 and 111, for which he requested 40 ducats each.[xv] In the event, Beethoven had to settle for the lower fee of 30 ducats for each sonata as is evident from a further letter he wrote to Schlesinger on 28 June in which he states: 'I could let you have [the] three completely new sonatas for the price you suggested ... of 30 ducats for each sonata – however, only to do business with you [this way] once, since I would have to stipulate higher prices in future dealings.'[xvi] Beethoven had clearly met his match in his business dealings with Adolph Schlesinger who was shrewd in mercantile matters. It was, for example, as a consequence of Schlesinger's persistent lobbying on the issue of copyright infringement, prompted by flagrant abuse (that caused Beethoven so much travail and loss of income) that was a major factor in the introduction of the influential Prussian copyright law of 1830 – too late though to benefit Beethoven who died in 1827. Schlesinger's Jewish origins led to unjust pejorative remarks about him from some other publishers and contemporary composers, including occasionally Beethoven himself who not infrequently referred to Schlesinger in less than complimentary terms.[xvii]

On 20 September Beethoven wrote to Schlesinger apologising for delays in fulfilling his obligations, notably regarding the 25 song settings, and promised: 'Everything will go more quickly in the case of the sonatas [Opp. 109, 110 and 111].'[xviii] This was not strictly true. In 1820 Beethoven was mainly working on the *Missa Solemnis* and, according to the pianoforte sketches, (see later) Beethoven only worked on his last two piano sonatas in the autumn and winter of 1821–22.[xix]

Early in the New Year (1821) Beethoven found himself in financial difficulties. We learn something of this from a letter he sent to the publisher Mathias Artaria (see Piano Sonata Op. 54) on 28 January that included a receipt for the loan of 150 florins he had received from him. In this letter he undertakes to repay the loan 'very soon' or to reimburse him with a composition for his [Artaria's] own use. In the event Beethoven never repaid the loan nor did he write a composition for the publisher. Artaria's loan was finally repaid in 1828 out of his estate.[x] Anton Schindler, then acting as Beethoven's assistant, informs how Beethoven had incurred high legal costs in the litigation relating to the custody of his nephew Karl. Furthermore, with Karl's eventual adoption his domestic expenses increased substantially. Beethoven's annual income then stood at 900 florins, derived from his annuity (see Piano Sonata Op. 26), and, according to Schindler, 'fell far short of defraying his expenses, especially as the piano works brought in very little in comparison with other musical forms'. In fact, Beethoven composed few large-scale works between 1815 and 1822. Moreover, thirty or forty ducats were about the highest sums he was ever paid for a single sonata that took an average of three months to compose.[xi]

To add to his difficulties, Beethoven had been seriously unwell from the previous summer when he had contracted jaundice, possibly induced by consuming seafood of which he was fond but which may have been contaminated.[xii] On 7 March he had to apologise to Schlesinger following a further period of illness: 'You have probably formed an unfavourable opinion of me. But you will soon think better of me when I tell you that for six weeks I have been laid up with a violent attack of rheumatism. However, I am better now [and] I shall soon make up for lost time ...'.[xiii] He gave an undertaking the Op. 110 Piano Sonata and its companion Op. 111 would soon be completed. This proved to be too optimistic as we learn from yet a further letter to Schlesinger of 7 June intimating 'he will send the Op. 110 soon'.[xiv] In the autumn of 1821 Beethoven was at last able to commence serious work on the A-flat major Sonata, expressing his relief from illness to Schlesinger in a letter of 14 November in which he states: 'Thank God my health is improving every day, and I hope that my mental powers will also become stronger.'[xxv] Reflecting on the effect illness had upon Beethoven's experience of abating and returning powers, Brendel observes how previously, in the *Hammerklavier* Sonata, the composer had 'gathered up new musical energy' and would do so in the Op. 110 and later still in the Op. 132 String Quartet in the score of which the composer inscribed the words 'feeling new strength' in the passage 'Heiliger Dankgesang' ('Holy Song of Thanksgiving').[xxvi]

On 12 December, Beethoven was in a position to reassure Schlesinger he was indeed making progress with both the Piano Sonatas Opp. 110 and 111.[xxvii] This time he was as good as his word. The completed autograph score of Op. 110 bears the date 25 December 1821 and was despatched to Schlesinger in Berlin two weeks later.[xxviii] Beethoven duly received Schlesinger's payment in the form of '30 full-weight ducats in gold' the receipt of which he acknowledged on 11 January 1822.[xxix] He made some revisions to the last movement but the subsequent publication does not appear to have posed any further difficulties and the A-flat major Piano Sonata was subsequently published later in the year.[xxx]

Beethoven was largely immune to flattery but he may have been touched by a letter he received on New Year's Day, 1822. This was from the President and Secretary of the Graz-based Music Society of Steiremark, admitting him to its membership together with a lithograph Diploma bearing the composer's name in gold script. The citation reads: 'through the development and perfection of the art of music, strives in the flower-strewn path of spiritual pleasures, to attain the sublime objective of moral refinement [and] of religious elevation of minds in the Fatherland, has the honour to appoint you, Herr Ludwig van Beethoven, recognised through merit as the greatest composer of the present century ... herewith made known through the present Diploma.'[xxxi] Another honour, albeit of an indirect kind, came to Beethoven in a letter of 13 May from his friend the publisher Nikolaus Simrock (see Piano Sonata Op. 28). Simrock gave an undertaking to publish the composer's first six symphonies in full score on the grounds: 'I wanted to dedicate to my old friend a worthy monument.'[xxxii]

Beethoven's health was now improving but the extent to which illness still weighed upon him is evident in a letter he sent to his friend Franz Brentano on 19 May. In this he reflected philosophically: 'We are destined once and for all to have both joy and sorrow, if only our share of sorrow does not become too large.'[xxxiii] A month later (6 July) he wrote in similar terms to his former pupil Ferdinand Ries, now resident in London: 'I am entirely devoted to my Muses, as I have always been; and in this alone do I find the joy of my life.'[xxxiv]

Although the subject of our present narrative is the A-flat major Piano Sonata, we are reminded, by the correspondence he had with the Leipzig publisher Carl Peters, that this composition was subordinate to his major creative work at this period, namely the *Missa Solemnis*. Peters had approached the Beethoven earlier in May with a view to publishing some of his works.[xxxv] This prompted him to reply on 5 June: 'The *greatest* [Beethoven's emphasis] work which I have composed so far is a grand Mass with choruses, four obbligato voices and a large orchestra [the *Missa Solemnis*, Op. 123].' Beethoven wanted payment for this of 1000 gulden, remarking that he had already been offered 100 'full weight Louis d'or' for this work; Beethoven in fact attempted to sell the Mass to several publishers.[xxxvi] Our main point here, however, is that this exchange of letters serves as a reminder that the Piano Sonatas Opp. 109—111 were written almost co-incidentally against the gestation and evolution of this great work.

Peters appears to have suggested the possibility of his publishing-enterprise bringing out a comprehensive edition of the composer's works. He also appears to have been aware of Beethoven's straightened financial circumstances, since on 3 July he expressed his wish to assist the composer alleviate his financial position 'in any way possible'. He comments: 'Earth should long ago have placed you in a completely worry-free position, so that you would no longer have to live *from* Art, but only *for* Art.' He adds, it is little consolation for a great artist to live in hardship during his lifetime only to be compensated in death by having a statue erected in his honour![xxxvii] Beethoven responded with alacrity to Peters' proposal that was dear to his heart: 'I should like to hear soon about your projected plan to publish my collected works, for I am bound to have such an undertaking very much at heart.'[xxxviii] Nothing came though of this projected enterprise. In fact Peters became disenchanted with the composer after he later sent him a set of bagatelles that he considered to be too trifling and had them peremptorily returned.

Of related interest is the circumstance that the art and music dealer Tobias Haslinger and the music publisher Sigmund Steiner also contemplated a projected publication of Beethoven's collected works. In a memorandum, thought to date from sometime in June 1822, they compiled a price list for each of the categories of the composer's compositions — as they might appear in a collected edition. They anticipated a symphony would retail for 60—80 ducats, piano concertos, 60 ducats, piano trios 50 ducats, string quartets 40 ducats, and piano sonatas 30 ducats. Beethoven was to receive a copyright payment. This plan, like that of Peters', came to nothing.xxxix

On 2 July, Schlesinger confirmed the Piano Sonatas Opp. 110 and 111 were to be engraved in Paris where his son Moritz (Maurice) had established a branch of the family business. He reassured the composer: 'They will be truly superlative when they appear.' By way of added reassurance he confirmed the texts would be proofread by non other than the celebrated pianist Ignaz Moscheles.xl The following day Moritz sent a letter to the composer expressing his pleasure that his business was now collaborating with Beethoven in the publication of his works. Moritz confirmed he was now established in Paris and hoped this would facilitate 'the better distribution of the composer's works so that they will also be endowed externally according to their inner value'.xli

Eager to earn an additional fee from an English publisher, Beethoven wrote to his former pupil Ferdinand Ries on 6 July — Ries then being resident in London. Beethoven informed him: 'I have composed two new sonatas [Opp. 110 and 111] for pianoforte solo which [he considered] are really not very difficult.' Adopting his business style he adds: 'I should be glad if you could obtain the same sum [as he had received for previous compositions] of 26 pounds sterling for these ... *if you can get more, all the better* [Beethoven's italics].' There is almost an element of desperation here in Beethoven's remarks — evidence of his anxiety to improve his financial position whatever the financial terms. Beethoven further exhorted Ries, 'that any money ... should be sent to Vienna as soon as possible'.xlii As Alan Tyson comments: 'Beethoven's bargaining position was weak [particularly in his later years]; his works were not commercially tempting to an English publisher, and there was always the risk that the ones which he did not sell would be printed anyway.'[xliii]

Despite Schlesinger's reassurance to bring out 'truly superlative' editions of Beethoven's works, the Paris edition of the Piano Sonata Op. 110 was marred by errors. Consequently Beethoven wrote to Schlesinger on 31 August requesting a proof copy of the composition before it was to be finally released for publication. He took up an all too familiar theme in his negotiations with publishers: 'For it is very unpleasant for me if my works come out full of mistakes.'[xliv] Beethoven appears to have corrected any remaining textual errors and the Piano Sonata in A-flat major, Op. 110 was published shortly thereafter.

1822 closed as it had opened with a further honour being conferred upon the composer. On 28 December the President and Secretary of the Royal Swedish Music Academy of Stockholm wrote to Beethoven conferring its Membership on him in recognition of 'its obligation to recognize and ... to embrace unto itself persons who have, with success or in a distinguished manner, pursued praiseworthy music'.[xlv]

Sketches for the Piano Sonata Op. 110 are contained in the so-called Artaria 197 Sketchbook; these occupied Beethoven from about March to December 1821. It originally formed part of the collection of the art dealer and music publisher Mathias Artaria and eventually passed to the Berlin Royal Library (Staatsbibliothek) in 1901. Today it consists of 44 leaves (88 pages) that Beethoven appears to have assembled somewhat randomly, as was his occasional habit, from available sheets of music paper. Reflecting the composer's pre-occupation at the period under consideration with the *Missa Solemnis*, the first 63 pages of the sketchbook are taken up with ideas for the *Agnus Dei* and the *Dona nobis pacem*. Beethoven then appears to have started work on the A-flat major Sonata to which some 25 pages are devoted bearing on the work's first two movements. Preliminary thoughts at the end of the sketchbook relate to the fugue of the final movement with brief sketches for the first movement of the finale of the Piano Sonata Op. 111.[xlvi]

From his study of Beethoven's drafts the American pianist and scholar-musicologist William Kinderman remarks: 'These sketches outline the basic concept of the new sonata [Op. 110] even before the thematic material and keys have been established ... As these sketches show, Beethoven seems to have begun his compositional process of Op. 110 with the finale, which exploits contrast in remarkable ways, its double presentation of a mournful lament in the minor balanced against fugal sections in the major.' Kinderman finds a strong kinship here with what he describes as the 'the duality' of the *Agnus Dei* and the *Donna nobis pacem* of the final movement of the *Missa Solemnis*. He concludes: 'Beethoven allowed compositional preoccupations derived from the Mass to infiltrate this final sonata trilogy [Opp. 109–111] composed concurrently with his work on the *Missa Solemnis*.'[xlvii]

Given the Paris connection with the Piano Sonata Op. 110, through the publishing house established there by Moritz Schlesinger, it is fitting today that a small collection of sketches relating to this work now reside in the Bibliothèque Nationale. These are catalogued as MS 80 and MS 51/3 and date from August to November 1821 and from December of that year to January or February 1822. They variously include sketches for the second and third movements and the fugue of Op. 110. These sketches have a complex ownership history. They consist of unstitched pocket 'gatherings' (miscellaneous manuscript sheets) that originally belonged to Mathias Artaria. He sold them to the collector Johann Kafka who in 1881 disposed of them by auction to the Paris dealer Charles Malherbe. It was from him they were subsequently donated to the Paris Conservatory and later transferred to the Bibliothèque Nationale.[xlviii]

A copy of the manuscript of Op. 110 with revisions by Beethoven, once owned by Brahms, is now in the collection of the Gesellschaft der Musikfreunde, Vienna. In his discussion of these sources, musicologist John Cockshoot remarks: 'They give a good insight into Beethoven's way of thinking in the final stages of composition. His highly self-critical standards are always present in his attempts to reach perfection.'[xlix]

With regard to the structure of the A-flat major Piano Sonata, Philip Radcliffe finds Beethoven returning to the general scheme he had adopted in his Op. 101 remarking 'a fairly short and intimate first movement, a fast movement ... and a short *Adagio ma non troppo* leading straight into a great fugal finale'.[l] Despite these conventional three movements, Matthew Rye perceives what he likens to 'a "disintegration" of accepted sonata norms enhanced in the final movement that incorporates both slow movement and finale in alternation'.[li] Alexander Ringer describes the composition as being 'essentially monothematic', also ranking it 'among the most sublime studies in thematic expansion and intention'.[lii]

Given Beethoven's predilection for dedicating his piano sonatas to those whom he particularly favoured, or who had rendered him some valued service, it is, in the words of Eric Blom, 'curious that so deeply personal a work as this sonata should bear no dedication'.[liii] This, however, does not appear to have been the composer's original intention. In a pencilled note to his assistant Anton Schindler, Beethoven remarks cryptically: 'The two sonatas in A flat and C minor are to be dedicated to Frau Brentano, née Edle von Birkenstock — nothing to Ries.'[liv] Frau Brentano was

Johanna, the wife of Franz Brentano to whom we have made previous reference. Beethoven frequently expressed his affections to the Brentano family in such endearing terms as: 'I recall to my mind with pleasure the hours I spent in the company of both of you.'[iv] However, despite Beethoven's instruction to Schindler, his intentions were not fulfilled and the A-flat major Sonata was published without a dedication simply as: '*Sonata für das Pianoforte von Ludwig. van Beethoven. 110 Werk.*'

It is clear from Beethoven's instruction to Schindler, that at some point he had contemplated making a dedication to his former piano pupil Ferdinand Ries. That he did not do so is one of the regrettable omissions in the context of Beethoven's list of dedicatees. Ries rendered many services to Beethoven. As a composer he may be said to have helped advance the public's familiarity with Beethoven's music through the many transcriptions of his works. These include: arrangement's for piano trio of the six String Quartets, Op. 18 and the three String Trios, Op. 9; a piano arrangement of the Second Symphony; and string-quartet arrangements of the Piano Sonatas Op. 10, No.3, Op. 28 and Op. 31, No. 3. Furthermore, in his capacity as a Director of the Philharmonic Society of London, it was Ries who helped to bring about the Ninth Symphony that Beethoven promised to dedicate to him but who once more failed to carry out his intention. Perhaps Ries's compensation is the legacy he left — in addition to his own large musical output — in the study he co-authored with Franz Wegeler that was published in 1838 under the title *Biographische Notizen über Ludwig van Beethoven*. It is still valued today and read in the English version, *Remembering Beethoven: the biographical notes of Franz Wegeler and Ferdinand Ries.*

Following Ries's endeavours on Beethoven's behalf, an English edition of the Piano Sonata Op. 110 was eventually registered as Stationer's Hall, London on 2 July 1823 — in accordance with the copyright procedures then in force regarding published works (see Piano Sonata Op. 78).[lvi] This edition was published by Muzio Clementi as: 'Sonata,/FOR THE/piano forte,/COMPOSED/BY/L. V. Beethoven./Ent. Sta. Hall — Op. 110, Price 4s, [shillings]/London, Published by Clementi & Co. 26 Cheapside./NB. This Sonata is Copyright./Hewitt sculp [engraver].'[lvii] Two copies of these first editions are preserved today at the Beethoven House, Bonn and can be viewed on their Digital Archives.[lviii]

In the early part of the nineteenth century, the manuscript score of the A-flat major Piano Sonata appears to have been in the possession of the London publisher Charles Letts since it is recorded as having been sold at auction, as part of his effects, in January 1912 for 90 pounds sterling — the equivalent in today's money values of about 8,000 pounds and only a fraction of the sum it would doubtless command if it ever appeared on the market again.[lix] Beethoven's Death Mask was also sold at the same auction.

As we draw our prefatory remarks concerning the creation origins of the A-flat major Piano Sonata to a close, we pause for a moment to consider how Beethoven appeared to his contemporaries at the period in question.

The reader will recall from our study of the Piano Sonata Op. 109, that the writer and music teacher Dr. Wilhelm Christian Müller of Bremen met Beethoven with his daughter — a gifted pianist — in October 1820; they were journeying to Italy at the time. Recalling this experience in 1824, Müller writes: 'Beethoven is perhaps the greatest aesthetic artist. His profound works are far in advance of their time, and just as Sebastian Bach's compositions have been revived a hundred years after they were written, so will Beethoven's be. Many of his earlier works are much appreciated by the fashionable world ... He seems less understood in Vienna ... They do certainly express unfavourable opinions about his peculiarities and strange manners, but they all agree that he is a genius, although few are acquainted with him. Those who know the soundness of his understanding and the purity of his heart, entertain the sincerest friendship for him. This much is certain: he is a stranger to the world, the court, politics, and the art of dissimulation. He lives in his own art-world like a monarch in the kingdom of music.'[lx]

The horn player and composer Friedrich Starke first made Beethoven's acquaintance in 1812 and later on was trusted to give piano lessons to his nephew Karl; Starke in fact published a piano tutor for which Beethoven contributed his five Bagatelles Op. 119. Starke recalled the occasion when he dined with Beethoven sometime in 1821. On their way home they passed a chapel that prompted Beethoven to recall his youthful days when he regularly played the organ. This prompted Starke to persuade Beethoven to play for him. Beethoven agreed, and played for nearly half-an-hour — two preludes, the first *con amore* and the second a fugue. Starke relates: 'What a pity that those strains could not have been preserved and perpetuated; but they passed away.'[lxi]

Wilhelmine Schröder-Devrient was young opera singer who by all accounts had a phenomenal voice — Beethoven once described it as being 'as big as the side of a house'! In 1821 she established her reputation in Vienna as a highly acclaimed dramatic artist in the role of Pamina in Mozart's *Die Zauberflöte*; she was just seventeen at the time. The following year she appeared to considerable acclaim as Agathe in Weber's *Der Freischütz* — earning warm praise from the composer himself. Later that year she took on the challenging role of Leonora in Beethoven's revised opera *Fidelio* that had not been performed for several years.

Beethoven himself insisted on directing the dress rehearsal from which occasion Wilhelmine left the following account: 'Beethoven sat in the orchestra and waved his baton above the heads of us all, and I never had seen the man before! At that time the Master's physical ear already was deaf to all tone. With confusion written on his face, with more than earthly enthusiasm in his eye, swinging his baton to and fro with violent motions, he stood in the midst of the playing musicians and did not hear a single note!' She further describes how Beethoven's best efforts served merely to throw singers and orchestra into confusion and to put them entirely off beat, Beethoven all the while being unaware of the ensuing circumstances but apparently content with the rehearsal, 'for he laid down his baton with a happy smile'. Schröder-Devrient recalls it fell to the lot of the violinist-conductor Michael Umlauf to tactfully suggest he should take charge of the actual performances. This he subsequently did, Beethoven apparently being consigned to having to sit behind Umlauf – 'lost in profound meditation'.[lxii]

In the years 1820–22, the English statesman Sir John Russell travelled extensively in Europe and published an account of his journeys in *A Tour in Germany and Some of the Southern Provinces of the Austrian Empire.* In this he makes reference to Beethoven's appearance: 'The carelessness of his dress gives him a savage appearance; his features are marked and prominent; his eyes expressive; his hair, which looks as if it had not been touched by comb or scissors for some years, falls over his broad brow in a disorderly mass, being comparable only to the serpents on Medusa's head.' Russell heard the composer perform on the piano once, commenting 'it required no little tact to induce him to play, so great is his dislike of anything like a pressing request'. When he was finally induced to perform, Russell comments: 'Left to himself, Beethoven sat down at the piano. At first he struck a few short chords ... but soon he forgot his surroundings, and for about half an hour lost himself in an improvisation, the style of which was exceedingly varied, and especially distinguished by sudden transitions ... he revelled rather in bold stormy moods than in soft and gentle ones.'[lxiii]

The writer, composer and editor Friedrich Rochlitz — an influential figure in the inception and production of the journal *Allgemeine musikalische Zeitung* — met Beethoven sometime between May and early August 1822. He alleges he succeeded in engaging the composer in conversation — despite the difficulties imposed by his deafness. Our caution here is that some authorities, e.g. Barrie Cooper (*Compendium*) and Maynard Solomon (*Beethoven Essays*), consider Rochlitz may have embroidered his recollections. However, if we place our trust in Rochlitz this is what he has to say: 'Picture to yourself a man of approximately fifty years of age, small rather than of medium size, but a very powerful, stumpy figure ... a red, healthy complexion; restless, glowing, and when his gaze is fixed even piercing eyes ... intelligent and full of life ... in his whole attitude that tension, that uneasy, worried striving to hear peculiar to the deaf ... such is the man who had given happiness to millions, a purely spiritual happiness.' Rochlitz claims Beethoven gave a rare, albeit brief, insight into his thoughts concerning his compositional process: 'I am busy with three large ... works. Much is already cut out, in my head at least ... two great symphonies and what is more, an oratorio. And these will take a long time, for latterly I have not written easily. I sit and think a long time before my ideas will come out on paper ... When I have begun, it is all right ...'. The three works in question are thought to be the Ninth and Tenth Symphonies and the Oratorio *The Triumph on the Cross*.[lxiv]

Our final pen-portrait of Beethoven at the period of

composition of the Piano Sonata Op. 110, is derived from the meeting Gioacchino Rossini had with the composer in 1822. Rossini was then being lionised in Vienna through the popularity of his *Il Barbiere di Seviglia*. He states he was familiar with some the composer's string quartets, that he regarded 'with admiration', and, likewise, 'a number of his piano compositions'. Notwithstanding, he describes how he could barely master his emotions as he mounted the stairs to Beethoven's lodgings. He continues: 'When the door opened, I found myself in a sort of attic terribly disordered and dirty ... The portraits of Beethoven which we know, reproduce fairly well his physiognomy. But what no etcher's needle could not express was the indefinable sadness spread over his features — while from under heavy eyebrows his eyes shone as from out of caverns and, though small, seemed to pierce one.'[lxv]

Before turning to a consideration of the individual movements of the A-flat major Piano Sonata, we close our prefatory remarks with reference to a selection of impressions bearing upon the interpretation of the composition. These relate to keyboard artists of acknowledged standing drawn from different time periods.

Marie Lipsius has left an account of a performance of the Piano Sonata Op. 110 that Liszt gave to a small circle of admirers. Marie was a musicologist of recognised attainments, being the author of some twenty biographies — including one of Beethoven. She enjoyed a close friendship with Liszt over period of thirty years and published an edition of his correspondence. Writing of his interpretation she enthuses: 'I was later to hear the sonata performed by [Hans von] Bülow and [Anton] Rubinstein, and others — but as rendered by Liszt, *never again*! We were all enraptured.' E. F. Wenzel, the pianist-teacher friend of Mendelssohn and Schuman, was present and Marie remarks how 'he stood there as though turned to stone'. She recalls him exclaiming: "This playing is a miracle ... We know every note, but under these hands it is something never before heard, a revelation. An unparalleled inspiration makes something newly created arise before us, as though formed out of the universal abyss."[lxvi]

Clara Schumann had a close friendship with the celebrated violinist Joseph Joachim. Clara valued his musical judgements and the opinion he expressed of her interpretations of Beethoven's works. This is evident in a letter she wrote to him in which she enthuses: 'Nothing can teach me more than your comments, nothing can so stimulate me.' She concludes her letter: 'Lately, I have been studying Sonatas Op. 109 and Op. 110, for the first time, with much enjoyment. The A-flat major, which used to seem to me chaotic in places, has now become clear.'[lxvii]

The American composer and music critic Virgil Thomson heard Artur Schnabel perform on March 28 1944. His programme included the Piano Sonata Op. 110. By then Thomson had earned a reputation for his wit, candour and independent-minded judgement in his capacity of music critic for the *New York Herald-Tribune*. Notwithstanding that by then Schnabel had also earned a reputation for his interpretations of the piano works of Beethoven, and, we may add, for the 'rediscovery' from years of neglect of the piano sonatas of Franz Schubert, Thomson was clearly not in awe of Schnabel's performance. In his review of the concert, Thomson reflected on Schnabel's many years of study of Beethoven and of his standing as an artist of distinction: 'He passes, indeed, and with reason, for an expert on the subject, by which is usually meant that his knowledge of it is extensive and that his judgements about it are respected ... His readings about Beethoven's piano music in general, whether or not one finds his readings convincing, are not to be dismissed lightly.' We should add here, by way of amplification of Thomson's remarks, that in 1932 Schnabel had just completed the first recoding ever of Beethoven's complete set of piano sonatas and at about the same time had published a meticulously thorough performing edition of these works.

Of Schnabel's interpretation, Thomson commented: 'For all the consistency and logic of his musicianship, there is too large a modicum of late-nineteenth-century Romanticism in Mr. Schnabel's own personality to make his Beethoven – who was after all, a child of the late eighteenth – wholly convincing to musicians of the mid-twentieth.' Thomson elaborates on Schnabel's style of playing that he considered unduly emphasized what Thomson regarded as the composition's 'secondary material': 'Mr. Schnabel does not admit, or plays as if he did not admit, any difference between the expressive functions of melody and passage work. The neutral material of music – scales, arpeggiated basses, accompanying figures, ostinato chordal backgrounds, formal cadences – he plays as if they were as intense communication, as if they were saying something as important as the main thematic material. They are important to Beethoven's composition, of course; but they are not directly expressive musical elements. They serve as amplification, as underpinning, frequently as mere acoustical brilliance. To execute them all with climactic emphasis is to rob the melodic material, the expressive phrases, of their singing power.'[lxviii]

Throughout our series of narratives relating to the creation origins and reception history of Beethoven's piano sonatas, we have made reference to the occasions when they were performed at the series of recitals held in London during the Second World War at The National Gallery. Our next such recollection renews this connection with these recitals and a much-respected interpreter of Beethoven who contributed generously of her time to them. Musicologist Thomas Lewis, in conversation with the composer Raymond Leppard, asked if he had ever heard Dame Myra Hess perform. Leppard responded: 'Yes ... I heard her play at the National Gallery ... She was a big woman and a pretty tough one. She was a very remarkable pianist. I remember her almost at the very end of her life when she played Beethoven's Opus 110. I knew the piece because I was learning it with a pianist called Solomon ... She was very famous for these late Beethoven sonatas and she played almost nothing else. She loved Beethoven's music, but she had almost recomposed them! There were funny extra notes, and different tempi. It was strange, but lovely and beautiful playing.'[lxix] The Piano Sonata Op. 110 was in fact performed at the National Gallery recitals on no fewer than 17 occasions (a record), bringing solace to many during those dark days.

We now direct our comments to a consideration of the A-flat major Piano Sonata's individual movements.

In the construction of the first movement, commentators acknowledge the extent to which Beethoven adopts 'clearly defined sonata form'[lxx] even to the extent that 'everything is ... orderly and predictable'.[lxxi] Notwithstanding Beethoven's conformity with sonata-form principles, Eric Blom describes the compositional structure as being 'curiously softened, its main features smoothed and its connecting links rounded so that its divisions melt into each other almost imperceptibly'. He believes: 'It is no longer possible to say quite decisively how far the first- and second-subject groups extend and what is in the nature of transition.'[lxxii]

A hundred years ago, Romain Rolland felt disposed to describe the first movement as being 'handled with great freedom'.[lxxiii] Musicologist F. E. Kirby finds Beethoven's procedures here consistent with what he describes as the composer's propensity, in the later sonatas, 'to shift around the various forms in the piano sonata that had an effect on the structural type that had long been the mainstay of the genre of the sonata form'. Of the Op. 110 he maintains: 'The Sonata in A-flat major ... shows sonata form appears in the first movement, but Beethoven has given it a lyrical interpretation, emphasising cantabile themes and reducing the significance of the development with a lyrical Allegretto ...'.[lxxiv] It has been suggested at bars 5–8 Beethoven may have looked back briefly, in self-quotation form, to his Violin Sonata, Op. 30, No. 3.[lxxv]

More radically, Paul Lang believes a compelling connection exists with Beethoven's Op. 110 and the E-flat major Sonata of the English composer George Pinto. His teacher Johann Salomon — a name we normally associate with Joseph Haydn and his London Symphonies — said of him: 'If he had lived [he died in his mid twenties] ... England would have the honour of producing a second Mozart.' As it is, in the few years spared to him, Lang believes Pinto's pianoforte style went a long way towards the transformation of the keyboard idiom of such pianistic contemporaries as Jan Dussek and even had a later bearing on 'the musical language of nineteenth-century Continental Romanticism'. Although operating at a lower level of sophistication than Beethoven, Lang believes the measures 34–7 of Pinto's E-flat Sonata, 'read almost like a blueprint of Beethoven's measures 18–19'. In particular, he identifies such features as 'identical chordal descents ... wide skip[s] in the bass ... [and] nearly identical figuration patterns in the treble'. He also cites other 'more striking similarities' in their relative 'melodic, harmonic and textural details'.[lxxvi] Lang is not alone in holding these beliefs. They are shared, for example, by Alexander Ringer.[lxxvii]

With regard to what we may refer to as the nuts and bolts of Beethoven's construction, Brendel characterises the main themes of the sonata as being derived from the hexachord — the first six notes of the diatonic scale — and intervals of the third and fourth that divide it. He also singles out for special mention Beethoven's adoption of 'contrary motion [combining] ascending and descending lines' that impart 'a notion of excitement'.[lxxviii] Charles Rosen expresses similar views: 'The sonata is based on two kinds of motifs ascending or descending parallel fourths, and rising or falling sixths in scale motion.' He adds: 'The contrasts of these two-kinds of musical material is important in establishing the variety of textures within the work.'[lxxix] In his discussion of Beethoven's constructional procedures, Martin Cooper remarks on the care taken by Beethoven in the fully writing out of the appoggiaturas at bars 25 and 26 by way of emphasising the expressive treatment Beethoven required. In his words: 'They herald a characteristic crisis of intensity, in which the two hands move further and further apart, opposed not only in direction but in character, and separated by over four and a half octaves of empty keyboard.' He also comments on Beethoven's exploitation of what he describes as 'the extremes of pitch'. In the A-flat major sonata he considers these are used 'for purely expressive purposes' unlike in the work's predecessor, the Op. 109, in which he maintains Beethoven's intention 'was often to create a remote, ethereal atmosphere'.[lxxx] Denis Matthews regards much of Beethoven's writing as having 'a quartet texture' but which is nevertheless 'purely pianistic' especially in what he describes as the movement's 'fluttering arpeggios'.[lxxxi]

Beethoven designates the first movement *Moderato cantabile molto espressivo* which may be taken to mean 'at a moderate speed in a singing style, very expressively'.

Writing about the composer's instructions to the performer, Blom makes the observation that Beethoven is more explicit in this respect in his later compositions than in his earlier ones. He reasons: 'The less he was able to hear, it seems, the more anxious he grew to let the player know how his music should sound, not only in the matter of tempo and dynamics, but in that of meaning.'[lxxxii] To give added significance to the expressive qualities Beethoven wished the performer to contribute to his music, he adds the expression *con amabilità* ('with loveableness') at the very opening of the movement. Thereby he wished the music to sound 'amiable' and to reveal 'warmth and depth of feeling'.[lxxxiii] Writing of Beethoven's opening more than a century ago, the influential musicologist Ernst von Elterlein had the following to say: 'The opening ... is only to be described as "freundlich-hold" [amiably lovely]; it has a distant assonance with the motive of the canon in the second finale of Mozart's *Cosi fan tutti*. After a close, a song of deep even ardent yearning commences, then suddenly, harp-like strains are heard, and the most laughing images flit around the soul.' He concludes the passage: 'Happy forms arise in gay multiplicity, that song of yearning and the first motive which, in the so-called fantasia part is so conspicuous, re-appear.'[lxxxiv] In Gordon's estimation, the opening ideas, inherent in the first movement, leave as their hallmark a 'high-flown, lyrical quality' so pronounced in mood its lyricism is taken as the basis for the short development section.[lxxxv] In the manuscript score the word *sanft* has been added by another hand, it is thought probably at Beethoven's dictation, and is intended to assist in the interpretation of the expression *con amabilità*. Donald Tovey remarks: '[sanft] does not mean "soft" but, as nearly as may be, "gentle" in the most ethical sense of the word.'[lxxxvi] For Matthews the expression *con amabilità* serves as a sufficient guide to convey 'the warmth of heart in all the first-movement themes'.[lxxxvii] Rosen concurs: 'The first movement begins *con amabilità* and never completely loses that quality.'[lxxxviii] Rye goes further and suggests the opening theme 'forms the basis for much of the motivic working of the whole sonata'.[lxxxix] For Cooper, the movement's chordal introduction and first theme have a vocal character that he likens to 'a cloud of fine spray' that vanishes, as it were, to give way at bar 12 to the arpeggio demisemiquavers that follow.[xc]

From the time of the appearance of the A-flat major Piano Sonata, commentators have remarked on — have even marvelled at — Beethoven's skill in making something of musical significance from seemingly modest and unpromising material. Writing in the *Berliner Allgemeine musikalische Zeitung*, Friedrich Bernard Marx remarked: 'The first movement shows what a great composer can make out of the simplest material.'[xci] Von Elterlein also cites Marx who found in the first movement the sentiment of 'the parting from a beloved instrument in the Ossian-like sense'. This disposed von Elterlein to offer the rejoinder: 'Who would dispute that a touch of deep sadness prevails throughout.'[xcii] Mindful of the personal tribulations and illness that bore down upon Beethoven at the period of composition of his Op. 110, Fischer felt disposed to write: 'The childlike simplicity of the main subjects warms the heart as one remembers all the vicissitudes that the composer had to overcome before he could reach this point.'[xciii] His sometime-pupil Brendel expressed similar sentiments: 'In the first movement there is a new simplicity, which also comes with the new complexity in the late works, and it's nowhere more simple and loveable than here.'[xciv]

Carl Dahlhaus finds the lyricism that he believes 'shapes and colours' the thematic material in some of the composer's later works, is manifestly evident in the Piano Sonata

Op. 110.[xcv] Paul Bekker considers 'grace and sensibility dominate the movement' with 'very little dark shading' whose effect 'resembles the dawn of a brilliant day, the course of which is still unknown'.[xcvi] In the movement's exposition, Rosen detects Beethoven looking back to Haydn but with an overlay of some of his own original features.[xcvii] Writing of the period when Beethoven composed his Piano Sonata Op. 110, Peter Charleton remarks: 'Beethoven's heaviest cross was loneliness.' He draws attention to the composer's failure in marriage and his filial rejections in the manner in which his adopted nephew Karl sought to escape from his uncle. We may also add the social isolation imposed upon Beethoven by his deafness. Notwithstanding, Charlton adds: 'Yet the man who wrote the first movement of this work [Piano Sonata Op. 110] expresses the kindliest human warmth that is constant and a striving that is ardent.'[xcviii] In his estimation of the first movement Matthews also draws attention to its 'warm-hearted character' that he considers Beethoven achieved almost despite what he describes as its 'more normal sonata form' and likening it as being 'a law unto itself'.[xcix] Returning once more to the 1927 writings of Sir John B. McEwan (see above) he enthused: 'Movements like the opening movement of the Sonate in A flat, Op. 110 ... combine the noble symmetry and exquisite proportions of a Greek vase with the expressive significance of a Shakespeare sonnet ...'.[c] Igor Stravinsky was more succinct: 'The Allegro molto movement [is] a masterpiece in and by itself'.[ci]

Turning to questions of interpretation, Carl Czerny characterises the movement as being, 'A very lovely piece, and replete with feeling.' He urges the performer to play the tranquil passages 'very *cantabile* and expressively' and 'the roulades [the elaborate embellishments] extremely light and by no means brilliant.' Of interest also are his suggestions bearing on the appropriate fingering to adopt with particular emphasis on the role of the thumb, something he had learned directly from the composer himself.[cii] Von Elterlein exhorts: 'The whole movement demands much gentle tenderness, with a soft, singing expression.'[ciii] In his words of guidance to the would-be interpreter of the movement, Fischer reminds us that whilst the music may have initially have emanated, as it were, from the spirit of the composer, in its performance 'it should be remembered that the primal roots of every rhythm are to be found in breathing, the heart-beat, or the dance-step'.[civ] Tovey regarded the Op. 110 Piano Sonata to be technically the easiest of the composer's final trilogy. Perhaps it was with this in mind that he urges the young not to put off attempting to play the piece on the grounds: 'Those who recognise that they are unready for it must remember that experience cannot come except by experience, and therefore its foundations must be well and truly laid in youth.'[cv] Martin Cooper, however, urges caution: The works of Beethoven's last years, including all five of the last piano sonatas, should be regarded, like great operatic roles, as something that no physical, or even intellectual gifts, however exceptional, justify a young artist in attempting.' He then adds: 'A pianist of seventeen who attempts Op. 110 should be regarded as no less presumptuous than a singer of twenty-five who attempts Brünnhilde.' Cooper concludes his remarks by invoking thoughts about interpretation expressed by the musicologist Hermann Wetzel: 'In late Beethoven one must weigh every note until one has realized its motivic significance ... Not a single note is superfluous, and there is no passage ... that can be treated as you please, no trivial ornament.' (Herman Wetzel, *Beethoven Sonate Op. 110*, in Theodor Frimmel, *Beethoven Handbuch*, 1926.)[cvi]

Beethoven marks the second movement *Molto allegro*,

an indication to play the movement in a quick, lively tempo — 'very swift'. Not surprising, therefore, although not designated as such, the movement has the character of a scherzo; Beethoven in fact identified only one movement of his late piano sonatas with the term *scherzo*, namely the second movement of the *Hammerklavier* Sonata, Op. 106. As with it, we encounter dramatic contrasts of dynamics. In von Elterlein's words: 'We meet again, although in another form, the same wild hurrying and anxious hunting and crowding as in the *scherzi* of some of the last-named sonatas.'[cvii] Consistent with the composer's designation *Molto allegro*, the movement plays for just over two minutes disposing Rolland to describe it as, 'somewhat puzzling ... somewhat florid ... a remarkable *recitative* bridge' and 'one of those fast pieces, somewhat fantastic, with which Schuman has made us familiar at a later period'.[cviii] In much the same spirit Kinderman views the second movement as being in the manner of 'a transition' and draws attention to Beethoven's notation that in passages is 'partly without bar lines and with a profusion of tempo and expressive directions'.[cix]

'Here we have the quintessence of a playful, frolicsome *scherzo*,' states von Elterlein.[cx] Rosen is in agreement, contending: 'The Scherzo is humorous, folksy, sometimes brutal, and even sardonic.'[cxi] To Brendel's ears the second movement recalls Beethoven's late bagatelles 'dominated entirely by contrary motion'. He also recalls the views of a pianist of an earlier generation, namely, the Scottish-born German composer-pianist Eugen d'Albert. Among his many accomplishments, d'Albert edited a critical edition of Beethoven's piano works in which, as Brendel remarks, 'd'Albert tried to read into [the second movement] a gavotte with accents on every second bar'. For Brendel, however, 'the capricious character of the piece ... [stems] from its frequent changes of accentuation, and from the fact that the bar pattern ... becomes confused in a manner half burlesque and half mysteriously modal'.[cxii]

On 18 March 1820, Beethoven wrote to the publisher Nikolaus Simrock offering him accompaniments to two frivolous Austrian folk songs which respectively contain the words, *Unsa Kätz häd Katzlan ghabt* ('Our cat has had kittens') and *Ich bin lüderlich, du bist lüderlich* which may politely be translated as: 'I am a slovenly person, you're a slovenly person.' Commentators believe aspects of the melodies Beethoven composed for these songs may have infiltrated into the Scherzo of the A-flat major Piano Sonata. The reasoning is that at about the same time that Beethoven wrote his letter to Simrock he was probably working on the sonata.[cxiii] The nineteenth-century composer and music-theorist Adolf Bernard Marx was one of the first to make this connection and remarked philosophically: 'Did there ever come over the pure singer a dissatisfaction with the life that he was leading, a scorn of the foolish play which they call life?' — an indirect reference to the composer's personal circumstances at this time.[cxiv] Marx's approximate contemporary Hans von Bülow adopted a moralistic stance and was careful to warn players against what he considered to be 'the trivialization of this popular idea'. He conveys the impression that if it were possible he would have preferred Beethoven 'not to indulge his naïve sense of humour in this way'.[cxv] Kinderman's remarks are mediatory: '[The] main artistic significance lies in Beethoven's assimilation of this lowly, droll, and commonplace into the work, where such material proves complementary to the most elevated of sentiments.'[cxvi]

The terse Scherzo functions as a minuet and trio imbued with a 'jovial, witty quality'[cxvii] that is perhaps almost 'comic'.[cxviii] Von Elterlein enthuses: 'How fantastic and aerial, how interwoven with bright streaks of light!'[cix] Cooper describes Beethoven's writing here as being 'deliberately awkward'.[cxx] This observation reminds us of the composer's letter to Ferdinand Ries claiming the composition to be 'really not very difficult' (see above). Was Beethoven perhaps being just a little facetious? Matthews, a performing artist of standing, discussing the character of the movement remarks: 'Its quirks continue in the Trio, where abrupt leaps are followed by perilous descents of quavers, and where the left hand, crossing over, tends to mask the right hand's subsequent leap — a matter of importance for the player to adjust.'[cxxi] Gordon has similar things to say: 'The middle section is famous for its tricky, descending passagework, combined with a syncopated, cross-hand accompaniment.'[cxxii] With interpretation in mind, Fischer observes: 'The Trio shows that the whole movement must be taken fairly steadily, so that the Chopinesque filigree figuration in the right hand can achieve its full poetic effect.'[cxxiii] Czerny is more prosaic being content to remark: 'Very quick, energetic and humorous but earnest.'[cxxiv]

The movement ends with a coda of fifteen bars, five of which are silent. 'And how expressive [is] the Coda with those full powerful chords, separated by pauses which only make them more impressive and the final gentle dying away in the major!'[cxxv] Thereby, the movement comes to rest via a four-bar arpeggio in the base. The *Allgemeine musikalische Zeitung* of April 1824 contains a review of the last three Piano Sonatas, Opp. 109, 110 and 111. Despite regarding Beethoven's compositions with some scepticism, writing of the second movement of Op. 110 the reviewer captures the psychology inherent in the music: '[It] paints in tones, one after another: despondency ("Munthlosigkeit"), reassurance ("Ermuthigung"), transport by a higher power ("Fortgerissenwerden durch eine höhere Gewalt"), hesitation before a resolve ("Schwanken vor dem Entschluss"), full encouragement once more, and finally, after a cry of despair, total collapse ("gänzliches Zusammenstürzen").[cxxvi]

The final movement of Op. 110 is considered to be one of the composer's most original conceptions for the medium of the piano sonata. It is in effect a double movement insofar as it combines two slow and two fast sections of markedly different character and within which cross-references and allusions to each other occur. Barry Cooper suggests, thereby, 'Beethoven solved the problem of abandoning the four-movement structure which he had been so reluctant to give up entirely'.[cxxvii] The third movement is passion music — a complex of Baroque forms in which *ariosi* and fugues are interwoven. Musicologist David Dubal invited Brendel to comment on Beethoven's adoption of fugal writing in the Op. 110, prompting the following response: '[The] complexity of the last two movements of ariosos and fugues that return and interlock has Baroque features. Beethoven was not only an innovator in his late years, he also went back to earlier periods of music and took as much as he could from them, transforming the material to serve his purpose. In a way, these two interlocking movements are "passion" music, they remind me of Bach's Passions.'[cxxviii]

Philip Downs discerns Beethoven recalling the compositional manner he adopted at the outset of his final piano-sonata trilogy: 'The third movement resembles Op. 109 in that it too seems to set the heart, represented by songful melody, and the head, represented by fugue.'[cxxix] Also reflecting on the composer's previous style of writing for the keyboard, Bekker recalls how, in the Piano Sonata Op. 106, 'both grief and consolation' assume proportions of 'supernatural magnitude'. In the Op 110 he finds these features are also present but: '[The] scale of things is less tremendous, the sorrow is the sorrow of a man, not a super-human being, and the consolation has not the soaring sublimity of Op. 106, where titanic emotions oppose each other.' The reader will recall Bekker likened the first movement to 'dawn on a brilliant day' (see above). In his discussion of the final movement he adopts further imagery: 'The veil is lifted ... with the opening of the solemn and mournful *adagio* in B-flat minor. The instrument begins to speak as it spoke in the D minor Sonata [Op. 31, No. 2 *The Tempest*].'[xxx]

Rye places the final movement at the very heart of the sonata.[xxxi] In the same spirit, Matthews contends Beethoven reserves the 'full emotional depths' for the final movement of his Op. 110 and for him: 'No summary description can convey the intense personal involvement that this music commands and deserves.' As he argues, even if we discount or mistrust what he describes as 'Beethoven's extra-musical inspirations', he considers at this period in his life '[Beethoven] regarded the piano on the one hand, and the quartet on the other, as the confidants of his most intimate thoughts'.[xxxii] Beethoven's manner, as expressed in the A-flat major Piano Sonata, disposed Maynard Solomon to reflect more generally on the composer's style and ideals as exemplified in his late period: 'In the late works, his archetypal patterns retain their impress: struggle is sublimated into ecstasy ... chaos strives for lucid formation ... victorious conclusion are incessantly sought after and discovered as in the *Grosse Fuge*, the Piano Sonata Op. 110 and the finale of the Quartet in C-sharp minor, Op. 131.' At this stage in his life — nearing the apogee on his compositional trajectory — Solomon maintains: 'Beethoven had now found the accepted scheme of organization which he himself had brought to perfection ... and therefore endeavoured to find new types of form and to revive sundry earlier types of organization and combine them in various ways which departed from the essential principles upon which composers had been working for generations.'[cxxxiii] Also reflecting on Beethoven's compositional procedures, Rosen reflects that the final movement of the Op. 110 'is the first time in the history of music where the academic devices of counterpoint and fugue are integral to a composition's drama'. Moreover, he further observes in this movement: 'Beethoven does not simply represent the return to life, but persuades us physically of the process.'[cxxxiv]

We have described the third movement as being characterised by slow and fast sections, but this is an oversimplification. As the music unfolds it progresses through no fewer than six episodes that may be said to be a part of its highly original construction. The opening bars take the form of an introduction that commentators liken to a recitative. These are followed by a passage Beethoven's marks *Arioso dolente*. A fugue disrupts the contemplative mood but may be regarded as forming a part of the movement's exposition. The *Arioso* returns once more only to be superseded by the fugue in its inverted form.[cxxxv] The final bars bring the movement to its memorable conclusion. We now consider each of these sections of the music in turn.

With the *Adagio ma non troppo* of the third movement, 'we leave the humour of the Scherzo far behind'.[cxxxvi] The first three measures have the character of 'a vocal idiom transferred into instrumental music'. Thereby, at the outset, Beethoven 'evokes the human voice in [what will become] a dramatic situation'.[cxxxvii] Donald Tovey described the manner of the first three bars as being 'that of an extempore modulating passage'.[cxxxviii] Other commentators liken the entire 26 bars of the opening to a *scena* — a sort of scene-setting characteristic of the recitative part of a vocal number within an opera typical of the eighteenth century. Beethoven in fact writes the expression *recit* (recitative) immediately following the three opening bars. Von Elterlein described this passage as 'the wonderfully tragic entrance of the *Adagio*, as profound and touching a *scena* as Beethoven ever conceived'.[cxxxix] Moreover, it is a '*scena* and recitative full of pain'.[cxl] The prevailing mood is 'very solemn and grave, interwoven with a recitative full of unspeakable secret woe ... In this plaintive song, the soul fully but quietly pours out all its sorrow'.[cxli]

As the movement progresses, the idiom continues to be improvisatory and for a moment appears to look back to earlier times. Pairs of notes are repeated successively that to some authorities suggest Beethoven is expressing – imitating – the technical device of the *bebung*. We let Fuller-Maitland explain: 'In the fifth bar there is a succession of repeated notes, mostly tied together in pairs ... I think there must have been in Beethoven's mind some remembrances of the clavichords he probably knew in his youth and of their characteristic effect, known as the *bebung*, by which a note could be reinforced without being actually struck again.'[cxlii] Beethoven's procedures are no mere anachronism or pianistic idiosyncrasy. The music becomes suggestive of 'deep contemplation'[cxliii] with perhaps even 'a cry of pain'.[cxliv] In these first eight bars Beethoven resorts to an ever-changing sequence of indications to convey the depth of feeling that he wants the performer to impart to the music – *Adagio, ma non tropo/Più adagio/Andante/Meno adagio/Adagio/Adagio ma non troppo*.

The recitative 'gropes its way through remote keys' before reaching the passage he describes as 'plaintive'[cxlv] and which Beethoven marks *Arioso dolente* – to be played melodically in the style of an aria but sad/mournful. For Rolland this was 'one of the most beautiful airs ever penned by Beethoven'.[cxlvi] Reverting to the native German he desired to adopt in his later compositions, Beethoven inscribed the Autograph with the words *Klagender Gesang* – 'Song of

Lamentation'.[cxlvii] Commentators are fulsome in their appreciation of this passage. It has been perceived as expressing: 'Beethoven's innermost thoughts';[cxlviii] 'a lament that is literally choked with despair, [going] through a condition close to death';[cxlix] 'achingly beautiful';[cl] and 'a song of sorrow ... with dull palpitating harmonies'.[cli] Cooper's assessment is: 'No voice could give their full value to the anticipation which gives the melody its heartrending character, anymore than it could compass the wide span that is part of the design.'[clii] Reflecting on Beethoven's achievement, and mindful of the illness and personal tribulation that burdened him at the period when he was composing the music in question, Brendel hypothesises: 'In a movement for which Beethoven has left us such specific and meaningful instructions as "wearily lamenting", one may assume a large psychological context.'[cliii] Downs similarly conjectures: 'The question may be asked whether, here, Beethoven is more concerned with expressing the feeling of lamentation or with making a musical impression of breath caught between sobs.'[cliv]

The melodic contour of the *Arioso dolente* hovers above no fewer than 17 bars of incessant gently repeated semiquaver chords that are marked to be played 'very softly'. We have mentioned previously that the innovatory writing for the piano by the young English composer George Pinto may have exerted an influence on Beethoven in his composition of this piano sonata (see above). His influence has also been detected here in the *Arioso dolente*. Lang believes Pinto anticipated both Beethoven's melodic contour and his repeated chord accompaniment. By way of evidence, he compares Pinto's bars 17–19 from the third movement of his E-flat major Piano Sonata with Beethoven's bars 24–28 in the Op. 110.[clv] Commenting on this passage Cooper remarks: 'The accompaniment of repeated chords, though conceived for the lighter instrument of Beethoven's day and more difficult to manipulate successfully on today's fuller-toned pianoforte, emphasizes the forlorn character of the melody, which is further enhanced by its frequent accompaniment.'[clvi] Von Elterlein is almost poetic in his exhortation to the would-be interpreter of Beethoven's deeply felt music: 'One *must* have some mental picture when playing or listening to this sublime movement; a suitable one is the Prison Scene in Schiller's *Joan of Arc*: "Hear me, O God, in mine extremity/In fervent supplication up to Thee/Up to Thy Heaven above, I send my soul".'[clvii]

As remarked, the third episode in the third movement is a fugue. Whereas the *Arioso dolente* is 'achingly beautiful in its utter despair' it is 'soothed by the fugue theme — carved out of marble in its perfection'.[clviii] It contributes to both the construction of the sonata and its emotional content. With regard to the former, John Cockshoot states: 'Beethoven wanted to overcome the inherent division between an adagio and a finale and raise them to a powerful unity. He solves the problem by making the fugue the truly dominating section and embodying in it the desired unity at the same time.'[clix] As Brendel remarks, the fugue remains part of the exposition, retains the key of A-flat major and serves to counteract the 'lamenting song' that has gone before.[clx] Kinderman regards the *Arioso dolente* and the fugue — that he describes as 'spiritualized' — as working together as a 'framework and sees parallels in their alternation to those of the *Agnus Dei* and *Dona nobis pacem* in the last movement of the *Missa solemnis* — a reminder of the composer's disposition to transfer musical ideas and processes from one composition to another.[clxi]

In the context of the 'spiritualized' mood Beethoven is creating, the fugue fulfils 'a subjective emotional' role and one of 'gathering of confidence after illness or despair ... a translation into music of a personal experience'.[clxii] There is perhaps a foreshadowing of the 'Heiliger danksagung eines genesenen an die Gottheit' (Holy song of thanksgiving of a convalescent) that the composer inscribed in the third movement of his String Quartet, Op. 132.[clxiii]

According to Rolland, Vincent d'Indy was given to comparing Beethoven's concentration of expression in this movement with the A minor String Quartet and its celebrated 'Song of gratitude to God for his goodness'.[clxiv] Cockshoot remarks on the manner in which Beethoven's writing is 'very thrilling' in its 'upward striving' and 'so very occupied with spiritual matters'. He remarks one is tempted to believe Beethoven is even putting 'emotion above reason'. He concludes: 'At all events, this passage carries out the aspiring nature of the [fugal] subject to its logical and inevitable conclusion, which satisfies our strongest musical demands.'[clxv] 'From its last breathed tones [i.e. the close of the *Arioso dolente*] ascends the fugue, the great law of nature. Once again the lament, broken helpless, dashing is the fugue, embracing all, truth with its disregard of the individual. Thus does Beethoven express his pantheism.'[clxvi]

The fugue grows with hardly a pause from the *Arioso dolente* in answer, as it were, to its lament.[clxvii] It is as though Beethoven is releasing 'the intensity of his innermost thoughts'.[clxviii] For a moment, Beethoven appears to recall the aria 'It is finished' from Bach's *St. John Passion*.[clxix] Brendel likens the *Arioso dolente* to 'a unit' that work together. Quoting his former teacher Edwin Fischer, he comments: 'We are led to the brink of death and then witness "the gradual resurgence of the heartbeat" in the crescendo on the repeated G major chords.'[clxx] Kinderman makes similar observations and recalls the influence once more of the contemporaneous *Missa Solemnis*: 'The pairing of the *Arioso dolente* with the fugue in A flat has no precedent in Beethoven's earlier piano music; its closest affinity is with the *Agnus Dei* and *Dona Nobis Pacem* of the *Missa Solemnis* ... The *Agnus Dei* is burdened by an overwhelming awareness of the sins of mankind and the fallen state of earthly existence; by contrast, the *Dona Nobis Pacem* represents the promise of liberation from the endless cycle of suffering and injustice'.[clxxi]

D' Indy remarks that Beethoven's adoption of the form of the fugue helped, as he puts it, 'to revivify the languishing form of the sonata and this was the point of departure of a new system of musical structure, which was, however, solidly based upon classical tradition'. Writing of which he adds: '[The] fugue had enjoyed, with J. S. Bach and his predecessors and contemporaries, a moment of ineffable splendour.'[clxxii]

With the publication of the *Hammerklavier* Sonata, a number of Beethoven's contemporaries cavilled over his fugal writing. His assistant Anton Schindler, ever eager to defend his master, attempted to set the record straight by writing: '[The] B-flat major, Op. 106, has an impressive three-part fugue, whose like is to be found in no other piano work. If the master indicates that it is to be played with "certain liberties" [a reference to Beethoven's instructions to the performer, *con alcune licenze*], he merely wishes to show that he is quite familiar with the rules he has ignored.' Schindler continues: 'Later on, in the sonata in A-flat major, Op. 110, we find a three part fugue that contains neither "shocking passages" nor "certain liberties" [a dig at the critics who had disparaged the work] ... but is full of charm and beauty.'[clxxiii]

Just as he had taken care with his indications to the performer in the Piano Sonata Op. 106, Beethoven is so minded — even more so — in the directions he sets out in the fugue (first part) in the Piano Sonata Op. 110. These are: *Allegro ma non troppo/L'istesso tempo di*

Arioso/Listesso tempo della Fuga/poco a poco di nuovo vivente/popc a poco tutte le corde/ and *poco a poco più mosso*. Commenting on this aspect of his instructions to the performer, Rolland remarks: 'The Italian indications to this sonata are fuller and more unusual, and show that Beethoven was aiming at the deepest possible expression ... and the insertion of the *Arioso Dolente* into the fugue, show what a struggle Beethoven underwent in the conquest of his feelings.'[clxiv] Additionally, we recall Blom's previously cited observation: 'The less he was able to hear, it seems, the more anxious he grew to let the player know how his music should sound, not only in the matter of tempo and dynamics, but in that of meaning.'

In his youth Beethoven had become familiar with the preludes and fugues of Bach's *Well-tempered Clavier* through the instruction he gained from his teacher Christian Gottlob Neefe; he was proficient in their performance from about the age of twelve. He augmented this youthful experience by undertaking numerous exercises in counterpoint for his Viennese teachers Haydn and Johan Albrechtsberger (see Piano Sonatas Op. 2, Nos. 1–3). In a letter to the violinist and conductor Karl Holtz he once wrote: 'To write a fugue is no great art; I wrote dozens of them when I was a student. But the imagination also insists on its rights ... nowadays'.[clxv] We have also seen Beethoven further developed his skills in the art of counterpoint in the pedagogical studies he prepared for his composition pupil the Archduke Rudolph (see Piano Sonata Op. 106). Cooper reflects: 'Beethoven's musical style was inevitably founded in the musical language of the time [and was] shaped by the influences of a great variety of music from Bach ... to ... works by such contemporaries as Clementi and Cherubini [who Beethoven considered to be one of the greatest living composers].'[clxvi] The Fuge in the third movement 'shows the power of the composer's imagination [and] also exhibits ... the force of his intellect'.[clxxvii]

The first subject of the fugue is derived from the opening notes of the first movement, disposing Downs to reflect philosophically 'that epigram of eternal musical truth here stripped of its rhythmic profile and now on notes of equal length emphasising the melody'.[clxxviii] Paying tribute to Beethoven's powers of imagination, Rye comments: '[The] genius of Beethoven's scheme becomes clear when the fugue subject recalls the outline of the opening melody of the first movement – a subtle association by suggestion rather than outright imitation.'[clxxix] 'It draws its character [in three voices] from the combination of steadily progressing dotted crotchets, persistent quaver movement and most importantly, the idea of syncopation and suspension ... The dramatic contrasting and combining of these elements produce that fundamental unity within apparent diversity which is one of the clearest evidences of Beethoven's intellectual power.'[clxxx] 'The counterpoint in the fugue is smoother and more euphonious than in that of the three previous sonatas; its subject is related to the theme of the first movement and is sufficiently melodious in character to form the basis of a magnificent, non-contrapuntal peroration which sums up the whole sonata with an air of complete inevitability.'[clxxxi]

The surviving sketches and autograph score reveal Beethoven had difficulty in finding a solution to combining the fugue with the preceding Adagio. The autograph, initially intended to be a fair copy, became a composing score. Beethoven's emendations and second thoughts became so extensive that he felt obliged to write out a fair copy.[clxxxii] Having found a solution to the structure of the fugue, he then made a new manuscript of the third movement, known today as the Bonn Autograph score.[clxxxiii] Further ensuing doubts caused him to return to correct the text that, as previously remarked (see above), is now preserved in the Staatsbibliothek. Beethoven's labours were soon recognised for their artistic accomplishment. A contemporary review of the composition in the *Berliner Allgemeine musikalische Zeitung* remarked: 'it proves that counterpoint need not be an academic exercise; it can be made to live in its own right and sound as visibly as the other movements of the sonata.'[clxxxiv]

After eighty-eight bars, Beethoven recalls the *Arioso dolente* in a passage marked *L'istesso temo di Arioso*. The forward march of the fugue is checked 'in faltering accents as though grief-stricken'.[clxxxv] The mood is anguished and in the autograph score is marked 'ermatte, klagend' — 'exhausted, plaintive'. The agitation of the fugue subsides but the music 'expresses a yet deeper feeling and breathes more profound sighs'.[clxxxvi] Brendel describes the melodic line as becoming porous, 'expressing, with its continual sighs, the reduced resistance of the sufferer'.[clxxxvii] Rosen considers the G minor tonality in this section imparts to the music 'a flattened quality befitting exhaustion ... a lament that is literally choked with emotion'.[clxxxviii] At the close of the *Arioso* reprise, a nine-times repeated chord creates 'a cloud of sound'[clxxxix] suggestive of sobs (Tovey) and 'like a reawakening heartbeat' (Fischer). Through a crescendo, these chords increase in strength allowing the fugue to return once more.

Beethoven designates the return of the fugue, *L'istesso tempo della Fuga* and inscribed the score with the words 'Nach und nach wieder auflebend' — 'Little by little reviving to life' or 'gaining new life'. The three voices enter 'one by one, reflecting sentiments of revival and strength'.[cxc] Von Elterlein describes the transition as 'masterly' and the animation of the fugal figures as 'weben hin, weben her, fluthen hin, fluthen her' — with ever-increasing energy — to the end where harp-like strains are heard, a clever imitation, an expressive souvenir of the spirit of the first movement'.[cxci] 'Little by little life and joy return ... suffering disappears ... fantastic cleverness comes to the fore with the subject in contrary movement.'[cxcii] In his commentary Czerny proclaims: 'Another fugue, which by constantly increasing motion is carried to a rushing and brilliant conclusion.'[cxciii] Stravinsky, whom we have cited previously, is once more full of admiration for Beethoven's workmanship: 'The Fuge is the pinnacle of the sonata, but the marvel of it is in the substance of the counterpoint and cannot be described.'[cxciv]

Taking up the challenge of describing the fugue, Matthews comments: 'Through various complexities of diminutions and augmentations ... [the Fuge] finds its way back to the home [key of] A flat, gathering momentum and confidence, and losing its contrapuntal texture and becoming purely melodic in the last triumphant bars.'[cxcv] In Downs' analysis: 'Fugal devices of various kinds ... give way to a concluding, ecstatically manic extension of the fugue subject treated now homophonically as each stretch of endless melody with each cadence becoming the start of the next phrase.'[cxcvi] Gordon expresses similar views: 'Passing through a section marked both *Mento allegro* and its German equivalent *Etwas langsamer*, the fugue subject is transformed by free diminution into an accompaniment figure ... the fugue becomes virtually homophonic, its subject enters anew in an ecstatic, lyrical statement and continues to expand, reaching a glorious climax at the final cadence of the work.'[cxcvii]

Tovey shared Stravinsky's high estimation of Beethoven's achievement: 'Like all Beethoven's visions this fugue absorbs and transcends the world.'[cxcviii] '[The] work throws off "the chains of music itself".'[cxcix] As throughout the sonata, Beethoven takes particular care in his instructions to the performer to ensure the interpretation he envisaged, citing: *poco a poco di nuovo vivente/sempre una corda/poco a poco tutte le corde/Meno allegro/poco a poco più mosso/Animato.* These words of guidance disposed Rolland to remark: 'The Italian indications to this sonata are fuller and more unusual, and show that Beethoven was aiming at the deepest possible expression.'[cc] Reflecting on the pain and angst in the preceding part of the third movement, Neumayr adds: 'The way the fugue in three voices develops out of this dirge and ascends to triumphant transfiguration is a masterpiece of the art of counterpoint found elsewhere only in the last movement of Mozart's *Jupiter* Symphony and in the finale of Anton Bruckner's Fifth Symphony.'[cci]

As we draw our discussion of Beethoven's Piano Sonata in A-flat major, Op. 110 to a close, we call to mind a recollection by Isodore Philipp of the playing of the virtuoso pianist and composer Charles-Valentin Alkan. Philipp was himself an exceptional pianist and was familiar with the playing of the greatest pianists of his era from Liszt to Busoni. He had occasion to hear Alkan play at the Maison Érard in Paris, whose studios were reserved exclusively for the practice and lessons of only the most accomplished pianists. Observing that Philipp was eavesdropping on his practice, Alkan remarked: 'Listen well, I'm going to play for you alone, Beethoven's Opus 110 – listen.' Philipp recalls: 'What happened to the great Beethovenian poem beneath the skinny, hooked fingers of the little old man I couldn't begin to describe – above all in the *Arioso* and the fugue, where the melody, penetrating the mystery of Death itself, climbs up to a blaze of light, affected me with an excess of enthusiasm such as I have never experienced since.'[ccii] What Philpp has to say here is indicative of the high estimation in which this composition is held. We close with a selection of further testimonies. 'The working-out is a triumph: the return to life is gloriously ecstatic.'[cciii] 'The conclusion is ethereal.'[cciv] 'The piece triumphs in an enthusiasm of good feeling.'[ccv] The closing bars signal 'the emergence of the triumphant ascent'.[ccvi]

Mindful of the temptation to invest music with 'meaning' and 'extra-musical associations', Ernst von Elterlein cautions: 'A certain reserve is advisable if we would not lose ourselves in capricious phantasmagoria. Instrumental music often offers riddles, which perhaps will never be fully solved, as the next and last of Beethoven's sonatas gives reason to observe.'[ccvii]

---

[i] Marion M. Scott, 1940. p. 79.

[ii] David Wyn Jones, 1998, p. 147.

[iii] Edwin Fischer, 1959, p. 114.

[iv] Donald Jay Grout and Claude V. Palisca, editors, 1988, p. 648.

[v] Anton Neumayr, 1994–1997, p. 277.

[vi] Stewart Gordon, 1996, p. 190.

[vii] Charles Rosen, 2002, p. 235.

[viii] As quoted by Robin Wallace, 1986, pp. 53–4.

[ix] Alfred Brendel in conversation with Martin Meyer, in: Alfred Brendel, 2002.

[x] Bernard Shaw, 1937, pp. 60–1. In another account of this concert, originally published in the *The World* of 25 June 1890, Shaw considered Madame Haas had made the work so thoroughly her own he considered that Ignaz Paderewski – her distinguished pianist contemporary – should have been there to take a lesson in the work's interpretation from her. As recorded in: Bernard Shaw, *Music in London*, 1890–94, 1932, p. 25.

[xi] John A. Fuller-Maitland writing in the special issue of *The Musical Times*, London: Vol. VIII, No. 2, 1927, pp. 222–3.

[xii] (Sir) John B. McEwan writing in: *Music & Letters, Beethoven: special number*, London, 1927, p. 162.

[xiii] Nicholas Delbanco, 1985, pp. 171–2.

[xiv] Barry Cooper, 1990, p. 41.

[xv] Emily Anderson, 1961, Vol. 2, Letter No. 1021, pp. 891–2.

[xvi] Theodore Albrecht, translator and editor, 1996, Vol. 2, Letter No. 274, pp. 188–90.

[xvii] For a summary account of the life and work of Adolph Schlesinger, including details of the various works of Beethoven that he and his son published, see Peter Clive, 2001, pp. 316–18.

[xviii] Emily Anderson, 1961, Vol. 2, Letter No. 1033, p. 902.

[xix] See: Beethoven House Digital Archives, Library Document Samlung H. C. Bodmer, HCB Br 210. This includes an audio recording of the letter of 20 September together with the German text.

[xx] See: Beethoven house, Digital Archives, Sammlung H. C. Bodmer, HCB Br 8.

[xxi] Anton Felix Schindler, edited by Donald W. MacArdle and translated by Constance S. Jolly from the German edition of 1860, 1966, p. 239.

xxii Beethoven had his first attack of jaundice during the summer of 1820 and it persisted well into August. Writing of this, the medical authority Anton Neumayr has the following observations. 'Beethoven liked fish and was particularly fond of oysters. In the conversation books, we read time and again about oysters having freshly arrived ... by special mail. It could have been his fondness for fresh oysters that gave him viral hepatitis with jaundice. According to present-day scientific understanding, oysters are a common source of infection for Hepatitis A virus, present in [contaminated] seawater.' See: Anton Neumayr, 1994–1997, pp. 276–7.

xxiii Emily Anderson, 1961, Vol. 2, Letter No. 1050, pp. 915–6.

xxiv See: Beethoven House Digital Archives, Library Document NE 88. This includes an audio recording of the letter of 7 June 1821 together with the full German text.

xxv Emily Anderson, 1961, Vol. 2, Letter No. 1061, pp. 929–931.

xxvi Alfred Brendel, 2001, p. 86.

xxvii See: Beethoven house, Digital Archives, Sammlung H. C. Bodmer, HCB Br 50. This includes an audio recording of the letter of 12 December together with the German text.

xxviii See: Beethoven House *Sonata für Klavier (As-Dur) Op. 110*.

xxix Theodore Albrecht, translator and editor, 1996, Vol. 2, Letter No. 283, p. 201.

xxx See: Beethoven House *Sonata für Klavier (As-Dur) Op. 110*. Some authorities give a publication date of August. Alan Tyson suggests Schlesinger's Berlin and Paris editions may have been published as early as July 1822. See: Alan Tyson, 1963, pp. 17–20.

xxxi Theodore Albrecht, translator and editor, 1996, Vol. 2, Letter No. 282, p. 200.

xxxii *Ibid*, Vol. 2, Letter No. 285 and note 8, pp. 203–4.

xxxiii Emily Anderson, 1961, Vol. 2, Letter No. 1077, pp. 943–4.

xxxiv *Ibid*, Vol. 2, Letter No. 1084, pp. 953–5.

xxxv Peter Clive, 2001, p. 260.

xxxvi Emily Anderson, 1961, Vol. 2, Letter No. 1079, pp. 947–50.

xxxvii Theodore Albrecht, translator and editor, 1996, Vol. 2, Letter No. 294, pp. 220–1.

xxxviii Emily Anderson, 1961, Vol. 2, Letter No. 1083, pp. 952–3.

xxxix Theodore Albrecht, translator and editor, 1996, Vol. 2, Document 288, pp. 207–10.

xl *Ibid*, Vol. 2, Letter No. 292, pp. 216–8.

xli *Ibid*, Vol. 2, Letter No. 293, pp. 218–20. For a discussion of Beethoven's late Piano Sonata and their publication, see: Beethoven house, Digital Archives, BH 218.

xlii Emily Anderson, 1961, Vol. 2, Letter No. 1084, pp. 953–4.

xliii Alan Tyson, 1963, p. 15.

xliv Emily Anderson, 1961, Vol. 2, Letter No. 1095, pp. 965–6. For a facsimile reproduction of this letter and its edited text see: Beethoven House, Digital Archives, Sammlung H. C. Bodmer, HCB BBr 141. Anton Schindler remarks that Beethoven was still not entirely satisfied with the Paris edition of the Op. 110, even after two proof-readings, and requested third. See: Anton Felix Schindler, Beethoven as I knew him, edited by Donald W. MacArdle and translated by Constance S. Jolly from the German edition of

[xlv] Theodore Albrecht, translator and editor, 1996, Vol. 2, Letter No. 301, pp. 332–3.

[xlvi] Derived from, Douglas Porter Johnson, editor, *The Beethoven sketchbooks: history, reconstruction, inventory*, 1985, p. 73 and pp. 265–72.

[xlvii] William Kinderman: *Contrast and continuity*, in: Scott G Burnham and Michael P. Steinberg, editors, *Beethoven and his world*, 2000, pp. 214–8.

[xlviii] Douglas Porter Johnson, editor, *The Beethoven sketchbooks: history, reconstruction, inventory*, 1985, pp. 377–89.

[xlix] John V. Cockshoot, 1959, p. 99. Cockshoot illustrates his contention regarding Beethoven's self-critical standards by quoting selected musical examples from the sources he has identified.

[l] Philip Radcliffe, *Piano music* in: *The age of Beethoven*, The new Oxford history of music, Vol. VIII, Gerald Abraham, editor, 1988, p. 340 and pp. 349–50.

[li] Matthew Rye, *Notes to the BBC Radio Three Beethoven experience*, Friday 10 June 2005, www.bbc.co.uk/radio3/Beethoven

[lii] Alexander A. Ringer, *Beethoven and the London Pianoforte School*, in: Paul Henry Lang, *The creative world of Beethoven*, 1971, p. 254.

[liii] Eric Blom, 1938, p. 229.

[liv] Emily Anderson, 1961, Vol. 2, Letter No. 1118, p. 983. This document is undated but probably derives from early (January?) 1822.

[lv] For an extended commentary on Beethoven's relationship with the Brentano family, see: Peter Clive, 2001, pp. 47–52.

[lvi] See: Alan Tyson, 1963, p. 111 and Pamela J. Willetts, 1970, p. 29.

[lvii] *Ibid*, pp. 17–20.

[lviii] See: Beethoven House, Digital Archives, Sammlung J. Van der Spek C Op. 110.

[lix] As listed in the *London Auction records*, 'from the Collection of Charles Letts', pp. 358–9.

[lx] Ludwig Nohl, 1880, pp. 185–6.

[lxi] *Ibid*, pp. 195–6.

[lxii] Oscar George Theodore Sonneck, 1927, pp. 129–30. See also: Peter Clive, 2001, pp. 325–6 and p. 374.

[lxiii] Ludwig Nohl, 1880, pp. 200–1. See also: Oscar George Theodore Sonneck, 1927, pp. 114–16 and Peter Clive, 2001, pp. 298–99.

[lxiv] Friedrich Rochlitz quoted in Ludwig Nohl, 1880, p. 210. See also: Oscar George Theodore Sonneck, 1927, pp. 120–9 and Peter Clive, 2001, 288–9.

[lxv] Quoted in: Oscar George Theodore Sonneck, 1927, pp. 116–20. When Rossini took leave of Beethoven, he encouraged his young contemporary 'to compose some more barbers'. Rossini's visit to see Beethoven so seized the mind of Richard Wagner as to dispose him to meet the Italian composer in Paris in 1860. The meeting subsequently took place in the presence of a number of others including the wealthy amateur pianist-composer Edmond Michotte. He took notes of the ensuing conversation that he subsequently published in 1906 as *La visite de Wagner à Rossini*. This is available today as *Richard Wagner's visit to Rossini* (Paris 1860) and *An evening at Rossini's in Beau-Sejour (Passy)* (1858), translated by Herbert Weinstock (1968.) In this work, Michotte's text is of interest in providing an insight into Wagner's theories about music drama and, relevant to the present study, Rossini's impressions of Beethoven.

[lxvi] As quoted by Adrian Williams in: *Portrait of Liszt: by himself and his*

[lvii] *contemporaries*, 1990, pp. 422–3.
[lvii] Berthold Litzmann editor, *Clara Schumann: an artist's life, based on material found in diaries and letters*, 1993 pp. 150–1.
[lviii] Virgil Thomson, 1968, pp. 192–3.
[lix] Thomas P. Lewis, editor, *Raymond Leppard on music: an anthology of critical and personal writings*, 1993, p. 325.
[lx] This is the description of Ernst von Elterlein, 1898, p. 118.
[lxi] Denis Matthews, 1967, p. 53.
[lxii] Eric Blom, 1938, p. 230.
[lxiii] Romain Rolland, 1917, p. 163.
[lxiv] F. E. Kirby, 1995, p. 129.
[lxv] Philip Radcliffe, *Piano music in: The age of Beethoven, The new Oxford history of music, Vol. VIII*, Gerald Abraham, editor, 1988, p. 349.
[lxvi] Paul Henry Lang, 1971, p. 252.
[lxvii] See, by way of illustration, musical example 13 in: Alexander Ringer, editor. *The early Romantic era: between revolutions; 1789 and 1848*, 1990, p. 254.
[lxviii] Alfred Brendel, 2001, p. 87.
[lxix] Charles Rosen, 2002, p. 235.
[lxx] Martin Cooper, *Beethoven: the last decade, 1817–1827*, 1970, p. 188. Cooper numbers the bars in question as being 23 and 24.
[lxxi] Denis Matthews, 1985, p. 98.
[lxxii] Eric Blom, 1938, p. 230.
[lxxiii] Matthew Rye, *Notes to the BBC Radio Three Beethoven experience*, Friday 10 June 2005, www.bbc.co.uk/radio3/Beethoven
[lxxiv] Ernst von Elterlein, 1898, p. 116.
[lxxv] Stewart Gordon, 1996, p. 190.
[lxxvi] Harold Craxton and Donald Francis Tovey, *Beethoven: Sonatas for pianoforte, Piano Sonata in E-flat major, Op. 110*, [1931], p. 214.
[lxxvii] Denis Matthews, 1967, p. 53.
[lxxviii] Charles Rosen, 2002, p. 235.
[lxxix] Matthew Rye, *Notes to the BBC Radio Three Beethoven experience*, Friday 10 June 2005, www.bbc.co.uk/radio3/Beethoven
[xc] Martin Cooper, 1970, p. 188.
[xci] Quoted by Robin Wallace in: *Beethoven's critics: aesthetic dilemmas and resolutions during the composer's lifetime*, 1986, pp. 53–4.
[xcii] Ernst von Elterlein, 1898, p. 116.
[xciii] Edwin Fischer, 1959, p. 114.
[xciv] Alfred Brendel in: David Dubal, *The world of the concert pianist*, 1985, pp. 110–11.
[xcv] Carl Dahlhaus, 1991, p. 215.
[xcvi] Paul Bekker, 1925, p. 138.
[xcvii] Charles Rosen, 2002, p. 236.
[xcviii] Peter Charleton, *website* text, *The works of Ludwig van Beethoven*.
[xcix] Denis Matthews, 1985, pp. 98–9.
[c] (Sir) John B. McEwan writing in *Music & Letters, Beethoven: special number*, London, 1927, p. 161.
[ci] Igor Stravinsky, 1972, p. 273.
[cii] Quoted in: Paul Badura-Skoda, Carl Czerny: *On the Proper Performance of*

all Beethoven's Works for the Piano, 1970, p. 66. Czerny makes particular mention of the role of the thumb that he received in Beethoven's instruction in the art of piano playing which he (Czerny) said was then innovative for the period in question (the first decade of the nineteenth century).

[ciii] Ernst von Elterlein, 1898, p. 147.
[civ] Edwin Fischer, 1959, p. 114.
[cv] Harold Craxton and Donald Francis Tovey, *Beethoven: Sonatas for pianoforte, Piano Sonata in E-flat major, Op. 110*, [1931], p. 214.
[cvi] Martin Cooper, *Beethoven: the last decade, 1817–1827*, 1970, p. 187.
[cvii] Ernst von Elterlein, 1898, pp. 116–7.
[cviii] Romain Rolland, 1917, p. 163–4.
[cix] William Kinderman, *[Beethoven] The late sonatas*, in: Larry R. Todd, editor, *Nineteenth-century piano music*, 2004, pp. 72–83.
[cx] Ernst von Elterlein, 1898, p. 148.
[cxi] Charles Rosen, 2002, p. 235.
[cxii] Alfred Brendel, 1985, pp. 110–11 and 2001, p. 87.
[cxiii] See, for example: John South Shedlock, 1918, p. 31 and Ernst von Elterlein, 1898, p. 148.
[cxiv] *Ibid*, von Elterlein, pp. 116–17.
[cxv] Derived from: Martin Cooper, 1970, pp. 190–1.
[cxvi] William Kinderman, 1997, p. 226.
[cxvii] Stewart Gordon, 1996, p. 191.
[cxviii] William Kinderman, *The piano sonatas [of Beethoven]*, in: Glen Stanley, editor, *The Cambridge companion to Beethoven*, 2000, p. 121.
[cxix] Ernest von Elterlein, 1898, p. 117.
[cxx] Martin Cooper, 1970, p. 191.
[cxxi] Denis Matthews, 1967, p. 54.
[cxxii] Stewart Gordon, 1996, p. 191.
[cxxiii] Edwin Fischer, 1959, p. 114.
[cxxiv] Quoted in: Paul Badura-Skoda, Carl Czerny: *On the Proper Performance of all Beethoven's Works for the Piano*, 1970, p. 66.
[cxxv] Ernst von Elterlein, 1898, p. 117.
[cxxvi] Robin Wallace, 1986, p. 39.
[cxxvii] Barry Cooper, 1991, p. 242. See also: Martin Cooper, 1970, p. 191.
[cxxviii] Alfred Brendel in: David Dubal, *The world of the concert pianist*, 1985, pp. 110–11.
[cxxix] Philip Downs, 1992, p. 610.
[cxxx] Paul Bekker, 1925, p. 138.
[cxxxi] Matthew Rye, *Notes to the BBC Radio Three Beethoven Experience*, Friday 10 June 2005, www.bbc.co.uk/radio3/Beethoven
[cxxxii] Denis Matthews, 1972, p. 181.
[cxxxiii] Maynard Solomon, 1977, p. 294 and pp. 300–1. The words quoted in this passage are in part derived from the writings of Sir Hubert Parry (see Piano Sonata, Op. 10, No. 2).
[cxxxiv] Charles Rosen, 2002, p. 240.
[cxxxv] With acknowledgement to Alfred Brendel, 2001, p. 87.
[cxxxvi] Charles Rosen, 2002, p. 238.
[cxxxvii] Philip G. Downs, 1992, p. 610.
[cxxxviii] Harold Craxton and Donald Francis Tovey, [1931], *Beethoven: Sonatas for*

pianoforte, *Piano Sonata in A-flat major, Op. 110*, p. 216.
[cxxxix] Ernst von Elterlein, 1898, p. 148.
[cxl] Charles Rosen, p. 2002, p. 235.
[cxli] Ernst von Elterlein, 1898, p. 117.
[cxlii] John A. Fuller-Maitland writing in the special issue of *The Musical Times*, London: Vol. VIII, No. 2, 1927, pp. 222–3.
[cxliii] Stewart Gordon, 1996, p. 192.
[cxliv] Charles Rosen, 2002, p. 238.
[cxlv] Denis Matthews, 1967, pp. 54–5.
[cxlvi] Romain Rolland, 1917, pp. 163–4.
[cxlvii] See, for example, the commentary by Philip G. Downs, 1992, p. 610.
[cxlviii] Barry Cooper, 1991, p. 242.
[cxlix] Charles Rosen, 2002, p. 235.
[cl] Peter Charleton, *website* text, *The works of Ludwig van Beethoven*.
[cli] Paul Bekker, 1925, p. 138.
[clii] Martin Cooper, 1970, p. 192.
[cliii] Alfred Brendel, 2001, p. 87.
[cliv] Philip G. Downs, 1992, pp. 610–11.
[clv] Paul Henry Lang, 1971, p. 252.
[clvi] Martin Cooper, 1970, p. 192.
[clvii] Ernst von Elterlein, 1898, p. 148.
[clviii] Peter Charleton, *website* text, *The works of Ludwig van Beethoven*.
[clix] John V. Cockshoot, 1959, pp. 95–6.
[clx] Alfred Brendel, 2001, p. 87.
[clxi] William Kinderman, *The piano sonatas [of Beethoven]*, in: Glen Stanley, editor, *The Cambridge companion to Beethoven*, 2000, p. 121.
[clxii] Denis Matthews, 1967, p. 54.
[clxiii] A view shared by Edwin Fischer, 1959, p. 114.
[clxiv] Romain Rolland, 1917, p. 164.
[clxv] John V. Cockshoot, 1959, p. 120.
[clxvi] Oskar Bie, 1966, p. 181.
[clxvii] Martin Cooper, 1976, p. 192.
[clxviii] Barry Cooper, 1991, p. 242.
[clxix] As remarked, amongst others, by Alfred Brendel, 2001, p. 87.
[clxx] *Ibid*, pp. 55–6.
[clxxi] William Kinderman, *[Beethoven] The late sonatas*, in: Larry R. Todd, editor, *Nineteenth-century piano music*, 2004, pp. 72–83.
[clxxii] Vincent d' Indy, discussing Beethoven's contribution to contrapuntal writing in: *César Franck*, 1965, p. 85.
[clxxiii] Anton Felix Schindler, edited by Donald W. MacArdle and translated by Constance S. Jolly from the German edition of 1860, 1966, p. 214.
[clxxiv] Romain Rolland, 1917, p. 164.
[clxxv] See: Martin Cooper, 1970, p. 192.
[clxxvi] Barry Cooper, 1990, p. 59.
[clxxvii] Martin Cooper, 1970, p. 192.
[clxxviii] Philip G. Downs, 1992, pp. 610–11. See also: Denis Matthews, 1967 and William Kinderman in: Larry R. Todd, editor, *Nineteenth-century piano*

  music, 2004.

[lxxix] Matthew Rye, *Notes to the BBC Radio Three Beethoven experience*, Friday 10 June 2005, www.bbc.co.uk/radio3/Beethoven

[lxxx] Martin Cooper, 1970, p. 192.

[lxxxi] Philip Radcliffe, *Piano music in: The age of Beethoven, The new Oxford history of music, Vol. VIII*, Gerald Abraham, editor, 1988, p. 340.

[lxxxii] See: Barry Cooper, *The compositional act: sketches and autographs* in: Glen Stanley, editor, *The Cambridge companion to Beethoven*, 2000, p. 35. See also: Douglas Porter Johnson, 1985, p. 386.

[lxxxiii] This is preserved in the Beethoven House, Digital Archives as, Sammlung H. C. Bodmer HCB BMh 2/42.

[lxxxiv] Robin Wallace, 1986, pp. 53–4.

[lxxxv] Denis Matthews, 1967, pp. 54–5.

[lxxxvi] Ernest von Elterlein, 1898, p. 118.

[lxxxvii] Alfred Brendel, 2001, p. 87.

[lxxxviii] Charles Rosen, p. 2002, p. 235.

[lxxxix] Denis Matthews, 1967, pp. 54–5.

[xc] Barry Cooper, 1991, p. 242.

[xci] Ernst von Elterlein, 1898, p. 118.

[xcii] Romain Rolland, 1917, p. 164.

[xciii] Quoted in: Paul Badura-Skoda, Carl Czerny: *On the proper performance of all Beethoven's works for the piano*, 1970, p. 66.

[xciv] Igor Stravinsky, 1972, p. 274.

[xcv] Denis Matthews, 1967, pp. 54–5.

[xcvi] Philip G. Downs, 1992, p. 611.

[xcvii] Stewart Gordon, 1996, p. 191.

[xcviii] Quoted by William Kinderman, in: *Liner notes to: Beethoven, The complete sonatas*, Alfred Brendel, Phillips 446 909–2.

[xcix] *Ibid*. The words in double quotation marks are derived from Alfred Brendel

[c] Romain Rolland, 1917, p. 164.

[ci] Anton Neumayr, 1994–1997, pp. 277–8.

[cii] As recalled in: Ronald Smith, *Alkan*, 1976, pp. 100–1.

[ciii] Charles Rosen, 2002, p. 242.

[civ] William S. Newman, 1983, p. 534.

[cv] Romain Rolland, 1917, p. 164.

[cvi] William Kinderman, *The piano sonatas [of Beethoven]*, in: Glen Stanley, editor, *The Cambridge companion to Beethoven*, 2000, p. 121.

[cvii] Ernst von Elterlein, 1898, p. 118. A performance of the A-flat major Piano Sonata, Op. 110 was recorded by Jörg Demus on Beethoven's Conrad Graf piano of 1825. See: BASF KHF-20328. It was also recorded on: Musical Heritage Society, MHS 3039 (same instrument) and by Elly Ney on Harmonia Mundi 1C 047-29 (once more on the 1825 Conrad Graf). Source: Ann P. Basart, The sound of the fortepiano: A discography of recordings on early pianos: Berkley, Fallen Leaf Press, 1985.

PIANO SONATA IN C MINOR, OP. 111

'[This] Beethoven sonata stands unrivalled in original beauty, an inexhaustible well of the purest wonderment, a glittering crown of stars to all who seek after pure musical forms.'

Ernst von Elterlein, *Beethoven's Pianoforte Sonatas: explained for the lovers of the musical art*, 1898, p. 125.

'[In] this sonata we have left the first ones completely out of sight.'

Romain Rolland, *Beethoven and Handel*, 1917, p. 165.

'Op. 111 is Beethoven's farewell pianoforte sonata. It is hard to estimate the possibility of his return to the pianoforte after the completion of the great string quartets and the projected tenth symphony, even if longer life had been granted him.'

Paul Bekker, *Beethoven*, 1925, p. 141.

'This is, next to Op. 106, technically the hardest of the last five sonatas; but it is so dramatic in its first movement and so unmistakably sublime as a whole that it is less discouraging to the student than any other of Beethoven's later works.'

Harold Craxton and Donald Francis Tovey, *Beethoven: Sonatas for Pianoforte*, [1931], p. 237.

'The last sonata sums up the whole experience gathered by Beethoven throughout all the sonata writing that had occupied him on and off for twenty-six years.'

Eric Blom, Notes to: *The Beethoven Society, Volume 1*, The Gramophone Company, Ltd., London (c. 1935). See also: Eric Blom, *Beethoven's Pianoforte Sonatas Discussed*, 1938, p. 236.

'The Sonata in C minor, Op. 111, came ... in 1822. It was as if Beethoven had felt with Browning: "I was ever a fighter, so — one fight more/The best and the last!".'

Marion M. Scott, *Beethoven: The Master Musicians*, 1940, p. 146.

'In Op. 111 we are taken to realms where the drama or "argument" is spiritual or metaphysical. If old-fashioned language may nowadays be used without apology ... Beethoven exploited tone as Shakespeare exploited language; to give spiritual account of himself.'

Neville Cardus, *Talking of Music*, 1957, p. 290 and p. 292.

'[We] find in it [Op. 111] a summing-up of Beethoven's whole nature, a testament of his spiritual world which left nothing for him to say in the form of the piano sonata. At least, that is how it appears to us poor mortals. The two movements of this work symbolize this world and the world to come.'

Edwin Fischer, *Beethoven's Pianoforte Sonatas: a guide for students & amateurs*, 1959, p. 116.

'All one might say briefly of Op. 111 in C minor is that it resolves the minor-major conflict on the sublimest scale imaginable. An introduction sets the scale, dynamically and tonally. As Tovey might have put it, it views the solar system of keys with awe before attending to the strife of earthly affairs and passions ... Two movements say everything that has to be said'.

Denis Matthews, *Keyboard Music*, 1972, p. 181.

'Beethoven the man had his limitations and frailties, but as a composer he encompassed and mastered nearly everything that is human. And

> of course the last sonata is an essence of this humanity; it is a true conclusion of the series.'

Alfred Brendel in conversation with David Dubal in: *The World of the Concert Pianist*, 1985, p. 111.

> Op. 111 epitomizes Beethoven's late style. It is literally and figuratively a lifetime away from the Op. 2 group. Words are inadequate to convey the range of emotions — the tension, the despair, the sublimity — expressed therein.'

Barry Cooper, *The Beethoven Compendium: a guide to Beethoven's life and music*, 1991, p. 242.

> 'It's so extraordinary, you know, it's all about acoustics. Everything is vibrating. The low notes vibrating with the top notes on the piano. Beethoven is relishing the sheer acoustic phenomenon of the instrument.'

Michael Tilson Thomas, *Viva Voce: conversations with Edward Seckerson*, 1994, p. 80.

> 'Beethoven's last piano sonata is a monument to his conviction that solutions to the problems facing humanity lie ever within our grasp if they can be recognised for what they are and be confronted by models of human transformation ... Op. 111 has three principal moments: the acceptance and resolution of conflict embodied in the *Allegro* and transition; the rich, dynamic synthesis of experience projected in the ensuing variations; and the surpassing inner climax in

E-flat major.'

William Kinderman, Liner Notes to, *Beethoven: The Complete Sonatas*, 1996, Philips 446 909-2, pp. 54–5.

'Beethoven's thirty-second and last piano sonata remains one of the great musical challenges for performers, its presence in his output like that of a mountain range visible from afar and growing more ominous the closer one gets to it.'

Conrad Wilson, *Notes on Beethoven: 20 crucial works*, 2003, p. 99.

'The Sonata in C minor challenges not only the structure of sonata form, but dramatic time itself.'

Stephen C. Rumph, *Beethoven after Napoleon: political romanticism in the late works*, 2004, p. 125.

Beethoven's later years had been relatively unproductive – by the standards of his formative 'heroic period' – but, as we have seen, the emergence of the Piano Sonata Op. 109, in 1820 and the Piano Sonata Op. 110, in 1821, saw a resurgence in his creativity. This was further consolidated by the completion of the Piano Sonata in C minor, Op. 111 in 1822. We have also seen, in our commentaries to the Piano Sonatas Opp. 109 and 110, that they form a trilogy with what would be the composer's final sonata – the Op. 111. More than that these sonatas, alongside the *Diabelli* Variations Op. 120 and the Bagatelles Op. 126, are considered to form 'one of the pillars' of Beethoven's creative achievement in his last years: 'It was in them that he first worked out the fusion of fugue, variation form, and sonata form which is fundamental to the formulation of his new musical thought.'[i]

The three final sonatas are unified not only by the circumstances of their creation and publication origins, to which we make reference in due course, but also by such musicological considerations as their shared key interrelationships.[ii] The composition of Beethoven's last three piano sonatas is all the more astonishing since they evolved at a period when he was gestating his Ninth Symphony and — what he considered to be his greatest work — the *Missa Solemnis*. Writing to the publisher Carl Peters on 5 June 1822, Beethoven stated: 'The *greatest* [Beethoven's emphasis] work which I have composed so far is a grand Mass with choruses, four obbligato voices and a large orchestra.' [The *Missa Solemnis*, Op. 123.] This is a reminder that the Piano Sonatas Opp. 109–111 were written, almost co-incidentally, against the gestation and evolution of these great works.[iii] Moreover, Beethoven's health at the period in question was marred by persistent illness, notably jaundice, rheumatism and eyesight problems, over and above the almost total loss of hearing that disposed him to withdraw into himself in ever-greater isolation. Charles Rosen makes the case that Beethoven's loss of hearing may account for the deeply personal nature of the music found in the Op. 111 Piano Sonata, especially in its closing pages.[iv] In addition, Beethoven's composure was undermined by concern over his financial affairs — he had to borrow money from friends and publishers. Writing in November 1821 to his friend Franz Brentano, he complained how he had had to renounce his art for almost two years adding: 'In order to keep myself alive I had to finish off several *pot boilers* (unfortunately I have to describe them as such)'. Beethoven's so-called *pot boilers* (his italics) are non other than the epochal trilogy Opp. 109, 110 and 111.[v]

Reflecting on Beethoven's self-deprecating remarks, Barry Cooper comments that if the three final piano sonatas were indeed written out of the shear necessity to stay alive, they are 'the most remarkable potboilers ever written!' and, furthermore he argues, they demonstrate how even in adversity Beethoven 'would not compromise his style, and considered only how to make the best of the work in question'.[vi]

In the Op. 111 Sonata, Beethoven reverts once more to the key of C minor with which so much of his dramatic music is associated. It can be argued, in the context of his writing for the piano, that the first movement of the *Pathétique* Sonata, written years previously, provides a distant glimpse of what lay ahead and what we now find in the first movement of Op. 111. However, in the work's second movement we also have the key of C major — where the music remains through most of the *Arietta*. In Conrad Wilson's words: 'In no sense is there a contest between the two keys, or an element of transition, or any suggestion that the ending is a triumph of light over darkness. The two movements — the two metaphysical slabs of Beethoven — are simply juxtaposed, the one the obverse, as well as the resolution, of the other.'[vii] In the estimation of Denis Mathews 'contrasts' lie at the heart of the work in 'the fieriest of allegros' (first movement) and 'the most serene of adagios' (second movement), which for him contain 'the material world and the spiritual, C minor and C major'.[viii] Barry Cooper makes similar observations likening the contrasts on the one hand to 'stormy and gentle' and on the other to 'fast and slow' even between 'Earth and Heaven'.[ix]

For William Kinderman such symbolism as is implicit in the foregoing has three principal episodes in the Op. 111 Sonata: '[The] acceptance and resolution of conflict' as embodied in the *Allegro*; 'the rich, dynamic synthesis of experience' in the ensuing variations of the second movement's *Arietta*; and 'the surpassing inner climax in E-flat major'.[x] Cooper lists the Piano Sonata Op. 111 as being amongst the composer's works that contain 'a sense of struggle' that, in its various ways, is finally overcome as, for example, 'triumph' (Overture *Egmont* and the Fifth Symphony), 'joy' (Ninth Symphony), 'thanksgiving' (*Pastoral* Symphony) and, regarding Op. 111, 'peace'.[xi] Writing about Beethoven's last piano sonata, musicologist Henry Edward Krehbiel remarks 'there is less intimation of a drama playing on the stage of the individual human heart than of a projection of the imagination into the realm of cosmic ideality'. He believed that whilst the composer was, as he puts it, 'frequently transfigured' he was never more so than in certain moments of the Piano Sonata Op. 111 in which he said almost his last word on the pianoforte.[xii]

Two modern-day anecdotes bear testimony to the high regard in which the C minor Sonata is held. Beethoven occupied a place of special honour in the estimation of the Spanish composer Enrique Granados. Although somewhat macabre, he was given to wearing a leather band on his wrist bearing a metallic reproduction of Beethoven's death mask. He described the Op. 111 as 'a work of inexplicable beauty' that could not readily be put into words. Attempting to do so, he considered the Piano Sonata Op. 111 to be 'nothing less than an allusion to death and the soul's journey to heaven'.[xiii] In his *Themes and conclusions,* Igor Stravinsky refers to Beethoven's piano sonatas as being 'part of our daily bread' and the three final sonatas in particular he regarded as representing what he describes as 'a great ventilation in style'. By this he means 'a rediscovery of the classical spirit' but one in which 'compression is more evident than expansion' and in which 'a more controlled emotion' replaces what he describes as 'the inconsolable feelings' of the *Adagio* in Op. 106. Although Stravinsky was not fully convinced regarding the construction of the first movement — he considered its repeat to be a Beethoven 'miscalculation' — he regarded the composition's 'rhythmic innovations' to be 'astonishing', especially in the final movement's variations. He cites Beethoven's 'new aspect of time itself', as exploited in the variations' ever more subtle metrical divisions and sub-divisions, disposing him to quote Hamlet's line: 'My pulse as yours doth temporarily keep time.'[xiv] Further evidence of Stravinsky's admiration for the C minor Sonata is evident from the recollections of his friend the American conductor Robert Craft. He recalls an evening spent in the composer's company in January 1974. After dinner they listened to a recording of the C minor Piano Sonata, at the same time following the music with the printed score before them. A measure of Stravinsky's admiration of the music is conveyed in Craft's observation of the composer's demeanour: 'His head was bent over the score ... half conducting, indicating by finger on the page important entries ... Stravinsky's concentration was so complete and consuming I felt in the presence of an act of creation.'[xv]

The Piano Sonata in C minor, Op. 111 is, like its predecessors Opp. 54, 78 and 90, conceived in two movements. As we shall later narrate, at the time of its composition this provoked considerable questioning — that reverberates still in discussions about the piece. Notwithstanding these former misunderstandings, the sonata has found favour with pianists who consider the work well-suited to the keyboard: 'The two movements have a perfection of balance and contrast that justifies the claim that Beethoven here set the limits of the piano sonata in amplitude of conception, perfection of design, vigour of movements and rightness of detail.'[xvi] Matthew Rye believes in his Op. 111

Beethoven found the ultimate solution to the problem of unity of form 'by resolving in one movement the conflicts of the other'.[xvii] In her commentary to Beethoven's adoption of a two-part format, Jane Coup elaborates on the manner in which the ensuing music unfolds in a palette of contrasts, to which, as we have just seen, Matthews also makes reference: 'The contrasts between the two mammoth foundations [i.e. movements] are striking: fiery allegros versus serene adagios; tightly-knit sonata form versus exploratory variations; the dark key of C minor versus the tranquil key of C major; compressed fugal writing versus improvisatory wandering; in essence, the concrete world of man versus the ethereal realm of spirituality.'[xviii] And to quote Rye once more: 'The two movements contrast on a number of planes: major/minor, allegro/adagio/*semplice*, sonata form/variation form/ecstatic serenity/ earthly/spiritual.'[xix] Within this scheme of contrasts Stewart Gordon also discerns unifying order: 'Here [Beethoven] presents a two-movement work in which the movements provide a balance for each other, both being strong, lengthy, serious compositions. At the same time, they offer the ultimate contrast, the first acting as an expression of turbulent drama and the second as an essay in transcendentalism.'[xx]

Beethoven's adoption of a two-part format for his design is known to have exerted an influence on the young Sergei Prokofiev. Writing to his friend Boris Vladimirovich on 23 May 1925, he revealed he had just completed his Second Symphony, acknowledging a debt to Beethoven: 'In its form the Symphony is similar to the last sonata of Beethoven: a sombre first movement, and a theme and variations for the second and final movement.' Despite Prokofiev's homage to Beethoven, critics have likened the parallels between the two compositions as being superficial, criticising Prokofiev for aiming at 'novelty pure and simple' — an allegation that later in life Prokofiev himself conceded was not without foundation.[xxi]

We direct our attention now to the creation origins and publication history of the C minor Piano Sonata.

In our commentaries to the piano sonatas Opp. 109 and 110, we have seen that the final piano sonata-trilogy had its origins in a request from the Berlin-based music publisher Adolph Martin Schlesinger — a founder member of the influential *Berliner Allgemeine musikalische Zeitung*. Beethoven, ever in need of income, responded in a letter of 30 April offering Schlesinger three piano sonatas that would subsequently become the Opp. 109, 110 and 111. He initially hoped to secure a fee of 40 ducats for each work but Schlesinger, an astute business man, subsequently bargained the composer down to the lower fee of 30 ducats for each composition.[xxii] We shall see in due course that Schlesinger's Jewish origins would later attract pejorative remarks, bearing on his prowess in mercantile dealings, and with accusations of nefarious complicity concerning pirate editions of the Op. 111.

Throughout the early months of 1820 Beethoven endeavoured to make progress with his work on the three sonatas but was hampered by the illnesses to which we have previously referred. On 20 September he sought to reassure Schlesinger, telling him his health was improving and that he was making progress with his obligations: 'I am working uninterruptedly on the other two [Opp. 110 and 111].'[xxiii] What Beethoven told Schlesinger, however, was not strictly true; he was then working mainly on the *Missa Solemnis* and the Bagatelles Op. 119. He did not commence serious work on the Piano Sonata Op. 111 until late the following year.[xxiv]

On 7 March 1821 Beethoven once more had to apologise to Schlesinger. He had been laid up with a violent attack of rheumatism for six weeks, but, feeling better, he resolved the Sonata Op. 111 'will soon follow'.[xxv] Despite this reassurance, on 7 June Beethoven had to inform Schlesinger his health 'was still very shaky' and would probably remain so until he could seek relief at a 'watering place' (health spa) as directed by his doctor.[xxvi] Through November Beethoven was preoccupied with correcting the many errors in Schlesinger's publication-copy of the Piano Sonata Op. 110. Nonetheless, he gave the publisher a further reassurance that the Op. 111 would soon follow, exonerating himself that a severe attack of jaundice had debilitated his powers.[xxvii] On 12 December Beethoven confirmed with Schlesinger the Piano Sonata Op. 110 would be sent to him 'very soon' (in effect in the New Year), adding 'also a third one' — Op. 111. This time his reassurance had some foundation, since the sketches reveal he had indeed been working on both the Op. 110 and Op. 111 together.[xxviii]

The two primary sources for Op. 111 are Beethoven's surviving desk sketchbooks. These are the so-called Artaria 197, that the composer used over the period March–December 1821, and Artaria 201 that followed on for the period December 1821 until October 1822.[xxix] Artaria 197 once formed part of the collection of the music publisher Mathias Artaria. In 1901 it passed to the Berlin Royal Library — today's Berlin State Library (Deutsche Staatsbibliothek). It consists of 44 leaves that Beethoven assembled from miscellaneous leftover manuscript sheets and then stitched together in his improvisatory fashion. The first and second movements of Op. 111 are represented with brief sketches that jostle with more extended ideas for the *Agnus Dei* and *Dona nobis pacem* of the *Missa Solemnis* and workings-out for the companion Piano Sonata Op. 110.[xxx] Artaria 201 is prized for being one of the few composer's sketchbooks to have survived intact. For this reason the number of leaves in the book today — 64 in a single gathering — is the same as that recorded on both of Artaria's covers. The elder Domenico Artaria purchased the manuscript at the 1827 Nachlass auction of Beethoven's effects. Like its companion Artaria 197, it now forms part of the *Special Collections* of the Deutsche Staatsbibliothek. The layout of the sketches indicate the composer was now (late 1821—early 1822) concentrating his mind on the Op. 111 Piano Sonata; Artaria 201 begins with sketches for the first movement that occupy pages 1 to 22 with the second movement following on pages 22—63. At the top of page 21 is the note 'am 13ten die neue sonate'.[xxxi] These sketches also jostle for space with further ideas for the *Missa Solemnis* and, what was a new commission, the overture *The Consecration of the House*. Sets of loose leaves are preserved in the Bibliothèque Nationale, Paris that also contain ideas for the Piano Sonata Op. 111; these may once have formed part of a larger collection. Although not strictly pocket sketchbooks, they are known as such with the catalogue designations Ms 51. One of the sets consists of 14 leaves that are thought to have been in use towards the end of 1821 and the first months of 1822. The companion set consists of two additional bifolia (four leaves) that contain sketches for the variations that form part of the second movement.[xxxii]

Early in the New Year (1822) Beethoven made progress with the composition of the C minor Sonata, dating his 'first concept' 13 January.[xxxiii] This manuscript bears the typical hallmarks of the composer's working method: 'It has been greatly revised ... whole sections have been crossed out or erased then written over again ... [changes include] single notes, articulation indications, modifications to sharp and flat signs, tempo markings and dynamics.' The text became so confusing that Beethoven had the autograph score copied out to form a more error-free basis for the engraver's model

— probably undertaken by the composer's copyist Wenzel Rampl.[xxxiv][xxxv] Beethoven read through this copy, corrected it and sent it to Berlin. However, he later reworked the score making major changes, in particular, to the second movement and its set of variations.[xxxvi] Anxious that Schlesinger should produce his composition from the corrected manuscript, he wrote to him on 9 April: ' ... *owing to a hold-up the fresh copy of the last movement of the third sonata* [Op. 111] is only being dispatched by tomorrow's mail coach. As soon as you receive it *please mark it at once so that this copy may not be mistaken for the one you already have; and destroy the latter immediately* [Beethoven's italics]'.[xxxvii] On 1 May he wrote once more to Schlesinger confirming he had sent him the last movement with the curious remark: 'You are at liberty to dedicate the third sonata [Op. 111] to anyone you like.' As we shall see, he later exercised his own judgement and made over the dedication to his patron the Archduke Rudolph.[xxxviii]

It is evident from a letter Beethoven sent early in July to his younger brother Johann, then resident at his country house in Gneixendorf, that he still had to take care of his health. He describes how, under doctor's orders, he must take four powders a day and 30 daily baths.[xxxix] However, his spirit was clearly in good shape since he writes that the publishers Breitkopf and Härtel had expressed an interest in his works and likewise the Schlesingers in Paris and Berlin and also Diabelli in Vienna. He concludes with a characteristic touch of irony: 'In short, there is a general scramble to secure my works. *What an unhappy, yet happy man am I* !!!.'[xl] His loss of hearing though still continued to affect his demeanour. Writing later in the year once more to Johann he complained: 'My poor hearing ... cuts me off to a certain extent from human society.'[xli]

We have remarked (Piano Sonata Op. 110) that Adolph

Schlesinger's son Moritz (Maurice) had established a branch of the family business in Paris.[xlii] Moritz had visited Beethoven in 1819, was warmly received by the composer and was given the autograph score of the Canon WoO 174 that Beethoven also dedicated to him; Moritz cherished this all his life 'like a relic'. On 3 July 1822 Moritz wrote to Beethoven reassuring him he would have his masterworks engraved and distributed 'externally according to their inner value'. Of the Op. 111 he remarks: 'Since I had the pleasure, a few days ago, of receiving your third sonata, [i.e. the third in the Opp. 109, 110 and 111 trilogy] ... which contains so many beauties that could only have been created by the great master, I take the liberty, before I have engraved it, to ask you most submissively if you wrote for the work only one *Maestoso* [first movement] and one *Andante* [second movement], or if perhaps the [final] *Allegro* was accidentally forgotten by the copyist. Moritz, relatively new to music publishing, was clearly eager to do things correctly as he further remarks: 'I consider it an obligation to ask you about this since every masterwork must be published strictly according to the will of its creator, it would therefore be an injustice to publish this work without asking you beforehand.'[xliii] Ten days later Moritz's father Adolph, writing from Berlin asked much the same question: 'For the present, I only wanted to ask, concerning, the second sonata [Op. 111] that you sent me [then, as we have just seen, in the hands of his son in Paris] ... if a third movement is not to be added, and the piece is thus ended.' Adolph requested the Beethoven to clarify his intentions with his son whom he describes as 'Bookseller and Music Publisher ... near the Boulevard's'. Of additional interest is that Adolph also asked Beethoven for the metronome markings for the Opp. 109–111 trilogy, an indication of the growing standing that Maelzel's system of tempo regulation was acquiring.[xliv]

As we have seen, there is no *Allegro* third movement to the C minor Piano Sonata and the Schlesingers have been chastised for doubting that a creation so whole and perfect in its two-movement format could ever have been conceived otherwise. It has even been suggested they may have suspected they had not received as much music for which they had paid, as expressed in terms of individual movements.[xlv] In their defence it may be argued that a music publisher, doing business in the early part od the eighteenth century, might well have expected a new piano sonata to consist of three movements. Evidence for this comes from the writings of the respected music theorist Adolf Bernhard Marx. He reflected on Beethoven's music in the May 1824 issue of the *Berliner Allgemeine musikalische Zeitung* — almost exactly contemporaneous with Beethoven's Op. 111. What he has to say is illustrative of the extent to which the three-movement piano sonata was then a part of accepted and expected musical culture. Marx first positions the role of the piano sonata in the music making of the period, characterising it as having three movements — 'one fast, one slow and another fast' — thereby to achieve 'fullness and variety' and a 'unified character'. He then commends this form as a medium 'for putting together one's ideas in a rich, diverse, yet unified way'.[xlvi]

The Schlesingers were not the only ones to fail to recognise the innovatory nature and perfection of Beethoven's two-movement format. Anton Schindler confesses: 'I ventured in my innocence to ask Beethoven why he had not written a third movement appropriate to the character of the first. He replied casually that he had not had time to write a third movement, and had therefore simply expanded the second.' Schindler justified himself: 'Since at that that time I had heard only fragments of the sonata as the composer was working on it, I was satisfied with this explanation. But later, when I had listened to the sonata, I began to wonder about the reason he had given me for not writing a third movement, and I must confess frankly that I still deplore it. I could not then understand how two movements of such sharply differing character could possibly produce an integrated and satisfying whole.'[xlvii]

In their consideration of Beethoven's alleged remark to Schindler, some commentators give Beethoven the benefit of the doubt recognising that perhaps he was indeed too busy to write a third movement as a consequence of the work on which he was engaged in connection with the Ninth Symphony and the *Missa Solemnis*. There is also the tantalising suggestion the idea of a third movement may have been in his head, early on in the work's creation. William Newman explains: 'Actually, Beethoven did seem to have a third movement in mind originally, for "3tes Stück presto" appears over a sketch of the main idea that eventually served for the first movement.'[xlviii]

Other commentators take a more sanguine view of Beethoven's justification to Schindler. Having regard to the character of the C minor Sonata as a whole, Paul Bekker remarks: 'It is clear that the two movements were not planned philosophically, but upon a purely artistic impulse.'[xlix] Hans von Bülow was withering in his condemnation of Schindler's story and dismissed him personally for being 'a jener strohkopf' – 'that straw head/addle-pate'. Martin Cooper attempts to reconcile the opposing views: 'The nineteenth century believed in the divine right of artists and preferred a mystical to a factual explanation of all aesthetic phenomena. It is indeed difficult to imagine any movement that could have followed the theme and variations of Op. 111, and there was the precedent of Op. 109 ending with a movement in this form. Beethoven himself, on the other hand, made no mystical claims for his music;

and he might well have given Schindler this very practical answer in perfectly good faith and not, as Bülow believes, in witheringly sardonic scorn for the incomprehension that could ask such an abysmally irrelevant question'.[i] Barry Cooper is content to observe: '[The Sonata's] two movements contrast with and complement each other, nothing else is required.'[ii] In the same spirit Conrad Wilson concludes: '[In] bringing the second movement full circle to something like its starting point, Beethoven created his own statement of finality ... and in so doing made history.'[iii]

On 31 August Beethoven wrote to Moritz Schlesinger in Paris requesting sight of the proof copy of the Piano Sonata Op. 111 before it was to be put out for sale. He was concerned its text still contained errors: 'For it is very unpleasant for me if my works come out full of mistakes.' He undertook to return the copy without delay, whereupon the Schlesingers would be free 'to circulate it throughout the world'. Beethoven was clearly unhappy though about the business side of his dealings when he discovered the payment for the two Sonatas Opp. 110 and 111 was short by 12 to 13 gulden. He remonstrated: 'I should have much preferred not to accept it [his payment] at all than *to have to put up with* such insulting niggardliness, the like of which I have *never* experienced [Beethoven's italics].'

In calmer mood he raised the question of the sonata's dedication. Earlier, as we have noted, Adolph Schlesinger had been given a free hand in dedicating the composition to a person of his own choosing, but Beethoven now had a change of mind. He remarks: 'And the *dedication* [Beethoven's italics] of the C minor Sonata is to be to his Imperial Highness the Cardinal [Archduke Rudolph] ... I have written it down for you and as soon as the proof copy arrives I will send you the dedication with the corrected copy.'[liii] This was in fact a two-fold change of mind on

Beethoven's part. In an undated memorandum from early in 1822, he had indicated to his assistant Anton Schindler that he wished to dedicate both the Piano Sonatas Opp. 110 and 111 to Antonie (Antonia) Brentano, the wife of his close friend Franz Brentano.[liv] This was still his intention as late as 18 February 1823 when he wrote once more to Moritz Schlesinger in Paris: 'The dedication of the C minor Sonata is to Antonie Brentano, née von Birkenstock.'[lv] Beethoven's intended dedication was doubtless in recognition of his feelings towards Antonie. Perhaps also he was mindful of the debt of gratitude he owed to her husband who had lent him quite large sums of money.[lvi] In the event, Antonie was not entirely denied her association with the Op. 111 Sonata. She received the dedication to the English edition (see later) and, moreover, was favoured with the dedication to the monumental *Diabelli* Variations, Op. 120.

Beethoven's change of mind regarding the dedication may have been prompted by the enthusiasm his patron and pupil the Archduke Rudolph had apparently shown for the composition. This conjecture is supported by Beethoven's letter to Rudolph of 1 July 1823 in which he states: 'As Y.I.H. seemed to enjoy hearing the C minor Sonata [Beethoven must have played it though for him], I thought I should not be too presumptuous if I gave you the surprise of dedicating it to Your Highness.'[lvii] Also worthy of remark is that in this letter Beethoven gives a rare insight into his working method when composing at the piano — we recall the Archduke was his only composition pupil. He advised him: '[You] should have a small table beside the pianoforte. In this way not only is one's imagination stimulated but one learns to pin down immediately the most remote ideas. You should also compose without a pianoforte; and you should sometimes work out a simple melody ... according to the laws of counterpoint ... This will ... afford you real enjoyment when you find yourself in the very swim of artistic production.' In support of these remarks we learn from Schindler: 'While composing music for the pianoforte, the master would often go to the instrument and try difficult passages, especially those that might present difficulties in performance ... To this circumstance I owe my acquaintance with the complete sonatas Op. 106, 109, 110 and parts of Op. 111.'[lviii]

It is also from Schindler we learn that errors persisted in the Paris edition of the Op. 111 such that they had to be sent twice to Vienna for Beethoven's approval, the outcome of which was still not to his complete satisfaction. When he requested a third reading the publisher refused leaving Beethoven 'beside himself with exasperation and despair'.[lix] Of equal concern to him was the realization that pirate editions of the Op. 111 Sonata were being prepared for publication in Vienna by Anton Diabelli and Saur and Leidesdorf. Suspecting (Moritz) Schlesinger of complicity, he wrote sarcastically to him on 3 June: 'Apparently you know how to choose your friends ... As a striking incident, someone has sent me two copies [of the sonata] in order to show me, strange though it be, how far one can succeed in imitating.' He complained the pirate texts were apparently 'so identical in every respect that neither can be distinguished from the other'.[lx]

The (Ignaz) Saur and (Marcus) Leidesdorf music-publishing partnership was founded in July 1822 and was, doubtless, like Schlesinger in Paris, eager to do business with the most eminent composer of the day. In fact, Leidesdorf had plans to bring out a collective edition of Beethoven's works — ever dear to the composer's heart — but nothing came of this. In due course the Saur-Leidesdorf enterprise did publish the two Piano Sonatas Opp. 110 and 111, but apparently without any involvement on the part of the composer.[lxi] Beethoven was, however, more vigilant in keeping a watchful eye over the progress of Diabelli's proofs.[lxii] This was the period we recall when he was collaborating with Diabelli in the publication of the Variations Op. 120 bearing his name. This circumstance may have disposed the composer, at least in some measure, in Diabelli's favour. More probable, however, is that Beethoven's motivation to assist Diabelli was prompted by his wish to safeguard his reputation in the sanctioning of a work bearing his name – a work which, as we have seen, he was strenuously attempting to make as free of errors as humanely possible. As Thayer puts it: 'Once the damage was done to Schlesinger by Diabelli, the composer in Beethoven asserted himself and every instinct of artistic self-protection in him demanded that he undo the damage done to him as the creator of the sonata by Schlesinger with so very faulty an edition.'[lxiii] Schindler remarks here on the importance Beethoven attached to the correctness of the presentation of his works and that he expected similar care of others. Beethoven was therefore Schindler felt obliged – almost forced, to collaborate with Diabelli in bringing out an unauthorized but corrected edition of his composition.[lxiv]

To help things along Beethoven wrote to Diabelli in late May 1823 advising him to make his own engraving of the Piano Sonata Op. 111 from the Paris edition of Moritz Schlesinger – over which, as we have seen, he had been taking such pains. He cautioned Diabelli from having anything to do though with the Saur and Leidesdorf text. An inference of Beethoven's willingness to assist Diabelli can also be inferred from this letter. He asked him for the loan of 300 gulden (quite a large sum) to tide him over for the next few weeks.[lxv] To put this into context, Beethoven had been suffering for some time from an eye infection that had been interfering with his work and therefore his capacity to earn an income. Such was the severity of his condition that his physician, Carl von Smetana, required him to bind up his eyes at night and to be very sparing with them. He cautioned Beethoven if he did not follow his advice he would 'write but few more notes'.[lxvi]

To further protect the integrity of his work, Beethoven enlisted Schindler's help. Writing to him in late May he urged: 'As to the mistakes in the sonata [Op. 111] — well, *you* must see from the engraved copy the places where it is being sold *here* [i.e. in Vienna]. But do everything immediately and then inform the publishers ... make haste ... We are dealing with the mistakes we marked *and which Schlemmer* [Beethoven's copyist] *copied* [Beethoven's italics].'[lxvii] In late June Beethoven sent Diabelli a list of corrections for his Vienna edition of the Op. 111 Sonata that he had discovered in the Paris edition of the work. He was clearly riled and refers disparagingly to Moritz as 'the rag and bone Jew Schlesinger'.[lxviii] Another letter quickly followed urging Diabelli to proofread the manuscript himself to finally ensure its accuracy — Diabelli had a formidable reputation in this regard.[lxix] Later on Beethoven promised to send Diabelli his metronome markings for the C minor Sonata but he appears not to have kept this promise.[lxx]

On 27 May 1823, the *Wiener Zeitung* cryptically announced a sonata as 'newly arrived' — taken to be a reference to Beethoven's Op. 111.[lxxi] The precise date of publication of Moritz Schlesinger's Paris edition of the Piano Sonata in C minor, Op. 111 is not known but it probably followed soon after in July.[lxxii] Copies of both Schlesinger's and Diabelli's first editions of the Op. 111 are preserved today in the Beethoven House Archives in Bonn. The Title Page to Schlesinger's first edition carried the following wording, with slight variations: 'SONATA/pour le/Piano-Forte/Composée *et trés respecteusement Dediée*/à Son

Altesse Impériale Monseigneur/L'Archduc Rodolphe d'Autriche/*Cardinal Prince Archevêque d'Olmütz etc., etc.*/par' L: van [Louis De] BEETHOVEN/ *Oeuvre 111.*'[lxxiii]

To close our account of the publication history of the Piano Sonata Op. 111, we briefly turn our attention to the origins of the English edition. Eager to earn an additional fee from an English publisher, on 6 July 1822 Beethoven wrote to his former piano pupil Ferdinand Ries, then residing in London, that he was at work on new piano compositions: 'I have composed two new Sonatas (Opp. 110 and 111) for pianoforte solo which [he considers] are really not very difficult [!]. I should be glad if you could obtain the same sum [as he had received for pervious compositions] of 26 pounds sterling for these ... *if you can get more, all the better* [Beethoven's italics].'[lxxiv] Several months passed before Beethoven raised the prospect once more with Ries, namely of seeing his work published in England. Writing to him on 25 February 1823 he first of all asked about the progress his Ninth Symphony was making with its sponsors the Philharmonic Society of London — a further reminder that the composer's final piano sonatas were created amidst the gestation of other great works. Turning to the sonatas, he asks: 'I hope you have *received the two sonatas* [Opp. 110 and 111]; and again I beg you to drive *a hard bargain* for these.' He explains how the rigours of the winter and his poor health have taken their toll, adding 'it is not easy to have to live entirely by my *pen*'. Beethoven anticipated being in London himself the next year adding, affectionately, that he looked forward to kissing Ries's wife! — this long anticipated visit to London, however, never took place.[lxxv]

Delays in the composer's dealings with Ries appear to have occurred since Beethoven wrote to him once more on 22 March asking: 'Well, have you not received two sonatas, one in A major and one in C minor?' Of interest is that in this letter he reassured Ries that work was progressing well on the Ninth Symphony that he hoped would be finished in the next two weeks. Ries needed to know this since he was himself negotiating on Beethoven's behalf with the Philharmonic Society concerning the publication of this work.[lxxvi] On 25 April, Ries received a further exhortation from Beethoven 'do see that the C minor Sonata is engraved immediately'. The reason for this urgency is apparent from the next part of the letter: 'I promise that the C minor Sonata will not appear anywhere else first. And, if necessary, I will also send him [the intended publisher] the copyright for England.'[lxxvii] Having given this undertaking, Beethoven was doubtless anxious to see progress made with the English edition of his work since, as we have seen, events regarding publication of the C minor Sonata were also progressing in Paris, Berlin and Vienna.

It was something of a privilege for a publishing house to announce a first edition of a work by Beethoven — then internationally recognised as being the foremost of composers. Doubtless Ries used this cachet in his negotiations with potential English publishers but the Beethoven-Ries correspondence is silent on this. Suffice it to say, the English edition of the Op. 111 was entered at Stationers Hall on 25 April 1823, following the copyright-registration procedures of the period. Ries appears to have negotiated the publication rights with Muzio Clementi.[lxxviii] This is not surprising since Clementi's London-based publishing house had already brought out the first English editions of the piano sonatas Opp. 78, 79 and 81a as well as other of Beethoven's compositions. Clementi duly announced his edition as: 'GRAND SONATA/Composed for the/Piano Forte/and Dedicated to/Madame Antonia de Brentano/ By/L. v. BEETHOVEN/ ... /London/ Published by Clementi & Co.

... /N.B. This work is Copyright.' We see here, as anticipated in the earlier part of our narrative, that Antonie (Antonia) Brentano finally received her due as the originally intended dedicatee of the C minor Sonata. Of interest also is the reference to the work being 'copyright'. This was emphasised when the work was reviewed in the August 1823 edition of *The Harmonicon*. It contained the caution: 'The publishers have, in their title, deemed it necessary to warn off all pirates, by announcing the sonata as "copyright".'[lxxix] The authority Alan Tyson, from whom we have just quoted, praises the Clementi edition of the C minor Sonata for being perhaps the most accurate edition of Beethoven's Op. 111 ever to have appeared. It was quite independent of its continental equivalents and, Tyson considers, a 'far superior' and 'a very careful one'.[lxxx] In 1835, Ignaz Moscheles published the C minor Sonata as Op. 17 in his 'Complete Edition' of Beethoven works, thereby helping to promote further awareness of the composition in England.[lxxxi]

Before we proceed to other considerations bearing on the origins and creation history of the C minor Piano Sonata, to gain a more rounded picture of Beethoven at the period under consideration we briefly reflect on other aspects of his life and work. In this regard, of particular interest are the circumstances that helped to redirect his attention away from the medium of the piano sonata to that of the string quartet.

On 18 May 1822, the Leipzig music publisher Carl Peters wrote to Beethoven expressing an interest in the composer's works, including a list of the particular compositions he wished to have. He rather grandly states 'for I seek your association not from self-interest but from honour'. Among Peters' wish list he cites string quartets.[lxxxii] It is tempting to infer this request provided a stimulus to Beethoven's imagination and disposed him to think seriously about writing for the medium of the string quartet.

Beethoven did indeed reply to Peters on 5 July stating, among other things, he could have a string quartet 'very soon' for 50 ducats.[lxxxiii] The words 'very soon' may be interpreted two ways; were they a typical Beethoven-style promise or was he in fact turning his mind already to writing for the string quartet? Ten days after receiving Beethoven's offer, Peters responded. He remarked that although he would like to have a quartet from Beethoven 'very much' he considered the asking price was too high since the most he had ever paid for such a composition was 150 florins (roughly 40 ducats) — a reminder Beethoven had a reputation for demanding top prices for his work.[lxxxiv] The following month (12 July) Peters felt obliged to apologise to the composer for declining the possibility of him publishing one of his string quartets. He did not blame him and, in any event, he explained he was already fully committed in publishing four new string quartets by Louis Spohr. He concluded 'I had better hold off' and nothing more, therefore, came of the venture.[lxxxv] However, a few months later Providence called from another quarter that would indeed precipitate Beethoven into writing for the string quartet and, moreover, would elevate the medium to unprecedented heights — many would say seldom equalled and never surpassed.

Prince Nikolay Galitzin was a Russian nobleman domiciled in St. Petersburg and had family connections in Vienna with the Russian ambassador to the Austrian court. Galitzin was an accomplished cellist and on 9 November 1822 he wrote to Beethoven introducing himself as 'a great admirer' of the composer. More significantly, he requested two or three new quartets for which he would be honoured to receive the dedication.[lxxxvi] In the New Year, on 25 January 1823, Beethoven responded writing in French through an intermediary: 'Etant contraint de vivre des produits de mon esprit, il faut que je prenne la liberté de fixer l'honoraire de 50 ducats pour un quatuor.' Beethoven's French-language letters were often written by a third party and only signed by the composer himself; it can be seen he was still seeking 50 ducats for a string quartet.[lxxxvii] Galitzin could hardly contain his delight. He replied on 23 February: 'Your letter of 25 January ... filled me with joy by making me hope I shall soon enjoy a new product of your sublime genius.' He arranged for the payment of 50 ducats to be made with the promise of a further 100 for the two others.[lxxxviii] Over the next few months Galitzin appears to have established a bond of friendship with the composer such that on 3 August he wrote to him remarking how his wife Elena, a talented pianist, shared his love of music and 'is one of your great admirers' and how she looked forward to receiving and performing his latest piano sonatas.[lxxxix] In due course Galitzin received the three string quartets Opp. 127, 130 and 132 and Beethoven received his payment — although delayed by several months as a consequence of misunderstandings. His commissioning of the three mentioned quartets, and their consequent standing in the repertoire, has justly earned Galitzin a place of distinction among the composer's patrons. Also worthy of mention is Galitzin's promotion of Beethoven's *Missa Solemnis*; on 30 December 1823 he wrote about his plans for its rehearsal. In the course of his letter he pays tribute to Beethoven's tempo indications that he had expressed in terms of Maelzel's metronome markings. He enthuses: 'I urge you very much to perform this same operation ... for all the works you have composed, because I have frequently observed great variants in the manner in which your music is performed'.[xc]

From Beethoven's putative exchanges with Peters, and his more conclusive negotiations with Galitzin, we can infer they must have encouraged the composer in his personal resolve to redirect his musical expression away from the medium of the piano sonata to that of the string quartet. Little wonder then, if such speculation has any foundation, that the C minor Piano Sonata, Op. 111 should be his last.

In November 1822 Louis Schlösser made Beethoven's acquaintance. He was then a twenty-two year old musician residing in Vienna receiving instruction in composition from Salieri. Beethoven came to regard Schlösser 'as a young and talented artist' possessed of 'a cordial and friendly manner'.[xci] Years later Schlösser left an account of his first meeting with the composer. Although Beethoven scholars view Schlösser's recollections with some caution – he may have embroidered his accounts – if they are taken at face value they offer insights into the composer's living conditions and personal circumstances at the period when he was at work on the Piano Sonata Op. 111. Beethoven was then living in a relatively poor district of Vienna known as the *Wiedener* suburb. Schlösser describes Beethoven's apartment as being rather undecorated with a large, four-square oak table and various chairs presenting a somewhat untidy aspect. On the table lay books, pens, pencils, music-paper a metronome and an ear trumpet. In another room Schlösser noticed the Broadwood piano Beethoven had received a few years previously as a personal gift from the English piano maker John Broadwood. On its music rack rested a volume from the complete works of Handel that he had also received as a gift in recognition of his admiration for his works; towards the end of his life Handel displaced Mozart as Beethoven's most respected composer. On entering the apartment, Schlösser found Beethoven preoccupied at his writing desk and he had to stamp with his feet to secure his attention. He writes of the composer's 'characteristic head' with its 'surrounding mane of heavy hair ... the furrowed brow of a thinker ... profoundly serious eyes ... [and] ... the amiably smiling expression'. Schlösser attempted to convers with the composer using the ear trumpet but Beethoven laid it aside complaining 'it agitated his nerves too greatly'. Conversation between the two continued by Schlösser writing his thoughts on paper — as by then had become Beethoven's custom. Schlösser records he left the composer feeling 'the day felt like a beautiful dream'.

On a subsequent occasion Beethoven favoured Schlösser with thoughts concerning his working method. He described his ideas as coming to him 'uninvited, directly or indirectly, such that he could almost grasp them in his hands ... when in the open woods ... during his promenades ... in the silence of the night ... tones ... that take shape for me as notes'. In composing he described how he made many changes, rejecting until he was satisfied adding: 'I am conscious of what I want, the basic idea never leaves me ... It rises, grows upward, and I hear and see the pictures as a whole take shape and stand forth before me as though cast in a single piece, so that all that is left to me is the work of writing it down.'[xcii]

When Schlösser took leave of Beethoven, aware he was planning to visit Paris, asked him to convey two letters on his behalf — Beethoven had a mistrust of the post. One was intended for Moritz Schlesinger, to inquire about his progress with the publication of the C minor Sonata, the other was for Luigi Cherubini. The latter is of interest insofar as it reveals Beethoven's high estimation of Cherubini. He had made his acquaintance years previously in 1805 and esteemed him above all living writers of dramatic music. In particular, he admired Cherubini's operas copying out excerpts in order to study them more closely. The reason for Beethoven writing to Cherubini was to try to enlist his help with the publication and performance of his *Missa Solemnis* in France. However, in his letter, notwithstanding that almost twenty years had passed since their first meeting, Beethoven wrote: 'Quite often I am beside you in spirit, for I value your works more highly than all others [composing] for the theatre.' He then gave expression to one of his typical utterances to a fellow artist: 'True art is immortal, and the true artist finds deep satisfaction and pleasure in the true and great creations of genius.'[xciii] Regrettably, despite Beethoven's precautions in sending his letter via Schlösser, Cherubini does not appear to have received it and his possible response can only be conjectured. What is known though is that he that had reservations about Beethoven. In his person he considered him to be boorish and in his music he harboured doubts about his setting of texts, particularly with regard to *Fidelio* that he thought was not very well done.[xciv]

Despite the fact that at the period of composition of the Piano Sonata Op. 111, Beethoven was at the height of his creative powers, he still felt financially insecure. He had a pension and his compositions helped to supplement his income but, at the age of 53, he was still in search of an official appointment. Such an opportunity appeared to present itself at the close of 1822 when Beethoven learned of the death of Anton Teyber. He had occupied the desirable post of Imperial and Royal Chamber Composer with the additional responsibility of being teacher of music to the Imperial children. On 1 January 1823, Beethoven to wrote to Count Moritz von Dietrichstein: 'I hear that the post of Imperial and Royal Chamber Composer ... is again to be filled, and I gladly apply for it, particularly if, as I fancy, one of the requirements is that I should occasionally provide a composition for the Imperial Court. Seeing that I have composed, and am still composing, works in all branches of music, I do not consider that I can be accused of taking too great a liberty if I recommend myself to your Excellency's favour.' He elaborates, reflecting his current position was 'not exactly brilliant', how his health was poor and how he might have left Vienna years ago in order 'to lead a life free of anxiety for the future'.[xcv]

Beethoven's association with Dietrichstein was primarily professional rather than personal. The two had collaborated in the past when Dietrichstein had responsibility for court music. Although Beethoven had had differences of opinion with Dietrichstein — almost an occupational hazard in Beethoven's relationships even with those disposed to help him — for his part, Dietrichstein revered Beethoven. Aware the appointment he was seeking was not going to be filled, Dietrichstein could not bring himself to inform Beethoven directly. Instead he enlisted the help of the composer's friend and benefactor Count Moritz Lichnowsky. Writing to him on 7 January he pleaded: 'I do not want to write this [bad news] to Beethoven because I do not want to disappoint a man whom I so sincerely respect, and therefor I beg you to let him know'.[xcvi] Not for the first time then, Beethoven had to rely upon his own creative resources to secure his financial position.

Perhaps Beethoven was cheered up later in the month when, on 28 January, he received a letter from Carl Maria von Weber. Weber recalled the occasion in 1814 when he had directed a performance of *Fidelio* in Prague. Although his own opera *Der Freischütz* was then taking Europe by storm, he praised *Fidelio* for being 'this mighty stage work testifying to German greatness and depth of feeling'. His primary purpose though in writing to Beethoven was to request a copy of the score of *Fidelio* for a further projected performance of the work in April at the Royal Opera house in Dresden.[xcvii] On 26 June the Director of the Royal Opera, Hans von Könneritz, confirmed with Beethoven his opera had indeed been preformed 'with decided success' and, doubtless more to the composer's liking, he included the copyright-performance fee of 40 ducats.[xcviii]

In the autumn of 1823, Weber had occasion to call on Beethoven and on 5 October he wrote to his wife of their meeting: '[Beethoven] received me with the most touching affection; he embraced me at least six or seven times in the heartiest fashion, full of enthusiasm ... We spent the noon hour together, very merrily and happily.' Later in life Weber's son Max recalled his father telling him how he had entered a bare, almost poverty-stricken room: 'The chamber was in the greatest disorder. Music, money, articles of clothing lay on the floor ... the grand piano, which was open, was thick with dust'. Weber likened Beethoven in appearance to King Lear: 'His hair was thick, grey and bristly, here and there altogether white ... like in his [later] portraits ... beneath the bushy eyebrows ... small radiant eyes beamed mildly out'. Weber, like Beethoven, was small in stature but he describes how the eminent composer 'towered cyclopean' above him.[xcix]

To these pen-portraits of Beethoven, at the period of composition of the C minor Piano Sonata, we can add a painterly likeness. In January 1823 the publisher Gottfried Georg Härtel wrote to Ferdinand Georg Waldmüller requesting he should make a portrait of Beethoven. Doubtless this was to form the basis for a subsequent engraving with which to adorn one of his forthcoming sets of musical works, as was then the custom. Waldmüller was a respected genre and portrait painter and on 18 April he responded to Härtel's request, undertaking to attend on the composer in this capacity 'with the greatest pleasure'. Although Beethoven subsequently promised Waldmüller several sittings, in the event the artist had to make do with only one hurried session. Under these circumstances it can be assumed Waldmüller had time only to portray Beethoven's face, adding the details of his clothes retrospectively. Anton Schindler disliked Waldmüller's study condemning it for being 'further from the truth than any other'. At a later date, Waldmüller prepared a more carefully considered version of his original study, this time for the Leipzig publisher Friedrich Kistner. In Alessandra Commi's study *The Changing Face of Beethoven* (New York, 1987), contrary to Schindler's opinion, she defends Waldmüller's study for its accuracy.[c][d]

To complete our depiction of Beethoven in the early 1820s, we call to mind the recollections of Johann Andreas Stumpff. He is described as being a Thuringian harp manufacturer but who earned his living in London as a piano tuner to John Broadwood. The reader may recall (Piano Sonata Op. 106) Stumpff had travelled to Vienna in 1816 to regulate the fine Broadwood piano the English manufacturer had presented to Beethoven. In the autumn of 1823, Stumpff once more had occasion to meet the composer. This time he found him 'unhappy looking' and 'considerably changed in appearance' since their last meeting. However, he comments on Beethoven being 'a capital walker' disposed to 'ramble for hours through wild, romantic country'. He perceived nothing pleased him so much as the music of Handel of whom he remarked, 'Handel is the greatest composer who ever lived'. He spoke 'with sublimity' of the *Messiah* adding: 'I would uncover my head and kneel at his [Handel's] grave.' Stumpff relates Beethoven could not endure hearing his earlier works praised and in particular would allow no compliments to be paid to his Septet that by then had become universally popular. Stumpff concludes his account: 'The portrait you see in the music shops is not like him now, but it may have been eight or ten years ago.'[cii]

The portrait to which Stumpff refers is thought to be the crayon study of Beethoven created by the fashionable

French artist Louis Letronne that had been commissioned by Artaria & Co at the time of the Congress of Vienna (see Piano Sonata Op. 109).[ciii] Regarding Waldmüller's portrait of the composer, this was favourably reviewed in the Stuttgart *Morgenblatt* and later in the Vienna *Theaterzeitung*. It describes it as 'very good' recalling 'Ossian's grey-haired bards of Ullin' — the latter being 'the stormy god of war' in the epic poem. Beethoven is then acknowledged as being honoured 'not only in Vienna and Germany, but by Europe and the whole civilized world'. His fondness for strolling about the countryside is once more noted, prompting the reviewer to remark: 'No wonder then, that his works are glorious like herself, and that in contemplation of them, we are drawn nearer to the spiritual world.'[civ]

Although Beethoven was largely immune to flattery, two honours came his way at the period under consideration that may have helped to elevate his self-esteem; in his later years, with his enforced withdrawal from public life, he was inclined to feel neglected. On 28 December the Royal Swedish Academy, Stockholm wrote to him of its intention to confer on him its honorary membership in recognition of its obligation to acknowledge 'persons who have with success, or in a distinguished manner, pursued praiseworthy music'.[cv] In 1799 Joseph Haydn had been similarly honoured. Doubtless the Academy's letter took time to reach Vienna and it was not until 1 March 1823 that Beethoven sent his response, drafted in French by another hand: 'C'est avec bien du plaisir ... que je recoit l'hommage que l'Academie royale suédoise de Musique rend à mes médiocres mérites.'[cvi]

The following year Beethoven received further recognition of his achievements in music, this time from nearer home. On 24 February 1824, twenty-eight signatories sent the composer a fulsome letter expressing their esteem of him and his works. The signatories include several names that have appeared in our foregoing pages such as: Artaria & Co., (one of the composer's first music publishers), Carl Czerny (Beethoven's former piano pupil and pianistic pedagogue), Anton Diabelli (composer and music publisher), Prince Eduard and Count Moritz Lichnowsky (respectively nephew and brother of Prince Carl Lichnowsky, Beethoven's friend and patron), and Andreas Streicher (piano manufacturer and long-time friend of Beethoven). We can only imagine how eagerly Beethoven's ardent admirer Franz Schubert would have added his name to this list had he been invited to do so. Collectively, Beethoven's devotees remark: 'Out of the wide circle of reverent admirers that surround your genius in your native city, a small number of disciples and lovers of art approach you today to express long-felt wishes.' They place him on a level with Haydn and Mozart, regret his enforced retirement from public life and look forward to 'new blossoms' of his art and 'rejuvenated life'. In this context they reveal their awareness that 'a new flower grows in the garland of your glorious, still unequalled symphonies' (a reference to the Ninth Symphony, Op. 125) and of a 'grand sacred composition' (the *Missa Solemnis*, Op. 124). Beethoven's admirers take leave of him by anticipating the spring in the hope that it will bring forth 'a twofold blossoming-time for us and the entire world of art'.[cvii]

We recall in his letter of 6 July 1822 to Ferdinand Ries, Beethoven had declared his new piano sonatas to be 'really not very difficult'. This remark must be taken as more indicative of the composer's sense of humour and irony, than a serious estimation of the challenges with which his work confronts the pianist. In this context Donald Tovey has words of support for the would-be performer of the C minor Piano Sonata, Op. 111: 'Its technical difficulties are positive encouragements; we know that practice can overcome them.'[cviii] Tovey's words of reassurance lead us to conclude our prefatory remarks about the Piano Sonata Op. 111 with reference to two interpreters of the music who assuredly did have it under their fingers.

It may surprise the reader to reveal the first of these is Gustav Mahler, who today we remember primarily for being a symphonist. This overlooks the fact that he studied piano intensively at the Vienna Conservatory in the years 1875–8. Among those privileged to hear Mahler at the height (almost) of his powers was his archaeologist friend Friedrich Löhr. In July 1885, when Mahler was then aged 25, he stayed with Löhr who has left the following account: 'How few people there are today who know what it meant then to hear Mahler play at the piano! True, he said himself that five or six years earlier he had been a more able pianist.' Of his interpretation, Löhr enthuses: 'I have never before or since heard such de-materialization of the human, the technical, process. Mahler rose inexpressibly above what he did; every thought of technical difficulty was utterly cancelled out; all was disembodied, purely contemplative, passionately and spiritually concentrated on all that, without conscious physical contact, passed from the keys into his being.' Löhr continues: 'In a way all his own, comprehending it with the energy and accomplishment of genius, bringing out every nuance, every shade of expression, he caused the music to ring out with all the force with which it had gushed forth from the soul of the creator.' Löhr heard Mahler perform the C minor Sonata of which he recalls: 'In Beethoven's Sonata Op. 111, for instance, the storm at the beginning broke out in a terrible *maestoso*, shatteringly intense, with a wild ferocity such as I have never heard again; and similarly the finale faded out, pure, utterly luminous, in loveliest beauty, softly and softlier still, from the closest touch with this earth out into eternity.'[cix]

Our second reference to an acknowledged accomplished performer of the C minor Sonata draws us nearer to our own time. In fact we have two remembrances of the artist in question, namely Artur Schnabel. In March 1944 the American composer and music critic Virgil Thomson heard Schnabel perform in an all Beethoven performance. By then Thomson had earned a reputation for his wit, candour and independent-minded judgement in his capacity of music critic for the New York Herald-Tribune. Of the celebrated pianist's rendering of the Op. 111 he responded in a more measured demeanour: 'Here Mr. Schnabel achieved in the first movement a more convincing relation than one currently hears between the declamatory and the lyrical subjects. And in the finale he produced for us that beatific tranquillity that was a characteristic part of Beethoven's mature expression.'[cx]

A few years later it was the privilege of the distinguished British music critic Neville Cardus to hear Schnabel gave a recital in Manchester that included the Op. 111. As an interpreter of Beethoven, Cardus regarded Schnabel being 'like a spiritual medium as though the composer were speaking through him'. He found Schnabel's rendering of the C minor Sonata so profoundly moving that in his review of the recital in *The Manchester Guardian* (23 March 1974) he devoted his attention almost exclusively to the music — making only a passing reference to Schnabel himself. Consider his surprise then when, the following day, Schnabel phoned him to say — disarmingly: 'This is just what I wanted to achieve. I want an audience to listen to Beethoven, and to go home thinking about Beethoven — not Schnabel!'[cxi]

Beethoven designates the first movement of the Piano Sonata Op. 111 *Maestoso* that can be taken to mean 'stately, dignified and majestic'. With regards to its interpretation, he adds the tempo marking *Allegro con brio ed appassionato*, 'at a fast tempo, with spirit and energetic/expressive'. The opening five bars have been likened to 'a cry of agony' to which Beethoven responds with five further bars where he seems to be looking 'with tender amazement at his own human wretchedness, turning it in his hands as though to discover its meaning'.[cxii] Ernst von Elterlein describes the opening chords as 'deep lacerations of the heart', exclaiming: 'What titanic power! What a volcanic outburst![cxiii] Another commentator has compared the intensity of passion of the opening to a 'lightening-bolt' that sets the character of the whole movement 'one of torment and strife, carried along by hard, driving energy'.[cxiv] The defiant opening bars invite comparison with those of the *Pathétique* Sonata, but elevated to an even higher level of intensity.[cxv] 'Its opening notes stop you in your tracks, which was surely Beethoven's intention. Not even the mighty *Hammerklavier* Sonata, that Everest of a work ... contains anything as threatening as those terse opening notes in C minor, and their thunderous progress into the succeeding *Allegro con brio*, the music filled with suggestions of cliff faces, chasms, torrents and avalanches.'[cxvi]

The emphatic opening chords to the C minor Piano Sonata convey an impression of immense breadth in much the same manner as do those that herald the opening to the Ninth Symphony. In the sonata they also set the stage as it were by preparing the way for the 'energy and conflict' of the main Allegro.[cxvii] There are also unsettling feelings of uncertainty and ambiguity; in which key will the movement find resolution?[cxviii] C minor is established but only to be disrupted amidst the movement's 'restlessness, dramatic pauses and the tossing about of fragments of themes between all registers of the piano'.[cxix]

The C minor Sonata is one of the few amongst the

composer's thirty-two that open with a slow movement, the others being Opp. 13, 78 and 81a. The musicologist Wilhelm von Lenz, however, argued the case that the *Maestoso* in Op. 111 is the only *true* introduction in all of Beethoven's sonatas.[cxx] The music critic John Fuller-Maitland, writing about the work on the occasion of the composer's death centenary, found it possessed of 'Aeschylean grandeur' — a reference to the work of the Athenian tragic poet Aeschylus.[cxxi] Romain Rolland characterises the movement's stormy, singing phrases as 'leonine' — imposing/majestic.[cxxii] Alfred Brendel considers the manner of the opening to be one of 'angry revolt' that at the same time provides 'a thematic seed' for the whole sonata. He also finds a parallel 'psychologically and materially' with Schubert's song setting of Heine's *Der Atlas*.[cxxiii] The reader will recall Atlas was the Titan who was condemned to bear the burden of the world upon his shoulders throughout all eternity. Brendel's suggestion is doubly appropriate, considering that at the time Beethoven was composing the C minor Sonata, his mind was also occupied with the *Choral* Symphony with its moving evocation of mankind and joy to its millions.

Joy does not infiltrate the first movement of Op. 111. In the words of Neville Cardus: 'The stamping notes shatter attempts towards peace and appeasement.'[cxxiv] Instead, we have 'a sombre image of passionate agitation'.[cxxv] In nineteenth-century style imagery, Oscar Bie calls to mind the Titans once more: 'From the dominant grows a theme of savage grandeur, of Titanic power, all-embracing in its widening grasp, its Medusa-locks flying in the air, crushing out all sweetness and softness, till, as it came, it sinks terribly to earth.'[cxxvi] In Op. 111, Beethoven is no longer hurling defiance at the world and his creator, as may be detected in the C minor Sonata, Op. 13. As Martin Cooper reflects: 'It is significant that in Op. 13 Beethoven engages in a manifest dialogue, with fortissimo chords in the bass answered by an eloquently pleading phrase in the treble, while in Op. 111 we have a monologue.' He elaborates: 'Whereas the young man exteriorized the struggle in himself, dramatizing his "opponent" as a force outside himself, one whom it was possible to defy or placate, middle age brought the knowledge that this opponent was his own dark shadow, a rejected aspect of his own, self-sharing with him a common identity.' In short, Beethoven had outgrown the days of being Prometheus defying the almighty.[cxxvii] Barry Cooper expresses much the same idea: 'This is not the defiant, "heroic" figure of earlier works; the subsequent quiet, despairing journey, but never resting on, distant keys, reveals it to be the tormented, confused questioning of the introvert.'[cxxviii]

In his commentary to the C minor Sonata, Donald Tovey reminds the would-be performer that Beethoven's tempo indication is not to be taken as that of a slow movement.[cxxix] Also with this in mind, Brendel gives expression to his Puckish sense of humour: 'With his tempo marking *Allegro con brio ed appassionato* Beethoven indicates that he is not enthroned on Olympus.'[cxxx] In other words, despite the gravitas — 'grim pathos' — within the music, and its heavenly associations with the pantheon of the gods, the music must move along.[cxxxi] Indeed, Charles Rosen argues that the contour of the theme of the first movement resembles, in some respects, the waltz that Diabelli sent to many European composers in 1819, asking each of them to contribute one variation. Although Beethoven at first scornfully rejected Diabelli's proposition, in due course it came to seize his imagination. Rosen comments: 'Beethoven profoundly reshaped Diabelli's theme for his sonata.'[cxxxii]

In his *Talking of Music*, Cardus directs attention to the

constructional procedures at work in the C minor Sonata: 'Beethoven shapes his motifs into the stuff and texture of the whole movement. It is action and reaction of mind and spirit.'[cxxxiii] Von Elterlein viewed what he called 'the matter of the movement' to be 'superbly grand' and the formal construction to be 'simplicity itself' being nothing more than two-part sonata form: 'It affords a striking illustration of how the greatest ends are attainable with the smallest means.'[cxxxiv] Cooper reminds us that at the period of composition of the C minor Sonata, Beethoven was particularly interested in counterpoint and that this had a direct bearing on the manner in which he manipulated his material. He also reflects on the challenges its realization poses for the performer — despite what Beethoven said to Ries about the work being 'not very difficult'. Cooper is more realistic: 'This movement ... has a number of virtuoso traits — the semiquaver passages in octaves, the dizzy climbs and descents over the whole range of the keyboard — but these are always subordinate to musical, expressive consideration.'[cxxxv]

Despite Beethoven's desire to promote the German language in the designations to his works (see Piano Sonata Op. 106), in the trilogy Opp. 109, 110 and 111 he reverts to the use of Italian, prompting Eric Blom to comment: 'Beethoven's growing international reputation [may have] had something to do with his reverting to what was then, and still is, the musician's universal language.'[cxxxvi]

We have remarked earlier of the occasion when Louis Schlösser made Beethoven's acquaintance. Schlösser records the composer telling him how he could recall a musical idea in his head years after its origination.[cxxxvii] This is corroborated in the case of the theme Beethoven adopted for the first movement of the C minor Sonata. It appears to have occurred to him some twenty years previously and is found in sketches dating from 1801–02 in connection with the Violin Sonata Op. 30, No.1.[xxxviii] Of related interest is that musicologist John Shedlock has found a resemblance in the sketches to the opening of the *Maestoso* with the measures Handel uses in the fugal chorus to 'And with His stripes' as found in the Oratorio *The Messiah* – a reminder of how Beethoven had become absorbed in Handel's music at the period in question.[xxxix]

In his later compositions Beethoven was disposed to incorporating fugal textures into his writing. In this regard he was subscribing to well-established musicological procedures of the day, nurtured by such masters as Haydn and Mozart with Bach as the fountainhead. As Rosen remarks: 'Combining fugue and sonata was a great classical preoccupation ... [It] was a learned technique and it gave prestige to the more sociable form of the sonata.' In our previous discussions, we have seen how this aspect of Beethoven's design came to the fore in the *Hammerklavier* Sonata. Similarly, in the Piano Sonata Op. 101 Beethoven adopts an extended fugal texture that, in the Sonata Op. 110, becomes even more profound – no less than 'a rethinking and humanization of all the most basic devices of fugue in order to create a scenario of dramatic power'.[cxl]

In the C minor Piano Sonata, Beethoven once more welds fantasy and fugue: 'Beethoven devised [a] hybrid creation and perhaps his most searching exploration of the tension between counterpoint and sonata form.'[cxli] For a few measures Beethoven conveys the impression the music is about to unfold in the guise of a regular fugue but this is set aside in favour of 'more homophonic-figural writing'.[cxlii] Notwithstanding, the music is possessed of unrestrained passion: 'The fugue opens like a veritable thunderstorm. There are short phrases in the major which answer to the second subject, a brief snatch of two celestial bars, and the agitated atmosphere again unfolds itself.'[cxliii] With performance in mind, Tovey first treats us to an example of his wry humour: '[There] is a tradition from the Dark Ages (*circa* 1840), which inculcates that in fugues the subject should be played as on a trombone, while all countersubjects should be decorously concealed.' He than adds the encouragement to regard the fugal passages as one of the main themes of the movement, and 'see that you miss none of the passion which inspires each detail of its progress'.[cxliv]

With regard to the interpretation of the C minor Sonata more generally, Carl Czerny writes: 'This first movement of Beethoven's last sonata, belongs to his greatest, and must be performed with all power, bravura and impassioned emotion, which the tragic character, as well as the difficulty of the passages requires.'[cxlv] Edwin Fischer exhorts: 'The first movement, *Maestoso*, should be begun in the grand manner ... something approaching the opening of the Piano Sonata Op. 106.' He invites the performer to regard the music as the embodiment of life's struggle and for its relentless figuration to be 'chiselled out with steely fingers'.[cxlvi] Rosen urges the performer to resist the temptation to play this profound movement too slowly even though, as he puts it, 'that is a way of convincing a docile public that it is listening to something spiritual and sublime'.[cxlvii]

We catch a glimpse of how Franz Liszt may have sounded in his performance of the C minor Piano Sonata in a letter Richard Wagner wrote on 15 February 1857 to the daughter of Princess Wittgenstein. Wagner first pays tribute to Liszt's power of endowing music with his own personality: 'Whoever had frequent occasion to hear Liszt play Beethoven ... must surely have always been struck with the fact there was no question here of re-production, but of genuine production.' He then exemplifies his remark: 'I ask all who have heard, for instance, Op. 106 or Op. 111 of Beethoven's ... played by Liszt in a private circle, what they previously knew of these creations and what they discovered in them? ... [It] was at least of infinitely greater worth than all the sonatas, reproducing Beethoven, which have been "produced" by our pianoforte-composers in imitation of those still badly-understood works.'[cxlviii]

Nearer to our own time Joseph Horowitz had occasion to discuss questions of interpretation with the Chilean-born pianist Claudio Arrau. In particular, Horowitz asked Arrau what his position was concerning the redistribution of notes between the hands in performance to facilitate evenness or accuracy. Arrau acknowledged that an audience may not notice such things but he maintained 'one should play for the *ideal* listener'. He believed the ideal listener will notice the difference, citing passages in the first movement of Op 111: 'People play it with two hands because they don't want to risk dirty octaves. Well, first of all, it sounds different played with one hand, as written. And then technical difficulty has itself an expressive value.' On another occasion in the 1970s, the pianist Philip Lorenz assisted Arrau to conduct a series of master classes; these were in connection with the Beethoven Bicentennial. It was a first-time experience for Arrau. Students attended from, Europe, Japan and America. One student elected to perform the Op. 111 Piano Sonata. Lorenz recalls how, in guiding the pupil, Arrau did not play a single note. Instead he encouraged her with his views about the composition, remarking on 'the emotional world the music occupies and how to realise the work's technical challenges'. At the close of the student's performance there was thunderous applause. Lorenz remembers: 'I think a lot of people were moved to tears ... it wasn't so much for her playing, although she played very well. It was for [Arrau].'[cxlix]

The pervasive atmosphere of the first movement of Op. 111 has captivated audiences from the time of its inception.

Writing of the work in the April 1824 edition of the *Allgemeine musikalische Zeitung*, the reviewer commented on the work's 'powerful, passionate impulsiveness that hardly stops for a moment ... and which drives everything restlessly forward'.[d] Henry Krehbiel adopts loftier imagery: 'With the first movement of this sonata [Beethoven] carries us to the theatre in which the last scene in Goethe's *Faust* plays – the higher regions of this sphere, where earth and heaven meet as they seem to do at times in the high Alps.'[cli]

In the Op. 111 Paul Bekker finds Beethoven from the outset standing upon the heights to which his earlier creations had pointed. The work's opening chord he describes as 'the most agonised dissonance in Beethoven's musical vocabulary ... A phrase [that] rings like a groan from the palpitating *sforzati* base'. Of the music's ensuing passion, he characterises it as 'unprecedented in Beethoven's work since Op. 57'. Regarding the movement as a whole, Bekker finds similarities exist between it and the Overture *Coriolanus* insofar, he considers, both portray 'head-strong energy' in the form of 'dramatic monologues'. In the sonata, Bekker perceives: 'The will, worn by earthly conflict, is translated to realms of light, its strength purified and transfigured.' In this context Bekker alludes to the views of earlier writers. He cites Wilhelm von Lenz's take on the music as expressed in terms of 'defiance and submission' and von Bülow's characterisation of the movement's contrasting moods, oscillating between *samsara* (the cycle of birth, death and rebirth) and *nirvana* (peace and happiness).[clii]

Although Chopin was not one of Beethoven's foremost champions, it is known he admired the C minor Sonata, passages of which appear to have found expression in his own *Revolutionary Etude*. As Wilson remarks of the Op. 111: 'With its stormy semiquaver passages ... and its restless closing bars ... surely a decade later, inspired Chopin's

Revolutionary study in the same key, this movement might seem the essence of nineteenth-century romanticism.'[cliii] We have noted that the young Sergei Prokofiev drew inspiration for his Second Symphony from Beethoven's Op. 111. Twenty years later its influence may also have been at work in his mind as evident in his Sixth Symphony, premiered in Leningrad on 11 October 1947. Although its main sources of influence are known to have been the harrowing events of the war years, Arnold Whittall maintains: '[The] the titanic conflicts which are expressed so uncompromisingly [in the Sixth Symphony] may owe at least as much to an intention of Prokofiev's to dedicate the Symphony – his Op. 111 – to the memory of Beethoven: although Prokofiev makes no attempt to match the Olympian serenity of the *Arietta* of Beethoven's Op. 111, the C minor Piano Sonata, the terse forcefulness of the Sonata's opening *Allegro con brio ed appassionato* can be sensed behind the more expansive but no less tragic character of the Symphony's *Allegro moderato*.'[cliv]

With passion and fervour spent, Beethoven closes the first movement with a softly expressed ending that he marks *pp* – pianissimo. Thereby, in Barry Cooper's words, the ending 'prepares the ear for the serenity of the *Arietta*' that is to follow and thereby 'we now enter a new world – one of inner, spiritual contemplation'.[clv]

This 'new world' is the second movement that Beethoven designates *Arietta*. Taken literally as the diminutive of the Italian *aria*, the term can be understood to mean a song on a small scale that has particular associations with eighteenth-century operas and operettas, often of a quasi-pathetic or light and frivolous nature. Here, in the Op. 111, however, it does not possess any such suggestions of lightness or flippancy: 'Beethoven's theme is a short song, certainly, but neither light nor gay. Still, a song, and one of the most heart easing ever sung by a musical instrument.'[clvi] In the *Arietta* there is no conflict, 'tension is exchanged for sublimity'[clvii] within 'a sublime synthesis of slow movement and finale'.[clviii] In the Op. 111 Sonata 'the simplicity and static quality of the *Arietta* ... suggests a spirit completely at rest, at peace with itself, not so much resigned to suffering as willingly accepting and transfiguring it into something that is indistinguishable from joy'.[clix] We are presented with 'a study in suspended harmonic motion with almost a quarter of an hour of the purest C major'.[clx] In strictly formal musicological terms, Beethoven's design consists of a theme, the *Arietta*, and a concluding set of variations.

Beethoven's contemporaries appear to have been divided on the merits of his most recent creation for the keyboard. In 1824, an extract from a review in the Leipzig *Allgemeine musikalische Zeitung* reads: 'The devices that the composer has seen fit to deploy for the development of his beautiful material are so artificial that we find them quite unworthy of his great genius. In his use of this musical material he is like a painter who uses a miniature brush and a single colour to execute a whole alter piece.' The second movement, however, inspired the critic of the sister journal the *Berliner Allgemeine musikalische Zeitung* to view the music as 'a most extraordinary vision'. Entitling his interpretation of the music as 'The death of a great man' – namely Beethoven himself – he writes: 'Do not the harmonies of the theme swell like the music of a distant funeral procession echoing through the night? And in the second part we hear the sounds of the grave. Then the pall-bearers in long veils and friends, the friends weeping quietly come nearer and nearer ... I hear through the pealing bells the last heavy breathing of the dying man.'[clxi] Beethoven's confident Anton Schindler was of the view: 'Here we find almost unrestrained passion broken by a few lovely melodic passages, followed by a melodic figure tenaciously, even gloomily, held practically throughout, a new phenomenon in Beethoven's work at that time. It is as if in this movement he were vying himself to develop a multiplicity of devices and to contrive a mathematical labyrinth from the simple material of the *Arietta* — the theme of the variations.'[clxii]

Later nineteenth-century commentators were no less fulsome in their estimation of the depth of feeling Beethoven invested in the C minor Piano Sonata. Friedrich Bernard Marx speaks of the composition 'as a theme of deep feeling, overflowing with tender, profound melancholy, developed with the utmost regularity but with ever increasing richness, now subdued, now pleasantly stirred, but returning to the elegiac primary tone of feeling, then rousing up with new courage'. He elaborates: 'It seems as if we had an echo from the loftiest ideal and spiritual regions, the language, which is simply untranslatable into words, of the soul soaring to the heavenly regions with fervent and holy rapture.'[clxiii] In similar mood, von Elterlein was moved to comment: 'How wonderfully does the deep, fervent song of the *Arietta* ever aspire towards the heavenly spheres ...'.[clxiv] And likewise Rolland: 'Beethoven concludes his world contribution of sonatas with an air of celestial happiness, varied in the most lovely manner possible.' He likens the theme of the *Arietta* to 'a voice from above'.[clxv]

Sir George Grove had occasion to write to his pianist sister-in-law Miss Emma Bradley sometime in 1862. Grove had been seized with enthusiasm for Beethoven's piano sonatas years previously when he had heard the *Hammerklavier* Sonata for the first time when it was performed at a London recital by Arabella Goddard — in what was one of the earliest public renderings of the work in England. In his letter he enthuses to Miss Bradley in the following terms: 'There is no doubt whatever, it is she [Arabella Goddard] we have to thank for Beethoven's latest and most difficult sonatas having become so popular as they are. But the gem of them all (and playable too) is the *Arietta* which is the subject of the last movement of Op. 111. You will find no difficulty in playing the *Arietta* itself and the first two variations, and if they don't make you cry I shall be astonished ... the tenderness of this little air is most overcoming.'[clxvi]

From Cosima Wagner's Diary of 25 September 1877, we gain as insight into the intellectual nature of their relationship and of Wagner's estimation of the C minor Sonata's second movement: 'In the evening ... [Richard] reads me ... Voltaire's article on Aristotle in the *Dictionnaire philosophique*. The boldness of its flights of imagination leads to Beethoven, and R. says that were he to try to visualize Beethoven "in all his starry glory", he would surely think of the second movement of Op. 111 (*Adagio* with variations); he knows nothing more ecstatic, he says, yet at the same time it is never sentimental.'[clxvii]

Turning to our own times, modern-day authorities have been no less moved than their predecessors to bestow praise on the feeling Beethoven enshrined in the *Arietta* passages of the Op. 111. Marion Scott is succinct: '[No] words can describe the serenity and light of the *Arietta*'.[clxviii] Eric Blom, writing in the 1930s, expressed much the same: 'To write about this farewell to the sonata for the piano is to come as near an attempt at describing the indescribable as anyone can possible be faced with ... No idea can be given of the theme on which Beethoven bases his variations except by writing out the whole of it.'[clxix] Wilfrid Mellers compares Beethoven's achievement with Wagner's *Tristan*: 'Like Beethoven's last piano sonatas and quartets, Wagner's *Tristan* ... expresses the end and inversion of humanism. The distinction between them lies in the fact that Beethoven entered his paradise in the sublime melodic proliferations of the *Arietta* of Op. 111, whereas Wagner, performing a mystical act in dissolving time, consciousness and sexuality, does not completely achieve this lyrical consummation.'[clxx]

The British writer and music critic Alec Robertson is remembered today, by an older generation of music lovers, for his broadcasts about music. He was also religiously inclined and contributed writings to *The Catholic Herald* and *The Tablet*. In this latter capacity, in January 1954 he contributed to the BBC *Epiphany* broadcast *Ways to God*. In his text he argued one of the roles of music was to show ways to God and to inspire help on that difficult journey. To substantiate his point of view he recalled Beethoven's alleged remark to Elisabeth (Bettina) von Arnim that music 'was a higher revelation than all wisdom and philosophy'. Commenting on this somewhat sweeping utterance, Robertson offered the defence: 'It may seem an exaggerated claim: but what other art could sum up in terms so simple as to be understood by any child, so profound that they are inexhaustible matter for contemplation what Beethoven reveals in the *Arietta* of his last piano sonatas? Here indeed is music testifying to something inexpressible, something beyond itself, and fulfilling also Bach's reported saying that: "The aim and final reason of all music is the glory of God and the refreshment of the spirit".'[clxxi]

A dissentient voice is heard from an unexpected quarter. In his student days at the Leningrad Conservatory, Dmitri Shostakovich learned the *Moonlight* and *Appassionata* Sonatas under the direction of Leonid Nikolayev, professor of piano. With the encouragement of fellow piano student Maria Yudina, he later mastered the taxing *Hammerklavier* Piano Sonata. Reflecting on the C minor Piano Sonata, Op. 111 he confessed he found the second movement 'extremely long and extremely boring'. (Taken at a spacious tempo it does in fact have a performing time of almost twenty minutes.) The day came, however, when he heard Yudina play through the composition that, Shostakovich later acknowledged, helped him to modify his opinion.[clxxii]

In his *In Pursuit of Music*, Denis Matthews considers the string quartet to be the most perfect and satisfying of all instrumental mediums. He also acknowledges the solo piano has two series of masterpieces that he held to be 'so comprehensive as to be inexhaustible', namely, Bach's forty-eight preludes and fugues and Beethoven's thirty-two piano sonatas — in former times characterised as being respectively music's *Old Testament* and *New Testament*. Continuing in this spirit, Matthews pays tribute to Beethoven having encompassed in his piano writing a whole 'gamut of experience' that for him culminated in the two movements of the Piano Sonata Op. 111. Of this he remarks: 'This, to me, is the pianist's greatest moment, and especially towards the end of the *Arietta*, when his strivings, reflecting those of the composer, take the apotheosis of the C major theme into ethereal regions.'[clxxiii]

In his essay *The Greatness of Beethoven*, the British composer, pianist and teacher Alan Bush discusses Beethoven's treatment of melancholy, despair and resignation that characterise much of the music of the composer's final years. He emphasises Beethoven was intent not on merely giving expression to them but of overcoming them through such procedures as 'a joyful, liberating finale'. Bush maintains the composer's intention thereby is to convey the expression of 'inner peace', not of passive resignation but 'lofty calmness' and 'inner energy'. He cites the final movement of Piano Sonata Op. 111 as evidence of these procedures.[clxxiv]

Maynard Solomon perceives the *Arietta* within a wider framework of the composer searching for new styles of musical language with which to express his evolving musical idealism. He cites the manner in which 'chaos strives for lucid formation' in the transition to the fugue of the *Hammerklavier* Piano Sonata and how a 'victorious conclusion' brings the Piano Sonata Op. 110 to a close. In the *Arietta* of the Op. 111 Piano Sonata, he considers 'struggle is sublimated into ecstasy'.[clxxv] Barry Cooper describes the whole of the second movement of the C minor Sonata as 'enormous, unfathomable and uplifting' and possessed of 'an extraordinary visionary quality, transcending all previous piano music and even challenging the limits of the notational system in which it was written ... creating notational peculiarities that bewildered some of his contemporaries' (see later).[clxxvi]

In the construction of the *Arietta*, Marx refers to what he describes as the music's 'strangely dissevered melodies' that for him recalled elegiac funeral songs.[clxxvii] Theodor Adorno similarly argues that in attempting to understand melody in late Beethoven, we need to think of song that he considered to be manifest in the *Arietta* of Op. 111.[clxxviii] Matthews, with others, considers that in his working out of the *Arietta*, Beethoven may have absorbed influences from his own material when at work simultaneously on the *Diabelli* variations.[clxxix] Amongst those sharing this opinion is Cooper who states: 'The *Arietta* theme is deceptively simple, with a cantabile whose opening ... recalls that of the *Diabelli* Variations.'[clxxx] What is evident from the surviving sketches is that Beethoven rejected many versions of the Adagio theme before resolving upon its final, simple — and sublime — shape.[clxxxi]

As a guide to the interpretation of the second movement, Beethoven writes at the head of the score *Adagio molto semplice e cantabile*. This may be translated as 'slowly, very simply and songlike'. As Rosen argues, this is not a description of the music but a direction to the performer to bear in mind that 'simplicity is necessary to bring out what is already there'.[clxxxii] In Matthews' reflections on performance, Beethoven's instruction serves as 'a touchstone for the interpreter'.[clxxxiii] For Brendel, the words *molto semplice e cantabile* aim 'to show to performers the way' but he adds: 'What they imply is not ingenuousness or simple-minded sweetness, but simplicity as a result of complexity – distilled experience.'[clxxxiv]

In his notes to the interpretation of the movement, Carl Czerny urges the adoption of a *cantabile* and *legatissimo* to bring out its 'beautiful, touching and simple theme'.[clxxxv] Tovey contends: 'The whole movement should give an impression of being in one tempo without even a moment's slackening or hurrying from beginning to end ... The *Arietta* and its variations put a great strain upon the player's capacity to keep his tone quiet without losing warmth. But no work of Beethoven is better calculated to convince the player of the wisdom of playing what is written there.' Reflecting on the performance-practice of his day he adds: 'On the whole, as those who have heard Schnabel play this sonata will agree, the slowest tempo is here the most impressive.'[clxxxvi] Virgil Thomson attributes the challenges confronting the performer to what he describes as the 'knottiness' found in the music arising from Beethoven experimenting with new pianistic dispositions that are expressed in unusual and intricate time signatures such as nine semiquavers to the bar – all painstakingly and scrupulously devised. In a review of a concert given by Josef Hofmann on 7 November 1940, Thomson reflected: 'The Beethoven Op. 111, despite the rival claims of various bravura compositions, remains, in my opinion, the most difficult piano piece in the world. Not only because the trills and tremolos and stretches are ungratefully placed and unconscionably tiring to play, but because the work presents as great a difficulty to the mind as to the hand. To make anything consistent out of it is both an intellectual and a technical achievement ... I am simply saying that the work is hermetic, complex and knotty from every point of view.'[clxxxvii] For Fischer, the *Arietta* represented 'the transcendental' that he considered 'should be played with a touch dematerialized as not to seem to be of this world'. To achieve this he adds: 'It is the spirit that creates for itself the body to dwell in; it is the idea that discovers the necessary technique ... Be completely conscious of the eternal laws that rule the stars, and then your fingers will become "magnetic" and conjure up transcendental light from wood and strings.'[clxxxviii]

The *Arietta* is followed by a set of variations that unfold progressively in a sequence of transformations that elevate the music to 'a higher plane of consciousness'.[clxxxix] Beethoven had given expression to his musical ideas in the language of the piano variation from the time of his youth. When only twelve years old he had published nine variations in C minor (WoO 63) on a theme by Ernst Christoph Dressler, given to him as an exercise by his then teacher Christian Gottlob Neefe.[cxc] In these, he adopts the standard technique of the day of elaborating figuration, to a greater or lesser degree of virtuosity, over a fixed harmonic and metrical framework — nonetheless, remarkable for a child. At the outset of his career as a virtuoso pianist in Vienna though, the piano variation in his hands — elevated by his powers of improvisation — had become his veritable calling card in the musical salons of the nobility. Beethoven was no longer content to simply transform the physiognomy of an original theme: '[We] overhear, as it were, the composer while he meditates on his theme, finding with each meditation new depths of insight, gradually leading us into a realm where the music takes on a luminance and transcendent quality of mystical revelation.'[cxci] In this context mention may be made of the variations dedicated to Prince Lichnowsky (WoO 69, 1795) and to Countess Browne (WoO 71, 1796–7). These were followed in due course by even greater sets of variations that Beethoven considered worthy of opus numbers, namely those dedicated to Princess Odescalchi (Op. 34, 1802), to Prince Karl Lichnowsky (Op. 35, 1802/3 – the so-called *Eroica* Variations) – and to Franz Olivia (Op. 76, 1809). Beethoven would crown his achievement in 1819–20 with the publication of the *Diabelli* Variations, Op. 120, composed as we have seen contemporaneously with the Piano Sonata Op. 111.

It has been estimated that by 1820, Beethoven had written more than sixty sets of variations. Many of these were settings of popular tunes of the day such as WoO 65/66/68/69/70/71/72/73/75/76 and 77. Others were patriotic such as WoO 78 on the theme of *God save the King* and WoO 79 on the theme of *Rule Britannia*. In his later adoption of the piano variation form, however, Beethoven imbued it with 'a "transfigured", almost ecstatic content and a profundity of expression which indicated he had found in this basic musical form a new vehicle for his most imaginative musical thought' and turned to it for 'the expression of his deepest meditations'.[cxcii]

We have seen in the Piano Sonata Op. 109, Beethoven had established a precedent for the adoption of the variation form to close a final movement. In the C minor Sonata he extends this principle even further. In his estimation of Beethoven's achievement, Henry Krehbiel invokes imagery from Goethe's *Faust*: '[We] hear the song of *Pater Profundis*, and thence we begin the ascent to the celestial realms above. The variations are the songs of the *Pater Ecstaticus, Blessed Boys, Penitents* and *Angels*, who soar higher and higher, carrying with them the immortal soul of *Faust*.'[cxciii]

Oscar Bie invokes a similar picture: 'After a movement of wild outcry [the declamatory opening movement] come the simply resigned variations, which finally mount from dull earthly devotion to angelic harmonies, to end in the glitter of their smile, in the bright sphere of their unearthliness.'[cxciv] Kinderman is more succinct but no less expressive: '[The] tension of the first movement is resolved ... as the unfolding variations on a lyric *Arietta* in C major achieve a synthesis of Being and Becoming.'[cxcv]

For the British music critic Samuel Langford, the variations that draw the C minor Piano Sonata to a close were the embodiment of perfection: 'The final variations approach so nearly to a mechanical perfection that the contemplation of its neatness almost brings a shudder ... where shall we find music more divinely separated from the mechanical than in those first variations? ... Those various transitions and ranges of emotions for the height and parallel of which we could go nowhere in poetry but to the *Paradiso* of Dante.'[cxcvi] Henry Krehbiel elevates Beethoven to an even higher plane and compares him, as he 'soars heavenward like a skylark in the rapture of the variations', with the Evangelist St. John of Patmos writing *The Book of Revelation*.[cxcvii] Also with the divine in mind, William Newman suggests '*sublimation* or *transfiguration* ... come [close] to the spiritual sense of the variations.'[cxcviii] In the variations, Paul Bekker finds Beethoven 'striving for the heights ... with the wishes and hopes of an indestructible personality.' He elaborates: 'The song [of the *Arietta*] is heard, increasingly spiritualized, dematerialised ... High notes call up a vision of ideal unapproachable heights, the accompanying rhythms flow along, sweeping, harp-like; high above all, a trill suggests the glitter of the stars, while the melody like a silver thread – the thread woven between earth and heaven by the inspiration of a great soul.'[cxcix]

As the variations soar effortlessly heavenwards, they convey none of the difficulty they gave the composer in their creation. Beethoven's sketches, however, reveal him exercising his characteristic process of rigorous selection from potential ideas until he finally resolved on the finished versions.[cc] It is a tribute to his workmanship that the variations selected for final inclusion then 'proceed seamlessly, gaining in momentum and colour'.[cci] '[They] grow logically one from another, with subdivisions of increasing complexity.' In this way 'the celestial calm' of the *Arietta* theme yields to 'a mood of tremendous exaltation'.[ccii]

Whilst the spirit of Beethoven's music aspires to the heavenly spheres, his workmanship is firmly grounded in established musicological procedures. In the working-out of the variations he adopts the traditional procedure of ever decreasing note values, so that bars in successive variations employ eighths, sixteenths, thirty-seconds and sixty-fourth notes. At the same time, in order to accommodate these sub-divisions, Beethoven employs unconventional — almost mathematically worked-out — time signatures including 9/19 and 12/32 — and this from a composer who, although possessed of business acumen, was hopeless at arithmetic.[cciii] Beethoven's contemporaries initially failed to appreciate the significance of the composer's departure from musicological convention. When the composition was reviewed in England in the 1820s, the reviewer in *The Harmonicon* was sharply critical of passages that he considered to be written in complex notation.[cciv] It has of course long been recognised that Beethoven's rhythmical diminutions — what Brendel describes as 'progressively rhythmic foreshortening'[ccv] — transforms the original tempo of the music, imbuing it with a sublime quality that, as it approaches its close, is elevated further into the heavenly spheres by the adoption of sustained trills.

The first three variations conform to the formal pattern of foreshortening as just described, increasing the music's sense of forward motion. Speaking of this in conversation with Joseph Horowitz, Claudio Arrau remarked: 'There is ... a tremendous evolution of the *Arietta* from the first variation to the second and from the second to the third. Particularly from the second to the third.'[ccvi] The rhythmic values double in variation one from eighths to sixteenths, in variation two from sixteenths to thirty-seconds, and in variation three sixty-fourth notes are used. Adorno argues one of Beethoven's most splendid formal compositional means, when adopting the variation form, is what he calls the *shadow*. He considered the first variation of the *Arietta* from Op. 111 to be such a shadow adding: 'The animated voice hardly dares stir after the compelling appearance of the theme.'[ccvii] Rolland's insight is similarly inclined: 'The first variation gently stirs the rhythm of the [*Arietta*] theme.'[ccviii]

Beethoven cautions against slowing the tempo of the opening variation by writing the instruction *L'istesso tempo* – at the same tempo as the preceding *Arietta*. This does not preclude it, however, from expanding its register 'in an unfolding of passionate melody of an almost operatic character'.[ccix] Rolland likened the effect of the increased tempo in the second variation to a 'doubling of its momentum'[ccx]. Kinderman draws attention to the second variation's 'expressive trills' that come to the fore with even greater effect later in the movement. In this more flowing variation, Kinderman discerns a 'tripartite structure' that serves as a basis for 'varied structural repetition' and changes of musical 'texture'.[ccxi]

With an increase in tempo in the third variation, 'celestial calm' gives way to ecstatic exultation'.[ccxii] By ever more complex subdivisions of metre, the calm of the original theme is transformed 'into euphonic abandonment',[ccxiii] to the 'almost giddy joyous and back to the sublime'.[ccxiv] To quote Arrau once more: 'It is a joyful assertion of life on earth ... I find it wonderful ... this attachment to life.'[ccxv] To some ears the music here possesses a modern, dance-like character perhaps even suggestive of the jagged, accented rhythms of ragtime.[ccxvi] Cooper offers the proposition: 'If the mood of this variation is violent, it is a violent joy, a stamping dance of triumph.'[ccxvii] Finding the precise musical language with which to give the desired expression to the music clearly did not come readily to the composer. Mention has been made of Beethoven's adoption of challenging time signatures and note values. Cooper also draws attention to the shear density of this variation's musical notation – that must have presented a formidable challenge to Beethoven's copyist: 'There are few pages in classical piano literature that present to the eye so many notes, so many black lines and so many ties.'[ccxviii] In this variation, Beethoven exalts in the entire range of the keyboard available to him, in counterpoint that is expressed in syncopated accents with suggestions of two-voice Bach-style invention.[ccxix]

In his discussion of Beethoven's late manner of exploiting extreme musical registers, Alfred Brendel refers to these as 'a new "geographical" awareness of sound – not spatial depth, as in the *Waldstein* Sonata – but "deep down" and "high above", or, indeed, "subterranean" and "stratospheric".' He considers the fourth variation from Op. 111 provides 'a magical example' of these procedures.[ccxx] Matthews remarks in similar vein: '[This] double variation explores the lower and higher reaches of the keyboard with a magic alternation of darkness and ethereal lightness;'[ccxxi] dark bass colours alternate 'with ethereally light passagework in the treble'.[ccxxii] Cooper describes this variation as having 'a timeless feeling'[ccxxiii] and for Rosen it embodies a sense of 'perpetual motion'.[cxxiv] In his estimation of the mood that prevails, Arrau calls to mind Goethe's *Faust*: 'I think [of this variation] as the breathing of nature ... Then comes this marvellous ascent to mystical ecstasy. There is a phrase in Goethe that describes it — "der Fall nacho ben", "the fall upward".'[cxxv]

We have remarked on the care Beethoven exercised in the working out and writing down his musical notation in the variations, and this aspect of his musicology appears once more in the fourth variation. Repeats are carefully written out, not only making the variation a double one but also permitting further, figural patterns and a new sound atmosphere. In a pianissimo episode the two hands move progressively upwards in the treble range of the keyboard executing delicate demisemiquaver figures over a supporting staccato that recalls the outline of the *Arietta*. Von Bülow described this passage as 'a dance of the sylphs'. Cooper, from whom this quotation is derived, adds: 'If this were in some sense a dance, than it is the morning stars [and] the notes sunbeams'.[cxxvi] It is as if 'Beethoven were loth to leave these ecstatic heights.'[cxxvii] The accented rhythms of variation three are further reshaped and convey 'an even faster yet suspended, inward pulsation'.[cxxviii] Figuration takes on an 'improvisatory nature',[cxxix] the process of foreshortening continues and a sustained trill portends the final variation.

Rumph likens the progress of the motion in the variations section of the *Arietta* to a 'rhythmic quest' that in his words 'reaches consummation in the fifth and final variation'.[cxxx] The original theme is heard taking on 'greater breadth and richness without losing simplicity'[cxxxi] and is expressed in 'simple contours'[cxxxii] with an accompaniment of demisemiquaver figures and triplets — a legacy from the preceding variation. 'Thus, through a rigorous process of rhythmic acceleration and registral expansion, the slow cantabile theme virtually explodes from within, yielding, through a kind of radioactive break-up, a fantastically elaborate texture of shimmering, vibrating sound.'[cxxxiii] High in the uppermost register the music 'interweaves itself becoming ever more ethereal'.[cxxxiv] It finally descends in an extended cadence 'exploring long, wave-like figures in the base to counter the high oscillations of the treble that have occupied the ear for so long'.[cxxxv] A trill of unprecedented proportions heralds the end of the variation.

Stewart Gordon's assessment of Beethoven's achievement in the variations to the *Arietta* movement captures the spirit of the feelings expressed by other commentators: 'A description of what happens in this set of variations does not begin to touch upon the effect the movement can produce, for it has the potential of creating a musical experience that incorporates both profound meditation and exalted revelation. It is not possible to know if Beethoven consciously wrote this movement as a capstone to the body of works for solo piano in sonata form, but it seems almost as if he planned for this movement to be a summation of his spiritual energy and his creative life.'[cxxxvi] Wagner likened the variations to 'innumerable butterflies',[cxxxvii] Rolland to 'waves caressing sands on a beautiful day'[cxxxviii] and Scott to 'a theme of light and peace everlasting'.[cxxxix] Bie likens the variations to spreading themselves out into 'a world-embracing grandeur' possessed of 'wisdom ... deep internal ardour and ethereal brightness'. With his powers of invention, Beethoven's forms have become 'a twilight dream', a realm where 'our soul meets the Master-Soul'.[ccxl] In his more formal commentary, von Elterlein views the variations as resolving into 'a sort of fantasia'. That said, he does not regard them as being mere 'ordinary variations': 'They were not written by Beethoven the musician, but by Beethoven the tone-poet. They are creations such as he alone could produce, such, for example, as he has given us in the Sonata Op. 57 ... [In Op. 111] the formal aspect of the variation retreats, and the free, spontaneous play of imagination creates an ideal dénouement.'[ccxli]

Igor Stravinsky writing about the variations that close the C minor Sonata, remarks on Beethoven's ingenuity in the management of what he calls 'time itself': '[It] seems to me that the listener's subjective reckonings of time-passage, his apprehensions of its pressures, limits, inevitabilities, are more apparent and more urgent factors here than ever before in music.' His enthusiasm in recognition of the composer's genius disposed Stravinsky to quote lines from Shakespeare's *Troilus and Cressida*: 'The Heavens themselves, the Planets, and the Centre/Observe degree, priority and place.' He amplifies his meaning by suggesting Beethoven is manifesting in time 'an evolution from linearism to an ever more versatile relativism'. He considers Beethoven has reached a point 'where powers of tonality (powers of music) are a power of and over time'.[ccxlii]

In the interests of objectivity, it is necessary to interject an opposing point of view alongside the foregoing laudatory remarks. When musicologist Murray Schafer asked Benjamin Britten as to his sympathies towards Beethoven and Brahms, Britten responded: 'I'm not blind to them. Once I adored them. Between the ages of thirteen and fourteen, I knew every note of Beethoven and Brahms. I remember receiving the full score of *Fidelio* for my fourteenth birthday. It was a red letter day.' Of his present-day feelings toward Beethoven, he added: 'I certainly don't dislike all Beethoven but sometimes I feel I have lost the point of what he's up to. I heard recently [1963] the Piano Sonata Op. 111. The sound of the variations was so grotesque I just couldn't see what they were about.'[ccxliii] There is a distant echo in Britten's dismissive comments, from one hundred and fifty years previously, when the reviewer in the *Allgemeine musikalische Zeitung* rejected Beethoven's endeavours as 'a commonplace place set of variations'.[ccxliv]

Beethoven enthusiasts and detractors alike are agreed, however, that the *Arietta* variations present a considerable challenge to the performer. Czerny acknowledged this: 'The variations [to be played] with constantly increasing warmth. The concluding ones are extremely difficult, and require all the player's perseverance in order to master theme.'[ccxlv] When in conversation with the American composer Roger Sessions, fellow American musicologist Andrea Olmstead raised the proposition: 'There are passages in Beethoven which sound awkward, perhaps because they were meant to.' Sessions responded: 'Writing for an instrument doesn't mean that the music is always easy to play, it means that it really makes that instrument sound the way it can sound. Anybody who could make the piano ring out, the way for instance the last movement of Op. 111 does in the variations, wrote pianistically.'[ccxlvi]

The coda that finally draws the sonata to a close emanates from the variations and assumes an identity of its own in which Beethoven makes unprecedented use of the trill. The trill makes a first appearance in the third bar of the first movement, but only as a mere flourish, it subsequently evolves transcendentally at the close of the second. In Rumph's memorable phrase: 'The sonata takes birth from the pulsating womb of the trill, and it returns thence at the end of the *Arietta* ... Paradise lost is regained.'[ccxlvii] To add to the previous imagery we have invoked, '[The] trills of high notes suggest vibrations of light'.[ccxlviii] For Matthews they constitute 'one of the most daringly inspired effects in music' and for Tovey they were nothing less than 'an ecstatic vision'.[ccxlix] In Philip Radcliffe's estimation the trills and shimmering demisemiquavers elevate the music 'to the empyrean' — the highest heaven in ancient cosmologies occupied by the element of fire.[ccl] Beethoven gives us 'ethereal textures that music had never known before' and 'time seems to stand still'.[ccli]

Adorno considers the close of the *Arietta* variations have a force of 'backward-looking' or 'leave-taking', such that what has gone before is 'immeasurably enlarged'. He maintains the music's inherent sense of form 'changes what has preceded' in such a way that 'it takes on a greatness, a presence in the past which, within music, it could never achieve in the present.' Quoting from Stefan George's poem *Haus in Bonn* (Beethoven's birthplace) Adorno admires Beethoven's capacity here to make us 'dream in stars eternal'.[cclii] Fuller-Maitland was disposed to exclaim: 'Words are poor things to describe the ineffable beauty of this ending.'[ccliii] Commentators are alike in describing Beethoven's ending as one of 'calm contentment'[ccliv] that closes his sonatas 'in a heavenly peace'.[cclv] The movement as a whole has been described as 'a miraculous capsulization of Beethoven's musical essence and as such stands as a fitting closing statement to the thirty-two sonatas.'[cclvi] 'The sublimity of the ending is unique in piano literature and it is hard not to sense a valedictory note.'[cclvii]

The last page is written almost entirely *pianissimo* 'with a sonority of diaphanous delicacy and refinement' and ending with Beethoven's sparingly used *pp* — 'very soft'.[cclviii] 'The first strain of the *Arietta* seems to be evaporating gently into space ... and one of the most complex and difficult movements in the whole range of piano music has ended in simplicity — the simplicity which only a child or a master-mind dare express with the perfect assurance of being understood.'[cclix]

As Kinderman observes, various commentators have perceived 'a philosophical and even religious dimension in this great work'. He cites Maynard Solomon who has argued that 'masterpieces of art are instilled with a surplus of energy — an energy that provides a motive force for changes in the relations between human beings — because they contain projections of human desires and goals which have not yet been achieved (which indeed may be unrealisable)'. Kinderman's own view has no less resonance: 'Among Beethoven's instrumental works Op. 111 assumes a special position as an "effigy of the ideal" in Schiller's formulation; and every adequate performance must re-enact something of this process, reaching as it does beyond merely the aesthetic dimension to touch the domain of the moral and ethical.'[cclx] In his commentary to the C minor Piano Sonata Op. 111, Gordon similarly identifies Beethoven's achievement as aspiring to the highest attainable: 'The perception of this development in the composer's style has built a firm, well-founded belief among musicians and listeners that "late Beethoven" is music of great depth and spirituality, representing in music the eternal enigmas of life itself.'[cclxi] Edwin Fischer considered in his final years Beethoven possessed within himself 'the creative power of nature herself' and that 'he raised the personal to the level of the typical and the universal and gave us an example of how it is possible, in spite of material and human limitations, to reveal the eternal and temporal'.[cclxii]

In his novel *Doktor Faustus*, Thomas Mann has the fictional character Wendell Kretzschmar describe the end of the *Arietta* movement as 'an end without any return' comprising nothing less than a farewell to the art of the sonata in general.[cclxiii] Ernst von Elterlein identifies Beethoven's 'leave taking' with the words Shakespeare gives to Prospero in his soliloquy in the final pages of *The Tempest*: '[Beethoven] finished his course as a sonata-maker, and like Prospero, broke and buried fathoms deep the magic wand of his tone-poetry'.[cclxiv] The reader will recall, Prospero's lines in question are: 'Some heavenly music, which even now I do/To work mine end upon their senses that/This airy charm is for, I'll break my staff/Bury it fathoms in the earth/ And deeper than plummet sound/I'll drown my book.'

As we finally take leave of the C minor Piano Sonata, Op. 111 we can do no better than recall further words written in the composer's honour on 24 February 1824 by 28 distinguished signatories:

> 'Beethoven's name and his creations belong to all contemporaneous humanity and every country that opens a sensitive heart to art.'[cclxv]

---

[i] Maynard Solomon, 1977, p. 299.

[ii] Barry Cooper, for example, argues: 'The three sonatas Opp. 109, 110 and 111 form a set as coherent as any of his previous groups of three works, and they contain many subtle links: for example, just as Op. 110 moves to E major (the key of Op. 109) during the first movement, Op. 111 includes a second subject in A flat (the key of Op. 110).' Barry Cooper, 2000, pp. 288–9.

[iii] Emily Anderson, 1961, Vol. 2, Letter No. 1083, pp. 952–3.

[iv] See: Charles Rosen, 'The last piano sonatas', in *Beethoven's piano sonatas: a short companion*, 2002.

[v] These circumstances are discussed in Beethoven House, Digital Archives, Library Documents BH 24 and the composer's letter to Franz Brentano in: Emily Anderson, 1961, Vol. 2, Letter No. 1059, p. 926.

[vi] Barry Cooper, 2000, p. 296.

[vii] Conrad Wilson, 2003, pp. 100–1

[viii] Denis Matthews, 1985, p. 99.

[ix] Barry Cooper, 2000, pp. 288–9.

[x] William Kinderman, Liner Notes to *Beethoven: The Complete Sonatas*, 1996, Philips 446 909-2, p. 54.

[xi] Barry Cooper, 1990, p. 21.

[xii] Henry Edward Krehbiel, 1971, p. 158.

[xiii] Walter Aaron Clark, *Enrique Granados: poet of the piano*, 2006, pp. 69–71.

[xiv] Igor Stravinsky, 1972, pp. 274–5.

[xv] Paul Horgan, *Encounters with Stravinsky: a personal record*, 1972, pp. 194–5.

[xvi] Conrad Wilson, 2003, p. 101. The remarks quoted in the main text are in marked contrast to what is frequently said of the Piano Sonata Op. 106 – *The Hammerklavier* – a creation more suited, in the estimation of some, to being interpreted by the full orchestra. Consider, for example, the remarks

of this kind expressed by Richard Wagner (see Piano Sonata Op. 106).

[xvii] Matthew Rye, *Notes to the BBC Radio Three Beethoven Experience*, Friday 10 June 2005, www.bbc.co.uk/radio3/Beethoven

[xviii] Jane Coup, website text: *Ludwig van Beethoven, Sonatas No. 30 and No. 32.*

[xix] Matthew Rye, *Notes to the BBC Radio Three Beethoven Experience*, Friday 10 June 2005, www.bbc.co.uk/radio3/Beethoven

[xx] Stewart Gordon, 1996, p. 193.

[xxi] Harlow Robinson, editor and translator: *Selected letters of Sergei Prokofiev*, 1998, pp. 98–9.

[xxii] Emily Anderson, 1961, Vol. 2, Letter No. 1021, pp. 891–3. In his response to Schlesinger, Beethoven agreed to accept the lower fee of 30 ducats but added the stipulation: 'However, only to do business with you [this way] once, since I would have to stipulate higher prices in future dealings.' For the exchange of letters between Beethoven and his publisher, see also: Theodore Albrecht, translator and editor, 1996, Vol. 2, Letter No. 274, pp. 188–90.

[xxiii] Emily Anderson, 1961, Vol. 2, Letter No. 1033, p. 902.

[xxiv] Beethoven's letter of 20 September 1820 is available in the form of an audio letter with supporting text on the Beethoven House, Digital Archives, Library Document, Sammlung H.C. Bodmer, HCB Br 210.

[xxv] Emily Anderson, 1961, Vol. 2, Letter No. 1050, pp. 915–6.

[xxvi] See: Beethoven House, Digital Archives, Library Documents NE 88 and Emily Anderson, 1961, Vol. 2, Letter No. 1052, pp. 918–9.

[xxvii] Emily Anderson, 1961, Vol. 2, Letter No. 1060, pp. 927– 8.

[xxviii] See: Beethoven House, Digital Archives, Library Documents Sammlung H.C. Bodmer, HCB BBr 50 and Emily Anderson, 1961, Vol. 2, Letter No. 1063, pp. 932–3.

[xxix] Barry Cooper, 1991, p. 186. Artaria 201 may have in fact have been in use beyond October 1822 extending possibly into 1823.

[xxx] Douglas Porter Johnson, editor, 1985, pp. 265–72.

[xxxi] *Ibid.* See also: Martin Cooper, 1970, p. 187 and p. 196.

[xxxii] Douglas Porter Johnson, editor, 1985, pp. 384–90.

[xxxiii] A fair copy of the Autograph of Piano Sonata Op. 111 is reproduced on the Beethoven House, Digital Archives, Document, H.C. Bodmer, Mh 54. See also: Elliot Forbes, editor, *Thayer's life of Beethoven*, 1967, p. 781.

[xxxiv] For this aspect of the composition history of the Piano Sonata Op. 111, see: Beethoven House, Digital Archives, Library Documents BH 71 and the text to H. C. Bodmer, HCB Mh 54.

[xxxv] Wenzel Rampl was Beethoven's most faithful copyist after the similarly named Wenzel Schlemmer – Beethoven's most reliable copyist. Rampl is known to have undertaken work for Schlemmer in 1822 when Beethoven was at work on the Op. 111. See: Peter Clive, 2001, pp. 276–7.

[xxxvi] Douglas Porter Johnson, editor, 1985, p. 389.

[xxxvii] Emily Anderson, 1961, Vol. 2, Letter No. 1074, pp. 942–3. See also: Beethoven House, Digital Archives, Library Documents NE 213.

[xxxviii] Emily Anderson, 1961, Vol. 2, Letter No. 1075, pp. 943–4.

[xxxix] Beethoven's doctor at this period was probably the distinguished Viennese physician Jacob Staudentheim. See: Peter Clive, 2001, pp. 349–50.

[xl] Emily Anderson, 1961, Letter No. 1086, pp. 956–7.

[xli] *Ibid*, Letter No. 1101, pp. 971–2.

xlii Adolph Schlesinger reassured Beethoven the Piano Sonatas Opp. 110 and 111 would be engraved in Paris and would be 'truly superlative' when they appeared. See: Theodore Albrecht, translator and editor, 1996, Vol. 2, Letter No. 292, pp. 216–8.

xliii *Ibid*, Vol. 2, Letter No. 293, pp. 218–9.

xliv *Ibid*, Vol. 2, Letter No. 296, pp. 225–6. See also: Beethoven House, Digital Archives, Library Documents BH 218.

xlv Elliot Forbes, editor, *Thayer's life of Beethoven*, 1967, p. 786.

xlvi Derived from Wayne M. Senner, Robin Wallace and William Meredith, editors, 1999, Vol. 1, pp. 61–2.

xlvii Anton Felix Schindler, *Beethoven as I knew him*, edited by Donald W. MacArdle and translated by Constance S. Jolly from the German edition of 1860, 1966, p. 232.

xlviii Newman makes the additional observations: 'That idea [the thematic motif mentioned in the main text] is another of the recurring motives in Beethoven's music. It originally appeared in his sketches some twenty years earlier and variants can still be found as late as the String Quartets Opp. 131/ii/1–4 and 135/iv/15–18 (the "Es muss sein!" motive).' William S. Newman, 1963, p. 536.

xlix Paul Bekker, 1925, p. 140.

l Martin Cooper, 1970, p. 196.

li Barry Cooper, 1991, p. 242.

lii Conrad Wilson, 2003, p. 102.

liii Emily Anderson, 1961, Vol. 2, Letter No. 1095, pp. 965–6. See also: Beethoven House, Digital Archives, Library Documents H. C. Bodmer HCB BBr 141.

liv Emily Anderson, 1961, Vol. 2, Letter No. 1118, p. 983.

lv *Ibid*, Letter No. 1140, p. 1003.

lvi Commenting on Beethoven's intended (altruistic) dedication to Antonie, Maynard Solomon remarks: 'Beethoven no longer indulged in his love pretences ... and in relation to making dedications to young women for whom he felt some deep attachment.' Maynard Solomon, 1977, p. 262.

lvii Emily Anderson, 1961, Vol. 3, Letter No. 1203, pp. 1054–6.

lviii Anton Felix Schindler, *Beethoven as I knew him*, edited by Donald W. MacArdle and translated by Constance S. Jolly from the German edition of 1860, 1966, p. 270.

lix *Ibid*, pp. 231–2.

lx Emily Anderson, 1961, Vol. 3, Letter No. 1190, pp. 1045–7 and Beethoven House, Digital Archives, Library Documents H. C. Bodmer HCB Br 212.

lxi Peter Clive, 2001, pp. 304–5.

lxii As discussed by Martin Cooper, 1970, p. 196.

lxiii Elliot Forbes, editor, *Thayer's life of Beethoven*, 1967, p. 861.

lxiv Anton Felix Schindler, *Beethoven as I knew him*, edited by Donald W. MacArdle and translated by Constance S. Jolly from the German edition of 1860, 1966, p. 69 and editor's note 43 at p. 85.

lxv Emily Anderson, 1961, Vol. 3, Letter No. 1182, pp. 1039–40. See also: Beethoven House, Digital Archives, Library Documents H. C. Bodmer HCB Br 115 for the text and an audio recording of this letter.

lxvi Elliot Forbes, editor, *Thayer's life of Beethoven*, 1967, p. 859.

lxvii Emily Anderson, 1961, Vol. 3, Letter No. 1187, pp. 1042–3.

lxviii *Ibid*, Letter No. 1190a, pp. 1047–9. Martin Cooper attempts to exonerate Beethoven of his indiscretion saying: 'In this matter he was very much a man of his age and the place where he lived.' Martin Cooper, 1970, p. 196.

lxix Emily Anderson, 1961, Vol. 3, Letter No. 1197, p. 1051.

lxx *Ibid*, Letter No. 1201, p. 1053.

lxxi Elliot Forbes, editor, *Thayer's life of Beethoven*, 1967, p. 859.

lxxii Alan Tyson suggests a publication date for the Op. 111 as 'early summer of 1823' (Alan Tyson, 1963, p. 110). This is consistent with that given in: Beethoven House, Digital Archives, Library Documents BH 71.

lxxiii See: Beethoven House, Digital Archives, Library Documents: C 111/3 (Paris, Berlin, Vienna and London), C 111/19 (Paris, Berlin, Vienna and Lyon); and J. van der Spek C Op. 111 (Paris, Berlin, Vienna and London). An edition by Cappi and Diabelli is reproduced at the Beethoven House Digital Archives, Library Document C 111/1.

lxxiv Emily Anderson, 1961, Vol. 2, Letter No. 1084, pp. 953–4.

lxxv *Ibid*, Letter No. 1143, pp. 1006–7. See also: Beethoven House, Digital Archives, Sammlung H. C. Bodmer, HCB Br 200.

lxxvi *Ibid*, Letter No. 1159, p. 1012.

lxxvii *Ibid*, Letter No. 1167, pp. 1026–7.

lxxviii Elliot Forbes, editor, *Thayer's life of Beethoven*, 1967, p. 861. Ries was also responsible for negotiating the fee Beethoven was to receive in England for the C minor Sonata.

lxxix Alan Tyson, 1963, pp. 110–13. A facsimile reproduction of the Title Page to Clementi's edition appears facing p. 112.

lxxx Whilst the evidence suggests Clementi's edition of the C minor Sonata was indeed the first to be published in England, Tyson also points out that in the May 1823 issue of *The Harmonicon*, the publishing house of Boosey & Co. also listed the Piano Sonata Op. 111 as being 'among their recent importations'. Alan Tyson, 1963, p. 26.

lxxxi Alan Tyson, 1963, p. 110.

lxxxii Theodore Albrecht, translator and editor, 1996, Vol. 2, Letter No. 286, pp. 204–6.

lxxxiii Emily Anderson, 1961, Vol. 2, Letter No. 1079, pp. 947–50. In this long letter, Beethoven lists several types of composition he could offer Peters and the prices he wanted for them.

lxxxiv Theodore Albrecht, translator and editor, 1996, Vol. 2, Letter No. 290, pp. 211–14. This letter is dated 15 June 1822.

lxxxv *Ibid*, Letter No. 295, pp. 222–5.

lxxxvi *Ibid*, Letter No. 299, pp. 288–9.

lxxxvii Emily Anderson, 1961, Vol. 2, Letter No. 1123, pp. 988–9.

lxxxviii Theodore Albrecht, translator and editor, 1996, Vol. 2, Letter No. 310, pp. 244–5.

lxxxix *Ibid*, Letter No. 333, pp. 277–8.

xc *Ibid*, Letter No. 340, pp. 288–90.

xci Peter Clive, 2001, p. 318.

xcii Derived from: Oscar George Theodore Sonneck, *Beethoven: impressions of contemporaries*, 1927, pp. 132–48.

xciii Emily Anderson, 1961, Vol. 3, Letter No. 1154, pp. 1016–17.

xciv Beethoven House, Digital Archives, Library Documents H. C. Bodmer HCB BBr 51

[xv] Emily Anderson, 1961, Vol. 3, Letter No. 1121, p. 987.
[xvi] Theodore Albrecht, translator and editor, 1996, Vol. 2, Letter No. 311, pp. 245–7.
[xvii] *Ibid*, Letter No. 305, pp. 238–9.
[xviii] *Ibid*, Letter No. 325, pp. 265–6.
[xix] Derived from, Oscar George Theodore Sonneck, *Beethoven: impressions of contemporaries*, 1927, pp. 159– 61.
[l] Theodore Albrecht, translator and editor, 1996, Vol. 2, Letter No. 315, pp. 255–6.
[li] The Härtel portrait was destroyed during World War II and is now known only from reproductions. See, for example, the frontispiece to Emily Anderson's *The Letters of Beethoven* Vol. 3 and Beethoven House, Digital Archives Library Document B. 362.
[lii] Derived from: Ludwig Nohl, *Beethoven depicted by his contemporaries*, 1880, p. 239.
[liii] Elliot Forbes, editor, *Thayer's life of Beethoven*, 1967, p. 589.
[liv] Ludwig Nohl, *Beethoven depicted by his contemporaries*, 1880, pp. 240–4.
[lv] Theodore Albrecht, translator and editor, 1996, Vol. 2, Letter No. 301, pp. 232–4.
[lvi] Emily Anderson, 1961, Vol. 3, Letter No. 1149, p. 1011.
[lvii] Theodore Albrecht, translator and editor, 1996, Vol. 3, Letter No. 344, pp. 4–11.
[lviii] Harold Craxton and Donald Francis Tovey, *Beethoven: Sonatas for Pianoforte* [1931], p. 237.
[lix] Knud Martner, editor, *Selected letters of Gustav Mahler*, 1979, p. 392.
[cx] Virgil Thomson, 1968, pp. 192–3.
[cxi] Neville Cardus, 1957, p. 323. See also: Robin Daniels, *Conversations with Cardus*, 1976, p. 140.
[cxii] Martin Cooper, 1970, p. 197.
[cxiii] Ernst von Elterlein, 1898, p. 119.
[cxiv] Anonymous, website text: *Ludwig van Beethoven, Sonatas 30 and 32*.
[cxv] Philip Radcliffe, *Piano Music* in: *The age of Beethoven, The new Oxford history of music*, Vol. VIII, Gerald Abraham, editor, 1988, p. 150.
[cxvi] Conrad Wilson, 2003, p. 99.
[cxvii] See: Denis Matthews, 1967, p. 55
[cxviii] Eric Blom, 1938, p. 236.
[cxix] Matthew Rye, *Notes to the BBC Radio Three Beethoven experience*, Friday 10 June 2005, www.bbc.co.uk/radio3/Beethoven
[cxx] As cited and discussed by William S. Newman, 1963, p. 537.
[cxxi] John Fuller-Maitland, *Special Issue* [Death Centenary], *The Musical Times*, London, Vol. VIII, No. 2, 1927, p. 223.
[cxxii] Romain Rolland, 1917, p. 165.
[cxxiii] Alfred Brendel, 2001, p. 88.
[cxxiv] Neville Cardus, 1957, p. 292.
[cxxv] Ernst von Elterlein, 1898, p. 119.
[cxxvi] Oskar Bie, 1966, p. 181.
[cxxvii] Martin Cooper, 1970, p. 197.
[cxxviii] Barry Cooper, 1991, p. 242.
[cxxix] Harold Craxton and Donald Francis Tovey, [1931], *Piano Sonata in C minor,*

Op. 111, p. 237. Tovey commends a metronome reading of crochet = 54 for the *Maestoso* and minim = 63 for the *Allegro*.
[cxxx] Alfred Brendel, 2001, p. 89.
[cxxxi] The expression 'grim pathos' is used by William Kinderman, see: Liner Notes to *Beethoven: The Complete Sonatas*, 1996, Philips 446 909-2, p. 54.
[cxxxii] Charles Rosen, 2002, p. 246.
[cxxxiii] Neville Cardus, 1957, p. 291.
[cxxxiv] Ernst von Elterlein, 1898, p. 120.
[cxxxv] Martin Cooper, 1970, p. 198.
[cxxxvi] Eric Blom, Notes to: *The Beethoven Society, Volume 1*, The Gramophone Company, Ltd., London (c. 1935). See also: Eric Blom, 1938, p. 236.
[cxxxvii] Derived from: Oscar George *Theodore Sonneck, Beethoven: impressions of contemporaries*, 1927, pp. 132–48.
[cxxxviii] Elliot Forbes, editor, *Thayer's life of Beethoven*, 1967, p. 781, Denis Matthews, 1967, p. 39 and Barry Cooper, 1990, p. 67.
[cxxxix] John South Shedlock, 1918, p. 41.
[cxl] Charles Rosen, 2002, p. 246.
[cxli] Stephen C. Rumph, 2004, p. 125.
[cxlii] Gordon Stewart, 1996, p. 193.
[cxliii] Romain Rolland, 1917, p. 165.
[cxliv] Harold Craxton and Donald Francis Tovey, *Beethoven: Sonatas for Pianoforte* [1931], p. 237.
[cxlv] Carl Czerny in: Paul Badura-Skoda, *On the proper performance of all Beethoven's works for the piano*, 1970, p. 57.
[cxlvi] Edwin Fischer, 1959, p. 116.
[cxlvii] Charles Rosen, 2002, p. 243 and p. 246.
[cxlviii] As quoted in: William Ashton Ellis, *Richard Wagner's prose works*: Vol. 3, 1907, p. 240.
[cxlix] Joseph Horowitz, 1982, p. 21 and pp. 214–15.
[cl] Cited in: Robin Wallace, 1986, pp. 39–40.
[cli] Henry Edward Krehbiel, 1971, p. 159.
[clii] Paul Bekker, 1925, pp. 139–40.
[cliii] Conrad Wilson, 2003, p. 102. Compare for example, the opening bars of the two sonatas and bars 77–81 of Chopin's Etude with bars 150–2 in the first movement of Beethoven's sonata. As remarked by Wayne C. Petty, *Chopin and the ghost of Beethoven*, in: Beethoven, *19–Century Music*, XXII/3, pp. 281–99.
[cliv] Arnold Whittall, 1977, p. 79.
[clv] Barry Cooper, 1991, p. 142. The second quotation is derived from Jane Coup, website text: *Ludwig van Beethoven, Sonatas 30 and 32*.
[clvi] Eric Blom, Notes to: *The Beethoven Society, Volume 1*, The Gramophone Company, Ltd., London (c. 1935). See also: Eric Blom, *Beethoven's Pianoforte Sonatas Discussed*, 1938.
[clvii] Matthew Rye, *Notes to the BBC Radio Three Beethoven Experience*, Friday 10 June 2005, www.bbc.co.uk/radio3/Beethoven
[clviii] Conrad Wilson, 2003, p. 102.
[clix] Martin Cooper, 1970, p. 200.
[clx] Charles Rosen, 1976, as quoted by Conrad Wilson, 2003, p. 101.
[clxi] As quoted in Anton Felix Schindler, *Beethoven as I knew him*, edited by

dxii Donald W. MacArdle and translated by Constance S. Jolly from the German edition of 1860, (1966), footnote to p. 232. Schindler himself was dismissive of overly fanciful descriptions of Beethoven's music.
dxiii *Ibid*, p. 232.
dxiiii Derived from, Ernst von Elterlein, 1898, pp. 120–2.
dxiv *Ibid*.
dxv Romain Rolland, 1917, p. 165.
dxvi Derived from: Charles L. Graves, *The life & letters of Sir George Grove*, 1903, p. 93.
dxvii Gregor-Dellin and Dietrich Mack, editors, *Cosima Wagner's diaries*, Vol. 1, 1869 - 1877, 1978–1980, pp. 983–4.
dxviii Marion Scott, 1940, p. 146.
dxix Eric Blom, Notes to: *The Beethoven Society, Volume 1*, The Gramophone Company, Ltd., London (c. 1935). See also: Eric Blom, *Beethoven's Pianoforte Sonatas Discussed*, 1938.
dxx Wilfrid Howard Mellers, 1967, p. 38.
dxxi Alec Robertson, 1961, p. 229.
dxxii Solomon Volkov, editor, *Testimony: the memoirs of Dmitri Shostakovich*, 1981, p. 52.
dxxiii Dennis Matthews, 1968. Matthews considered Beethoven approached the sublimity expressed in the Op. 111 Piano Sonata once more in his piano music in the *Diabelli* Variations.
dxxiv Alan Dudley Bush, 1980, pp. 57–61.
dxxv Maynard Solomon, 1977, p. 294.
dxxvi Barry Cooper, 2000, p. 290.
dxxvii As quoted by Ernst von Elterlein, 1898, p. 120.
dxxviii Theodor W. Adorno, 1998, p. 128 and p. 171.
dxxix Denis Matthews, 1967, p. 56.
dxxx Barry Cooper, 2000, p. 290.
dxxxi As discussed by Martin Cooper, 1970, p. 202.
dxxxii Charles Rosen, 2002, p. 247.
dxxxiii Denis Matthews, 1985, p. 99.
dxxxiv Alfred Brendel, 2001, p. 89.
dxxxv Carl Czerny in: Paul Badura-Skoda, *On the proper performance of all Beethoven's works for the piano*, 1970, p. 57.
dxxxvi Harold Craxton and Donald Francis Tovey, *Beethoven: Sonatas for Pianoforte* [1931], p. 238. Denis Matthews is in agreement with Tovey, stating: 'Beethoven asks for *semplice e cantabile* and few have approached Schnabel here'.
dxxxvii Virgil Thomson, 1968, pp. 184–5.
dxxxviii Edwin Fischer, 1959, p. 116.
dxxxix Neville Cardus, 1957, p. 293.
cxc Beethoven's youthful experiments with the piano-variation form are outlined in Elliot Forbes, editor, *Thayer's life of Beethoven*, 1967, pp. 66, 72 and 133.
cxci Donald Jay Grout, and Claude V. Palisca, editors, *A history of Western music*, 1988, p. 646.
cxcii Maynard Solomon, 1977, p. 302.
cxciii Henry Edward Krehbiel, 1971, p. 159.

- ccxiv Oskar Bie, 1966, p. 173.
- ccxv William Kinderman, 1997, p. 122.
- ccxvi As quoted in, Neville Cardus, 1957, p. 293.
- ccxvii Henry Edward Krehbiel, 1971, p. 159.
- ccxviii William S. Newman, 1963, p. 537.
- ccxix Paul Bekker, 1925, p. 140.
- cc As remarked, for example, by William Kinderman, 1997, p. 223.
- cci Jane Coup, website text: *Ludwig van Beethoven, Sonatas No. 30 and No. 32.*
- ccii Denis Matthews, 1967, p. 56.
- cciii For commentary on this aspect of the variations to the C minor Piano Sonata, see: Barry Cooper, 1990, p. 290 and William Kinderman, 1997, p. 223.
- cciv As remarked in Alan Tyson, 1963, note 2 at p. 30.
- ccv Alfred Brendel, 2001, p. 88.
- ccvi Joseph. Horowitz, *Conversations with Arrau*, 1982, p. 164.
- ccvii Theodor W. Adorno, 1998, p. 70.
- ccviii Romain Rolland, 1917, p. 166.
- ccix William Kinderman, 1997, p. 223.
- ccx Romain Rolland, 1917, p. 166. The words in quotation marks have been slightly adapted from the original.
- ccxi William Kinderman, 1997, p. 223.
- ccxii Denis Matthews, 1985, p. 99.
- ccxiii Matthew Rye, *Notes to the BBC Radio Three Beethoven Experience*, Friday 10 June 2005, www.bbc.co.uk/radio3/Beethoven
- ccxiv Robert Cummings, website text, *Piano Sonata, No. 32 in C minor, Op. 111.*
- ccxv Joseph. Horowitz, *Conversations with Arrau*, 1982, p. 164.
- ccxvi William Kinderman, 1996, Liner Notes to *Beethoven: The complete sonatas,* Philips 446 909 2, p. 54 and Wikipedia article (anonymous*), Beethoven, Piano Sonata in C minor, Op. 111.*
- ccxvii Martin Cooper, 1970, p. 202.
- ccxviii *Ibid.*
- ccxix In the context of Beethoven's adoption of contrapuntal procedures, see: Barry Cooper, 1991, p. 242, and William Kinderman, 1997, p. 223.
- ccxx Alfred Brendel, 2000, p. 81.
- ccxxi Denis Matthews, 1985, p. 99.
- ccxxii Denis Matthews, 1967, p. 56.
- ccxxiii Barry Cooper, 1991, p. 242.
- ccxxiv Charles Rosen, 2002, p. 248.
- ccxxv Joseph. Horowitz, *Conversations with Arrau*, 1982, p. 164.
- ccxxvi Martin Cooper, 1970, p. 202.
- ccxxvii Barry Cooper, 1991, p. 242.
- ccxxviii William Kinderman, 1996, Liner Notes to *Beethoven: The complete sonatas,* Philips 446 909 2, p. 54.
- ccxxix Stewart Gordon, 1996, p. 195.
- ccxxx Stephen C. Rumph, 2004, p. 130.
- ccxxxi Barry Cooper, 1991, p. 243.
- ccxxxii Martin Cooper, 1970, p. 204.
- ccxxxiii William Kinderman, 1996, Liner Notes to *Beethoven: The complete sonatas,* Philips 446 909 2, p. 54. In Kinderman's somewhat enigmatic expression:

'Being and Becoming are merged here into a unified structure.'

[cxxxiv] Matthew Rye, *Notes to the BBC Radio Three Beethoven Experience*, Friday 10 June 2005, www.bbc.co.uk/radio3/Beethoven

[cxxxv] Martin Cooper, 1970, p. 203.

[cxxxvi] Stewart Gordon, 1996, p. 195.

[cxxxvii] Gregor-Dellin and Dietrich Mack, editors, *Cosima Wagner's diaries*, Vol. 1, 1869 - 1877, 1978–1980, p. 527.

[cxxxviii] Romain Rolland, 1917, pp. 165–6.

[cxxxix] Marion Scott, 1940, p. 146.

[cxl] Oskar Bie, 1966, p. 181.

[cxli] Ernst von Elterlein, 1898, pp. 123–4.

[cxlii] Igor Stravinsky, 1972, pp. 274–5.

[cxliii] The original source for the quotation is: Murray Schafer, *British composer's interview*, 1963, pp. 113–24. See also: Paul Kildea, editor, *Britten on music*, 2003, p. 228.

[cxliv] As quoted in: Robin Wallace, 1986, pp. 39–40.

[cxlv] Carl Czerny in: Paul Badura-Skoda, *On the proper performance of all Beethoven's works for the piano*, 1970, p. 57.

[cxlvi] Andrea Olmstead, *Conversations with Roger Sessions*, 1987, pp. 99–100.

[cxlvii] Stephan Rumph, 2004, p. 130.

[cxlviii] Neville Cardus, 1957, p. 293.

[cxlix] Denis Matthews, 1967, p. 56. The words attributed to Donald Tovey also come from this source.

[cl] Philip Radcliffe, *Piano Music* in: *The age of Beethoven, The new Oxford history of music*, Vol. VIII, Gerald Abraham, editor, 1988, p. 150.

[cli] William Kinderman, 1997, p. 122.

[clii] Theodor W. Adorno, 1998, pp. 175–6.

[cliii] John Fuller-Maitland, *Special Issue* [Death Centenary], *The Musical Times*, London, Vol. VIII, No. 2, 1927, p. 223.

[cliv] Romain Rolland, 1917, p. 166.

[clv] Matthew Rye, *Notes to the BBC Radio Three Beethoven Experience*, Friday 10 June 2005, www.bbc.co.uk/radio3/Beethoven

[clvi] Stewart Gordon, 1996, p. 195.

[clvii] Denis Matthews, 1985, p. 99.

[clviii] Charles Rosen, 2002, p. 249.

[clix] Eric Blom, Notes to: *The Beethoven Society, Volume 1*, The Gramophone Company, Ltd., London (c. 1935). See also: Eric Blom, *Beethoven's Pianoforte Sonatas Discussed*, 1938.

[clx] William Kinderman, Liner Notes to *Beethoven: The Complete Sonatas*, 1996, Philips 446 909-2, p. 55.

[clxi] Stewart Gordon, 1996, p. 180.

[clxii] Edwin Fischer, 1959, p. 118.

[clxiii] Adapted from: William Kinderman, Liner Notes to *Beethoven: The Complete Sonatas*, 1996, Philips 446 909-2, p. 53.

[clxiv] Ernst von Elterlein, 1898, p. 124.

[clxv] Theodore Albrecht, translator and editor, 1996, Vol. 3, Letter No. 344, pp. 4–11. A performance of the C minor Piano Sonata, Op. 111 was recorded by Elley Ney on Beethoven's Conrad Graf piano of 1825. See: Harmonia Mundi 1C 047 1936. Source: Ann P. Basart, The sound of the fortepiano:

BIBLIOGRAPHY

The author has individually consulted all the publications listed in this bibliography and can confirm that each makes reference, in some way or other, to Beethoven and his works. It will be evident from their titles which of these are publications devoted exclusively to the composer. Others that make only passing reference to Beethoven and his compositions, nevertheless unfailingly bear testimony to his genius and humanity. The diversity of the titles listed also testifies to the centrality of Beethoven to western culture and, indeed, beyond; the mere survey of these should be of itself a rewarding experience for the typical lover of so-called classical music. The entries are confined to book publications only, reflecting the scope of the author's researches. The cut-off date for this was 2007; consequently no works after this date are listed, notwithstanding the author is mindful that Beethoven musicology, and related publication, continue to be a major field of endeavour.

Abraham, Gerald. *Beethoven's second-period quartets*. London: Oxford University Press: Humphrey Milford, 1944.

Abraham, Gerald. *Essays on Russian and East European music*. Oxford: Clarendon Press: New York: Oxford University Press, 1985.

Abraham, Gerald, Editor. *The age of Beethoven, 1790-1830*. London: Oxford University Press, 1982.

Abraham, Gerald. *The tradition of Western music*. London: Oxford University Press, 1974.

Abse, Dannie and Joan. *The Music lover's literary companion*. London: Robson Books, 1988.

Adorno, Theodor W., Translator. *Alban Berg: master of the smallest link*. Cambridge: Cambridge University Press, 1991.

Adorno, Theodor W. *Beethoven: the philosophy of music; fragments and texts*. Cambridge: Polity Press, 1998.

Albrecht, Daniel, Editor. *Modernism and music: an anthology of sources*. Chicago; London: University of Chicago Press, 2004.

Albrecht, Theodore, Translator and Editor. *Letters to Beethoven and other correspondence*. Lincoln, New England: University of Nebraska Press, 3 vols., 1996.

Allsobrook, David Ian. *Liszt: my travelling circus life*. London: Macmillan, 1991.

Anderson, Christopher, Editor and Translator. *Selected writings of Max Reger*. New York; London: Routledge, 2006.

Anderson, Emily, Editor and Translator. *The letters of Beethoven*. London: Macmillan, 3 vols., 1961.

Anderson, Martin, Editor. *Klemperer on music: shavings from a musician's workbench*. London: Toccata Press, 1986.

Antheil, George. *Bad boy of music*. London; New York: Hurst & Blackett Ltd., 1945.

Appleby, David P. *Heitor Villa-Lobos: a bio-bibliography*. New York: Greenwood Press, 1988.

Aprahamian, Felix, Editor. *Essays on music: an anthology from The Listener*. London, Cassell, 1967.

Armero, Gonzalo and Jorge de Persia. *Manuel de Falla : his life & works*. London: Omnibus Press, 1999.

Arnold, Ben, Editor. *The Liszt companion*. Westport, Connecticut; London: Greenwood Press, 2002.

Arnold, Denis and Nigel Fortune, Editors. *The Beethoven companion*. London: Faber and Faber, 1973.

Ashbrook, William. *Donizetti*. London: Cassell, 1965.

Auner, Joseph Henry. *A Schoenberg reader: documents of a life*. New Haven Connecticut; London: Yale University Press, 2003.

Avins, Styra, Editor. *Johannes Brahms: life and letters*. Oxford: Oxford University Press, 1997.

Azoury, Pierre H. *Chopin through his contemporaries: friends, lovers, and rivals*. Westport, Connecticut: Greenwood Press, 1999.

Badura-Skoda, Paul. *Carl Czerny: On the Proper Performance of all Beethoven's Works for the Piano*. Universal Edition: A. G. Wien, 1970.

Bailey, Cyril. *Hugh Percy Allen*. London: Oxford University Press, 1948.

Bailey, Kathryn. *The life of Webern*. Cambridge: Cambridge University Press, 1998.

Barenboim, Daniel. *A life in music*. London: Weidenfeld & Nicolson, 1991.

Barlow, Michael. *Whom the gods love: the life and music of George Butterworth*. London: Toccata Press, 1997.

Barrett-Ayres, Reginald. *Joseph Haydn and the string quartet*. New York: Schirmer Books, 1974.

Bartos, Frantisek. *Bedrich Smetana: Letters and reminiscences*. Prague: Artia, 1953.

Barzun, Jacques. *Pleasures of music: an anthology of writing about music and musicians.* London: Cassell, 1977.

Bauer-Lechner, Natalie. *Recollections of Gustav Mahler.* London: Faber Music, 1980.

Bazhanov, N. Nikolai. *Rakhmaninov.* Moscow: Raduga, 1983.

Beaumont, Antony, Editor. *Ferruccio Busoni: Selected letters.* London: Faber and Faber, 1987.

Beaumont, Antony, Editor. *Gustav Mahler, letters to his wife.* London: Faber and Faber, 2004.

Beecham, Thomas. *A mingled chime: an autobiography.* New York: Da Capo Press, 1976.

Bekker, Paul. *Beethoven.* London: J. M. Dent & Sons, 1925.

Bellasis, Edward. *Cherubini: memorials illustrative of his life.* London: Burns and Oates, 1874.

Bennett, James R. Sterndale. *The life of William Sterndale Bennett.* Cambridge: University Press, 1907.

Benser, Caroline Cepin. *Egon Wellesz (1885–1974): chronicle of twentieth-century musician.* New York: P. Lang, 1985.

Berlioz, Hector. *Evenings in the orchestra.* Harmondsworth: Penguin Books, 1963.

Berlioz, Hector. *The musical madhouse (Les grotesques de la musique).* Rochester, New York: University of Rochester Press, 2003.

Bernard, Jonathan W., Editor. *Elliott Carter: collected essays and lectures, 1937-1995.* Rochester, New York; Woodbridge: University of Rochester Press, 1998.

Bernstein, Leonard. *The joy of music.* New York: Simon and Schuster, 1959.

Bertensson, Sergei. *Sergei Rachmaninoff: a lifetime in music.* London: G. Allen & Unwin, 1965.

Biancolli, Louis. *The Flagstad manuscript.* New York: Putnam, 1952.

Bickley, Nora, Editor. *Letters from and to Joseph Joachim.* London: Macmillan, 1914.

Bie, Oskar. *A history of the pianoforte and pianoforte players.* New York: Da Capo Press, 1966.

Blaukopf, Herta. *Mahler's unknown letters.* London: Gollancz, 1986.

Blaukopf, Kurt and Herta. *Mahler: his life, work and world.* London: Thames and Hudson, 1991.

Bliss, Arthur. *As I remember.* London: Thames Publishing, 1989.

Block, Adrienne Fried. *Amy Beach, passionate Victorian: the life and work of an American composer, 1867–1944.* New York: Oxford University Press, 1998.

Bloch, Ernst. *Essays on the philosophy of music.* Cambridge: Cambridge University Press, 1985.

Blocker, Robert. *The Robert Shaw reader.* New Haven; London: Yale University Press, 2004.

Blom, Eric. *A musical postbag.* London: J. M. Dent, 1945.

Blom, Eric. *Beethoven's pianoforte sonatas discussed.* London: J. M. Dent, 1938.

Blom, Eric. *Classics major and minor: with some other musical ruminations.* London: J. M. Dent, 1958.

Blum, David. *The art of quartet playing: the Guarneri Quartet in conversation with David Blum.* London: Gollancz, 1986.

Blume, Friedrich. *Classic and Romantic music: a comprehensive survey.* London: Faber and Faber, 1972.

Boden, Anthony. *The Parrys of the Golden Vale: background to genius.* London: Thames Publishing, 1998.

Bonavia, Ferruccio. *Musicians on music.* London: Routledge & Kegan Paul, 1956.

Bonds, Mark Evan *After Beethoven: imperatives of originality in the symphony.* Cambridge, Massachusetts; London: Harvard University Press, 1996.

Bonis, Ferenc, Editor. *The selected writings of Zoltán Kodály.*

Bookspan, Martin. André Previn: a biography. London: Hamilton, 1981.

Boros, James and Richard Toop, Editors. *Brian Ferneyhough: Collected writings*. Amsterdam: Harwood Academic, 1995.

Boulez, Pierre. *Stocktakings from an apprenticeship*. Oxford: Clarendon Press, 1991.

Boult, Adrian. *Boult on music: words from a lifetime's communication*. London: Toccata Press, 1983.

Boult, Adrian. *My own trumpet.* London, Hamish Hamilton, 1973.

Boult, Adrian with Jerrold Northrop Moore. *Music and friends: seven decades of letters to Adrian Boult from Elgar, Vaughan Williams, Holst, Bruno Walter, Yehudi Menuhin and other friends.* London: Hamish Hamilton, 1979.

Bovet, Marie Anne de. *Charles Gounod: his life and his works.* London: S. Low, Marston, Searle & Rivington, Ltd., 1891.

Bowen, Catherine Drinker. *Beloved friend: the story of Tchaikowsky and Nadejda von Meck.* London: Hutchinson & Co., 1937.

Bowen, Meiron, Editor. *Gerhard on music: selected writings.* Brookfield, Vermont: Ashgate, 2000.

Bowen, Meirion. *Michael Tippett.* London: Robson Books, 1982.

Bowen, Meiron, Editor. *Music of the angels: essays and sketchbooks of Michael Tippett.* London: Eulenburg, 1980.

Bowen, Meiron, Editor. *Tippett on music.* Oxford: Clarendon Press, 1995.

Bowers, Faubion. *Scriabin: a biography.* Mineola: Dover; London: Constable, 1996.

Boyden, Matthew. *Richard Strauss.* London: Weidenfeld & Nicolson, 1999.

Bozarth, George S., Editor. *Brahms studies: analytical and historical perspectives; papers delivered at the International Brahms Conference, Washington, DC, 5-8 May 1983.* Oxford: Clarendon Press, 1990.

Brand, Juliane, Christopher Hailey and Donald Harris, Editors. *The Berg-Schoenberg correspondence: selected letters.* Basingstoke: Macmillan, 1987.

Brandenbugh, Sieghard, Editor. *Haydn, Mozart, & Beethoven: studies in the music of the classical period: essays in honor of Alan Tyson.* Oxford: Clarendon Press, 1998.

Braunstein, Joseph. *Musica Æterna, program notes for 1961–1971.* New York: Musica Æterna, 1972.

Braunstein, Joseph. *Musica Æterna, program notes for 1971–1976.* New York: Musica Æterna, 1978.

Brendel, Alfred. *Alfred Brendel on music: collected essays.* Chicago, Iliinois: A Cappella Books, 2001.

Brendel, Alfred. *The veil of order: Alfred Brendel in conversation with Martin Meyer.* London: Faber and Faber, 2002.

Breuning, Gerhard von. *Memories of Beethoven: from the house of the black-robed Spaniards.* Cambridge: Cambridge University Press, 1992.

Briscoe, James R., Editor. (Brief Description): *Debussy in performance.* New Haven: Yale University Press, 1999.

Brott, Alexander Betty Nygaard King. *Alexander Brott: my lives in music.* Oakville, Ontario; Niagara Falls, New York: Mosaic Press, 2005.

Brown, Alfred Peter. *The symphonic repertoire. Vol. 2, The first golden age of the Viennese symphony: Haydn, Mozart, Beethoven, and Schubert.* Bloomington, Indiana: Indiana University Press, 2002.

Brown, Maurice John Edwin. *Schubert: a critical biography.*

London: Macmillan; New York: St. Martin's Press, 1958.

Broyles, Michael. *Beethoven: the emergence and evolution of Beethoven's heroic style.* New York: Excelsior Music Publishing Co., 1987.

Brubaker, Bruce and Jane Gottlieb, Editors. *Pianist, scholar, connoisseur: essays in honor of Jacob Lateiner.* Stuyvesant, N.Y., Pendragon Press, 2000.

Buch, Esteban. *Beethoven's Ninth: a political history.* Chicago; London: University of Chicago Press, 2003.

Burk, John N., Editor. *Letters of Richard Wagner: the Burrell collection.* London: Gollancz, 1951.

Burnham, Scott G. *Beethoven hero.* Princeton, New Jersey: Princeton University Press, 1995.

Burnham, Scott G and Michael P. Steinberg, Editors. *Beethoven and his world.* Princeton, New Jersey; Oxford: Princeton University Press, 2000.

Burton, William Westbrook, Editor. *Conversations about Bernstein.* New York; Oxford: Oxford University Press, 1995.

Busch, Fritz. *Pages from a musician's life.* London: Hogarth Press, 1953.

Busch, Hans, Editor. *Verdi's Aida: the history of an opera in letters and documents.* Minneapolis: University of Minnesota Press, 1978.

Busch, Hans, Editor. *Verdi's Falstaff in letters and contemporary reviews.* Bloomington: Indiana University Press, 1997.

Busch, Marie, Translator. *Memoirs of Eugenie Schumann.* London: W. Heinemann, 1927.

Bush, Alan Dudley. *In my eighth decade and other essays.* London: Kahn & Averill, 1980.

Busoni, Ferruccio. *Letters to his wife.* Translated by Rosamond Ley. New York: Da Capo Press, 1975.

Byron, Reginald. *Music, culture, & experience: selected papers of John Blacking.* Chicago: University of Chicago Press, 1995.

Cairns, David. *Responses: musical essays and reviews.* New York: Da Capo Press, 1980.

Cardus, Neville. *Talking of music.* London: Collins, 1957.

Carley, Lionel. *Delius: a life in letters.* London: Scolar Press in association with the Delius Trust, 1988.

Carley, Lionel. *Grieg and Delius: a chronicle of their friendship in letters.* London: Marion Boyars, 1993.

Carner, Mosco. *Major and minor.* London: Duckworth, 1980

Carner, Mosco. *Puccini: a critical biography.* London: Duckworth, 1958.

Carroll, Brendan G. *The last prodigy: a biography of Erich Wolfgang Korngold.* Portland, Oregon: Amadeus Press, 1997.

Carse, Adam von Ahn. *The life of Jullien: adventurer, showman-conductor and establisher of the Promenade Concerts in England, together with a history of those concerts up to 1895.* Cambridge England: Heffer, 1951.

Carse, Adam von Ahn. *The orchestra from Beethoven to Berlioz: a history of the orchestra in the first half of the 19th century, and of the development of orchestral baton-conducting.* Cambridge: W. Heffer, 1948.

Casals, Pablo. *Joys and sorrows: reflections by Pablo Casals as told to Albert E. Kahn.* London: Macdonald, 1970.

Casals, Pablo. *The memoirs of Pablo Casals as told to Thomas Dozier.* London: Life en Español, 1959.

Chappell, Paul. *Dr. S. S. Wesley, 1810–1876: portrait of a Victorian musician.* Great Wakering: Mayhew-McCrimmon, 1977.

Chasins, Abram. *Leopold Stokowski, a profile.* New York: Hawthorn Books, 1979.

Charlton, Davi, Editor and Martyn Clarke Translator. *E.T.A. Hoffmann's musical writings: Kreisleriana, The Poet and the*

Composer. Cambridge: Cambridge University Press, 1989.

Chávez, Carlos. *Musical thought.* Cambridge: Harvard University Press, 1961.

Chesterman, Robert, Editor. *Conversations with conductors: Bruno Walter, Sir Adrian Boult, Leonard Bernstein, Ernest Ansermet, Otto Klemperer, Leopold Stokowski.* Totowa, New Jersey: Rowman and Littlefield, 1976.

Chissell, Joan. *Clara Schumann: a dedicated spirit; a study of her life and work.* London: Hamilton, 1983.

Chua, Daniel K. L. *The "Galitzin" quartets of Beethoven: Opp.127, 132, 130.* Princeton: Princeton University Press, 1995.

Citron, Marcia, Editor. *The letters of Fanny Hensel to Felix Mendelssohn.* Stuyvesant, New York: Pendragon Press, 1987.

Clark, Walter Aaron. *Enrique Granados: poet of the piano.* Oxford, England; New York, N.Y.: Oxford University Press, 2006.

Clark, Walter Aaron. *Isaac Albéniz: portrait of a romantic.* Oxford; New York: Oxford University Press, 1999.

Clive, Peter. *Beethoven and his world.* Oxford University Press, 2001.

Closson, Ernest. *History of the piano.* Translated by Delano Ames and edited by Robin Golding. London: Paul Elek, 1947.

Cockshoot, John V. *The fugue in Beethoven's piano music.* London: Routledge & Kegan Paul, 1959.

Coe, Richard N, Translator. *Life of Rossini by Stendhal.* London: Calder & Boyars, 1970.

Coleman, Alexander, Editor. *Diversions & animadversions: essays from The new criterion.* New Brunswick, New Jersey; London: Transaction Publishers, 2005.

Colerick, George. *From the Italian girl to Cabaret: musical humour, parody and burlesque.* London: Juventus, 1998.

Coleridge, A. D. *Life of Moscheles, with selections from his diaries and correspondence by his wife.* London: Hurst & Blackett, 1873.

Colles, Henry Cope. *Essays and lectures.* London: Humphrey Milford, Oxford University Press, 1945.

Cone, Edward T., Editor. *Roger Sessions on music: collected essays.* Princeton, New Jersey: Princeton University Press, 1979.

Cone, Edward T. *The composer's voice.* Berkeley; London: University of California Press, 1974.

Cook, Susan and Judy S. Tsou, Editors. *Cecilia reclaimed: feminist perspectives on gender and music.* Urbana: University of Illinois Press, 1994.

Cooper, Barry. *Beethoven:* The master musicians series. Oxford: Oxford University Press, 2000.

Cooper, Barry. *Beethoven and the creative process.* Oxford: Clarendon Press, 1990.

Cooper, Barry. *Beethoven's folksong settings: chronology, sources, style.* Cambridge: Cambridge University Press, 1991.

Cooper, Barry. *The Beethoven compendium: a guide to Beethoven's life and music.* London: Thames and Hudson, 1991.

Cooper, Martin. *Beethoven: the last decade, 1817–1827.* London: Oxford University Press, 1970.

Cooper, Martin. *Judgements of value: selected writings on music.* Oxford; New York: Oxford University Press, 1988.

Cooper, Martin. *Ideas and music.* London: Barrie and Rockliff, 1965.

Cooper, Victoria L. *The house of Novello: the practice and policy of a Victorian music publisher, 1829–1866.* Aldershot, Hants: Ashgate, 2003.

Coover, James. *Music at auction: Puttick and Simpson (of London), 1794–1971: being an annotated, chronological list of sales of musical materials.*

Warren, Michigan: Harmonie Park Press, 1988.

Copland, Aaron. *Copland on music.* London: Deutsch, 1961.

Corredor, J. Ma. *Conversations with Casals.* London: Hutchinson, 1956.

Cott, Jonathan. *Stockhausen: conversations with the composer.* London: Picador, 1974.

Cottrell, Stephen. *Professional music making in London: ethnography and experience.* Aldershot: Ashgate, 2004.

Cowell, Henry. *Charles Ives and his music.* New York: Oxford University Press, 1955.

Cowling, Elizabeth. *The cello.* London: Batsford, 1983.

Crabbe, John. *Beethoven's empire of the mind.* Newbury: Lovell Baines, 1982.

Craft, Robert. *An improbable life: memoirs.* Nashville: Vanderbilt University Press, 2002.

Craft, Robert, Editor. *Stravinsky: selected correspondence.* London: Faber and Faber, 3 Vols. 1982–1985.

Craw, Howard Allen. *A biography and thematic catalog of the works of J. L. Dussek: 1760–1812.* Ann Arbor: Michigan, 1965.

Crawford, Richard, R. Allen Lott and Carol J. Oja, Editors. *A Celebration of American music: words and music in honor of H. Wiley Hitchcock.* Ann Arbor: University of Michigan Press, 1990.

Craxton, Harold and Tovey, Donald Francis. *Beethoven: Sonatas for Pianoforte.* London: The Associated Board, [1931].

Crichton, Ronald: Editor. *The memoirs of Ethel Smyth.* New York: Viking, 1987.

Crist, Stephen A. and Roberta M. Marvin, Editors. *Historical musicology: sources, methods, interpretations.* Rochester, New York: University of Rochester Press, 2004.

Crofton, Ian and Donald Fraser, Editors. *A dictionary of musical quotations.* London: Croom Helm, 1985.

Crompton, Louis, Editor. *Shaw, Bernard: The great composers: reviews and bombardments.* Berkeley; London: University of California Press, 1978.

Csicserry-Ronay, Elizabeth, Translator and Editor. *Hector Berlioz: The art of music and other essays: (A travers chants).* Bloomington: Indiana University Press, 1994.

Curtiss, Mina Kirstein. *Bizet and his world.* London: Secker & Warburg, 1959.

Cuyler, Louise Elvira. *The symphony.* New York: Harcourt Brace Jovanovich, 1973.

Dahlhaus, Carl. *Ludwig van Beethoven: approaches to his music.* Oxford: Clarendon Press, 1991.

Dahlhaus, Carl. *Nineteenth-century music.* Translated by J. Bradford Robinson. Berkeley; London: University of California Press, 1989.

Daniels, Robin. *Conversations with Cardus.* London: Gollancz, 1976.

Daniels, Robin. Conversations with Menuhin. London: Macdonald General Books, 1979.

Day, James. *Vaughan Williams.* London: Dent, 1961.

Davies, Peter Maxwell. *Studies from two decades.* Selected and introduced by Stephen Pruslin. London: Boosey & Hawkes, 1979.

Dean, Winton. *Georges Bizet: his life and work.* London: J.M. Dent, 1965.

Deas, Stewart. *In defence of Hanslick.* London: Williams and Norgate, 1940.

Debussy, Claude. *Debussy on music.* London: Secker & Warburg, 1977.

Delbanco, Nicholas. *The Beaux Arts Trio.* London: Gollancz, 1985.

Demény, Janos, Editor. *Béla Bartók: letters.* London: Faber and Faber, 1971.

Dent, Edward Joseph. *Selected essays.* Edited by Hugh Taylor. Cambridge; New York: Cambridge University Press, 1979.

Deutsch, Otto Erich. *Mozart: a documentary biography.* London: Adam & Charles Black, 1965.

Deutsch, Otto Erich. *Schubert: a documentary biography.* London: J.M. Dent, 1946

Deutsch, Otto Erich. *Schubert: memoirs by his friends.* London: Adam & Charles Black, 1958.

Dibble, Jeremy. *C. Hubert H. Parry: his life and music.* Oxford: Clarendon Press, 1992.

Dibble, Jeremy. *Charles Villiers Stanford: man and musician.* Oxford: Oxford University Press, 2002.

Donakowski, Conrad L. *A muse for the masses: ritual and music in an age of democratic revolution, 1770–1870.* Chicago: University of Chicago Press, 1977.

Dower, Catherine. *Alfred Einstein on music: selected music criticisms.* New York: Greenwood Press, 1991.

Downs, Philip G. *Classical music: the era of Haydn, Mozart, and Beethoven.* New York: W.W. Norton, 1992.

Drabkin, William. *Beethoven: Missa Solemnis.* Cambridge: Cambridge University Press, 1991.

Dreyfus, Kay. *The farthest north of humanness: letters of Percy Grainger, 1901–1914.* South Melbourne; Basingstoke: Macmillan, 1985.

Dubal, David, Editor. *Remembering Horowitz: 125 pianists recall a legend.* New York: Schirmer Books, 1993.

Dubal, David. *The world of the concert pianist.* London: Victor Gollancz, 1985.

Dvořák, Otakar. *Antonín Dvořák, my father.* Spillville, Iowa: Czech Historical Research Center, 1993.

Dyson, George. *The progress of music.* London: Oxford University Press, Humphrey Milford, 1932.

Eastaugh, Kenneth. *Havergal Brian: the making of a composer.* London: Harrap, 1976.

Edwards, Allen. *Flawed words and stubborn sounds: a conversation with Elliott Carter.* New York: Norton & Company, 1971.

Edwards, Frederick George. *Musical haunts in London.* London: J. Curwen & Sons, 1895.

Ehrlich, Cyril. *First philharmonic: a history of the Royal Philharmonic Society.* Oxford: Clarendon Press, 1995.

Einstein, Alfred. *A short history of music.* London: Cassell and Company Ltd., 1948.

Einstein, Alfred. *Essays on music.* London: Faber and Faber, 1958.

Einstein, Alfred. *Mozart: his character, his work.* London: Cassell and Company Ltd., 1946.

Einstein, Alfred. *Music in the Romantic era.* London: J.M. Dent Ltd., 1947.

Ekman, Karl. *Jean Sibelius, his life and personality.* New York: Tudor Publishing. Co., 1945.

Elgar, Edward. *A future for English music: and other lectures,* Edited by Percy M. Young. London: Dobson, 1968.

Elkin, Robert. *Queen's Hall, 1893–1941.* London: Rider, 1944.

Ella, John. *Musical sketches, abroad and at home: with original music by Mozart, Czerny, Graun, etc., vocal cadenzas and other musical illustrations.* London: Ridgway, Vol. 1., 1869.

Ellis, William Ashton. *The family letters of Richard Wagner.* Edited and translated by William Ashton Ellis and enlarged with introduction and notes by John Deathridge. Basingstoke: Macmillan, 1991.

Ellis, William Ashton. *Richard Wagner's prose works: Vol. 1, The art-work of the future.* Edited and translated by William Ashton Ellis. London: Kegan Paul, Trench, Trübner, 1895.

Ellis, William Ashton. *Richard Wagner's prose works: Vol. 2, Opera and drama.* Edited and translated by William Ashton Ellis. London: Kegan Paul, Trench, Trübner, 1900.

Ellis, William Ashton. *Richard Wagner's prose works: Vol. 3, The theatre.* Edited and translated by William Ashton Ellis. London: Kegan Paul, Trench, Trübner, 1907.

Ellis, William Ashton. *Richard Wagner's prose works: Vol. 4, Art and politics.* Edited and translated by William Ashton Ellis. London: Kegan Paul, Trench, Trübner, 1895.

Ellis, William Ashton. *Richard Wagner's prose works: Vol. 5, Actors and singers.* Edited and translated by William Ashton Ellis. London: Kegan Paul, Trench, Trübner, 1896.

Ellis, William Ashton. *Richard Wagner's prose works: Vol. 6, Religion and art.* Edited and translated by William Ashton Ellis. London: Kegan Paul, Trench, Trübner, 1897.

Ellis, William Ashton. *Richard Wagner's prose works: Vol. 7, In Paris and Dresden.* Edited and translated by William Ashton Ellis. London: Kegan Paul, Trench, Trübner, 1898.

Ellis, William Ashton. *Richard Wagner's prose works: Vol. 8, Posthumous.* Edited and translated by William Ashton Ellis. London: Kegan Paul, Trench, Trübner, 1899.

Elterlein, Ernst von. *Beethoven's pianoforte sonatas: explained for the lovers of the musical art.* London: W. Reeves, 1898.

Engel, Carl. *Musical myths and facts.* London: Novello, Ewer & Co.; New York: J.L. Peters, 1876.

Eosze, László. *Zoltán Kodály: his life and work.* London: Collet's, 1962.

Etter, Brian K. *From classicism to modernism: Western musical culture and the metaphysics of order.* Aldershot: Ashgate, 2001.

Ewen, David. *From Bach to Stravinsky: the history of music by its foremost critics.* New York, Greenwood Press, 1968.

Ewen, David. *Romain Rolland's Essays on music.* New York: Dover Publications, 1959.

Fay, Amy. *Music-study in Germany: from the home correspondence of Amy Fay.* New York: Dover Publications, 1965.

Fenby, Eric. *Delius as I knew him.* London: Quality Press, 1936.

Ferguson, Donald Nivison. *Masterworks of the orchestral repertoire: a guide for listeners.* Minneapolis: University of Minnesota Press, 1954.

Fétis, François-Joseph. *Curiosités historiques de la musique: complément nécessaire de la Musique mise à la portée de tout le monde.* Paris: Janet et Cotelle, 1830.

Fifield, Christopher. *Max Bruch: his life and works.* London: Gollancz, 1988.

Fifield, Christopher. *True artist and true friend: a biography of Hans Richter.* Oxford: Clarendon Press, 1993.

Finson, Jon and R. Larry Todd, Editors. *Mendelssohn and Schumann: essays on their music and its context.* Durham, N.C.: Duke University Press, 1984.

Fischer, Edwin. *Beethoven's pianoforte sonatas: a guide for students & amateurs.* London: Faber and Faber, 1959.

Fischer, Edwin. *Reflections on music.* London: Williams and Norgate, 1951.

Fischer, Hans Conrad and Erich Kock. *Ludwig van Beethoven: a study in text and pictures.* London: Macmillan; New York, St. Martin's Press, 1972.

Fischmann, Zdenka E. *Janác̆ek-Newmarch correspondence. 1st limited and numbered edition.* Rockville, MD: Kabel Publishers, 1986.

Fitzlyon, April. *Maria Malibran: diva of the romantic age.* London: Souvenir Press, 1987.

FitzLyon, April. *The price of genius: a life of Pauline Viardot*. London: John Calder, 1964.

Forbes, Elliot, Editor. *Thayer's life of Beethoven*. Princeton, New Jersey: Princeton University Press, 1967.

Foreman, Lewis. *Bax: a composer and his times*. London: Scolar Press, 1983.

Foreman, Lewis, Editor. *Farewell, my youth, and other writings by Arnold Bax*. Aldershot: Scolar Press, 1992.

Foster, Myles Birket. *History of the Philharmonic Society of London, 1813–1912: a record of a hundred years' work in the cause of music*. London: Bodley Head, 1912.

Foulds, John. *Music today: its heritage from the past, and legacy to the future*. London: I. Nicholson and Watson, limited, 1934.

Frank, Mortimer H. *Arturo Toscanini: the NBC years*. Portland, Oregon: Amadeus Press, 2002.

Fraser, Andrew Alastair. *Essays on music*. London: Oxford University Press, H. Milford, 1930.

Frohlich, Martha. *Beethoven's Appassionata' sonata*. Oxford: Clarendon Press, 1991.

Gal, Hans. *The golden age of Vienna*. London: Max Parrish & Co. Limited, 1948.

Gal, Hans. *The musician's world: great composers in their letters*. London: Thames and Hudson, 1965.

Galatopoulos, Stelios. *Bellini: life, times, music*. London: Sanctuary, 2002.

Garden, Edward and Nigel Gottrei, Editors. *'To my best friend': correspondence between Tchaikovsky and Nadezhda von Meck, 1876–1878*. Oxford: Clarendon Press, 1993.

Geck, Martin. Beethoven. London: Haus, 2003.

Gerig, Reginald. *Famous pianists & their technique*. Washington: R. B. Luce, 1974.

Gilliam, Bryan. *The life of Richard Strauss*. Cambridge: Cambridge University Press, 1999.

Gilliam, Bryan, Editor. *Richard Strauss and his world*. Princeton, New Jersey: Princeton University Press, 1992.

Gillies, Malcolm and Bruce Clunies Ross, Editors. *Grainger on music*. Oxford; New York: Oxford University Press, 1999.

Gillies, Malcolm and David Pear, Editors. *The all-round man: selected letters of Percy Grainger, 1914–1961*. Oxford: Clarendon Press, 1994.

Gillies, Malcolm, Editor. *The Bartók companion*. London: Faber and Faber, 1993.

Gillmor, Alan M. *Erik Satie*. Basingstoke: Macmillan Press, 1988.

Glehn, M. E. *Goethe and Mendelssohn : (1821–1831)*. London: Macmillan, 1874.

Glowacki, John, Editor. *Paul A. Pisk: Essays in his honor*. Austin, Texas: University of Texas, 1966

Gollancz, Victor. *Journey towards music: a memoir*. London: Victor Gollancz Ltd., 1964.

Good, Edwin Marshall. *Giraffes, black dragons, and other pianos: a technological history from Cristofori to the modern concert grand*. Stanford, California: Stanford University Press, 1982.

Gordon, David. *Musical visitors to Britain*. London: Routledge, 2005.

Gordon, Stewart. *A history of keyboard literature: music for the piano and its forerunners*. Schirmer Books: New York: London : Prentice Hall International, 1996.

Gorrell, Lorraine. *The nineteenth-century German lied*. Portland, Oregon: Amadeus Press, 1993.

Goss, Glenda D. *Jean Sibelius: the Hämeenlinna letters: scenes from a musical life, 1875–1895*. Esbo, Finland: Schildts, 1997.

Goss, Madeleine. *Bolero: the life of Maurice Ravel*. New York: Tudor, 1945.

Gotch, Rosamund Brunel, Editor. *Mendelssohn and his friends in Kensington: letters from Fanny and Sophy Horsley, written 1833–36.* London: Oxford University Press, 1938.

Gounod, Charles. *Charles Gounod; autobiographical reminiscences: with family letters and notes on music; from the French.* London: William Heinemann, 1896.

Grabs, Manfred, Editor. *Hanns Eisler: a rebel in music; selected writings.* Berlin: Seven Seas Publishers, 1978.

Grace, Harvey. *A musician at large.* London: Oxford University Press, H. Milford, 1928.

(La) Grange, Henry-Louis de. *Gustav Mahler.* Oxford: Oxford University Press, 1995.

Graves, Charles L. *Hubert Parry: his life and works.* London: Macmillan, 1926.

Graves, Charles L. *Post-Victorian music: with other studies and sketches.* London: Macmillan and Co., limited, 1911.

Graves, Charles L. *The life & letters of Sir George Grove, Hon. D.C.L. (Durham), Hon. LL.D. (Glasgow), formerly director of the Royal college of music.* London: Macmillan and Co., Ltd.; New York: The Macmillan Co., 1903.

Gray, Cecil. *Musical chairs, or, between two stools: being the life and memoirs of Cecil Gray.* London: Home & Van Thal, 1948.

Gregor-Dellin and Dietrich Mack, Editors. *Cosima Wagner's diaries.: Vol. 1, 1869 - 1877.* London: Collins, 1978-1980.

Griffiths, Paul. *Modern music: the avant-garde since 1945.* London: J. M. Dent & Sons Ltd., 1981.

Griffiths, Paul. *Olivier Messiaen and the music of time.* London: Faber and Faber, 1985.

Griffiths, Paul. *Peter Maxwell Davies.* London: Robson Books, 1988.

Griffiths, Paul. *The sea on fire: Jean Barraqué.* Rochester, New York: Woodbridge: University of Rochester Press, 2003.

Griffiths, Paul. *The string quartet.* London: Thames and Hudson, 1983.

Grout, Donald Jay and Claude V. Palisca, Editors. *A history of Western music.* London: J. M. Dent, 1988.

Grove, George. *Beethoven and his nine symphonies.* London: Novello, Ewer, 1896.

Grover, Ralph Scott. *Ernest Chausson: the man and his music.* London: The Athlone Press, 1980.

Grover, Ralph Scott. *The music of Edmund Rubbra.* Aldershot: Scolar Press, 1993.

Grun, Bernard. *Alban Berg: letters to his wife.* Edited and translated by Bernard Grun. London: Faber and Faber, 1971.

Gutman, David. *Prokofiev.* London: Omnibus Press, 1990.

Hadow, William Henry. *Collected essays.* London: H. Milford at the Oxford University Press, 1928.

Hadow, William Henry. *Beethoven's Op. 18 Quartets.* London: H. Milford at the Oxford University Press, 1926.

Haggin, Bernard H. *Music observed.* New York: Oxford University Press, 1964.

Hailey, Christopher. *Franz Schreker, 1878–1934: a cultural biography.* Cambridge: Cambridge University Press, 1993.

Hall, Michael. *Leaving home: a conducted tour of twentieth-century music with Simon Rattle.* London: Faber and Faber, 1996.

Hall, Patricia and Friedemann Sallis, Editors. (Brief Description): *A handbook to twentieth-century musical sketches.* Cambridge: Cambridge University Press, 2004.

Hallé, C. E. *Life and letters of Sir Charles Hallé: being an autobiography (1819–1860) with correspondence and diaries.*

London: Smith, Elder & Co., 1896.

Halstead, Jill. *The woman composer: creativity and the gendered politics of musical composition.* Aldershot: Ashgate, 1997.

Hamburger, Michael, Editor and Translator. *Beethoven letters, journals, and conversations.* New York: Thames and Hudson, 1951.

Hammelmann, Hanns A. and Ewald Osers. *The correspondence between Richard Strauss and Hugo von Hofmannsthal.* London: Collins, 1961.

Hanson, Lawrence and Elisabeth Hanson. *Tchaikovsky: the man behind the music.* New York: Dodd, Mead & Co, 1967.

Harding, James. *Massenet.* London: J. M. Dent & Sons Ltd., 1970.

Harding, James. *Saint-Saëns and his circle.* London: Chapman & Hall, 1965.

Harding, Rosamond E. M. *Origins of musical time and expression.* London: Oxford University Press, 1938.

Harman, Alec with Anthony Milner and Wilfrid Mellers. *Man and his music: the story of musical experience in the West.* London: Barrie & Jenkins, 1988.

Harper, Nancy Lee. *Manuel de Falla: his life and music.* Lanham, Maryland; London: The Scarecrow Press, 2005.

Hartmann, Arthur. *'Claude Debussy as I knew him' and other writings of Arthur Hartmann.* Edited by Samuel Hsu, Sidney Grolnic, and Mark Peters. Rochester, New York; Woodbridge: University of Rochester Press, 2003.

Haugen, Einar and Camilla Cai. *Ole Bull: Norway's romantic musician and cosmopolitan patriot.* Madison: The University of Wisconsin Press, 1993.

Headington, Christopher. *The Bodley Head history of Western music.* London: The Bodley Head, 1974.

Heartz, Daniel. *Music in European capitals: the galant style, 1720–1780.* New York; London: W. W. Norton, 2003.

Hedley, Arthur, Editor. *Selected correspondence of Fryderyk Chopin: abridged from Fryderyk Chopin's correspondence.* London: Heinemann, 1962.

Heiles, Anne Mischakoff. *Mischa Mischakoff: journeys of a concertmaster.* Sterling Heights, Michigan: Harmonie Park Press, 2006.

Henderson, Sanya Shoilevska. *Alex North, film composer: a biography, with musical analyses of a Streetcar named desire, Spartacus, The misfits, Under the volcano, and Prizzi's honor.* Jefferson, N.C.; London: McFarland, 2003.

Henschel, George. *Personal recollections of Johannes Brahms: some of his letters to and pages from a journal kept by George Henschel.* Boston: R G. Badger, 1907.

Henze, Hans Werner. *Bohemian fifths: an autobiography.* London: Faber and Faber, 1998.

Henze, Hans Werner. *Music and politics: collected writings 1953–81.* London: Faber and Faber, 1982.

Herbert, May, Translator. *Early letters of Robert Schumann.* London: George Bell and Sons, 1888.

Heyman, Barbara B. *Samuel Barber: the composer and his music.* New York: Oxford University Press, 1992.

Heyworth, Peter. *Otto Klemperer, his life and times.* Cambridge: Cambridge University Press, 2 Vols. 1983–1996.

Hildebrandt, Dieter. *Pianoforte: a social history of the piano.* London: Hutchinson, 1988.

Hill, Peter. *The Messiaen companion.* London: Faber and Faber, 1995.

Hill, Peter and Nigel Simeone. Messiaen. New Haven Connecticut; London: Yale University Press,

2005.

Hiller, Ferdinand. *Mendelssohn: Letters and recollections.* New York: Vienna House, 1972.

Hines, Robert Stephan. *The orchestral composer's point of view: essays on twentieth-century music by those who wrote it.* Norman: University of Oklahoma Press, 1970.

Ho, Allan B. *Shostakovich reconsidered.* London: Toccata Press, 1998.

Hodeir, André. *Since Debussy: a view of contemporary music.* New York: Da Capo Press, 1975.

Holmes, Edward. *The life of Mozart: including his correspondence.* London: Chapman and Hall, 1845.

Holmes, John L. *Composers on composers.* New York: Greenwood Press, 1990.

Hopkins, Antony. *The concertgoer's companion.* London: J.M. Dent & Sons Ltd., 1984.

Hopkins, Antony. *The seven concertos of Beethoven.* Aldershot: Scolar Press, 1996.

Holt, Richard. *Nicolas Medtner (1879–1951): a tribute to his art and personality.* London: D. Dobson, 1955.

Honegger, Arthur. *I am a composer.* London: Faber and Faber, 1966.

Hoover, Kathleen and John Cage. *Virgil Thomson: his life and music.* New York; London: T. Yoseloff, 1959.

Horgan, Paul. *Encounters with Stravinsky: a personal record.* London: The Bodley Head, 1972.

Horowitz, Joseph. *Conversations with Arrau.* London: Collins, 1982.

Horowitz, Joseph. Understanding Toscanini. London: Faber and Faber, 1987.

Horwood, Wally. *Adolphe Sax, 1814–1894: his life and legacy.* Bramley: Bramley Books, 1980.

Howie, Crawford. *Anton Bruckner: a documentary biography.* Lewiston, N.Y.; Lampeter: Edwin Mellen Press, 2002.

Hueffer, Francis. *Correspondence of Wagner and Liszt.* New York: Greenwood Press, 2 Vols. 1969.

Hughes, Spike. *The Toscanini legacy: a critical study of Arturo Toscanini's performances of Beethoven, Verdi, and other composers.* London: Putnam, 1959.

Hullah, Annette. *Theodor Leschetizky.* London and New York: J. Land & Co., 1906.

Le Huray, Peter and James Day, Editors. *Music and aesthetics in the eighteenth and early-nineteenth centuries.* Cambridge: Cambridge University Press, 1988.

D'Indy, Vincent. *César Franck.* New York: Dover Publications, 1965.

Jacobs, Arthur. *Arthur Sullivan: A Victorian musician.* Aldershot: Scolar Press, 1992.

Jahn, Otto. *Life of Mozart.* London: Novello, Ewer & Co., 1882.

Jefferson, Alan. *Sir Thomas Beecham: a centenary tribute.* London: World Records Ltd., 1979.

Jezic, Diane. *The musical migration and Ernst Toch.* Ames: Iowa State University Press, 1989.

Johnson, Douglas Porter, Editor. *The Beethoven sketchbooks: history, reconstruction, inventory.* Oxford: Clarendon, 1985.

Johnson, Stephen. *Bruckner remembered.* London: Faber and Faber, 1998.

Jones, David, Wyn. *Beethoven: Pastoral symphony.* Cambridge: Cambridge University Press, 1995.

Jones, David Wyn. *The life of Beethoven.* Cambridge: Cambridge University Press, 1998.

Jones, David Wyn. *The symphony in Beethoven's Vienna.* Cambridge: Cambridge University Press, 2006.

Jones, J. Barrie, Editor. *Gabriel Fauré: a life in letters.* London: Batsford, 1989.

Jones, Peter Ward, Editor and Translator. *The Mendelssohns on* honeymoon: the 1837 diary of Felix and Cécile Mendelssohn Bartholdy, together with letters to their families. Oxford: Clarendon Press, 1997.

Jones, Timothy. Beethoven, the Moonlight and other sonatas, Op. 27 and Op. 31. Cambridge; New York, N.Y.: Cambridge University Press, 1999.

Kalischer, A. C., Editor. Beethoven's letters: a critical edition. London: J. M. Dent, 1909.

Kárpáti, János. Bartók's chamber music. Stuyvesant, New York: Pendragon Press, 1994.

Keefe, Simon P. The Cambridge companion to the concerto. Cambridge, New York, N.Y.: Cambridge University Press, 2005.

Keller, Hans. The great Haydn quartets: their interpretation. London: J. M. Dent, 1986.

Keller, Hans, Editor. The memoirs of Carl Flesch. New York: Macmillan, 1958.

Keller, Hans, and Christopher Wintle. Beethoven's string quartets in F minor, Op. 95 and C minor, Op. 131: two studies. Nottingham: Department of Music, University of Nottingham, 1995.

Kelly, Thomas Forrest. First nights at the opera: five musical premiers. New Haven: Yale University Press, 2004.

Kennedy, Michael. Adrian Boult. London: Hamish Hamilton, 1987.

Kennedy, Michael. Barbirolli, conductor laureate: the authorised biography. London: Hart-Davis, MacGibbon, 1973.

Kennedy, Michael, Editor. The autobiography of Charles Hallé; with correspondence and diaries. London: Paul Elek, 1972.

Kennedy, Michael. Hallé tradition: a century of music. Manchester: Manchester University Press, 1960.

Kennedy, Michael. The works of Ralph Vaughan Williams. London: Oxford University Press, 1964.

Kemp, Ian. Tippett: the composer and his music. London; New York: Eulenburg Books, 1984.

Kerman, Joseph. The Beethoven quartets. London: Oxford University Press, 1967, c1966.

Kerman, Joseph. Write all these down: essays on music. Berkeley, California; London: University of California Press, 1994.

Kildea, Paul, Editor. Britten on music. Oxford: Oxford University Press, 2003.

Kinderman, William. Beethoven. Oxford: Oxford University Press, 1997.

Kinderman, William. Beethoven's Diabelli variations. Oxford: Clarendon Press; New York: Oxford University Press, 1987.

Kinderman, William, Editor. The string quartets of Beethoven. Urbana, Illinois: University of Illinois Press, 2005.

King, Alec Hyatt. Musical pursuits: selected essays. London: British Library, 1987.

Kirby, F. E. Music for piano: a short history. Amadeus Press: Portland, 1995.

Kirkpatrick, John, Editor. Charles E. Ives: Memos. New York: W.W. Norton, 1972.

Knapp, Raymond. Brahms and the challenge of the symphony. Stuyvesant, N.Y.: Pendragon Press, c.1997.

Knight, Frida. Cambridge music: from the Middle Ages to modern times. Cambridge, England.: New York: Oleander Press, 1980.

Knight, Max, Translator. A confidential matter: the letters of Richard Strauss and Stefan Zweig, 1931–1935. Berkeley; London: University of California Press, 1977.

Kok, Alexander. A voice in the dark: the philharmonia years. Ampleforth: Emerson Edition, 2002.

Kopelson, Kevin. Beethoven's kiss: pianism, perversion, and the mastery of desire. Stanford, California: Stanford University Press, 1996.

Kostelanetz, Richard, Editor. *Aaron Copland: a reader; selected writings 1923–1972*. New York; London: Routledge, 2003.

Kostelanetz, Richard. *Conversing with Cage*. New York; London: Routledge, 2003.

Kostelanetz, Richard. *On innovative musicians*. New York: Limelight Editions, 1989.

Kostelanetz, Richard, Editor. *Virgil Thomson: a reader ; selected writings, 1924–1984*. New York; London: Routledge, 2002.

Kowalke, Kim H. *Kurt Weill in Europe*. Ann Arbor, Michigan: UMI Research Press, 1979.

Krehbiel, Henry Edward. *The pianoforte and its music*. New York: Cooper Square Publishers, 1971.

Kruseman, Philip, Editor. *Beethoven's own words*. London: Hinrichsen Edition, 1948.

Kurtz, Michael. *Stockhausen: a biography*. London: Faber and Faber, 1992.

Lam, Basil. *Beethoven string quartets*. Seattle: University of Washington Press, 1975.

Lambert, Constant. *Music ho!: a study of music in decline*. London: Faber and Faber, Ltd. 1934.

Landon, H. C. Robbins. *Beethoven: a documentary study*. London: Thames and Hudson, 1970.

Landon, H. C. Robbins. *Beethoven: his life, work and world*. London: Thames and Hudson, 1992.

Landon, H. C. Robbins. *Essays on the Viennese classical style: Gluck, Haydn, Mozart, Beethoven*. London: Barrie & Rockliff The Cresset Press, 1970.

Landon, H. C. Robbins. *Haydn: chronicle and works/Haydn, the late years, 1801–1809*. Bloomington: Indiana University Press, 1977.

Landon, H. C. Robbins. *Haydn: his life and music*. London: Thames and Hudson, 1988.

Landon, H. C. Robbins. *Haydn in England, 1791–1795*. London: Thames and Hudson, 1976.

Landon, H. C. Robbins. *Haydn: the years of 'The creation', 1796–800*. London: Thames and Hudson, 1977.

Landon, H. C. Robbins. *Mozart: the golden years, 1781–1791*. New York: Schirmer Books, 1989.

Landon, H. C. Robbins. *1791, Mozart's last year*. London: Thames and Hudson, 1988.

Landon, H. C. Robbins *The collected correspondence and London notebooks of Joseph Haydn*. London: Barrie and Rockliff, 1959.

Landon, H. C. Robbins: Editor. *The Mozart companion*. London: Faber, 1956.

Landowska, Wanda. *Music of the past*. London: Geoffrey Bles, 1926.

Lang, Paul Henry. *Musicology and performance*. New Haven: Yale University Press, 1997.

Lang, Paul Henry. *The creative world of Beethoven*. New York: W. W. Norton 1971.

Laurence, Dan H., Editor. *Shaw's music: the complete musical criticism in three volumes*. London: Max Reinhardt, the Bodley Head, 1981.

Lawford-Hinrichsen, Irene. *Music publishing and patronage: C. F. Peters, 1800 to the Holocaust*. Kenton: Edition Press, 2000.

Layton, Robert, Editor. *A guide to the concerto*. Oxford: Oxford University Press, 1996.

Layton, Robert, Editor. *A guide to the symphony*. Oxford: Oxford University Press, 1995.

Lebrecht, Norman. *The maestro myth: great conductors in pursuit of power*. London: Simon & Schuster, 1991.

Lee, Ernest Markham. *The story of the symphony*. London: Scott Publishing Co., 1916.

Leibowitz, Herbert A., Editor. *Musical impressions: selections* from *Paul Rosenfeld's criticism.* London: G. Allen & Unwin, 1970.

Lenrow, Elbert, Editor and Translator. *The letters of Richard Wagner to Anton Pusinelli.* New York: Vienna House, 1972.

Leonard, Maurice. *Kathleen: the life of Kathleen Ferrier: 1912–1953.* London: Hutchinson, 1988.

Lesure, François and Roger Nichols, Editors. *Debussy, letters.* London: Faber and Faber, 1987.

Letellier, Robert Ignatius, Editor and Translator. *The diaries of Giacomo Meyerbeer.* Madison: Fairleigh Dickinson University Press; London: Associated University Presses, 4 Vols., 1999–2004.

Levas, Santeri. *Sibelius: a personal portrait.* London: J. M. Dent, 1972.

Levy, Alan Howard. *Edward MacDowell, an American master.* Lanham, Md. & London: Scarecrow Press, 1998.

Levy, David Benjamin. *Beethoven: the Ninth Symphony.* New Haven, Connecticut; London: Yale University Press, 2003.

Leyda, Jay and Sergi Bertensson. *The Musorgsky reader: a life of Modeste Petrovich Musorgsky in letters and documents.* New York: W.W. Norton, 1947.

Lewis, Thomas P., Editor. *Raymond Leppard on music: an anthology of critical and personal writings.* White Plains, N.Y.: Pro/Am Music Resources, 1993.

Liébert, Georges. *Nietzsche and music.* Chicago: University of Chicago Press, 2004.

Liszt, Franz. *An artist's journey: lettres d'un bachelier ès musique, 1835–1841.* Chicago: University of Chicago Press, 1989.

Litzmann, Berthold, Editor. *Clara Schumann: an artist's life, based on material found in diaries and letters.* London: Macmillan; Leipzig: Breitkopf & Härtel, 2 Vols. 1913.

Litzmann, Berthold, Editor. *Letters of Clara Schumann and Johannes Brahms, 1853–1896.* New York, Vienna House. 2 Vols. 1971.

Lloyd, Stephen. *William Walton: muse of fire.* Woodbridge, Suffolk: The Boydell Press, 2001.

Locke, Ralph P. and Cyrilla Barr, Editors. *Cultivating music in America: women patrons and activists since 1860.* Berkeley: University of California Press, 1997.

Lockspeiser, Edward. *Debussy: his life and mind.* London: Cassell. 2 Vols. 1962–1965.

Lockspeiser, Edward. *The literary clef: an anthology of letters and writings by French composers.* London: J. Calder. 1958.

Lockwood, Lewis, Editor. *Beethoven essays: studies in honor of Elliot Forbes.* Cambridge, Massachusetts: Harvard University Department of Music: Distributed by Harvard University Press, 1984.

Lockwood, Lewis and Mark Kroll, Editors. *The Beethoven violin sonatas: history, criticism, performance.* Urbana: University of Illinois Press, 2004.

Loft, Abram. *Violin and keyboard: the duo repertoire.* New York: Grossman Publishers. 2 Vols. 1973.

Longyear, Rey Morgan. *Nineteenth-century romanticism in music.* Englewood Cliffs: Prentice-Hall, 1969.

Lowe, C. Egerton. *Beethoven's pianoforte sonatas: hints on their rendering, form, etc., with appendices on definition of sonata, music forms, ornaments, pianoforte pedals, and how to discover keys.* London: Novello, 1929.

Macdonald, Hugh, Editor. *Berlioz: Selected letters.* London: Faber and Faber, 1995.

Macdonald, Malcolm, Editor. *Havergal Brian on music: selections from his journalism: Volume One, British music.* London:

Toccata Press, 1986.

MacDonald, Malcolm. *Varèse: astronomer in sound*. London: Kahn & Averill, 2003.

MacDowell, Edward. *Critical and historical essays: lectures delivered at Columbia University*. Edited by W. J. Baltzell. London: Elkin; Boston: A.P. Schmidt, 1912.

MacFarren, Walter. Memories: an autobiography. London: Walter Scott Publishing Co.,1905.

Mackenzie, Alexander Campbell. *A musician's narrative*. London: Cassell and company, Ltd, 1927.

McCarthy, Margaret William, Editor. *More letters of Amy Fay: the American years, 1879–1916.* Detroit: Information Coordinators, 1986.

McClary, Susan. *Feminine endings: music, gender, and sexuality*. Minneapolis: University of Minnesota Press, 1991.

McClatchie, Stephen, Editor and Translator. *The Mahler family letters*. Oxford: Oxford University Press, 2006.

McVeigh, Simon. *Concert life in London from Mozart to Haydn*. Cambridge: Cambridge University Press, 1993.

Mahler, Alma. *Gustav Mahler: memories and letters*. Enlarged edition revised and edited and with and introduction by Donald Mitchell. London: John Murray, 1968.

Mai, François Martin. *Diagnosing genius: the life and death of Beethoven*. Montreal; London: McGill-Queen's University Press, 2007.

Del Mar, Norman. *Orchestral variations: confusion and error in the orchestral repertoire*. London: Eulenburg, 1981.

Del Mar, Norman. *Richard Strauss: a critical commentary on his life and works*. London: Barrie & Jenkins. 3 Vols. 1978.

(La) Mara [pseudonym]. *Letters of Franz Liszt*. London: H. Grevel & Co., 2 Vols. 1894.

Marek, George Richard. *Puccini*. London: Cassell & Co., 1952.

Marek, George Richard. *Toscanini*. London: Vision, 1976.

(De) Marliave, Joseph. *Beethoven's quartets*. New York: Dover Publications (reprint), 1961.

Martin, George Whitney. *Verdi: his music, life and times*. London: Macmillan, 1965.

Martner, Knud, Editor. *Selected letters of Gustav Mahler*. London; Boston: Faber and Faber, 1979.

Martyn, Barrie. *Nicolas Medtner: his life and music*. Aldershot: Scolar Press, 1995.

Martyn, Barrie. *Rachmaninoff: composer, pianist, conductor*. Aldershot: Scolar, 1990.

Massenet, Jules. *My recollections*. Westport, Connecticut: Greenwood Press.1970.

Matheopoulos, Helena. *Maestro: encounters with conductors of today*. London: Hutchinson, 1982.

Matthews, Denis. *Beethoven*. London: J. M. Dent, 1985.

Matthews, Denis. *Beethoven piano sonatas*. London: British Broadcasting Corporation, 1967.

Matthews, Dennis. *In pursuit of music*. London: Victor Gollancz Ltd., 1968.

Matthews, Denis. *Keyboard music*. Newton Abbot: London David & Charles, 1972.

Mellers, Wilfrid Howard. *Caliban reborn: renewal in twentieth-century music*. London: Victor Gollancz, 1967.

Mellers, Wilfrid Howard. *The sonata principle (from c. 1750)*. London: Rockliff, 1957.

Mendelssohn Bartholdy. *Letters from Italy and Switzerland*. London: Longman, Green, Longman, and Roberts, 1862.

Mendelssohn Bartholdy, Paul. *Letters of Felix Mendelssohn Bartholdy, from 1833 to 1847.* London: Longman, Green, Longman, Roberts, & Green, 1864.

Menuhin, Yehudi and Curtis W. Davis. *The music of man.* London: Macdonald and Jane's, 1979.

Menuhin, Yehudi. *Theme and variations.* London: Heinemann Educational Books Ltd., 1972.

Menuhin, Yehudi. *Unfinished journey.* London: Macdonald and Jane's, 1977.

Messian, Olivier. *Music and color: conversations with Claude Samuel.* Portland, Oregon: Amadeus, 1994.

Miall, Antony. *Musical bumps.* London: J.M. Dent & Sons Ltd, 1981.

Michotte, Edmond. *Richard Wagner's visit to Rossini (Paris 1860): and, An evening at Rossini's in Beau-Sejour (Passy), 1858.* Chicago; London: University of Chicago Press, 1982.

Mies, Paul. *Beethoven's sketches: an analysis of his style based on a study of his sketchbooks.* New York: Johnson Reprint, 1969.

Milhaud, Darius. *My happy life.* London: Boyars, 1995.

Miller, Mina. *The Nielsen companion.* London: Faber and Faber, 1994.

Milsom, David. *Theory and practice in late nineteenth-century violin performance: an examination of style in performance, 1850–1900.* Aldershot: Ashgate, 2003.

Mitchell, Donald, Editor. *Letters from a life: the selected letters and diaries of Benjamin Britten 1913–1976.* London: Faber and Faber. 3 Vols., 1991.

Mitchell, Donald and Hans Keller, Editors. *Music survey: new series 1949–1952.* London: Faber Music in association with Faber & Faber, 1981.

Mitchell, Jon C. *A comprehensive biography of composer Gustav Holst, with correspondence and diary excerpts: including his American years.* Lewiston, New York: Edwin Mellen Press, 2001.

Moldenhauer, Hans. *Anton von Webern: a chronicle of his life and work.* London: Victor Gollancz, 1978.

Monrad-Johansen. *Edvard Grieg.* New York: Tudor Publishing Co., 1945.

Moore, Gerald. *Am I too loud?: memoirs of an accompanist.* London: Hamish Hamilton, 1962.

Moore, Gerald. *Farewell recital: further memoirs.* Harmondsworth: Penguin Books, 1979.

Moore, Gerald. *Furthermoore: interludes in an accompanist's life.* London: Hamish Hamilton, 1983.

Moore, Jerrold Northrop. *Edward Elgar: a creative life.* Oxford: Oxford University Press, 1984.

Moore, Jerrold Northrop. *Elgar, Edward. The windflower letters: correspondence with Alice Caroline Stuart Wortley and her family.* Oxford: Clarendon Press; New York: Oxford University Press, 1989.

Moore, Jerrold Northrop. *Elgar, Edward. Edward Elgar: letters of a lifetime.* Oxford: Clarendon Press; New York: Oxford University Press, 1990.

Moore, Jerrold Northrop. *Elgar, Edward. Elgar and his publishers: letters of a creative life.* Oxford: Clarendon, 1987.

Moreux, Serge. *Béla Bartók.* London: Harvill Press, 1953.

Morgan, Kenneth. *Fritz Reiner, maestro and martinet.* Urbana: University of Illinois Press, 2005.

Cone, Edward T., Editor. *Music, a view from Delft: selected essays.* Chicago: University of Chicago Press, 1989.

Morgan, Robert P. *Twentieth-century music: a history of musical style in modern Europe and America.* New York: Norton, 1991.

Morgenstern, Sam., Editor. *Composers on music: an anthology of composers' writings.* London: Faber & Faber, 1956.

Morrow, Mary Sue. *Concert life in Haydn's Vienna: aspects of a developing musical and social*

institution. Stuyvesant, New York: Pendragon Press, 1989.
Moscheles, Felix, Editor and Translator. *Letters from Felix Mendelssohn-Bartholdy to Ignaz and Charlotte Moscheles.* London: Trübner and Co., 1888.
Mudge, Richard B., Translator. *Glinka, Mikhail Ivanovich: Memoirs.* Norman: University of Oklahoma Press, 1963.
Munch, Charles. *I am a conductor.* New York: Oxford University Press, 1955.
Mundy, Simon. *Bernard Haitink: a working life.* London: Robson Books, 1987.
Musgrave, Michael. *The musical life of the Crystal Palace.* Cambridge: Cambridge University Press, 1995.
Music & Letters. *Beethoven: special number.* London: Music & Letters, 1927.
Musical Times. *Special Issue.* John A. Fuller-Maitland London: Vol. VIII, No. 2, 1927.
Myers, Rollo H., Editor. *Twentieth-century music.* London: Calder and Boyars, 1960.
National Gallery (Great Britain). *Music performed at the National Gallery concerts, 10th October 1939 to 10th April 1946.* London: Privately printed, 1948.
Nattiez, Jean-Jacques, Editor. *Orientations: collected writings — Pierre Boulez.* London: Faber and Faber, 1986.
Nauhaus, Gerd, Editor. *The marriage diaries of Robert & Clara Schumann.* London: Robson Books, 1994.
Nectoux, Jean Michel. *Gabriel Fauré: a musical life.* Translated by Roger Nichols. Cambridge: Cambridge University Press, 1991.
Nettl, Paul. *Beethoven handbook.* Westport, Connecticut: Greenwood Press, 1975.
Neumayr, Anton. *Music and medicine.* Bloomington, Illinois: Medi-Ed Press, 1994–1997
Newbould, Brian. *Schubert and the symphony: a new perspective.* Surbiton: Toccata Press, 1992.
Newlin, Dika. *Schoenberg remembered: diaries and recollections (1938–76).* New York: Pendragon Press, 1980.
Newman, Ernest. *From the world of music: essays from 'The Sunday Times'.* London: J. Calder, 1956.
Newman, Ernest. *Hugo Wolf.* New York: Dover Publications, 1966.
Newman, Ernest, Annotated and Translated. *Memoirs of Hector Berlioz from 1803 to 1865, comprising his travels in Germany, Italy, Russia, and England.* New York: Knopf, 1932.
Newman, Ernest. *More essays from the world of music: essays from the 'Sunday Times'.* London: John Calder, 1958.
Newman, Ernest. *Musical studies.* London; New York: John Lane, 1910.
Newman, Ernest. *Testament of music: essays and papers.* London: Putnam, 1962.
Newman, Richard. *Alma Rosé: Vienna to Auschwitz.* Portland, Oregon: Amadeus Press, 2000.
Newman, William S. *The sonata in the classic era.* Chapel Hill: University of North Carolina Press 1963.
Newman, William S. *The sonata in the Classic era.* New York; London: W.W. Norton, 1983.
Newmarch, Rosa Harriet. *Henry J. Wood.* London & New York: John Lane, 1904.
Nicholas, Jeremy. *Godowsky: the pianists' pianist; a biography of Leopold Godowsky.* Hexham: Appian Publications & Recordings, 1989.
Nichols, Roger. *Debussy remembered.* London: Faber and Faber, 1992.
Nichols, Roger. *Mendelssohn remembered.* London: Faber and Faber, 1997.
Nichols, Roger. *Ravel remembered.* London: Faber and Faber, 1987.
Niecks, Frederick. *Robert Schumann.* London: J. M. Dent,

1925.

Nielsen, Carl. *Living music.* Copenhagen, Wilhelm Hansen, 1968.

Nielsen, Carl. *My childhood.* Copenhagen, Wilhelm Hansen, 1972.

Nikolska, Irina. *Conversations with Witold Lutoslawski, (1987–92).* Stockholm: Melos, 1994.

Nohl, Ludwig. *Beethoven depicted by his contemporaries.* London: Reeves, 1880.

De Nora, Tia. *Beethoven and the construction of genius: musical politics in Vienna, 1792–1803.* Berkeley: University of California Press, 1997.

Norton, Spencer, Editor and Translator. *Music in my time: the memoirs of Alfredo Casella.* Norman: University of Oklahoma Press, 1955.

Nottebohm, Gustav. *Two Beethoven sketchbooks: a description with musical extracts.* London: Gollancz, 1979.

Oakeley, Edward Murray. *The life of Sir Herbert Stanley Oakeley.* London: George Allen, 1904.

Lucas, Brenda and Michael Kerr. *Virtuoso: the story of John Ogdon.* London: H. Hamilton, 1981.

Oliver, Michael, Editor. *Settling the score: a journey through the music of the twentieth century.* London: Faber and Faber, 1999.

Olleson, Philip. *Samuel Wesley: the man and his music.* Woodbridge: Boydell Press, 2003.

Olleson, Philip, Editor. *The letters of Samuel Wesley: professional and social correspondence, 1797–1837.* Oxford; New York: Oxford University Press, 2001.

Olmstead, Andrea. *Conversations with Roger Sessions.* Boston: Northeastern University Press, 1987.

Orenstein, Arbie, Editor. *A Ravel reader: correspondence, articles, interviews.* New York: Columbia University Press, 1990.

Orenstein, Arbie. *Ravel: man and musician.* New York: Columbia University Press, 1975.

Orledge, Robert. *Charles Koechlin (1867–1950): his life and works.* New York: Harwood Academic Publishers, 1989.

Orledge, Robert. *Gabriel Fauré.* London: Eulenburg Books, 1979.

Orledge, Robert. *Satie remembered.* London: Faber and Faber, 1995.

Orledge, Robert. *Satie the composer.* Cambridge: Cambridge University Press, 1990.

Orlova, Alexandra. *Glinka's life in music: a chronicle.* Ann Arbor: UMI Research Press, 1988.

Orlova, Alexandra. *Musorgsky's days and works: a biography in documents.* Ann Arbor: UMI Research Press, 1983.

Orlova, Alexandra. *Tchaikovsky: a self-portrait.* Oxford: Oxford University Press, 1990.

Osborne, Charles, Editor and Translator. *Letters of Giuseppe Verdi.* London: Victor Gollancz, 1971.

Osmond-Smith David, Editor and Translator. *Luciano Berio: Two interviews with Rossana Dalmonte and Bálint András Varga.* New York; London: Boyars, 1985.

Ouellette, Fernand. *Edgard Varèse.* London: Calder & Boyars, 1973.

Paderewski, Ignacy Jan and Mary Lawton. *The Paderewski memoirs.* London: Collins, 1939.

Page, Tim: Editor. *The Glenn Gould reader.* London: Faber and Faber, 1987.

Page, Tim. *Music from the road: views and reviews, 1978–1992.* New York; Oxford: Oxford University Press, 1992.

Page, Tim and Vanessa Weeks, Editors. *Selected letters of Virgil Thomson.* New York: Summit Books, 1988.

Page, Tim. *Tim Page on music: views and reviews.* Portland, Oregon: Amadeus Press, 2002.

Palmer, Christopher. *Herbert Howells, (1892–1983): a celebration.* London: Thames, 1996.

Palmer, Christopher, Editor. *Sergei Prokofiev: Soviet diary 1927 and*

other writings. London: Faber and Faber, 1991.
Palmer, Fiona M. *Domenico Dragonetti in England (1794–1846): the career of a double bass virtuoso*. Oxford: Clarendon, 1997.
Palmieri, Robert, Editor. *Encyclopedia of the piano*. New York: Garland, 1996.
Panufnik, Andrzej. *Composing myself*. London: Methuen, 1987.
Parsons, James, Editor. *The Cambridge companion to the Lied*. Cambridge: Cambridge University Press, 2004.
Paynter, John, Editor. *Between old worlds and new: occasional writings on music by Wilfrid Mellers*. London: Cygnus Arts, 1997.
Pestelli, Giorgio. *The age of Mozart and Beethoven*. Cambridge: Cambridge University Press, 1984.
Peyser, Joan. *Bernstein: a biography: revised & updated*. New York: Billboard Books, 1998.
Phillips-Matz, Mary Jane. *Verdi: a biography*. Oxford: Oxford University Press, 1993.
Piggott, Patrick. *The life and music of John Field, 1782–1837: creator of the nocturne*. London: Faber and Faber, 1973.
Plantinga, Leon. *Beethoven's concertos: history, style, performance*. New York: Norton, 1999.
Plantinga, Leon. *Clementi: his life and music*. London: Oxford University Press, 1977.
Plantinga, Leon. *Romantic music: a history of musical style in nineteenth-century Europe*. New York; London: Norton, 1984.
Plaskin, Glenn. *Horowitz: a biography of Vladimir Horowitz*. London: Macdonald, 1983.
Pleasants, Henry, Editor and Translator. *Hanslick, Eduard: Music criticisms, 1846–99*. Baltimore: Penguin Books, 1963.
Pleasants, Henry, Editor and Translator. *Hanslick's music criticisms*. New York: Dover Publications, 1988.
Pleasants, Henry, Editor and Translator. *The music criticism of Hugo Wolf*. New York: Holmes & Meier Publishers, 1978.
Pleasants, Henry, Editor and Translator. *The musical journeys of Louis Spohr*. Norman: University of Oklahoma Press, 1961.
Pollack, Howard. *Aaron Copland: the life and work of an uncommon man*. New York: Henry Holt, 1999.
Poulenc, Francis. *My friends and myself*. London: Dennis Dobson, 1978.
Powell, Richard, Mrs. *Edward Elgar: memories of a variation*. Aldershot, Hants, England: Scolar Press; Brookfield, Vermont, USA: Ashgate Publishing. Co., 1994.
Poznansky, Alexander, Editor. *Tchaikovsky through others' eyes*. Bloomington: Indiana University Press, 1999.
Praeger, Ferdinand. *Wagner as I knew him*. London; New York: Longmans, Green, 1892.
Previn, Andre. *Antony Hopkins. Music face to face*. London, Hamish Hamilton, 1971.
Prieberg, Fred K. *Trial of strength: Wilhelm Furtwängler and the Third Reich*. London: Quartet, 1991.
Procter-Gregg, Humphrey. *Beecham remembered*. London: Duckworth, 1976.
Prokofiev, Sergey. *Prokofiev by Prokofiev: a composer's memoir*. London: Macdonald and Jane's, 1979.
Rachmaninoff, Sergei. *Rachmaninoff's recollections told to Oskar von Riesemann*. London: George Allen & Unwin, 1934.
Radcliffe, Philip. *Beethoven's string quartets*. Cambridge: Cambridge University Press, 1978.
Radcliffe, Philip. *Piano Music in: The Age of Beethoven, The New Oxford History of Music, Vol. VIII*. Gerald Abraham, (Editor), 1988, p. 340.
Ratner, Leonard G. *Romantic music: sound and syntax*. New York:

Schirmer Books, 1992.
Raynor, Henry. *A social history of music: from the middle ages to Beethoven.* London: Barrie & Jenkins, 1972.
Rees, Brian. *Camille Saint-Saëns: a life.* London: Chatto & Windus, 1999.
Reich, Willi, Editor. *Anton Webern: The path to the new music.* London; Bryn Mawr: Theodore Presser in association with Universal Edition, 1963.
Reid, Charles. *John Barbirolli: a biography.* London, Hamish Hamilton, 1971.
Reid, Charles. *Malcolm Sargent: a biography.* London: Hamilton, 1968.
Rennert, Jonathan. *William Crotch (1775-1847): composer, artist, teacher.* Lavenham: Terence Dalton, 1975.
Rice, John A. *Antonio Salieri and Viennese Opera.* Chicago, Illinois: University of Chicago Press, 1998.
Rice, John A. *Empress Marie Therese and music at the Viennese court, 1792-1807.* Cambridge: Cambridge University Press, 2003.
Richards, Fiona. *The Music of John Ireland.* Aldershot: Ashgate, 2000.
Rigby, Charles. *Sir Charles Hallé: a portrait for today.* Manchester: Dolphin Press, 1952.
Ringer, Alexander, Editor. *The early Romantic era: between Revolutions; 1789 and 1848.* Basingstoke: Macmillan, 1990.
Roberts, John P.L. and Ghyslaine Guertin, Editors. *Glenn Gould: Selected letters.* Toronto; Oxford: Oxford University Press, 1992.
Robertson, Alec. *More than music.* London: Collins, 1961.
Robinson, Harlow, Editor and Translator. *Selected letters of Sergei Prokofiev.* Boston: Northeastern University Press, 1998.
Robinson, Harlow. *Sergei Prokofiev: a biography.* London: Hale, 1987.
Robinson, Paul A. *Ludwig van Beethoven, Fidelio.* Cambridge: Cambridge University Press, 1996.
Robinson, Suzanne, Editor. *Michael Tippett: music and literature.* Aldershot: Ashgate, 2002.
Rochberg, George. *The aesthetics of survival: a composer's view of twentieth-century music.* Ann Arbor, Michigan: University of Michigan Press, 2004.
Rodmell, Paul. *Charles Villiers Stanford.* Aldershot: Ashgate, 2002.
Roeder, Michael Thomas. *A history of the concerto.* Portland, Oregon: Amadeus Press, 1994.
Rohr, Deborah Adams. *The careers of British musicians, 1750-1850: a profession of artisans.* Cambridge: Cambridge University Press, 2001.
Rolland, Romain. *Goethe and Beethoven.* New York; London: Blom, 1968.
Rolland, Romain. *Beethoven and Handel.* London: Waverley Book Co., 1917.
Rolland, Romain. *Beethoven the creator.* Garden City, New York: Garden City Pub., 1937.
Roscow, Gregory, Editor. *Bliss on music: selected writings of Arthur Bliss, 1920-1975.* Oxford: Oxford University Press, 1991.
Rosen, Charles. *Beethoven's piano sonatas: a short companion.* New Haven, Connecticut: London: Yale University Press, 2002.
Rosen, Charles. *Critical entertainments: music old and new.* Cambridge, Massachusetts; London: Harvard University Press, 2000.
Rosen, Charles. *The classical style: Haydn, Mozart, Beethoven.* London: Faber and Faber, 1976.
Rosen, Charles. *The romantic generation.* Cambridge, Massachusetts: Harvard University Press, 1995.
Rosenthal, Albi. *Obiter scripta: essays, lectures, articles, interviews and reviews on music, and

other subjects. Oxford: Offox Press; Lanham: Scarecrow Press, 2000.

Rostal, Max. *Beethoven: the sonatas for piano and violin; thoughts on their interpretation.* London: Toccata Press, 1985.

Rostropovich, Mstislav and Galina Vishnevskaya. *Russia, music, and liberty.* Portland, Oregan: Amadeus Press, 1995.

Rubinstein, Arthur. *My many years.* London: Jonathan Cape, 1980.

Rubinstein, Arthur. *My young years.* London: Jonathan Cape, 1973.

Rumph, Stephen C. *Beethoven after Napoleon: political romanticism in the late works.* Berkeley; London: University of California Press, 2004.

Rye, Matthew Rye. *Notes to the BBC Radio Three Beethoven Experience, Friday 10 June 2005,* www.bbc.co.uk/radio3/Beethoven.

Sachs, Harvey. *Toscanini.* London: Weidenfeld and Nicholson, 1978.

Sachs, Joel. *Kapellmeister Hummel in England and France.* Detroit: Information Coordinators, 1977.

Saffle, Michael, Editor. *Liszt and his world: proceedings of the International Liszt Conference held at Virginia Polytechnic Institute and State University, 20—23 May 1993.* Stuyvesant, New York: Pendragon Press, 1998.

Safránek, Milos. *Bohuslav Martinu, his life and works.* London: Allan Wingate, 1962.

Saint-Saëns, Camille. *Outspoken essays on music.* Westport, Connecticut: Greenwood Press, 1970.

Saussine, Renée de. *Paganini.* Westport, Connecticut: Greenwood Press, 1976.

Sayers, W. C. Berwick. *Samuel Coleridge-Taylor, musician: his life and letters.* London; New York: Cassell and Co., 1915.

Schaarwächter, Jürgen. *HB: aspects of Havergal Brian.* Aldershot: Ashgate, 1997.

Schafer, R. Murray. *E.T.A. Hoffmann and music.* Toronto: University of Toronto Press, 1975.

Schafer, R. Murray, Editor. *Ezra Pound and music: the complete criticism.* London: Faber and Faber, 1978.

Schat, Peter. *The tone clock.* Chur, Switzerland; Langhorne, Pa.: Harwood Academic Publishers, 1993.

Schenk, Erich. *Mozart and his times.* Edited and Translated by Richard and Clara Winstin. London: Secker & Warburg, 1960.

Schindler, Anton Felix. *Beethoven as I knew him.* Edited by Donald W. MacArdle and Translated by Constance S. Jolly from the German edition of 1860 London: Faber and Faber, 1966.

Schlosser, Johann. *Beethoven: the first biography, 1827.* Edited by Barry Cooper. Portland, Oregon: Amadeus Press, 1996.

Schnabel, Artur. *My life and music.* London: Longmans, 1961.

Schnittke, Alfred. *A Schnittke reader.* Bloomington: Indiana University Press, 2002.

Scholes, Percy Alfred. *Crotchets: a few short musical notes.* London: John Lane, 1924.

Schonberg, Harold C. *The great pianists.* London: Victor Gollancz, 1964.

Schrade, Leo. *Beethoven in France: the growth of an idea.* New Haven; London: Yale University Press, H. Milford, Oxford University Press, 1942.

Schrade, Leo. *Tragedy in the art of music.* Cambridge, Massachusetts: Harvard University Press, 1964.

Schuh, Willi. *Richard Strauss: a chronicle of the early years 1864—1898.* Cambridge: Cambridge University Press, 1982.

Schuh, Willi, Editor. *Richard Strauss: Recollections and reflections.* London; New York: Boosey & Hawkes, 1953.

Schuller, Gunther. *Musings: the*

musical worlds of Gunther Schuller. New York: Oxford University Press, 1986.

Schumann, Robert. *Music and musicians: essays and criticisms.* London: William Reeves, 1877.

Schuttenhelm, Editor. *Selected letters of Michael Tippett.* London: Faber and Faber, 2005.

Schwartz, Elliott. *Music since 1945: issues, materials, and literature.* New York: Schirmer Books, 1993.

Scott, Marion M. *Beethoven: (The master musicians).* London: Dent, 1940.

Scott-Sutherland, Colin. *Arnold Bax.* London: J. M. Dent, 1973.

Searle, Muriel V. *John Ireland: the man and his music.* Tunbridge Wells: Midas Books, 1979.

Secrest, Meryle. *Leonard Bernstein: a life.* London: Bloomsbury, 1995.

Seeger, Charles. *Studies in musicology II, 1929–1979.* Edited by Anne M. Pescatello. Berkeley; London: University of California Press, 1994.

Selden-Goth, Gisela, Editor. *Felix Mendelssohn: letters.* London: Paul Elek Publishers Ltd, 1946.

Senner, Wayne M., Robin Wallace and William Meredith, Editors. *The critical reception of Beethoven's compositions by his German contemporaries.* Lincoln: University of Nebraska Press, in association with the American Beethoven Society and the Ira F. Brilliant Center for Beethoven Studies, San José State University, 1999.

Seroff, Victor I. *Rachmaninoff.* London: Cassell & Company, 1951.

Sessions, Roger. *Questions about music.* Cambridge, Massachusetts: Harvard University Press, 1970.

Sessions, Roger. *The musical experience of composer, performer, listener.* New York: Atheneum, 1966, 1950.

Seyfried, Ignaz von. *Louis van Beethoven's Studies in thoroughbass, counterpoint and the art of scientific composition.* Leipzig; New-York: Schuberth and Company, 1853.

Sharma, Bhesham R. *Music and culture in the age of mechanical reproduction.* New York: Peter Lang, 2000.

Shaw, Bernard. *How to become a musical critic.* London: R. Hart Davis, 1960.

Shaw, Bernard. *London music in 1888–89 as heard by Corno di Bassetto (later known as Bernard Shaw): with some further autobiographical particulars.* London: Constable and Company, 1937.

Shaw, Bernard. *Music in London, 1890–1894.* London: Constable and Company Limited, 3 Vols., 1932.

Shedlock, John South. *Beethoven's pianoforte sonatas: the origin and respective values of various readings.* London: Augener Ltd., 1918.

Shedlock, John South. *The pianoforte sonata: its origin and development.* London: Methuen, 1895.

Shepherd, Arthur. *The string quartets of Ludwig van Beethoven.* Cleveland: H. Carr, The Printing Press, 1935.

Sheppard, Leslie and Herbert R. Axelrod. *Paganini: containing a portfolio of drawings by Vido Polikarpus.* Neptune City, New Jersey: Paganiniana Publications, 1979.

Short, Michael. *Gustav Holst: the man and his music.* Oxford: Oxford University Press, 1990.

Shostakovich, Dmitry. *Dmitry Shostakovich: about himself and his times.* Moscow: Progress Publishers, 1981.

Simpson, John Palgrave. *Carl Maria von Weber: the life of an artist, from the German of his son Baron, Max Maria von Weber.* London: Chapman and Hall, 1865.

Simpson, Robert. *Beethoven sym-*

phonies. London: British Broadcasting Corporation, 1970.

Sipe, Thomas. *Beethoven: Eroica symphony*. Cambridge: Cambridge University Press, 1998.

Sitwell, Sacheverell. *Mozart*. Edinburgh: Peter Davies Limited, 1932.

Skelton, Geoffrey. *Paul Hindemith: the man behind the music; a biography*. London: Victor Gollancz, 1975.

Smallman, Basil. *The piano trio: its history, technique, and repertoire*. Oxford: Clarendon Press; Oxford; New York: Oxford University Press, 1990.

Smidak, Emil. *Isaak-Ignaz Moscheles: the life of the composer and his encounters with Beethoven, Liszt, Chopin, and Mendelssohn*. Aldershot, Hampshire, England: Scolar Press; Brookfield, Vermont, USA: Gower Publishing Co., 1989.

Smith, Barry. *Peter Warlock: the life of Philip Heseltine*. Oxford: Oxford University Press, 1994.

Smith, Joan Allen. *Schoenberg and his circle: a Viennese portrait*. New York: Schirmer Books, London: Collier Macmillan, 1986.

Smith, Richard Langham, Editor. *Debussy on music: the critical writings of the great French composer Claude Debussy*. London: Secker & Warburg, 1977.

Smith, Ronald. *Alkan*. London: Kahn and Averill, 1976.

Snowman, Daniel. *The Amadeus Quartet: the men and the music*. London: Robson Books, 1981.

Solomon, Maynard. *Beethoven*. New York: Schirmer, 1977.

Solomon, Maynard. *Beethoven essays*. Cambridge, Massachusetts; London: Harvard University Press, 1988.

Solomon, Maynard. *Late Beethoven: music, thought, imagination*. Berkeley; London: University of California Press, 2003.

Solomon, Maynard. *Mozart: a life*. London: Hutchinson, 1995.

Sonneck, Oscar George Theodore. *Beethoven: impressions of contemporaries*. London: Oxford University Press, 1927.

Spalding, Albert. *Rise to follow: an autobiography*. London: Frederick Muller Ltd., 1946.

Spohr, Louis. *Louis Spohr's autobiography*. London: Longman, Green, Longman, Roberts, & Green, 1865.

Stafford, William. *Mozart myths: a critical reassessment*. Stanford, California: Stanford University Press, 1991.

Stanford, Charles Villiers. *Interludes: records and reflections*. London: John Murray, 1922.

Stanley, Glenn, Editor. *The Cambridge companion to Beethoven*. Cambridge; New York: Cambridge University Press, 2000

Stedman, Preston. *The symphony*. Englewood Cliffs, New Jersey; London: Prentice-Hall, 1979.

Stedron, Bohumír, Editor and Translator. *Leos Janácek: letters and reminiscences*. Prague: Artia, 1955.

Stein, Erwin, Editor. *Arnold Schoenberg: letters*. London: Faber and Faber, 1964.

Stein, Erwin. *Orpheus in new guises*. London: Rockliff, 1953.

Stein, Jack Madison. *Poem and music in the German lied from Gluck to Hugo Wolf*. Cambridge, Massachusetts: Harvard University Press, 1971.

Stein, Leonard, Editor. *Style and idea: selected writings of Arnold Schoenberg*. London: Faber and Faber, 1975.

Steinberg, Michael P. *Listening to reason: culture, subjectivity, and nineteenth-century music*. Princeton, New Jersey: Princeton University Press, 2004.

Steinberg, Michael. *The concerto: a listener's guide*. New York: Oxford University Press, 1998.

Steinberg, Michael. *The symphony: a listener's guide*. Oxford; New York: Oxford University Press, 1995.

Sternfeld, Frederick William. *Goethe and music: a list of parodies and Goethe's relationship to music; a list of references.* New York: Da Capo Press, 1979.

Stivender, David. *Mascagni: an autobiography compiled, edited and translated from original sources.* New York: Pro/Am Music Resources; London: Kahn & Averill, 1988.

Stone, Else and Kurt Stone, Editors. *The writings of Elliott Carter: an American composer looks at modern music.* Bloomington: Indiana University Press, 1977.

Stowell, Robin. *Beethoven: violin concerto.* Cambridge: Cambridge University Press, 1998.

Stowell, Robin: Editor. *The Cambridge companion to the cello.* Cambridge: Cambridge University Press, 1999.

Stowell, Robin: Editor. *The Cambridge companion to the string quartet.* Cambridge: Cambridge University Press, 2003.

Stratton, Stephen Samuel. *Mendelssohn.* London: J.M. Dent & Co.; New York: E.P. Dutton & Co., 1901.

Straus, Joseph N. *Remaking the past: musical modernism and the influence of the tonal tradition.* Cambridge, Massachusetts: Harvard University Press, 1990.

Stravinsky, Igor. *An autobiography.* London: Calder and Boyars, 1975.

Stravinsky, Igor. *Themes and conclusions.* London: Faber and Faber, 1972.

Stravinsky, Igor and Robert Craft. *Conversations with Igor Stravinsky.* London: Faber and Faber, 1959.

Stravinsky, Igor and Robert Craft. *Dialogues and a diary.* London: Faber and Faber 1968.

Stravinsky, Igor and Robert Craft. *Memories and commentaries.* London: Faber and Faber, 2002.

Strunk, Oliver. *Source readings in music history, 4: The Classic era.* London: Faber and Faber 1981.

Sullivan, Blair, Editor. *The echo of music: essays in honor of Marie Louise Göllner.* Warren, Michigan: Harmonie Park Press, 2004.

Sullivan, Jack, Editor. *Words on music: from Addison to Barzun.* Athens: Ohio University Press, 1990.

Symonette, Lys and Kim H. Kowalke, Editors and Translators. *Speak low (when you speak love): the letters of Kurt Weill and Lotte Lenya.* London: Hamish Hamilton, 1996.

Swalin, Benjamin F. *The violin concerto: a study in German romanticism.* New York, Da Capo Press, 1973.

Szigeti, Joseph. *With strings attached: reminiscences and reflections.* London: Cassell & Co. Ltd, 1949.

Tanner, Michael, Editor. *Notebooks, 1924–1954: Wilhelm Furtwängler.* London: Quartet Books, 1989.

Taylor, Robert, Editor. *Furtwängler on music: essays and addresses.* Aldershot: Scolar, 1991.

Taylor, Ronald. *Kurt Weill: composer in a divided world.* London: Simon & Schuster, 1991.

Tchaikovsky, Peter Ilich. *Letters to his family: an autobiography.* Translated by Galina von Meck. London: Dennis Dobson, 1981.

Tertis, Lionel. *My viola and I: a complete autobiography; with, 'Beauty of tone in string playing', and other essays.* London: Paul Elek, 1974.

Thayer, Alexander Wheelock. *Salieri: rival of Mozart.* Edited by Theodore Albrecht. Kansas City, Missouri: Philharmonia of Greater Kansas City, 1989.

Thomas, Michael Tilson. *Viva voce: conversations with Edward Seckerson.* London: Faber and Faber 1994.

Thomson, Andrew. *Vincent d'Indy and his world.* Oxford: Clarendon Press, 1996.

Thomson, Virgil. *The musical scene.*

New York: Greenwood Press, 1968.

Thomson, Virgil. *Virgil Thomson*. London: Weidenfeld & Nicolson, 1967.

Tillard, Françoise. *Fanny Mendelssohn*. Amadeus Press: Portland, 1996.

Tilmouth, Michael, Editor. *Donald Francis Tovey: The classics of music: talks, essays, and other writings previously uncollected*. Oxford: Oxford University Press, 2001

Tippett, Michael. *Moving into Aquarius*. London: Routledge and Kegan Paul, 1959.

Tippett, Michael. *Those twentieth century blues: an autobiography*. London: Hutchinson, 1991.

Todd, R. Larry, Editor. *Nineteenth-century piano music*. New York; London: Routledge, 2004.

Todd, R. Larry, Editor. *Schumann and his world*. Princeton: Princeton University Press, 1994.

Tommasini, Anthony. *Virgil Thomson: composer on the aisle*. New York: W.W. Norton, 1997.

Tortelier, Paul. *A self-portrait: in conversation with David Blum*. London: Heinemann, 1984.

Tovey, Donald Francis. *A Companion to Beethoven's Pianoforte Sonatas*. Revised by Barry Cooper. London: The Associated Board, [1931], 1998.

Tovey, Donald Francis. *Beethoven*. London: Oxford University Press, 1944.

Tovey, Donald Francis. *Essays and lectures on music*. London: Oxford University Press, 1949.

Tovey, Donald Francis. *Essays in musical analysis*. London: Oxford University Press, H. Milford, 7 Vols., 1935–41.

Tovey, Donald Francis. *The forms of music: musical articles from The Encyclopaedia Britannica*. London: Oxford University Press, 1944.

Toye, Francis. *Giuseppe Verdi: his life and works*. London: William Heinemann Ltd., 1931.

Truscott, Harold. *Beethoven's late string quartets*. London: Dobson, 1968.

Tyler, William R. *The letters of Franz Liszt to Olga von Meyendorff, 1871–1886, in the Mildred Bliss Collection at Dumbarton Oaks*. Translated by William R. Tyler. Washington: Dumbarton Oaks, Trustees for Harvard University; Cambridge, Massachusetts: distributed by Harvard University Press, 1979.

Tyrrell, John. *Janácek: years of a life. Vol. 1, (1854–1914) The lonely blackbird*. London: Faber and Faber, 2006.

Tyrrell, John, Editor and Translator. *My life with Janácek: the memoirs of Zdenka Janácková*. London: Faber and Faber, 1998.

Tyson, Alan, Editor. *Beethoven studies 2*. Cambridge: Cambridge University Press, 1977.

Tyson, Alan, Editor. *Beethoven studies 3*. Cambridge: Cambridge University Press, 1982.

Tyson, Alan. *Mozart: studies of the autograph scores*. Cambridge, Massachusetts; London: Harvard University Press, 1987.

Tyson, Alan. *The authentic English editions of Beethoven*. London: Faber and Faber, 1963.

Underwood, J. A., Editor. *Gabriel Fauré: his life through his letters*. London: Marion Boyars, 1984.

Vechten, Carl van, Editor. *Nikolay, Rimsky-Korsakov: My musical life*. London: Martin Secker & Warburg Ltd., 1942.

Vinton, John. *Essays after a dictionary: music and culture at the close of Western civilization*. Lewisburg: Bucknell University Press, 1977.

Volkov, Solomon, Editor. *Testimony: the memoirs of Dmitri Shostakovich*. London: Faber and Faber, 1981.

Volta, Ornella, Editor. *A mammal's notebook: collected writings of Erik Satie*. London: Atlas Press, 1996.

Wagner, Richard. Beethoven: *With [a]*

supplement from the philosophical works of A. Schopenhauer. Translated by E. Dannreuther. London: Reeves, 1893.

Wagner, Richard. *My life*. London: Constable and Company Ltd., 1911.

Walden, Valerie. *One hundred years of violoncello: a history of technique and performance practice, 1740–1840*. Cambridge: Cambridge University Press, 1998.

Walker, Alan. *Franz Liszt. Volume 1, The virtuoso years: 1811–1847*. New York: Alfred A. Knopf, 1983.

Walker, Alan. *Franz Liszt. Volume 2, The Weimar years: 1848–1861*. London: Faber and Faber, 1989.

Walker, Alan. *Franz Liszt. Volume 3, The final years, 1861–1886*. London: Faber and Faber, 1997.

Walker, Bettina. *My musical experiences*. London: Richard Bentley and Son, 1890.

Walker, Ernest. *Free thought and the musician, and other essays*. London; New York: Oxford University Press, 1946.

Walker, Frank. *Hugo Wolf: a biography*. London: J. M. Dent, 1951.

Walker, Frank. *The man Verdi*. London: Dent, 1962.

Wallace, Grace, [Lady Wallace]. *Beethoven's letters (1790–1826): from the collection of Dr. Ludwig Nohl. Also his letters to the Archduke Rudolph, Cardinal-Archbishop of Olmutz, K.W., from the collection of Dr. Ludwig Ritter Von Kolchel*. London: Longmans, Green, 2 Vols., 1866.

Wallace, Robin. *Beethoven's critics: aesthetic dilemmas and resolutions during the composer's lifetime*. Cambridge; New York: Cambridge University Press, 1986.

Walter, Bruno. *Theme and variations: an autobiography*. London: H. Hamilton, 1948.

Warrack, John Hamilton. *Writings on music*. Cambridge: Cambridge University Press, 1981.

Wasielewski, Wilhelm Joseph von. *Life of Robert Schumann: with letters, 1833–1852*. London: William Reeves, 1878.

Watkins, Glenn. *Proof through the night: music and the Great War*. Berkeley: University of California Press, 2003.

Watkins, Glenn. *Pyramids at the Louvre: music, culture, and collage from Stravinsky to the postmodernists*. Cambridge, Massachusetts; London: Belknap Press of Harvard University Press, 1994.

Watkins, Glenn. *Soundings: music in the twentieth century*. New York: Schirmer Books London: Collier Macmillan, 1988.

Watson, Derek. *Liszt*. London: J. M. Dent, 1989.

Weaver, William, Editor. *The Verdi-Boito correspondence*. Chicago; London: University of Chicago Press, 1994.

Wegeler, Franz. *Remembering Beethoven: the biographical notes of Franz Wegeler and Ferdinand Ries*. London: Andre Deutsch, 1988.

Weingartner, Felix. *Buffets and rewards: a musician's reminiscences*. London: Hutchinson & Co., 1937.

Weinstock, Herbert. *Rossini: a biography*. New York: Limelight, 1987.

Weiss, Piero and Richard Taruskin. *Music in the Western World: a history in documents*. New York: Schirmer; London: Collier Macmillan, 1984.

Weissweiler, Eva *The complete correspondence of Clara and Robert Schumann*. New York: Peter Lang, 2 Vols., 1994.

Whittaker, William Gillies. *Collected essays*. London: Oxford University Press, 1940.

Whittall, Arnold. *Exploring twentieth-century music: tradition and innovation*. Cambridge; New York: Cambridge University Press, 2003.

Whittall, Arnold. *Music since the First World War.* London: J. M. Dent, 1977.

Whitton, Kenneth S. *Lieder: an introduction to German song.* London: Julia MacRae, 1984.

Wightman, Alistair, Editor. *Szymanowski on music: selected writings of Karol Szymanowski.* London: Toccata Press, 1999.

Wilhelm, Kurt. *Richard Strauss: an intimate portrait.* London: Thames and Hudson, 1999.

Will, Richard James. *The characteristic symphony in the age of Haydn and Beethoven.* Cambridge: Cambridge University Press, 2002.

Willetts, Pamela J. *Beethoven and England: an account of sources in the British Museum.* London: British Museum, 1970.

Williams, Adrian, Editor and Translator. *Liszt, Franz: Selected letters.* Oxford: Clarendon Press, 1998.

Williams, Adrian. *Portrait of Liszt: by himself and his contemporaries.* Oxford: Clarendon Press, 1990.

Williams, Ralph Vaughan. *Heirs and rebels: letters written to each other and occasional writings on music.* London; New York: Oxford University Press, 1959.

Williams, Ralph Vaughan. *Some thoughts on Beethoven's Choral symphony: with writings on other musical subjects.* London; Oxford University Press, 1953.

Williams, Ralph Vaughan. *The making of music.* Ithaca, New York: Cornell University Press, 1955.

Williams, Ursula Vaughan. *R.V.W.: a biography of Ralph Vaughan Williams.* London: Oxford University Press, 1964.

Wilson, Conrad. *Notes on Beethoven: 20 crucial works.* Edinburgh: Saint Andrew Press, 2003.

Wilson, Elizabeth. *Shostakovich: a life remembered.* Princeton, New Jersey: Princeton University Press, 1994.

Winter, Robert, Editor. *Beethoven, performers, and critics: the International Beethoven Congress, Detroit, 1977.* Detroit: Wayne State University Press, 1980.

Winter, Robert. *Compositional origins of Beethoven's opus 131.* Ann Arbor, Michigan: UMI Research Press, 1982.

Winter, Robert and Robert Martin, Editors. *The Beethoven quartet companion.* Berkeley: University of California Press, 1994.

Wolf, Eugene K. and Edward H. Roesner, Editors. *Studies in musical sources and style: essays in honor of Jan LaRue.* Madison, Wisconsin: A-R Editions, 1990.

Wolff, Christoph and Robert Riggs. *The string quartets of Haydn, Mozart and Beethoven: studies of the autograph manuscripts: a conference at Isham Memorial Library, March 15–17, 1979.* Cambridge, Massachusetts: Department of Music, Harvard University, 1980.

Wolff, Konrad. *Masters of the keyboard: individual style elements in the piano music of Bach, Haydn, Mozart, Beethoven, Schubert, Chopin, and Brahms.* Bloomington: Indiana University Press, 1990.

Wörner, Karl Heinrich. *Stockhausen: life and work.* London: Faber, 1973.

Wright, Donald, Editor. *Cardus on music: a centenary collection.* London: Hamish Hamilton, 1988.

Wyndham, Henry Saxe. *August Manns and the Saturday concerts: a memoir and a retrospect.* London and Felling-on-Tyne, New York, The Walter Scott Publishing Co., Ltd., 1909.

Yastrebtsev, V.V. Edited and Translated by Florence Jonas. *Reminiscences of Rimsky-Korsakov.* New York: Columbia University Press, 1985.

Yates, Peter. *Twentieth century music: its evolution from the end of the harmonic era into the present era of sound.* London: Allen & Unwin Ltd., 1968.

Young, Percy M. *Beethoven: a Victorian tribute based on the papers of Sir George Smart.* London: D. Dobson, 1976.

Young, Percy M. *George Grove, 1820–1900: a biography.* London: Macmillan, 1980.

Young, Percy M. *Letters of Edward Elgar and other writings.* London: Geoffrey Bles, 1956.

Young, Percy M., Editor. *Letters to Nimrod: Edward Elgar to August Jaeger, 1897–1908.* London: Dennis Dobson, 1965.

Young, Percy M. *The concert tradition: from the middle ages to the twentieth century.* London: Routledge and Kegan Paul, 1965.

Young, Rob, Editor. *(Brief Description): Undercurrents: the hidden wiring of modern music.* London; New York, N.Y.: Continuum, 2002.

Yourke, Electra Slonimsky, Editor. *Nicolas Slonimsky: writings on music.* New York, N.Y.; London: Routledge, 4 Vols. 2003-2005.

Slonimsky, Nicolas. *The great composers and their works.* Edited by Electra Slonimsky Yourke. New York: Schirmer Books, 2 Vols. 2000.

Ysaÿe, Antoine. *Ysaÿe: his life, work and influence.* London: W. Heinemann, 1947.

Zamoyski, Adam. *Paderewski.* London: Collins, 1982.

Zegers, Mirjam, Editor. *Louis Andriessen: The art of stealing time.* Todmorden: Arc Music, 2002.

Zemanova, Mirka, Editor. *Janácek's uncollected essays on music.* London: Marion Boyars, 1989.

INDEX

Index to the Piano Sonatas Op. 90 to Op. 111 and a Beethoven timeline of significant musical and related events.

The order adopted for the listing of the individual entries in this index, for each of the piano sonatas under consideration, is chronological – according to the sequential unfolding of events under discussion. Thereby, the reader is provided with both a guide to the contents discussed in the main text and a timeline of the principal events bearing on Beethoven's life and work.

OP. 90 PP. 1-35
Time interval between previous sonatas
To which creative period does Op. 90 belong?
Beethoven's revitalised impulse to compose
Op. 90 a transitional work
Op. 90 a programmatic work
Beethoven's connections with Lichnowsky family
Count Moritz Lichnowsky
Op. 90 a contest between head and heart
Anton Schindler's fabrications
A metaphor to contrasting relation-

ships of mood
Caspar Karl (Carl) Beethoven
Beethoven's health
Publisher Sigmund Anton Steiner
Dessauer Sketchbook
Archduke Rudolf
Publication announcement
Wenzel Schlemmer, costs of copying
Tobias Haslinger
Beethoven's quasi military-terms
Title Page designation
Allgemeine musikalische Zeitung, critical reception
Napoleon Bonaparte
Beethoven's adoption of German expressions
Two-movement structure
Critical evaluations of Op. 90
Sound-world of Schubert
Congress of Vienna
Wellington's Victory – Battle Symphony
Cantata *Der glorreiche Augenblick*
Johann Nepomuk Mälzel
Panharmonicon
Ernst Theodor Hoffman
Revision of *Leonora – Fidelio*
Beethoven's portraits
Louis Letronne
Blasius Höfel
Joseph Mähler
Johann Christoph Heckel
Franz Klein
Archduke Trio, Op. 97
Beethoven's worsening deafness
Johann Wenzel Tomaschek, recollections of Beethoven
Beethoven's hearing aids
German headings to movements
First movement, interpretation of
Nineteenth-century Romanticism
Performance and interpretation
Final movement
Schubertian feeling
Performance and interpretation

OP. 101 PP. 41-95
Beethoven on threshold of last creative period
Deeper levels of expression and intensity of spiritual expression
Invention linked with memory
Op. 101 a fantasy-sonata
Influence of folksong arrangements
A new intimate tone
An evolving musical style
Beethoven's wish to make use of German language
Evolving disposition to romantically conceived music
Impact on Romantic composers
Fusion of fugal writing and variation form
Caspar David Friederich
Beethoven's absorption in fugue
Allgemeine musikalische Zeitung concert review
Few public performances of piano sonatas
Significance of German language
Influence of transformation of keyboard
Baroness Dorothea von Ertmann
Ertmann's style of performance
Scheide Sketchbook
Miscellaneous leaves
Associated compositions
Beethoven's originality
Exploitation of extended keyboard
Period of composition
Origins of *HammerKlavier*
Ideas for dedication
Wilhelm Hebenstreit
The 'difficult to perform' Piano Sonata
Publication February 1817
Title Page announcement
Allgemeine musikalische Zeitung of 1817
Nineteenth century neglect
Contextual circumstances relating to Op. 101

Effects the loss of hearing
Search for sonorous instrument
Johann Mälzel (Maelzel)
Ear trumpet
Death of brother Casper Carl
Depression
The Philharmonic Society, London
Demeanour restored
Countess Anna Maria Erdödy
Guardianship of nephew Kaspar
Dr. Karl von Bursy
Schnyder von Wartensee
Freedom of the City of Vienna
Allgemeine musikalische Zeitung review
Franz Schubert, diary entry
Susan Salzer, sonnet
First movement, *Allegretto ma non troppo*
Subjective and poetic mood
Influence of Romantic composers
Transcendental lyricism
Metronome
Nikolaus Winkel
Johann Maelzel
Beethoven's metronome markings
Powers of invention
Allgemeine musikalische Zeitung review
Carl Czerny, on performance
Cosima Wagner, recollections of Josef Rubinstein
Artur Schnabel on a concert tour
Veronica Jochum, recollections of Vladimir Horowitz
Glen Gould
Second movement, *Vivace alla Marcia*
String quartet like
Ethereal effect
Rhythm of drumbeat
Back to Bach
Robert Schuman, influence on
Allgemeine musikalische Zeitung review
Carl Czerny on proper performance

Third movement *Adagio ma non troppo, con affetto*
Yearning quality of music
Soft pedal — *una corda*, importance of
Parallel with Cello Sonata Op. 102, No. 2
Concept of thematic recollection
Allgemeine musikalische Zeitung review
Carl Czerny, on performance
Influence of Bach's Chromatic Fantasia and Fugue, BVW 903
Final movement *Allegro*
New poetic feeling in piano-sonata writing
Spiritualized counterpoint
Inherent exuberance
A profusion of ideas
Exploration of compass of new keyboard
Accommodation of low E
Fugato writing
Cumulative fugal development
String quartet like character
Beethoven's use of trill
Allgemeine musikalische Zeitung review
Carl Czerny on performance

OP. 106 PP. 103-203
Standing of work in repertoire
Keyboard metamorphosis
Return to four-movement structure
Expanded scale
Stamp of originality and boldness
Hammerklavier terminology
Beethoven's preferred sonata
Estimations of composition
A triumph over adversity
Critics, *King Lear*-like
Vehicle for the professional pianist
Technical and emotional challenges
Melancholic and gloomy
Ultimately unplayable
Nature of great art

Tonal landscape
Boldrini Sketchbook
Vienna A 44 and Vienna A 45 Sketchbooks
Sketches for Ninth and Tenth Symphonies
Unconventional order of movements
Beethoven's constructional procedures
Evidence of musicological pedagogy
Schindler on Beethoven striving for pianistic effect
Dedication to Archduke Rudolph
Viennese publisher Mathias Artaria
Wiener Zeitung announcement
Title Page
Review of 1826
Negotiations for English edition
George Thomson and folksongs
English publishers
London transactions with Ferdinand Ries
Wenzel Schlemmer, copyist
English edition, controversial suggestions for revised order of movements
Beethoven's financial needs
Publication in England
Title Page, English edition
Beethoven's metronome marks
Johann Nepomuk Hummel, Piano Sonata in F-Sharp minor, Op. 81
Maelzel's metronome
Uncertainty regarding Beethoven's metronome indications
Carl Czerny, first performance
Henri Mortier de Fontaine, early performance by
Cipriani Potter and Sterndale Bennett
Ignaz Moscheles, early performance by
Nineteenth century performances
Arabella Goddard, early performance by

Camille Saint-Saëns and Eugène Gigout
Franz Liszt, recollections of
Otto Klemperer as pianist
Arthur Rubinstein, recollections of
Dmitri Shostakovich, recollections of
Olivier Messiaen, recollections of
Wilhelm Backhaus, estimation of
Symphonic conception
Felix Weingartner's orchestration
Interpretations of the Piano Sonata Op. 106: Carl Czerny, Donald Tovey, Alfred Brendel, Charles Rosen
Beethoven's personal circumstances at period of composition
London visit postponed – later abandoned
Hydrotherapy, need for
Worsening hearing
Conversation books, reliance on
Piano Concerto in E-flat, Op. 73, unable to perform
Custody of nephew Karl
Legal proceedings
George Thomson, negotiations with
Domestic affairs
J. S. Bach, interest in and debt to
Carl Maria von Weber, adverse view of Beethoven
Allgemeine musikalische Zeitung, review of 26 December 1818
Streicher's 6 1/2 octave piano
Thomas Broadwood, gift of piano to B Beethoven
Beethoven's portrait taken by August von Kloeber, Ferdinand Schimon, Joseph Carl Stieler

FIRST MOVEMENT:
Large-scale structure
Opening chords, significance of
Symphonic in conception
'Vivat, vivat Rudolfus', Cantata origins
Challenge to the pianist

Carl Czerny, anecdote
Strategies to aid performance, doubts concerning
Psychology of performance
Felix Mendelssohn, influence on his Piano Sonata in B-flat major
Johannes Brahms, influence on his Piano Sonata, Op. 1
Vincent Novello, origins of Beethoven sketch
Opening chords, role of
Michael Tippett, extract from 1938 lecture
Vincent d'Indy, views of
Alfred Brendel, value of word-imagery
Drama of movement
'Chains of thirds', significance of
Beethoven's tempo indications
Artur Schnabel, adherence to Beethoven
Beethoven's metronome indications, Brendel, Arrau, Rosen, Wiengartner, Badura-Skoda
Hector Berlioz on Franz Liszt
Wendelin Weissheimer on Franz Liszt
Siegfried Ochs and Liszt master-class
Carl Czerny, views on interpretation
Donald Tovey, views on interpretation

SECOND MOVEMENT:
Ninth Symphony, precedent
Light-hearted character
Restless, unstable character
Goethe's Faust, intimations of
Strangely whimsical
Sketch drafts
Preoccupation with accented upbeat
Scherzo that breaks bounds
Carl Czerny on interpretation

Third Movement
Heart of Sonata
Transcend limits of piano
Profound spiritual expression
Stream of consciousness
Hugo Riemann, views of
Wilhelm von Lenz, views of
J. W. N. Sullivan, views of
Song-like character
J.S. Bach, reminiscences of
Chopin's anticipation of Ballades
Mozart's A major Concerto, K. 488, parallel with
Sketches
Keyboard, fullest exploitation of
Igor Stravinsky, views of
Luciano Berio, views of
Additional opening bar
Significance of additional notes
Function of link
Franz Liszt, interpretations of
Wendelin Weissheimer, recollections of
Margaret Chanter, recollections of
Felix Weingartner as pianist
Arthur Rubinstein, recollections of
Hans von Bulow, views of
Carl Czerny on interpretation
Modern-day performance
John Fuller-Maitland, reflections from Death Centenary

FOURTH MOVEMENT
Ethereal-like introduction
Ninth Symphony, parallel with
Ferruccio Busoni, views of
Prelude to great Fugue
Transitional passage
Fuga a tre voci, con alcune licenze, significance of
Fugue not contrapuntal exercise
Power and grandeur of Finale
Grosse Fuge, parallel with
Nature of fugal writing
Critics of Fugue
André Hodeir, views of
Christopher Headington, views of
Challenge to performer
Sketches

Sense of strain, value of
Landsberg 9 Sketchbook
Roger Sessions, Spencer Trask Lecture
Role of trill
Beethoven's early instruction in fugue
Beethoven's respect for Bach
Departure from traditional fugue writing
Large-scale conception
Bars 250–278, moment of tranquillity
Sanctus of Mass in D, parallel with
Wendelin Weissheimer, recollections of Franz Liszt
Technical challenges
Metronome settings
Donald Tovey, noblest work of man

OP. 109 PP. 222-257
Return to fantasia style sonata
Piano Sonatas Opp. 109, 110 and 111, Beethoven's last will and testament
Composition contemporaneous with *Missa Solemnis*
Exploration of terse, aphoristic statements
Finale centre of gravity
One of 'profoundest things in music'
A mixture of styles
Wittgenstein Sketchbook, compositional origins
Aloys Fuchs, collector of Beethoven autographs
Artaria 197 Sketchbook
Adolph Martin Schlesinger and composition origins
Beethoven's poor health, consequences of
Maximiliana Brentano, dedicatee
Copyists errors, problems of
Piano Sonatas Opp. 110 and 11, related work on
Franz and Antonia Brentano
Title Page, details of
Innovatory nature of Beethoven's achievement
Artur Schnabel, anecdote
Franz Liszt, recollections of
Stuttgart *Morgenblatt für gebilete Stände*, estimation of Beethoven
Allgemeine musikalische Zeitung, estimation of Beethoven
Per Daniel Atterbom, recollections of Beethoven
Portraits and likenesses of Beethoven: Joseph Weidner
Joseph Daniel Böhm
Joseph Karl (Carl) Stieler
Beethoven honoured:
Philharmonic Society of Laibach
Styrian Musical Society
Carl Friedrich Zelter, recollections of Beethoven
Dr. Wilhelm Christian Müller
Thomas Alsager and Queen Square Select Society: English performances of Beethoven
Franz Olivia, service to Beethoven
First movement:
Irregular structural features, dream-like, wave-like figures, dual character – *Vivace Adagio*, brevity, influence of Friedrich Starke's piano tutor studies, *Fantasie* quality, study in contrast of textures, influence of J. S. Bach, *Allgemeine musikalische Zeitung* – assessment, Carl Czerny, views of, performance and interpretation
Second movement:
Prestissimo – rare use of, imaginative, transformational processes, character of restlessness, manner of late Mendelssohn, *Allgemeine musikalische Zeitung* – assessment, diverse rhythms, contrapuntal thought, passionate restatement of opening subject, interpretation

Third movement:
Most radical — theme followed by six variations, wide-ranging use of variation form, originality and depth of expression, opening elegiac theme, feeling of holy devotion, like a prayer, subsequent transformation
Variation I:
Songful melody, prayer-like, a solemn mazurka, anticipation of pianistic waltz, Sir George Grove — recollections,
Variation II:
Reminiscence of first movement, hints of polyphony, unearthly trills, Carl Czerny on performance
Variation III:
Brilliant technical study, double counterpoint, Bach-like two-part invention, Carl Czerny and performance
Variation IV:
An extraordinary inspiration, four-voice textures, Hans von Bülow — intimations of *Faust*, rebirth of fugue from spirit of sonata, Czerny and Tovey on performance and interpretation
Variation V:
Canonic writing to the fore, march-like fugue, Stravinsky's estimation
Variation VI
Tribute to the *Goldberg* Variations and Emanuel Bach, suggestions of Handelian Doubles, power of relentless trills —transcendental, polyphonic and ethereal character.

OP. 110 PP. 264-313

Reflections on Beethoven's late period works
Beethoven's preoccupation with *Missa Solemnis*
Implications of Beethoven's illness
Op. 110 likened to quasi una fantasia
Review in Berliner Allgemeine musikalische Zeitung
'extra-musical' influences
Bernard Shaw, review of Op. 110
1927 Centenary recollections
Sir John B. McEwan, recollections of
Menahan Pressler, recollections of
Adolph Martin Schlesinger, inception of Op. 110
Summary of creation origins of Op. 110
Prussian copyright law of 1830
Mathias Artaria and Beethoven's financial difficulties
Beethoven's jaundice
Beethoven's extensive negotiations with Schlesinger
Graz Music Society, Beethoven elected member
Franz Brentano
Carl Peters and Tobias Haslinger, plans for a comprehensive edition of Beethoven's works
Moritz Schlesinger, Paris publishing business
Ferdinand Ries, plans for an English edition of Op. 110
Problem of errors in text of Op. 110
Royal Swedish Music Academy of Stockholm, Beethoven elected Member
Artaria 197 Sketchbook, compositional insights
Bibliothèque Nationale, sketches of Op. 110
Gesellschaft der Musikfreunde
Op. 110 dedication, omission of
Publication of Op. 110
Ferdinand Ries, neglect of
English publication by Clementi
Charles Letts, London auction of Autograph

Recollections of Beethoven's contemporaries: Dr. Wilhelm Christian Müller, Friedrich Starke, Wilhelmine Schröder-Devrient, Sir John Russell, Friedrich Rochlitz, and Gioacchino Rossini
Marie Lipsius, recollections of Franz Liszt
Clara Schumann, influence of Joseph Joachim
Virgil Thomson, recollections of Artur Schnabel
Raymond Leppard, recollections of Dame Myra Hess
First movement:
Sonata-form, great freedom
George Pinto, influence of
Hexachord, use of
Quartet texture
Cosi fan tutti, parallels with
Friedrich Bernard Marx, review by
Critical assessments by Carl Dahlhaus, Paul Bekker, Peter Charleton, and Denis Matthews
Questions of Interpretation, Carl Czerny, Ernst Von Elterlein, Martin Cooper,
Second movement:
Character of scherzo
Eugen d'Albert, recollections of
Austrian folk songs, influence of
Adolf Bernard Marx, views of
Technical challenges
Coda
Beethoven's performance designations
Final movement:
Structure
Comparisons with Op. 109
Movement at heart of Sonata
Struggle sublimated into ecstasy
Episodes in third movement"
Recitative;
Arioso dolente
Fugue
Return of Arioso
Inversion of the Fugue
Homophonic conclusion
Estimations of Beethoven's achievement

OP. 111 PP. 320-385

Reflections on Beethoven's later years
Opp. 109, 110 and 111 as a trilogy
Beethoven's pre-occupation with Ninth Symphony and *Missa Solemnis*
Persistent illness
Significance of key of C minor
Roll of contrasts
Enrique Granados, estimation of Op. 111
Igor Stravinsky, estimation of Beethoven and his concept of time
Concept of two movements
Sergei Prokofiev, influence on Second Symphony
Creation origins of Op. 111
Adolph Martin Schlesinger, request for piano sonatas
1820, compositional progress hindered by illness
1821, pre-occupation with Piano Sonata Op. 110
Primary sources for Op. 111: Artaria 197 and 201
Bibliothèque Nationale sources: MS 51
1822 progress with C minor Sonata
Wenzel Rampl, copyist
Archduke Rudolph, dedication
Moritz Schlesinger, Paris publishing house
Third movement, confusion regarding
Adolf Bernhard Marx views in *Berliner Allgemeine musikalische Zeitung*
Anton Schindler, views regarding a

third movement
Contemporary responses to concept of a third movement
Proof reading, problems with
Archduke Rudolph, confirmation of dedication
Antonie (Antonia) Brentano, née von Birkenstock, original dedicatee
Beethoven's views on composition
Pirate editions, Anton Diabelli and Saur and Leidesdorf
Diabelli edition, Beethoven's care with
Wiener Zeitung, announcement 27 May 1823
English edition of Op. 111
Ferdinand Ries, negotiations with
Muzio Clementi, English edition
Carl Peters, string quartet proposals
Nikolay Galitzin, string quartet proposals
Louis Schlösser, meeting with Beethoven (1822)
Beethoven's insights into creative process
Luigi Cherubini, Beethoven's estimation of
Imperial and Royal Chamber Composer, Beethoven seeks appointment to
Carl Maria von Weber, meeting with Beethoven
Ferdinand Georg Waldmüller, takes Beethoven's portrait
Johann Andreas Stumpff, meeting with Beethoven
Royal Swedish Academy, honours Beethoven
Twenty-eight signatories honour Beethoven
Gustav Mahler, recollections of performing Op. 111
Artur Schnabel, recalled by Virgil Thomson and Neville Cardus
First movement, description of
Aeschylean grandeur
Titanic power
Beethoven's tempo indication, significance of
Virtuoso traits
Sketch origins
Fugal textures
Fantasy and fugue combined
Carl Czerny, on interpretation
Franz Liszt, recalled by Richard Wagner
Claudio Arrau in conversation with
Claudio Arrau in conversation with Joseph Horowitz
Allgemeine musikalische Zeitung, review of Op. 111
Overture *Coriolanus*, comparison with
Frederick Chopin, influence on
Sergei Prokofiev, influence on
First movement close
Second movement, description of
Arietta, nature of
Allgemeine musikalische Zeitung, views of
Friedrich Bernard Marx, views of
Sir George Grove, views of
Cosima Wagner, Diary recollections
Contemporary views of *Arietta*: Marion Scott, Eric Blom, Wilfrid Mellers, Alec Robertson, Dmitri Shostakovich, Denis Matthews, Alan Bush, Maynard Solomon
Arietta, construction of
Adagio molto semplice e cantabile, interpretation of
Carl Czerny, views on interpretation
Josef Hofmann, recollections of
Beethoven and variation form
Piano Sonata Op. 109, importance as precedent
Samuel Langford, views of
Paul Bekker, views of
Beethoven's sketches
Time signatures, unconventional

The Harmonicon, reference to
Claudio Arrau, views on *Arietta*
Variations, introductory remarks
Variations 1–3
Fourth variation
Fifth variation

Beethoven's achievement in the variations: Stewart Gordon, Wagner, Rolland, von Elterlein, Igor Stravinsky, Benjamin Britten,
Challenge of performance
Valedictory remarks

ABOUT THE AUTHOR

Terence M. Russell graduated with first class honours in architecture and was a nominee for the coveted Silver Medal of the Royal Institute of British Architects. He is a Fellow of the Royal Incorporation of Architects in Scotland (retired), was formerly Reader in the School of Arts, Culture and Environment at the University of Edinburgh, a Fellow of the British Higher Education Academy, and Senior Assessor to the Scottish Higher Education Funding Council. Alongside his professional work in the field of architecture – embracing practice, teaching and research – he has maintained a lifetime's interest in the music and musicology of Beethoven. He has an equal admiration for the work of Franz Schubert and was for many years an active member of the Schubert Institute, UK. His book writings in the field of architecture include the following:

The Built Environment: A Subject Index, Gregg Publishing (1989):
- Vol. 1: Town planning and urbanism, architecture, gardens and landscape design
- Vol. 2: Environmental technology, constructional engineering, building and materials
- Vol. 3: Decorative art and industrial design, international exhibitions and collections, recreational and performing arts
- Vol. 4: Public health, municipal services, community welfare

Architecture in the Encyclopédie of Diderot and D'Alemebert: The Letterpress Articles and Selected Engravings, Scolar Press (1993)

The Encyclopaedic Dictionary in the Eighteenth Century: Architecture, Arts and Crafts, Scolar Press (1997):
- Vol. 1: John Harris, Lexicon Technicum
- Vol. 2: Ephraim Chambers, Cyclopaedia
- Vol. 3: The Builder's Dictionary
- Vol. 4: Samuel Johnson, A Dictionary of the English Language
- Vol. 5: A Society of Gentlemen, Encyclopaedia Britannica

Gardens and Landscapes in the Encyclopédie of Diderot and D'Alemebert: The Letterpress Articles and Selected Engravings, 2 Vols., Ashgate (1999)

The Napoleonic Survey of Egypt: The Monuments and Customs of Egypt, 2 Vols., Ashgate (2001)

The Discovery of Egypt: Vivant Denon's Travels with Napoleon's Army, History Press (2005)

www.ingramcontent.com/pod-product-compliance
Lightning Source LLC
Chambersburg PA
CBHW010021130526
44590CB00047B/3742